FROM BLAIR TO BROWN

Diaries: Volume 6, 2005–2007

FROM BLAIR TO BROWN
ALASTAIR CAMPBELL

DIARIES: VOLUME 6, 2005–2007

Biteback Publishing

First published in Great Britain in 2017 by
Biteback Publishing Ltd
Westminster Tower
3 Albert Embankment
London SE1 7SP

ISBN 978-1-78590-084-6

10 9 8 7 6 5 4 3 2 1

A CIP catalogue record for this book is available from the British Library.

Set in Palatino

Printed and bound in Great Britain by
CPI Group (UK) Ltd, Croydon CR0 4YY

MIX
Paper from
responsible sources
FSC® C020471

Contents

Introduction   *vii*

Who's Who   *xv*

THE DIARIES   1

Index   609

Introduction

The publication of these diaries has been a long, often agonising journey – much of the agonising going on inside my mind, which, as readers of previous volumes will know, is prone to creating trouble for itself. When that journey began well over a decade ago, in addition to my partner Fiona, the people I leaned on to help me with my agonising were publisher Gail Rebuck and her husband, Philip Gould, my brilliant agent Ed Victor, my former *Daily Mirror* boss turned diaries editor Richard Stott, and my co-transcriber and head researcher Mark Bennett. It is incredible, and incredibly sad, that the four men in that list have all since passed away, evidence not just of how long this journey has been, but also of the lottery of this wonderful thing called life, from which, during the period of this volume, Robin Cook, Mo Mowlam and Tony Banks were among those taken all too young.

Of my four diary colleagues, only Ed, who died earlier this year aged seventy-seven, got even close to a full life, and 'oh boy', as he might have put it, did he live life to the full. He was, as he promised he would be, working to the end, in the hospital bed where he breathed his last. He was so much more than an agent, and became a true friend, despite – perhaps because of – my becoming what he delighted in describing as 'my most complicated client'. Richard was taken by pancreatic cancer aged sixty-three, a full decade ago now, and was on his deathbed at home when I was finally able to take him one of the first copies of *The Blair Years*, the extracts of my diaries from 1994 to 2003, published in June 2007, the same month he died. He – his enthusiasm, professionalism, judgement and friendship – was a fundamental part of the success that book became, not least the editing processes that have continued since, including his idea of what we called the 'running feet', the few words at the bottom of each page saying what the page is about. Richard loved his running feet, almost as much as he hated, as you shall read, the fact that I chose to sanitise that first book to protect Gordon

Brown. With both Tony Blair and Gordon now former Prime Ministers, the full story can be told. I am just sad that Richard is not here to see it, and Labour out of power as it is told.

Philip Gould was my closest friend in politics, and five years after his death from cancer of the oesophagus aged just sixty-one, there is not a day I don't think of him, not least because we see so much of Gail and their two daughters, Georgia and Grace. He would be so proud that Georgia is now Camden Council leader aged thirty-one – and utterly stunned by much else that is happening in British and world politics, from Corbyn to May (neither of whom are even mentioned in the entries of this volume), Brexit to Trump (ditto, though the dread word 'referendum' – of the EU constitution – appears often enough).

Mark Bennett's death was the biggest shock of all, because it was so unexpected and, unlike the others, there was no preceding illness that we knew of. He just dropped dead aged forty-four, in February 2014. 'Researcher' does not even begin to describe his importance to me and to these diaries, and I want to start this, the eighth book based on my diaries, and the sixth full volume, by dedicating it

In Memory of Philip, Ed, Richard and Mark.

As to why there was so much agonising, it was not just a question of my troubled, sometimes catastrophising mind. It was my friend and colleague Ben Wegg-Prosser who, on publication of Volume 5, *Outside, Inside*, last year, was on good mickey-taking form at one of the periodic gatherings of the original Team TB '97: 'So now we have the diaries about the diaries … how long before we get the diaries about the diaries about the diaries?' Not long, Ben, not long. But the truth is, there were important personal and political judgements attached to the questions of whether, what, when and how to publish what I knew would become a significant part of the already enormous literary analysis of the Blair–Brown eras. As the running foot on page 523 puts it:

February '07: TB worries AC diaries 'posthumous suicide' for both of them

Though to be fair to him, he was a great support when push came to shove, and figures as varied as Cherie, Peter Mandelson, Jonathan Powell and assorted spooks, diplomats and civil servants were arguing strongly against some or all publication.

On the personal front, there was the question of just how far to go in setting out the mental health issues which, post my departure from Downing Street, perhaps with more time to think, seemed to crowd in more persistently than ever. The gaps between the depressions seemed to get shorter. It meant the hope Fiona and I both shared, that our lives would improve when I was out of No. 10, and my head out of the 'vice' in which I often felt competing demands of life, work and politics put it, took a long time to be fulfilled. I decided, as you shall see, and against TB's advice, for full disclosure, both about the continuing difficulties at home and about my attempts to get professional help to resolve my own issues, which were in large part causing those difficulties.

Journalist and broadcaster Steve Richards – a man of fine judgement on many things – said he found Volume 5 'even more interesting' than the previous four, not only because there was a little more distance from, and thus perspective on, the political events I was recording, but also, he said, because there were some interesting new characters closer to centre stage. He cited as an example my highly political, often searingly critical, GP, Tom Bostock, to whom visits to get a prescription could become full-on rows about Iraq or NHS reform. When I was interviewed by Steve about the book for *The Week in Westminster* on BBC Radio 4, I was able to tell him that Volume 6 gets even better, with the introduction of a totally new medical character, my psychiatrist David Sturgeon. 'That must be quite a gig, being Alastair Campbell's psychiatrist,' someone wrote in *The Guardian* when it first emerged I was seeing one. Well, DS (not to be confused with Downing Street, though that DS might be the reason I ended up needing the other one) is the man who got that gig. He too became part of my agonising advice squad, not least as first Tony Blair then Gordon Brown sought to get me back into Downing Street, both with very different reasons for doing so. He also, surely, is the person who inadvertently set me on the road down a very different path, when out of the blue, out on my bike one day, into my head popped the idea for a novel, *All in the Mind*, about the relationship between a psychiatrist and his patients. I never expected or planned to be a novelist, but that first one was anonymously dedicated to David and another psychiatrist, and I am now on my fourth novel, out next year, which is exclusively dedicated to Ed Victor – because it arose from a collaboration that was his idea. I am grateful to David Sturgeon also for the support he gives in the work I now do as an ambassador for Time to Change, trying to change attitudes to mental health and mental illness. My own mental health has been hugely helped by him, his advice and his medication, and also by my own openness and the feeling of being part of a campaign going in the right direction.

There are other new characters that hopefully Steve Richards will appreciate. Did I ever imagine I would be negotiating fairground rides with Cheryl Cole and Karren Brady, or being stabbed by Trinny for a Comic Relief version of *The Apprentice?* No. And did I expect to get drawn into the 'celebrity culture' against which I otherwise spend my time raging? No, but charity – and trying to adapt to a new life – can have strange consequences, and at least I managed to help get Piers Morgan fired – again. Less happily, 'Yates of the Yard' enters TB's life, when the combination of an SNP MP, Angus MacNeil, and a Labour treasurer, Jack Dromey, provoke what became one of the most difficult and unpleasant crises of TB's time – the police probe into 'cash for honours' (*sic*).

Many of the new characters come from sport. Indeed, readers of the first parts of this book might wonder if they shouldn't have found it in the rugby section, rather than politics, as I leave the aftermath of our 2005 election win and head for New Zealand with the British and Irish Lions. Both on and off the field, it was not the greatest success, but I was privileged to see people like Jonny Wilkinson working up close, I learned a lot, and I enjoyed it, even if being debagged and having my BlackBerry stolen by the players – while it had a note about TB–GB transition plans on it – was one of the more panicky moments of my life. I have stayed in touch with many of the players and coaches, and at times, as when I felt like a marriage counsellor, I wished TB and GB had taken me up on adopting some of the team-bonding techniques I learned from the world of rugby. The Lions having been back to New Zealand more successfully this year, it was frankly bizarre the extent to which I was still part of the media focus of that tour twelve years ago, not least because of the controversy over the infamous 'spear tackle' on our captain Brian O'Driscoll in the opening moments of the first Test. So though I was grateful to Clive Woodward for asking me to do it, that tour was what made me realise a 'normal comms job' was something I no longer could, should or wanted to do.

This book starts the day after Tony has been returned to office following a third successive – unprecedented for a Labour leader – election win, a clear majority, beyond the dreams of David Cameron, Theresa May and Jeremy Corbyn; and yet, as the very first of the running feet puts it, it was a time 'when a win feels more like a defeat'. Problems between TB and GB, largely settled during the campaign, emerged almost immediately. We are only three pages in when the TB–GBs get their first running foot:

May '05: GB furious over reshuffle

As we know from Mrs May's botched election earlier this year, expectations are so important in politics. She 'won', in that she survived as PM, but she lost much of her authority. Labour leader Jeremy Corbyn lost, yet found his position strengthened. Tony Blair won, again, but because the majority fell from three figures to two – what would May or Corbyn give for a majority of 66 – Labour MPs were out calling for his head, and some continued to do so until he was gone – see last page. *Funny old game, Saint* … and interesting that among those most appalled at the way TB was treated were friends from sport, Clive Woodward, Brendan Foster and Alex Ferguson all calling to register their shock and even disgust at how a winner was being treated like a loser. Compare and contrast, also, TB's speech after the election, about having listened and learned, with Theresa May's after her plans for a landslide had melted, which gave every indication that nothing much had changed.

Of course, for all the new characters – oh, and I should apologise in advance for the length of my entries on Diego Maradona, but meeting and playing football with him was one of the highlights of my entire life, and the footnote on page 339, about the fact that I mention it to someone every day, is true – there is one very old story that runs through this volume as through all others, and that is what alas has become known as the TB–GBs.

Here is where the agonising a decade ago was at its height, and why both Richard and Ed, who had read every word of my diaries from 1994 to 2003, were shocked that I would even consider protecting GB, let alone going back, as I did in the period of the previous volume, to help rebuild TB–GB relations sufficient to get them through a winning campaign focused on the economy. This détente came at the price of a TB commitment to leave some way through his third term, and support from both of us in GB taking over. Richard felt if I just published the whole lot back in 2006, it could have put paid to GB's chances. Maybe, maybe not. Then again, Richard admitted that he was looking at the material from the standpoint of a journalist who, though Labour like me, did not share my, Philip's and Mark's obsessive desire for Labour not the Tories to be in power. So, for all GB's faults, and for the many moments I, and more importantly TB, felt he might be a disaster as PM, there were many other moments when it was clear he remained a formidable figure, head and shoulders above most others home and abroad, and we shared a hope that once he was freed of the TB shadow, he would emerge to be as good a PM as he had been a Chancellor over a decade of growth, prosperity and record investment in public services.

Even now – and this volume records some pretty negative views of GB, with plenty of evidence to justify them – I am able to see a lot that is positive in him. That explains why even after all that is recorded here, up to and including some brutal tactics that both TB and Jonathan Powell at various points compare with the Mafia way of doing things – Dromey and Tom Watson spring to mind – I went back to try to help in the 2010 campaign (Volume 7, out next year, Ben) and though GB didn't win, he did at least manage to stop the Tories winning a majority. And though GB was definitely among those who felt I should not have kept, let alone published, my diaries, he always knew that I did and I would, and I feel privileged to have had many of the times and conversations I had with him, including after the point when he knew I intended one day to publish it all.

David Cameron and George Osborne are two more who move from bit players to central characters in the period covered here. My favourite text message of the period was from Tory MP Andrew Mitchell, who was running the leadership campaign of David Davis. Davis was something of an old pal of mine from my *Mirror* days, and TB had expected him to win, but he flopped at the Tory conference where Cameron shone. 'Are we completely fucked?' asked Mitchell on behalf of his boss. They were. Yet how strange is politics that today Cameron is history, on the back of the folly of his EU referendum, while Davis is the man entrusted by May with the near impossible task of making sense of the decision the British people took last June?

And how are these for running feet that resonate today?

44   *June '05: Dutch following French in rejecting constitution*
45   *June '05: EU constitution in trouble*
52   *June '05: GB threatens veto if others come after UK rebate*
63   *June '05: Juncker warns 'whole EU in crisis'*
69   *June '05: TB trying to open debate on EU renewal*

Most timeless of all, however...

169   *December '05: Europe still a problem for Tories*

Long may it continue, hopefully to the day that the madness of Brexit is rejected.

Just as David Cameron underestimated his Leave opponents in last June's referendum, so Theresa May underestimated her Labour opponent in the general election that her hubris provoked her to call. We always obsessed about our opponents. Cameron, however, became another source of disagreement between TB and GB as they tried to work out how to handle him, and came to different conclusions. I had forgotten

Introduction

– this is why it is good to keep a diary – some of my encounters with the new Tory leadership team. They worked out pretty quickly that an 'heir to Blair' strategy would be rejected by GB, and so they took it for themselves. GB, from the off, despite Philip and I, among others, pleading with him not to, defined himself as much against TB as against DC, and did so, I fear, out of personal antipathy to TB, rather than for reasons of cold, hard-headed strategy. It is sad. I am indebted once more to Richard – see the running foot on page 286 – for his description of the TB–GBs as 'Shakespearean'. Tragedy, not comedy. See also the running foot on page 198:

January '06: 'Is there any page of diary without TB–GB?' – Mark Bennett … Mmm, not many.

Or, earlier, page 111:

August '05: Fiona and Gail Rebuck fed up of TB–GB talk

I do understand their feelings, but hope that, for some readers at least, trying to understand this complex and politically hugely significant relationship is worth another long read. Also, Mark Bennett's point notwithstanding, there is of course a lot more to these times than the TB–GB story, though even I was shocked to be reminded that GB once told me he was thinking of going to the backbenches. Iraq continues to be a problem, though Saddam's execution brings that particular chapter to an end, even if the issue more generally will never close so far as the analysis of TB's legacy is concerned. Northern Ireland continues to have its ups and downs. The ups and downs of political life more generally could hardly have been more graphically set out than the winning of the Olympic bid for London 2012, followed by the horror of the July 7 bombings.

Through it all, despite our own considerable ups and downs, Fiona has stuck by me, endured my agonising and my wildly swinging moods, and for that, and for the love of our three children, Rory, Calum and Grace, I am more grateful than anything. There is a point in the book where TB and I discuss the damage politics does to relationships, and our shared sadness that Fiona so fell out with Cherie, and became so angry with him over Iraq and some of his domestic reform policies, that she would not even go to farewell events as he departed No. 10. He said he hoped that when things were less raw, she would look back more happily at our times together. I am pleased to say she does and, looking at UK politics now, also understands even better just how special and winning a leader TB was.

Finally, I want to thank Bill Hagerty, who stepped in to replace our mutual friend Richard – indeed, Bill delivered a brilliant eulogy at Richard's funeral – as editor of this and future volumes. Richard was a hard act to follow, but Bill has followed in style; and of the Biteback team, I would like to thank Iain Dale, Olivia Beattie, James Stephens, Isabelle Ralphs, Ashley Biles and Namkwan Cho.

I hope you enjoy reading what all of us, the dead and the living, have produced.

Who's Who

May 2005–June 2007

Tony Blair	Prime Minister (TB)
John Prescott	Deputy Prime Minister and First Secretary of State (JP)
Gordon Brown	Chancellor of the Exchequer (GB)
Alastair Campbell	Journalist, author, political aide, former Downing Street director of communications and strategy (AC)
Jack Straw	Foreign Secretary until May 2006, Leader of the House of Commons from May 2006 (JS)
Philip Gould	Political pollster and strategist (PG, Philip)
Peter Mandelson	European Commissioner for Trade, former Cabinet minister (Peter M)
David Hill	Tony Blair's director of communications (DH)
Andrew Adonis	Minister of State for Education (AA)
Peter Hyman	Strategist and speechwriter turned teacher (PH)
Geoff Hoon	Leader of the House of Commons until May 2006, Minister for Europe from May 2006 (GH)
Charles Clarke	Home Secretary until May 2006 (CC)
Robin Cook	Former Leader of the House of Commons (RC)
Lord (Bruce) Grocott	Government chief whip in the House of Lords
Jonathan Powell	Tony Blair's chief of staff (JoP)
Cherie Blair	Wife of TB (CB)
Fiona Millar	AC's partner (Fiona, FM)
Catherine Rimmer	Research and Information Unit (CR)
Lord (Charlie) Falconer	Lord Chancellor, Constitutional Affairs Secretary (CF)

Tessa Jowell	Culture, Media and Sport Secretary & Minister for the Olympics from July 2005
Michael Howard	Leader of the Opposition until December 2005 (MH)
David Cameron	Shadow Education Secretary until December 2005, Leader of the Opposition from December 2005 (DC)
George Osborne	Shadow Chancellor of the Exchequer
David Davis	Shadow Home Secretary
Ken Clarke	Tory MP, former Chancellor
William Hague	Former Leader of the Opposition
Charles Kennedy	Leader of the Liberal Democrats until 2006
Lady (Margaret) Thatcher	Former Prime Minister
David Blunkett	Former Home Secretary (DB)
Stephen Byers	Former Cabinet minister
John Reid	Defence Secretary until May 2006, Home Secretary from May 2006 (JR)
David Miliband	Communities and Local Government minister until May 2006, Secretary for Environment, Food and Rural Affairs from May 2006 (DM)
Ed Miliband	MP for Doncaster, North Minister for the Third Sector from May 2006
Bill Clinton	42nd President of the United States (BC)
George W. Bush	43rd President of the United States (GWB)
Jacques Chirac	President of France (JC)
Nicolas Sarkozy	French Minister of the Interior
Gerhard Schroeder	Chancellor of Germany until November 2005
Angela Merkel	Chancellor of Germany from November 2005
Douglas Alexander	Minister of State for Europe until May 2006, Secretary for Scotland and Transport from May 2006 (DA)
Neil Kinnock	Leader of the Labour Party, 1983–92 (NK)
Glenys Kinnock MEP	Wife of Neil Kinnock
Anji Hunter	Former director of government relations, BP director of communications from 2002
Ed Victor	AC's literary agent
Richard Stott	Former *Daily Mirror* editor, friend, editor of AC's *The Blair Years* (RS)

Ruth Kelly	Secretary for Education until May 2006, Secretary for Communities and Local Government and Minister for Women from May 2006
Ed Balls	Economic Secretary to the Treasury from May 2006 (EB)
Margaret Beckett	Secretary for the Environment, Food and Rural Affairs until May 2006, Foreign Secretary from May 2006 (MB)
Alan Milburn	Former Cabinet minister (AM, Alan)
Alan Johnson	Secretary for Trade and Industry until May 2006, Education Secretary from May 2006 (AJ)
Godric Smith	Former chief spokesperson for Tony Blair
Alistair Darling	Secretary for Scotland and Transport until May 2006, Secretary for Trade and Industry from May 2006 (AD)
Patricia Hewitt	Health Secretary
Charles Clarke	Home Secretary until 20 May 2006
Sir Clive Woodward	British and Irish Lions head coach (CW)
Bill Beaumont	British and Irish Lions manager (BB)
Brian O'Driscoll	Lions squad captain (BOD)
Gavin Henson	Welsh Lions player
Jonny Wilkinson	English Lions player (JW)
Ronan O'Gara	Irish Lions player (ROG)
Donncha O'Callaghan	Irish Lions player (DOC)
Louisa Cheetham	Lions press officer
Sir Alex Ferguson	Friend of AC, manager of Manchester United (AF)
Brendan Foster	Businessman and commentator, former athlete
Lord (Sebastian) Coe	Former athlete, former Tory MP, chair of Olympics organising committee
Diego Maradona	Argentinian legendary football star
Sir David Frost	Broadcaster, TV host
Betty Campbell	Mother of AC
Rory, Calum and Grace Campbell	Children of AC and FM
Audrey Millar	Mother of FM
Gail Rebuck	Publisher, wife of Philip Gould

The Diaries

Friday 6 May 2005

It was kind of crazy, to think that if this had been the majority back in 1997, we would have been reasonably OK with it, but because '97 and '01 were so big, 66 felt closer to disappointment than triumph. I didn't get much sleep, and when I went downstairs the day started with a bad row when the reporter on the radio said TB had seen his majority severely reduced and Fiona [Millar, AC partner] just snapped, 'Good.' I said, 'What on earth are you talking about?' She said she thought one of the reasons he had started to do more and more stuff that a lot of Labour people didn't like was because he thought the big majorities meant he could do what he wanted. Unbelievable, I said. We work our bollocks off and now you're saying it would be better if we didn't succeed in what we were trying to do, and it's time you stopped seeing everything in such a negative light. The first 'I'm not saying that' row of the third term.

I felt really, really tired today, cellular tired, and I slept on and off. TB called a couple of times, mainly to go over his words, but also for a bit of a whinge about the way victory was being presented as defeat. His speech was fine and in the end it went OK, essentially saying a win was a win but he understood the country wanted us back with a reduced majority, and that meant listening to some of the reasons why some people deserted us. He had listened and learned. He had heard what people were saying about asylum and immigration, and lack of respect in communities. And of course he knew Iraq had been a hugely divisive issue.

I thought he was being a bit optimistic when he said he thought people would now want to 'move on'. I crashed out most of the day, all a bit weird in that in the previous elections I had gone flat-out and then gone straight on after the event with a non-stop new full-on mode, but this time I was able to chill, give or take a few calls about the reshuffle. The big four stayed where they were – JP [John Prescott] still DPM, GB [Gordon Brown] still Chancellor, Jack Straw still Foreign Secretary, Charles Clarke Home Secretary, so with nothing much changing at the top, it was not terribly dramatic, but it still kept the media blathering all day with all the comings and goings. There was a lot of coverage of DB [David Blunkett, former Home Secretary] coming back, to Work and Pensions, and with pensions reform and incapacity benefit changes he was going to have a busy time of it. Good to see David M[iliband] in there for the first time, doing local government, along with Des Browne [Chief Secretary to the Treasury] and John Hutton [minister for the Cabinet Office].

Saturday 7 May

Fiona took Rory [son] to Cambridge to have a look around and see if he fancied the university so I was mainly looking after Grace [daughter] and talking to Calum [son] about this and that. Both TB and GB were calling me a fair bit, but I was kind of wanting to get away from it all now. I felt caught between them in a way I didn't really want to be. It was fine during the campaign because I had hands on levers, and a focus, but now it was not like that. I was not really in charge and so they looked to me to do things I could not deliver in the same way. It was about government now, and I wasn't going back. GB said he was pissed off at the way the reshuffle was done. I said he will maybe find out one day just how awful it is to do them, and they are not science. They are about people and difficult. He was back to his 'The problem is…' mode. He said he hadn't realised Blunkett was coming back to that job. Out and about with Calum, then we went out for dinner. I took part in the No. 10 conference call because I was doing TV in the morning. Loads of 'Blair must go' stuff, which was ludicrous.

Sunday 8 May

Up to do *Breakfast with Frost* and [Adam] Boulton on Sky and deal with the nonsense in the Sundays, re 'TB must go, say MPs'. It was incredible, that he deliver a third win and the third biggest Labour majority outside the landslides, and these people were saying either that he go, or that New Labour is dead. I was willing to accept that the vote is a rejection of the Iraq policy by some, but not a rejection of New Labour. At TB's behest I tried to get a briefing sorted with Ed Balls [GB advisor, newly elected Labour MP for Normanton] to get them on to the same page again, but GB repeated to Balls what he said to me yesterday – that he had not been aware re Blunkett's new job, not properly consulted on the reshuffle and it was back to the old days. I had been up for it up to

5 May but was feeling very fed up that I was still having to negotiate between the two of them to get lines agreed and put out. In the end TB had to be entitled to pick his own government, but GB was signalling that he considered him weakened by the vote and he was being told by his own people that in so far as we won, it was because GB came back in for the campaign.

I was beginning to feel resentful that I was still having to do this stuff, try to get them to work together and be in the same place publicly. It was hard not to feel sorry for TB, who had after all won the bloody election again, but equally I was now keen to move on. I felt I defended him well on TV and reminded people that self-indulgence cost us dear in the past, and we should not go back to it, particularly not now. Part of the problem was that our people had got used to winning and so they felt they could mess around now, like winning was the natural order of things. It wasn't, and losing would very quickly become the habit again if too many people carried on like all these MPs whining and moaning in the Sundays and on the airwaves.

I did a series of calls with TB, Ed B, David Hill [director of communications] to try to get it all sorted. TB called later and said he wanted a briefing that he was going to fight for the reforms, that it was ridiculous he was being portrayed as a villain, and he was going to be absolutely gung-ho about reform at the PLP. He said he was fed up with GB, that he only ever thought of himself. They had had a fairly difficult conversation this morning, when TB had said to GB that he would be best served by helping with the reform programme. Their interests actually coincided, if only he could see that. If he didn't support the basic thrust of the reforms, then when TB went it would be said New Labour went with him, and that would be a mistake for GB. GB was reverting to type. He said he was not going to sign up to briefings that were untrue... He said to me, 'I know you don't want to get involved, but you have to stop this Adonis appointment, it will be a total disaster.' TB was determined to get Andrew [Adonis, director, No. 10 Policy Unit] in at education, convinced he needed his drive and radicalism. I told GB he was overstating things, and that Andrew had a good brain and it was daft to make such a big deal of this. The public just will not understand if the infighting returns on the back of an election win.

Clive [Woodward, rugby coach] called, said he really wanted us to make big news, especially in New Zealand, about the fact that Jonny Wilkinson [rugby player] was fit and coming with us [on the British and Irish Lions tour] to NZ. He wanted to use it to send a message to

Graham Henry [All Blacks coach]. Jonny had described Clive as the best coach he ever worked with. I called Louisa [Cheetham, Lions' press officer] and we got out good words all round though the main focus was still the climax of the football season.

The Sundays having been full of it, the Mondays just carried on where they left off. You really would think the winners had lost, and the losers had won. In *The Times*, Phil Webster [political editor] did a good piece on the line I had used in the telly interviews yesterday about TB fighting back hard at the PLP and making clear there would be no backing down on reform. But the combination of a reshuffle that was a bit messy plus the direct calls on him to go were making things pretty tough for him at the moment. I was getting angrier and angrier at the notion you could be kicked in the slats for winning.

It was interesting how many of my friends in sport seemed to be really offended by it – Clive, Alex [Ferguson, Manchester United manager] and Brendan [Foster, former athlete, now businessman and commentator] all called at various stages during the day and said it was unbelievable this was happening. Brendan was absolutely raging. He said it is like you win an Olympic final by one second, but because you won the last one by two seconds, and the one before that by three, this one doesn't really count. CW said it was the first rule of teamship – play as a team and stick together. No slagging off. 'He must be absolutely gutted at this,' he said. 'I know I would be. In fact I can't think of any circumstances where I have seen this kind of thing before.'

What worried TB was the sense of his authority constantly being weakened. Pat McFadden [former special advisor, newly elected Labour MP for Wolverhampton South East] was doing a good job on the media pushing the pro-TB line, but there were so many voices on the other side causing trouble, on and off the record. A lot was also now focusing on Andrew Adonis, who was becoming a bit of a symbol of the divisions between Blairites and the rest. I know from discussions at home that he can be a real touch-paper personality, especially on education, but TB was adamant that if we were serious about reform, Andrew had the right approach on schools, he had guts and he would be a good education minister. He had mentioned it to Ruth Kelly [Education Secretary] that he might do it. She – or her spad – had told GB or Balls. So it was set up in the press as GB won't let it happen. The feeling was GB was at it again though that wasn't coming through the papers much. I had said to TB that I thought AA was too neuralgic for some and that particularly right now it might turn out to be a mistake, in that it would fire up even more antis to him staying as leader. I sent him a note saying fine if he is convinced he can't do the reform programme without him, but asking that he really think through whether it might turn out to be bad for both of them.

When we spoke later, I said the fact he would have to make him [as a non-MP] a peer overnight didn't help either. 'Oh, for fuck's sake,' he said. He felt now that he had no option. One, he said, it was the right thing to do. Two, these fuckers were basically saying, 'You may have won the election, but we are going to stop you doing the things you said you would, like reform public services. Well, bollocks to that.' Bruce [Grocott, Labour peer, formerly TB's parliamentary private secretary] was apoplectic about it. He called me just as I was getting back from a run. 'He cannot put Andrew into education,' he said. 'The comrades just won't wear it.' Well, they're going to have to, I said. His mind is made up. Alex called again. 'What the fuck is happening?' he said. 'I cannot believe the way he is getting treated. Do these MPs think people voted for them, rather than for Tony and the party as a whole?' He said the same thing as Clive said, that TB had every right to be furious. He just had to hold his head up and keep going.

I spent a lot of the day working on the stuff Clive had asked me to do when I joined the Lions for the next awayday session. Humphrey Walters [leadership consultant, friend of Woodward] sent through a note on his impressions of the players and he felt a lot of them were really quite shy and not forthcoming. Ben Wilson [press officer] thought they would be intimidated by me. Clive said he wanted me to give them a very basic education in the media, how it works, why it matters, how it can help them, how it can harm them. I did a piece basically trying to set out what we meant by communications. Maybe it will go over their heads but I don't think so. I was starting to worry about being away for so long on the trip to NZ especially as my return to the political fray these past few months had set things back with Fiona a bit. But also because Grace was pulling hard at the heartstrings and it was going to be less driven and demanding than what I had been doing. I sat down and spent a while writing a few handwritten thank-you letters for the campaign.

As well as the Adonis appointment, some of the antis saw Shaun Woodward getting a ministerial job, Beverley Hughes making a comeback, and Paul Drayson going into the Lords to do defence. But TB was clear that he needed good people in the right places and he could not be hemmed in by the nonsense people were trying to peddle out of the result last week. I did a bit of work on the speech I was due to be doing at RBS, then into town to get some new running shoes. In the papers, one or two voices were beginning to come out for TB a bit more. His mood was pretty low at the moment and I can't say I blame him. I met up with Parna [Basu, AC's assistant during the campaign] to thank her for her work and she said we ought to find a way of keeping me involved even if only part-time. She was really worried about the TB–GB thing just sliding right back. [TB political advisor] Sally Morgan's departure was announced so I did a bit of ringing round the hacks to talk her up.

The TB situation settled down a bit. I called him and said at the PLP tomorrow he should say the best route to opposition is to start behaving like we used to when we were in it. He felt things had swung back his way a bit in the last twenty-four hours, in part just out of most people's basic sense of decency. But GB was a little bit back to his old games, for example, when TB said he would like to run through the junior jobs in the reshuffle with him, GB said, 'No, no, it's your reshuffle not mine.' TB said that would be fine but then they go out and brief he has been monstrously excluded from all the key decisions. 'I tried to tell him, tried to involve him, promoted some of his people, like Yvette [Cooper, to housing minister] but it was obvious he had decided the line he wanted to run was that he was being excluded, that we had brought him in for the campaign because without him I am a liability, but now I'm back in No. 10, he is back out in the cold. It is monstrous.'

I was doing an interview for *The Times* tomorrow and we talked over a few lines for that. He said I needed to be more scalpel than fist, e.g., yes to saying RC [Robin Cook] had said Clause Four review would destroy the party* but no to saying some of our ministers were shit. Pat was doing well on media and he loved the fact Alex F called me to say who was this Pat McFadden he heard on the radio because he's excellent. TB said most of the new MPs were fine. Some said Iraq had been a

---

* In his first leader's speech at the Labour Party conference in 1994, Tony Blair had announced that Labour needed a new statement of aims and values. The new version, abandoning the public ownership principles of the original Clause Four, was adopted the following Easter.

problem, others that it was immigration that had really damaged us. He sounded a lot chirpier today than yesterday and felt he could see a way through. Michael Howard [Conservative leader] announced his shadow Cabinet. George Osborne [Tory MP for Tatton] shadow Chancellor at thirty-three. Howard having already announced he would be stepping down, TB felt fairly sure David Davis [shadow Home Secretary] would be next leader. He thought he was OK but limited. Someone sent me a big piece from a German paper on how TB had betrayed GB by not going after two terms, saying he would pay a heavy price.

Wednesday 11 May

I had a bad throat and was also feeling a bit depressed. I did a bit of work upstairs, then my interview with Robert Crampton for *The Times*. Sara Latham [communications consultant] popped round. What with Parna maybe doing Katie Kay's job as diary secretary in No. 10 and John Woodcock [Labour official] asking me re whether he should work for John Hutton, I seemed to be taking on a bit of a careers advice role. Sally called me after the PLP, said it had been tough but TB held his own. She said there was a lot of anger in there, mainly the usual suspects but not just them. Also there was a lot of anger among loyalists at the rebels and the mood was a bit nasty. She said GB had just sat there looking a bit sullen and morose. It was going to be rough for a while. Her own departure had not got massive coverage and she seemed quite pleased about that.

Crampton really pushed me on GB, clearly thought I was closer to him politically than I was to TB, keen to know whether I could ever work for him, how the deal to get him back in the campaign was put together etc. etc. But it was fine I think and hopefully a clear top line hitting back against those calling for TB's resignation, with maybe a GB subsidiary line. Jayne Woodward [Clive's wife] called very excited because the Palace had confirmed that Prince William was coming out for the last two Tests in NZ. Everyone was all of a twitter about it but it was not exactly rugby rebranded. Grace was getting very upset about me going and I was getting anxious about it at home generally. Even though I was coming home in the middle of the Tour, because I had a couple of things I couldn't move, it was a long time to be away after a busy period doing the election, especially as the main reason for quitting in the first place was to be able to have more freedom and more time with them.

And I wasn't yet totally sure the rugby thing was me, or that it would work out professionally. Clive was adamant I was the right man for the job, but a lot would depend on whether the media felt the same way. It did not need to be as adversarial as politics but if they decided to make it so, there would not be that much I could do about it. The workload on it was picking up a bit and I was looking forward to working with the players and the coaches. I had a bit of a logistical nightmare both getting down to Wales to do the session with the Lions next week and doing the RBS speech in London, but Humphrey [Walters] came to the rescue as his son is a helicopter pilot, and volunteered to take me.

Thursday 12 May

TB did a press conference focused on the respect and anti-social behaviour agenda. The topline seemed to be that he was backing a ban on hoodies, which was a classic, and not very good, example of the bigger and more important picture being shrouded by something more trivial. It was another odd day in which I felt half in and half out of things. They sent over his speech to me a couple of times and I fed in a few thoughts but not with great enthusiasm. Also Fiona was having a few people round from our local Labour Party branch and they were all to a greater or lesser extent in grungy mode so I was fucked off with that. I was getting a lot of conflicting advice and pressure. Tim Allan [AC's former deputy, now owner of his own PR firm] and Philip [Gould, pollster and strategist] – maybe put up to it by TB – were both on at me saying I really needed to go back in some form, that I had been central to holding them together during the campaign, and there was a real danger if I left them to it. Ed Balls was saying much the same thing, that I had managed to get them working together and there were not that many people that both of them respected and would work with.

I had only really been able to get through the last few weeks by having the election day as a cut-off point and it just hadn't happened, I was still trapped in there to a far bigger extent than I wanted. TB kept saying he was resigned to me not going back in, but he still knew how to press the buttons, and he did. It wasn't helping with Fiona. She said she had decided that the only way to avoid being hurt was to let me do what I wanted to do, and if she seemed indifferent to whatever decisions I took, that was my lookout. It meant I didn't really have anyone to talk to about it properly. Philip I suppose, but he had his own vested interest for wanting me more not less involved. I went to bed early, feeling like shit.

Friday 13 May

I left early for Putney and an all-morning meeting with Louisa Cheetham, Ben Wilson and Marcus Jansa [Lions media team]. Alex called halfway through, the papers full of Malcolm Glazer [US business family trying to gain control of Manchester United] being almost there with the takeover. He said he was going to sit tight and not declare any hand. If he got the boot he would get a big pay-off and there would be plenty of clubs would want him. If they wanted him to stay he was strengthened. So he wasn't planning to get publicly embroiled, even if the fans started to press on it. I was sure that was the right approach. He said the worst thing at the moment was that his players were not delivering.

The Lions meeting was OK, loads to do but they seemed on top of it. Louisa C was good and hard-working, though I think a bit surprised that I was interested in doing this. It seemed a bit weird that it was now so close. We had an OK day-by-day plan. It was nothing like as adrenalin-charged as planning an election or big diplomatic visits but hopefully it would get there. We were due to leave on my birthday, which apparently was the same as Jonny Wilkinson's [25 May]. I was getting really worried about Grace, who seemed properly upset about the whole thing, and I was worried too that the campaign seemed to have set me and Fiona back, and this might make it worse.

I got a message saying TB wondered if I could pop in so I headed there on the way home from Putney. He was out on the terrace going through a few boxes. It was warm and sunny, and the birds were singing away. He was wearing a beige suit which reminded me of the first time I ever met him, years ago, but at least this one vaguely fitted. I walked out and he looked surprised and pleased to see me. 'I didn't know if you'd be able to make it. Nobody seemed to know where you were.' We talked a bit about sport, and I passed on what some of the sports people had been saying. That's because they get the whole team thing, he said, and also it must seem a bit odd to reasonable people that I deliver a win in pretty tough circumstances and I have my own side turn against me. But he said he had recovered his equilibrium after a bit of a wobble and he was settled in his own mind – he knew what he wanted to do, particularly on public services. If he was knocked off his perch in the process, fine. But he knew what he wanted to do. Likewise if the party suddenly wanted him out and GB in, he would live with it. He was settled. He would rather do what he thought was right and get kicked out for it than play a compromise-consensus game on policies he didn't really believe in.

He said GB had slightly gone back to type. He was in no doubt at all now that he had gone out of his way to avoid TB telling him what he had been planning in the reshuffle so that he could then say he had not been consulted. TB said he tried to tell him three times. Also on some of the policy stuff, TB asked him why health was doing better here than in Scotland or Wales and he had some complex argument that was nothing to do with reform. He asked me what I was going to do workwise. I said I didn't know. I didn't feel I could come back but didn't know what else to do in terms of any full-time job. Part of me felt I didn't want one, that I needed a bit more freedom to diversify and be my own boss on things. He said, 'You were fucking awesome during the campaign. No other word for it. You totally gripped it and everyone knows it.' He said even GB said so, though not without sideswiping everyone else. TB said GB had said, 'There's only one person in your team of any talent at all.' He repeated that he thought that though GB had always retained a little fear about me, he had seen again during the campaign that I was willing to help him if he played ball, and he seemed to have got something out of that. His hunch was GB would want me around in some way.

He said he is almost certainly the best option to take over as PM, but God knows how he would deal with the pressure and all the personal attacks that come with the territory. We went over some of the things we'd been through and how GB might have reacted differently. I was there for an hour, maybe a bit more, and it was a nice, reflective chat. He seemed a lot more relaxed now. He said at one point in the run-up, he had been worried I wasn't engaging but suddenly I kicked in and after that it was all fine. Then he said if I ever wanted any job I just had to ask. He didn't think I should come back to a press job – he wanted Tim [Allan] to help out with comms if he could get him – but he felt I could do a big job in the party, remotivating and rebuilding. He felt the party had a basic instinct I was a good thing and I could rebuild. And he felt GB would approve.

He sort of felt GB was going to be OK. But he had put forward a paper for the next couple of years and GB told him it wasn't good enough – 'like I was a pupil and he was the pupil master'. So TB said, 'Why don't you come up with some ideas?' and GB said, 'That's not my job!' At least he was laughing about it but it was tough. He told a very funny story of how Nigel Griffiths [deputy leader of the Commons], who he was intending to put out, kept a job. Nigel had said to him he intended to go to the PLP and say these attacks on TB were monstrous and had to stop. Then he said, 'Now I've kept one job do I have another?' TB said I was thinking of sacking you but now I'm not so sure. He made him deputy to Geoff Hoon [Commons leader]. He felt the second part of the reshuffle, in which he had imposed his will a bit more, and also the press conference, had put him in a stronger position.

Saturday 14 May

The *Times* interview came out OK, though maybe I was a bit hard on Dobbo [former minister Frank Dobson] and Robin [Cook, former minister] but there was lots of positive feedback from our people. I went for a walk with Fiona to resume a discussion from last night and it was all quite emotional by the end. She just felt she couldn't cope with having to address it all again and again, and that our problems always flared up when I was immersed in that political hothouse atmosphere, with everyone putting me under pressures which necessarily took me away and played to my strengths and weaknesses at the same time. But she was the one left to pick up everything else, and she honestly thought it was going to stop but it never really did. I took Calum to play tennis with Philip [Gould], who was still saying we did well and I should not be down about the result. We could easily have lost, he said. TB was in big trouble at certain points and we held it up. Rory had a race and I went to see him. He ran well but came second and was a bit disappointed.

Sunday 15 May

Out to see the Goulds and I was in a better mood. I was worried about these waves of tiredness I was getting. It was great talking to Georgia [Gould, PG's daughter] about politics – she was so enthusiastic about the party and the future. I read Lindsay's book, *Living on the Seabed* [Lindsay Nicholson, widow of AC's best friend John Merritt, had written a memoir having lost both John and their daughter Ellie to leukaemia], which was really powerful, and had me in tears at more than one point. I emailed her to say I felt it showed an extraordinary honesty and self-awareness and that it would help people understand grief better. It was kind of odd to think I was going on a rugby tour to New Zealand quite soon. Philip thought it was a good thing to be doing, but I could tell Gail, who is so not a sports fan, thought it was really odd.

The *Independent on Sunday* diary ran a story based on someone in the RFU saying I knew nothing about rugby and was just doing it to promote myself. Little did they know I was half regretting going because I was going to miss the family, and I was feeling a bit guilty and worried about leaving the political scene. F and I were like a stuck record re TB. I spoke to him about it when we talked later and he felt that though she might have issues with some of the policy stuff, it was probably as much about me as about him. There might be something in that, though I think there was a bit of his wishful thinking too. He still had a lot of fondness for Fiona, and knew that she had had to put up with a lot as a result of me working for him, but he said he thought when finally we were all free of it, she would be glad I had done it.

Monday 16 May

Tessa [Jowell, Culture, Media and Sports Secretary] came round for a chat about the 2012 Olympics bid. She was fairly confident but felt they still had a lot to do. I felt they needed a change of gear and a new narrative to take them through the last stages. In a way, the ability of London to deliver it had to be a given, and instead get more focus on the fact that the whole world is here already. Also, there was mileage to be gained from what appeared to be a complacency and an arrogance in the French feeling that it was in the bag. The trouble of course with these big sporting venue races is that you could never really know whether people were not saying different things to different teams about who they intended to support. I was working on transcribing the '98 diary, through the Good Friday Agreement, and so much of the detail I had totally forgotten. There were parts of it that I had completely blanked as the days rolled into one another. But I felt really emotional when I got to the bit where it all came together. It was probably the best day of the lot, certainly one of them.

I had a nice lunch with Rory, so enjoying his company at the moment, partly because, of the immediate family, I think he was the one who most enjoyed and appreciated the stuff I did workwise, and we had a good chat re things before he went back to school. TB called asking for lines for his Queen's Speech debate tomorrow. He said he was really happy re the policy programme, and felt in some ways it was the best QS yet. I said you say that every year. He said, 'Maybe I have to think that but I do feel we are in the right place. I just feel now we have the three wins under our belt and I just have to go for it. If they kick me out, they kick me out. But there is no point being here if you don't do what you think you should.' I said it was important not to portray the whole thing as such a radical departure, because a lot of the changes did flow from the previous two terms.

He was very keen to press the education reform buttons, though, along with welfare, crime and the respect agenda, and I worked a bit on sharpening the lines he was planning to use. I had a worry he would push the choice theme too hard, partly as two fingers to the MPs trying to cause trouble. There was a lot of other stuff in there too, though, like the ID cards, smoking ban, preparing for the Olympics if we win the bid, knife crime, corporate manslaughter, charities, religious hatred etc. It was actually not a bad Queen's Speech, pretty ambitious.

Tuesday 17 May

Grace was really upset last night and I felt pretty wretched leaving, even though I would be back tomorrow briefly. Essentially I was now gone and with Calum really having to gear up for GCSEs, it was a bad time to be going. Also I had no idea whether I was going to enjoy it or whether I could make much of a difference. Ben [Wilson] picked me up at 8 and we headed off to the Vale of Glamorgan hotel. It was a little bit first day at school, people getting to know each other. We had to collect suits – mine didn't fit – then mountains of Adidas gear. Even the non-players were kitted out, so my massive bag contained loads of rugby shirts, shorts, socks, boots, tracksuits, the lot, all embossed with 'AC'. Clive did what he thought was going to be a little briefing, an informal chat, but it turned out to be a lot bigger than that, and he complained to Louisa that he had felt unprepared. So although I had mentioned the story about Prince William going out for the Tests, he felt he was on the defensive a bit too much. It wasn't that bad but he beat himself up about it pretty badly. He called me as I was going to bed and said he really felt it was the one part of the day that hadn't gone well for him. He was blaming Louisa but I felt I had to take some of the responsibility.

The rest of the day was taken up with admin meetings, lunch and dinner in the leisure room, and the first proper session, all dressed in red top and blue track bottoms. Bill Beaumont [Lions manager, former England captain] did yet another welcome, CW did a good spiel, his basic theme that winning was about inches not miles, they were going to the most rugby-obsessed nation in the world, with some of the greatest players, but one thing he was sure of was this would be the best-prepared tour ever, and above all if we get things right off the field we get them right on it. The players, in the main, sat still and silent, just listening. The English guys who were with him when they won the World Cup obviously knew him well, but for the others they were seeing him in this kind of action for the first time and it was interesting to watch their reaction. Hard to gauge but I felt they sensed something quite impressive. Ben may have been right that some of them found it a bit intimidating – or maybe just odd – that I was there, especially having just done the election.

The Irish were definitely the most relaxed and welcoming, I would say. Shane Horgan and Denis Hickie [Irish players] were totally fascinated about our politics, and just straight into picking my brains, asking about the election and then back a bit, to Northern Ireland, and lots about Iraq. Some of them were saying congratulations on the election. I sensed that Mike Ford [defence coach] was very pro-us, definitely pro-TB. I had lunch with Brian O'Driscoll and Ronan O'Gara [Irish players] and Ronan was joking about how he would hang around [Manchester United footballer] Roy Keane's door for his autograph when United checked in for the Cup Final. I think the hotel people were pretty excited too, having the Lions team and the United team, in Wales for the FA Cup Final, at the same time.

I was talking to United about maybe doing some pictures together, taking e.g. Keane with one of the Irish players, Darren Fletcher [Manchester United and Scotland footballer] with one of the Scots, Ryan Giggs [United and Wales] with a Welsh player, and maybe Rio Ferdinand [United and England player] with an English player. Iain Balshaw [England rugby player] had had to pull out through injury, and Mark Cueto [England player] was called up to replace him, and we got him to do some media. Nice guy, another United fan.

TB called later, said the Queen's Speech had gone pretty well. He had banged home the 'quintessentially New Labour' line. Most people seemed to be going on a mix of the respect agenda – 'The decent majority reclaiming the streets' – and the education and health reforms. He thought Howard's heart wasn't really in it.

Wednesday 18 May

I had breakfast with Richard Smith, the tour lawyer, Graeme Rowntree [England player], Michael Owen [Welsh player] and Bill Beaumont. Clive was pissed off last night at the lack of newspaper cuttings so I got Ben W to sort, which he did via media monitoring. At my first HOD [heads of department] meeting he got Louisa C to go over the day, then Otis [Dave Reddin, fitness coach] re what he needed for training, including wanting to fine players if they didn't take the right supplements. Clive said just warn them they could lose the series for us. But don't fine. We talked over press and he said he thought yesterday was really badly organised. I said the output was not bad. The important thing was only to do something like that when he had something proper to say. We agreed he, Owen and Ian McGeechan [coach] for the press conference before the Argentina match. I spent bits of the morning doing his words.

I was a bit surprised at the way he announced the team. I guess they just had to get used to it, but there were a lot of disappointed players given only fifteen could start. We had such a big squad and I could sense the frustration when he read out the names. He said those not picked for this pre-Tour game in Cardiff had to think of being in the first side in NZ. Those who were injured – there were five of them on the list at the moment – had to think the same. His approach was to tell everyone together and they just had to deal with disappointment. When I asked him later if he always did it like that, he said basically yes. You might have a special situation where you really needed to manage someone especially carefully, or when you worried that leaving someone out would affect the whole team mentally, not just the player, but they were in a tough environment and they knew there was no easy way. We took CW, BB, Michael Owen and Ian McGeechan up to the barn for the presser, which went OK.

Louisa was clearly a bit upset at yesterday. I told her not to worry, and later told Clive we all fucked up, not just her, and she was a bit down. He said, 'What, very, very down?' No, just very. He seemed to think that was OK, because yesterday had not been good enough. He smiled, but said he would have a word. Jonny Wilkinson came over to do his share of interviews and we had a really nice chat while CW was doing Sky. He was really friendly but incredibly intense. I asked when he would be doing columns. He wasn't sure, said he didn't like doing them around a match because he was so focused. The day after a match he just liked to be in his room. I asked if he liked doing the media. He said he understood he had to deal with it but he didn't like all the attention on him at the expense of the other players, e.g. he had played less than the others but was getting the most attention. It was wrong. He said he felt very self-conscious when the other players were there and yet the focus was on him. He hated that bit. He then did his round of interviews, then a gaggle where he was swarmed. The other players had maybe one or two people talking to them.

Mick Cleary [*Daily Telegraph*] and Peter Jackson [*Daily Mail*] were badgering me about the the the fact I would be doing a column for *The Times*. I defended myself, but I could see they had a point. I said I would try my best to make sure I did not use stuff that really I should be giving to all of them too. Shane Horgan and Denis Hickie wanted another chat about the election. They were a good double act; one would ask the question, the other would pile in during my answer. They were both bright though. Gavin Henson [Wales player, partner of singer Charlotte Church] seemed very much a loner and I wondered how he would cope without proper support if the media really went for him. The atmosphere among the hacks was better than yesterday. Did a note to CW re the press events and how we had to raise through the gears once we were there. I had to get back to London for the dinner I was speaking at.

Thursday 19 May

I had a tearful farewell with Fiona and the kids, with Grace really upset, and telling me she hadn't slept at all and she just didn't want me to go. So I felt pretty low heading out to Battersea to wait for Mark Walters and his helicopter. The weather was bad and so I had to hang around for almost two hours, during which I went through the big red folder with all the Lions info in it and also worked up a plan on how to deal with the various bids I was getting. It was pretty clear the New Zealanders were going to be interested in my role and Clive wanted me to use the profile to stir it a bit when we got there. The flight down was fine and we landed in Wales just after 2. The United squad had arrived for the FA Cup Final at the Millennium Stadium against Arsenal on Saturday and the first person I bumped into was Roy Keane, who was in cracking form, recalling the Eamonn Dunphy [broadcaster, former footballer] show we had done together in 2003, and not seeming terribly sad about its demise. As far as the Glazer takeover was concerned, he said the players just got on with it, there was no point worrying.

I saw Alex, who said he had one or two injury worries and looked and sounded a bit nervous about the whole thing. I fixed the Man U photocall for tomorrow, taking one player from each of the four nations from both teams. Then out to training, travelled with Ian McGeechan, who took me through the notes he had prepared, a new move called Overlord, which he reckoned they could launch six or more times during a match. There was a real passion about it as he explained it. He said he had kept all his notes from every training session he had ever done. I said that is auction treasure trove territory. The game was changing so fast, really advancing from the amateur years. He had little maps of where the players were meant to be at any point in a given move. Tony Biscombe [video analyst] took me through all the technology used to follow every player on the field of play, and the kind of data they could gather, and how they used it. All of the coaches, at the session and over dinner in Cardiff, were saying the level of players was higher than what they were used to. Eddie O'Sullivan [Irish coach] said he had some great players in the Ireland team but then after the top guys there were a few who were a level below. Here they were all quality.

It was interesting to watch Wilkinson, who was very different on the pitch to off it, full of confidence, incredibly commanding, giving out instructions, constantly engaging with the players and the coaches. Then the minute he came off, it was like he wanted to melt into the crowd. Fascinating guy. Nice day, maybe 200 people turned up just to watch. I was still grappling with how to establish the best use of my time. We had an informal management meeting at which CW said the only feedback from Brian O'Driscoll was the feeling of some of the players that they didn't know whether they were allowed to enjoy themselves. I raised the issue of photos at training and said we should try to engineer better pictures if we could, and get the press out of their hair earlier. Some days we may not want any pictures at all.

All aboard the bus and out for dinner, travelled up front with Clive, who was asking what I would do in the future. He suggested I set up a consultancy just to be on the end of the phone to various big-name clients, e.g. he said Andy Robinson [English coach] was complaining about his operation. Clive was always very intense whereas Gareth Jenkins [Welsh coach] and Eddie O'Sullivan started to let their hair down a bit. Gareth was really funny, very good with words and mega Labour. Eddie said his ambition was to take the next Lions tour and this was the blueprint. If we won, it would be deemed a success. If we lost by one point, everyone would say taking such a big party had been a mistake. TB called after getting back to Chequers [Prime Minister's country retreat] after his trip to the Royal Free [Hospital in north London] to get an injection for his slipped disc. To be fair to him, it was amazing he had lasted as long as he did, especially during the campaign. Earlier Grace gave me a little folder of pictures to take with me, and told me I couldn't look at them till later, and when I did it was major heartstring stuff.

Friday 20 May

At HOD, we went over whether to do the new picture approach straight away or let it bed down with the players first. The only real media issue was Neil Back [Leicester and England player] and whether he should appeal over the four-week ban he had been given for a punch in the Leicester–Wasps Cup Final. CW and Richard Smith saw him and agreed, though he was reluctant, to let it go. The truth is it was a bad punch, and Joe Worsley had needed thirteen stitches, but they felt there was a lot of politics in it and that the sentence was disproportionate, especially as it meant missing international matches too. I drafted a statement for CW and Neil, which they agreed and which we got out quickly. Clive was keen to emphasise that even if the old farts did not recognise Back's qualities, we did. BB told me there had been some real objections at the RFU to my invitation to the France match at Twickenham. CW was scathing of the RFU, and of the sport's general culture, and said there were still too many hangovers from the amateur era.

Gareth Jenkins filled me in on salaries. Young players starting out with Llanelli maybe 15k, average players maybe 30. The top could get up to 80. English players better off. Internationals depended on win bonuses. Very few made plans for after. Some of the guys playing in France could be on 100, 150k. Some of the top players in England closer to 200 but rare. So the Man U players were in a different league. I had a late breakfast with Alex and Carlos [Queiroz, Ferguson's assistant], joined by Albert [Morgan, kitman] and later some of the players wandered in. AF said he was fairly relaxed about Glazer, as did Keane later, who said people find it hard to believe but the players just don't get involved. AF was looking and sounding a bit nervous about the Final and was desperate to win. He wasn't a big rugby fan, didn't seem particularly interested in what they were up to. He asked how TB was coping with all the shit thrown at him since winning. Later we had our Man U–Lions photocall – Brian O'Driscoll with Keane, Rio with Lawrence Dallaglio [England], Fletcher and Chris Cusiter [Scottish rugby international], Owen and Giggs. The Man U guys were really friendly and Roy and BOD had a good old natter. As they went out, Roy yelled out 'Come on, Ireland' at all the English players.

He was telling everyone why he hated Arsenal. He and I had a chat after about Burnley, and he said he was definitely going to look to go into management. He reckoned he had another year as a player and then he was going for his other badges. He knew he would have to start low down, that just because he worked with Brian Clough [Keane's manager

May '05: When the Lions meet Man United

when he played at Nottingham Forest] and Ferguson meant nothing. Giggs was very friendly too, said he was really pleased to see TB up in Manchester. Good pictures. CW had a problem after training, with Simon Taylor [Scotland player] and Mal O'Kelly [Ireland player] both picking up injuries. He thought it was because everyone, including the coaches, was trying too hard to impress. Taylor looked pretty fed up at dinner, and clearly sensed he was in trouble. Clive got in all the coaches, medics and fitness guys and bollocked them, said this was not necessary and counterproductive. He said the players were so competitive they had gone wild in the conditioning sessions, and were over-tired and so picking up injuries.

The other thing I had to do was my first so-called masterclass on the media. I went through my spiel on comms, then gave them some case studies to do. How would they have handled Robin Cook's affair exposé; the time NATO bombed the Chinese Embassy;* then a couple of sports ones, which they did better. Eddie O'Sullivan was pretty quick. Steve Thompson [England player] was at a forwards' table who didn't really get into it but they were having a laugh by the end. CW said, as did Jayne, in their nice OTT way, that it was brilliant. He said, you had JW and BOD hanging on every word and when you said you would help with ghosted columns, there was a huge sigh of relief. JW got into the discussions after a while and could get very animated. The Irish, though, were the ones who really got into it, plus some of the Welsh too. I enjoyed it and I think most of them did.

Afterwards CW said he was convinced I should set myself up as a sports consultancy. He had mentioned me to Rupert Lowe [Southampton FC chairman] and said he wanted me to go down there. What was interesting in the Q&A was how little some of them knew – e.g. on Robin Cook, only one of the five groups remembered the story. One or two asked whether NATO was the UN. But they were a pretty good bunch and the feedback was good. JW said he found it really interesting, that he had never really looked at it from the other side. I went to collect Rory from Cardiff then back for a drink with CW, Jayne and one or two others in the bar. CW had three or four pints of Guinness. He and Jayne

---

* In 1997, AC explained to the then Foreign Secretary that the press was about to reveal the extramarital affair Cook was having with a member of his staff, Gaynor Regan. About to go on holiday with his wife, Cook announced from Heathrow Airport that he was to leave her and marry Gaynor. In 1999, during NATO bombing of Yugoslavia, five US-guided bombs erroneously hit the Chinese Embassy in Belgrade, killing three journalists and enraging the Chinese public.

were at me again re doing more sports stuff in the future. He said he was definitely going to Southampton and he knew there was a lot of opposition in football. Re Dave Aldred [kicking coach], he said he was not necessarily a great team man but he was a superb one-on-one coach, the best there was at what he did. Rory enjoyed the night but shame he hadn't been there earlier with the Man U lot before they went to bed. Nice chat with Micky Phelan [Manchester United coach, former Burnley player] re his time at BFC. Also a good laugh with Paddy Crerand and Lou Macari [former United players], who were there commentating for MUTV [club channel]. Crerand was about as Labour as they come.

The issue of the UK rebate* looked like it was back on the table again, which would just add to TB's problems with the EU rotating presidency coming up.

Saturday 21 May

I couldn't sleep so went out for a run at half-five over the hotel golf course. At the HOD meeting, the team doctor, James Robson, said Simon Taylor's best-case scenario was three weeks out; worst-case was off the tour. O'Kelly was not so bad. He and Otis were a bit fed up because O'Kelly had done a training routine outside the one agreed with him. Humphrey Walters was there to watch and raised the subject of Gavin Henson. There was a feeling he was not engaging at all, and that some of the players would not put up with it for ever. CW wanted to come to my masterclass at 9 rather than sending Humphrey because he was going to take a close look at him with the others. I did my spiel, and felt today's group was much more engaged, and also maybe saw more than the guys yesterday what they might be able to get out of a better understanding of this stuff. I did two groups the same as yesterday – RC marriage and also a training ground punch-up. But I also did Euan [Blair, TB's son] being found drunk in Trafalgar Square, and a *Sun* undercover team setting up a player to admit match fixing. Lawrence Dallaglio, target of the tabloids over drugs, laughed halfway through and said, 'Do you want me to carry on from here?'[†] It was a great ice breaker.

---

* In 1984, Margaret Thatcher won a rebate on the UK's contribution to EU funds. French President Jacques Chirac, supported by Germany and Poland, was now asking for this to be reviewed. Tony Blair claimed the rebate was 'fully justified'.

† In 1999, Dallagio had resigned as England captain after newspaper allegations of boasting of drug use and drug dealing in the past. The player 'categorically denied' the drug dealing and said he had been the victim of a 'set-up'.

Josh Lewsey [England player] was very bright, and spiky, got to the point very quickly. Hickie seemed really bright too. Dallaglio and Richard Hill [England player] engaged a fair bit. One or two probably thought it was a waste of time, but the feedback from most was really good, and some realised it could help with their own media and, in some cases, their own futures. Matt Dawson [England player] said straight out he wanted advice on his own future media career. The section on the match-fixing scenario led to a really interesting discussion on morality and the limits of individual conduct. CW came in with a pretty heavy line, said that if they got set up doing something really stupid because they were so pissed they couldn't keep control, he would probably put them on the first plane home. Shane Byrne [Ireland player] came up to me afterwards and said quietly, 'Does that mean we can't have a drink?' I felt today went better than yesterday and that most of them now thought there probably was a purpose to me being there. I told Ronan O'Gara I would help with his *Irish Times* column. By the end even Dave Aldred – who had wanted to take his kickers out of the master-class – thought it was worthwhile and was engaging.

I had a brief chat with Alex and Rory in the foyer. He was on good form and the players seemed pretty psyched up by it all. He had a real intensity about winning this one. I did a Sky interview with Brian O'Driscoll on the Cup Final, and the mood was good. CW, me and four others had to go to the FA lunch. Nice enough do. On the way, CW sent me a text message he had received from the Garforth Town guy he had mentioned he was going to take to Southampton [Simon Clifford, owner and manager]. He said that he was a huge fan of mine, saw me as a winner who would not let Labour come second. Previously Labour had let the media roll over them. We had turned them and then controlled them. I said I didn't always feel like that. The first person I saw at the lunch at the stadium was Nancy [Dell'Olio, Italian lawyer who came to prominence in Britain as the girlfriend of former England football manager Sven-Göran Eriksson]. She was very flirty and funny, happy we had won again, wanting to meet up, asking me what I was doing with all these big rugby men. She was pressing me not to leave politics. 'Toneee neeeeds you, dahling,' then her big sexy laugh.

David Davies [FA executive] was there with Susan [wife], and felt I would enjoy the Lions but end up feeling it was all second best. 'Your problem is that everything is going to be second best.' The Iraqi Ambassador was there and was with an Iraqi who came over to say Iraq owed its future to TB and history would judge him kindly. Tom Pendry [Labour peer] was sitting next to Richard Smith, who later told me Tom gave him the usual angry stuff that I was to blame for him being the only member of the shadow team in 1997 not to go into government, as sports minister. He said TB had dropped him a note because he had spoken out against those calling for his resignation, but could not resist adding, 'They at least had the chance.'

The match was pretty pulsating, really exciting at times, and the result unjust because United should have walked it, but Arsenal won on penalties. In so far as the Lions players were supporting anyone, I'd say most were backing United. Alex looked very hacked off at the end. Rory said he had rarely seen him so intense pre-match as when we saw him this morning. He had so wanted this one and even though he normally got over these defeats quickly, he looked absolutely gutted. There was also an amazing little spat with Arsene Wenger [Arsenal manager] and Gary Neville [Manchester United player] when Neville was trying to get drinks to players. Wenger was trying to stop him and water got flung around. I saw Cathy [Ferguson, AF's wife] afterwards, philosophical as ever, who said, 'Someone has to win, so someone has to lose.' TB called, said he had seen me in my nice blazer with CW. He wanted me to tell Alex that they totally deserved to win. He sounded on good form, felt he could see a plan for a way forward and wanted to talk to me about it on my return. 'I've been thinking how you can stay involved without being submerged,' he said, which sounded a bit ominous.

I had a good chat with Brian and Gary O'Driscoll [BOD's cousin, one of the Lions tour doctors] re the match, the election, the media. Matt Dawson signed up to doing a column for an NZ paper, which could be great fun. Dinner with Lewis Moody [England], Wilkinson, Chris Cusiter, Dave Campbell [chef], Gordon D'Arcy [Ireland]. JW had quite an interesting analysis of the game. They knew less about football than I thought they would, like not knowing who some of the players were. But all felt – apart from the Arsenal supporters – that it was totally unfair and wrong. But sometimes sport is like that. Some were doing computer games, watching match videos on laptops, table tennis, reading the papers. I did a press release re the new Lions anthem with Louisa, then drink in the bar and bed. Felt better about things today. CW said the players loved the media masterclass. I felt they were buying into it a bit. Martin Corry [England] seemed a pretty good bloke, I thought.

The papers were full of FA Cuppery, but also the Lions stuff was growing. The chat with *The Indy* came out OK, but the issue of my *Times* column was picking up a bit with some of the hacks, the idea that there had to be a conflict between being a communications advisor, there in part to help the press, and also a writer and commentator. Clive was completely relaxed, felt it was just one more useful vehicle for the Lions, but I could see they were going to keep having a go. Also the *Mail on Sunday* had a vile Patrick Collins piece on CW being mad to get me and Prince William involved. The *MoS* were also on to the Olympics theme, saying Prince William had snubbed the 2012 bid by deciding to go to NZ. I said to Clive that was the angle I was worried about. If we were to lose narrowly on the Olympics bid, then there were bound to be people saying if William had gone it might have made a difference, blahdiblah. But I don't doubt they had thought that all through before deciding he was definitely going to NZ, and of course he was signalling the interest by coming to the Argentina match before we left. I felt it might work out fine, but there was a risk from their perspective they were heading for a lose–lose situation which could also impinge on us once the pressure really rose.

I called Paddy Harverson [Prince Charles' press secretary] and asked whether he thought William going to Singapore for the Olympics meeting was reopenable, even if just a flying visit. He thought not. Prince Charles himself had decided it was too charged and high-profile, and NZ was a better option. I said the worst-case scenario was that we narrowly lost the bid, lack of high-level presence got blamed, and meanwhile back with us there was a circus around the royals on the tour, and it started to affect performance. I spoke also to Jamie Lowther-Pinkerton, the ex-SAS guy who was now William's private secretary. He said Singapore was no-go, and was not going to be reopened, but we agreed he, Louisa and I should meet up at the Millennium Stadium tomorrow – with William due to come, even though nobody knew about it till today – and go over the range of options. There was going to be the risk that William would be presented, whether we liked it or not, almost like he was part of the squad, so it was important we agreed both on the messaging and also when and how he would get publicly involved, e.g. at training sessions, visits and so forth.

I think re the Lions we were broadly on the same page, but I was fairly frank with him about the Olympics. I did feel they were making a mistake re the bid, especially as London's key theme was youth and the future. Paddy H said he had really tried but been overruled. Mike

Lee [Olympics bid advisor] and Tessa [Jowell] were also both pressing me to try to press them to change. Tessa said she remained confident we could win the bid, but it was very close and everything we could do just to get one more person over, we should do it. She said TB was going to be key, and asked if I could press for him to have as much Olympics time carved into his diary as possible. But she felt William would be a real positive for some of the votes they were targeting.

On the royals and the tour, I did Clive and Louisa a note saying we had to start to work out clarity about it all. One of the problems was it was all being done a little bit ad hoc through Jayne. After reading the papers, I did a quick *Times* column on the United–Arsenal match. HOD was fairly low key. James Robson said Taylor's injury had healed up a lot, and things were not as bad as they seemed yesterday. Maybe ten days. We went over community stuff, and also the need for pictures to go with the story about the new Lions anthem, 'The Power of Four', so Ben was organising the Lions choir to come down. Louisa, Ben and I set off for the Millennium Stadium. The roof was on. The kickers arrived first and both JW and ROG were pretty impressive to watch. How many thousands and thousands of times had they done this, and yet they took it as seriously as though it were the first time. Dave Aldred had also loosened up a lot with me, and we were discussing good picture ideas. They liked the Wilko pictures and TV got some good stuff when the players were practising their movements in lines. It all looked very technical and very impressive.

The staff at the stadium complained the kickers had come too early and JW and ROG had to leave to go to the Cardiff Blues pitch nearby. CW was livid when he heard and when he arrived, complete with baseball cap again, he looked pretty steamed up. 'Welcome to British sport,' he said. 'The greatest sportsman we have is not allowed to practise because he arrives too early. What kind of message does that send?' The rest of the players came, four did a picture with the Lions choir. We watched for a bit, then set off back to the hotel. Run, cycle, then dinner with Martin Corry and Bill B. I liked Corry. I asked him why he was writing a column for the most evil paper in the world. We had a good laugh about what he might say in it – 'Dear *Daily Mail* … AC is now in charge of my column, and here is today's. Had breakfast. It was nice. Trained. It was good. We have a match soon. I hope we win. Clive is fab and Alastair is fab. Having a lovely time, wish you were here.' He said the problem with these ghosted columns was that they were bland. I said we had to unbland them.

We had a good chat about what it was like being away so much when you had kids. A lot of these guys had young kids and spent a fair amount of time away from them, and I sensed for some of them it was easily the worst part of their life. He was also asking what Cherie [Blair] was like. He said he had talked to her a bit when they went to No. 10 after England won the World Cup, and he felt she was a bit nervy and not quite sure what it was all about. I said I felt sorry for her, the way she got treated by the media in a way Tory wives of PMs tended not to be. We had the anthem ready and we got BOD, then CW and Ben Kay [England] to hear it. Pretty good reaction really. I wasn't totally convinced about it myself, but with the four countries coming together you couldn't do a national anthem, so this was a good second best.

Monday 23 May

I didn't sleep well. The papers were OK, with some terrific pictures from the JW kicking session. Also, as Ben W said, the best pictures were the players just laughing while they trained and warmed up, and there were plenty of them. The *Mail* was the only paper to do the anthem big, but again with a dig at me, and at Prince William. We were becoming the two symbols of CW's alleged OTT-ness. *The Guardian* did a fairly straight piece on my role on the news page. Ben did an instant summary for HOD, which had better news on injuries. Louisa went through the day and again CW emphasised the importance of the community side of things, something he hammered home to the players later. I persuaded Clive it would be odd if he did not do the media after the match, but he still wanted Ian McGeechan to take the lead. I drafted words for Ian and for Bill's dinner speech, then worked on transcribing 1998 diary – our first major visit to Middle East. Parna sent through some stuff for the trip and said she was anxious about her new job lined up with TB and was still up for doing a job for me.

After a swim, I joined some of the players at lunch. It was interesting to see the different moods and approaches. JW said he always, always got nervous, no matter what the match. Corry said wouldn't it be great if we could bring the kick-off forward. JW said no, because once he knew it was an evening match, that was how he prepared. He said he tended to lie down for most of the afternoon, try to sleep, then wake up in a panic. He asked if politicians got nervous and I told them a few stories, like Bill Clinton before a press conference during the Lewinsky scandal when he seemed to have three phases – sort the detail in his mind, then have a joking-around couple of minutes, then withdraw; similar with TB e.g. at PMQs, conference, before a big meeting, but generally we used nerves to try to enhance performance, much as he did. They loved the story of TB having worn the same pair of shoes for every PMQs. Jonny said he would be terrified of something like a TV debate. Isn't it scary to kick a penalty that the match depends on with thousands in the stadium and millions on TV? He said the practice helped you push it out of your mind, and all you had was you, the ball and the posts.

I said it was not dissimilar for the politicians when they were under real pressure, in a parliamentary or a TV thing. They had to learn to focus on what they had to focus on. Steve Thompson was much friendlier than before, talking about football fans. I think they had sussed, if they didn't already know, that I was much more a football man than rugby, and that in England especially, there was still a sense that rugby saw itself as being a middle-class sport and looked down on football, and even more on Rugby League. But at the United–Arsenal match, a lot of them had been struck by the noise the United fans made, and an atmosphere that was a lot better than they tended to get at rugby. I asked him his neck size. 22. After lunch, we had the first of the community visits, which both Clive and Bill wanted to get noticed. Ben had one group of players, which he took to the barn, LC and I had the other – BOD and Paul O'Connell from the Irish boys, Matt Stevens, Dawson, Lewsey from England, Gordon Bulloch the Scot, Gethin Jenkins and Martyn Williams for Wales, one or two others – to a charity launch of Schoolchildren for Children.

I had a good chat with Matt Stevens [English player] on the way about his course in politics, and he was thinking of doing a dissertation on affirmative action. I liked him, and he seemed to have a good feel for politics and how it worked. Ditto Josh Lewsey, who was very bright but maybe more cynical. He kept asking me what I would do next with my life. He was definitely one of those of the more surprised end of the market about me being there. He said later, as did O'Connell, that a few weeks ago I was pushing around some of the most powerful people in the world. Now I was telling five-year-old kids to run around with players. They were both friendly, though. Josh said a man of your magnitude must have a lot of things on the go, and of course you have a lot of dirt on people!

Louisa and I headed for the stadium, I did an interview about the anthem, then we hung around waiting for the players. They arrived off the bus, most with earphones in, in total silence. Michael Owen was pretty stunned that Clive had asked him to be captain against the Pumas. We got him and Ian [McGeechan] out for quick interviews. J. J. Williams [former Welsh rugby international] came over for a chat, first about his son [an athlete] but then he was the latest to warn me that nothing prepares you for the intensity of rugby in NZ. 'If you think football is big here, wait till you see how they treat rugby out there,' he said. 'It is a religion.' I was really impressed at the operation in the dressing room. In so many ways, I was seeing the kind of attention to detail that more in politics should get a handle on. It was also such a big logistical operation to get all the different things they needed, for the warm-up, for the medical treatment, diet, supplements. Then there were personal nameplates and badges on every spot so they all knew immediately where they were meant to go. Two shirts for each of them, so that they could start each half clean and fresh. Also so they had one to keep and one to swap with an opponent.

It was quite exciting now to see the whole thing swing into action. Stacks of kit being moved in. The physios working away. Players going through their own routines as well as the stuff they had to do together. And seeing the different personalities come out, some quiet and methodical, some a bit more charged and pumped up. I went out for a feel of the stadium and chatted with Miles Harrison and Stuart Barnes [Sky TV commentators], who again seemed fairly friendly, though Barnes' commentary was a bit negative. Les Cusworth, part of the Argentina coaching set-up, was pretty clear it would be a walkover. Ditto Eddie O'Sullivan. The kick-off was delayed fifteen minutes for traffic. Ben called about a story that Jim Smith [football coach] had said he was not being retained at Southampton to make way for CW next year. Had to put together a line on that. Anthem went OK, but could have done with a male voice rather than the lovely Katherine Jenkins [singer].

The match was all a bit a weird. The Pumas scored a try in the fourth minute, Federico Todeschini's kicking was superb, and though the Lions kept looking like they were going to start to stamp their authority, they never did. The big plus was JW played well and bravely, and kicked well. But there were a lot of mistakes made and they never really gelled. Half-time came, they were 19–16 down, and we thought there would be such a bollocking that they would be re-fired up but it didn't really happen. It took a JW kick to draw the match in the last minute. Not exactly the start we wanted. Everyone said Ian's team talk had been absolutely inspirational – that people bought the shirt for the badge but you guys made the badge. Make history. Be part of it etc. CW said he knew Ian had a reputation for his talks but this was superb. However, they all seemed pretty disappointed with the performance. CW was so proud of his attention to detail, and had been hoping for a decent start, not least for the mood. But it all looked a bit ragged as we came off having drawn to a sub-standard Pumas side.

We got together with Clive before his interviews and agreed he had to emphasise it was a tough and proper start and lots to build on. Nobody should underestimate how hard it was for four countries to come together and gel. We got Michael Owen and Jonny out for interviews. Michael was too downbeat, JW got the balance right. They took so long to change we started the presser with just Ian and Clive. The press were not as aggressive as I thought they would be. Ian looked a bit down. Prince William came down to the dressing room with a couple of mates and his private secretary, Jamie LP. CW took them through and everyone would have loved a picture of the scene that followed – Michael Owen standing there bollock naked shaking his hand and William blushing like mad.

I had a preliminary chat with Jamie LP re NZ. They were definitely alive to some of the sensitivities. JW and Owen presser OK, again mood not that negative. Back told me some of the players were surprised coaches said kick for touch a few minutes before the end. CW said it was the right thing to happen, get their feet on the ground, but a few of them had let themselves down. There was no angst though. He told me Jason Robinson [England player] was staying home for a week with his pregnant wife and that would become a media thing. Then the official dinner. I was next to Donncha O'Callaghan [Ireland player], who is a very good laugh and was gently taking the mick out of the speeches, translating what they said to what they meant, so that 'good sportsmanlike match' became 'you dirty bastards', 'thanks to the referee' was 'you useless one-eyed messer', and so on. On the coach back I was chatting to Mark Cueto about United. Will Greenwood [England player] was asking re the press. Tony Biscombe asked me to do a clip for the in-house film on how I was not going to be associated with defeat. Pretty good mood considering.

Tuesday 24 May
The papers were not as bad as I thought they would be, with only the *Mail* really going for them – and for the anthem, which both CW and Jayne wanted to get rid of, and Louisa and I had to argue against. There

May '05: Prince William shakes hand with naked captain

was lots of 'Wilko saves the day'. I drafted CW words for the presser, then waited for William's advisors to arrive – Paddy Harverson, Jamie Lowther-Pinkerton and Patrick Harrison [press secretary]. We went up to the team room and planned out the visit. They clearly wanted him totally immersed in the tour but by the end I think we had the balance right, with a mix of public and private, and also some days he was away from us. We agreed kicking practice with JW was probably the best photo, and we should maybe think about community stuff too. I was surprised they wanted to make the rugby the main focus, with the other stuff added on, rather than the other way round.

JLP kept emphasising William was quite nervous and did not want to be a burden. Also I'm not sure they had taken kindly to the line from Matt Dawson yesterday, saying William was the team pet or some such. They did say they had had a very good laugh afterwards at his handshaking Michael Owen while bollock naked. William had said it was a first. We had lunch with them which became a much more general chat, the election, current stuff. Then all off to the local castle for official photos. Good mood. I argued politics with Will Greenwood, who said he voted Tory because he can't stand GB, and he didn't like the idea that TB was going to go and GB take over. He felt the Tories should have made far more of that. He seemed a bit shocked when I said we had actually deliberately brought GB in centre stage. The pictures were fairly painless. As the tallest member of the management/backroom, I was plonked right in the middle and felt a bit of a fraud but they seemed to be OK.

Jason Robinson was there but was then going home to be with wife Amanda. CW had agreed he could stay with her an extra week, and we worked on a press notice for it, that he would be coming out on 7 June. I got a call from Amanda Docherty [communications director] at Arsenal, who had read my piece about Wenger and the water bottle and wanted me to know that Wenger's anger was at the official, not Neville. Then the players had to do a load of pictures for sponsors. I was in charge of the Eden Park photo, jackets inside out, walk in the park, mean and moody. Henson, Dallaglio, Cusiter, O'Callaghan, Thompson and Geordan Murphy [Ireland player]. Donncha O'C was without doubt one of the funniest, and had worked out he had a rich vein of new laughs in taking the piss out of me. He was a bit like me in deciding to work out a line on someone and then keep banging on about it, and he had decided that the line was that I was 'fucking loaded', and Geordan said why would he care about being loaded when he ran the fucking country, and DOC said the country was but a vehicle for his wealth. Then when someone mentioned they had seen me arriving in a helicopter... away he went.

Gavin Henson was coming out of himself a bit, but still fairly quiet. Lawrence D was very calm, a cool guy, and wanting to be nice to everyone. Steve Thompson was much nicer than advertised. Several of the hacks had warned me he would give me a hard time. The sponsorship stuff was comic at times. Ben sent me a text message saying, 'I am a whore and you have ruined my life ... I am having to tell Jonny Wilkinson to run up and down a golf fairway pretending a laptop is a rugby ball.' Back on the bus and after a stint in the gym there was a barbecue, where Jayne bent my ear about the anthem. I said the key was to get a paper behind it, though I accepted that might be tricky.

Lots of wives and girlfriends there, the Irish the best laugh. I worked on CW words, plus Q&A for players doing media, then ended up at the bar with Josh Lewsey and Shane Horgan for a good hour or so of political argument, JL coming at me from the right, SH from the left. Josh was very bright but needed to get his views centred a bit. SH was really clued up on UK politics, as was Hickie. Lawrence D suggested we had a debating society. I told Richard Hill that Rory was surprised he had four pints the other night. He said it was only two. But tonight quite a few of them were tanking it, and half a dozen went off into town at midnight. I was quite surprised by how many seemed to be off to hit the town, but they did all the stuff about being able to train it out etc.

Wednesday 25 May

I couldn't sleep well, probably a bit of guilt about going away, more self-doubt about whether it was the right thing. Also, an odd thing to be doing on my birthday. I went to the gym early. JW was one of the first people I met in the foyer. It was his birthday, and it was mine. He said keep it quiet or else they will get up to something. I suspected they already were. I had breakfast with him, Mark Cueto, Dwayne Peel [Welsh player] and Charlie Hodgson [England player]. We were talking about how awful the press were. JW had quite a few examples of stuff that was completely untrue, like the time a paper said he paid a lap dancer, and there was absolutely nothing in it. I told them the story of the *Mail* saying Dad was dead when he wasn't, but that unless it was stone wall like that it was like pulling teeth to get them to admit to errors. It was interesting how little the players seemed to mind if there were no papers there to read. There were none at breakfast. I asked JW if he liked doing the sponsors' work, and showed him Ben's text that he felt like a whore asking him to pretend a laptop was a rugby ball. JW laughed but then said he liked to do everything he did to the best of his ability, and sponsors put money in and they were entitled to something back. He seemed such a transparently nice bloke.

They were all picking up on how ghastly the papers were about me and, for example, Martin Corry and Paul O'Connell, who had never really noticed it before, both asked, 'How on earth do you put up with it?' This morning the *Today* programme allowed Peter Oborne [journalist who wrote an unofficial biography of AC] to do an open letter to the people of NZ on what badness to expect from me. Heaven knows how they justified it as a *Today* programme item. Corry was asking if it wasn't an abuse of their position. I worked on CW's script for today and for NZ, along with BB and BOD. Jayne was still at me over the anthem. The players were mixed in their views on it. Some liked, some were indifferent, some hated. CW rehearsed the words for the press conference a couple of times. He was still a bit nervous doing it but I thought did fine. Then BOD did a bit, then the ludicrous scene where all the players came up and had to do all their requests. They had allowed this system to develop where essentially on a press day like this the media could talk to whoever they wanted. I talked to Lewis Moody, Geordan Murphy and others and agreed we ought to try to change it if we could.

They didn't seem to enjoy it, at least most of them didn't, and it was frankly embarrassing that a small number were mobbed and others stood around looking – and more importantly feeling – like spare pricks. I said if they wanted to change things I was happy to do it and take the flak. The players who went out last night got back at 4 a.m., and Gordon D'Arcy said he couldn't remember anything about it. Lawrence D said it was a good blow-out but they behaved. He was late for the press but did it fine. It was an odd scene, though, all these players hanging round like waiting for a date. Gavin Henson came up and we organised a little gaggle for him. I couldn't decide whether he was arrogant, nervous or not very sharp. Maybe a bit of all three. Stephen Jones [*Sunday Times*] was shocked that he was late and that he said to me he was only staying for fifteen minutes. But he was just a bit gauche, I think, and though he had a bit of attitude, I thought he was OK. He thanked me for the gaggle idea so he didn't have to do lots of one-on-ones.

Lots of the players were now asking me about their columns, and I was happy to help. The system seemed to be working OK. Quick lunch with Eddie O'Sullivan, then packed and up for the final meeting. Nice warm words from BB, then CW did another little talk. He said again that we had to get everything right on the pitch by getting it right off the pitch. Lots of F words in there. Lots of let's go and do it, up and at them, make history, be part of something great. LD laughing, no doubt because he had heard it all so many times, but some of the younger ones clearly hanging on every word. We organised a CW–BOD snap on the way out and then on to the coach that was taking us to Heathrow. I was next to Gavin Scott, the Scottish video analysis guy, who was editing a Bay of Plenty [Lions' first opponents] match on his laptop. It was incredible what he was doing there, and really interesting to watch how quickly he put together the bits he thought the coaches and individual players would need to see. Gavin H and Shane Williams [Wales player] were playing PlayStation. LD got the driver to put on a *Little Britain* video and they started to call me Sebastian [a comic character devoted to a Prime Minister in the TV show]. Good craic, I guess, though I am not sure I want Sebastian to stick as a nickname.

I was joshing again with Josh re politics. He was constantly banging on at me about hunting now. Later he slept on the floor. They all looked a bit tired and were clearly desperate to get going. I did a note on William's visits and also was trying to fix *The Sun* re the anthem. But Hammonds, the Lions' lawyers, had been on to *The Sun* for calling themselves the official paper. They could get behind us but not claim official support as it suggested a financial relationship. Rebekah Wade [*Sun* editor] asked me to do a stand-in for Richard Littlejohn's column. I probably would have done it but by the time the flight got there the deadline would be gone. Talked lots to F and the kids through the day and was really going to miss them. Grace called a couple of times with different friends to sing happy birthday. Rory called for a really nice chat about the football, with Liverpool playing AC Milan in the Champions' League final in Istanbul, and then about the rugby.

We spent an hour or so in the first-class lounge and then off. I showed the Oborne piece to a few of them, and they were basically on my side. We took off just after 10. Really nice message from Fiona. The captain announced that Liverpool had fought back to win. Amazing comeback, 3–0 down, back to 3–3, and then they won on penalties as we were about to go airborne. It was funny how even the ones who didn't really like football that much just loved the drama. Clive was totally fired up by it, said he would start the first presser by saying something about it, and how if they could do that when everyone wrote them off, then we could beat the mighty All Blacks. I got more signs on the flight of the extraordinary attention to detail, like the note the medics gave out on sleep, diet, vitamin C, zinc. The biggest players got the first-class seats, the rest in club. They also gave us a note on how to avoid jetlag, with a scientific explanation. I worked, read, listened to music to try to follow Otis' advice not to sleep on the first leg.

I reckon Wilkinson and I were the only ones in our bit who heeded the advice to try to stay awake on the first leg and we ended up having a two-hour chat at the bottom of the stairs. We got on to the subject of obsessiveness. He said the first time he felt sick before a game was when he was seven and it has never gone away. On a match day he will just lie on his bed thinking. After a match, internally he just focuses on his own game, things he should have done differently. We had an interesting chat about Mark, his brother, who went a different route – state sixth-form college, university – but who he thinks is an equal rugby talent in many ways. He said relationships can be hard because they have to live with his ups and downs, and his obsessiveness. We spoke at length re my breakdown and how it came about and he described a time when he felt he was close to that kind of thing because things were so on top of him. He said it passed. He never read about himself and didn't watch rugby on TV. If he read a paper he would stop at the racing page in case there was anything about him in the sports pages. He didn't have much time for the media but recognised they were part of his world.

He was saying yes to some sponsorship deals etc. but would not do anything unethical or embarrassing. He asked a fair bit about politics and had roomed with Shane Horgan and they had talked politics and he found himself more interested. He hoped to play to thirty-four and didn't know if he was more or less likely to have a longer career having been so injured so often. He had a very straightforward manner – ask a question, get a fairly long answer – and always very open about how he felt, e.g. how he would find it hard to handle playing badly, sometimes cry, not knowing what it was in him that drove him, anxieties about the future, a hatred of being drawn out from the crowd. He said he did *A Question of Sport* when he was nineteen and he felt humiliated and small and vowed never to do it again. I really liked talking to him, and admired his single-mindedness and his focus. There was also an extraordinary integrity that came through. He was clearly different to most of the others, not really into the banter in the same way, and often seeming very much in his own world, but they clearly respected him.

Quite a few echoed the thing Brian O'Driscoll had said to me in Dublin, when I did him for *The Times*, that Jonny was special. Like Richard Hill, 'There is Jonny and there is the rest.'

We landed in Bangkok, where CW and I worked on the script, then chatted to some of the journalists. I slept most of the second leg, we had a brief stop in Sydney, then a three-hour flight to Auckland, again mainly working on scripts. Chatted to Lewsey about bloody hunting again – he was another one who was really funny when he got going – and BOD about how the media was changing public life. Josh was really into winding me up over the hunting ban, and how little we understood the countryside. We landed and after a fair old bit of faffing around organised OK pictures of the players arriving. A few dozen Lions fans there, good mood, lots of focus on JW and BOD, then on to the bus and to the Hilton. It was nice and bright, and we had lots of space set aside just for us. I had a nice room with a lovely view out over the sea. The pool wasn't up to much, effectively a single lane, but I had a little swim before the team meeting. More jetlag advice. Another pep talk from BB, another from Clive. He also said he wanted to see real standards set in public and he didn't want to see any of the players on mobiles in public spaces. Only the media team could use mobiles in the public spaces, he said.

Clive was unusually nervous about the press conference, and in particular about reading script, but he did it fine. One of his main lines was that he had respect but no fear. We had all the players there, and all the coaches, as a show of strength. Brian O'Driscoll also said a few words and was OK except for constantly rubbing the side of his face. The NZ media were not there in the numbers I had expected but as an event it would carry fine. I was feeling pretty shagged by the time I got to bed.

Saturday 28 May

The fitness guys' advice seemed to pay off, as I slept straight through, and felt fine. At breakfast Ben came in and said Graham Henry had just been on NZTV and he thought he was crap, which CW loved to hear. We got good NZ coverage for yesterday's arrival, and I was pleased when Neil Back said to me later, 'All our messages have definitely got through.' HOD was fairly low key and it was a weird time, with no games for a while, and just gentle working into things. We had the official Maori welcome tomorrow and I was working on words for BB and BOD. The first media event was the launch of the new Adidas commercial, which was based on Lions and New Zealanders playing without a ball and enjoying it. I had a brief meeting with the four guys going over to it, JW, BOD, Ben Kay and Gareth Cooper, and said they must not be put in the position of doing dozens of interviews, or doing nose to nose, head to head, back to back. JW seemed relieved. He said he hated doing that kind of thing.

We ran through some of the main messages. Ben Kay said if we kept saying 'Respect not fear', they would think we feared them. The event itself was less sleazy than these things sometimes are, very well organised, and the NZ media loved the access early on. Small world – Stewart Binns [Burnley fan, friend of AC] was there for Octagon [sports agency]. I wanted to shower the NZ media early on, and some of them were already noticing, including an old guy who said professionalism had put barriers between players and press, and this kind of thing, even if it was driven by corporate interests, helped bring them down. Next stop the gym, where Getty Images and an NZ agency did snaps of the players with Otis on conditioning, including the sight of Andy Sheridan [England prop] with 40kg strapped to his waist. Then to the hotel to collect Andy Robinson and Eddie O'Sullivan [coaches] to take them to North Harbour Stadium, where we were to promote Tuesday's planned public training session.

Eddie and Andy were much more growly than CW and Ian McG, and didn't much like the press. Eddie slapped down David Hands [*Times*] when he asked whether Simon Taylor's hamstring was a recurring problem. 'It's his first time,' he snapped back. He said afterwards that was how rumours started and he wasn't having it. But they did some one-on-ones, nice pictures in the stadium and I'm sure it was worth it. On the drive back we had another discussion about the difference between media in politics and rugby. Then to lunch and another political discussion, this time Martin Corry going on about Europe taking over our lives, Labour not being patriotic enough, asylum seekers etc. I said just because you write for the *Mail* doesn't mean you have to talk like them. Tommo [Steve Thompson] joined in a bit and Andy Robinson ditto. Matt Stevens was fairly quiet, though later he said he hated the way people took arguments from the press. Josh joined us and was now banging on about the need to bring back some kind of national service idea.

Ben Kay said they had had a Cabinet in the England team: Martin Johnson [England World Cup-winning captain] was PM, he was Chancellor. His most radical idea was an ID card with DNA and biometrics, which also had all your cash and benefit entitlements on it. It was not as barmy as it sounds, and one day might happen, but I tried to explain some of the practical problems – topical, as back home we were hearing the first rumblings of opposition against ID card plans. But they were certainly getting into the mood for arguments. BB and CW were off playing golf. I worked on the Maori speeches, dinner with Neil Back and Dave Campbell talking about nutrition. Back filled me in on the amount of protein he ate every day, and also on the change in the game over the last few years. Bed at 10. UK news was mainly focused on the French referendum tomorrow, on the adoption of the new EU constitution. Not looking good.

Sunday 29 May

I woke up at 3 a.m., like a light pinging on, so I had not got away with the jetlag after all. I tried to get back to sleep but it was hopeless so I got up to do some work. There was an email from Tina Weaver [*Sunday Mirror* editor] saying Prince Charles wanted to hire me. I sent her a message saying I didn't believe it for one second. I suspect they had heard something about the meeting with Paddy Harverson and co, had put two and two together and made a few hundred. I had been warned that the NZ press would turn pretty quickly, and today there was a definite gearing up. There was a CW dartboard picture in one of the tabloids; a broadsheet had a front-page spoof interview with me saying Jonny W's comeback was the greatest since Lazarus. Another had a line saying it was the first time a touring party outnumbered the population of the country being visited, which to be fair was funny. CW loved it all. He felt we should use it to show the players how edgy and scared the All Blacks and their supporters were getting.

He asked me to speak to the players because some of them had been followed by a snapper, and I said they should just call us and we would sort. He told them who was in the team for the first match against Bay of Plenty so we agreed we would it put out straight away, prompting another bout of old-woman-itis from the rugby writers, who were expecting it on Wednesday. I made the point they would be pissed off if it had leaked out through a player's column or some such. Louisa and I had breakfast with the group of four she had put together – she called them her spin group – Greenwood, Cusiter, Henson and O'Connell – who we wanted to represent the players, tell the media team what they wanted by way of support, things that annoyed them, things they thought we could help with. I said they should be totally frank. Greenwood was friendly, Cusiter seemed quite quiet but bright, O'Connell was bright and a hoot, Henson was still a bit distant.

The basic pitch was that most of them would like to do as little media as possible but understood they had to do some. They felt the column system was going OK and found it helpful to be able to use us if they wanted to. They were fine about a new approach to pictures and giving access to the media to some of their leisure stuff. But generally I sensed they were a bit down and negative and BB and Louise Ramsay [tour manager] had the same thing from a group of others who felt there was going to be too much spare time and they needed a bit more organisation around how it might be spent. Paul O'C did say they felt it was best we were on the front foot all the time, and keep them at bay. Henson was a bit more open. He said his problem was he had had a couple of issues with Clive for saying what he thought so he was now terrified of saying anything. He didn't really want to do much media because of that. They went through the ones in their countries who were OK at it, and who didn't mind doing it. We selected four for later, including Martyn Williams, who was excellent and a top bloke, one of those guys you just took to. Mal O'Kelly had decided not to do the column for the *Sunday Times* Ireland because they only wanted slag-off stuff.

We got a bus out to the airport. I was sitting with Dave Campbell, who was reading a paper. Jonny and Richard Hill were behind us, I was turning to talk to them, and when Dave turned to a page with a picture of Jonny, I could see Jonny turn away. We got the plane down to Rotorua [230km south-east of Auckland], planning Tuesday's public training session. Then a long day. Great welcome at the airport, especially for Jonny. Sulphur springs, a smell that really got into you. Some poor housing but lovely scenery. To the official welcome. BB and BOD accepting the challenge sticks. Some of the players were like kids but quite funny – Donncha pretend farting to say he wanted to mingle in with the local smells, and his farts smelled like sulphur, Tommo and Danny Grewcock [English player] pinching Lewis Moody the whole time in front. Good pictures. Inside, the speeches were too long and despite our coaching BB fucked up the pronunciation of Tena Koutou [Maori for 'Hello to you'] – he said Koo-koo, which got picked up. We sang 'Bread of Heaven' very badly. We still hadn't decided what to do about our anthem. The trophy was unveiled.

Out to do media with Gordon Bulloch, O'Connell, Cueto and Martyn Williams. In for a cup of tea and a chat with CW, saying we needed to get out, saying in future a tour would be even bigger, maybe take A and B teams and play exhibitions and make it a proper tour promoting the game, rather than just focusing on the Tests as the be-all and end-all. We did a museum visit, more larking around from some of them, then the flight back. Dinner with Eddie O'S and Dave Aldred, who was very much into the CW view of the RFU. Francis Baron [RFU CEO] seemed to be fairly widely hated, but that did seem to go with the territory of sports bodies and their relationship with the people who actually performed.

I chatted with some of the English players about Clive. They said views were mixed. There was a lot of respect but, more than in football, rugby players liked to think they not the coaches were the ones who really counted. One or two felt Clive got too much of the credit for the World Cup, that yes, they didn't underestimate his role, but the cult of the coach was a relatively new thing. I asked if they listened carefully to all the stuff in team talks. Some said yes, some said no. All said that if a coach talked too much it could be a problem. They also had mixed views about how much they had to do on the commercial side of things. The number of players who could get their own deals with sponsors was relatively small, but they all had to do stuff, and they felt, as with media duties, that they should let the ones who like doing it do more and the ones who don't do less.

Monday 30 May

We were doing a daily thought for the day on top of the printed schedule that went to all members of the party, and today's we lifted from a paper, *NZ Truth,* a columnist saying maybe people should realise we were indeed a professional outfit and the old clichés were history. The Sundays were mixed. Will Carling [former England captain] had a go at all the usual stuff. But there was a lot of positive stuff too. The 'has-been syndrome', former players slagging off the current lot, was pretty strong in rugby. The French lost the referendum on the EU constitution, 45 to 55 per cent, which was dominating everything at home, and setting off a mini-crisis. One or two of the players asked about it. TB was in Italy and I got a message to call him. He ran a few lines by me, but it was all really holding stuff while people took stock. The news went on him saying it was 'too early to say' if we would also hold a referendum, and that people needed to reflect on the French vote. He was clearly worried about the Dutch being next, and also we were about to take on the rotating presidency so there was a danger this thing dominated the next few months. He sounded generally OK otherwise.

I visited the Lions shop with John Feehan [Lions CEO] to plan an event for later in the week. Then a few interviews to promote the training session tomorrow, including with a broadcaster called Paul Thomas from Prime TV, who was odd. He was a bit brash, constantly trying to be funny, and the interview weaved between sport and politics, serious and trivial, though when I saw it later it wasn't as bad as I feared. Some of the players saw it and agreed it was odd – Corry: 'What a twat', D'Arcy: 'Can you teach me how to look down my nose at interviewers like you did there? You were a genius looking down your nose at him like that.' But we were still getting NZ brownie points for the charm offensive, as evidenced by the questions in a couple of interviews I did. NZTV was wall-to-wall rugby. News and chat programmes had stacks of it, and the rugby channel was showing old Lions Tests.

I did a couple more press interviews while working on 1998 diary, the Wim Duisenberg episode [a long struggle at a European summit before the Dutchman was finally confirmed as President of the European Central Bank]. Interesting that I was recording one of the great Chirac fiascos, when he was desperately trying to stop Duisenberg, just as the French were saying no to the constitution. Paul Keating [former Australian PM] called, asked if I would do a speech in Australia and also get involved in some company whose boss wanted an in to TB–GB, as did Paul. He was in full flow about the relevance of his own experience to TB (re polishing legacy) and GB (re maintaining momentum). It was great to hear from him, though and I said I would try to get there but couldn't guarantee. We had a good laugh recollecting the time in opposition when he accompanied us to Hayman Island, for the [Rupert] Murdoch [chairman and CEO News Corporation] editors' conference.

Tuesday 31 May

There was more antsy stuff in the NZ media. CW wanted us to start pasting stuff on message boards in the team room, which Louisa and I did when the players were out training. The main event media-wise was the public training session. After HOD, I prepared a note to brief the players. I gave them the line from the stadium that 10,000 were expected, so when it was half that later, I got a fair bit of ribbing from them. Donncha went off on a riff about how we calculated our majorities.

'You get ten thousand votes but you tell everyone it was twenty. You get a majority of fifty seats, but you tell the world it's a hundred.' Jonny was a bit pissed off we made him one of the four players to do pitchside interviews. He told Clive later that he didn't like being the one always singled out. It was hard, in that he hated it, but there was no getting round the extra interest in him. I had a chat, said I would say no as a default position, but it would be good if he would do some but not all. He said what he hated was the idea that he was above and separate from the rest of the team. The problem was that that was how most of the media saw him.

The players entered into the spirit, though, with the possible exception of DOC, who when a kid ballsed up told him, 'Get out of the fucking way, you little prick.' I'm not sure the kid was on the same humour wavelength. I had tried to tell the players it was a normal session designed not to disrupt. CW told them it was purely for PR but he wanted them to get engaged and by and large they did. I did a couple of pitchside interviews, including one where the guy said, 'It is very hard to be cynical when you see so many kids enjoying this.' Eddie O'S said that in rugby terms it was as useful as a chocolate fireguard, and the players told [Dr] Gary O'D that they'd had enough of the stuff they had to do. Lawrence and Dwayne did the media afterwards and both did it well. Good pictures on NZ media later and they were starting to say that the charm offensive was real.

CW said the real training session in the afternoon was hopeless. Ian said they were all trying too hard to impress and were making mistakes. I was trying to persuade Louisa to use me to change the system whereby the players had to meet the press every week if selected. They were also whingeing that we put out the team when we did. I was struck by how little respect the rugby people had for their media, either because they knew nothing or because they were in the bitter 'has-been' fraternity. The other media event was a little press conference for Stephen Jones [Wales player], who had arrived late. He was a lovely bloke. I took to him instantly, warm and funny. 'Was I on message?' he asked. Apart from not saying vote Labour, totally, I said. 'Don't worry, I do.' Good bloke, another one who felt the press knew nothing but understood you had to deal with them. Over dinner Martin Corry said he didn't care what any of the papers said and he felt we were trying too hard on the PR front. We were still messing around re the anthem. For a week now we had been saying do we go for it or not and we still hadn't decided.

Wednesday 1 June

We got good press out of the training session, with BOD and the kid dressed as a lion the main picture. Plus some good snaps of a line of players signing autographs. HOD – CW asked BB to speak to French contacts about trying to get Gareth Thomas [Wales player] released from his club, Toulouse. We had yet another chat re the anthem and agreed to go ahead with it with a choir rather than expect the players to sing it. Our main media event was the CW–BOD–LD presser to talk pre-Bay of Plenty and then what I had called the whorehouse – all the players coming in and doing a dating agency job round TV, radio and print. I was trying to change the system but Louisa was worried it would just offend too many and it wasn't worth it. I did words for CW, including a whinge about security stories, but basically setting up Bay of Plenty as the real start of the tour. As he got back from training, he said today was a lot better than yesterday when there were too many involved and too much headless chickenry. He was a bit hyper this morning but had calmed down for the presser, which went fine, though I pointed out he was saying 'erm' more than usual. He and BOD did one-on-ones while the players came down. All fine, and though they hated doing it, they did it pretty well.

Gavin H was pretty truculent but in an interesting way and with a smile. He told me again he was just terrified of saying something daft and getting bollocked by Clive. I hadn't realised CW had totally lost it with him after he said he hadn't much enjoyed the first Vale session at the Vale of Glamorgan hotel. He had a whack at Peter Jackson. 'I've already answered that question.' PJ said he wasn't there. 'Ask one of your mates then.' The main thing we were pushing was the line that we were ready for a match and desperate to get the tour started properly. Josh good on message. Matt Stevens pretty popular. Baby-faced, him and Gethin [Jenkins] both. Some of the media threw a wobbly because we didn't bring down Ronan O'G who had got back late and I had told him he could slope off. I got him down after a while – after he called me a langer [popular Irish insult] and had a laugh with BOD re what it meant. Apparently it started as something Dubliners said of anyone from Cork, but sounded like it was on the wanker scale of things. Ronan did his bit and was fine but this system – that they all had to do stuff – was bonkers.

I did an interview with *NZ Herald* – pretty straightforward – then to the UK Consulate-General's for an event in Auckland to promote UK media. I took BB, who was very good at these things. There were a few old All Blacks there for him to talk to, including Andy Haden [controversially outspoken ex-player]. I was asked to do a speech and did a light-hearted number on my relations with the UK media, but then quite a serious thing about the importance of media as an export market. I was taken aback in the Q&A and mingling by how much a certain type of New Zealander knew about me – e.g. row with BBC, relations with press, specific incidents, bagpipes, Burnley.

Nice enough evening, then out for a management dinner at Euro restaurant – as it happens, just as the Dutch were in the process of following France in dumping the new constitution in their referendum. According to the polls, it looked like the margin would be even bigger. Lovely chat with Grace before she headed to Norfolk. She sent me an email saying she didn't like talking long on the phone because it made her upset and sad and she missed me more if we spoke. I was also having nice chats with Calum re his golf and his studies. My first *Irish Times* column appeared.

Thursday 2 June
Day off for everyone. We had tried to generate some interest in a media-funded boat trip but there was no take-up, prompting Donncha to go around shouting, 'Boat for one, anyone?' He was hilarious, and emerging as one of the characters and, according to those in the know, someone who might just emerge as a star during the tour on the playing side too. The Irish were far more laid back than the others. ROG kept saying he couldn't take me seriously because I was a double for his uncle. I noticed again how much ketchup Jonny had with his omelette. I couldn't quite bring myself to tell him about my ketchup phobia. I had a chat with Josh re MPs and their earnings, and tried to persuade him that most politicians were actually OK. He was also giving me a guide to what kind of behaviour was and was not considered OK on the field. Stamping on a body if it was in the way – fine. Stamping on head – not fine. It happened to him on the last tour.

We had lined up Phil Larder [coach] and James Robson the doc to do a briefing. Phil and I had a pre-chat and he said he often ended up in trouble because he shot from the lip and said what he thought. He didn't want to slag Graham Henry because he thought he was a good coach and did OK for the Lions last time. In the event he was good, detailed and technical and obviously expert. I was surprised at how open the doctor was, for example making clear Mal O'Kelly could be off the tour. He was also very jokey with them. I raised the Mal story afterwards and he defended the openness, saying they would find out in the end and the reality was that he could be off the tour. He also gave figures about how many players had had treatment – thirty-eight out of forty-five – which although he explained it was open to real misinterpretation, he insisted it was the best way to deal with them on the injury front. Mal was to see another specialist this afternoon.

On the Rugby Channel there was a discussion about the media coverage, with endless references to me. I was watching with Louisa and Louise, who let out a loud cheer when one of the presenters said how good we had been at setting the agenda so far. He said in particular that the media training session had been like nothing seen before. Alastair Hignell [commentator, former England international] was on and said CW hiring AC was a masterstroke because it signalled how big it was going to be, which was much better than most of the written press were saying. We only put a few of the cuttings around the press room because a lot of them were trying to build up rivalry between JW and Stephen Jones, as to who the No. 1 half-back was.

The Dutch referendum was dominating the news and the EU constitution was looking pretty damaged. Needless to say, as with all bloody referendums, the constitution was not the main focus for a lot of the opposition. [Jan Peter] Balkenende [Dutch Prime Minister] was making a lot of cuts to public spending, and also, as with the French, part of it was just giving the establishment a kick up the arse. I hadn't realised this one was only advisory, not binding, but so many countries were promising referendums, the two so far were both lost, others would be. It was hard to see how it limped along.

I was getting too many interview bids, but did a few before going out for a run, then back to meet Mal O'Kelly in the team room. He was back from the NZ doctor and basically said he had had it. 'Off the tour.' He had his usual huge friendly smile so I assumed he was joking. He said, 'No, it's serious, I am out.' There was the slight possibility a steroid injection would help but he had had two already this season and a third could be career-threatening. I guess injury was just a part of their life, but it was incredible, and impressive, how philosophical he was. 'You have no option, you've just got to come to terms with it.'

He said he had had lots of good moments in his career and this was a bad moment. There was no point hanging around now. He intended to see Clive when he got back from golf, and he felt he would want a replacement out straight away, and said it was best for the tour he went home straight away. He would just get frustrated hanging around. He was a lovely guy and probably hurting a lot more than he let on. He said at least I got here and there were times during the season I didn't think I would. Yes, I said, but wouldn't you rather not have come at all than come all this way only to fly back home without playing. 'For sure, it's tough, but cookie crumbles and all that.' We knocked out a statement with words from Mal, CW and BOD. It was all very sad but they were very matter of fact about it. Some of the players went turkey shooting and came back to regale us with stories of Josh wringing the their necks and Mark Cueto hitting two with one shot.

Friday 3 June

The Dutch vote was lost by an even bigger margin than had been predicted. Over 60 per cent, and turnout way above expectations too, also over 60, when they had been predicting less than half would bother to vote. The domino effect from France may have had something to do with it, but the EU leaders had a big problem on their hands. I spoke briefly to TB, who called re 'tone and body language'. I said it was probably sensible to say it couldn't be left to one country to declare the whole thing dead, but he should be pointing that way. He said Chirac would be reluctant to kill it off. But it was not a good scene that only the Spanish had won a referendum, all the others who had ratified so far had done so with parliamentary support only, and more than half of those still to do had promised a referendum.

HOD – we were still trying to pin down Toulouse re Gareth Thomas. CW was picking up vibes re the players not getting the point of the community stuff and he planned to lay it on them at the team meeting before we left. I did an NZTV interview, another fairly quirky one, and then a bit of work upstairs. The cuttings board was coming on really well and most of the players seemed to take a look most days, though not Jonny. He really did have an aversion to reading about himself. After lunch we had a pre-departure team talk in which the sheer scale of the technical side of things became clearer as they went through really quite complicated calls for line-outs and phases of play. On the flight down to Rotorua I gave BOD a couple of Vince Lombardi [legendary American football coach] quotes for his team talk, the ones I had used at the event for party staff a few months before the election.

There were no crowds to greet us this time as we headed straight to the International Stadium, which was a bit bleak and desolate because of the cold. Also thousands of the crowd were to be packed on grass banks which if it was wet would be an HSE [health and safety] disaster area. The players had been told by Dave Aldred to go to the edges and visualise the play, and also to sit in the stands and imagine the match. They were very good at this kind of thing. I loved all the visualisation stuff, and the different little mental and physical tics they had. Equally CW wanted everyone there when the shirts were handed out and he wanted Ian McG to do the handing out, as a bit of a Lions legend. I noticed too at the morning meeting Clive doing handwritten cards to everyone playing. Each shirt had a monogram with date and match. The mood on the bus to the hotel was good. Everyone was just saying they wanted to get on and play. We had a management meeting where again the technical side came through as they worked out who was to be on a microphone and who was to carry messages out to the players during the match. The substitutes were to be out in the elements on chairs on the far side because they would be in front of sponsors' hoardings on this side.

We then took Andy, Eddie and Richard Hill to the convention centre for the press conference. All three did well. Richard was definitely one of the all-round nice guys. Great reputation with players, fans and media. The England players talked about him as one of the World Cup-winning unsung heroes. And he was a total team player. He said most players would not want to do press the night before a match, but if we needed someone, he was fine. Over dinner we watched the All Blacks' trial. They seemed pretty impressive to me but the players said they were making a lot of mistakes. After a run I did RTE [Ireland channel], in bed by 11. Ian called to say Jonny had picked up a stinger – dead arm – in training, and would not travel tomorrow, which would be big news when the media noticed.

Saturday 4 June

I had a good chat with Dave Aldred over breakfast where he was slagging off the RFU, saying a lot of CW's work had been undone because of their basic amateurism. He was scathing of the lot of them. He was an interesting, clever guy, e.g. said at one point in JW's life he advised him to learn a language or instrument as a way of sharpening the mathematical side of his mind. He feared rugby players would become like footballers – driven to it too young, unable to be properly educated or take responsibility for themselves. 'You have to teach them to learn – and not just the sport they play.' He was doing a DVD for dads to teach kids to kick. The pre-match news was going to be JW and Shane Byrne [Ireland player], who were not going to be travelling because both had picked up injuries in training. CW was irritated, said that whenever he wasn't there they went a bit wild in training, and he was not happy about it. We agreed we should say JW was staying for physio to be in the best possible shape for the Taranaki match.

There was a different mood and rhythm to match days. No morning meetings, breakfast later than usual, the place generally quieter. The atmosphere was very different, less banter, quieter, fewer of the players around, most off resting or doing their own thing. The hotel overlooked a beautiful lake whose circumference was a marathon. It was tempting but when I went out I struggled to get going. I had a meeting with Louise and Marcus Jansa to try to get some strategy into the next phase, and later did a note to CW taking forward the professionalism and community themes. We needed to open up a bit behind the scenes. We spread the word among the supporters that we were leaving for the ground around five, so a crowd built up around the hotel. The players gathered in the team room, a mix of players and non-players, all much quieter than usual. Clive did a little speech and said 'fucking' seven times, which was not him really. But the general thrust was powerful – we've been nice off the field now let's go and hit them fucking hard. Stressed good start, focus, concentration.

Ian McGeechan was meant to hand out the shirts but his trip was delayed so Clive asked Gareth Jenkins, who made a really powerful and emotional speech, saying he had played with Lions but never been one, how it was a huge honour but with it came responsibilities. He talked about how we were a group of seventy special people who shared a great purpose and if we got it right, you players were going to be legends. He went on for a few minutes, then said he was getting emotional and he stopped. The players were clearly moved and there was applause for all of them as they went up. Then it was on to the bus through a fairly big crowd and off. The stadium was filling out. It wasn't as cold as yesterday and the players seemed up for it.

Three tries in the opening minutes had the crowd quietened, then a big blow when Lawrence D went down injured and clearly wasn't going to come back on. I was sitting next to Dave Aldred. That is a fucking big blow, he said – exactly the words CW used at half-time. It was a dislocation and fracture of the ankle and he was out of the tour. They were leading 17–0 at half-time, but then they seemed to lose direction and concentration for a bit, Bay of Plenty were fast and furious and put in some crunching hits, and pulled it back to 17–17. In the second half Lions settled down better and the final score was OK, at 34–20. 'At least we're playing after all the hype and the build-up,' said Josh Lewsey, who could have had a hat-trick of tries. The atmosphere was good, though yet again the anthem bombed and it was clear the players didn't like it.

In the dressing room, Clive, effing a few times again, said well done, ditto Eddie and Andy. Fairly easy media stuff – win's a win, grim re LD. Josh was man of the match and in his live interview had a friendly dig at me standing there, said I liked them doing hearts and minds but we were there to play rugby. The mood at the press conferences was OK in the rather dingy below stand press room. Clive said as we came off that losing LD was a massive blow. He asked Louise to track down Simon Easterby [Ireland player at home on standby] and we had announced that he would be flying out to join us by the time we left for the dinner.

We were also dealing with some piece of bollocks by one of their Sundays that they had had a reporter wandering around our secure area in the hotel. We played it down, but I was beginning to see what people meant about their press being like a sixteenth man. There was a lot of LD talk at the press conference but Clive took a fairly brutal line – these things happen, we have to move on and not let it affect everyone else. On the bus the players were fairly subdued. It was fascinating to watch the ups and downs in team mood, the waves of tiredness and energy that came at different times, and also to be in this world where one man's mishap was someone else's opportunity. Josh asked if it was like that in politics? 'Are people hoping a minister to fail so they might get a chance of promotion?' I said it wasn't maybe as crude as that, but there was always a part of everyone that had a little part of their mind for their own ambition. It was a question of degree. 'Do subs hope their team-mates get injured?' 'No,' he said, 'but if they do, they are going to do what they can to seize a chance.'

At the reception I chatted mainly to ROG, who was his usual piss-taking, have-a-laugh self, but was clearly beating himself up a bit. He had kicked badly at goal and he had missed a few tackles. The speeches were the usual thing, then we met for a drink downstairs and I ended up going to a bar with Richard Hill and some of the staff. Josh, ROG, BOD, Paul O'C, Martyn Williams, Dwayne Peel and Matt Dawson already there, all mixing with the supporters, perfectly happy. I guess this was what football used to be like, players much closer to the fans. RH was casting an eye over the younger guys starting to get a bit wild. The fans were pretty friendly. He was taking the mick re some of them wanting to be photographed with me, not the players, and especially the woman who started lobbying me about the tampon tax.* 'Do you get that all the time?' asked RH. 'What?' 'People asking you about random stuff like that and expecting you to sort it?' 'Yeah, I guess.' 'It would do my head in,' he said. Then she came back at me again, and he said, 'Hey love, give him a break.' I stayed till about two, good atmosphere but worried it was getting a bit rowdy and boozy.

Sunday 5 June

CW was due to do a presser at 8.30 so I was up to do words, mainly focused on making a solid start, positives and negatives. Obviously Lawrence would take a lot of the coverage. Clive had been to see him at the hospital last night and said he was remarkably philosophical. He was going to have surgery tomorrow under general anaesthetic. Everyone was incredibly sad but they did move on fairly quickly and amid the sympathy there was a pretty hard-headed determination not to let it get them down. It reminded me a little of the mood the day after a ministerial resignation. People were sad but quickly put it behind them and got on with what they were doing. Just as TB got tougher doing reshuffles with time, so Clive said he had had to get a very tough approach to issues like selection and injury. Once the player was badly injured, you had to focus on the replacement and any other changes it meant making, and just let them get on with rehab and recovery.

He was asking me about what I had said about him sounding a bit odd when he was swearing so much in team talks. He said he was not even aware he was doing it and that he hated swearing as a rule. The papers were pretty wall-to-wall, masses of reports and analyses. The general feeling was that there were some good individual performances but we should not have let them back in the game. One of the NZ papers said Ronan Keating [Irish pop singer] would have tackled better than Ronan O'Gara and he was laughing about it, but I reckoned he was beating himself up a fair bit. We hung around the hotel until CW told us the team for the next match against Taranaki on the bus to the airport, plus Corry as captain. I worked on a piece for *The Times* re the tour generally and in particular the media and tried to start up this

* The EU classified tampons as a 'luxury item' and they therefore attracted VAT; lobbyists argued that as essential items for half the population, tampons should be free of tax.

June '05: Woodward and AC discuss excessive swearing

line re the NZ media being sixteenth man being a problem for them not us, because of the additional pressure it put on the All Blacks. I even believed it (I think).

There was a smaller crowd to see us away and then the flight home. I was seated next to BOD and we were talking politics, media management and security stuff. He was a lovely bloke, a good talker and seemed genuinely interested in TB, my old job, what I thought of stuff I was seeing. Another person emerging as good and clever to talk to, not just about sport but the way the world was changing, was Dave Aldred. Like a lot of people, BOD, ROG and PO'C wanted to know what TB was like, what Bush was like, how they coped with pressure etc. Back to the hotel in Auckland for team and management meeting. CW went through the team again, congratulated everyone about last night, then the coaches all spoke. Andy and Eddie said pretty much the same thing – they had to learn from it, understand that if they got the ball they were strong and we could not afford to give the ball away. Phil Larder said in the semis of the World Cup v France, England missed eight tackles; in the final against the Aussies it was five. Last night we gave away too many tackles. The number had to come down game by game. He said he and Mike Ford were there to help with technique but collectively and individually the players had to look to themselves. It couldn't be done for them. He said they all needed their own programme and schedule in their minds, but they had to patrol it themselves. CW delivered a public bollocking about the training schedule that saw JW hurt. He said, '9s and 10s are our quarterbacks and they have to be protected.' He did not want them doing contact and it was stupid they had been doing it. He said the coaches had argued about this but he was adamant.

For the later media event, I did notes for Martin Corry on the honour of captaincy before we brought down about six or seven players. I was in Gareth Cooper's good books because having first asked for him, I then agreed he didn't need to do it. He said he hated it. Some of the others – e.g. Geordan Murphy and one or two others – liked it. The hacks were pressing for access to Lawrence, who had just come out of surgery. James the doc thought they were scum for trying to contact him direct but we agreed we should do a pool fairly soon, maybe as early as tomorrow.

The next big event was the management five-a-side football at Auckland Grammar. I was in Andy's team. Ben in Clive's, who had Bill B in goal. Good fun but I didn't play well and we lost in the final to Ian's team. It got fairly competitive and the toughest players were probably

Gavin Scott and Richard Smith, who sent Andy flying at one point. CW was strangely uncoordinated and also loath to go in for tackles. I ended up with a big lump on my shin from a tackle by Gavin. But it was good fun and should become a regular thing of the tour. I had mixed feelings about leaving to go back to the UK. I was keen to see the family and help Calum with his exams but I had probably become more integral than I thought I would be. Clive in particular was always coming for advice but I think I was also beginning to make a bit of a difference with some of the players, and changing things enough to take some pressure off them. Will Greenwood was agitating about the anthem, which was probably going to have to bite the dust. They really did hate it. One of those bad ideas that should probably have been strangled at birth.

Monday 6 June

I got a lift to the airport at 6.30 a.m., limping a bit and with a massive bruise on my shin where Gavin the video guy had clattered me last night in the five-a-side. It was going to be a long journey home, but it was relatively painless. The four hours in Sydney passed with the help of me writing a piece for the *Irish Times* and doing some diary work from '98. In one of those 'small world' moments, Ross Harper [Scottish lawyer, former colleague and friend of Donald Dewar, deceased Labour politician] was next to me on the plane and we chatted away about Donald, about whom I was reading in [former Labour special advisor] Peter Hyman's book. We had a break in Singapore, from where I slept pretty much all the way. Into London by six, home just after seven and into bed. It was great to see them all, even though it would have been better in some ways to see the whole thing through.

Tuesday 7 June

GB was talking about using the veto if member countries came after the EU rebate. Spoke to TB, who said it would hopefully not come to that, but there was definitely a move on. Most of the others were also getting agitated at us putting a hold on the Treaty referendum. Peter Hehir [NZ agent] came round to chat over NZ speaking engagements. Ben and Louisa were keeping me in touch with events out there, which seemed to be taking care of themselves. We had only been seeing the tour cuttings, which gave a false impression, because there was still page upon page of other sports. It was picking up here but nothing like the scale of coverage in NZ. I'd brought home a few NZ profiles to show F et al how different the media were there vis a vis me. Flattering pictures and profiles and little of the nastiness of the media here, but there was still plenty of time for things to go wrong. TB was in Washington, with Africa and climate change the main issues and barely a mention of Iraq on the news. He called when I was out for a run, said GWB [President George W. Bush] was asking for me and complaining these visits were not nearly as much fun when I wasn't there to take the piss out of him [TB]. On the substance, he was pushing him as hard as he could, and said he was making progress, ahead of Gleneagles [TB was due to chair the G8 summit]. On MEPP [Middle East Peace Process], it was still hard to get them as engaged as they should be, but he thought Bush at least was keen to do more. But the stuff he was really pushing on ahead of the summit was climate change and Africa, and there, he said, 'It's not easy, because you have so many bloody Americans who won't even accept climate change is real.' At least he had Bush talking about alternative energies, but the way climate change had become a left–right thing in the States was grimsville. Where he did seem to have made real progress was on aid, Africa and debt. Bush was ready to wipe out $15 billion worth of debt, and join in big style with the general trend of huge increases in aid. He [TB] said he [GWB] was a bit sore that they gave so much and yet still got seen as mean and difficult. TB was sounding pretty chirpy, but knew that Gleneagles was going to take a lot of his time and maybe drag his focus from the domestic too much. I caught some of TB's White House stuff later and it was OK, if not quite as one-way as I had expected following what he had said. Most of our media seemed to be going down the line of whether TB was getting some kind of political Iraq dividend, getting Bush to help him deliver the priorities for the G8. He did announce all kinds of stuff TB had been pressing for, on aid especially, and humanitarian relief, but there was a lot of emphasis from both of them, especially Bush, on supporting those who were committed to reform and 'Western values'. And a fair few of the reports I saw focused on their differences on aid, not just climate change, rather than the closeness. The Marshall Plan for Africa idea was not really flying, I guessed.

Wednesday 8 June

Match day, and this time I was watching on Sky rather than there in person. I texted a few thoughts and also kept Ben and Louisa in touch with what the commentators and panellists were saying. They were all pretty down on us at half-time, when we were trailing 6–7, apart from Charlie Hodgson, who played really well, Cusiter, Corry and Owen. But the second half came good and they ran out comfortable winners in the end, 36–14. Clive called from the dinner, said it was great, they had put Saturday's team under real pressure to perform, and that was how this tour had to go. His one big beef was the officials. He felt the linesmen had over-influenced the ref; that the first-half try disallowance should not have been; that it was like having three refs out there not one. But he sounded on a high with the overall performance and the sense of progress and momentum.

Thursday 9 June

I spent most of the day up on the Heath for Grace's Camden sports day, getting sunburnt. TB back from the US yesterday and people reflecting maybe he didn't get as much out of it as he should. Richard Stott [friend and former editor, *Daily Mirror* and *Today*] had begun work on editing first volume of diaries, '94–'95, and said the NK [Neil Kinnock, former Labour leader] row on holiday [AC and NK had argued about Murdoch and at one point NK held a kettle close to AC's face] was the most searing political reportage he had ever read. I was worrying about all the people who might feel let down by me doing it. Richard felt if the quality was repeated throughout it was the best political diary he had ever read. *Esquire* sent round mag with CW article. I was talking to LC and Ben on and off as they prepared for the pre-Maori press conference. I did words for CW but he toned down a bit on the attack on officials.

Friday 10 June

Louisa called. She said the press were moaning about us changing schedules and also that they felt they were not getting real access to players. The snappers were moaning too. Most of them were getting a fair bit published though. Louisa felt the only legitimate whinge was that when they saw the players it wasn't for long. What the players never told them was that they hated doing it. She asked me to help draft a statement about Ryan Jones [Wales player] being called up, effectively because Simon Taylor's hamstring was still playing up but we didn't want to say it was a direct replacement. We had to prepare a statement which did not rule out Taylor for future selection, but clearly people would see Jones as a replacement. Meanwhile Taylor was replaced in Saturday's team by Michael Owen, who would then be heading home to see his child being born. Any doubts we had about the quality needed to beat New Zealand were dispelled by their match against Fiji, which they won 91–0.

Fiona and I had our first big row since getting back, but it was a big one. She had tickets for the opera with Neil [Kinnock] and I had not wanted to go. I dreaded the political debate at the moment. Against my better judgement I went and hated it. They were late, I was a bit depressed and bad tempered, NK was up for picking a fight re politics and it was just a bad night. Fiona and I had a right go at each other and I ended up getting out of the car in a rage and walking home.

Saturday 11 June

Another match day, and despite the motivational powers of Lawrence Dallaglio, who gave out the shirts, it just didn't happen. New Zealand Maori played better in virtually all departments and there were a lot of disappointed Lions trooping off the pitch at the end. In his post-match interviews, Clive made no bones about it – the best team won and if anything the score, 19–13, flattered the Lions. We stood by for an avalanche of criticism, though wiser souls were pointing out that this was not the Test side, while also saying we only had two matches before the first Test, on which so many hopes were hanging. The row with Fiona had settled a bit and we were at least talking about things. The main problem was mutual validation. I felt she did not validate my time with TB and what she thought was support was actually tolerance. She said she could not validate TB but that should not be taken as an attack on me and so it went on, round and round in the same old circles.

Sunday 12 June

The Sunday papers weren't very pretty, but we had the announcement of the side against Wellington on Wednesday to move things on and with Jonny Wilkinson, Jason Robinson, Gareth Thomas and Neil Back all making their first appearance on New Zealand soil, it had a very different look and feel to what had gone before. Simon Taylor was going home, a second successive Lions tour ruined by injury. The media perked up a bit with the arrival of Charlotte Church [singer], flying in to see her boyfriend Gavin Henson, also selected for the Wellington match.

Monday 13 June

Clive called after the public training session and sounded positively upbeat. He said he had pretty much settled on the Test side and as things stood only five of the fifteen against NZ Maori would be there. That was why it was daft to read too much into the match. He said if we stay free of any more injuries, we stand half a chance. He was not playing Hill or O'Connell until the Test. He railed at the idea in parts of the media that he should now play his Test side and stick to it. Some of them need games, some of them need rest. But I am not picking the Test side until the Test.

Tuesday 14 June

I was working on my diary for 1998. The big *plus ça change* was Europe, with TB currently on a tour of capitals, as he was in '98, trying to get the future of Europe and future financing sorted. He was due to see Chirac and it looked like it was going to be one of their testier meetings. Chirac had said he wouldn't do a joint press conference. I sent a note saying he should do one solo, which he did. Chirac's basic pitch was that we had to keep going with ratifying the treaty, pretty much whatever the referendums said. TB was up for saying he was living in the past and not facing up to the realities of a new world, the new constitution had no chance, and he intended to have the whole working of the EU on the agenda for the summit and also our Presidency. Fiona had a meeting with new MPs at the HoC and we met for dinner, which was fine and nice until again we got to the nub and it was like a bloody great elephant in the room. She could not say that the experience of the last decade had been positive for her, but that should not be seen as a negative re me. But it was how I took it and as hers was one of the small number of validations I needed and wanted, it was hard to move on.

Wednesday 15 June

Up for the Wellington match. A lot better but still not great and a sense JW was not quite firing yet. Clive moved him to the centre and put Stephen Jones in at fly half in the second half. 13–6 up at half-time, 23–6 full-time. The score slightly flattering. But it was a win in difficult circumstances and but for the conditions and a couple of errors there could have been a much bigger lead. Fiona and I went for a long walk to carry on last night's discussion and we went round the same circles. But we were talking fine and by and large getting on OK. There were just certain flashpoints on either side to be avoided. But to me it was beginning to feel like post my breakdown – I had thought that by stopping drinking, everything would work out fine, but then once not drinking became the norm, there was still other stuff going on in my head, the depressions especially, that she was sure had made me drink in the first place. Now, the equivalent was that I had stopped working in No. 10, and was hoping that would solve the problems that drove us both crazy, but again it was not as simple as that, and so the problems were still there. And it was probably best we didn't engage on them, at least not until we were in a better place psychologically with it.

Philip was convinced I should do some kind of deep therapy, otherwise he was worried I was heading for more trouble ahead, added to which he was worried Fiona would one day just say sod it, this guy is totally impossible to live with. The truth is we had got through worse than this, but I suppose there was a cumulative effect. In the afternoon I had a speech at an event on engagement marketing run by Octagon. I did my usual strategy speech but adapted to take in some of the points made during the earlier presentations, some of which were interesting. For example, they had done a massive 'Passion Drivers' [research tool] polling of sports fans to find out what factors made people support certain sports. Some of it was obvious, e.g. team attachment was most important in football and rugby, the fact that fans also played was more important in golf, nostalgia and talking about past players was important in cricket. But as I said in the speech, there was a lot in there that politics could learn from by way of the depth of sophistication of a project like that. Seemed to go OK. I took Rory to Watford for a race, his second sub-2 mins in four days but he was still a good few seconds behind the best and I think getting a bit worried about it.

Thursday 16 June
Clive called early, my time, and said he had torn a strip off the press over the so-called brawl story.* It turned out it was an accidental clash of heads in the public training session, and had been blown up by a Scots journo because it involved Bulloch, and then was picked up by the others. Mick Cleary [*Telegraph*] had met CW earlier and said things

---

* Initial British newspaper reports alleged that Gordon Bulloch and John Hayes came to blows which led to Bulloch needing stitches to a head wound.

were at crisis point. What total bollocks. CW made clear rugby had to come first, but we were getting whacked by our media because of perceived lack of access, and NZ because we were cutting back on planned community work as a result of the players complaining it was all a bit much. Clive said he went for Peter Jackson [*Mail*] in particular, who claimed he never wrote the brawl story, though it had his name on it. Clive said to him he had been negative the whole way through, e.g. re Prince William, re me, re JW etc. but he sounded a lot happier, as did LC and Ben.

Fiona and I went for another long walk with the dog, then I left to see GB at the Treasury, via a cup of tea with Bradders [David Bradshaw, Downing Street special advisor]. GB was in an odd state. He looked a bit dishevelled, had not lost much weight despite saying last time I saw him he was determined to, same suit, same shoes, same crumpled sock look. He was fairly effusive to start with, said that I had done a brilliant job during the campaign and that if I had not turned it around, the thing might easily have fallen apart completely. He said he didn't know how to get into the campaign and I got him in, and although we could not undo everything, we did make a difference. He said I had showed again I was one of a small number of people with the determination to make a difference, and that was why I should not be lost to the continuing challenge. He felt Tony did not have enough good people around him. I defended them, said actually he had a lot of good people in there, but the real lesson of the campaign was that when we all worked together, we were still very, very hard to beat. It shouldn't have taken all that grief and aggro to get to where we got to, and it was really important they did not descend back into it again.

He said that was not just down to him. TB would feel the need to retrench. Some of his people spent all their time undermining the Treasury team. I said that cut both ways and it really had to stop. He was more interested in the Lions stuff than Tony, I would say, keen to know what Clive was like, also what kind of systems we ran. We had lots of small talk about that, and about football. He said we should be worried that most MPs were so unfit, and most of our lot so complacent. I filled him in on some of the team-building stuff I had seen with the Lions and said while some of it was probably sports-specific, some of it at least could be translated. Their away days, for example, seemed so much better focused and prepared than ours. There also seemed to be a deeper honesty about what makes people tick and what annoys people. The big red folder we all had was the bringing together not just of information, but a set of values. The rules of teamship were also important in that they had flowed from a proper analysis of how to build the strongest possible team out of those individuals.

He was interested, but I said when I went through some of this with TB, he had said there was no way we could do that kind of thing because of the openness to parody, but also that GB would not engage. GB snorted, and I said, 'He's got a point though, hasn't he?' I would love it if we could get you guys to do some of this stuff, where we strip away all the shit and the baggage, and really try to get to the heart of why they were not as strong together and rebuild. He said it was probably too late, too much water under the bridge, too many broken promises, too much animosity and mistrust. I said it was never too late to get to the right place. But people needed to be honest with each other. The one thing I had felt during the campaign was that, with just a few exceptions, there had been a brittleness to their exchanges, certainly they had lost the easy flow that came with genuine camaraderie. But I said they would both get hurt, reputationally, if it all fell back to the old ways. He was listening, and nodding a fair bit, and admitted that on the political scene, things did not feel as they should after a third win.

He didn't say it in so many words, but he clearly sensed TB was on borrowed time. I said the best way he could secure the top job was for the two of them to operate as a team as much as possible and when TB went, it would be obvious. 'I have a lot of scars, Alastair,' he said. 'We all do,' I said, 'including him. Let's not pretend this is you as victim. I am just saying – and I can see you might think I am doing this from his perspective, but I'm not, I think this helps you both – that if you were to be solid with him in this next phase, that will benefit both of you.' But he said on policy, there were real differences. He worried TB was going too far. He worried he was trying to provoke. He worried some of his ideas were not thought through. I said, 'Try and make them work then. Don't resist them purely because he is the author.' He veered from being really engaged and energetic one moment, to a bit whingy the next. Then suddenly he said that from his own personal perspective he would be better off leaving the government and starting to prepare for the future from the backbenches. 'You're not serious, are you?', I asked. I'm not saying that's what's going to happen, he said, but he did say it two or three times, and in a way that made me think he was genuinely reflecting on it.

He said the problem was that people like he and I knew that the Labour Party had real problems that would take time to deal with and we could not begin to do it properly at the moment. 'Tony does not want a proper analysis done because it might say things he doesn't like. He wants his legacy, and his focus is on doing these things in the public services that make that happen, so he is not just seen as a foreign policy Prime Minister. But it means he is putting up in lights the very things we agreed should not be dominant in the election because in the end people wanted a simpler investment v cuts argument.' He was clear that the longer TB went on, the worse it became. But the worst thing for him was the lack of clarity. He was aware that he had to watch out for problems of his own – mainly that it would be seen as an old-fashioned leftie taking over from someone genuinely able to command support from centre and left of centre. 'Don't forget the right,' he said.

But if he was to plan properly for a transition at some point, how did he put together a plan on that? If he was making a series of big speeches, when was the best time to do that? How did he plan a personal strategy when there was no clarity about when? He said there was a sense of drift on the domestic agenda. TB was now taken up again with EU, G8 etc. and people would start to say, 'What is happening to the domestic front?' 'I know what will happen,' he said. 'He will be sucked into all the foreign stuff again, more and more, but will dip in and out of all the domestic, and won't necessarily understand all the implications.' He is quite a good multi-tasker, I said. Maybe what I could do is persuade TB that making sure the party is in good shape when he goes is part of the legacy, and that means making sure we learn the lessons and act on them. I felt TB should ask GB to chair a group that looks to do a proper thorough analysis. GB said he had had a similar idea but felt JP should chair it and he, maybe I, maybe people off the NEC should be on it.

I had been expecting him to be a bit less whingey and a bit more a man with a plan, but he seemed to think it was impossible to have one, because of TB. He said once the threat of a challenge receded, TB went back into his usual mode. They did not communicate, he was not consulted about things and even if TB gave him a date when he said he was going, he would be loath to believe it because he had been given plenty of false promises before. 'You know him as well as I do. You know how many promises he has broken.' I loved the way he threw out these statements as though we were on the same side of the argument. I said when I talk to TB about him, and then him about GB, it was like listening to parallel universes. He said he didn't think TB was as concerned about the future of the party as he was. There was a part of him [TB] that thought, 'Après moi, le déluge.' He was pretty scathing about the political operation around TB and said about the party we needed to think in new ways about it; we had to create a network or networks, not just a party machine; learn from the charities and other successful organisations.

He asked what I was going to do, and I said I didn't know. I didn't want to come back in full-time but I did not want to see the party fall now, and would help. He said he would want to work with me up to the election in some way or another. He was also keen to know if Fiona was interested in a seat. 'She is better on education than anyone, and should be more involved.' I said she had mixed views. She was passionate about some issues but she didn't like Parliament, like me was not really that bothered about status, and was unsure at the moment. Added to which it was fair to say she and I were still recovering from the pretty horrible ups and downs we had had over the last part of my time in No. 10. She hadn't particularly enjoyed me being back in the centre of things. 'You should both be there,' he said. He said the new blood was poor, and the stock of ministers was not great.

I said there were certain things we had to do – establish the extent of the Lib Dem threat; work out whether the position on tuition fees was recoverable; deal with disengagement among certain groups, including women; trust more generally; it all needed real in-depth analysis. But it was not being done. I said I felt he could do more than he thought. I said also that the story about him had to be one about his modus operandi changing not as a foil to TB – sofa government and all that crap – but as a foil to himself, emerging as a team player. I said one of my first rules of leadership – and the Lions had confirmed me in this – was that the best team leaders are also team players. He did not have that reputation and he needed to work hard and fast to try to get it. That was why I felt the team-building stuff was important. It wasn't enough just to pepper speeches with flattering references to other ministers. He had to engage with them genuinely, and stop killing those he felt were not 100 per cent signed up to him. He needed to broaden his base and his reach in part through how he did it.

It was a perfectly pleasant meeting. The only reference to books was when he asked whether I was doing one on the Lions. I was beginning to feel a bit between a rock and a hard place. I had done the deal on the diaries, money was coming in via the advance, but I might not be able to do it if I was still working for GB because basically I would feel it was totally dishonourable to publish anything that could damage him if he was still active, let alone PM. I was going at some stage to have to tell him, and in detail, but for now I was clear I would do nothing, other than get on with transcribing them. His assistant kept popping her head in to say the next meeting was waiting, but he appeared to want to carry on talking. I guess he had felt I had been able to get him and TB to where they needed to be for the campaign, and it had sort of worked, and now he hoped I could help him see that through to the next stage, which was TB going and him taking over. I said I genuinely believed the best way for that to be made to happen was genuine not phoney teamship. He walked me out, said keep in touch, regards to Fiona, enjoy New Zealand, and off I went.

I had lunch with Rory and Calum and then had a meeting with Gail [Rebuck, Random House publisher, wife of Philip Gould] Susan Sandon [also Random House] and Richard [Stott] re the book. Susan and Stott, who had seen parts of it, both thought it was brilliant but would obviously need editing. RS saw it as amazing reportage. Susan saw it as an intense historical document covering interesting events and people. But both felt it would go down a storm. I levelled with them about the GB situation and said it may not be possible as soon as she thinks. But I liked her OK, I liked Stott's enthusiasm and energy and I felt I was probably with the right editing team.

GB had been the usual mix of flattery, paranoia and brilliance, but I felt he was lacking confidence a bit, and he was still too prone to play the blame game, especially TB. I spoke to TB later, filled him in, and needless to say the whole 'parallel universe' thing just kicked off again. I had heard it so many times. All the undermining came from the other side. GB had to be cajoled to do even the most basic cooperation. He had a whole team of MPs feeding the line out that we were shit. Etc., etc., etc. I agreed to do TB a note re legacy/party. David Cameron threw his hat in the ring for the Tory leadership. David Davis was sure the Tories wouldn't go for an Old Etonian, but I had a chat with Phil Webster [*Times*], who thought Cameron was not to be underestimated.

Friday 17 June

On the last day at home, I tried to spend some time revising with Calum, swimming with Grace then after another tearful farewell with Fiona, Rory, proud new owner of a driving licence, drove me to Paddington to catch the Heathrow Express. I had a brief chat with Jonathan [Powell, TB chief of staff], and with TB, who was at what sounded like a particularly ball-saching EU summit on the new budget. He was coming under pressure on the rebate, also not happy about their plans on CAP [Common Agricultural Policy] reform – it didn't go far enough – and was in a position where he might have to block the whole thing. One of those moments where I was half glad I wasn't there and half wishing I was. He sounded like he felt a bit between a rock and a hard place. [Jean-Claude] Juncker [PM of Luxembourg] was setting it up as TB and others, but especially TB, trying to use the French and Dutch defeats to get changes they knew were impossible, and to steer Europe in a totally different direction. He was talking about how ashamed he was that the poorer countries were prepared to make concessions but richer countries – i.e. us – were not.

Chirac was also pissed off at TB making a push on the deal France got from the CAP. TB was pushing the message that if we didn't listen to what people were saying, we would end up in an even worse state. He asked if I was around and when I said I was about to get on a plane to NZ, the silence was his way of asking, 'Are you mad?' I said I was quite enjoying the Lions. 'Yeah, well, they probably talk a lot more sense than I am hearing.' We left home 7 p.m. Friday, UK time. By 1.30 p.m. NZ time, three flights later, I was in Christchurch, with a fair amount of '98 diary work and another *Irish Times* piece behind me. While I had been airborne, the Lions had chalked up another win, 30–19 against Otago after going behind early on, with Charlie Hodgson kicking five penalties out of five. It was mainly the second string, but late recall Ryan Jones was man of the match, pictures of his flowing locks all over the NZ papers, and lots saying he might have forced his way in. The BA pilot announced the score as we flew from Singapore to Sydney, but even he couldn't resist saying we won after a poor first-half performance.

During the stopover in Singapore I caught up with what was happening at the EU summit – it looked like it was heading for failure, and we were going to be getting the lion's share of the blame. Juncker was talking about the whole EU being in crisis. Overblown, but certainly tricky stuff. TB had held out and, given they all wanted to get home, it was not so urgent that they literally had to sort it now. But as TB said when we spoke just after landing, it meant there were a few who would be out to get him during our Presidency. 'The trouble is they think we can just carry on as though nothing has happened. I am as pro-European as they will ever have in Downing Street, but if we don't respond to these concerns, we end up in a worse situation.' [José Manuel] Barroso [Commission President] was being a bit more practical and pragmatic, he said, and realised we could come back to this and keep working at it. 'But it's not a happy scene.' It was a classic summit breakdown: we were blaming the French and the French were blaming us.

The tone in the NZ media was a lot more negative and aggressive than when I left, again a sign that things were hotting up for the Test match. I bumped into Andy Robinson, who was clearly pumped up being so close to the Tests. Bill Beaumont filled me in on the grief he was getting from the NZ media and sponsors about the cutbacks on the community side, but he had reached the view that whatever we did they would criticise. The feeling had grown that the local media had moved to straightforward bias mode. We were still doing more than any other Lions tour in history. I had a catch-up with the media team, which we did just before the team for the match against Southland was named, as a way of avoiding questions about those who were omitted – i.e. the ones likeliest to make Lions Test side. The UK press had stopped whining as much as before but there were still one or two. Louisa and I went for a coffee to plot out the next few days.

Tonight was a big moment in the tour, namely the all-comers meeting Clive had called for all players and management at 5.30 p.m. There was the usual chit-chat outside but it was maybe a bit more nervy than usual. He was announcing the team for the Southland match on Tuesday night, and it was a rare occasion where players were hoping not to be selected, because if they were in for Southland, it meant they were almost certainly not in the 23 being considered for a Test place on Saturday. Clive said that he had always prided himself on no bullshit with players. He could tell them they were fighting for a first Test slot but it would not be true. It did not mean they did not have a chance for future Tests, but they were not going to be in this time. The names went up, and you could sense the disappointment of those named, and the elation of those not named. Ian McGeechan, coach of the midweek side, made a little speech saying Lions Tests were won by squads not just the Test sides, and pointed out that in most series, a lot more players played in Tests than those picked for the first one. The most notable names, or at least those who had been written up as having a chance, were probably Gavin Henson, Geordan Murphy and Donncha O'Callaghan.

Then CW asked everyone to leave apart from the 23 still in Test contention, and the Saturday side coaches. It was a very public breach into A and B teams, but most managed a smile or a hello as they filed out. The one we were a bit worried about was Gavin. As we filed out, Clive asked me to stay in, presumably to hear what he had to say, which would help shape some of our communications plan in the coming days. Again, he said he didn't want to bullshit them, and he told them the side he had in mind. Jenkins, Byrne, White up front; O'Connell and Kay; Hill, Corry and Back; Peel and Stephen Jones at half-back with Wilkinson moved to 12, Brian O'Driscoll at 13, Lewsey and Thomas on the wings, Robinson at full back. On the bench, Rowntree, Thompson, Grewcock, Ryan Jones, Dawson, Greenwood, with the last slot undecided between Shane Horgan and Shane Williams. He had spoken to none of the players about selection apart from Brian [Test captain], so they were all taking it in for the first time, and also being expected to keep it quiet till Wednesday. I felt privileged to be present for this part of the tour, and quite surprised this was how Clive did it.

Jonny was sitting over from me taking notes into his red folder. Lewsey had a totally focused look on his face. The Welsh boys looked happy. He told them they were the best of the best. He was convinced we could win. He had picked a team to play a pressure match and this one was 'all about pressure. The New Zealanders were not great under pressure. We can beat them. I have no worries about that. My only worry is whether we go out and play. I want you to go out and play,' he said. 'Man for man, we are better than them.' This theme of pressure would become the staple diet of our communications.

He said he had had a New Zealander send him advice on how to deal with the haka [traditional war dance always performed by the All Blacks before kick-off] – send tribe leader to the front, and go down on one knee; put Dwayne Peel there to watch his back. The rest, track suits off, stare out their opposite number. At the end BOD throws some grass in the air. There was a lot of laughter and BOD said he and Peely got the short straws, but there was something in it, definitely. The players were sitting at a series of small tables and the intensity moved up another gear. There were no congratulations going on, but a growing sense of excitement. He said most of the bench would be used and explained why he was playing JR not Josh L at full back. He made clear Ryan Jones had stormed in on the back of one performance, that Back was in there because of how he handled himself through the ban and in his comeback. He urged them all to shout out if there was anything in training they didn't like, and urged them to be sensible and avoid injuries.

He asked Brian O'D to say a few words. He said this was going to be a very special week. He already felt butterflies and goosebumps just listening to that. How excited were they going to be by Saturday?

They looked and felt up for it. The mood around the place was pretty good and the Maori game felt a fair time away now. I had a cup of tea with CW to go over a few things. He said Henson wasn't close because he was too young and inexperienced. O'Callaghan did get close but he went for experience. One downside would be the charge it was based on the England World Cup squad, but once people saw Byrne, Jones at 10, O'Connell, Thomas, it was a bit more varied than that, though there were no Welsh forwards. The omitted one he was worried about was Gavin Henson. When I went out, Gavin was talking to a Welsh journalist in the foyer. I hung around, and got him to agree to a quote that was basically – disappointed but I will play on and keep challenging for a place.

He had that little smile on his face that managed to look both mischievous and totally gutted. He said it hadn't sunk in yet. 'The thing is I thought I would be in.' He said he didn't want to do any interviews. 'Trouble is, I'm not intelligent enough to lie.' Some of the Welsh players feared he would explode and he had to be managed carefully. The mood among the selected, not surprisingly, was very different. A real buzz, real excitement. I had a team meeting to plot out media and we were joined by Gethin Jenkins and Stephen Jones, followed by Peel, Lewsey, BOD and Shane H. Stephen J had very quickly joined the 'interested in politics' club. He would come in, big smile always on his face, sit down, clap his hands, 'Right, Alastair, today we want to learn about… how does Tony sack someone? What does he say? Does he do it by phone? Face to face?' Or something like, 'So, Alastair, what I need to know for my political education today, who is the biggest bullshitter you have ever met?' Lots of good-natured banter. Bed with help from Gary O'D's decongestants. Grace crying down the phone because it's Father's Day. But on the plus side I had fitted straight back into things and the excitement really was growing.

Monday 20 June

I slept OK and was taunting Otis about how his jetlag advice had been all wrong. He said we'll see if you're still saying that in three days' time. I went for a run around six but was not motoring at all. We had finally fixed for Clive to do *Campbell Live*, one of the big set-piece NZ shows, and John Campbell [broadcaster] joined me for breakfast to go over the interview. I had done a note for Clive saying we wanted to get into the whole argument about pressure and whether the ABs could handle it as well as the Lions. We did it upstairs and Clive was on good form, so much so that Campbell's last question was that he seemed relaxed and he was enjoying it. All the key messages were in there. I had breakfast with Josh, Simon Shaw and then Richard Hill, who was not training today to protect his knee. He was interesting on the subject of players' wives being there, obviously wished his was – she was working – but felt it posed some problems for those who had no partners there.

Josh was a bit mellower, relieved to know where he was playing. He said, 'I'd watch out for Gavin if I were you.' He said he had been going round saying he hated NZ. But my sense was a lot of the players didn't rate him as much as he rated himself – a couple of them openly said they didn't like playing alongside him. The HOD meeting, for the first time, was up in the team room, which Clive now wanted manned twenty-four hours a day. The security boys said they were stepping up, above all stopping any chance of being snooped on in training, but truth be told we did not have the personnel really to stop it. I persuaded Clive we needed a special picture on Wednesday and later Ben and the Getty snappers and I scoped out a few places round the city, settling on a riverside scene. Clive was worried about leaving the Test side for a day, fearing Andy and Eddie would let them go too hard in training and there would be injuries. The main story out of yesterday was Henson, and I suggested to Clive he had a word with him, which he did after training. Clive was keen the message was out there that just because he wasn't in this time, it didn't mean he would not make it in a later Test.

I did an interview with *L'Equipe* on the tour, then got ready for the plane to Invercargill. On the bus, Tom Shanklin [Wales player] put on *The Office* and I was winding up Clive about how David Brent's motivational speeches were like team talks. I worked on a piece for a NZ paper re the NZ media, which were getting more one-eyed than ever, particularly on the security, basically intimating we were totally paranoid, not doing enough community stuff and above all of course how crap we were at rugby. I also did CW a note on the tunnel and staring after he sent me his paper on the haka, and how we should respond to it – with BOD on one knee, Peel behind him as the young warrior, and the others hanging back staring at their opposite numbers. We were met at the airport by two men in yellow suits and gas masks giving out oysters – a reference to [former England player] Brian Moore's comment that Invercargill was like Chernobyl with oysters.

The stadium was pretty bleak, even in fairly mild weather. We had agreed the players would do mix and mingle with the media, which went fine, John Hayes [Ireland player] the star attraction because he used to live here for two years. John was right at the front of the queue of the guys who would be happy never to have to do media, and didn't particularly enjoy it, but he was a lovely bloke and handled it all fine. Clive asked me to speak to them in the dressing room, just to underline that the media would want stories about their disappointment and everyone had to be positive and focused on tomorrow's match. Gavin had asked yesterday that he do no interviews, but I could sense he was in a bit of a mood. He said, 'Did we put out that bullshit you wrote for me yesterday?' It was fine but he didn't believe it really. He didn't care if he did interviews. He said Clive had said he could say what he liked. I said I'm sure he meant up to a point.

It became immaterial when Dean Wilson of Hayters [sports news agency] grabbed him as he came off the pitch and he said a few words – gutted, devastated, didn't sleep all night etc. etc. It was fine on one level but we had told the rest of the media he would not be talking so it was a problem. Dean unsurprisingly wanted to put it all round as a Hayters' story, which we feared would piss off the rest, so in the end we did a deal with him and he agreed to send us the quotes, which we would put out. We had to watch it didn't look like Gavin was saying he wanted the Test team to do badly. It was in the dressing room with the other kickers that I realised his fellow players were slightly losing it with him. Back at the hotel I showed the Henson statement to Clive, who was OK with it and said don't bother showing it to him, just leave him now. He asked me to go out for dinner with him, Gareth and Ian as guests of Paddy O'Brien [former NZ referee and head of International Rugby Board's referee board] and some of his friends. Nice enough evening, lots of sport of course, but a lot of politics too.

Ian McG was interested in politics too and we talked about the differences – e.g. how it would be impossible for TB to announce a team as CW did yesterday; how we did not have enough time to groom talent. He liked TB though I doubt he was Labour, which was probably where most of them were. But I was feeling rough, and later the doctor put me on antibiotics for a chest problem, probably exacerbated by too much flying. I talked a lot of politics to a couple of O'Brien's friends, a policeman – specialist in child abuse – and a farmer who said one day NZ would be a state of Australia. The cop told me TB got a bad press here because of Bush and Iraq, but he felt the NZ people really liked him. CW had told the team for tomorrow their job was to 'keep the Test side honest', press them hard, make them feel they were breathing down their necks for a place. Paddy O'Brien gave me a lift back early. He thought the first Test would be tight, felt if the game was played at pace, NZ would win, but if it became tough and hard and slow, our experience might win out. Drink in the bar with Gary, John Feehan, Louise and Louisa and then to bed, and awake by 3 a.m., so maybe Otis was right. Added to which I was worried because Fiona fell down the stairs on the bus and Calum was worrying about his exams.

TB sent through a draft of his speech to the European Parliament [on Thursday] and we had a series of exchanges about that, especially on how to mesh the idea that social Europe and political project Europe were two parts of the same argument. He didn't have to burnish his pro-Europe credentials, but he did have to open up some space for real debate. He asked me to draft a section on the idea of the EU having helped deliver, peace, progress and prosperity, and get into the aftermath of WW2 a bit. Where I thought the speech was weaker was in the 'New Europe' or 'Europe renewal project' that he wanted. I agreed to work on that. He wanted to be pretty frank, that the referendums rejecting the Treaty were not based on millions reading the thing, or even of it not being well put together, but because people did not feel either close to, or represented by, Europe's institutions. And that had to be addressed. The UK rebate was picking up as an issue and he was going to have to address that in the speech itself, but wanted to do it in the context of everyone needed to do a fundamental reassessment of how things worked. He said he had not particularly enjoyed being in the traditional British spoiling position, but they were making a mistake if they thought they could just carry on as though nothing had happened.

Tuesday 21 June

I slept for two hours, waking up at three with jetlag, congestion, coughing, the lot. I knew I wouldn't get back to sleep and so got up and did some work. I was first up for breakfast, followed by Gavin Henson, my first of many, many chats during a day in which I seemed to become Clive's representative to Gav, and his hand-holder for the day. I – in common with Donncha – thought there was a touch of comic genius in Gavin, whereas most of the others thought he was a mix of shy, not bright and too flash and individual. But he had been the big story of the tour for two days now and we needed, as several of the players told me, to keep an eye on him. At HOD, Gary O'D went through the injuries, Clive was worried about not bringing down replacements. Later he said he was worried that too much of the focus at the moment was media and not enough on playing. I suggested Ian being at HOD as a remedy but he wasn't keen. We needed the players to get more humour going. On Gavin, he said the opposite of yesterday, when he had wanted to keep him off the media. He said he thought he should front it up. Both he and BB liked my NZ media analysis, which I offered to a defensive-sounding Wynn Gray [NZ journalist], who I liked.

I went with CW and Bill to their community visit, the children's ward of a brilliant local hospital which had a number of Brit staff. Clive's manner was good – he spent time talking to the kids and parents, including some very sad cases, and did a good media bit – clip on rugby tonight, clip on Michael Campbell, clip on community and he was good on all three. I got very emotional when they called me into see a young leukaemia patient whose demeanour was so like Ellie [Merritt, daughter of AC's best friend John. Both died of leukaemia in the 1990s]. They asked why I was involved in LRF [Leukaemia Research Fund] and I couldn't bring myself to talk about John and Ellie – said it was because of Sissy [Bridge, next door neighbour, friend of Grace], and told how she was now fully recovered, and didn't mention John and Ellie, whose graves we had visited last week on the anniversary of John's death.

Clive then went into town to do what he always does on match days – send a postcard to his kids. I was doing some '98 diary work plus drafting a joint TB–Bertie Ahern [Taoiseach of Ireland] letter for the Test match on Saturday. Then the kind of hanging about bit while Ian did his team talk, and we just killed time before going to the stadium. Gareth Jenkins had had a word with Gavin Henson, told him just to understand how he handled this would in part decide what kind of player and person he became. He was a good player but could be better. He had to learn from this, maybe for future tours. We set off for the stadium, and Louisa took care of pre-match interviews while I chatted to Miles Harrison [Sky] and alerted him that we may need to speak just before the Test – about the response Clive was planning to the haka.

The players looked pretty pumped up, and started well. But then mistakes crept in and at half-time the coaches were saying it was as if they had never played with each other. Southland pulled level then we ground out a 26–16 win but it was disappointing. In the immediate

June '05: Getting TB and Ahern to send good luck message

aftermath I had to get Gavin in the right place to do media because he was man of the match. He looked pained when I told him. Oh fucking hell, do I have to? I said he did. So what should I say? I said the basic line from the match was we did not play as well as we hoped but a win is a win, and he should talk up his own performance. There was no harm repeating he was devastated etc. but it was time to move on. It took me ten minutes to get him out there, and he did Sky, then NZ, then radio (after which he signed a handwritten book agreement with HarperCollins). He was OK, probably too much dwelling on yesterday, and saying it was now out of his hands if he got in or not – which I was worried sounded a bit like he wanted the others to fail.

Of course the Welsh media were in full cry about him being out of the Test side and the story had gone big everywhere. Also NZ were talking up their surprise at his omission, which was clearly a line to take for them. I then told him he had to do the after-match press conference, not just the interviews for broadcasters, and he seemed even more pained, swearing and screwing up his face like I had hit him. But by then Clive had taken me to one side and told me to hint to Gavin that he might reconsider him for a place on the bench for the first Test. Gavin looked like he assumed I was joking, but in fact CW had texted Will Greenwood with the idea, who had texted back that he saw the logic. Andy Robinson said he was happy enough with it. So Gavin was a bit more up about things.

After he went through to the toilet again to do his hair and pretty himself up, we finally got him in front of the media and he was almost comic – a bit monosyllabic but at times funny, e.g. when asked how he felt about all the support and sympathy at home – 'Is there – I don't know anything what's going on there.' Or when asked if it was down to 'off-pitch activities' that he hadn't been included – what a stupid question, he said. He asked me several times afterwards if he did OK. He was a mix of shy and cocky, needy and confident. ROG, Moody and Michael Owen were mesmerised as they sat alongside him at the press conference. All three were totally on message – though Michael was probably too nice, sounded almost priestlike at times, to be a captain – but when Gavin spoke you could see them on tenterhooks as to what he was going to come out with next. ROG looked at several points like he was about to burst out laughing. But in the end he did fine. Cusiter did the Scots' reporters then off we went.

Clive was going over Henson v Greenwood for the bench. Mike Ford, Scott Johnson (great bloke, Aussie advisor who arrived today and was a total stir-it-up merchant) all felt no, stick with Will and by the end of the day that was where Clive was. But when we got back to Christchurch he asked me to see Gavin one more time and tell him he was going to review the tapes, that he was impressed with the way he responded to disappointment and he was back in the frame, but if he did not push Greenwood out, he should understand he had done himself a lot of good. GH and I chatted by the lift on the ninth floor, which opened and a host of players came out, including Donncha, who pretended to be me. 'Bad move, Gavin, calling Clive a fucking knobhead on live TV, very bad move. No chance now, son.' Gav seemed more at ease in himself, said that sounded fine, he felt better about things. Earlier in the dressing room Clive had been talking to him and he said, 'Where's my shadow?' meaning me, so at least he was laughing about it.

ROG was not having Gavin at all. I liked ROG a lot. He was always asking me about my madness, and later told me his brother was a shrink in a London hospital. The mood lifted fairly quickly and by the time we got to the reception was good. They press-ganged John Hayes into making a little speech about his time in Invercargill. He was coming out of himself a bit too, joking to me that he knew the press all wanted him but he was hiding away. His and Donncha's mums and D's girlfriend were at the reception, real solid Irish folk. Singing on the bus later, led by Matt Stevens. Scott Johnson very funny – 'The bad news is I had to come to Invercargill. The good news it is the shortest day of the year.' Dave Rogers and others still moaning about photo access. Nice chat with Louise on the plane north re planning, security etc.

On the plane I watched an edited video with Gareth Jenkins and it was fascinating to go through it with someone who knew the game, explaining who was doing what right and what wrong. So technical and thousands of things going at once. He had been good at the presser too. We flew up in an hour, then CW asked me to sit with him on the bus and go over the Gavin situation again. It was probably right to stick with Will but he owed it to Henson to review overnight. I was feeling ill but had enjoyed today. I had also done a couple of emails to Fiona on the validation situation and I felt better for that too. David Hill was chasing the joint letter from TB and Bertie idea. CW loved it. Back by 1, planning press conference, sleep by 2, up at 4. Really needed to watch this jetlag. Also planning 'Audiences With' in NZ and they were sold out, just as players and others were showing an interest.

Wednesday 22 June

I had another bad night's sleep then breakfast, filled in Otis on last night before being joined by Gavin, who was much more open than before. We had a chat about yesterday, how he had reacted. I got the final Test team from Clive, which we agreed to put out as he was telling the players. LC and I did words, then to the all-squad meeting for him to set out the team formally. BOD spoke well, talked about the fact that it was win or lose for all, selected or not. Then a 22-only meeting in the war room – must have been horrible for the others to troop out, very much with a feeling of being second best, before I went with them on the bus for a photocall by the rock we had recced. Sebastian was starting up again as a nickname. The coaches were a bit pissed off at the media eating into their time but we were over in minutes. At training we had them nearer the snappers and it was fine. Lovely day, mood good, more security there. Donncha had us all in hysterics as he stood watching four blokes mending a door and went off on one about what kind of special door it must be that they needed four men to fix it. Matt Stevens, injured, said most people would break their neck in a scrum against Julian White.

I listened in to Clive's post-training talk, which again underlined how technical and analytical it all was. To a rugby virgin like myself, it was fascinating, all the codes, the combinations, the patterns. Did it feel like it was a winning environment? Pretty much. Clive was getting a bit narky and tense but the mood was OK. Thousands of fans were arriving. Lots of ex-players were hanging around the hotel. I was getting tired but still felt we were on top of things. Running the pressure line pretty hard. Having to sort a few too many things next week on other work side. Fiona was doing an education TV programme and sounded OK. Everyone too hot, she said. Calum OK, Grace still a bit weepy.

We had a press conference at six and Clive asked me to talk to the 22 at 5.45 to go over things. I thanked them for cooperation, said it was now about showing confidence and momentum, went over some of the tricky lines and the format for the press conference. As before, most would rather not be doing it but again Clive wanted to get good coverage, good pictures, show solidarity. We took them over, and they filed in to the new video, brief words from Clive then fairly obvious questions, then into the long round of interviews. They didn't like doing it but did it well. It went on for an hour or so, and the media were fairly happy. I had said before we went in for the presser that given what happened at Rotorua, when Danny Grewcock and Steve Thompson had spent the whole time messing about and making each other laugh, it might be a good idea if they didn't sit together. They all got their revenge later. As we were all filing out, Paul O'Connell whipped down my tracksuit bottoms from behind – thankfully without anyone filming it! but provoking plenty of laughter.

Worse than that, Tommo ran off with my BlackBerry as it fell from my pocket, putting me into a total panic until I got it back. There was a note on there about TB's Europe strategy, and also about his recent chats with GB and what we do about all that. I suppose it showed they were taking me as one of their own, but I was in a total panic. 'Come on, Tommo, don't be a cunt.' 'Don't know what you're talking about.' Then when I said there was stuff on there that was a bit sensitive, they just went into 'Sebastian' mode. I eventually got it back when I got the security guys to put the wind up him by saying the spooks were tracking it down! Off to the Gondola cable car restaurant for a press reception. Most management went out afterwards and Andy Robinson was pissed off I didn't but I was knackered.

Thursday 23 June

It was a rest day for everyone. Media-wise all we did was a little screening of the *Campbell Live* Europe interview. John Campbell had decided they would drop Graham Henry and make the whole show about the Lions. In the end it would be Clive, me and a barmy army package. Lots of the squad got a bit hammered last night, quite a few not back till 5 a.m. I still couldn't sleep, had breakfast with James [Robson], Stephen Jones and JW. Jones a lovely guy, really smiley and chatty and quizzing re anything and everything. Had an hour then arguing the toss with Josh on sports policy, Bush, TB, lots of different things. Most of the day I was just wandering around the hotel, didn't run or do much. The piece that I did for the *NZ Herald* came out fine, basically making the point that the NZ media saw its role less as one of covering the tour, more as doing what it could to help the All Blacks.

I was working a bit on TB's speech for the European Parliament, which after last week's row over the budget was going to be huge.[*] I called TB to go over the draft and said maybe after the Q&A he should point out that every time he has made any progress, it has been by facing up

---

[*] The EU budget talks had broken down after a bitter dispute between Britain and France over the bloc's long-term finances.

to the issues when they needed to. New Labour. Modernise economy. Now Europe. The speech was live on BBC and CNN and went down pretty well all round, with the usual noises against. He was still a very large cut above most of them when it came to these big set-piece events. He sounded pretty chirpy but said that last week had been the worst summit yet. But he had the bit between the teeth and was going for it. He read out a section about the lack of connection between leaders and people, and we strengthened it, taking apart some of the claims summits made about reconnection, and inserting a bit of a reality check on how we are seen, a wake-up call to what the public actually think about the way Europe is developing.

He said at the moment leadership was seen as much as a problem as it was a solution. The rows over the budget meant he had to get into that and didn't leave much doubt the recent summit had been pretty ugly. He also did a good defence of New Labour to rebut the idea that we were hellbent on some kind of ultra-Anglo-Saxon-US economic model that cared nothing for the poor and vulnerable. But ultimately he was telling Europe's leaders to start leading and stop thinking all was well in the relationship with the people of Europe because it was not, and the issues were going to grow in significance and the pressures they were under.

CW went off for a two-hour drive and called in very mad professor mode. He said he had just been reflecting whether he had made the right decisions. He thought he had. He was getting hammered in a lot of the media, especially by some of the old players. He was not really bothered, but I thought JW looked more tense and nervous than usual. We did a TV slot with the kit boys and used Donncha to do an interview, which was another hysterical job. He was incapable of not being funny. Lots of hanging around today. Coffee shop with Louisa C, Louise and her family and some friends of theirs. Dinner with a few of the lads then a political discussion with Shane and Scott Johnson, who was another major pisstaker and very bright. Two pills and bed. News going massive with TB's speech, pretty positive considering the backdrop.

Friday 24 June

I still wasn't sleeping well but was at least having some decent ideas while I tried to. Did a piece for *The Times* on man management. I had breakfast with the media team and we planned the various things for today. There was a fair bit of follow-up to the *Herald* article, which seemed to please some and provoke others. Then Clive asked me to go to the team talk, just him and the coaches, because he thought I would be interested. I was. He had written a number of bullet points, starting with 'Win the bully contest', basically just heavy out your opponents one by one, be really aggressive and physical, especially when with the ball. He said he felt we were the pressure side and that if we won those early skirmishes, they would crumble. He said he did not fear the side Henry had picked. Scott Johnson said he was not impressed by them. They were flat-track bullies – if they were against a crap side they would win 120–0 instead of 100, but against a good side, they would struggle.

Clive said you guys were hand picked for pressure, and you were there because man for man you were brighter. They had a vulnerability in the centre and we had to go for it. Kick to kill. I don't care how it looks as long as we have more points on the board at the end. NZ looked good against France but when Wales bullied them, they struggled. Richie McCaw their star player – don't let him settle, clear him out of the way. Go to the edge but not over it. Do not let the excitement get to you. Think clearly under pressure. TCUP [thinking clearly under pressure] was one of his obsessions. David McHugh [referee liaison] said talk to the ref, repeat his calls, show him we are playing with him. Jones and JW then went through the options from the scrum, SJ clearly in the lead. I barely understood what they were on about – knife, puma, kog. E.g. BOD: 'Are we generally going to play kog in the green zone?' Looking around the room, I saw a pretty impressive bunch of people.

Then to training in private at a new venue, where Ben and I went for a run. Back with CW, then lunch, which became a sports quiz with Dawson and Corry. 5 p.m. Clive and I saw Miles Harrison and Stuart Barnes [Sky] to explain the plans re our response to the haka, which they liked, then to the press conference, main point to keep talking it up as a pressure match. Jayne W there. Funny moment when someone asked if anyone high-profile had sent good luck messages – Clive said TB. 'Yes, but anyone high-profile?' No tough Qs, all coaches on message re pressure, and then a couple of one-on-ones. Then to the last team talk, first forwards and backs separately, then everyone, and again CW fairly low key, told them it was all theirs to win. Then a film of the 22 of them in action individually, and messages about who we were up against etc., strong stuff.

I had to run to do *Campbell Live*, which was fine. A few Brits out there. The interview was fine and again hit the pressure message. Met Ronan O'G's family, who said that Colin Meads [former NZ player, All Blacks icon] had a pop at me for having a pop at the NZ media. Back for dinner and then into what became a quiz night – me, Alfie [Gareth Thomas] and Martyn Williams v Stephen Jones, Dwayne Peel and Corry. Johnson setting questions, mainly geography. Ended with SJ, Martyn and Alfie (who said that when he first heard I was coming on the tour, he confused me with Trevor McDonald [broadcaster]) asking really direct questions re politics – Bush, WMD, the media, and ended up asking about my breakdown for some reason. Alfie said if we win can you get TB to speak to me on the phone? That would be just brilliant. He was texting his mates to say he was going to speak to TB. I was a fully fledged part of the banter team, with Scott's line that anyone called Alastair was a Tory and I was an infiltrator into the Labour Party. All good fun. I was telling them stories about Hutton etc.* But Corry said I should learn to turn a blind eye better, just turn away. Maybe. Really good night though.

Saturday 25 June

I guess the nearest feeling to today, for these guys, would be a general election. A long day of waiting. Nothing to do apart from logistics and waste time. The sense of pressure was enormous, so heaven knows what it was like for the players. At the various times in the team room, they were generally more quiet than usual, though some, e.g. SJ and Alfie, were incapable of being quiet for long. We had a HOD but it was pretty much going through the motions. CW was on edge, at one point snapping, 'Can we all just calm down a bit?' when nobody was uncalm. Some of the players were barely visible all day, others were hanging around a bit more, but they were all a lot quieter. The day dragged on and on. I had a run in the gym and chatted with Dave Aldred about leadership and pressure and learning. He said he was basically a teacher. He was always happiest making the bad pupil better. He felt too many were about themselves – 'I' had a good session, not 'the players'. Lunch and then around five all the players trooped in for the team talk and presentation.

The whole squad was in there, not just those playing, and it was not easy for the ones who had not been picked. I was sitting at the back with Martyn Williams, who admitted it was really tough for him and the other non-selected players. Everyone always thought they were in

---

* Lord Hutton chaired the 2003 judicial inquiry into the death of David Kelly, biological weapons expert and former UN weapons inspector in Iraq.

with a chance so to see the guys there all tense and getting the jerseys is hard. But you just have to get behind them, he said. Clive was pretty brief – just do what we have done in training, win the bully contest, fight them hard, kick to kill etc., very basic messages. Then Ian McG did a very moving speech about how when his mother died they went through her box of personal belongings and treasures and in there was 'Ian's first Test jersey – his dad would have been so proud'. Good moving little number about the heritage etc. The foyer was packed with cheering fans as we left, which was a very Clive thing. Earlier BOD told me he didn't like having all the fans around because you were trying to get in the zone and they just wanted autographs or to chat so you put your head down and they thought you were rude. We travelled out to the stadium, the rain pouring down in a 38,000-seater ground only half covered.

Brian really got them fired up in the dressing room beforehand, not that they really needed it. They did the walk-round, the warm-up, and it was all now just whizzing by. The anthem was sung well for the first time since we were here. They stripped off straight away, did the haka response well, on which we had done a briefing note to go out straight away. I was standing then sitting next to Gary O'Driscoll, who within seconds of the match starting was gone because BOD was hurt, and clearly seriously, out of the game, and possibly out of the tour. He was upended and hammered into the ground. It was horrible to see him disappearing on a cart. A tough challenge became tougher. In any event we never got going and you felt from early on it was not going to happen, with line outs terrible and no real fight going on, while the AB backs were pretty much on fire. We were lucky to be only 11 points down at half-time. The players trooped in, changed their strips, with Clive telling them re line outs and shape and Corry – now captain for the night with BOD off to hospital – saying we had to get into them more.

Ryan Jones did well after Richard Hill came off with another bad injury – also out of the tour – but it was never happening. 21–3. Louisa, Louise and I watched the last bit on the telly to work out who to put up for the interviews. Martin and Clive did the after-match rounds – no excuses, best team won etc., – and then the presser, first the coaches, then Paul O'Connell and Corry. Meanwhile Ben, who was hanging out with the press, was reporting they were saying they felt BOD was taken out by a spear tackle.* Henry and [Tana] Umaga [All Blacks captain]

---

* An illegal tackle in which a player lifts another into the air and drops him so that he lands on his back, head or neck.

had been pretty defensive about it at their presser. It was time to go on the front foot. I suggested to Clive to say we would review the tapes before deciding what action to take.

Gary was saying BOD, who had been in agony when they took him into the dressing room, was saying he definitely felt he was speared. Richard Smith was reviewing the tapes. He, Clive and I went to the Sky truck to look at their tapes. They had two clips which, put together, would show him being speared. We then went briefly to the reception but Richard now got the NZ tape, which we reviewed on the team bus. They both felt it was a red card offence. I said if we were taking it to the citing commissioner we should get that out now. Clive was up for it, RS a bit more cautious but after a while he agreed. This was now as much about the media war as the battle over the legality of the tackle. They were confident he would be cited, but when I talked to some of the players they were very much in 'see it when I believe it' mode. 'This is their territory, it won't happen,' said ROG. Richard put in the complaint against No. 2, Kevin Mealamu, and 13, Umaga. So it was captain against captain. The bus took us back to the team hotel, where CW got all players and management together, and asked BOD – now back from hospital – Hill, and Shanklin (out of the tour after being injured in training) to come in.

He vented his spleen a bit about Brian but basically said that we had to fight back, learn from defeat and go out among the fans in the hotel bar and smile. I was not sure about that bit, felt the fans needed to feel they felt it too. Indeed, a guy who said he was ex-SAS came up to me, said he had put his life on the line for years for people like them, why couldn't they do it for him? I interviewed Brian and put out a statement making clear in his view it was an illegal double spear [by two opposing players], that he was devastated etc. His parents and sisters had arrived and he was amazingly calm and mature about it. Arm in sling, sedated to kill the pain, but he was really looking pained. He talked me through the incident, said he was really shocked Umaga was involved, and that must be why he never came over – guilt. I put together a really strong statement and got it out. Clive and most of the players went to bed. But then news came through the citing commissioner was looking at an incident involving Danny Grewcock biting one of their players.

We looked at that and it seemed inconclusive but I could tell Richard Smith was worried. We had not seen anything on the video other than the NZ reaction. RS said if they proved it, it would be a long ban. Danny said their player grabbed his face and his finger went in Danny's mouth. He had a gumshield on. He was dealing with a different player at the time. As Richard made calls, I chatted to Danny, who said they just hadn't played tonight, none of them. NZ were good but not unbeatable. We then started to get media calls saying the Brian claim had been rejected. I wanted to put out a statement from Clive saying it was unfathomable and again go on the front foot. But Jayne – now 3 a.m. – said she could not wake him. I then had another session with Danny, who had such a big innocent face for a hard man, and who was a bit more worried than he was letting on, I think. Bed at four, up at seven.

Sunday 26 June

For the first time, the hotel put papers outside our doors. The headline 'Spin that one, Alastair' was staring me as I opened the door. I had breakfast with Jayne, who said we had to be big and inspire the players to be big. Clive knew we had to make changes. I called home and was struck by how worried Grace was about Brian. Rory, hard-headed as ever, just said Byrne, Kay, Back and the backs were shit and CW had to pick younger forwards and play Henson! BOD came down, and we agreed he should do media before he went for his scan. In the cold light of day he was if anything even more annoyed than before. I went in for the end of the coaches' meeting, where they were going through selection issues. They were clearly going to be bringing in more Welsh boys for the second Test. Alfie would be captain. Clive said he knew there would have to be changes now. The presser was strong. BOD very emotional but also measured and calm. He used the line I had not put in the statement last night about Umaga and guilt, the idea that he must have known he had done wrong or he would have come over and seen him when he was being taken off, because that is what most players do.

Most of the questions were on Brian, one on Danny, a couple on general play. I then did a background briefing on the night's events to pile it on, then said we would show all the video stuff later. Team talk – Alfie to be captain, so I put out a statement with words from both. Clive told them we did some things right but a lot wrong and he would use the match on Tuesday for a fight for Test places. They all went off training while we set up the day, then back for lunch, which turned on our table into a quiz session, going through the alphabet with singers and bands, and which at times got hysterical. The mood was lifting pretty quickly, but the players were all pretty shocked when they saw the tackle on

BOD again on video. Meanwhile Danny was off for what would be a seven-hour-plus hearing into a so-called 'bite' that did not even break the skin. The point we were making was that whether it was a spear tackle or not, there should at least have been an investigation. After another little team talk, we set off for the airport, Clive still wondering how hard to push the line about the 'spear tackle' incident. Another development: Alfie told us that when the touch judge saw the incident he shouted, 'Leave him alone, leave him, the ball has gone', and on the video we could see Alfie chasing to the touch judge three times after the incident, because he claimed not to see it. Alfie was steaming about it and agreed to do the press conference with Clive.

As we left the hotel, mad Donncha followed me into the toilet with his camera, filming me having a pee and asking me if TB washed his hands after having a piss! I was chatting to Ryan Jones on the bus, who said he was thinking re post-rugby already. The flight down to Wellington was fairly subdued, talking to Richard Hill, who was wondering whether to go home or not now that his knee had gone again. He, BOD and Tom Shanklin all out for the rest of the tour was a bit grim. We showed the video of the BOD incident to some of the hacks on the plane, which got them going even more. Mark Souster [*Times*] tracked down the citing commissioner, who went mad at him and another reporter but the amazing thing was there was nothing we could do about it now. It was done; no appeal; nothing.

We drove to the Intercontinental, Stephen Jones putting on *The Office*, and they started making jokes about it being like team talks. Brief team talk, saying we were delaying selection till we knew what was happening with Danny, then to a press conference with CW and Alfie to show them the video of the incident. Some of the former players were a bit dubious but lots of them definitely thought it was over the top. The line being run by some of them was that it was because we wound them up over the haka, and Clive got far too deep into the detail, and said it had come from a Maori chief and we would give them the email. As they went through the video frame by frame, Ben texted me to say Danny Grewcock was banned for two months. So they were going to get away with nothing for taking out our captain, and he was getting two months. We would have to do another doorstep [press announcement] at the end anyway. We had set it up, based on Richard telling us we were likely to lose, by saying we would take whatever sentence they imposed. Having tried to go for the moral high ground, it was not the best outcome but there we are. The media certainly had enough stories

– crap result, BOD, Hill out, citing commissioner, Danny, changes for the next match.

Clive just kept saying, 'I can't believe we lost. I was sure it was the right side. I made some mistakes and have to admit it. I played too many of the English guys I thought would be able to take the big pressure, and they didn't.' Later he told me the whole back row would be replaced, JW to 10, Henson in, maybe Shane Williams on the wing. Some would play in both the midweek match and the Test. I was speaking to TB at one point and, as Alfie walked by, and having said he wanted to talk to TB if we won, I put him on anyway. 'You fucking kidding me, yeah?' But then he took the phone, and just said, 'Hi there, butt, how you doing?' He was listening to whatever TB was saying, and telling passers-by he was talking to the PM, and then saying stuff like, 'How you been doing, you must be busy what with being Prime Minister and stuff, do you ever get a day off… anyway, I get up to London a fair bit, so we'll meet up for a drink, yeah? I'll get Posh Boy' – his new nickname for me – 'to fix it… You take care now, butt, I'll put you back on to your man.'

TB was laughing his head off. 'What the fuck? That guy is hilarious.' Alfie was now running down the street shouting to fans, 'I've just been talking to Tony Blair. Me and Tony, we're like that… best mates.' 'He'll hold you to having a drink when he's in London,' I said. 'He sounds a lot more fun than the ones I usually have a drink with.' He said the fallout from the speech was still ticking on, but he felt it made the right impact, both domestically and with other leaders, even if some didn't like what they heard. He said recent events had been pretty tough. But Europe speech had really hit a chord and he was more confident than before. He said GB was OK but no more. He was still not really cooperating, and was only really engaging on his own terms. But he was thinking it was OK-ish. A quick game of table tennis with SJ, who was quick-firing questions re me, TB the whole time and quick-firing laughs. Danny got back and we worked out a statement to put out for him – disagree with the decision but have to accept it and now move on.

Monday 27 June
I had breakfast over at the hotel with some of the Welsh guys, who were still the most upbeat and lively. SJ told me I was very important for morale at the moment! BOD described him as the most relentlessly positive man he had ever met. Brian O'D spoke to Grace and was really sweet with her. We had managed to get a fair bit of the focus on to the

Umaga tackle – several NZ and UK–Ireland front pages – and lots of pictures, but the line was creeping in that it was all a deflection operation from how badly we were outplayed. We had a full squad meeting at which Clive was much more outspoken than before, saying they just totally under-performed, and then Andy Robinson going even further, saying he took responsibility for a lot of what went wrong, but making clear he felt let down. He said he was embarrassed by the line out and so should they be. He ran through a bit of a horror series of clips showing where things had gone badly wrong. He was good at taking them through it – line outs and slow ball, allowing the defence to regroup, and also where the ABs were just harder and meaner and more up for it. He said it was time for more hatred and anger, which is exactly what I had been thinking.

I mentioned later to Clive and Ian that I felt there was too much of a comfort zone. I mentioned the soldier at the hotel who said to me he laid his life on the line for them, why did they not do it for him? I said re elections and wars there was always a moment when you had the knot in your stomach. In my view you cannot perform unless you have it. There has to be a bit of hatred and fear. We talked it over and eventually Clive said he might ask me to speak to the 22 on Wednesday and say all this. He said to Ian they are so used to our team talks but maybe we need to have a different take on it. I said I did not feel I was in a stomach-churn zone. I did not feel their lives depended on it. There was not a charge here. There was too much chumminess. The ABs clearly hated us. We had to hate them more. Clive said he had been moving to the same position and wanted me to lead a discussion, then he and Ian would speak too. Maybe it would help, maybe not, but it was worth a try, he said. I felt JW had the knot in the guts. BOD had it. Martin Corry had it. Some of the others had it. But I didn't feel it collectively. It had to be there by Wednesday. Gareth Thomas had it. He had got the players in a huddle earlier and drawn them together.

I then wrote a draft of what I might say. I also did a piece for the *Irish Times* on the whole BOD episode. I had lunch with some of the Irish guys and was trying out this approach. They seemed to buy it too. I wrote more on the bus to Palmerston North, a two-hour drive through some of the most beautiful scenery yet. The journey was quieter and maybe the players were beginning to realise, some of them, that their Test hopes were nil, and others that they had to fight for it. We went to the stadium, did the walk-around and then the media chats, which were OK, and I did a Radio 5 Live [BBC] interview. There was a team talk once we got there, Mike Ford doing a good presentation on Mana-watu and then re Saturday, and I was glad to hear him say he wanted to see them just stop them, whatever it took. They had to harden up, be tougher, be meaner.

Clive was taking the management out for dinner, but I had dinner with ROG – who invited me to his wedding but was generally down because he realised he was unlikely to make the Test team – Corry and Back. They asked me who they thought Clive was kidding when he said he hadn't decided. Martin C was clearly down. I asked Back his best team talk ever. He said Martin Johnson in the tunnel before the World Cup final. Normally he looked around and said something down the line to the players. This time he said nothing, and indicated he knew they were ready. Back said it was brilliant. He was a thuggish-looking but quietly spoken and thoughtful kind of bloke. I did a stack of work upstairs, including a piece for *The Times* on BOD too. I got both cleared through Richard Smith.

Tuesday 28 June

Fiona emailed to say there was a 'near-death picture' of me on the front cover of the sports section of *The Guardian* and a headline, 'Nice PR, shame about the rugby'. The NZ media had a lot of the same theme, and had turned a bit nasty. I said to Clive we had to use it to our advantage now, really start to get fired up etc. He was still of the view that the ferocity of the attacks – there were plenty more today – showed that we had been getting to them a fair bit. But we had to come back and win. We did the walk-through, then Richard [Smith], David McHugh and I went for a really nice run. I got back to do a bit of work on the diary before heading into town to generate a few fans to come and see the team off from the Rydges hotel. Mike Ford did the team talk, and it was one of the best yet. How do you want to be remembered? And he said at the moment they were remembered as losers. The press said they were pitiful, got rolled over, got given a lesson. What were we going to do about that?

He was pretty heavy but it was the right thing to say. He did not hold back at all. The players took it and left in silence. There was a good crowd outside again and thousands in the stadium when we got there. We were sitting up with the non-selected players and sat back to watch a total rout [109–6]. Five tries for man of the match Shane Williams. Charlie Hodgson and Chris Cusiter strong again. After the match they were all fine about doing stuff and the mood was a lot better, though the media – and Clive privately – were saying it was not much of a test. The post-BOD fallout was still running, and there was an undercurrent about me we had to watch now. There was a brief reception before we headed back, reaching the hotel around half-one.

Wednesday 29 June

Clive had selected the team for the Test, and he asked me to speak to the whole squad before he announced it. I had written something on the bus yesterday and he read it and said he thought it was brilliant, and what he needed. Louisa thought it the right thing to say – that the NZers had wanted it more, that you sensed more hung on it for them, that we needed more hatred and fear. Clive introduced me by saying I was a better speaker than him and he was interested in the take I had. I think I delivered it OK but I could sense a lot of resistance. Matt Dawson said later I should not have started by saying I don't know about rugby, and also some of them said to Clive I knew about pressure in a different world, not theirs. But he said he wanted to shake things up all round. If they got angry about it, fine. He wanted more anger. I thought some of them took it, but some didn't. I spoke maybe ten, fifteen minutes, and told the story of the soldier in the hotel, and of the coverage back home. I went through some of my experiences of crises and campaigns, and the fear of failure, and didn't feel that with the intensity I had expected here. I noticed Stephen Jones nodding, but BOD looking on quizzical and even alarmed. There was going to be a mixed reaction to this, for sure.

Clive then read out the team, and said how people dealt with disappointment was part of the tour. He would talk to people left out but they had to accept it, and deal with it. He was pretty heavy. He then asked Mike F to restate what he said yesterday, then Ian and Gareth, who again spoke very emotionally about how gutted he was on Saturday. The 22 stayed and had a players' meeting. Of the coaches, only Dave [Reddin] said anything to me about what I said – positively. Few of the players did. I don't think it had gone down well. We went off to training and I sat in on Phil Larder's defensive session.

Outside, I was talking to BOD, who said he didn't want to go to the parliamentary reception, because he thought the New Zealanders – who had spun phone contact with Umaga–BOD to suggest all was fine between them – would use it to say it was all over. He wanted to say he was having a scan and couldn't be there. Bill B was totally against, and insisted he went. Richard Hill said I would have to engage Clive to get BOD out of it. Louise was also pro a sort of snub. Bill then wanted Gareth Thomas to do it. CW against. Eventually we got Bill to agree neither would go. Louise, Louisa and I had a meeting with Prince William's people, who were keen for rugby pictures. Later the press conference, where Clive was a bit down. Clive said he was surprised how much vitriol and bile there was around. He admitted he had made mistakes. He said we would repeat the response to the haka. The questions were all predictable.

In interviews, Donncha, Gavin and Jonny got the biggest crowds. Josh Lewsey, Will Greenwood and Scott Johnson were taking the piss out of my speech to the players. Clive was still adamant it had been the right thing to do, but I was not so sure. I think they were fine when I was talking about things they knew I knew about, and related it to them; but it was a very different thing if they felt I was talking about their performance as players. Some were fine, some were positively enthusiastic and felt it had to be said, but others, I could tell, were pissed off, and thought it was wrong of Clive to get me to do his dirty work, I guess. Then to the parliamentary reception with Clive. We arrived as the speeches began. There was no mention of BOD in the remarks by Tana Umaga, so Clive and some of our players walked out. I was talking to Don Brash [National Party politician], former banker turned opposition leader, who was giving [Helen] Clark [Labour Prime Minister] a run for her money. She came over too, so briefly I was talking to both. She was picking my brains about the EU scene and also asking whether TB would go the whole term.

I got a good briefing from the High Commissioner [Richard Fell], who gave me a lift to [Clark's press secretary] Mike Munro's house for the dinner I has having with the PM. The Speaker was there too, plus a guy called Stephen who was her pollster. They were interested in how we did the pitch for the third term. Summed it up as economy plus leadership, and don't take the risk of change. It was very similar to her pitch and they did not have Iraq in the same way – economy OK, anti-politics mood, tax cuts v investment. Tax cuts part of a bigger argument. Brash, not a detail merchant. So economy plus experience plus leadership plus understand change. I sensed she doubted William – who she was meeting off the plane at eight tomorrow – would become King, that both NZ and Oz would become republics. She talked a lot about gay rights. Mike seemed fairly back seat. They also ran their own operation down a lot. But I sensed she was going to be OK – economy/experience/leadership and take Brash apart through third parties and then win on detail in the debates. Nice enough evening. Britain now only fourth or fifth market for them. Europe as a whole was now more important.

Back briefly to the management dinner. Clive told me BB had had a heart flutter – into hospital for twenty-four hours. So lots going wrong. And I sensed some of the players were getting edgy about some of Clive's decisions.

Thursday 30 June

I had mentioned to Clive that I wasn't sure whether my speech yesterday had been the right thing and at the HOD meeting, Bill raised it and said he had had a lot of feedback from players that it was inappropriate and made them angry. It might have been the right thing to say but I was the wrong person to say it. It should have come from Clive, not me. They felt that I did not know what it was like out there and for me to talk about not putting bodies on the line when e.g. Hill had lost his career possibly was not great. Clive defended the decision, and me, said it was his call and he felt it needed an outsider to say something to provoke. He was glad they were angry. They needed to be fired up. I said yes, but you wanted the anger focused externally not internally. He said the coaches felt it had been the right thing, that we had been too soft up to now, and had to toughen up. James Robson said there had been talk in the medical room too, like 'What did he know?' He said if I had spoken after the team announcement rather than before, some would have walked out. Otis said the same, adding that they felt they did all the stuff we asked for the media, which they hated, but then the media man turned round and attacked them. He was meant to be media manager not motivational speechmaker.

Richard Smith said he thought it was the right message but the wrong messenger. Clive defended it again, said he felt we needed a shake up all round, and he would do it again. I was not so sure. I was worried from a personal perspective that it would damage good relations with the players, and also that if it all went belly up, they would make a big thing of it. There was far too much on me in the press as it was, which I saw as a problem. Clive was worried by my reaction, asked me a few times if I was OK. I felt fine but was not happy if the effect was a negative one. He felt it was positive because it fired them up.

I felt fairly down about it, till later when Stephen Jones and Simon Easterby took me for a coffee and SJ said he felt Clive put me in an invidious position because they knew I didn't know what it was like to be a player in that kind of situation. But the sentiments I had set out were right, he said. There was too much comfort zone. He kept asking me the most basic questions, e.g. what have you done since 9 a.m. today? We went for a walk and to a café and he said not to worry. On balance it was the right thing. I think Corry and Back were the really pissed off ones.

Our main event was Prince William arriving and spending some time with the players. Arthur Edwards and Harry Page [*Sun* and *Daily Mirror* photographers] and I agreed the pictures and meanwhile we were trying to set up a decent shot for tomorrow, though it might be a problem because training was cancelled. Charlie Hodgson agreed he would do a kicking session with him. I sat around for a while just watching the comings and goings. The players seemed OK in the main but maybe they didn't say anything to me about how they felt about yesterday. William pictures were fine – BOD who looked a bit rough after a night out, Gareth, Gordon and Will G. The pix were fine, then up to the team room. Donncha saying we should have a fancy dress party and he would go for Superman in a wheelchair. Later had a sensible chat with him. Eddie and Andy did a very good press conference and were more upbeat than Clive yesterday. Eddie kept going on the BOD–Umaga incident, really strong words.

I was due to do a public event at the Te Papa Tongarewa national museum, nice event, nice venue, and went well. Not as abusive as UK audiences. Arthur Edwards was in the audience and asked me about the JP punch, which went down as well here as at home.[*] When someone had a go at Clive there was a bit of sympathy for him in the audience. I did the spear joke – there are a couple of players here [Horgan and Hickie] and I won't tell you where they are in case you go and spear them. I did the Senate dinner, which was OK, next to a reasonably interesting woman amid the suits, but I left after three of the six courses, feeling a bit knackered. As a public speaking event it was all fine, though Denis and Shane thought I should have been given a harder time.

---

* In 2001, Deputy Prime Minister John Prescott had famously retaliated at having an egg thrown at him in Rhyl, north Wales, by punching the protestor.

June '05: Prince William arrives for kicking session

Friday 1 July

Shane Horgan and Denis Hickie took the mick about the questions last night. They could not believe how soft the audience had been. The *Dominion Post* carried my *Times* piece which, allied to the Eddie comments, made it look like we were still stoking the BOD incident. But, as Clive had said, they kept asking, we kept answering, they said we stoked. I got a very positive reaction from some of the Lions fans outside the hotel. 'Keep at them, they hate it,' said one. The one-eyed NZ approach was beginning to grate with everyone. Our main media activity for the morning was Charlie Hodgson and Dave Aldred giving Prince William a lesson in kicking at a nearby cricket cum rugby ground. It was a beautiful sunny day. Charlie, who is a lovely bloke and who many thought was unlucky not to be in the Test 22, having been brilliant on tour so far, could not believe how many cameras were there. But they seemed to affect William more than Charlie. William's first few kicks were a tad awry.

I noticed a photographer taking pictures of me, not the Prince, the whole time. A friendly reporter meanwhile had texted me to say the *Mail* had put a photographer on my tail. It was the kickstart I needed to go on a long run I had been promising myself all week. The photocall took care of itself. Later I was able to make two people very happy. I was buying a coffee in a café when I got a message from the guy I met I had been planning to give my two complimentary tickets to, saying he and his son already had tickets from another source. At that very moment, a man from Manchester and his sixteen-year-old grandson came in and asked if they could have their picture taken with me. He said he was a big Labour supporter. His grandson had seen my attack on the media coverage of the O'Driscoll–Umaga affair and was urging me to keep at them. As we got chatting they said they were having a great time but hadn't yet found any tickets. Their faces as I pulled out my two and gave them to them were a picture to behold. The man said he believed in God and he was going to go to the cathedral to thank Him for having moved in this mysterious way.

I told them though I am an atheist, I can remember a similar thing once happening to me at an FA Cup semi final, when a policeman gave me a ticket he had taken off kids who had been fighting, so I know how the boy was feeling. I had lunch with SJ and a few others and later lost 3–2 to him at table tennis. I wrote notes to Ben Kay, Martin Corry and Neil Back about my talk to the team, making clear I never intended to question their commitment or professionalism. Coincidentally, before it went, Martin came to see me and said he wanted to clear the air. He was clearly someone who wore his heart on his sleeve. He said he had been harbouring a grudge, which was not like him, and he wanted to put it behind us. He said he felt a weight lift off his shoulders, as did I. I told him the background, how Clive had wanted me to relay what I had said about the intensity of the feeling and desire at home, but I could see how it might have come across. I told him who I had written to, and we shook hands.

He said he was once attacked by Dean Richards [former player, coach] about his mental strength and he felt really hurt. So for someone to suggest we weren't hurting enough wasn't on. Clive had spoken to all 22 and said that he understood some were angry at what I said, but it was dead right, we were at war with this country and we had to step up the ante a lot more. Clive had defended me totally. I was not so sure about some of the other management, but felt OK about the coaches. Gareth [Jenkins] made a point of saying he backed what I said totally. Graham Henry had a pop at me for keeping the spear tackle story going so long.

TB kicked off our EU Presidency and was definitely setting it up for differences with Chirac and [Gerhard] Schroeder [Chancellor of Germany], and pointing to another 'future of Europe' type summit with a focus on reform of the social model, and he had another pop at the need to reform the CAP. Hilary Benn [international development secretary] had been making speeches saying it was a moral issue.

Saturday 2 July

The hotel was besieged with fans for most of the day. We went out for the walk-through at the Basin Reserve cricket ground. There was definitely a sharper edge to them than last week. You could feel a greater intensity and a greater sense of how it mattered. The hours dragged until, in almost complete silence, we all gathered in the team room, where Bill Beaumont handed out the shirts. Bill's speech was good by his standards but he just didn't do emotion and they took the piss out of his constant 'you guys' references. Clive said we had to feel like we were going to war. He said what I had said on Wednesday was right. We were going to war with this country. The *Mail* had published a full-page comment piece having a go at me, and would be gearing up for even more. Also I guessed Corry would have told them before we spoke and patched up that he had been pissed off at some of the things I said.

John Feehan told me Peter Jackson was on the case about my team talk and trying to wind up the sponsors.

They walked out of the hotel to a roar of support, which Andy Robinson said was even greater than on the day of the World Cup final. Clive had dispensed with the final coach's talk at the stadium, and let the players organise themselves in their own way. Huge swathes of the stadium were a sea of red and the atmosphere was the best yet. Gareth [Thomas, captain] and Tommo got them wound up pretty well, and they looked totally up for it. I went up to the stand and took a fair bit of abuse from NZ fans on the way. I was right at the back with the players, seated next to ROG, and we had the best possible start, with Alfie scoring a great try before we had even got settled. We were 7 up. The place went demented. Jonny hit the post with a penalty. The players all fought their hearts out but bit by bit New Zealand got a grip on the game, and they were awesome going forward. A try shortly after the restart was close to being a killer blow. 48–18, with Dan Carter [NZ fly-half] scoring 33 points. A hammering. Their highest ever score against the Lions.

As we walked down in front of the crowd to make our way to the tunnel to greet the players coming off, first Clive and then I got a hail of abuse. 'Spin that, you cunt' was one of the more colourful jibes – and from a woman. Clive was being condemned as a loser who should go home. We knew the media wouldn't be pretty. Heads were down in the dressing room. Clive said he was proud of the way they fought. So did Gareth J, who had emerged as a good passionate speaker. He said he hates losing but I can take it if we fight and we fought all the way tonight. Dan Carter was deservedly getting rave reviews. I went round the players lining up people for the media – Lewis, Josh, Dwayne, Simon (who was being drug tested) Donncha and Gareth. They all did bloody well considering. Clive did fine at the press conference, though he was clearly fairly down. Two down, one to go is a pretty shit place to be. He suggested there was a conflict between Lions tours and a winning approach – he would rather have taken his Test side away for four weeks and just trained. Graham Henry had another little dig at me at the press conference, saying Tana Umaga had been subject to a lot of nonsense from someone who knew nothing about rugby – I assume he meant me.

The players fronted up really well when doing the press afterwards and Gareth Thomas came up with a great line. He was asked whether leading the Lions out was the proudest moment of his life. He said no, leading them off having fought to the end was. There was a fair bit of gloating at the after-match reception. Some of the players tried to get me out on the piss with them but after tidying up a few loose ends I just felt like going to bed, and felt pretty low. But the players were consoling themselves with the knowledge they had really fought for it, and lots of them went out on the piss. The noise in the streets was something else. You'd have thought we'd won. Grace was at Live 8 in Hyde Park.

Sunday 3 July

The press was grim, as expected. The NZ media had a fairly pitiless approach, particularly to Clive, and for some reason I was second in line. There was some really strong stuff. The *NZ Herald* had me as a 24-hour plumber down in the sewer stirring the raw sewage and trying to 'polish a turd'. Bryan Gould [New Zealand-born former Labour MP in UK] had a right old go, saying all I cared about was creating diversions to stop people telling the truth about how shit we were. One of them had quite a funny spiel about how we were more a traveling circus than a rugby team, with lion-tamers, monkeys and of course clowns. The attacks here were of course being echoed at home. Rory pointed out to Fiona that I was getting a bit of a hammering. I sensed Clive was taking it worse than he let on. He was losing a bit of weight and looked stressed. We did a morning press conference that was sparsely attended, and the questions fairly polite. I said to him at least the politicos give it to your face. This lot ask the soft questions and then write heavy. I had another politics chat with S Jones and Scott, then farewells to the hotel, then to the plane to Auckland.

Stephen sat down next to me, come on let's have a good chat. We did a bit more politics, TB and how he dealt with pressure, then rugby and also him thinking about setting up a business of some sort. Agreed to try to meet up during August. Back acknowledged my note. Ben Kay yet to do so. Earlier D'Arcy debagged me and Tommo nicked my BlackBerry again, but just for a few minutes. To the hotel and straight into another media round. Jackson asked me about my speech to the players and I said my experience of the *Mail* was it would say whatever it wanted whatever I said, so get on with it. I had dinner with Alastair Hignell, Ian Robertson and Eddie Butler of the BBC. Nice enough evening. They said the problem was in some ways I was too big a personality on the trip alongside Clive so I was always going to be targeted in the way I was. The line was becoming that I had been a negative, fired up NZ by going for Umaga and was too big a personality for a position like this. Maybe they had a point.

Monday 4 July

Clive had gone from hero to zero. I briefed him on the press, which was grisly both here and at home, and he was saying he would still have done the same, but I could tell he was hurting, and questioning himself. Two games to go, one Test, and it was going to be hard to get the players up for it. Having felt after the first Test that the players didn't feel the defeat enough, this time it felt more like a bereavement. One down two to go, there was always a chance; two down one to go meant it was all over, and it wasn't helped that there was such a feeling of gloating among the New Zealanders. Even the hotel staff just seemed a little bit more friendly but in a 'poor you' patronising kind of a way. Clive said it was really important the players felt we were keeping our heads up and emphasising there was still a lot to play for and a lot worth fighting for. At breakfast, Martyn Williams was saying Auckland were a really strong team and we would have to be at our best to beat them. I did NZ radio, who were pretty heavy, and I defended myself as best as I could but there was no doubt there was a mini avalanche on the way, here and at home. The *Mail* papers were of course leading the way but e.g. Austin Healey, Stuart Barnes [former players/commentators] and plenty more had a go.

Clive was copping about 70 per cent of the shit, and I was getting about 20. Wilko was being hammered a bit, but by and large the players were given a fairly easy ride. Stephen Jones said in front of some of the other players that they owed me, because having had nothing to do with failure on the pitch, I was copping a lot of the blame they should be taking. It was going to be hard to keep spirits up all week. Later Clive said he was OK but inside he was hurting. I had a long chat with Jayne. She said he and I were both tall poppies and people liked to bring us down. We were people who dared to challenge. But she said she was surprised just how much of the flak was coming my way. Clive had always dared to do things differently. He had dared to resign. He had dared to say he would try another sport. I had dared to challenge the media in politics and was now daring to take on a different sort of challenge here. She said too many people in Britain didn't like successful people who did things differently. They preferred to fail, and they preferred us to fail.

The important thing was that we had to keep our heads up and did not let a negative judgement settle with the public, she said. To be fair, the mood among the fans wasn't as bad as among the media. I think they realised the ABs were just too good, and would have blown away anyone. There was a guy from Long Eaton who said to me, 'The players need to know there is no shame in losing to those guys, and for me it was a privilege to watch them.' Work-wise we had a straightforward day, with the Auckland team training, then doing the stadium run and media. The players were getting close to saying what they thought re NZ, media and the rugby mentality. I suggested someone dropped in that they didn't think they should get the World Cup because of stadia and media one-eyedness. Over dinner with SJ and then Scott [Johnson] who told me he disagreed with my team talk because he felt you should never mix sport and life and death. Sport is only about life. Fair enough point. He said he felt sorry for Clive, and that maybe the other coaches should be doing more with the players off the field, that they were all a bit too intense and needed to lighten the mood a bit. Rory said the UK press were giving me a hard time but Clive was really getting it. Bill B back in hospital and Clive worrying he was putting himself under too much pressure to stay totally involved in the tour. I did an Irish radio show with George Hook [broadcaster] and David Walsh [*Sunday Times*] and gave both barrels, particularly to Hook.

TB called from Singapore, where he had wall-to-wall blitzing planned in the run-up to the final vote on the Olympics. The bookies still had Paris favourite but both Tessa and Dick [Caborn, sports minister], and [Lord] Seb [Coe, bid chairman] reckoned if everyone who might fall our way did so, we could still do it. David Beckham [Real Madrid player, bid ambassador] was there, and the French seemed a bit taken aback by just how many of our big sports names were there. I still thought Prince William should have gone. Chirac had cocked up again, though. Yet another food piss-take. He said that the only thing the UK had ever given to cuisine was mad cow disease, and also that we couldn't be trusted. It was a private conversation with Schroeder but got picked up. TB said he had already picked up that some of the delegates thought the French were being a bit too cocky around the place, and thought they had it in the bag. 'We are in for a penny, in for a pound on this one,' he said. Keith Mills [bid CEO] had put together a huge programme of meetings for him, Cherie, who was seeing lots of delegates and spouses, Becks, [Sir] Steve Redgrave [bid ambassador], Seb etc. etc. Seb was playing a blinder.

Tuesday 5 July

The sports commentariat getting even more stuck in. Paul Hayward in the *Telegraph*: 'Taking Campbell on a sports tour is like hiring the board of BP to perform an oil change on your car. It is an aberration from start to finish.' I guess there was a kind of back-handed compliment in there, but the general take, inevitably, was negative. I did a bit of radio, not whingeing, simply pointing out that if we had won the Tests, there would be none of this, and that is the difference in sport. It is all about what happens on the pitch but when it goes badly people like to cast around. We had a very low and subdued HOD meeting. I think Clive was a bit taken aback by how much vitriol he was facing. He was making clear that on Saturday he intended to say what he thought, e.g. re the NZ media, ours – he had now picked up on the notion I was to blame for defeat – their World Cup bid etc. We mentioned the WC situation at the morning meeting, which alarmed John Feehan. William the waiter said can you imagine what the mood would be like if we were drawing?

It was now a bit flat and time was dragging a bit. I had pretty much given up trying to get a better media or care what they were saying. I was also moving towards saying something to the effect that they had not really come at me positively, which I think was their loss, which was also Clive's view. The side of the job re players and coaches had gone pretty well, the side with the media had not so I was ducking out a bit. I did a note for Clive on the weekend and stressed he had to be dignified and not OTT, and while others were losing perspective, he needed to keep his. He agreed but really felt he needed to say a few things. In interviews I was making the point that we ought to be able to have some balance and perspective. I stayed low-profile at the match against Auckland, which we won in difficult circs, just 17–13.

I was watching it next to Josh Lewsey, who loathed the ref, Steve Walsh, who loved being the centre of attention. The words spoken about the referee in the dressing room afterwards were unprintable. They were really angry at some of the decisions – e.g. no punishment for the guy who gave Ben Kay the worst black eye I have ever seen. Nothing for the guy who stamped on Gordon d'Arcy's head. Clive had words with the ref at the after-match reception. We had a bit of a dust up with Sky because Matt Dawson, who cannot stand Sky commentator Stuart Barnes, did not want to do the after-match interview for the man of the match – him. Eventually he did it but not before Sky threatened to stop allowing us access to review their tapes, as they had done over the O'Driscoll–Umaga affair. There was a great atmosphere in the dressing room at the end. But there were even more injuries. James Robson said it was ludicrous to have a match in the last week pre third Test. Bill was ill again. Gareth Thomas had a throat infection. Stephen Jones was laughing at the media attacks on me: 'Why did you leak those five tries, Alastair?' The players had a cricket set, which for a while became the focus for the team room.

Wednesday 6 July

The team doctors submitted the longest injury list yet, so long that Clive decided to cancel training and we had to delay the announcement of the third Test team by twenty-four hours. Meanwhile Clive had to go to a hearing after Graeme Rowntree had been cited about a match incident picked up on camera last night. Several hours later he was cleared. Without a team to announce, Clive did a press conference with the medical team to set out the details of the injury list. Clive said it was totally beyond me how people could still question the decision to bring a large squad, because we had now lost thirteen players plus Danny Grewcock's suspension since the original 44 were named. The management team went out for dinner, which we left at a reasonable hour to get back to the hotel to watch the Olympics bid announcement from Singapore.

Tessa called me as the voting went on and even then she was thinking a London win was possible rather than probable. I had spoken to TB yesterday and he felt it was possible but Paris still felt like they had the edge. He was doing a lot of last-minute stuff with some of the swing voters which he hoped would make a difference. Tessa called twice, and said it was even more nerve-racking than an election. But she sounded quite confident. I said I really wished I was there. She was about to be made Olympics minister if we got it. I went up to my room to hear the result. The roar that went round the Auckland Hilton when IOC President Jacques Rogge fiddled with his envelope and said, 'London' was almost on a par with the one that greeted Gareth Thomas's try last Saturday. I don't think anyone had really thought it would happen and when it did there was a real sense of excitement and celebration. I popped back to the bar and there was a real celebration going on. Even Josh Lewsey said, 'You guys did well on this one!' It had been touch and go through the various stages of voting. The G8 at Gleneagles had started, and George Bush had apparently knocked over a copper while out riding a bike!

Thursday 7 July

The injury list had grown further with Charlie Hodgson and Simon Shaw now declared unfit for selection for the Test. People felt very sorry for Charlie, who had played well but been behind Jonny and Steve for selection. Clive made a couple of changes to the third Test side, giving a chance to Geordan Murphy and Mark Cueto, who had both impressed for the midweek side. With the enormous injury list, and non-selected players going off for a short break in the ski resort of Queenstown, Clive had to ask for volunteers for training to play against the Test side. In the team meeting, Bill made a joke about the fact that he said 'guys' the whole time. He changed it to 'gentlemen'. Later I went with Clive to the Maritime Museum, where he did another press conference, to be followed by the players arriving to do media. They came by bus, from which they refused to disembark until Ben Wilson sang to them. He sang, 'If I'd known you were coming I'd have baked a cake,' which did the trick. Apart from one or two e.g. Gill Douglas [BBC], David Walsh and Paul Ackford [*Telegraph*] because they wanted an interview, none of the press really engaged with me at all now. I explained to CW that I felt my side of the job re the players and coaches had gone well, but the media had just never wanted to engage because I challenged their comfort zone and so it was pretty much impossible to deal with them.

In the evening I spoke at my second charity Q&A session, which was a lot livelier than the one in Wellington. There was one question I had never really been asked before – did I always elicit an emotional response? – to which the answer did seem to be yes. At the dinner afterwards came news of the London bombings, and any joy from either the Olympic announcement or the fundraising public meeting quickly evaporated.* Fiona was out at a NFPI [National Parenting and Family Institute, of which FM was chair] meeting and the boys at home but she managed to get home later. I went back to the hotel, made a few calls, but was just watching it like any other member of the public, seeing TB react at Gleneagles, where he confirmed there had been deaths, said he was going back to London, and the summit would continue without him, with Jack Straw flying up to stand in for him, and [Sir] Michael Jay [FCO permanent secretary] taking TB's place at the lunch.

TB made the point that all of the countries present had been hit by terrorism at some point, did the usual point re the need to respond

---

* Four Islamist extremists separately detonated bombs in central London, targeting civilians using the public transport system during the morning rush hour.

to their twisted values with our own, and emphasised this happened exactly as the G8 was discussing Africa and how to help the poorest in the world. He called en route a couple of times, sounded totally on top of it all, and getting good support even from Chirac, he said. He made the second statement, echoing the same points really, but a bit more Churchillian, not least re the spirit of the London people, and also the idea that bombs would never defeat our values. He spoke well on both occasions, but it was all grim stuff. The death toll was thirty-seven already, hundreds injured. [George] Galloway [controversial left-wing MP] was out saying this was caused by us going into Iraq and we should respond by coming out. TB did a COBRA [Cabinet Office crisis Briefing Room A] meeting, saw [Michael] Howard and [Charles] Kennedy [Lib Dem leader], and went to Scotland Yard. He went back by helicopter and straight back into meetings where, according to Jonathan, Bush was getting stuck into Chirac on our behalf over agriculture subsidies.

Friday 8 July

We had a meeting with the NZRU to decide what action to take to mark the deaths and maimings in London. There was no question of cancelling the match. We agreed that there should be a joint statement of condemnation and the announcement of a minute's silence, and a separate statement from Bill Beaumont on behalf of the Lions. The mood at breakfast was pretty subdued and the incident led to the latest political discussion with some of the players. Josh and Stephen Jones leading the way in wanting to know exactly what would be happening, and how decisions would be made, so we ended up talking quite a lot about 9/11.

Clive did an interview for New Zealand TV with John Campbell in which he said that while this was a great country to visit as a tourist, he had doubts about it as a country in which to play rugby, because of the intensity of views about rugby here. I did a long chat with David Walsh and said a few things re the media. He pressed me hard about the Henson snap with Clive, which I sensed would become a mini frenzy because Dave Rogers [photographer] had clearly complained we asked him to do it without Gav knowing.* The players' views were becoming more marked re GH. I joined a chat with Charlie and Donncha, who

---

* Following Henson's omission from the Lions team for the first Test, he was photographed walking and in conversation with Clive Woodward, suggesting he was still on good terms with the coach.

were saying he was a total non-team player – hadn't even gone to the last midweek match – and even the Welsh no longer defended him. Charlie admitted he felt a bit down about not having made the Tests because he felt he deserved a shout earlier. Donncha had emerged as the undoubted number 1 joker in the team. Tony Biscombe wanted to use in the DVD DOC filming me peeing in the loo at Christchurch where he said did TB wash his hands and I said yes. 'No, you did it for him.'

TB's ratings going stratospheric at the moment after his handling of yesterday's events. JoP [Jonathan Powell, chief of staff] sent through a note on the outcomes and asked me to feed in some thoughts for TB's press conference statement. The bombings were still the main thing, obviously, but he had also managed to secure a fair bit on Africa, doubling aid, climate change, though the Yanks were difficult, even if Bush was playing that down, and help for the Palestinian Authority. He wrapped it all up in the language of hope v hate.

I was beginning to see the end of the tour now and it was on balance positive re players but negative because of results and media and the flak, which was unrelentingly negative now. It was a given among them that my appointment was a mistake. It was part of the no-balance situation Clive was suffering from. Some of the players, e.g. Jones, Josh, said they felt sorry for him, that he knew what he wanted but the other coaches hadn't really delivered for him. Walsh made a similar point to someone at last night's Q&A and said that I was someone who so elicited responses from people, and so was associated with baggage, that it was maybe impossible for me to do any job at all! I explained that there had been two sides to what I had been doing – dealing with the players and coaches and helping them deal with the media and public; and dealing with the media directly. The first part had gone well, the second had not because a lot of the media couldn't cope with change. Clive made the point on radio that he felt the media had missed a huge opportunity – I could have helped them get more and better access and output but they decided to go anti, so it never happened.

Once the non-Test players got back from Queenstown we had the final squad meeting, with presentations to the locals who had helped us, and summing up speeches from Bill and Clive. Bill's speeches had improved as the tour went on and he was popular because he was so transparently nice. He spoke warmly of Clive and of the players. Clive said he hoped everyone had learned something and that the players would go back as better people and better players. But amid all the kind words and the friendships forged over the past few weeks, nothing could take away from the fact that we had lost the series even before the final game, and very few people were giving us much chance of winning that.

Saturday 9 July

We had the last HOD. The doctor James Robson had more bad news – Steve Thompson had gone down with the same virus that hit Gareth Thomas earlier in the week, and was ruled out. Shane Byrne would step up and Gordon Bulloch would take Shane's place on the bench. Stephen Jones and I went for a coffee down the wharf to pass a bit of time. He said he had enjoyed it, but he was looking forward to getting home. He felt there was a problem with expecting all the players from the four nations to come together at the end of a season and perform at their best, and the injuries had shown how hard it was. It was probably different in the amateur era because the teams they were up against were not of the same kind of quality. The truth is we were probably never going to win this, but he had enjoyed it. He said again that even though some of the players might think what the hell was Alastair Campbell doing on a rugby tour, the vast majority of them had enjoyed having me there, and learned something. 'I can see why Tony liked having you around as a lightning conductor.'

These match days really dragged. I bumped into Jonny Wilkinson in the lift back at the hotel. He said they dragged when you weren't involved but when he was playing, he always wanted more not less time to prepare. There seemed to be more Lions fans at the ground than there were for the Auckland match. As we arrived, the skies opened. Gareth did the captain's pre-match interview and sounded terrible. He was clearly not over his cold but desperate to play. We started well and Stephen kicked us into a six-point lead. Then Tana Umaga was sin-binned. I was sitting next to Ian McGeechan, who said a one-man advantage for ten minutes is usually reckoned to be worth seven points. Instead, in the ten minutes he was off, we shipped two tries and were suddenly trailing badly. Though the Lions fought hard in the second half, we never really looked like winning after that. They ran in five tries to our one and it was a fairly dejected dressing room afterwards. 38–19, and it could have been worse.

As I walked down the tunnel, a Kiwi screamed at me, '107 to 40, Campbell,' which I worked out was the total score over the three Tests. Some of the players looked dead on their feet. And watching some of them remove all the strapping showed how much they needed to be held together. TB called for a chat, mainly about the summit, where he said the others had been brilliant in relation to the bombings but it didn't stop them being difficult on other stuff. But by and large it had gone well.

I put him on to Clive for a chat. They were able to swap notes about the media losing perspective, and I think Clive felt better for the chat. TB said the ones who shout from the sidelines shout partly because they are not in the arena, but he had the balls to take on a big challenge when others might have thought why bother when it is going to be so hard to pull off. They chatted a bit about the Olympics, and later I suggested to TB and Tessa that Clive was definitely worth getting involved. He had a very quirky mind and he loved complicated problems and trying to make them simple. He said to TB he was about to do a press conference. 'Why don't we swap scripts?' TB said. 'Get Ali to write my words and yours, and I'll do yours and you can do mine.' Going back to TB, I said it was pretty much the first time in ages that he had managed to get himself a decent press, what with a fairly successful EU summit, his role in winning the Olympic bid, where lots of people out there were saying he swung it, his chairing of the G8, and his handling of the London bombings. He was certainly getting a better press than me or Clive right now. The NZ media were pitiless and piss-taking, and the UK media much the same.

Bill, Clive, Eddie and Andy went through for the press conference, Clive's last as a rugby coach. The usual obvious questions were asked. Clive said again there was not much he would have changed. Bill was very supportive. Clive warned the New Zealanders not to get too carried away. The players were now looking forward to going home. They had very mixed views about New Zealand and there were a lot of doubts about the country's ability to stage a World Cup. All that went largely unsaid at the dinner afterwards. They were now going on the piss for a month was how the mood felt now.

Sunday 10 July

Some of the squad had to be up by six to make the earlier of two flights taking us back. There were some badly hungover people on both flights, but the mood remained pretty good. As we walked though Auckland Airport, headlines blared at us the scale of our defeat and the All Blacks' victory. At the airport I got more shirts signed then had a long chat about education with Josh, Shane and Easterby, Josh on the right, Shane and Simon more with me. On the flight to Sydney I sat with Andrew Sheridan, who had a look through the *Esquire* diary piece I was doing and corrected a couple of things. On the flight to Singapore Stephen J rounded up a few of the guys for a piss-up and chat in the galley – Josh, Alfie, Cueto, Neil Back doing magic tricks, Simon E, John Hayes. Good laugh, occasionally too loud for the stewards, once people were trying to sleep.

Lots of politics with Josh, Jones and Alfie; Josh who already knew what he thought, Stephen who loved to ask all the process questions, and Alfie who said he just wanted to be told what to think and if he needed to think about stuff that was political, he would call me up and ask me. As the drink flowed a bit, they started to open up a bit more on the tour, and the sense was that they felt the coaches didn't get it. Some of them got fairly legless but they all knew they were going home as losers and with lots of the media saying it was the worst ever. Alfie said despite losing it had been a good tour and they were all the better for it. He and Stephen Jones asked me to go down to France and see them, also to Wales. Those two plus Josh, Richard Hill and some of the Irish would be the ones I would stay in touch with. Clive came down for a chat and again said he would not have changed things. He was a bit worried I think that I regretted it, and was also looking more worried and strained generally. He wanted to go low-profile then start at Southampton and move on. I said if the football didn't work out, he should get involved in the Olympics.

Monday 11 July

We arrived at Heathrow at 6 a.m. and had to wait ages for bags. Josh was a few places ahead of me in the cab queue. He texted to say the last time he came back through here there were thousands out welcoming them. This time there were a handful of fans and loads of media, and as we emerged from airside, it suddenly dawned on me that a lot of them were there for me, because David Walsh had done a big number in the *Sunday Times* on the orchestration of the Gavin Henson picture, and some of them had decided that was the story to follow up. It would run for a day or two, I guessed. I ignored them and got into a cab – the traffic was dire post the bombings – the driver was [footballer] Scott Parker's dad. He was pretty clued up, knew a lot about my political life but had also been following the Lions stuff and had noticed I had copped it.

We had a good chat about sport generally and about the media. It was interesting how many top sports people seemed to hate the media but so many wanted to end up in it so they didn't push it too far. He asked me if I was glad I had gone, given the stick I was getting. I said that the stick didn't bother me, I had enjoyed the trip, made some good relationships, and some would definitely be sustained, had seen the insides of elite sport which had been interesting, but I am not sure I was able to give as much added value as Clive had hoped, and the media side of it had been pretty crap. But as I said to Fiona when I got home, the fact is when the election was over, I didn't want to get sucked back in and the chances are I would have been if I had been around in London the whole time. So on balance, glad I did it but it had gone on too long; learned a lot (and had some great stories for the speaking circuit) but not sure I added that much. It probably did a bit damage to my reputation and showed once more I could not do anything without parts of the media trying to kill it. Matt Dawson said he couldn't understand why people hated me but a lot of people did.

Tessa, who had called during the stopover, said Matthew and David [Mills, her son and husband] had both noticed how much shit I seemed to be taking on the sports pages. She said I was an anti-hero. She recalled John Sergeant [political broadcaster] who had been reviewing the papers on *Breakfast with Frost* when I came back to politics for the campaign, saying the media would all complain but they loved it really.

Mid-July through August holiday

On the political front TB was pretty well transformed. Events, dear boy, events, working in his favour. His row with Chirac, his role in winning the Olympic bid, G8 and his handling of the bombings had all developed to create a new mood dominated by the notion that he could do no wrong. It kind of underlined the point he made to Clive that the media could only do two tones: all shit, or all fantastic. Parna had called while I was away to ask me to a political strategy meeting at No. 10 on the Wednesday after we got back. I got in and TB was out on the terrace. We had a chat about the tour, him saying he had followed the coverage and I must not take it seriously. He kind of echoed Jayne's tall poppy point. He repeated the suggestion that I take up some big job in the party, going round trying to re-energise and also proselytise for the government. But it was all a bit unclear and I could not really fathom it, or how it would work. It was nice to have a chat but it was maybe on the basis that we should just keep in touch and pop in every now and then. I had quite fancied being in Singapore for the IOC meeting, but I hadn't really missed doing another G8 or handling the bombings and he clearly did absolutely fine without me.

But at the same time, I was still in need of something beyond books and speeches to keep me focused and driven. I was getting a fair old slagging in the sports pages and I think I was probably taking it worse than I admitted. I sensed it in No. 10 that the ex-staff felt it. Bradders' jokes as ever had a point. He had even memorised some of the better lines of attack. I was certainly heading for a downer, I think. Rory went off to Greece. Calum and I had a nice time playing and watching golf. Grace was consumed with her school play, Tyler [friend], ponies. On the TB strategy meeting, it was OK but a bit groundhog. Mark Penn [US pollster] was there, and presented a fairly upbeat picture of TB's position, and a sense that things had turned. He felt TB should use the National Policy Forum speech on Friday to keep on the same anti-terror messages, as this was redefining his leadership. He, and I and others, felt he would be better turning to a domestic message.

We went over a conversation we've had so many times before – what is the driving narrative, how do we bind in ministers, what is the economic message? I liked Ruth Turner [special advisor], who was arguing for a clearer message on public services. I was saying he defaulted to process when it should be rooted in values and delivery. Waheed Alli [Labour peer] said he was probably being advised to worry about legacy but he should be worrying about just going for it. [Baroness] Margaret McDonagh [Labour peer and campaigner] was saying council tax was the biggest thing on the doorstep. TB said he wanted to give as much energy to domestic as people felt he gave to international. The feeling in the media was clearly that he was back in charge of deciding when he went.

Work-wise, a bit of diary work. A bit of post-Lions but I had pretty much put it behind me. I did an overnight trip to St Etienne to do a stage of the Tour de France with Geoff Thomas [ex-footballer, ambassador for Leukaemia Research] for the charity. It was good fun, though hard work even though we were doing one of the easier stages. Geoff was in terrific shape, and loving it. He was doing the whole route of the entire Tour. I did possibly the shortest stage of the whole thing, and felt shagged out. Back home, I went to the Anglo-French colloque organised by Dennis Stevenson [businessman and peer] and spoke at that. A depression was deepening, though, and I wasn't really on form. I could feel it was possibly a big one. Clive sent me a message saying our media operation had been light years ahead of other sporting ventures, and he felt sorry that we had not been able to enjoy the success on the field that he had hoped for. He was starting at Southampton FC next week. When it came the anniversary of Dad's death, Mum seemed not too bad, but Donald was very down.

23 July – We went to Tessa and David's place in the Cotswolds and after he and I played golf we ended up having a massive argument about religion, he and Fiona totally arguing the anti-faith line, religion caused all the problems in the world; me as a pro-faith atheist. For some reason it got quite heavy and that sent me further down mood-wise.

24 July – Lance won his seventh Tour de France. I sent him a message and he sent one back saying this had been the sweetest. Tessa was asking me to think about taking the next Sport England job. We got home later and as we walked through the door, TB called, and Fiona was irritated, I could tell. I took the call upstairs. I told him I was seeing Ed Balls on Tuesday. He said GB was again not really working with him. 'As soon as I go up ratings-wise, GB goes into a panic.' He felt that there was an obvious strategy that GB ought to pursue – work to deliver TB's agenda, then say there are new challenges and a new PM and a new team can meet them. Maybe in the area of taking forward the respect/anti-social behaviour agenda, the new global economy, lifelong learning, preventative health. But if instead they felt the need to dump on TB's legacy, or reverse public service direction, or respect, or the international agenda, it will be a big mistake.

Re the bombings he said he felt we could turn round the Iraq argument by making clear that it was because these people were carrying on as they were that we had to see the job through. This was not a phenomenon caused by Iraq. It is part of the same phenomenon as Iraq, a deep-seated hatred of all we stood for. He said if I wanted to pass on a message via Balls, it was that GB needed to understand he was serious about going but also serious about not being done in. He sounded very chipper. Constantly asking me how I was, was I OK, how was the head – I said fine but I think he could tell that wasn't true – and what next and clearly wanting me to say yes to this party job. He was also asking if I was making decent money – presumably because he wanted me to work for nothing.

It was PG who had pressed me to see Balls, because he felt I would have to get closely involved in transition, and also on planning for a GB election campaign if and when that came. It was all very confusing and conflicting because of course the other project I was currently working on was Volume 1 of the diaries, which according to Stott, who had now read them, was 'absolutely devastating for GB … I don't know how you ever put up with him'. Added to which there was a little media flurry about Lance Price [former special advisor] and Jeremy Greenstock [former UK diplomat] being blocked from doing memoirs, which I was sure was in part about laying the ground for me. Anyway, TB said GB had to know he was serious about going but was still not sure Gordon would do anything other than undermine him and his legacy. He felt GB was just holding back now, that he had come back in line (ish) for the campaign, that me having been there had held things together for a while, but now it was back pretty much to status quo ante and maybe even worse. 'He is just waiting for his moment, I think.'

26 July – Meanwhile when I saw Ed and PG on 26 July, chez moi, we had what felt like a mirror image. Ed's version was that TB had pulled up the drawbridge once he had secured the election win; he had used me to get GB back in, that now that he had got the election behind him, it was back to how it was before – no shared agenda, no consulting, blah-di-blah. He said, 'It's true you got them working together, we thought it would continue after the election but it didn't and TB was doing his own thing, didn't consult about the reshuffle, and also people around TB – especially Jonathan and Sally – were making clear they didn't want GB around even as Chancellor, let alone as successor to TB.' I said they had to rise above it, stop exaggerating, understand the life TB had, be in his slipstream, help him deliver then all of us can be in a position to say TB did a great job but now there are new challenges requiring a new team. If they dump on him, it will rebound.

He didn't buy into it all, kept coming back with examples of non-cooperation, bad briefing, TB not honouring stuff, plus a bit of policy differences especially on public services, and he said the problem was if you had any argument with any line of policy it was as though you were totally against TB. We went round in circles for ages. Eventually I said they were using any excuse for inertia. They were pretending they could do nothing until TB gave a date for his departure and that was rubbish. They had to work back from an election with GB there as leader. What did they want it to be about? What were the policy areas they wanted to highlight? What would they do about those areas now, after TB went, and in the manifesto? What type of campaign did they want to run? Who would be running it? Then work backwards a bit more. What would a first GB Budget do? What would a first GB Queen's Speech do? Then work back and assume there might be a leadership election, even if they didn't want one. What kind of speeches? What kind of conference? What kind of campaign? Then work back to what TB needs to achieve in the interim. And plan it all out and give him a note.

Ed said if he did it, TB would not buy it, so we agreed I would do it. But after they left – and PG had been very much with me saying we had to get on and DO something, break through this fucking inertia – I felt it was a pretty bad scene again and wasn't sure how much I wanted to be involved. PG called later and said he had found it very depressing. He said he didn't get the feeling they had much in the locker by way of planning. It was clear GB has no plan, he said, and is just sulking and waiting for a TB departure date. Later I met up with Richard [Stott] to go through some of the Volume 1 material. It was all very, very difficult. I was not sure how I could publish some of this with these guys still around. I was losing sleep over it, and it was driving my mood down even further.

28 July – I met some business friend of Jerry Bridge [neighbour], who was possibly into helping the party but I took the judgement early on that it was more about what the guy could get out of it, and fobbed him off. Then to JLA [speakers agency] to meet some of the people who work there. A bit Sloaney but OK, and I guess I do need to get into the speaking market in a more concerted way if I want to raise the cash to be able to fund the other stuff pro bono etc. Up to Watford to see Rory race.

At the weekend I set off with Calum to Wheatley [parents' home]. TB called and said could I see him before we left for the holidays. He was very pleased at what was happening re the IRA, who had finally effectively announced the end of the armed struggle, and were promising total decommissioning, to be witnessed by churchmen on both sides. The statement was really strong, and while justifying the armed struggle, in terms of what was being announced it could not have been clearer. It also went through the extensive process of consultation there had been with units and volunteers throughout the organisation. It was a fantastic thing to read. He said he had heard it so many times before he hadn't dared believe it but it was real enough.

On party conference he was not sure what his plan should be. Re GB he said that PG had filled him in about our chat with Ed B and he was worried GB was not thinking right – basically looking to undermine rather than build, looking to divide not unite and looking to ensure the absence of a date for departure was an excuse not to do much at all. We discussed the idea of me helping with a transition strategy, which he seemed to think was a good idea. He said GB was clearly worried he was going to decide to stay ad infinitum, which he had no intention of doing. He said ministers were being called in and urged to go against reform and they were not taking it like they did before because GB's star had waned a bit and some of them were signalling no more bullying.

The 7/7 death toll had reached seventy, including the suicide bombers. On the terror front, the arrests were good news, and there would be more to come, but we shared a concern that the rolling news coverage and all the comment surrounding it risked endangering the trials if and when they happened. TB said the problem was that news values were now driven purely by a sense of how much impact could be generated. Also the 24/7 discussion of the same story led to a distortion of the reality. On the day we left for France, 26 July, he did his last pre-holiday press conference and announced new anti-terror measures including for three new offences, inciting terrorism, preparing an attack, or training terrorists. It was pretty tough and from what I could pick up on the drive down, seems to have gone down OK. He had met [Michael] Howard and Charles [Kennedy] to square them in advance. But he was also saying if the security services wanted more powers, e.g. longer detention, use of intercept evidence in court, we would look at it. And he said they'd be looking at the way the internet and publications were being used to generate terrorist sympathy and action. He called me after and said there was a fair bit of questioning on the line that Iraq had caused it, or contributed to it, but he felt he pushed back OK. Yes, the terrorists used that argument, but it could not justify what they did.

I was pretty glad to get away. We drove down to Puymeras on the Thursday. On the Friday I spoke to Peter M [Peter Mandelson, former Cabinet minister, then European Commissioner for Trade] who said he really thought I should stand as an MP. He thought if TB were to stand down as PM and MP at the same time, whenever that came I could maybe get his seat. He felt I was 'betwixt and between and it doesn't work'. I was certainly in need of a new project. The Lions thing had unsettled me a bit, certainly confirmed me in the view that media work was no longer my thing, though I had enjoyed the player side and the strategic side. I was beginning to lose sleep about the book deal. I had signed up to do it but the bottom line is that I am not going to publish anything in a way that fucks anyone over while we are still in power.

So what else? A seat in the Lords was still open to me, and both TB and GB had said there should be a ministerial role with it, but I just cannot see myself in there. Every time I look at the place, and all the flummery and the nonsense, I remember Jonathan's observation at

[Queen's private secretary] Robin Janvrin's farewell at the Palace: 'We have failed in our mission' ... in that we haven't really changed a lot of things and the Lords, for all we did on hereditaries, falls into that. Sport? That was definitely an area, but how and what? I had an up and down first week on the depression front. I was trying hard with Fiona but we were getting on each other's nerves a bit. I was doing a lot of exercise and playing a bit of golf with Calum. Rory came out with the Goulds. It was nice that we were all together, but I had a really quite severe dip, and at one point just went for a long run, stopped near Propiac, and realised I was crying, without really knowing why.

Saturday 6 August

I was sitting in the main room inside the house, just reading and avoiding the heat a bit, when Sky News called and said would I go on to talk about Robin Cook dying. I was totally taken aback, asked them what they knew and of course all they cared about was getting me on, said it was definitely true, confirmed, but I said I wouldn't do anything until I had found out a bit more. I made a couple of calls and it seems it was sudden and by and large unexpected. It was all so weird, and so final. I told Fiona and then agreed I ought to do stuff as the airwaves would just be full of it and we should at least have people on who would talk him up and talk up how clever he was, how tricksy, yes, but clever, and how he actually did a lot for the party and for the government. It was also important people realised that even though he resigned over Iraq, he had always been clear that he did so in a way that was not about damaging the government as a whole, but because of a genuinely principled position.

I did a stack of interviews, and lots of stories and anecdotes and memories came back to me as I talked about him. I was asked about the whole marriage thing and the Heathrow call and all that, and the myth that had developed that I told him to choose between his job and his marriage, and also the Gaynor [Regan] situation,* but I think I managed to steer a lot of the interviews to big stuff he was involved in. Partly I was drawing on the conversations we had at the time of his resignation when we had a few funny exchanges on the draft resignation letter and

---

* Cook married Gaynor in 1997, after being told by AC that the press was about to reveal his extramarital affair with her. He and his wife were at Heathrow, heading off on holiday, but RC stayed in London and decided to leave his wife to marry Gaynor.

TB's draft reply, when he felt I was trying to portray him as a kind of war hero – his role in the conflict in Kosovo etc. – and he was keen for more focus on the International Criminal Court, human rights, ethical foreign policy. I listened to a fair bit of other people while waiting to be interviewed and it was amazing how people who twenty-four hours ago would have seen him as a figure of fun or would have relished slagging him off were now going into overdrive about what a great statesman he was.

I felt really sad when we went out to dinner. We were never close, close buddies but RC always felt he could trust me, and more or less I him. There were a couple of secrets he had shared with me which I hadn't even told Fiona or TB. One was about a woman he had been involved with way back, and he was sure she was going to talk about it, and we put together a contingency plan but thankfully it never happened. He was also someone who was interesting in a world full of so many bloody bores, though he could beat the best on the pomposity front – I like to think he was partly taking the mick out of himself. I didn't sleep well, just mulling it all over. I worried also that it would lead to more leftist emotionalism. I was worrying re GB's ability and also any role my book would play in highlighting that. I want to believe he could do it, and certainly it is hard to see anyone else who might be able to step up. I didn't want to damage him, though as Fiona said I did not exactly owe him much.

Mo [Mowlam, former Cabinet minister] was also still very ill and she died during the third week we were away. Losing both her and Robin was awful. I had been out of touch part of the day, having gone out to a race with Rory, and so I missed all the media bids. When I caught up with them I decided against, worrying it looked a bit mawkish, especially as I had done so much about Robin. I felt sad though once more. We had never found a way really to harness Mo and her talent. She was not as great as the publicity she generated and she could at times be terribly silly and self-indulgent but she was a one-off and there had been moments when she had done things that were bold and brought results. I think she went off TB a fair bit latterly but in the early days she had been a constructive critical friend and had had a bit of reach to the party. I got hacked off when she or her people were constantly saying we were briefing against her. It became another of those myths that took hold and I am pretty sure she was the one pushing it out there, though I have no idea why. She was absolutely convinced Jonathan and/or I did her in, and it wasn't so. We had had some good times though, especially when the peace process was working, and she was a proper people's person.

Rory and I did a 10k at Cheval Blanc and got a great insight into French bureaucracy. We couldn't run without a licence or certificate. In the end they agreed we could run but not with a number, and if we got injured they couldn't be expected to look after us. Rory ran really well and they were panic-stricken when it became clear he was winning. I ended up doing a piece for *The Times* on France and regulation. *L'Equipe* did over Lance Armstrong re EPO [erythropoietin, protein hormone stimulant] again but I wasn't convinced. I had some good chats with PG re our respective futures. Both of us were in a way trying to get a bit freer from the political scene, yet both also wanted to help get through the next stages, which were going to be tricky. PG had the idea that I do a note to myself almost as if I were advising someone else, and it was helpful and quite therapeutic.

First I tried to work out how I spent my time, then how much I enjoyed the various things I did, how much I was able to achieve, how much it felt relevant or interesting, how much money we made, how much we needed, what gaps were left in time work-wise. He and Gail had got into walks and day trips and we ended up calling it the grid. We saw them most days, which was nice, though I think both Fiona and Gail got irritated by all the yak re TB–GB blah. Gail was also picking up on my nervousness about the book doing in GB. The cricket [England v Australia] was fantastic, and at one point we thought about going back for a couple of days but ended up following via the media. I spoke to TB a few times, his holiday getting the usual negative attention. Mind you, he did go to Barbados, and until he did a couple of public things, the media had been pretty good at respecting a request from No. 10 not to reveal where he was on security grounds. In fact, it became a bit of a piss-take thing, people speculating where he might be, when in fact they knew.

We saw a fair bit of the Kennedys. Good moment when Calum's GCSEs came through via Audrey [Millar, Fiona's mother] and he did really well. Grace was really nagging me about getting a pony. After a few chats with Philip, Fiona and Gail, I did the note in the last week.

Overall objectives:

- To ensure long-term family, political, financial and reputational strength and stability;
- To maintain and develop AC brand as one of the country's and the

developed world's leading political and strategic voices, rooted in past reputation but with increasing emphasis on advice and input re the present and the future;

- To maintain good relations with leading Labour figures, develop new role within party to be in a position to help shape transition and election strategy;
- To continue to press ahead with the preparation of diaries for publication ASAP, consistent with the desire to protect reputation and limit any damage to the government or party, especially GB;
- To devise new ways of raising funds and profile for LRF. Also to advise mental health charities;
- To maintain and develop knowledge, expertise and profile in sport.

To this end, I will concentrate on the following:

- Public speaking. This will take up around 20 per cent of work time, rising to 25 if overseas visits plan is seen through, but will generate bulk of income. Other than pro bono party, educational and charity speeches, I should be in higher pay bracket. I should work up a programme of speech visits overseas and build around them political, media and other visits. I should generate new thinking and material and use some of these speeches to make public interventions in the political and media debate.
- Book. I should devote 25 per cent of time to this and maintain contact with ongoing editing process.
- Press. I should not seek to renegotiate the *Times* deal as a near weekly contributor but instead make occasional contributions, mainly but not exclusively with *The Times* and *Irish Times*, and also develop own website/blog for most political contributions.
- TV. I should make occasional serious contributions but resist run of the mill punditry. Not interested in full-time TV show. None of the semi-permanent offers to date are worth taking. I envisage media and TV as a whole taking up to 10 per cent of workload.
- Party. I should agree with TB, GB and others a semi-official role, with a small retainer, and the expectation of around one day a week, rising as transition and election near. This could be a vice-chairmanship, or an ad hoc committee role, tied in with motivational work. I should explore the possibility of working with PG and Mark Penn to put this kind of work on a professional footing. Around 20 to 25 per cent of time devoted to politics. I should see Bruce Grocott,

Neil K and others re parliamentary route but unlikely to lead anywhere.

- Charity. I should make better and more strategic input to LRF. I should also devise a new sporting challenge event to raise funds and profile for the charity. I should map out a strategy for engagement with mental health campaigns. 10 per cent.
- Related to this, I should continue to maintain a profile in sport. 5 per cent work time.
- Family/personal. I should continue to spend as much time as possible with the family. I should see a specialist re depression and work harder at the most important relationships.

Reading it back, I realised it was the first time I had written down in black and white that I needed to get help on the depression front. I had been limping along for too long, and the resistance of help and probably medication was almost certainly making it worse. I started to put feelers out, but Philip said he knew someone he thought was right for me.

Once we got back to London I was finding it quite hard to get back into work. I was plugging away on the diaries, but resisting the political pressure, intense at times, especially from TB, to get re-engaged. I had to accept the depression was really quite bad at the moment. On and off for weeks. I hadn't really felt right for some time, and sometimes it was as bad as it had ever been. Fiona and I had just gone round in circles all summer, her not thinking I had changed, me not thinking she was being supportive, her seeming to think there was some kind of easy solution if I went off and talked to someone, me insisting I could do it all myself. I talked to Philip a fair bit and eventually I agreed to see the guy he knew. Apart from me being a problem, Fiona was pretty well sorted at the moment, doing enough of what she wanted to, definitely glad to be out of the centre, and feeling freer to say what she thought. I had kind of got over the idea that she should always be on-message, I guess. She said she underestimated how much I needed validation from her and also from outsiders. I said sometimes I felt she made the depression worse because she didn't understand it. Tim Allan inadvertently got me embroiled in a row about John Humphrys [*Today* programme presenter] which ended with Humphrys being rebuked by the BBC top brass. He used an after-dinner speech to slag off politicians as liars and had a particular pop at TB.

TB was in China and India, looking a bit tired. I was reading Lance Price's diaries. David Hill thought I should maybe have a go at trying to persuade Lance not to publish until after TB had gone. But Anji had spoken to him and she felt if we tried that they would go ahead anyway and just use it to generate a bit of publicity. The book was very self-orientated, and though it was a pain I didn't really feel it was as bad as David [Hill] and Hilary [Coffman, special advisor, also DH partner] seemed to feel. Though it would get a fair bit of media play, I'm not sure it would have any long-term impact.

Thursday 8 September

I was watching the Test match, working on a piece for the *Irish Times* on what a proper fan was and for *The Times* on the Tory leadership. TB called and we had a very long chat about things. Someone had clearly told him I was a bit down because he asked how I was and when I said OK, he asked, 'Is that OK or OK?' I went over some of the issues – not sure what I wanted to do professionally, still rebuilding with Fiona and not wanting to upset that, mutual bitterness in there, and a feeling that I didn't really want to be in the media world. He said he thought I would get more and more depressed if I didn't sort out a long-term plan for myself, and he felt that the key to it would be one job or one big task. He felt I was a big-challenge person and for now it was all too bitty. Equally I was unable – even if I wanted to – to escape the TB shadow. He said that I had done the most arduous high-pressure job I would ever do. A handful of us carried the whole show and I took a lot of the burden so it was hard to adjust.

He said I needed something very big and difficult – he said he had spoken to [Ayad] Allawi [Iraq Vice-President] and wanted me to go and help run the Iraqi operation. Mmmm. That would go down well. Nice chat, and I think he was genuinely concerned. I suspect Philip had said something to him. I could tell by how often PG was phoning that he was worried. Half in jest, TB asked if I fancied being general secretary of the party. He asked after the kids and of his own he felt they doing fine and coming out strong. He often wondered whether his kids would have turned out different if he had been around more, but it's done. Likewise, he regularly wondered if he should have taken on GB direct by sacking him and done what he needed to do, but we will just never know. You just have to get on with it.

He said he would need me to get involved in the succession issue whenever that came – I sensed it wasn't going to be any time soon. He said he was dubious as to how GB would operate. I said a transition

September '05: Career advice – and odd suggestion – from TB

project would be interesting but I'm not sure I could take too much of the TB–GBs. He said he was due to see him on Monday, but they hadn't spoken at all through the whole holiday. He felt GB's handling of RC and the latter-day closeness was sadly indicative. GB loathed Robin for much of the time he was in government, but the moment he felt he could be used in the battle against TB, he used him. He felt GB – or certainly his people – were moving to a very anti-New Labour programme and approach. TB felt he was in a pretty good place internationally. He had enjoyed the trip, particularly India, and he felt he was listened to and respected for what he said more than ever. There was some pretty good trade stuff out of the trip, but a fair few rows on tariffs, also human rights.

Monday 12 September

The finale to the Ashes was absolutely fantastic, about as exciting as it gets, and the public response to England's win [2–1 in Ashes series v Australia] extraordinary. I watched the whole of the final day with PG, Rory and Grace Gould. Grace went to the celebrations the next day. Jamie Rubin [former US administration official, AC personal friend] had landed a programme with Sky and we chatted a fair bit about that. It sounded a bit highbrow for Sky, but he seemed up for it. Lance's diaries were causing a bit of a problem and I really went for him when I learned they were going in the *Mail on Sunday*. He sounded very sheepish, said it was the publisher's choice not his, which is what they always say. It would actually dent the credibility even more. The psychiatrist I was due to see had had a bad fall on holiday so the appointment was cancelled. It was odd how it added to my lowness. Having resisted it for so long, now I wanted to get on with it.

I did a piece for *The Times* taking apart Ken Clarke [Tory MP, former Chancellor]. Andrew Mitchell [shadow international development secretary] called for a chat about it. I like Ken but I doubted he could do it [leadership of party]. I thought his tobacco links would come back to harm him, he was daft to have worked with John Redwood [right-wing Tory MP, ex-minister] way back then, and though I thought he was on the right side of the argument on Europe, the Tories as a whole weren't. One or two pundits picked up on it and said Clarke was the man we feared and so this was all part of a strategy to stop him. It was hard to see who was emerging out of this. It was hard to see much in [David] Cameron [shadow Education Secretary] beyond the Tory toff, though he might be the one coming through the middle. I said in the piece [David] Davis lacked the emotional and political skills to take the Tories to the centre.

Monday 19 September

I did the Great North Run again but the build-up was marred by a row with Fiona on the morning I set off for Newcastle, so I was in a bad mood. Then I forgot my bloody glasses so couldn't read on the train. My mind was whirring, and I was actually feeling a bit on the edge. I met up with Brendan [Foster] at the Copthorne Hotel and he felt I was in an OK place, but I didn't feel it. At the dinner at the Sage I was next to Simon Lee of Leeds Met University and his very nice wife. He knew [Lord] Hutton, both having been at Balliol. It was a nice enough do though I was being stalked a bit by someone from Cancer Research. Lance's first instalment appeared in the *MoS* but it didn't really fly. TB called and asked how the run had gone. I said it's tomorrow! Out of touch or what? I said you know we won the Ashes… The what?

He felt re conference that the focus had to be domestic and the message had to be New Labour. The TUC had given GB's speech a cool reception and he should have gone further with a New Labour message, but had chosen not to. TB was tired after all the travelling. He was raging about the BBC coverage of Bush's reaction to Hurricane Katrina.* He was clearly very down on Schroeder [whose Social Democratic Party had failed to achieve an overall majority in Parliament]. He felt the grand coalition was the worst option. He wanted me to go in next week to go over the conference planning. The GNR was fine but I found it tougher than last year. The first nine miles were OK and I finished pretty well but miles 9–11 were shit and at one point I was even thinking about calling it off because my knee and hip were hurting a lot. I was glad I did it, though. The helicopter ride out was great, but getting off a nightmare because my legs were seizing up.

Tuesday 20 September

I went in to see TB in the flat. Leo [Blair's youngest child] was playing in the hall, very chatty and funny. Five now, and very sweet, wanting

---

* The US President had been criticised at home and abroad for not returning from vacation to Washington for more than a day after the hurricane struck in August. The costliest natural disaster in US history, it caused devastation along the Gulf coast from Florida to Texas.

to show me toys and books and things he had been drawing. TB and I went through to the sitting room and he started by asking, 'How are you, then?' with that quizzical 'I think things are not quite right' look. I said I was fine but very up and down. You're like me, he said, if you have no driving purpose you are in bother or if you're not in bother, you create some. He felt I needed two separate parts to my life – money and a cause. Money could come from speeches etc. but he also felt I needed a regular column in a broadsheet to show I was around on the political scene and because I would do it better than most. I said I thought that was more about him than me. Maybe, he said, but he felt it was possible to be both interesting and basically supportive and not many could do that like I could or would.

He also thought I should take up serious TV offers because there was a need for a clever progressive voice out there. There are not that many of them outside the actual Westminster bubble. He said the Lions job had shown I was too big a figure for that kind of role, but I needed a cause, something serious and heavy. He thought the Sport England thing wasn't big enough. He felt on the diaries that I should worry less about the impact on GB's reputation than anything that might hurt my own. I said they were linked. He nodded, yes that's what makes me think you'll do the right thing. People know you for your loyalty and you won't put that at risk. He felt I should try to maintain good relations with GB but said there comes a point where if you are not part of the sect you are excluded. He thought though that I should – 'must' – be around for the transition. GB and he had met that morning. GB was still asking for clarity, which was code for a fuck-off date. But TB was probably staying until 2007. He said GB said he understood he would need to maintain a centrist political position but he had given too much credence to groups like Compass [left-wing pressure group] and was publicly and privately espousing the outlines of what was essentially an election-losing position.

TB felt people round GB lacked the depth or understanding of people needed to plan and win elections. I asked if he thought GB could win two elections. No, he said straight away, 'because the flaws will emerge'. He felt next time we could lose or we could win big. It was all down to us. Sometimes he thought GB would be fine. Other times not. He felt GB remained head and shoulders above the rest. If it was not for the basic flaw in his character, he would be very special, but the flaw is real. 'Though I say so myself, we are both very special politicians, but I have the character for this level of pressure that he does not.'

We went over the outlines of the conference speech. The main arguments were about public service and criminal justice reform. The world of change was the key. Many not the few still a vital message. He said he would like me to go down to Brighton if I could and help with the speech. He sounded like he was slightly dreading it, as was I. Re his own future he said the stuff he found the most interesting in terms of work he was plotting out in his mind, once he had left, related to the inter-faith work. He felt it was central to the way the world was going to develop in the next phase of history. I think we both cheered each other up a bit. I said it was very nice of him to give me advice about me, the central planks of which all had the remarkably coincidental effect of ensuring I did more to help him. He laughed, said I should see him as a personal doctor who always knew the remedy to my problems. I went to see Bradders afterwards who felt I would not do the diaries while GB was still in power. Probably right.

Sunday 25 September

I was doing bits and bobs on TB's conference speech but he was doing the bulk himself and was pretty clear about the argument. I met JoP at Victoria and we set off for Brighton on a very crowded train. Jonathan felt the speech was in good shape apart from the usual weaknesses at this stage. The backdrop to the conference though was TB–GB and in particular GB saying he was New Labour and reform would go on. But also Tessa, Charles Clarke and David Miliband [communities and local government minister] all did interviews saying it was obvious GB would be the next leader and suddenly there was a sense of moving plates again. Tessa had pushed a bit hard, having been trying to avoid sounding anti-GB, but because several of them were saying the same thing, the media saw it as concerted. We were set for TB–GB the soap dominating again.

We got there and though TB was going through the motions of nerves, he seemed less wound up than usual re the speech itself. There were some strong passages and the argument was clearer. There were a few themes clanking against each other. New Labour renewed. Power to the people. Solidarity. Pace of change. In the course of the next twenty-four hours we stripped it down a lot to New Labour renewed being the answer in a world of change. It was also the only way to deal with the GB situation – to show he was the true moderniser with the real agenda for change plus experience etc. TB was pretty exasperated with GB again. They had not spoken properly about their plans for conference. Come Monday and GB's speech, we had not seen a text. He didn't hit the New Labour buttons as hard as they had done in the briefing. He did the touchy feely stuff on values but nothing really challenging or breaking fresh ground. TB said to me later, 'What more does he want? How do you deal with him? I say I'm not standing at the next election. I endorse him as successor. I say if he cooperates I would be happy to fuck off now. And he still wants more. No other PM has had to put up with something like this.'

He also had the problem of JP who had gone offside again and had also cooperated with Colin Brown [*Independent*] on an updated book which had the line that TB did give a date for departure and that JP was pushing for him to go. Added to which, JP was throwing a wobbly about NEC seating on the platform for TB's speech on Tuesday and Jo Gibbons and Ruth Turner got me to speak to him to try to calm it down. I did so but found him far from being in a pro-TB place. He said he had given up on him; he was sure he and GB had done a deal and he was being carved out of it. I said that was far from the truth, but clearly TB had not been managing him, and GB was working on him all the time. JP said I had been missed because there was nobody in there who could speak to both of them, and give it to them straight. He was worried about the longer-term impact. TB's speech was going along fine. GB as ever had overreached and TB was set up to make a strong speech. He and I went through it on the Monday night/Tuesday morning to tighten up the language and the flow was good. Neil had an interesting take – he thought GB's speech assumed leadership without showing it and he felt TB's was his best yet.

I basically stayed in the hotel while I was there. On the rare occasions I ventured out, I didn't enjoy it. I didn't like being recognised, which was often the case when I was feeling down. When people came up to talk to me, I tried to engage but felt a desire to move on the whole time. The party asked me to do a little speech at the event for CLP [Constituency Labour Party] chairs, and I got a really good reception. Both Ian McCartney [party chairman] and Matt Carter [general secretary] said very nice things about the role I played in the last and previous campaigns and in keeping going with work for the party. I popped into *The Times* and *Guardian* receptions but whereas I didn't mind the party people, I found most of the media people a bit of a pain. That was the part of the job I wanted nothing to do with. I also felt there were too many almost-big people around TB. It was interesting that he had seemed so keen to get Sally [Morgan] and me back. Phil Collins [special advisor] seemed OK but not really big hitter I don't think. Not sure about David Bennett [head of policy unit]. Liz Lloyd was doing well as deputy chief of staff. The speech day itself was relatively painless. TB and I ended up doing only a minor rewrite. The themes were clearer. Bruce and I went through it for better claplines.

TB was at me again to go back to No. 10 and also get a seat for next time. I did a bit of media pre and post the speech, both solo and also with Bob Marshall-Andrews [Labour MP] who needless to say didn't like it. Did a bit with Roy Hattersley [former deputy leader] who was in the studio and was backing my analysis that the media were obsessing re TB–GB and ignoring the more important policy debates. Fiona and Audrey [Fiona's mother] watching at home both thought I looked happy for the first time in ages and that it meant I should go back and do more, but actually I felt quite pleased to be getting away. I was pleased the speech had gone well but I didn't have the same feeling of ownership. But it went well and he was strengthened after – plus the Tories were rejecting Howard's plans for change. I saw Rebekah Wade for a drink and took her to see TB. She seemed more settled but it was all the gossipy stuff she was interested in. She did say GB had been asking her in what she thought was a genuine spirit of concern what I was going to do with myself. I think a lot of people were beginning to sense I was not really fulfilled. And they were right of course. But at the same time I was glad to get away. Parts of it I really missed. A lot of it I hated. But I was drifting.

The week following the conference was fairly quiet. Mark Bennett [former assistant to AC] came round to do a couple of days' work on the diaries. F and I had another bad scene but got over it quickly. I was running but putting on weight still. The main political story was the Tories and a sense they were getting their act together, with the right wing going for GB a bit more. David Cameron and Ken Clarke did well on the Monday, David Davis less so on the Tuesday. He just wasn't a great speaker and, particularly at conference, that was so important to shaping the mood.

Wednesday 5 October

I ran over to PG's house in Regent's Park for a meeting with him and Ed Balls. Ed arrived and we both had a bit of fun taking the piss out of the house, which I said was like a small country's Embassy. Georgia had left for Oxford [University] which was terrific on one level but PG was going to miss her a lot. Once we got a fair bit of small talk out of the way we went upstairs and got down to the serious business of talking through where we were. The analysis was that things were pretty much all bad. Even worse than before. Ed felt there was no cooperation at all, that TB was just stringing him along. GB was really fearful he would successfully be painted as Old Labour and he knew that would damage him. Also they felt both the right-wing press and people around TB were giving out the sense that the next Tory leader, rather than GB, was the real successor to TB. I said the problem on TB's side was that he did not feel supported on the policy agenda. Ed said GB tried to support him but they had genuine differences over some issues and every genuine argument became a charge of 'You're not supporting me'.

He said he felt I was ambivalent re GB becoming leader – that meant GB did. I said I sometimes worried that GB did not fully understand how big the job was, because he had always seen himself as doing a job of similar stature, and it was so much harder, so much bigger. I said I did think he could do it, but sometimes I worried that he didn't have the temperament for a situation in which balls were coming at you from every direction, you couldn't just dip in and out for the big moments, and it was much harder to pursue a strategic path. I also worried that he would act as a foil to TB, and use TB as the template for a different operation, rather than the Tories or the idea of new challenges. I said I was also ambivalent about going back in at all, but I knew both TB and GB felt I ought to be involved in the transition planning, and so I was happy to be so. I said I felt like I had been through twenty train crashes and lived and did I want to risk a few more?

He said they accepted there was a GB core team and sometimes they had been too focused on GB rather than the whole government. He knew PG and I were primarily TB people but he said GB trusted us because of our ability and because he felt we were straight, both with him and with TB. He didn't rate a lot of the other TB people and he never would. I said that was unfair. We had a lot of talented people. He said GB also felt that Peter M, Alan Milburn, Stephen Byers, John Reid [all former Cabinet ministers] and a lot of the people around TB were actively working to ensure GB did not follow TB. I said provided TB was on his own agenda, that didn't matter, and they should stop being so paranoid about it all. We needed to get back to how things had been in the election. He said it all fell apart the day after the election – there had been no discussions on the reshuffle, or the choice of general secretary, no shared analysis or even discussion about the election. He said the minute I left the relationship stopped. They clearly thought the next conference should be TB's last. Ed said GB had real worries about the direction of policy on pensions, health and schools – he was going with it for now but he was not convinced.

PG and I had agreed before the meeting that we would try to get them to accept the line that GB should project himself into the future as being about 'continuity plus change'. I said if he was change without continuity, it would not work. If he was only continuity, likewise, people would question what was the point of the change. Ed said GB got that but I am not sure he did. TB called later when I was at the charity triathlon awards. I filled him in on the chat with Ed. On the one hand, he felt it was good they were engaging and understood – or said they did – the problem from both sides. But on the other he said he could not really trust them. He felt maybe they should have a TB–GB meeting with me, PG and Ed there. He said I am willing to give this a go but the temperamental issues may be insurmountable. He said let's fix a meeting and see if we can get into a better place.

Thursday 6 October

I went in to do media on Howard's speech at the Tory conference. It was a bit redundant as the real interest was in Davis and Cameron. Davis had done really badly yesterday, bad speech, bad delivery and there was a real roll to the Cameron bandwagon now. I had a few OK exchanges with Tim Bell [PR man, former advisor to Margaret Thatcher] and then Andrew Neil [BBC broadcaster], whose teeth were whiter than his shirt, and then watched and commented on the Howard speech. There for two hours and all a bit unsatisfactory, and at end Neil asked about Lance Price's book in relation to me calling TB a dickhead.* I saw a student for a thesis he was doing, then Matthew Doyle [special advisor] re David B. He was finding it hard and was clearly part wishing he had never gone, part wishing he was doing something else. I advised shutdown, only do policy, nothing that sets up the soap side, and David needed to stop thinking people cared about his personal life. Twice now he had been seemingly targeted and he had made mistakes and he needed to get a grip of himself or he was finished. MD said it reminded him of

---

* Among the revelations that Downing Street considered a betrayal, Price reported that AC had used the term to TB's face.

October '05: David Davis speech flops, Cameron bandwagon rolls

Peter M second time around.* The media didn't give him the benefit of any doubt now. He needed to do policy and nothing else. Then to TB strategy meeting, fairly big cast who went through party renewal, and also forward plans. PG had done a good note on TB and Cameron being the winners of the conference season, but there was something odd about the meeting – GB was the elephant in the room; we were not talking about him, but we had to involve him in all these plans – party, policy, transition, all interlinked. TB said to me and PG, 'That's your job.' Later he agreed to the idea of a joint dinner. I told Parna she should fix it – TB, GB, PG and I, maybe Ed B – and she looked surprised. Let's see if he'll do it. TB headed off to a Chirac dinner to mend a few fences and plan the Hampton Court meeting on the future of Europe.

Sunday 9 October

TB called re Chirac, laughing, and I said, 'I know what you're going to say.' 'What?' 'I know he's a rogue but I do like Chirac.' He laughed even louder. 'Correct.' He said it went a lot better than expected, no hard feelings on the Olympics or some of the harsh things said on both sides, and they agreed a fair bit on the future of Europe debate. Chirac had accepted that there was a different mood out there that had to be responded to. The divisions on social and economic models were real though, and he said JC went very, very sniffy when TB suggested all our economies needed reform.

I went out for a run and bumped into Andrew Adonis on the Heath who said what about Alan Johnson [Secretary of State for Trade and Industry], or David Miliband as next leader? His worry was that GB would never change. He felt we were all sleepwalking towards something we knew was likely to be a disaster. We had been ground down by him. He felt both AJ and DM were possibles but that neither filled the gap completely and while that was the case GB would exploit it. I also bumped into George Osborne [shadow Chancellor], who was out with his family. They had been seeing friends on the other side of the Heath. His wife said she would love to live there. Osborne said it had been a crazy week, that Davis just blew it. He made the oldest mistake in the book – believed his own propaganda, got complacent, got exposed as second rate, and Cameron moved in where the gaps were. He said DD

---

* Mandelson had twice resigned from Cabinet positions following accusations of financial and then departmental indiscretions.

had very little goodwill in the bank so when he slipped, the tendency of the majority was to help push him down rather than hold him up.

Cameron had spoken well and he related more to the Tory grassroots than Davis realised. I said I was reading all the stuff saying Osborne was the brains of the operation and I was studying him closely so we could work out how to destroy him. He laughed, then said, 'You should destroy GB – it'd be easier because he gives his destroyers so much help.' I said so how is it being his shadow? He rolled his eyes. We are lower than vermin, he said. It was a perfectly friendly talk, a mix of banter and serious chat. He warned me not to underestimate Cameron, said there was a lot more to him than the posh boy thing. Osborne's wife seemed very friendly as well. He was clearly very cocky, and I sensed they felt last week had been a big staging moment for them. He said they had learned an awful lot from watching how we did things, and reading anything they could, and he felt I was making a mistake if I thought Cameron lacked either the toughness or the strategic mind. He said they both talked and strategised all the time, and unlike TB–GB they were genuine friends not rivals. I said so were they once. He said yes, but I didn't think I should go for the leadership, because I know David will do it better. I managed a two-hour-plus run, and felt OK, so I was beginning to think seriously about the 50 at 50 idea [a fifty-mile run on 50th birthday].

Monday 10 October

I was working on plans for a Nelson Mandela interview, then out in the afternoon to Deloitte, doing a pitch for Leukaemia Research. Seb Coe was speaking when I arrived, and I chatted to him before my speech, not least about adapting to post-pressure life. He seemed to have got a pretty good balance going for himself. We had a bit of a gas about the TB–[William] Hague [former Tory leader] campaign.* He said it had been quite odd for him. As an athlete he always had a sense of his own possibilities, and he knew if he was likely to win or not. In the campaign, he felt pretty much outclassed the whole time and though he was trying to keep Hague's spirits up, deep down he kind of knew where it was going to end. He said I should try to persuade TB to stay longer.

The leukaemia speech went well, trying to make a pitch for them to

---

* Coe, a former Tory MP, had been William Hague's chief of staff from June 1997 until the September following Blair's second general election victory.

October '05: 'Don't underestimate Cameron' – Osborne to AC

become a strategic partner. I became quite emotional towards the end and it seemed to go down well. Angela Merkel took over as Chancellor of Germany, with half of Cabinet jobs going to the SDP [Social Democratic Party] in a coalition government. It was such an odd system. I got a call out of the blue from Madrid about seeing Spanish government and advising on a new comms sytem. I did another long session on the diaries, mainly Northern Ireland. I had forgotten just how up and down the whole thing had been, even when it was good.

Wednesday 19 October

I went for a long walk with Fiona before going to see David Sturgeon [psychiatrist]. Her main point was that whatever else I was doing, there was always an underlying dissatisfaction and unhappiness and when it tipped over into depression it was very hard for me and very hard for her. I had to be open to the idea that there were things in me that needed addressing, and I had to be honest with this guy. PG said he was a lovely man, really warm and human. It also turned out he was a close friend of Michael and Alison Farthing [neighbours, and Michael Farthing had also been the specialist who looked after AC's colitis]. She felt the main thing to get into was the addictive personality, and the fact I always seemed to find ways of sabotaging my own happiness.

I felt the basic problem was that I had gone from a full on meaningful existence to this rather bitty existence now, but she said it was just the same when I was full on, and it was the same when I was at the *Mirror*. I always went in waves of manic energy and activity and obsessions, and then crashed at regular intervals in between. David had suggested I see him at his house rather than his clinic, so I walked round. I took to him. He had a nice, kindly manner, a bit of a stoop, a nice smile. He listened rather than take too many notes.

I had to head to the Belfry afterwards, Seb [Coe] having asked me to stand in for him at a speaking event. It was one of those where I felt slightly I was prostituting myself. Was I doing it as a favour for Seb? Yes. Was I doing it because I wanted to? No. Would I have done it without being well paid? No. Did I say anything useful for the audience? No idea. Did I feel better or worse leaving for home? A bit worse. I was only enjoying these speeches where there was at least the semblance of a purpose beyond money or entertainment. Prior to all that I had been very down. David S had asked me to write a long narrative for him, about my own life, key moments etc., so I worked on that. I also had a long chat with Kate Garvey, and told her I had finally decided to get help, and try to confront whatever it was that dragged me down so often. David talked a lot about demons, and he felt for me the demons were variously work, drink, obsession.

Thursday 20 October

I had breakfast with Philip at the Honest Sausage [café in Regent's Park] and went over my session with DS. He was convinced this was the best approach for me. He was also, however, convinced I had to get more involved not less with TB. But I was sure that was one of the reasons I had been dipping even more recently, the sense now I was back in the UK that I got dragged in almost on a daily basis. David had asked me if I dreamt much about TB–GB and the truth is I did. PG and I were also discussing the meeting later with TB. We agreed that if Cameron won, and it was looking likely, he might be a trickier opponent for GB if and when he took over. He would definitely change the climate and more than ever we needed a plan to get TB–GB in a better place. I think the Tories, or the cleverer ones, may have decided that though TB would handle Cameron fine, GB might not. Generational. Class. He would hate the Tory toff bit and wouldn't be able to hide it.

As we were winding up, David Davis called, ostensibly to lobby me about getting someone a knighthood – I did my usual rant about the honours system – but I sensed it was an excuse to call and pick my brains about the [Tory leadership] campaign. He was doing his best to sound reasonably up about it all, but I could tell he was a bit down. Cameron clearly had momentum. He had done that classic thing of coming from low expectations and surpassing them, whereas David had confirmed what most people thought, so those who liked him and liked his politics were fine with it, but he hadn't really made inroads on new support. I told him I had seen Osborne last week and they were very cocky. He said they definitely felt they were favourites now but they were still playing the underdog a bit. He sounded a bit lost, and I felt his strategy was to hope Cameron fucked up, which wasn't really a strategy at all. Also TB had said to me the other day he felt Cameron had more than the others, and he had a good touch. I went into No. 10 with PG, and we watched the second ballot result. Ken Clarke having already gone first time around, now Liam Fox was gone and it was Davis v Cameron and although Davis had led on the first round, momentum looked like it was with Cameron. Now down to the members though and I have never fully understood them.

Then PG and I to the meeting with TB, just the three of us. We said our pitch – from our outside/inside position, we had no sense of a plan. We saw lots of policies, and lots of energy, but no clarity about where it was all leading. We also sensed the public mood shifting a little. Cameron would give the Tories change and we needed to be in a better place when it happened, otherwise there would be a real sense we were the end of an era and DC was the beginning of a new one. If we were going to help GB, then part of helping had to be about finding ways that he could be change as well as continuity.

TB rolled his eyes. He said he was close to despairing re GB. He said that it was nonsense he didn't try to engage him on all the big policy decisions, but GB was operating on one level and with only one demand, clarity – in other words, 'When are you going?' What's more, they were putting the line round the whole time that TB was useless, the party was in crisis, there was no clear direction and they had a big agenda for the party and the country which could only happen if TB fucked off. For example, TB had said he wants the next wave of party reforms this year. GB said no because he should do them when he becomes leader. Yet then he says to JP it is all about TB wanting to scrap the union block vote and GB being against it, and he doesn't want to do this kind of thing at all. TB wants to do in the party; he wants to build it up. TB said he was worried GB didn't have the judgement and the temperament for the job. It was obvious where he should be heading if the Tories were going to try to move closer to the centre. He ought to be New Labour, tied to the hip with TB, giving real unequivocal support to the reform agenda, showing he is helping to drive it, not letting the Tories anywhere near that space, let TB stay a while so we can all work out DC, then he takes over, shows ferocious energy, then calls an election and do GB experience and strength v DC risk and lightweight.

TB said of Cameron, 'I am not sure yet whether he is good or very good but he is definitely good. And with the media determined to lift him that's all he needs right now. He may be crap but we should not bank on it. He looks to me like he might have it, and he looks to me like he could get to Gordon. He said our plan should be to test him on policy. He makes all the centrist modernising noises, just like the others did, but then set him policy tests the Tories won't let him make. And if we move off the New Labour pitch, we vacate the ground to him, and he will take it.' I said none of that negates what we are saying – there has to be a plan with him and GB. I said if he was having overall doubts, and really felt this whole strategy of trying to get GB in on continuity and change was a mistake, we needed to know now. If we were going for it, we had to go for it. And if we weren't, we had to pull back and he had to confront what that meant. He said he was happy to sit down with GB and agree to it all, and he was happy to agree a date provided it was kept between them. PG was against that; he felt the dealing had gone on long enough.

We needed a strategy, and that was not dependent on a date. I said if we did it that way, it just becomes a negotiating lever for GB. TB said the mood around GB was changing fast. For example, at education. At the white paper meeting, they went round the issues, a lot of detail, and GB said literally nothing, sat scribbling, and left early, silently indicating dissent. What kind of leadership is that? I said so are you saying we pull the plug? TB sighed, shook his head, he said whatever kind of doubts he had, and he had a lot, he still felt he was probably the best but he was making it harder. People were beginning to see DM in a different light, he was becoming tougher, sharper, more political. CC [Charles Clarke] was impressive and perhaps up to it as well. But TB was ready despite everything to say GB was still the right person even though he knew those people would go mad about it. His worry was GB showing up weaknesses – e.g. in the people he gathered around him and also in lack of leadership.

He reeled off examples of him being difficult and obstructive. He had asked him to pop into a meeting with City Academies people, just show his face and give them encouragement. He didn't do it. That's how people get judged. But also, he should be out there now closing off flanks they would open on him, like he just doesn't get the crime and respect agenda. The Tories would be on to it like a shot, and GB should pre-empt it now, by being with him on it. We agreed to try to fix a dinner with GB and Balls and work through it. Most people, said TB, would be amazed how much he had endured from GB – he had said publicly he wasn't standing again; he had all but confirmed GB as his candidate to take over. Yet even that was not enough for him. 'He has only one thing on his mind – when do I fuck off and let him get on with it?'

TB asked me at the end how I was in a tone that assumed not good. I don't know if Philip or Kate had talked to him before, and told him that I was seeing a shrink. Maybe. I felt OK about going back in today, but glad to leave. I was still ambivalent. I had a good chat with JoP, who was filling me in on some of the policy stuff going on and also saw Gus O'Donnell [Cabinet Secretary], and filled him in on my current thinking on the diaries. He felt GB was handling himself badly at the moment and agreed with my analysis that GB ought to be bombing TB with support and love! I went round to talk to the press office team who seemed fine, but the mood re GB was not great. Cameron was handling himself fine but I could see him becoming very irritating. The desire for change will be strong though and we need to adapt too. If we treat him like he is IDS or another Howard, we will be making a big mistake.

To Streatham for a school prizegiving, a school I had visited before with TB. There was a very nice atmosphere and the kids were great. I did a no-notes speech about how if anyone had said to me when I was their age that I would meet people like Mandela, US Presidents, work in Downing Street etc. etc., I'd never have believed it. But though we were still far too class-based as a society, it was possible to do things you never expected to, and they should all aim high. I got a really nice reception at the start, and the loudest applause when I said we used state schools for our kids because they got a better and more rounded education by mixing with all classes, all nationalities, all faiths, and how we would never become a meritocracy while a self-perpetuating elite used private schools and ran down the state schools. Mum was down for a few days and she was picking up on my volatile moods.

Saturday 22 October

I had a brief chat with JP who called first thing. I filled him in, partially, on the chat with TB, and asked how GB was behaving. He seemed to be in 'both as bad as each other' mode, and repeated his line about how TB felt guilty about screwing over GB, and GB just wanted to destroy him. But he said he was not going to let the party be destroyed. He asked if TB was having second thoughts. I said he was, but not sufficiently to go back on his word. JP laughed. 'I've heard that one before.' He was actually calling to speak to Fiona so they could have a moan about the education white paper. It was pretty obvious JP was closer to GB on this one, though more for policy reasons than because he was pressing for TB to go. In the afternoon I felt a massive plunge coming on, went to lie down for a bit to chase it away, and failed. We were meant to be going out but I just couldn't face it, so in the end Fiona went on her own.

Sunday 23 October

TB called while I was at the LRF event with Fiona and Grace. He said GB was being very iffy about the idea of a dinner (which I doubted). Also the papers were full of JP being on the rampage about the education white paper. TB said he didn't think that would be coming from JP direct but I wasn't so sure. He sounded pretty offside when he called yesterday. I told TB he had called to ask Fiona how mad she thought the ideas in it were. 'Oh Lord!' he said. He was totally of the view that we needed to be very New Labour on the policy reform agenda, so that Cameron echoed us in sentiment and rhetoric, but was then unable to meet us on policy. He sounded on good form and said it was important not to overreact about Cameron.

But he said the GB situation wasn't great. He described one conversation where GB said, 'You told me Davis would win' – like TB was in charge. I told him of a text message Andrew Mitchell [Tory MP, Davis campaign manager, friend of AC] sent me – 'Are we completely fucked?' I told him that Cameron had momentum and he was doing well at looking the part, sounding the part, hiding his toffness and so minimising the benefit DD had been getting from his own background and being a different kind of Tory. I sent him and Davis a message saying be Mr boring policy v Mr glib photocall. But the media were loving Cameron's PR campaign, and he was looking unstoppable to me.

I had a nice time with Rory on his birthday (which he celebrated by winning a poker tournament) and gave him a pile of books from upstairs to read for his Oxford interview. In one was a letter from Alan Clark [deceased Tory MP, fellow diarist, friend of AC] joking that our problem was we were both addicts and the addictions included politics. It was very funny in light of current visits to David S to discuss my addictive personality. There was also one from GB inside his book on [James] Maxton [socialist politician of the interwar period] thanking me for all the help I have given him down the years. Rory seemed a bit unsure about whether Oxford was really going to be his thing.

Monday 24 October

Ed Balls called to say GB was being rebuffed by TB on the idea of a dinner to thrash everything out so fuck knows what's going on. He also said that Cameron backing us on reform was a disaster. I said this is like a fucking family drama where nobody is taking anyone else at face value. TB says to me he wants a dinner. GB says to me he wants

October '05: Balls claims GB being rebuffed by TB

a dinner. Then when we try to fix it, both say they have spoken to the other and the other doesn't want it to happen. PG and I were tearing hair out at the inability to make headway and fix a meeting. I was cracking on for a couple of days with Mark [Bennett] on the diaries, into 2000 and loads of TB–GB problems.

Fiona was doing telly in the morning on the education stuff, which was fine but then later she said she was doing loads tonight and the plunge took another dive. The depressions were getting more frequent, worse, and lasting longer. It was good I was finally seeing someone I guess, and David seemed a really good guy, and saw me at his house so I wouldn't be seen, but I was finding the process quite hard. It was definitely making me even more introspective. It was stirring all kinds of stuff, which I suppose was partly the point, but I was waking more days than most feeling empty and listless, and when I couldn't sleep I was feeling something closer to suicidal, and I was imagining my funeral over and over, and trying to persuade myself that Fiona and the kids, Mum and the rest, would be OK with it, and it would relieve them of a big stress. Around half-five this morning for example, I was lying there awake and just looking at Fiona who looked totally at peace and calm, and I was telling myself it was because when she slept I was out of her life, and the second she woke up she would have this mood of mine affecting her and it wasn't fair.

Tuesday 25 October
I was finding the process with David S really hard because it just made me so introspective. He was asking me to write down too much stuff – good feelings, bad feelings, also go into greater detail on some of the key moments in life, and I was finding I had little space for other stuff; or, when I was doing other stuff, I was seeing it in a different context. Calum and I set off for the Villa match. We had a very good chat on the way back. He had a lot of empathy and understanding for someone of his age. It made me a little worried he might have the same gene on the depression front. Lost 1–0.

The white paper on schools was published. But the news was also going big on a Cabinet rift on the smoking ban.* The worst thing was that it was being briefed in real time, virtually as the discussion was

* The government was about to announce it would press ahead with plans to ban smoking in almost all public places in England and Wales.

taking place, and it was leading to a load of talk about 'Is TB's authority waning?' across the media. Breakfast meeting with the Association of Colleges and what I might be able to do for them. On the rugby front Brian O'Driscoll's book was out and he was reasonably OK re me. Matt Dawson and Gareth Thomas both did interviews saying I a good bloke etc. It was mainly the Welsh and Irish I had kept in touch with. I was doing a note for DS recording the best and worst moments day by day and things done to help Fiona, which was one of the little exercises he had given me.

Wednesday 26 October

I was doing bits and bobs through the day and then saw DS at 4. We went through the long note I had done for him. It kept going back to Fiona, and my feeling that she forced me out from doing something really worthwhile, but then also the feeling that part of me knew it was right to leave, part of me wanted to be in, part of me wanted out, but the pressures to get me in were on me all the time, from virtually all the main players. I found it hard to see it as flattering. It felt like a fucking great burden, a big guilt factory. I explained why I found Fiona's 'I'll say what I like' media stuff hard because I felt I'd been taken out of the frontline and now she was doing loads – to my eyes – of slagging off the government. He clearly thought we had just become settled in very negative patterns towards each other and asked me to do something for her every day that I had never done before, and make a note of it and send it to him. I told him that I had been sneaking in a few surreptitious drinks at the Albert Hall charity do the other night. Just two or three, but in a way that nobody would notice. He said it was a slippery slope and I should be very careful. I felt like I could control it but if something really bad happened, it could kick off again.

Helle [Thorning-Schmidt, wife of Stephen Kinnock and now leader of Danish Socialist Party] and her PR guy came round for a chat. I had taken a look at the polls and some of the coverage and I would say she was not in great shape. The government were going for her hard on inexperienced and incompetent, also out of touch, trying to make her out as some kind of wealthy socialite which was bollocks but their press, if not as bad as ours, was pretty tough. She had definitely lost support. She had next to no resources and the whole scene was really tough for her. I gave her a plan based on a detailed policy development process so that each major policy would have several different points at which she could hopefully set the agenda. She also needed a good 'on your side' strategy, so I agreed to do a separate note on that. I went into town with her, and in the car talked about whether she ever imagined it was just too tough to do this, to win, and to have a young family, and all complicated by Steve living in two different places. Fairly convincingly, she said she felt she could do it. She definitely has something a bit special, and though I am sure she has low moments she seems to have a pretty good 'triumph or disaster treat them both the same' mentality, and she has definitely got resilience.

Then to Brighton for a speech. It wasn't a great venue and a bit flat but OK. A couple of women came up at the end and said they were big fans and wanted me to get a seat and lead the party. A man came up and said he had no view earlier but now he really disliked me quite passionately and violently! Tim Kerr-Dineen [university friend] came and we went out for dinner. It was a really nice chat, much of it in the crazy language we had invented at Cambridge.

Thursday 27 October
We had the builders in. Mark Bennett was also here all day. Fiona doing Andrew Neil and seeing Melissa Benn [educational campaigner and friend]. I was plunged again. I went out for a run and on the suggestion from David S that every day I do something I have not done before, I ran over to the other side of the Heath, bought Fiona some flowers and ran back to meet her. We were fine for a bit but were then into usual political row. It was sparked by a Neal Lawson [Compass pressure group activist] piece saying Cameron moving to the centre means we should move left, and she seemed to agree with this election-losing approach. She went on and on, ranting about things she felt we had got wrong. I went silent. She kept going. I said TB, PG and I knew a thing or two about political strategy, these people just give recipes for defeat the whole time. She said so why did you lose seats at the election? On and on it went and eventually I stormed out and I went for a run for over an hour or so, the first half of it in a real rage.

I bumped into Andrew Morton [journalist and author]. He told me he and Lynne had broken up. Irony time – he said they had always looked at Fiona and me as a couple who seemed able to have similar but also different lives and views and yet still be strong together. Maybe he was right. He used a phrase later, 'This was the universe speaking', when someone knocked on the door and offered a huge price for the house, and it was time to split. I felt that meeting him, and hearing him say what he said about separate lives, it felt maybe he was 'the universe speaking' and I went home thinking maybe it was time to call it a day. We resumed the chat hoping the mood would be better and it got really heavy very quickly. I said I was really trying but it was hard, it felt like a kind of deep loss going on, like a bereavement, the depression was worse than ever, and it wasn't helped when she appeared to fly off the handle at the slightest thing. She felt I had not involved her in the discussion with Helle, though she had things she could contribute, and I said I couldn't win. Damned if I do, damned if I don't. Also, the reality is that Helle wanted to see me because she wants to put together as New Labour a campaign as she could, and she would have been arguing in another direction and it would be a waste of time. So that made it worse. Grace cut my hair which gave us all a good laugh.

Friday 28 October

More universe speaking moments, though God knows what it was saying. I was talking to Mark re Bob Mills [comedian] for some reason and out of the blue Mills then phoned. Also I had been talking about Charles Reiss [*Evening Standard*] and then he suddenly appeared outside Tootsies [restaurant] where I was having lunch with the boys. *Time* magazine had asked me to write an obit of George Best [former footballer] so I worked on that for a bit. Mark was in all day and we transcribed to the end of December '99. Loads of TB–GBery, Ireland, and a row with Schroeder – fitting because all over the news today was another one, Schroeder having spiked TB's guns at the EU summit at Hampton Court. TB had been banking on Angela Merkel being in place, but the German election result was still being sorted out. Schroeder knew TB was trying to push on a globalisation adjustment fund, and was determined to present it as a neoliberal thing, not progressive. The general view was that the summit was a bit of a damp squib.

I went for a run then TB called. He said the summit had not gone as well as it might have done. There was a feeling that they were not really getting down to the stuff that mattered. He said Schroeder had been pretty bitter and unpleasant. 'What they hate is that I am still standing.' He said the Cabinet row over the extent of the smoking ban had been a case of eyes getting taken off the ball. Patricia [Hewitt, Health Secretary] and John Reid had got themselves into a big argument, PH wanting to go further than the manifesto, JR [now Defence Secretary] sticking to what he had thought sensible at Health. Then others piled in, and before you knew it, there were arguments all over the place on it. Jack [Straw] had said he would sort it but then got into a wood for trees mindset. The problem was a sense among some that TB's authority was starting to wane.

Re TB–GB, through the week I'd been pressing for a TB–GB plus 3 – me, Philip, Ed Balls – dinner but EB was saying TB was stalling, then that TB was saying we would only discuss Cameron, not work back from the election. Ed had totally been giving me the argument that we needed to move to the left. TB said they were lying if they said he was stalling. Of course he was happy to conspire in this plan to get GB in there but he really did wonder whether he had the psychological make-up needed for the job. 'If anyone had been at my meeting with him last week they would have said he was mad,' he said. 'Quite mad.' TB said eventually he gave him a date, just the other side of halfway through the term, but then that wasn't enough. He was also worried GB wanted to call an election as soon as he took over. TB felt it was a bad idea. Re the idea of moving to the left from the centre he said it was quite mad, totally wrong and would lose us the election.

He had been following the Lions stuff and said he thought BOD had really helped me, and Henson was coming over really badly. Nice chat. Agreed we just had to make the dinner happen. He said Balls was lying. TB said the office people went in to see him today really worried that Cameron was picking up and he was slightly losing his grip. TB said to them we had been here before. JoP said Labour people just did not feel born to rule. Watched Burnley v Hull [1–0].

Sunday 30 October

More about me and the Lions in the Sundays, ridiculous it was still going on. To Sky to do Adam Boulton's programme, where he was trying out also having a sports section. It was OK but too bitty. Andy Gray [sports commentator] was also on, good as ever, though very loquacious. I went for a run then to see Ed Victor post his chemo [leukaemia treatment] for a chat re book timings. I also saw Philip who had been in Paris. He felt re the GB lot that there was so much anger and hatred in them that there would be a problem when Cameron was marketing himself as hope, optimism etc. In *The Guardian* there was loads of stuff about how TB didn't want GB to take over, clearly fed out by his lot. It was all victim mode, hopeless. PG was losing faith in both of them, in TB to see it through with GB, and in GB to get the politics right.

Tuesday 1 November

Working on the diaries all day, then out to a speaking gig at the Hilton. I had a nice chat with Sean Fitzpatrick [former All Blacks captain] who thought the focus on me was crazy. He said in the end the Lions were beaten by a much stronger team and that was it. Jimmy Carr [comedian] was also performing and it was fascinating to see how, even when not on stage, he had an obvious need to make people laugh, all the time. I asked him if he could live without making people laugh every few moments. Even the question seemed to freak him out. My speech was OK but not brilliant.

Wednesday 2 November

To Whitehall Place, speaking at a PR summit so-called. My main theme was that PR, or at least strategic comms, was not in crisis, in fact it was in stronger shape than the media, which could only operate at the level of frenzy. Good Q&A, good question on Serbia and how the Kosovo conflict comms played out, and also interest in how we could get messages out to the Muslim community home and abroad. Unbeknown to me TB was seeing David Blunkett who was about to go*. DB had basically applied his own smell test, and decided he should go. No. 10 had been holding the line that it had been a mistake, but not a hanging offence, not to get watchdog permission for all the commercial stuff he lined up in trying to sort his post-Cabinet life after the first resignation, but it was clear he hadn't followed all the procedures and that was enough to get the frenzy going. It was such a shame, and as with Peter M, it wouldn't be easy to come back after two resignations.

I called David Hill pre-PMQs, where TB was very warm about DB, and I did a stack of media doing the DB fallout. I got a lot of nice messages about content and tone; I was warm about David, but also making the points that TB is strategic and keeps going whatever problems get thrown his way. I was sad for DB, but it was not the end for the government.

---

* Blunkett resigned as Work and Pensions Secretary after breaking ministerial rules over a directorship in a DNA testing company. Earlier in the year, while outside government, he had accepted three jobs without consulting a Whitehall committee.

John Hutton took over. I was heading home when I realised I had left my phone at ITN. Panic time. But it turned out Alex Salmond [leader, Scottish National Party] had handed it in after we had been doing a slot together and he had seen I had left it. Good of him. Home and to a session with David Sturgeon, this time with Fiona. She liked him and he basically took her side in terms of setting out how difficult I could be to live with. This was what living with an addictive personality was like, he said. This was my fourth week with him.

I'd done a long emotional narrative history after week 1, best and worst moments each day for week 2, doing something new every day for week 3 and now he wanted a gratitude list plus he wanted the two of us to do something new together each week. I said I was finding the whole process quite disturbing. He said it was meant to be. I was probing myself in a way I hadn't done before. He said the addict in me had been responsible for a lot of the good I had done, in terms of work and achievement, but there is a price to pay, for the addict and for those living with the addict. He said Fiona was bound to put up barriers because when you live with the addict you imagine sometimes that it is you who are mad. The addict cannot see the self-destruction in a way others can. It was hard work probing away at this stuff, and at times I was close to tears, I just couldn't hold back from these waves of emotion coming over me.

We discussed whether to tell the kids I was seeing him. He said he believed my situation was totally salvageable. I felt maybe I could see a route map though Fiona said she often felt like she had lost the will because I was so difficult to live with. She said I operated at such a pace that is was like living with a whirlwind and then when I crashed it was like a slow death. I felt there were two possible ways of this thing panning out – either we get through it and end up closer than ever, or we just come to see we find each other too difficult to live with. We didn't really get into the guts of things today, in terms of my feeling that Fiona had essentially made it impossible for me to stay in the job at No. 10, and me loading my own guilt on her when things didn't go well. I did Channel 4 with Chris Grayling [Tory MP] and went for him for the way they were now pretending they had not been gunning for DB. Having tried as hard as they could to get him out, now they were pretending not to be that fussed. I also went for him on the way they went for Cherie the whole time. I did Sky with Matthew Parris [former Tory MP turned commentator] and later *Newsnight*, again Grayling. He struck me as bright and quite steely. Jeremy Paxman took my side of the argument against Grayling far too much I thought.

Lots of messages after – Anji, Margaret McDonagh, Fraser [Kemp, MP] saying go to the Lords and be the Cabinet enforcer. Then a nice woman came and persuaded me to do *Up All Night* with Rhod Sharp on Five Live. Quite a good discussion. TB called earlier, jokey enough but he did say it wasn't good. He was sorry for DB but he felt he had fucked up. He said GB changed his assessment of how TB was almost day by day. Immediately after the election they saw him as a lame duck, then after he landed the Olympics and dealt well with 7/7, GB went into 'You're cock of the north, can do not wrong, will never go' mode, then the weekend before conference he was a goner but by the end of the week he was cock of the north again. Now he was a goner again because he had lost a minister. He said what GB didn't realise was that the public could suss this stuff. They know. They are sassy about politics but also about the media. The big difference between his own political management issues and Major's towards the end of his time is that there is an agenda here. It's difficult because he's doing difficult things. TB was due to do an interview with *Football Focus* and we had a chat about who he would pick as unsung heroes.

Thursday 3 November

The papers were all going on TB's authority draining away. I got loads of bids and did Sky on the way to the airport. I hit back and felt the general argument about TB knowing what he was doing and able to survive this and more was OK. On the flight to Aberdeen I was sandwiched between a woman vomiting and a woman who was quizzing me the whole time about people I had met – what was Diana like, what is Bush like, had I ever met Paul McCartney [rock star]? I was met by Sarah Deacon from Unison who drove me to the hotel. En route I heard the news that Rebekah Wade had been arrested for assaulting Ross Kemp [then husband]. A bit of a jaw dropper. To the hotel then to a cinema bar for a party meeting. I did a good passionate speech on why it was right to support TB and the government, an OK Q&A and a merit award to Sheila Jones [longstanding member]. TB called from Manchester to go over his plans for the next few days. I could tell he was worried.

He had to deal with the notion he was not of the party or didn't care if we won or not once he was gone. He said this is going to be a difficult phase and we have to keep our nerve. He said some of our MPs were beyond caring about whether we won or not. And GB was giving them licence to cause trouble. Rory phoned and said one of his teachers had said, 'Tell your dad he was great on TV and absolutely right that a media frenzy should not drive out TB.' TB though was feeling a bit shaky. I could tell that from the volume and the tone of the calls. GB just was not there for him, in any way, just now.

Friday 4 November

TB said he had spoken to Murdoch who raised GB in the context of not being there when the going got tough. I texted Balls to say on the back of the Cameron-Davis TV debate last night, when they were both weak on terrorism, that GB should get out backing TB on terror and saying this is a test of leadership for them. Balls replied that *The Sun* and *The Times* had a line of attack on the issue and it would be seen as being about GB–TB not GB–the Tories. I said it would cover all bases but he didn't get it. Milburn called, said he was quite worried, felt TB was more vulnerable than people might imagine. I said don't worry, he knows how vulnerable things are, the question is what he does.

The dinner at the hotel was black tie and with Jackie Bird [Scottish broadcaster] compering. It was a good audience, the speech went well, the right mix of funny and serious, and one or two trying to have a go in the Q&A, one or two re the Lions tour, which I dealt with via humour, and then laying into a guy who asked why people were not honest in politics, and then a row with a bloke about Iraq. When I asked him, 'What would you have done, if you had to make a decision rather than just have an opinion?' most of the audience applauded. I stayed up late to watch a re-run of the Davis–Cameron debate. I thought Cameron came over as a bit of a lightweight, but Davis was treating it too much like a policy debate, whereas I thought Cameron was doing better on general positioning.

Saturday 5 November

Annoyingly the plane back was delayed. Alex called while I was at the airport, and sounded very down. The Rebekah Wade story had at least knocked David Blunkett off some of the front pages. TB called before and after *Football Focus*, which he thought went pretty well. I went out to see Grace horse riding and ended up having a lesson. Grace and Tyler [friend] having a good laugh about it. I enjoyed it and did pretty well.

The trainer, Janey, said I was the first pupil she'd had who cantered on the first lesson. I decided to quit while I was ahead but spent the rest of the day telling anyone and everyone, with a funny posh voice, 'I cantered on my first lesson, don't you know?'

Then I headed over to Luton for the Burnley match. I told Calum, in a little café near the ground, and later also told Rory, that I had decided to see someone for my depression, and how they needed to understand it was nothing to do with them, it was just an illness I needed to get sorted. They were both really good about it, said they could see when something was wrong and if I thought someone else could help sort it, why wouldn't you? Calum wondered if it had got worse because I had less pressure on a day to day basis, most of the things I was doing I could do easily, and it meant I had too much time to think. Rory felt likewise that I should never have left. TB called just before kick-off saying what a self-serving arrogant lying shit Chris Meyer* was. Meyer had not even been there. He said someone had said to him [TB] that Meyer was bitter because we didn't help him enough. 'Rubbish. Him and his ghastly wife.' Great match, 3–2 win with ten men and no goalie after forty minutes.

Sunday 6 November

Out for a long run in pouring rain. The Sundays had a fair bit of follow-through from the media round I'd done, for example [Andrew] Rawnsley [*Observer*] saying the number of AC interviews was an indication of the level of TB panic. I did a piece for *The Times* saying that Cameron was the new me not the new TB. I felt Cameron had absorbed a lot of the stuff we did on comms but I wasn't clear, other than in very general terms, what he had by way of an overall strategy. TB called after Man U beat Chelsea to pass a message to Alex. He felt actually there was an attempt to link the decline of us and them. He said he'd asked GB, as I had asked Ed, to get involved in the terrorism argument. GB had said it would be misinterpreted. Why? The problem was he was again not rising to a leadership challenge but disappearing when the going got tough. TB was nagging me again to get a regular column. He lacks courage, he said of GB.

---

* Former Ambassador to US, now chairman of the Press Complaints Commission, who had written a gossipy book, *DC Confidential*, and was making claims TB had done a deal with Bush at Crawford, Texas, in 2002.

November '05: Anger over Meyer gossip book

Monday 7 November

Up at the crack of dawn for the train to Liverpool to interview Steven Gerrard [footballer] for *GQ*. On the way reading cuttings and preparing a few upcoming speeches. I met Tim Lewis from the magazine at Lime Street and we headed to the training ground at Melwood, pretty modern though a lot of barbed wire around, and overlooked by terraced houses. Gerrard's agent was full of tips about how to get the best out of him. It became irritating after a while. But I liked Gerrard. He seemed pretty decent and relatively unspoilt considering. It would make a strong interview and there were some decent lines in it. They asked me to do a clip on him for a DVD they were making about him. TB was shifting things on the terror moves, sticking to ninety days [allowing police to detain suspects for that long without charging them] but with a sunset clause. He was surprised that Cameron was trying to cause problems on it. The sense was developing Cameron is not all he's cracked up to be, but I reckoned he was going to win. Davis was too expectable in a way.

Tuesday 8 November

Wrote the Gerrard piece, went for a fancy haircut – Fiona's David S thing for me – and then lunch with her before heading to see GB. TB had called a couple of times and was clearly very anti at the moment, felt he was in total obstruction mode. Ed B had made clear that GB was really wound up just now, felt things had gone backwards with TB. It did cross my mind that TB–GB ought to see someone like DS the way Fiona and I were. It was definitely like listening to two sides of a failing marriage. Fiona and I were blissfully happy compared with them! PG had lunch with Spencer Livermore [GB aide] and was of the view that what they wanted was to hear TB saying convincingly that he wanted a big Labour win with GB as the next leader. The trouble was they wanted all this on their terms. PG said they spoke of TB as though he was just an obstacle, hanging on for no real reason. They convinced themselves that the good the government did was all the work of GB. They just couldn't see the positive in TB at all. It all suggested a pretty poor perspective or grip of reality. I intended to say to GB – again – that his best way to the top job was to hug him close, support him on reform, stop undermining.

I saw him and Ed Balls at 4.30 at the Treasury. The usual small talk re sport, Burnley, Lions, Fergie. Then GB got pretty much straight into it. Things were terrible. There was no strategy and precious little discussion of one. TB was using the rise of Cameron to reposition, trying to send a message to the party that with Cameron trying to move the Tories to the centre, we had to make sure the party stayed bang in the middle. I said that was surely sensible. He said it was conceding that Cameron was centrist. I said he may or he may not be, but you cannot deny that is where he wants to go, if you take what he is saying at face value. 'Why should we take him at face value?' he asked. 'Because if he wins the leadership, he will be able to make the change. Then we can test it. There is no point us saying what he is unless it fits with what he is and does.' He shook his head, and said TB was on a solo kamikaze mission.

GB had advised against John Hutton going to DWP because he had no base in the party. He felt Alan Johnson should have done it. He had advised on lots of policy stuff but TB wanted to do it all on his own. Cooperation had ended on the day of the election. 'I don't care what Tony is saying to you, that is the truth. The minute he won, the minute you left, it was back to the old ways.' 'But that is exactly what he says about you, that the minute he won, you were asking when he was going and that was all, nothing else, no desire to work together.' 'That is rubbish,' he said. 'Well, all I can do is go on what you both say and it is not easy when what you say is so diametrically opposed.' I said it was like advising a married couple who wanted to stay married but hated each other. 'Listen,' he said, 'Tony has stopped discussing anything with me. With you not here full-time there is nobody strong enough to police it.' The others around TB only saw things from his perspective, and I was the only person capable of getting it done and ensuring TB would stick to a plan, he said.

He said he was fed up of TB reneging on deals. There was a deal and JP knows it and he knows TB reneged on it. Last time TB said he was going to go in 2006 but then, 'You're not working with me so it's 2007 and if you don't cooperate then it could be longer.' GB said fuck off then, I can't work on that basis. TB was only thinking of himself, not the party at the next election. Why did he go for Ray Collins [senior trade unionist] as general secretary? 'That was an appointment more relevant to me than him because he would be key at the election. Tony won't be there.' He was looking tired, the bags under his eyes bulging, his hair greyer, ink on his shirt as per. He was about to go to Israel. He said if the planned dinner on Friday was just more of the same then it was pointless because it was just more promises – there had to be a plan and it had to be seen through. He was not going to put up with lies and deceptions and reneging on deals any more. We had to be able to plan.

He felt he had ideas on the next phase for education, health, the environment etc. but he didn't trust TB not to nick the ideas. He said he had mentioned to TB that he was thinking we could get rid of DTI [Department of Trade and Industry]. TB stole the idea. GB begged him not to go for a change to the block vote system because it was best he did it – he just went ahead. It was a pretty bad state of affairs. I said things only really worked if they were together and they had to sort it. They had to get to common interests. TB legacy plus a good result for GB. We also had to develop a stronger GB narrative that was not about his differences with TB but with the Tories, and about the challenges for the country. I said he should use Cameron's arrival to shape a new agenda so that GB becomes the candidate of change as well as the force of stability and continuity. Ed and I were at least trying to get to the same place but they both said that while some of us want cooperation on the transition many in No. 10 didn't and Peter M and Cherie B in particular were 'at it'.

GB went through education, health, environment and elsewhere and said TB was getting us into the wrong position. Don't let Cameron into the centre. I said he should have been up against the Tories on terror earlier. He did it today. But he said he was tired of bailing TB out at the last minute. Also TB was spending too much because he was desperate to make an impact now – 'He has just spent £450 million on Afghanistan. Why so much? What did he promise Bush?' But we kept coming back to no plan. 'We don't have a plan. What is it? We don't know. Nobody knows.' He was a mix of calm and wound up. He said he could see how to get dividing lines in the right place but TB wanted the argument to be on this narrow strip of ground called 'choice'. On schools we could not really put the dividing line on selection. I said I didn't believe that was where TB wanted to go. 'What does choice mean then?'. I said TB was worried he would do his legacy in. GB agreed it had to be continuity plus change. But I said they were like a marriage gone wrong.

Talking to one or the other gave you a totally different story. GB was wronged and fed up of lying and never involved. When TB called later it was a totally different story – TB sent him a draft strategy paper but because it didn't have a date for leaving GB didn't see it as strategy paper at all. He tried to involve him in the reshuffle but he went AWOL. He asked for names and they never came. Added to which he has been diddling on policy. TB said he was happy to go with my plan to help him because there was no clear alternative but he was not at all sure it was the right thing because of GB's basic psychology. And GB had to understand he had to go to Charles Clarke, Tessa, John Reid types and say you should support him. He reckoned 95 per cent of the Cabinet thought GB would get it and 95 per cent thought it was the wrong decision. GB said he had had lots of these TB dinners. Promises made then broken and if that happens again he'd have to make his own decision. Party in decline, membership falling, local government weakening, what's the fucking point inheriting that? Not a threat just a reality. TB and I also discussed Meyer. *Telegraph* leader today saying how can he stay on at the PCC. TB thinking I should rebut re Iraq in particular.

Wednesday 9 November

In its own way, quite a big day, with TB losing his first ever vote in the Commons – not bad to go eight years without, mind you – on the move to let the security forces hold terrorism suspects for ninety days without charge. 322 to 291, with almost fifty of our MPs voting against, and a load more abstaining. So it was quite a rebellion, for sure. Then later they voted for the amendment limiting it to twenty-eight days, which was up from the current law, fourteen. It was going to unleash a whole load more of 'waning authority' stuff. Michael Howard was out saying TB should resign – God he is ridiculous – whereas Charles Kennedy was on the better line, that he was a lame duck PM. TB called before he did a BBC clip, where he said the cops felt they needed it, he was clear they had the arguments on their side, and he hoped MPs didn't rue the day. But it was all feeling a bit ragged right now.

I had another session with David Sturgeon. He wanted to go over the breakdown in the '80s, and also my relationship with drink, both then and now. He said he was worried that even the occasional drink was not sensible. It was fine when things were OK, but it could flare up again. I said might it be possible I am an addict, and the addiction then was alcohol but now it is other things, like work, sport? He didn't seem convinced. He said he thought I was playing with fire. He was very fond of setting me 'homework' and this time it was to do a long list of all the things in life I felt gratitude for, so I worked on that a bit.

Thursday 10 November

I was getting loads of bids to do stuff re the idea that this was the beginning of the end for TB. I decided against, and instead settled down with

Mark B for a morning working on the diaries. I felt the papers were going over the top, but Clare Short [former international development secretary] was out saying the sooner he went the better, and Frank Dobson was saying there would be big rebellions on the public service reforms too. PG and I were due to have a meeting with him at 5 p.m. He was in a meeting with the top guys from SOCA [Serious Organised Crime Agency] when we arrived. He was chirpier than I expected him to be. He said he knew what we had to do on terrorism; and he was going to do it and if he went down he went down. He had deliberately gone for this as an issue to fight to the hilt – one, because it was not part of the core programme and second, because it was one where he felt we had the public on side. He felt he had done GB a big strategic favour because Cameron and Davis were on the wrong side of the argument for the sake of politics.

He said he could not afford a defeat on a key issue and they knew that. And we had a fair number now who were lost causes. He said he would rather go than have to do the wrong thing. He had to turn them round but it would be hard. He said that the real problem with GB was that when it came to the difficult stuff, he gave MPs an argument against what we were doing, and then when he tried to turn them at the end of the process it was too late. I gave him some of the GB arguments that he had been putting to me, but he was having none of it. He had virtually anointed him, he said. 'I didn't have to say I wouldn't be standing but I did. And he always wanted more.' He said GB's ambivalence had grown, he was happy to go along with this when e.g. Cherie, Peter M, Sally and Anji all thought it was wrong – ditto JoP – but he was really worried he didn't have the necessary leadership qualities. He felt he had to let it happen as the party would want it but he was not at all sure it was the right thing. Most of the Cabinet thought so too.

The terror situation and the ninety days issue was a classic situation. He only came out for ninety days' possible detention when it was clear the public was there. He wanted it all easy. He didn't get the New Labour thing. Didn't *feel* crime, anti-social behaviour and terrorism. He couldn't understand why they mattered so much as issues, didn't have the instincts for it. He kept saying he would go along with it so long as I was fully aware of the possible impact of going back into the whole TB–GB drama. He felt if there were other clear contenders it would be very different. There was a feeling growing among some that Charles Clarke was emerging as a possibility. We were there for an hour or so at the end of which we agreed we needed specifics tomorrow – plans to get a government narrative focused on TB getting his stuff through and a GB narrative on the lines of him almost shadowing TB for the whole thing and becoming more prime ministerial. But he was clear he would not do anything to sacrifice New Labour. If that happened he would go down fighting. And he still believed GB did not want to embed his legacy but reverse it.

Friday 11 November

There was loads more TB losing authority in the media. Lots of GB-ology going on too. I was shocked to learn that GB hadn't actually needed to come back from Israel [to vote on terror laws] as he had been paired by the whips with Vince Cable [Lib Dem Treasury spokesman].* Also, on the way into Westminster, I noticed a story in the *Standard*, on the lines that GB would not challenge TB directly for a departure date, but that it was a matter for MPs. It was a pretty clear invitation to rebellion, all set in the usual context of 'not wanting to make life more difficult for TB'. Then in at 7 for the dinner that TB was totally dreading. I met up with PG first. He said No. 10 was a bit sepulchral. Up to see TB in the flat who was in 'Do we have to do this?' mode. But he went through what he intended to say. That we should see this as a parliament in two halves. Him pushing through his agenda then preparing for the handover. But it all had to be on the basis that GB worked with him. He said again that he was going to go along with all this but he didn't have any doubts it was a risk for the country.

PG and I went down to No. 11 dining room. Maureen and Juliette [No. 10 staff] were looking after us. No starter. Lasagne, salad, fruit and cheese. TB came down, impatient and irritable because GB and Ed were late. They were heading from a visit somewhere and Ed had texted from the train train to ask, 'Anything we should ignore?' I said I should steer it to the long term. GB arrived, bustle, bustle, loads of papers, which he dumped on a desk, said hello to me, then PG, then TB, into a bit of small talk about his trip to Israel, saying he got on with [Ariel] Sharon [Israeli PM], sent regards etc. We went through to the little dining room, waited till they had served us and left, and then TB laid it out. He said we have to get his reforms through and have the party in good shape for the next election with transition and time for GB to establish. He

---

* Brown led a delegation from the European Union and the G8 countries for talks on the West Bank and how to regenerate Israel's economy. He returned to Israel following the vote.

November '05: TB–GB dinner to try to resolve difficulties

emphasised that he felt New Labour being firmly entrenched had to be part of it. He was really calm and clear and ended by saying it could all happen but it needed them to work together. 'If I am somehow levered out and people think you are involved that is bad in one way and if I run someone against you that is bad in another way.'

The 'run someone against you' point led to both GB and Ed giving each other a little look. TB spotted it. 'The truth is, Gordon, that we are in a situation of mutually assured destruction and we have to stop it. We need to get back to the kind of working relationship we had during the election, or else we are fucked. So are we agreed: we work together to get plans through, and then we work together to ensure transition?' GB said thanks for focusing on the long term not the short term. He said I don't think any of us have fully realised the extent of the problem in the party and how renewal of New Labour is an even bigger project than creating New Labour. He was saying there were three areas – globalisation, terror and security and also the state of society – where he wanted us to have a different agenda and to have different answers to the questions we face. As he went through it he kept emphasising that he was in need of a proper framework with greater clarity. We pressed as to whether 'clarity' meant nothing more than a date for TB's departure, and though he kept trying to dress it up in terms of big strategic questions I said, 'Come on Gordon, this is really just about the date.'

TB said at one point, 'What more do you want? I am the first PM to be clear at one election that I won't be here for the next. I have virtually anointed you when plenty of people think I shouldn't, and some think I am mad even to think about it given all that has gone on. What more do you want? Is it just a date?' GB couldn't bring himself to say, 'Yes.' He kept trying to take it to these bigger questions. He said there were big questions working back from the election and, 'It is not you that would be doing a lot of these things but me.' Yet on things like nuclear power, some of the public service reforms, some of the personnel issues, 'you didn't even fucking consult'. He said he was livid about John Hutton. He had wanted Johnson. TB said one thing he would learn if he became PM was that the PM had to be able to make the final call. There would be plenty of different people giving lots of different advice, but in the end he had to make a call. Did it really make that much difference? Or was it just an excuse to be able to say he had not been 'consulted'. And then GB was back off on one, about how they worked together during the election, but the minute he won, and I went, it was back to the way it had been.

He then said the problem with the two halves concept was it didn't give enough time for him to set his own agenda. I said the two agendas had to be marry-able. Why should there be any difficulty in this? As ever, I said, we – I meant GB – were making difficulties when none needed to exist. TB said, 'This is only a problem if you are planning to do something radically different, fundamentally at odds with what we are doing now' (which of course is what TB suspected). The first exchanges had been perfectly friendly and civil but before long they were at it. GB said he was unlikely to believe promises about the future given the broken promises of the past. TB smiled, said, 'We have very different memories of that, Gordon. There was no deal and no date.' GB said JP would testify differently. TB sighed loudly. I said if we were just going over old ground like this we will get nowhere. We had managed to get everyone working together in the election and we had to do it again now, and we knew the basis on which we could do that. The modus operandi had to change all round. TB said to him there were people on both sides who were at it but they could stop it. If people felt there was division between them they would exploit it.

Their take was that we used him for the campaign but then the minute we didn't need him TB went back to solo working. They were also obsessed with the notion that Peter M and Alan M were briefing against him all the time. The truth was they were briefing far more. There was one genuinely funny moment of light relief when we were discussing the Tories and Cameron. TB said the thing about politics today is, 'It's a very quick game.' GB: 'It's a very slow game where I'm sitting.' Real laughter all round. We had a few laughs through it all. TB said one of the best things in the election was that there was some personal warmth again after all the angst. Why can't we just operate like that all the time? GB kept insisting the non-cooperation came from TB and TB denied it. TB also said GB had to show definitively he was New Labour. 'I AM – and I resent the suggestion I'm not. It is not just what we say. It is what we do and I have been driving a lot of the difficult reform.'

TB said, 'I've done you a massive strategic favour this week. Murdoch was going to shift to the Tories and because of the terror stance has not.' GB said he felt we had allowed Cameron into the centre on education. TB said you can't stop people trying to get to different places. We had to make clear he couldn't do it, put him at odds with his party. If he said he supported us fine but we could not play the same tunes. TB felt he was not quite what he was cracked up to be. He could win – but we could win big against him, provided we had the right strategy. But that had to be based on what he was, not what we wanted him to be. GB kept making the same point –we had to have a bit of time to let him shape his own agenda. PG said the public did not want TB to go and GB's best interests were to have a short honeymoon then go for an election. That said late not early. GB said at the end he believed he could persuade us taking over earlier was better than later. He said he would do a note to that effect. There were a few flashpoints – over the truth about previous deals, over whether GB really supported reform, over whether they authorised briefings one against the other.

GB kept saying, 'You mustn't allow Cameron into the centre,' as though we were arguing for it. TB said, 'Look, I don't want anyone to be my successor but you. I don't want anyone to win but Labour. I don't want to be seen as some kind of aberration of history. I want us to sustain this for the long term.' We kept going back to basic points – lots of problems but surmountable if they work together. GB in OK humour though occasionally got up to close the door whenever voices started to rise. We agreed there had to be a new modus operandi. I asked GB if there was anyone in No. 10 he trusted as there had to be someone to drive this. He said, 'Why don't you come back?' I made clear I was willing to help but I would not go back full-time. He and TB then had an argument about the EU financing deal, GB saying they could not afford what TB wanted and instead we should go for the French re CAP spending. It all ended reasonably amicably, but afterwards, when PG and I went up to the flat with TB, he said, 'People would not believe what I have to put up with.' Jonathan called when I was in the car home, to ask how it went. I said Monty Python would have had a field day.

Saturday 12 November

I woke up feeling really low, seven out of ten depression low. I could feel it the second my eyes opened, that feeling that I just wanted to go back to sleep, but also a sick feeling inside. I had been starting to feel like this a few days ago, had pushed it off, but it was in me big time now. I think a combination of the David Sturgeon process, which inevitably was making me even more introspective than usual, and an erosion of TB's position, added to the role I was being expected to play in the transition, was making for a depressing combination. I was very down all day.

Sunday 13 November

I really wasn't well. We were supposed to be going to Neil and Glenys's for a lunch for Michael Foot [former Labour leader] and I didn't feel up to it but Fiona was badgering me. I could really feel the physical manifestation of the mental side of things going wrong. I felt wretched internally, no energy, no appetite, feeling sick in my head and my stomach, and we had a major flare-up as we set off. I said, 'Why do you want me to go when you know I am going to end up feeling worse?' She said, 'Why can't you just do it for me?' I said because I know I am going to end up feeling even worse, and it has nothing to do with anything else. It just is. I went later with Calum and got through it fine, but I knew I was not well. It felt like this was going to be a really bad one. On the one hand, Fiona had wanted me to get help, but the help I was getting was clearly stirring all sorts of stuff, and making me worse if anything. Michael was on good form, very funny – and dismissive – about Cameron; sympathetic re TB, told me he hoped I was still in there helping him because he was going to need it. I wasn't engaging much with the political side of the discussion. I was feeling emptier and emptier inside.

Monday 14 November

Out for a walk with Fiona and we ended up having a big flare-up over the political side of things. She was going at it again about the education white paper [*14–19 Education and Skills*], and I was saying she was trying to provoke me the whole time, and why, when she knew I felt like shit? She said I felt like that because I probably agreed but I had got myself into this position where I felt I couldn't say anything that disagreed with the official line. There was a real bitterness to the way we were speaking to each other at the moment. I got back, still feeling like shit, and did a bit of work on the diaries. I was up to almost 600,000 words from May 1997 to April 2000.

Stephen Jones and Alfie [Gareth Thomas, Welsh rugby players] called from their team bus. Alfie was calling Gavin Henson a cunt for having a pop at me and slagging off everyone in his book, and he said I ought to have a go back. It was good to hear from them, they were both such amazing characters in very different ways. My name finally seemed to be fading from the rugby scene. I think I traced the current dive back to the ninety-day terror vote so maybe this was about an era coming to an end. Or maybe it was just cyclical. But the gaps between the downs were getting too fucking short. The papers were calming down a bit but a combination of what TB called 'the rejected, the dejected and the ejected' MPs were going to make it tough for him now.

Tuesday 15 November

All day with Mark B on the diaries. I called Parna. One of the things we had agreed out of our meeting on Friday was that TB and GB should have a pre-Cabinet meeting, but it wasn't happening.

Wednesday 16 November

Bad night. Central Unit [government security] guy came for a security review. He said I was down to level 5, there was no specific IRA threat but they still wanted to put more stuff on the house. Another session with Fiona at David Sturgeon's. I explained that my head had been in a bad way, really depressed, unable to function in many ways, and also we had not been getting on at all well. I got very tearful at points. He said it was bound to make a lot of bad stuff come to the fore, and I had been wrestling for a long time with a lot of difficult things. I was also feeling trapped, and unsure if I wanted to be doing all the things I was doing. Fiona admitted that she had become more withdrawn, but it was because she had to, because she couldn't understand what was happening in my head sometimes, and it could be scary. She was worried I could totally flip out sometimes, become a totally different person almost. She had to protect herself from the hurt that could cause.

She said she never worried about me becoming physically violent, but the mental side was so hard to deal with. She just couldn't predict what kind of mood I would be in. She said she tried to be sympathetic about the depression, but it was hard, because she felt she was the one who bore the brunt of it. I asked why she had insisted on me going out with her to the lunch for Michael when it was obvious I was so down, and she said because sometimes getting out and about got me out of it. Sturgeon said part of the process was to become more introspective and see depressive things in there. I went over some of the political stuff that I took as her expressing hostility to me personally, and also saying I felt she didn't really try to understand what the depression was like, and also what it was like having pressure piled upon me by others. She said, 'But that is a choice you make.' She said I had left but in truth I had never left, and 'these people' could pull me in any time they wanted, and they did. He said he felt I was genuinely torn, between wanting to do the right thing for myself and the family, and a sense of service to a bigger project that meant a lot to me, and which I worried would fall apart if I wasn't there nurturing it.

There was definitely something in that. Fiona felt I should just move on from it, move away, also that I kept busy to avoid having to confront whatever the demons were that drove me down. I said I had not felt truly supported at the time of the David Kelly suicide, and all the pressure that brought on me, because I knew a big part of her felt I had brought it on myself. She said, 'But you did.' I said I felt I had to rely on the kids as my rock back then and that was unfair on them. I said when I am like this, really depressed, only the kids can even begin to lift me. She said my assessment of her feelings was accurate, in that she did feel angry about a lot that had gone on, and about the way I had cared more for the job than for her, and not been there even when I was there, but she had no desire for revenge. She wanted us to be able to get to a better place and for me to sort out the issues that made me so depressed.

I felt she had neutered me in a way, got me out of something that meant something, and making me feel I could not do anything similar ever again. She said that was my feeling, not hers. I said I needed a sense of direction and right now I didn't have it. I needed purpose and didn't have it, and when I had no purpose or direction I tended to depression and when it got really bad I felt sometimes overwhelmed by suicidal thoughts, and I was worried one day I would. Sturgeon said he knew I didn't like medication but he really felt I needed to be on anti-depressants. He said I had to understand Fiona had moved to a tough love posture because she had to protect herself. It was impossible to expect her to do all she had to do in terms of the family, the kids, her own life, and also be taking all this too. So I shouldn't be surprised if she put up barriers to protect herself, it was very human, and it didn't mean she loved me less. Maybe he was right about medication. Whenever I had used it in the past, it had been OK. But I had a real thing about it.

Friday 18 November

Out first thing to do an interview with June Sarpong [broadcaster] for a film she was making for Children In Need. Then to see Richard [Stott] to go over the diaries, which he was loving, and on which he was doing a good job. I had to break out to do a conference call on an upcoming speech in Dublin and Paul Allen [boss of Dublin-based PR firm] said, 'What about Keano [Roy Keane] then?' 'What about him?'

'He's gone.' I spoke to Alex later who said it was the right time. I said you used to say he was the most intelligent player you'd had, and the one likeliest to be a top manager. 'He went wrong. There is something not right there.' I asked if it all went back to the MUTV interview Keane did, slagging off the players. He said it had started before that, when he was slagging off pre-season training and the like. He didn't want to get into detail but he sounded very down, as he had the last couple of times I spoke to him. He, Keane and David Gill [Man U CEO] had all put out the kind of diplomatic statements I knew well from ministerial resignations, but it was clear it had been a long-running row which had to be brought to a head. He kept trying to turn the subject to politics and especially raging at former ministers speaking out the whole time.

Saturday 19 November

Really nice day with Calum at England v the All Blacks. He had suddenly said last week he fancied going to it, even though Burnley were playing Leicester. We had lunch in a Richmond restaurant, surrounded by real forces of conservatism all around us, which led to a bit of banter, some political, some about the Lions tour. A couple of New Zealanders came over to rub things in a bit. For once, I was really hoping England won, but it never happened [19–23]. I met a guy from Sky on the way in who said Jamie Rubin's new show was struggling to get the ratings they had wanted. Met up with Matt Dawson and his lovely girlfriend and also Richard Smith [lawyer] and Tony Biscombe [video analyst]. Another win for Burnley [1–0] – from bottom to fifth in no time.

Sunday 20 November

I spoke to Michael Kennedy [Roy Keane's agent/lawyer] to get an address for Keano to give him a few thoughts on the pitfalls for obsessive addictive personalities leaving an all-consuming job for an uncertain future. I remember when we met in Dublin Keano and I got into a chat about being driven and addictive, and I could see him going on a real old dive if he didn't get back into something pretty quickly. I also said to Michael I was interested in writing a piece, maybe an interview, at some stage, and he said, 'Funny you should say that. Roy is planning on doing a book, and your name came up as someone who might want to write it with him.' It was tempting, though Fergie would doubtless not be happy, and also I wasn't sure I would be able to give it enough time. I said I would think about it. He said you're both similar characters and it could turn out to be something special, not your standard footballer life story told to make a few bob at the end of a career. He said Roy was totally unfazed by Friday's denouement, he had seen it coming, while he [Kennedy] was really sad about it, felt he deserved a better departure than this.

I worked on my Dublin speech, then TB called as we were leaving to go out for dinner with PG and Grace. He sounded very low and said we desperately needed another GB meeting because things were going backwards. He said it was obvious GB had dropped the story of him blocking a new ministerial plane in the Sundays.* The Sundays had also been enlivened by the letter from JP to Christopher Meyer suggesting that he leave the PCC. He had a point. How can the head of the PCC be doing private serialisation deals with newspapers whose standards he was meant to be overseeing? TB said things were bad again and we had to sort them. The good news was that he and GB were speaking. The bad news was that all GB did was shout and basically demand a date. He felt it was as clear as day the next government would be new New Labour or Tories. He felt the party was one problem but there was a real danger the public was shifting because TB was going. He sounded very keen to get something sorted this week if he could which was difficult for me. PG and I didn't talk much politics over dinner – sport, family, and also my head. He had been sure I would get on with David S, which I was, and the pills did seem to be working, though they were making me tired, and I couldn't stop yawning all the time.

Monday 21 November

I called Ed Balls but they had the moral high ground because of the *Times* splash, which was immediately leading the news, which was TB backing the next wave of nuclear power. As Ed said, it was a classic case of something GB not TB would be taking through. We repeated our basic points and I agreed to press for a meeting. For once it was my diary that was the problem but we fixed on Wednesday p.m. Then Brucie [Grocott] called, really worried, said TB could not see the trains charging down the track, and that education was going to make the terror vote look like a walk in the park. I agreed to meet him on Wednesday too. I had a long chat with Pat [McFadden] who said he didn't know how the basic loyalists should

---

* Brown had refused to fund up to three aircraft to transport senior members of the royal family and ministers when travelling on official business.

be pitching things at the moment. The waverers were getting a sense of TB trying to provoke them. I worked most of the day with Mark – up to August 2000, and we had a little light relief halfway through with an invitation from the Public Administration Select Committee [PASC] to give evidence about public service and memoirs. My initial reaction was what a pain, but Mark said I should see it as an opportunity to generate pre-publicity, and suggested I take in a few of the most revealing bits – hopefully involving some of the MPs on the committee – and just read them out.

Tuesday 22 November

Up very early and off to Dublin. I read lots of Stott stuff during the day. He had written a very good analysis of the main themes, but agreed with me a straightforward diary was the best way to publish. The plane was on time, but then a long drive to the hotel, which was like something out of the Middle East. Fake marble, lots of glitzy glittery furniture. But they had a nice pool and I managed to get in a swim before the speech. It was for Royal Sun Alliance, eighty or so middlemen. I did a pretty basic standard speech, with an OK Q&A, slow to warm up but fine. I got a lift up to the airport with Paul Allen, chatting about the Fergie/Keano scene, and also planning a few more gigs out there. He said he was amazed how popular I was in Ireland, and the more the UK papers slagged me, the more the Irish seemed to like me, He gave me Brian O'Driscoll's book, which I read on the flight home. He was nice enough about me, certainly didn't go along with the general media flow on that one. I landed to news we had lost at Leeds [2–0]. Home by 11.

Wednesday 23 November

A long walk with Fiona and Molly [the dog], then solo to see David S. I had given him long written answers to loads of questions and we went over them. He was probing away about my childhood and seemed a bit frustrated that I couldn't find much bad to say about it. Then about relationships more generally, history with women, motivations, all sorts of stuff. I was definitely feeling a bit better, which he said might be the medication, but which I felt might just have been the cycle blowing itself out. I was feeling better though, and not being so introspective, other than when he asked me to be. We talked a lot about this idea of the demon inside me, and he said it was always there, and it would love me to do things that wouldn't be good for me – go back on the drink, go back to full-time work. I said but what if it is the demon that makes me creative, makes me clever, makes me do things other people can't do? He said, 'That is your demon speaking.'

I went for a really good run to think about what he had been saying, also because I had not been exercising much when I was in the throes, and then in to No. 10. The whole place seemed a bit down, low mood, lacking in energy. JoP was not very well but struggling on. Liz and Matthew Taylor [head of No. 10 policy unit] were saying there were no lines out to GB at the moment. I knew what that meant, and I said I don't want to be sucked in full-time. PG and I had a pre-meeting with TB where we tested his statement that he still wanted GB to get the job. I'd been doing the diaries for 2000 and was struck by how much our time then was taken up with all this bollocks and how down we sometimes were. Also, Richard [Stott] said people would be gobsmacked by just how bad things were between them at times, including early on. But TB said it was clear the party wanted GB and also that there was nobody in his league ability-wise. But he is flawed. As Chancellor the genius hides the flaw. As PM there is a danger the flaw will hide the genius. He was really keen to get some kind of progress though.

PG and I went through to the No. 11 dining room, the thinking being it's better to do this where he feels more comfortable. A bit of small talk for a matter of seconds then GB read through a note he had written, but which he didn't want to hand over. He said again that renewal of New Labour was an even bigger challenge than its creation. The party is in bad shape. We are losing support in key policy areas. We are ceding ground to the Tories for example in education. The story of this period is Blair v the party. Spin is still a big problem. New challenges require a new agenda. He felt we were in bad shape on all of it. He didn't exactly say it was all because of TB still being there but body language indicated that's what he meant. The mood was not bad but he was quickly into 'The problem is...' mode. He was complaining there had been no proper consultation about nuclear power, which he not TB would have to take forward. The money TB was demanding for Afghanistan was also a problem. But the one he was really steamed up about was pensions and the recommendations of the Turner report.[*]

***

[*] The Pensions Commission Report, chaired by Lord [Adair] Turner and published in November, recommended a gradual rise in the state pension age to between 67 and 69, a basic pension linked to earnings and a 'national pension savings scheme' into which workers would be automatically enrolled but could then opt out if they wished.

November '05: GB runs through the TB problems

He said that it would cost £35 billion over a parliament; and again he complained re lack of consultation. 'I have warned him [TB] of all this but his "lunatics" are putting it to Turner that we could do it.' He said he went in, sat down with him, laid out all the fiscal charts showing hard facts, and TB just said that 'wasn't my understanding'. I said the key thing was they had to get a strategy agreed between them and work it through. GB sort of agreed but they both kept coming to difficulties not solutions. He was in more open and communicative mood but the truth was they didn't have any real empathy at all. Ed B and PG were exchanging gloomy looks. I said TB felt that he thought of GB's situation the whole time but there was no vice versa. As I listened to GB on the Tories, there was divergence there too. TB felt we had to go with the flow a bit, we could not pretend Cameron was far right if he genuinely moved to the centre. We had to get our dividing lines down properly. GB felt we had let him get credibility on education.

I said to GB/Ed they had to stop planning according to the world as they want it and instead work with it as it is. GB clearly felt in his impatience for legacy TB was on a kind of kamikaze mission to do crazy things and hang the expense. He said there was no strategy or discussion about the education reforms, for example, and where it took us for the election. It was madness. I was on both their sides really, could see it from both. But TB had been PM during a period when he had had to deal with this the whole time and it was no wonder he got a bit fed up with it all. TB had to see RUC widows on the day we were announcing OTRs [prisoners on the run] could return and had to go to defend that decision, and deal with all the grief that entailed. I warned GB he was going to have to do all this stuff and have a million things to deal with and all the time pressures. I said don't underestimate how much harder his job is than yours. He said he knew that, but I said I don't think you do. I think you imagine it is similar to what you do now, but it's not. The pressures you feel on the big days are the pressures he is dealing with every day, not least because of the scrutiny. He said, 'I understand, I understand.'

I said you are going to need to start well, and you are going to need goodwill and support, so don't sacrifice that now. Then he was off again, about TB's EU financing plan. It was clearly going nowhere. Hampton Court [EU summit] had been a disaster. He should leave it to him. He was really showing the worst side today – presenting problems without solutions and not facing up to a few realities. I said he had to be really careful because Cameron was going to capture hope and optimism, youth and the future, and he was in danger of looking like age and misery. He reacted badly to that. I said you mustn't take this stuff personally, I am telling you the truth, about how you risk being perceived against Cameron. He didn't like that kind of directness whereas TB was fine about being told stuff like that. We agreed at the end the five of us should meet again soon but when I saw TB later as I left for home he was doubtful things would improve. I saw the press office people then spoke to Anji re Sue Nye [GB special advisor] who had been saying I was the only one GB would speak to or trust at all. How things change. Anji's take was interesting – TB should do two years then go and he should not interfere, help GB win but then let him do what he wanted.

To the Old Vic, to see *Richard II*. Fantastic. Kevin Spacey [actor, Old Vic supremo] reminded me of Peter M in resignation when he was being unkinged. Bolingbroke looked like Jose Mourinho. Then we went to Livebait for dinner with Kevin and a French guy. He seemed really happy here, said the Old Vic was turning round well, the press were largely leaving him alone, London was just a great city to live. He was planning on being here for at least ten years. He was spending a lot of his time doing fundraising, and also had loads of his own professional work going on, but he felt more motivated than ever. He was still in touch with Bill and Hillary [Clinton], and he was sure HC was going to go for the Presidency, and he was confident she would win. He looked a bit tired, but said that the energy required for the performance was draining, yet it also took him a while to come down to earth. He was on great form though, and such a good addition to life in London. We talked a bit about our own political scene. I sensed he liked both TB and GB. I couldn't bring myself to relive the meeting earlier with GB.

Thursday 24 November

Up at half-six, and got the train up to Newcastle. I met Alan Milburn and we chatted most of the way about our various adaptations to a new life. He felt I had to get back into something, maybe running something big, outside politics. I said I was feeling OK, but I knew I was drifting a bit and maybe something would emerge and maybe not but in the end I wasn't sure it really mattered that much. I was always going to be defined by recent times with TB, and in a way I had to try to rebuild a new life that accepted that but also tried to move on. He said the difference between us was that I had real edge and controversy, and he felt I used that well. I said the other difference was that I wasn't being allowed to escape it, because I seemed to be the only one that both of them felt they could talk to about the other. We chatted for ages about TB–GB. He felt GB taking over was inevitable, even if so many people thought it the wrong move, and what we had to do was make sure he felt he had to be New Labour. He said he'd called him after the election and suggested they meet but it never happened.

He was fairly relaxed with life but was starting to think about policy long-term. He wanted to stay involved on the policy side of things from the back benches. He was interested in the stuff I was doing on speeches and how much the market was worth, but he said he lacked my controversy and so felt he would not be as much in demand. He felt we were teetering on the brink a bit and it was possible that GB would lose us the election, if DC was as good as people imagined him to be. He thought Cameron might be a dud, but he might not be. It was hard to read. Also GB was strong in the party but weak in Cabinet.

Some of the problems we were talking about came to a head today, over pensions. GB had it briefed through the *FT* (I knew he was seeing Lionel Barber [*FT* editor] yesterday) that the Turner pensions report's main proposals were unacceptable. So the news was massive on him sabotaging it. TB was doing a press conference with Angela Merkel after their first meeting since she was confirmed as Chancellor and, on the defensive, he did a clip on it. Turner needless to say was outraged. I think he could see he was now just being used in this TB–GB battle. Overall it was a pretty dire impression. PG was saying the sense of drift and decay was really getting through in focus groups. Newcastle, lunch with Mincoffs law firm, couple of interviews, nice crowd, good reception and Q&A. Nice to see Brendan [Foster] and his crowd. Good event, felt on form.

To Darlington, out for a run, then with AM to the venue for the party event we were doing, mix and mingle, an odd venue, a bit like a wedding marquee, and it was bloody cold so it was quite hard to lift the mood but it went fine. Alan was very nice about me in his introduction, the speech went OK, really going pro-politics and anti-media. But Alan was thinking the big picture scene re TB was bad and getting worse. He felt with me, SM and AH all now gone it was really hard. The new people were all a bit second order. I called TB to check out how the meeting with Merkel went. He said she was impressive, very calm and clear. She was being diplomatic about the future funding stuff, not as hard over as the French, but hard to read on whether she thought we could get a deal done under our Presidency. She said she didn't have a 'crystal ball', which was a neat way of not getting drawn into others' speculation. But given the summit was three weeks away, he knew it was going to be tough to get a deal. He said it was pretty obvious she thought Schroeder got way too close to [Vladimir] Putin [President of Russia].

Friday 25 November

I got the train back, working a bit, but feeling tired. Too many late nights and another one ahead. The papers were really bad on pensions and there was a danger the TB–GB thing was reaching tipping point. TB was off to CHOGM [Commonwealth Heads of Government meeting] in Malta and so was mainly focused on international stuff again. But pensions was becoming a disaster area – Alan Johnson's U-turn on public sector retirement age had set off the private sector. [Sir] Digby Jones [director-general, Confederation of British Industry] was on the rampage pre the CBI conference. There was definitely a feeling that the mood was turning against us. GB had kyboshed Turner while blaming No. 10. To Copthall [driving range] with Calum to hit a few golf balls then out to the Park Plaza Riverbank for Allianz Cornhill [insurance company] dinner. I was OK without being brilliant. I was getting tired of my own voice, and getting tired of being asked the same things all the time. They were all assuming I would do something else major. Alan said something interesting – people in politics looked on people like us with pity.

George Best died. Enormous coverage. The hype of death was now a huge part of the media age – being nice when someone is dead gives media and people permission to be vile when alive. Awful.

Saturday 26 November

Burnley v Crewe. 3–0. Excellent game. Steve Cotterill [Burnley manager] decided we should have a minute's applause for George Best. Home by half-eight. Watched a crap kids' film with Grace.

Sunday 27 November

The papers were full of stories about the fallout on pensions. These things were on autopilot now. Once the touchpaper was lit, the media knew where to go to keep it going. The overall impression wasn't just of TB losing authority but of the government becoming more dysfunctional.

Alex called, because he had a ticket for Rory for the United game at West Ham. 'What is Gordon up to?' he asked. It was interesting that though the papers tended either to put it as six of one/half a dozen of the other, and some of them invariably took GB's side, he saw it very much as GB trying to cause trouble. Fiona and I went to Lindsay's [Nicholson] new house then for a long walk with the dogs, she too saying I needed a big challenge, or I would go mad – again. Tessa and David said much the same when we went out for dinner. I was avoiding political talk. I didn't particularly want it widely known that I was doing these TB–GB 'Relate meetings'. Tessa was saying I was best out of it but also that I needed to be there.

Monday 28 November

Tessa was flying to Lausanne, and her plane was around the same time as mine so she gave me a lift, and we chatted about the TB situation. She was picking my brains re TB–GB and was very down about TB's chances of surviving that much longer. She felt there was a section of the PLP we had lost for good. Also, Ruth Kelly [Education Secretary] was the wrong person to be selling the education reforms. She [Tessa] felt GB was going to get TB's job but 'we will be trading a total star with talent and manners and a great, warm, positive personality for something very different'. She asked if I thought she should go for the deputy leadership. She didn't fear GB any more since she stood up to him over the Olympics when he was basically just buggering about. She was not fussed she claimed and not keen on what would be needed but she was thinking about it. Not sure if TB could last to 2007.

Tessa was clearly worried things were even worse than they seemed. She asked if I thought we could prop him up much longer. She said virtually everyone had given up any thought it would be anyone but GB. She felt that all she, JR, AM, Hilary Armstrong etc. could do was bind him in to a New Labour policy position. But it was going to be hard.

She was even thinking – and saying – it could just be that TB has reached the end of the road and so have we as a government for now. She said there was a distinct lack of energy in Cabinet these days. On the flight to Madrid I did a bit of work, and also tried to do the latest homework for David S, who had asked me to write down ten things I wanted, and ten things I needed. Though I was there for a conference, I was supposed to be seeing [Prime Minister José Luis Rodriguez] Zapatero's team but they had been delayed in Barcelona.

There was a pre-conference dinner at the Real Madrid ground, where I was given a stadium tour, then dinner with a mix of politicians, media and business. Out on the pitch, and with a crowd behind one of the goals, they were making a feature film – *GOAL*. I had a chat with Steve McManaman [former England international footballer], who was there as an advisor. He seemed a good bloke, very bright and positive, clued up, asking about politics, also about the Lions, and did I learn anything from it? He said he was doing bits and bobs, having lots of holidays. He said, 'We'll probably meet in a year and we'll be in the same boat then, still deciding what to do with our lives.' He had loved his time with Real Madrid, said they were treated like kings.

Tuesday 29 November

The Madrid conference itself was poor. They'd got me and some good people from the US but audience-wise it was low grade. I was therefore fairly desultory and ambled through it, then short Q&A, quick interview with one of the broadsheets and off. It really wasn't worth the time, effort or money. I worked on an article for AOL and tried to read some of the Spanish coverage of [Brazilian star with Barcelona] Ronaldinho's Ballon d'Or [world football award]. But in truth the tour of Real's stadium was the best bit, but I wouldn't have gone all that way for it. TB was in Barcelona for a Euromed [Euro-Mediterranean] summit which didn't seem to be going that well. It was an idea of Zapatero and [Prime Minister Recep Tayyip] Erdogan but most of the Muslim country leaders stayed away, and they had an argument about the definition of terrorism. He said it was an unusual grouping, good idea but didn't quite work. Some of the Arab countries had wanted to exempt anything to do with Palestinian resistance from the suggestion it was terrorism which, with Israel there, was never going to fly. He was heading back for a strategy meeting which PG called me after. He said he realised they were in trouble when someone said straight-faced that they were planning for TB to go to the first gay wedding as part of his 'reconnection strategy'.

Wednesday 30 November

Long walk with Fiona then David S. His basic take was that I expected people to be what I wanted them to be. It was impossible for anyone to live up to that. He was back on to whether there was anything in

November '05: Euromed conference the latest not to go well

childhood that made me not trust people. Fiona was saying things had been better since I started taking the medication but she felt the underlying problem was still there. He said the demon would want me to say it was all hopeless but it wasn't hard to persevere. I was good at perseverance, he said, and I had to persevere with this. But Fiona said for the first time that she thought it possible after the kids grew up and moved away, there would be nothing left. I said that was a choice, and it was up to both of us to make it or – hopefully – not make it. I suppose there was a danger all this emotional analysis just made things worse, but David felt confident we would end up in a much better place. I was struggling with deciding what response to give to the PASC about the memoirs inquiry. I was also dealing with Louise Plank [Channel 5 PR] who wanted to make a big thing of me guest editing 5 News, but I explained I didn't want to be in the papers for the sake of it.

Thursday 1 December

In for a meeting with Channel 5 people to go over a draft schedule for tomorrow. All pretty straightforward. Back for a repeat argument with Fiona because she said she saw no point in her coming to the sessions with DS because it made it all about us not me. So far as she was concerned, she didn't have a problem, but I did, and that was what we were meant to be trying to sort out. I went to collect Josh Lewsey, who had agreed to do a talk at the boys' school [William Ellis, Highgate]. He was excellent. Good role model stuff.

Friday 2 December

TB was at a meeting in Estonia, and the papers full of stories about him 'surrendering' the EU rebate. It was one of those totemic things but the reality is if we were going to get a deal on EU financing for an enlarged EU we would have to give something somewhere. The Tories were out pretty hard on it though. I spent most of the day at 5, as guest editor, being looked after by a girl from Blackburn called Laura. We agreed to lead on a football salary survey, then a story on leukaemia, which was a bit of an abuse of me doing the editing but so what? We did the rebate instead of a story we had planned on face transplants, then the Muslim converts piece, but we lost the radical edge we had had earlier because one of them who was pro-September 11 was involved in legal proceedings. I was doing a few interviews through the day to promote my doing it. OK day though and they were a nice crowd to work with. Home to another dip into a bad depression.

Saturday 3 December

All day with Calum and Charlie [Enstone-Watts, friend of Calum] for Southampton v Burnley. Clive Woodward was working there now and had invited me in for lunch with him and Rupert Lowe [Southampton owner], who was so right-wing it was untrue. All the buzz issues. I couldn't work out if he was just winding me up, but Clive said no, he really does believe all that stuff he comes out with. He was both right-wing and anti-politics, one of those people who thought 'common sense' was enough (provided it matched his definition of what common sense meant). I met Steve Cotterill's family, who still lived down south. The match was poor [1–1] but there was a good turnout from Burnley and the atmosphere was OK.

Sunday 4 December

Took Rory down to Oxford for his interviews at Balliol. He had a pretty good take on it. If he got in, fine, if he didn't, just as fine, because he had a feeling it wouldn't be for him. We met Philip and Georgia for lunch. One of the best things if he got in would be Georgia being there already. They have a very special friendship. PG noticed I seemed quite down, and assumed it was about Rory leaving home. That probably wasn't helping, but I explained that the David S process was stirring a lot of stuff. He said to stick with it. We left Rory at 6 and he was a bit more edgy than usual.

Monday 5 December

David had asked me to make a note of any dreams I could remember and some days there were stacks of them, and TB and GB were often in there, with violence involved. Maybe it was the effect of the medication. Another day waking up feeling down and also sleeping in again. Many dreams last night. Did I always dream so much, or was it that because he had asked me to record them I was remembering them more? I even had a moment during one dream where part of my mind was saying I must remember this one to write it down; and then I woke up, 4.20 a.m., and wrote it down. The TB scene was not great, as he recognised when he called. The pensions row, the row over the rebate, the internal briefings that were going on, and no real strategy re DC.

Out for a dinner at Shepherd's hosted by the FA – Brian Barwick [CEO], David Davies regaling us about staying at Hillsborough Castle in NI when they went over for the George Best funeral, Sven [Göran Eriksson] sleeping in the Queen's bed. Had quite an interesting discussion with David Gill about Keane, and then with him and Andy Burnham [junior minister] about the way the game was developing. Fair to say Andy and I less confident that it was going in the right direction. David Frost [TV presenter] on good form, Michael Peat [advisor to royal family] quite otherworldly but with a sharp mind and a good sense of humour. He claimed Prince Charles never read newspapers. Roger Mosey [director of sport] very BBC in everything he said. Barwick pretty full of himself. DD keen to be away. Gareth Southgate [Middlesbrough player] fairly bright and receptive to ideas. A lot of talk about the way the media culture was changing sport, not just politics.

Tuesday 6 December

Big day politics-wise. Cameron was elected Tory leader by more than two to one. Not bad for someone who has been an MP for just four years. I wasn't sure yet whether he really had it. TB thought he was 'good enough', and he was certainly going to be a bigger challenge than David Davis would have been. I watched his acceptance speech, which was OK, but felt like it was a bit sub-TB. The press, though, were determined to give him big licks. I got loads of bids but decided just to do *Newsnight* with Oliver Letwin [shadow Environment Secretary] and David Laws [Lib Dem MP]. Everyone seemed to think it was fine. I was basically pushing the idea that DC was trying to present himself as heir to Blair but it was all positioning no policy. What was clear, though, was that the Labour Party hadn't really put together a strategy for him. I called TB on the way to *Newsnight* and he felt DC had done fine, but the jury was still out and he felt we had to lay down tests for him on the policy change needed to match all the warm words. It was pretty clear the press were going to give him a big lift, though. He was getting easy hits all over the shop. His win also showed how speeches could still make a difference. The reality is that the turning point was the Tory conference and the fact that he spoke well and Davis didn't.

Wednesday 7 December

Cameron's first PMQs. Jeff Ennis [Labour MP] very funny in first question, asking TB how he intended to deal with a young, clever, handsome, charismatic politician 'such as myself'. Cameron looked reasonably confident, though he was a bit hesitant and over-prepared at times, and his best line, 'He was the future once,' felt a bit forced. Ditto when, in his first or second question, he had a go at Hilary Armstrong [government chief whip] for 'shouting like a child ... Have you finished?' But he didn't look ridiculous in the way I sometimes felt IDS and Howard had done. Good move to have David Davis alongside him, next to Osborne, Andrew Mitchell on the other side. He went on the education reforms, obviously trying to highlight the fact that he and the Tories supported TB more on this than a lot of our MPs. He threw back TB's 'at our best when at our boldest' line from conference quite well. But TB also upped his game, and took it to investment v cuts, GB gesticulating happily at Osborne.

I had loads of bids and decided to do a few, Jeremy Vine [BBC Radio], Sky, the Beeb and Channel 4. TB upped his game a bit, but the media were determined to go goo-goo-goo with DC. I asked TB afterwards how he came over close up. He said he certainly has confidence. I felt comfortable with the line that Cameron looked good but had to show he could deliver on policy, and that was the hard bit. He was doing and saying the right things, though, and there was a danger that we looked tired by comparison. Meanwhile I saw David S and went through the dream log. He said there was loads going on in there. 'Is that not normal?' 'There is more going on than in most people.' He felt there were hints of suicidal thoughts. He also thought there were hints that I wanted more space and was trying to sort things out too quickly. He thought the dreams involving Fiona revealed a deep need and love, and fear of loss. Another theme he said came through was fear of exclusion. We talked a bit about how I never felt I fitted in at Cambridge, and maybe that explained the heavy drinking – though in truth it had already set in by then – which was all quite fitting with what was going on with Rory and his Oxford application. After PMQs, media then a bit of work. Rory v. down, back from St Peter's [College] after Balliol and felt he had blown it.

Thursday 8 December

Rory was called back to Balliol tomorrow to do a politics and history interview. He felt they were on a power kick and partly it was about being vile to Fiona because of all her education campaigning stuff, and to a lesser extent me. I doubted that, but he was not enjoying the process. To Philip's for a meeting with him and Ed Balls. I saw Gail briefly and told her – and later Ed Victor – that I had said no to the PASC invite re memoirs. I think I had done enough select committees for a while, and this one sounded ridiculous. Ed arrived and we were straight into 'The trouble is...' stuff. He said the pensions row had been a debacle. JoP had told me GB's people had leaked the GB letter opposing Turner, which is what kicked it off. Ed did his aghast face, said no way, it was Turner – 'He has a massive ego' – or Matthew Taylor. PG and I both sceptical. I said there is no point going on about where it came from, it accurately reflected a big difference in opinion at a time when we should be trying to get them to work together. I also said that DC was changing the weather whether we liked it or not, and we had no proper strategic response.

TB did fine with him yesterday, but let's not pretend Cameron cannot get the Tories to a different place. The media are desperate to give him a lift, and if he is any good, he will use that time to force us to make some difficult choices. PG said it was quite alarming to see how well DC was going down in focus groups. The posh boy thing didn't seem to bother people at all. They saw him as young, fresh-faced, energetic and a bit different. 'We can't let him divide us,' said Ed. 'Exactly. But that means an agreed strategy.' We agreed that for our meeting on Monday we had to stop the 'Who did what to whom?' stuff, which was just a total waste of energy, and I should say there is 'no trust, no strategy and no operation and those three have to be addressed or we are in deep shit'. 'The problem is...' began almost all of Ed's contributions. But back at No. 10 they were all adamant the Turner briefing had come direct from the Treasury and then they blamed Matthew Taylor, who ended up threatening to sue unless they gave an assurance that they accepted the leak did not come from him.

PG was adamant it was as much about organisation as anything – that there was no me, no Ed to liaise on tricky politics and media stuff 24/7, no Jeremy who could say to TB with authority what was going on, and no real operation to push through a plan. But also they all lied to each other and didn't work together. And meanwhile the Tories were giving out a sense of energy and dynamism and DC was getting a total blowjob from the media. Back home briefly then out to do a really good conference on change. Really well organised, I was on form and gave a detailed analysis of how change actually happened in government and how people had more power to effect it than they realised. Back to get Mum down for Grace's school play. We went for the second night. Even better second time around.

Friday 9 December

Rory was off to Oxford again. I felt there was someone there really rooting for him but his statement lacked any real interest in the philosophy and economics part of PPE and they clearly worried he was more interested in sport and asked him outright if that was the case. 'Don't worry, Dad, I didn't tell them the truth!' I did a bit of work then took Mum to the station, then a longish run. Later to Wimbledon CLP at CWU [Communication Workers Union], OK speech and Q&A, then to a fundraising dinner at businessman Bill Botterill's place. Working-class boy made good. Five really nice kids but his friends who were paying a grand a head a bit grim. One, a bit of a wide boy, lost it over Iraq and I lost it back. Turned a bit nasty.

There was a very nice woman called Pat and she and her very pretty daughter, and one of Botterill's daughters, stuck up for me, and for TB. Over Iraq and then another pain in the ass drama bloke kicking off on human rights. All of them just wanted to mouth off, and felt because they had paid a few quid they could get tanked up and be rude. What was clear, though, was that there was still lots of anger out there re TB and Iraq. I called PG on the way home, said it had been quite weird for a fundraiser, in that it just turned into various massive arguments. I wondered whether they were even Labour, some of them. He had just done some groups, and he said the door was definitely opening for the Tories again, in that people were prepared to hear what Cameron had to say.

Saturday 10 December

Train up to Sheffield United v Burnley with Calum. Crap match, lost 3–0. Met by Dick Caborn, who said that things on education were worse than ever. He said even some of the reasonable ones felt TB was going too far, and it didn't help Cameron coming in behind him. I said but that is what they are bound to do. He is trying to move to the centre, he knows we have a problem with some of our own, so why wouldn't he? It fits with what he is trying to do. Yes, said Dick, but does TB have to make it so easy for them? Dick was a total loyalist in many ways so I fed back to TB what he was saying. I later discovered via Sally M that

TB was thinking of making Dick chief whip. We arrived back, Rory picked us up and we headed to Andrew [political journalist] and Sally Gimson's house for local Labour Party dinner. The main course was there then we all trooped to [local party organiser] Mick Farrant's house over the road for puddings. I don't know how they managed it... Sally G married to a Tory, Mick to a Lib Dem. Unbelievable. It was a nice enough evening, though, and Audrey really enjoyed it.

Sunday 11 December

Long run, then into ITV to do [Jonathan] *Dimbleby* with David Davis. I was basically doing it as a favour to James Macintyre, who was producing. DD was fairly relaxed and discreet for him. I showed him the text Andrew Mitchell had sent me a while back. 'Are we completely fucked?' He laughed, said, 'Well, now we have the answer.' He was putting the line about DC being OK, the right guy, the next Tory PM, but I was not sure he believed it at all, and I sensed he could be trouble ahead for Cameron. As we waited, Ken Clarke was on BBC1 *Politics Show*, and making clear he would be up for trouble too, from the other side of the European debate. He was pissed off at the Tories saying they would withdraw from the EPP grouping [European People's Party, composed of other political parties of member states] in Strasbourg. Europe was not going away as a problem for them. An oil refinery fire [Buncefield depot, near Hemel Hempstead] was wiping out most news. We went to [David's son] Isaac Miliband's 1st birthday, then watched BBC Sports Personality of the Year, as Geoff Thomas [former footballer turned leukaemia survivor and campaigner] was getting a special award.

Monday 12 December

Into Leukaemia Research to do an interview with Brian Viner [*Independent*] on sport, mainly about the Lions, but also Burnley, and weaving in a bit of charity stuff. We did some running shots outside. Then to the Hilton Park Lane for something called the Aircraft Golfing Society, 706 people in aerospace. A fairly boozy do, so I played it mainly for laughs, charity and a bit of politics v media, which seemed to go down really well. There was a very nice guy next to me who was very down on GB, just couldn't see him as PM. I was also picking up a few vibes that the public was not that convinced about Cameron but they were nudging ahead in polls. Then into No. 10. I arrived as TB was getting back from a visit on ASBOs [anti-social behaviour orders]. JoP and Liz Lloyd had done a note arguing for why GB should wait for the top job a bit more. Also suggesting that there was no need to rush in agreeing a line of attack on DC. I was waiting for TB in his office and when he came in, we had a little chat pre the GB meeting, where I sensed he was losing patience. Then Matthew Taylor and Ruth Turner came in and said [chairman, Home Affairs select committee] John Denham's 'alternative white paper' on education would get support from 100 of our MPs.* TB was saying, 'Be relaxed in public', but he was anything but.

He said if we allow the Tories to be the party of reform in public services, and we are just money, we go back to the old right–left divide which they always win. I met up with PG and we went through to No. 11. Football small talk mainly while we waited for TB. When he arrived, he sat down to complete silence. GB looking at his notes. Ed looking stern-faced. 'Shall I say something?' I said. GB nodded. I said there were three big problems – trust, strategy and operation. Lack of all three. That kicked us off into exactly the kind of argument I had been hoping to avoid, how did we get to where we were, who briefed what, who promised what, and eventually I said, as I had said to Ed earlier, that if we danced around on this stuff, we would get nowhere, and could we at least try to resolve things and make some decisions? We were there for around an hour. TB said this boiled down in the end to GB feeling he couldn't take over in two years because he felt he needed more time to put forward his own agenda before an election; and him feeling that one, having been elected for a full term he had to serve a good part of it, and two, the worry that GB would want to take the party in a different direction, which he did not believe would help us win, particularly with Cameron now there.

TB felt, as did PG and I, that if they worked together, genuinely and with impact, we could arrest any decline and be in good shape for GB v DC. TB wanted to get reforms through as GB started to shape a different agenda and then we had to watch and wait re DC. GB wanted to get in early to do party renewal, policy renewal and take on the Tories with all that going on. He repeated the view – which had become a fact in GBland – that TB had called him in when he needed him and then

---

* Blair's plans to make every school an independent 'trust' school provoked the alternative 'white paper' calling for a code of practice on school admissions to prevent selection by the back door and also arguing that there should be no financial advantage for schools with 'trust' status.

dumped him after the election. And later he said to me, 'Why should I believe he will go mid-'07? Last year he was going this year. Before the election he was going before the election.' During the meeting itself TB was much firmer than last time. He said to GB he would be making a big mistake if he thought he could only start to define himself once he got the job. He had a lot to do before he got there. I backed him up on that. I said people knew TB was leaving before the election – cue GB eye-rolling – and so they were already looking at GB in a different way, and making up their minds.

He got very agitato about Philip's note suggesting people were looking at him differently and seeing him as old-fashioned. I said we had to be honest. There was no point shaping strategy according to a world as we wanted it. We had to be in the world as it is. Cameron is seen as young and new and fresh. He has been around a long time. Experience good, but also there are dangers in that, and we had to be able to tell him what people were saying without him taking it personally. This was one of the things TB had in mind earlier when he said he just worried GB did not have the psychological bandwidth to take all the pressures. I said one thing I will say for TB was that he never wanted us to gloss what the public were saying. And nor should he. I said he could only see TB as part of the problem but he was also part of the solution. Likewise, GB's team could only see him as the solution but he may also be part of the problem. I was now looking him straight in the eye and he was looking back, and I said, 'Gordon, you cannot just will the right circumstances into being. The Tories will get a honeymoon for Cameron, we will go through a bit of turbulence, so what? It is always tough, you've just got to keep going. And we've got to work together.'

He felt that he was the target but he felt we couldn't hit back adequately. We kept coming back to the lack of a date. TB said, 'This is not complicated. Gordon doesn't think he can do this if I am here. But halfway through a parliament is not that far. And we can take the shine off DC and work him out.' TB, PG and I were all saying he was wrong to want to get in soon, from his own perspective, never mind TB's, but he just got angry at that, insisted it was not just about a date. 'Come on, Gordon,' I said. 'It is. There are no differences on policy so big that you cannot bridge them.' Ed was mainly raising health and education policy, saying we were ceding ground to the Tories. TB said he was not going to allow our policies to get hijacked so they were sub-Dave Spart [*Private Eye*]. Ed looked really hurt by that. TB later apologised but he said they were saying silly things about what he was actually trying to do. As ever, the left was taking the right's assessment of our policy, not our own.

GB was adamant later that his ratings were better than TB. But they fall under pressure, I said, and in any event they are always relatively higher because people see him in part as a foil to TB. When he is at the top, someone else will play the role he is playing to TB now. TB and I both said he should not worry about his ratings going up or down. He should keep his focus on getting things done and on planning for the election. GB would not bring himself to say he wanted TB to go now or soon but, as TB said, that was what it was about. GB summed up TB's approach, pejoratively, as 'Let's keep going, let me support you in all these positions and see what happens.' He also said he had trouble with some of the policies and felt we only had a two-year programme. TB summed up GB's position as 'I am the target of the Tory attacks yet I cannot fight back, I cannot define myself till I am in the job.' TB said the latter was a fundamental error, that he had doubts to overcome in some people's minds and should be doing it now.

GB was not happy about PG being so direct in his note that he was not as strong as TB in some quarters. At one point I said on trust, strategy and operation they were weak but GB could not set strategy according to what he willed. He had to be honest with himself, should accept the good and build on the rest but he needed to broaden his appeal. TB also said, 'Don't panic' at one point, and GB said loudly, 'I am not panicking. I am simply telling you that we are going to go down and it's time we had a proper strategy.' TB kept coming back to the same stuff and at one point he just had his head in his hands, clearly pretty fed up with it all.

We went round for hour or so, agreed again the need for a written strategy, plus people on both sides to implement modus operandi. He was not at all sure of the way forward but was more and more convinced GB underestimated his problems. TB had to leave after just over an hour. GB was also supposed to be going for a meeting at the Treasury, where IMF [International Monetary Fund] officials were waiting for them, and one of his people kept coming in but he waved them away. He said to us he understood his weaknesses but it wasn't true that he had all these negatives. PG was simply saying he was seen as more old-fashioned than DC and that TB still had a big lead on all of them for understanding the modern world, and for charisma. We were back to the need for a plan. GB said we two had more influence with TB than anyone else and we had to persuade him that there was a different way forward. I said the issue is that we can see it from TB's perspective and he can't. He is actually saying he is willing to go halfway through a parliament, having been elected to serve the whole term, and yet he – GB – can't see that as being good enough.

Tuesday 13 December

Out to the '94 TB leadership team dinner. Jonathan was pretty obsessive re GB. He said I don't see how you can continue to think he is the right person to take over. 'He gets worse not better.' As we were talking, the phone went and it was GB, weirdly asking if I was interested in being editor of *The Scotsman*. He said this was meant in a friendly not malevolent way. I said I was unplugging from journalism. He said, 'In which case you have a duty to stand for Parliament. You can't be both politics and media.' I said there were times I wished I was neither. I moved into the corner of the restaurant, and we chatted a bit about yesterday. I said he had to try to see it from TB's perspective. Most of TB's team felt he – TB – was being ridiculously accommodating. I didn't tell him where I was, but God, if he heard the things some of the people there said about him… I said he just couldn't expect for him to treat then like shit, and then they all support him. It was a perfectly friendly chat; he was more reflective than yesterday. I don't know what the *Scotsman* thing was about, though he didn't come back to it. He did come back to the MP thing, though, and mentioned Fiona too, said we should both get seats.

I went back and was chatting to Kate Garvey and Pat McF, telling them I was feeling like a Relate counsellor, when TB called. He said he was not moving from Plan A, despite the pressures from others to dump on GB, but, 'It was pretty bad yesterday, wasn't it?' GB just didn't want to admit there was any good in what we did. He said I had been very good with GB and it had been right to lose it a bit with him because he never heard it from his own people. Re DC he said GB wanted us to kill him but we had to bide our time a bit and see the weaknesses first. The dinner was OK but the mood was a bit flat compared with other years. Liz said it was like the recent film she had seen about Hitler's bunker in the final days. I think some of them were angry that I was still helping GB, but I made the point that I was doing so at TB's behest. Peter M, though, felt it was akin to colluding with bullying.

Wednesday 14 December

Fiona dropped in that she was thinking of trying to get a seat and becoming an MP and why don't I do the same? How weird was that, GB having raised the same last night? I was not sure about it, for either of us. In to have lunch with Catherine Rimmer [head of research] and David Bradshaw. They felt TB was weak at the moment. I don't think anyone in there, with perhaps the exception of Jonathan, knew quite how much TB–GBery was going on right now. I stayed in for a bit of his PMQs preparation. He did fine, he was tougher than last week. He used Clinton's old line about compassionate Conservatism – we don't care for the poor but we're really sorry about it. DC was too stilted and over-rehearsed. The story, though, was Charlie Kennedy's latest leadership crisis, with the drink stories doing the rounds again. I sent him a message saying if he wanted to chat about it, I was around. He had mentioned to me a couple of times that he might one day want a chat about how I stopped drinking, and it was pretty obvious he needed to. He sent a very non-committal reply, just thanks for being supportive.

The feelings in the media were growing against GB, who was getting some decent advice from some of the hacks amid the bile. But he needed to change his ways, for sure. To a PST [political strategy team] meeting. Huw Evans [special advisor] had done a six-month grid and there was at least some good forward planning work going on. But the huge and evident gap was real strategy implementation involving TB and GB. TB said the overall message had to be doing the right things for the long term. The problem he felt was the PLP. He had just met some of them and he was even more alarmed than before. They just didn't see the traps being laid by the Tories, though the loyalists were at least fighting back. On the education white paper, fifty-plus backbenchers and others, including [Baroness] Estelle Morris [former Education Secretary], had put together an alternative white paper which allowed Cameron to do another 'We will help get it through' line of attack presented as support, but TB was clearly not for changing. He said he didn't want any of his people putting it out we were up for compromise. We had to see it through. He said the best option was that we win the vote with our people, second best we win with the help of theirs, third we lose it.

Ruth Kelly was sure the Tories would find a way not to help. TB said doing it with the Tories was election-losing stuff. It was an OK meeting but I couldn't help feeling there was a slight mix of bunker and kamikaze in him at the moment. He took me and Sally through at the end to discuss GB. JoP said he wouldn't be joining us because his blood pressure soared whenever he contemplated Plan A, if it ended with GB taking over when we all knew it was madness. TB said the GB problems were growing and it would fall to me and him [AC and TB] to explain what he had to do. He had to hug TB tight. He could not establish New Labour credentials without him. But Sally was not convinced GB could change. I felt maybe that was so, but he would need a really honest appraisal, the likes of which he didn't really go for, and which his team tended to avoid.

TB was still very human and humorous. GB had to lighten up, not be so angry the whole time. What the press knew about him, and played down because he was a better story when undermining TB, was starting to move into their domain because they knew he was likely to be the next big target after TB went. TB said, 'I am sorry to drag you into this so much, but you are going to have to do the heavy lifting. He won't speak to anyone else.' 'We are all PNG [persona non grata] with GB,' said Sal.

I had to leave for another session with David S and Fiona. I ran there, and was feeling physically a lot better than when the last depression was on. I was feeling mentally better as well, so maybe the pills were helping. Fiona accepted I was trying to change. He felt that her saying maybe we should both become MPs would set off all the demons. I felt I was really trying and she had to understand how hard it was at the moment. He asked me straight out, 'So you have just come from Downing Street? Yet you left two years ago. So why do you keep going back?' I said partly out of duty. It is hard to say no when the PM or the Chancellor ask you, and they think you can help. But also because I don't want to see what we built up destroyed?' He said, 'But is it also because you want to be wanted?' I said maybe, but it didn't feel like that. Sometimes I was happy in there. Other times my heart sank.

He said, 'Maybe you need to think more about yourself, and less about them.' Fiona said, 'He can't. He can't let it go.' 'The addict,' said David. 'The demon.' 'I think you are both being harsh,' I said. 'But if your heart sinks at the thought, why do it?' I said I do think the duty thing kicks hard on me, and I sometimes felt bad I had left, and bad that, for example when GB asked me to get a seat, I just didn't want to. David said, 'I think power is very hard to give up, if there is nothing in its place.' I said I didn't have power. I only had power as an extension of TB. 'Not so sure about that,' he said.

We went later to the *Guardian* comment party via a drink with Melissa

Benn [daughter of Tony and Caroline]. I had a long chat with Tony Benn about his diaries. He had a total of 17 million words, plus – or was it including? – half a million words a year of taped interviews. He had only published 10 per cent of the whole so far. We chatted about whether writing it, as I did, or speaking it, as he often did, led to a different style. He said he hoped I kept on keeping a diary, because he felt having been there at the centre I might now start to get a different perspective. I said at the moment I felt I hadn't left at all. I had been there virtually every day recently. Yes, he said, but it is different. He was asking if I had become more reflective since leaving. Not yet, I said. 'It will happen, I am sure.' I said are you suggesting I will end up thinking New Labour was a dreadful mistake? 'I wouldn't go that far, no.' He said he would love to meet up and have a proper long chat about my diaries.

Ed Miliband was there, came over and asked me how the GB meetings were going. I said not great but I felt we would get there. He said I was key to TB–GB transition, as GB felt he could not trust anyone else in No. 10, including TB. I said they had to de-paranoia their whole operation. TB had said he was going, and he said he wanted GB to take over. Roll with it, for heaven's sake. Let's take our time, get the transition done effectively, and then let GB do what he needs to do to win the next election. It is possible but not if we carry on like this. Ed said he knew GB could be difficult, but he had no doubt when he took over we would see a very different kind of politician, the one they saw at the Treasury, not the one we saw from No. 10. I said I hoped so. The do was the usual mix of left-leaning hacks and MPs, and I said to Martin Kettle, if you bottled all the political wisdom in the room, you would have the perfect election-losing strategy. He agreed – '199 out of 200 not a clue,' he said. Andrew Marr [BBC presenter] was there as Mr Jackie Ashley [Marr's journalist wife] and asked me to go on his show again.

Thursday 15 December
Christopher Meyer and Lance Price were getting a hard time at PASC on memoirs. Andrew Turnbull [recent Cabinet Secretary and head of civil service] referring to me as 'the big C'. I got a few bids but generally avoided. Out for lunch with Calum then Mark round to work on the diaries. I mentioned the chat with Tony Benn. Mark thought Tony and I should do events together.

December '05: 'GB only trusts you in TB team,' Ed M to AC

Friday 16 December

Out for a long walk with Fiona then back to collect the garden bench I had ordered for Christmas, commemorating our dads. It arrived flat pack so I had to stamp my feet a bit until they agreed to put it together. Later to [public relations executive] Matthew Freud's party. We arrived fairly early because we wanted to leave fairly early. I bumped into James Murdoch [son of Rupert] on the way in, who was quizzing me about what I thought of the Tories under Cameron. He said he thought Cameron could not beat TB, but he could beat GB because he was 'an unreconstructed socialist'. I suggested he'd been listening to his dad too much. He felt TB was exceptional home and abroad but GB was not. Courage was a problem – he hid when things got tough, whereas real leaders showed themselves at that point. Maybe there he had a point, but 'unreconstructed socialist'! He said he was at a dinner recently of city and media and every one of them said they had problems with GB. He said, 'What you should worry about is that the ones who had more actual experience of him felt the most strongly.' There was definitely a new mood for the Tories developing.

George Osborne arrived and sought me out. We went to the landing and had a long chat, largely uninterrupted. He said their strategy was to talk up TB and present GB as being not just anti-reform but old-fashioned, of another age. He said he was sure that once TB went, Labour would be seen as the past and they could seize the future. He said the most powerful opposition message was always 'time for a change' and their youth plus GB as old and tired was a very powerful package. He said their biggest fear was a switch to Hilary Benn or David Miliband. He said they didn't fear John Reid. They thought TB had something very special, Hilary and David had a bit of it. 'GB is our Labour candidate of choice.' He was very relaxed, calm and poised, clever without a doubt. The posh thing could grate with both him and Cameron, but there was something quite authentic about him, and I sensed they had the measure of GB and would know how to get to him. I asked him if they were worried at all, or embarrassed, that Merkel had written to Cameron as she had about their decision to take their MEPs out of the EPP. He said, No, they value the EPP grouping – we don't. But why make Europe such a big deal from the off?

Today, as TB was up to his neck in rebate negotiations in Brussels, Cameron was cashing in on Charlie Kennedy's problems with a direct appeal to Libs to come over. He was surrounded by orange posters, Libdemsforcameron. They were enjoying themselves, but I thought it was low. Cameron arrived, Samantha clearly pregnant. There was a mild honeypot effect, though he didn't fill the room. Kate Garvey said she thought Osborne filled it more. [Baroness] Valerie Amos [leader of the House of Lords] came over and whispered to me that we had to talk. We went downstairs. She said Cabinet yesterday had been the worst ever – even though GB was not there. On judicial pensions and greater surveillance powers for the security services, TB was effectively turned over.* Even Douglas [Alexander, Europe minister] spoke against! She said it was almost painful. Sad. She felt like crying. 'You could actually see the authority seeping away.' But worse, she said, there had been no operation like there would have been in the old days. 'He looked drained, and people could feel the weakness.' Les Hinton [executive chairman, News International] came through – he said I was mad not to do a bidding war with HarperCollins for the diaries. He said they would have definitely gone higher than Random House. I said yes, but friendship matters too, and I trust Gail totally in a way I wouldn't trust someone else.

I went upstairs and Kate pointed out Cameron on the arm of a sofa. His wife gave him a little nudge as I went over and he stood up, keen to talk. A bit of small talk then he said, 'Why do you keep attacking me?' Nothing personal, I said. 'I know, the problem is you do it rather well, can't you get some of your numpties to do it?' He said he had been shitting himself pre-PMQs, felt he had been OK first time but TB got the measure of him this week. 'He really is quite formidable, isn't he?' 'Yep.' 'That's why we need Gordon in there as soon as possible.' Then Osborne joined us. Cameron said Hague had advised him to take tea with six sugars just before PMQs. He asked if TB had any rituals. Only that he wears the same shoes every time. GO said it was good to have Hague around because he had tried all sorts of different approaches and he was good on what would or wouldn't work. I said Hague had made a mistake in allowing us to stop him using humour because we kept attacking him as 'all jokes no judgement'. Once he stopped being funny, he stopped being effective. He should have stayed funny but worked on the judgement.

It was pretty obvious to me they both totally rated TB in terms of his capacity. Cameron said even between this week and last, he noticed that

---

* The Constitutional Reform Act 2005 had provided for a Supreme Court to take over responsibilities, including various measures relating to the judiciary, from the Law Lords and the Privy Council's Judicial Committee.

TB had made subtle adaptations, and was definitely better. 'I couldn't believe how nerve-racking it was first time around. Even if you have been in there, and seen it so often, nothing prepares you.' I said TB had been the same. Even if you know what you are going to say, it is so much harder than people imagine. 'How long before he stopped being nervous?' he asked. 'Never,' I said. 'Once you feel no nerves in there, you stop doing the things you need to do to get it right. He takes it very seriously.' He said he could not believe the noise. He also wanted to have a chat about his wife and kids. I suggested he make an approach to the PCC around the birth to sort some kind of deal. He said he had posed with his son for local media when writing to save a school and they kept using it. I said that is what they did, they found something that gave them a spurious justification for any intrusion in the future.

He felt it was a bit open season and I sensed he was a little worried. There was definitely a shift to them, no doubt, even though we were still the government. DC said something similar to what Osborne had said to me, that he was very proud to be seen as TB's successor and serious about helping get reforms through. He was amazingly young-looking but seemed very confident and assured. Lots of people were watching us talk, but leaving us to it. I said I would keep on whacking at him, but don't take any of it personally. I wanted to help TB cement his legacy, and I wanted GB to beat him next time. 'Good luck with the first bit,' he said.

Ben Wegg-Prosser [director of strategic communications, 10 Downing Street] arrived; he clearly knew both of them well. Ben said Cabinet had been dreadful. Also he and Liz were desperate to see me to work out how to improve the operation. TB was having to give fair bit on the rebate in his meetings out in Brussels. As we left, Cameron and Osborne were talking to Piers Morgan [former editor, *Daily Mirror*] and Celia Walden [*Daily Telegraph* journalist]. They said Morgan was the new AC and they were hiring him. Defintely an anti-GB mood around. Rebekah [Wade] and Andy Coulson [editor, *News of the World*] were asking me about what Cameron had been saying. Ditto Jamie Theakston [broadcaster] and Tim Bevan from Working Title. Gail [Rebuck] said it was revolting to see people licking DC's arse who had been up ours. Ben really worried. It was interesting that Cameron said I attacked him well, and I felt talking to them both that they really did think it was all about the media. I'm still not sure he has a really strong strategy. But he has good messaging and a good way about him, and good tone. It's not enough, though. That being said, as I said to Philip later on, they are definitely thinking of how to tackle GB, and they don't think they need to do much more than positioning and tone.

Saturday 17 December

Matthew Doyle sent me an interesting Electoral Commission report on media coverage. Bias and distortion definitely getting worse. *Telegraph* front pages joining others now in becoming total news as comment on the anti-Blair line. Really nice walk with Grace and Molly then hour-plus run. To Tessa and David's via stables. Not really wanting to engage but generally things not good. Ate there in between watching them watch *X Factor* and *Strictly Come Dancing* and raging at Tessa for voting the whole time for someone called Andy. The EU deal was the main story, and funnily enough seemed to be calmer now the decisions were being reached, but the Sundays were bad – JP v TB on schools, GB v TB on the rebate.

I went with David to [former Tory Cabinet minister, Lord] Geoffrey Howe's Christmas party a few miles away. He was looking a bit frail, his voice weak, but he was as bright as ever mentally, and asking me what I thought of Cameron, and whether TB would last the whole parliament. I was a bit of a curio in there among all their country friends, but he and Elspeth [Lady Howe] were both friendly, and I sensed he actually saw TB as a pretty good PM. He felt GB would not know how to handle Cameron. I chatted mainly to him before the chair of the local Tories and his wife came over. He was an Old Etonian – they get everywhere – and his son was a friend of DC's. He said he would give us a run for our money 'because he is so, so polite. I think that is such a quality in a politician, you know.' TB called, said the final denouement of the budget talks had been tough, Chirac difficult as ever, Merkel helpful, he would get whacked on the rebate, but he felt all in all the deal was good, and the French were also giving more than they wanted to. I filled him in on DC and he was straight on to their main point ... 'They have the same interest as GB, get me out quickly and him in as soon as possible.'

Sunday 18 December

Out for a long walk and Tessa was constantly quizzing me re TB–GB. I think she knew something was going on, but I so didn't want to talk about it. Long drive back via the stables to collect Grace. Then out for a run. GB called about *The Scotsman* again and, even more definitively, I said no. He said he thought I might have found it interesting to take a paper and move it right to left 'unlike the fucking *Guardian* going the other way'. So what are you doing then? he asked. Different things, I said. 'What do you make of things?' Bad, I said. We're divided and stale. The Tories look lively and interesting. The Libs are dead and the Tories are exploiting that better than we are. He said it was not unity that was the problem but the lack of a long-term agenda. I said they were related, because the disunity made it hard to get agreement on a long-term agenda, or any agenda at all.

He said the schools white paper was a short-term plan for a few schools, not a long-term plan for all schools. He was back on his 'not being consulted' kick, said TB had not called about the deal he did on the rebate despite him trying to reach him. He flatly denied briefing the papers on his stance on the rebate, which was a bit far fetched. He said that there had been no contact since our last meeting. He said I had more influence with TB than he did and I had to make him see this short-term approach was failing. He said he was not asking for special favours but anyone with an interest in the Labour Party could see what had to be done. Went to [neighbours] Michael and Alison Farthings' party. David S was there and I sensed Michael F knew I was seeing him.

Monday 19 December
A combination of JP stirring on the schools white paper, GB agitating on the rebate, polls shifting a bit on the back of DC, and the week was starting badly for TB. The media was actually not as bad as the reality, though. Ed B sent me a text saying things were getting worse not better: 'No discussion on rebate, education WP badly handled and is there anything we can do?' I called him, said I wasn't sure there was anything we can do, it was up to those two to sort themselves out and if they don't they're both fucked. I'm fed up of having to deal with all the crap. I spoke to PG, who agreed it was time to take a tough approach. We were both really beginning to wonder if GB was right for it. The Balliol letter arrived. Good news and Rory was pleased enough. Then a call from the Heath because the dog was misbehaving and driving Fiona crazy and that set things off later, to the full works again, culminating in I fell out of love with her and TB relations filled the gap. She said he had blown it and I should stop helping him. I said she was just waiting to be able to say he failed and I was determined not to let that

happen. If we managed to turn our most successful ever leader into a failure, it would be madness. Not great again, though the good news was we calmed down quicker than usual.

Tuesday 20 December

I met Liz Lloyd and Ben W-P to go over the script for TB's press conference tomorrow. TB needs to be chilled, even bigger picture, bring people into his confidence more re how he operates, what he has learned, be more conversational. I had noticed recently that he was much more defensive when doing interviews. He needed to get more of the PMQs mode into his media interactions, light and clever again. In terms of the office operation, I felt they had been allowing themselves to get dragged down and accept second best. There was not enough being put down on paper. They needed to revive the 'next week in strategic context' notes that I used to do. Liz said there was still no Plan B, it was all about makings things work with Gordon, but his people were a nightmare to work with so things were not getting better.

They both seemed quite down. I said they had to keep going, keep trying to get TB's head up, and above all try to get more strategy and organisation into the system. Without it, they would just being diddling day to day, being busy but ineffective. TB was in Brussels doing the usual reporting to MEPs on the end of the UK Presidency, and it was a lot livelier than expected, because he really went for UKIP, and Nigel Farage in particular. He said he sat there with the British flag but he didn't represent Britain's interests. And he also had a pop at the way the media covered Europe, and said they too didn't represent opinion. Most of the assessments of the Presidency – in Europe – were fairly positive, on future financing especially, but our politics and media were fixated on the rebate. Hague's line of attack was that he gave up a lot and got nothing in return. I watched a bit of TB on the news and I could sense the frustration.

Wednesday 21 December

Lie in after a bad night's sleep. TB called just after eight. 'Have I woken you up?' For once I could say yes. He had his press conference at twelve and had a new GB problem. He had asked him to delay putting out the financial analysis on the rebate sums but the Treasury had put them out in answer to a Parliamentary Question from John McFall [chair, Treasury

Select Committee], and it was running second on the news. TB said GB gave him some bollocks – echoed to me by Balls later – saying he was under real pressure to get the figures out. So much so that DC never even asked yesterday!! TB said they had a long session yesterday and though he was still committed to plan A he said there is a big problem here, the guy's psychology. It was obvious he needed to be close in there on reform, there when the going gets tough, not just agitating about the job. But he was if anything worse and it all stemmed from his inability to see that New Labour and TB had delivered progress. He wanted to hide behind a shield of blame. TB was sounding amazingly chirpy considering. He said he had gone zen Buddhist as a way of dealing with it. 'Otherwise I would go mad.'

I told him what I told Ben and Liz – be chilled, use experience, remind them that whenever we delivered real change it was tough. Tuition fees was supposedly our poll tax but we got through it; foundation hospitals would break up the NHS but they didn't. He said he never felt clearer about what needed to be done, but had a problem with the PLP. Some of them were off the radar now. About the summit, he said Merkel had been good to work with, really thorough and calm, always willing to listen, and importantly she was far from being up Chirac's backside. In fact he felt that Chirac had found it irritating that she didn't seem to want to side with him the whole time, but instead play the honest broker role. There was another poll with the Tories ahead.

Long run then David S. He had asked me to write down negative thoughts and then explain how each of them could be turned into a positive. 'Is this psychiatric spin doctoring?' I asked. He laughed. He had a very good sense of humour which was one of the reasons I didn't mind seeing him. He said the purpose was so that I could see things from a new perspective, and also work out why certain things pressed buttons in me. He said I did the same with Fiona, certain things I said and did pressed buttons in her and I had to understand more why.

We went through dreams again. There had been one where a guy kept trying to hit me with a bottle and I was dodging and weaving, but resisting the urge to grab the bottle and use it against the guy, and wondering why. He thought the man wanting me to hit with a bottle was my demon. TB and GB were both in there a lot as well. He said I had to see why Fiona might see my relationship with work in the way some women would see an affair. It was all consuming, took me away at times she needed support, felt to her like I found it all so much more exciting. 'But I gave it up.' Yes, he said, but she doesn't feel you have.

He said he wanted me to write him an essay on humility. He felt I was seeing myself as indispensable, because though my heart sank when I got dragged in, the demon in me was being made to feel indispensable, like the whole thing would come crashing down unless I responded when they asked me to help.

TB called after his press conference. He seemed to think it had gone OK. He said he felt confident and although they had been pressing on two flanks – internal opposition to reform, and Cameron giving the Tories a lift – he brought the two together as we had discussed, reforms always difficult, and Cameron's only strategy seemed to be to try to be more like us. We were making the weather. I told him about GB's *Scotsman* gambit. He said at least he's thinking of you, and still a bit scared of you. He was due to head to Basra tomorrow. Mark came round later to do more diary stuff and it was amazing how much of what was going on now was in the '01 diaries. Me agonising about my future. Depression. Fiona angry about the office. TB–GB. Europe. Foot and mouth was the big thing though. What a nightmare that had been. John Simpson [BBC foreign correspondent] had a book out and as well as spelling my name wrongly, he had facts wrong re the whole [Andrew] Gilligan [journalist] episode.*

Thursday 22 December
I caught a bit of TB in Iraq on the news. The troops brilliant as ever, lots of good vox pops, and the mood seemed OK considering. There were hints they'd be home sooner than they thought. I went out for a good run in the freezing cold. My head was feeling OK but the side effects were piling up, including a bit of memory loss. I was forgetting names of people I knew really well. Plus I was craving carbs the whole time. Weird. We went to Helena Kennedy's Christmas bash, which was a slight risk given how many would have been anti-Iraq War, and some of them anti-New Labour. Audrey gave a right doing over to Jon Snow [Channel 4 newsreader] over something he had said about me on screen. Neither he nor I could remember it but she was well into him, said he had no right to doubt me on anything at all, and all the more effective because she said it with a smile. The Kennedy family all saying how

---

* In 2003 Gilligan had broadcast on BBC Radio's *Today* programme that a British government document on Iraq and weapons of mass destruction had been 'sexed-up'. In his report, Lord Hutton questioned the reliability of Gilligan's evidence.

nice Calum was. Alan Rickman [actor] was telling me about a play he'd been working on and his research made him much more critical about politicians. Will Hutton [journalist, author] was telling me all about his book on China.

Friday 23 December

Viner's *Independent* interview came out fine. Good picture and good publicity for LRF. I went for a long walk with Calum who was quizzing me about Tony and Gordon, why they didn't get on, what it used to be like, how I dealt with both of them the way I did. He was very sensitive to the politics of it all, and had an ability to see it from both sides. But ultimately he said what he picked up from hearing me on the phone was that Tony could do the job and he wasn't sure I was sure about Gordon. Alex called to congratulate Rory and also to say he could go to Carrington [Man U training academy] for a week's work experience.

Over Christmas, I was trying to chill out. TB was off to Egypt for another controversial holiday.* Not working that much, just a few hours most days, mainly on diaries and future speeches. The dreams were coming thick and fast, and I was writing reams about them. Alex called a couple of times, including to have a rage re a story in the press that Bob Geldof was advising Cameron. He said he didn't like the look of Cameron at all, too posh, too grand. Rory wrote me a fantastic letter on Christmas Day. He said he knew I didn't go for presents much so instead he wanted to write why he thought I was such a great dad, and how he knew he owed me and Fiona so much. It was really warm and also incredibly insightful about all sorts of things. I was trying to keep up on the exercise front but I was overweight because the medication was making me hungry the whole time. I saw Ed Victor on Christmas Eve and we agreed to put together an annual LRF event given he had come through it. We saw the Kinnocks. Neil asked straight out, 'When is TB going?' and I said it's going to get worse not better. Where are you on doubt re GB? 3 out of 10, he said. They were all thinking Fiona should go for a seat. Glenys was very down on the idea of me doing my diaries.

---

* Blair had previously been criticised for accepting hospitality from private individuals and foreign governments on holidays.

Wednesday 28 December

To Norwich v Burnley [2–1]. Freezing cold. I had a long chat with Charles Clarke. He and Carole had had lunch with Ed Balls and Yvette [Cooper, his wife] and said what was striking was how they basically saw TB as separate from the party, and its success as separate from him. CC shared my view that the longer TB played in DC the better but they were of the opposite view. Also he said he reckoned the Cabinet were almost united in thinking GB would get it but at least half thought it was the wrong thing to do. He said our relationship was a good example of how these relationships in politics could work. You don't have to be especially close. You can have ups and downs but that's part of it. With GB though, it is all or nothing. He cannot do balanced relationships. You are for him or against him. A supporter or a threat. He said GB had more worries than most – does he have what it takes, what if the economy goes pear shaped – plus DC who, he said, is not to be underestimated. We may hate that Old Etonian thing, but it gives people like him a real confidence and he is already showing signs that he can do the job. CC wanted to meet in the New Year to talk more.

Thursday 29 December

JP called, mainly to talk about his (near incomprehensible) council tax problems, which seemed to revolve around a muddle inside his department about what was his primary and what was his secondary residence. It was classic JP, and I didn't have a clue what the issue was by the end of it. But first we got through football small talk. He had been to Brighton v Hull where Brighton fans were singing, 'He's fat, he's round, he's given us a ground' [JP had given the go-ahead for a new Brighton stadium after a long campaign and planning process] and then into TB–GB. He felt things were as bad as ever, and there was a total lack of trust. He felt TB was in choppy waters in the next few months, education was still a problem, and he felt he had to speak out as he had; health was a lesser problem but a problem nonetheless, and GB having shaken the apple loose was now letting others shake the tree. But JP agreed that if TB was forced out it was bad for everyone, not least GB. He felt that in the coming year, he should indicate he will be gone by '07 and then a transition. Till then GB had to help with reforms.

He asked what I was doing with myself and I was more and more conscious that apart from the diaries, speeches, charity, TB–GB and trying to sort out my mind, I was not doing much. I was sleeping loads but I was no less tired. Running loads but I was no fitter. All a bit odd. I said I am cogitating, and trying to work out what to do with the rest of my life. It was a good chat and he seemed calmer than the last time we spoke. He told me he would not be standing again but would not announce till last minute. He felt he needed a bit of rest and time out from the whole thing. He had been spending too much time and energy sorting these things. 'Tell me about it.' I said I felt TB still wanted to make it work but he grew more and more ambivalent because of the way GB treated him. He felt Cherie was bound to be winding him up a fair bit about GB having made his job so much harder. The point about the apple tree was well made. GB had shaken the tree and was now waiting for others to shake it free. He did not want to be Brutus himself, said JP.

On the education stuff, he said he let his own concerns come out because he had asked TB to reflect on where everyone stood and he hadn't so he needed to send a signal. He didn't like doing it publicly but he felt he had to. TB was so hitting the reform message that we were losing the benefits of our record, which was phenomenal. It was as if we were saying ourselves we hadn't done enough in eight years. He went through the things on the record we should be highlighting. I said I agreed with that but TB's point was that the record must always be allied to plans for the future. We will not win if we just make it about the past. He then had another go at explaining his council tax problem. We agreed to speak again tomorrow before he spoke to TB.

Friday 30 December

I was working on the diaries for '01, JP trying to resolve problems on the tube, when the phone rang and it was switch [Downing Street switchboard] with JP. He wanted a chat pre his call with TB. First we had another long explanation about his council tax muddle which he had spent days trying to grip because Caroline Spelman [Tory MP] had been pursuing him with PQs [parliamentary questions]. I said he needs to appoint someone to drill down on the facts, and get them all out before Parliament is back. Re TB–GB he said his approach was going to be that he intended to give it one last shot, get them to agree to a plan and if either went off it he would go public and say that's it, I've tried my best. He felt it was worse than ever which in many ways it was.

Saturday 31 December

Dinner with Philip, Gail, Rory and Georgia at Odin's. PG was totally hyper and OTT, and I was heading into my usual New Year's Eve dive.

Sunday 1 January 2006

Cameron seemed to me to be doing all the right things from his perspective. A big ad in the *Sunday Telegraph* on change and with a clear pitch to the centre. A big attack on GB in the *Sunday Times,* very much on the lines he and Osborne had said they would. PG called as he was working on a note and wanted to set out the need for GB to develop a whole new operation and TB a new gameplan too. He sent over the draft and I hardened it up a bit in places. It was definitely easier working with TB in that we never felt the need to sugarcoat, whereas with GB you were always wondering about not giving him excuses to take it personally. I took Rory and Calum out to Gerrards Cross for dinner with Steve Cotterill. It was always interesting to see the players en masse away from a match. They looked smaller, younger, shyer. He was interesting about the different approaches he used for players according to their own psychology. Some could cope with bollocking, some couldn't, but it was a tough environment and they had to be able to adapt.

He is quite a character, very intense and focused. He was convinced Clive Woodward would not hack it at Southampton. He felt football people are too different. Partly about class. Football is working class, the players are trickier, not mannered like rugby boys! The money was changing everything, not for the better. Managers liked to think they are all-powerful but they're not. He was interesting on all the skimping and saving he had to do, but with Clive Holt [Burnley director] there too it cramped his style a bit but we had a nice time and he was excellent with the boys.

PG sent me a copy of the revised note he had done for GB. The last poll showed people were feeling the economy had bottomed out and they were starting to feel a bit better off. The polls were closing again. He said that Cameron went down well with the one group he had done on him – youth, energy and a new optimism. He was considered to have done well at PMQs. Osborne like Cameron is considered to be modern and energetic, he said. GB would hate that. He laid it out straight on division, said the public now saw us as divided as the Tories and a lot of that came from TB–GB. He was pretty frank – not totally – about how people saw GB. 'People's view of you in groups is as someone they respect and but also as someone who tends to exemplify an old politics. People see you as a trustworthy but traditional politician. The YouGov poll today did show some erosion in your satisfaction levels since the election and I think this is because people are seeing you for the first time as the next Prime Minister, which is a harder test. Your emergence as the next Prime Minister has only happened recently.'

It would be interesting to see how GB reacted. There were a few warnings in there. PG set out the 'cluster of issues' he thought would decide the next election – security; economy; public services and the new politics, and the mood for change. He said the mood for change was where we would be vulnerable. That would worry GB, make him think he had to be the change himself. PG's point 9. 'I have said this before but will repeat it, the mood for change at the next election will be very strong and is your biggest enemy. To defeat it you will have to become the force for change in British politics, channelling the mood for change away from Cameron and towards you.'This does require as you said at our last meeting a huge project of political renewal, but it will also require a project of personal renewal. When you become Prime Minister you need to embody a new approach to politics, as well as leading a party that is renewed. You will need to embody openness, inclusiveness, and a relaxed self-confidence.'

He tried to tie together TB, handover, GB, but as I read it, as I said to him later, it was hard to see it all coming together like that. There was so little trust now. PG felt only he and I could really bridge the gap between the teams. I added a couple of final points, hammering home the need for an agreed strategy, and emphasising that the best way to brush Cameron aside was for TB to take the shine off the ball, grind him down, work him out, and then GB come in all guns blazing and shoot him down.

Monday 2 January

We did Fiona's birthday presents then out for QPR v BFC. Collected Georgia and had lunch at a pub. A random bloke came up and said it was time I was back in government – 'They're losing direction without you.' This kind of thing was happening more and more. I think Labour people were feeling a bit edgy about Cameron. We should have won, easily the better side, but it finished one all. We went to PG's afterwards and ended up looking at old pictures, including the holiday with Peter M in Majorca, when I was pretending to make a film about how he was engineering [former Labour leader, died 1994] John Smith's downfall to get Gordon in. How times change. Now PG and I were the villains for wanting GB to take over. PG was saying we had to decide pretty soon whether we were going to see this through. David M called for a chat. He asked what was going on, aware I had been seeing the two of them together. I said it is not easy, and if I were him, I wouldn't rule anything out. TB was still committed to going at some point and helping GB, but at times he is almost overwhelmed by it all, and totally unconvinced GB can change enough.

DM felt we had zero strategy and zero operation and it was not clear what TB was up to. All sorts of people were suggesting to him he had to make a move and try to stand against GB, rather than just have a coronation whenever TB went. He feared a steamroller assassination if he went for it. He didn't think it was a serious option to stop GB. He said the problem was that the TB–GB thing was just not operating at all, and affecting everyone. The last few Cabinets before Christmas had been awful, he said. Nobody was sure what they were meant to be thinking or doing. TB looked becalmed. GB looked odd. Everyone else looked confused. He echoed what several others had said, that there was a sense of inevitability about GB, and a shared sense that it was the wrong thing. I said he needed to keep his options open. Strange things can happen. But he didn't sound very sure.

Tuesday 3 January

TB sent through a note in advance of the meeting at Chequers tomorrow. He pointed out the irony of it being said we were running out of steam at a time everyone else felt the need to come on to our ground. It was a long note but as before everything came down to sorting out the future with GB and working together meanwhile. Plan A – work with GB. Plan B – work round him. Plan C – go down guns blazing. He felt the option of over-compromise on basic reforms was not worth it. He said he would rather go down than be emasculated and weak. Reform was the key still. The need for an agenda that connects. I had a dreadful cold, so didn't run. I weighed myself, and was up to sixteen stone, so the side effects kicking in. Went to see Alex before their match at Arsenal, fixing Rory for his work experience at the academy. He was asking if things with Tony and Gordon were as bad as they seemed from the media. Worse, I said. I bumped into Terry Neill [former Arsenal player and manager], reminiscing on the times he used to come in to do my Radio Five late night show. He was wanting to get back into doing more media work. It was a poor match [0–0] and Chelsea were cruising to the title now.

Wednesday 4 January

Another session with David S. He had asked me to write something on humility and he said he was deeply moved by it. Felt it was a fine piece of writing. I asked him his assessment so far. He felt I had been a bit lost and wandering towards an edge somewhere. He was really worried about me falling back on the drink. He felt now I was confused and that came through in my dreams, that I was really ambivalent about what to do. I said sometimes I felt our chats were a bit meandering but he said there was a process and I was doing fine, way better than a lot of his patients. As I left he asked me what I was doing for the rest of the day. I laughed. 'I was hoping not to have to tell you.' 'Oh my God, what now?' 'I'm going to Chequers for a strategy meeting.' He patted me on the back, laughing. 'I trust you are feeling ambivalent.' Indeed.

I drove down to Chequers. The security was noticeably heavier since the last time I was there. Loads of new gear around. More visible cameras and bollards etc. I arrived as Ruth Kelly was leaving. She seemed a bit surprised to see me, and we had a little chat about the white paper. She said TB was having a rethink of one or two things, but on the big picture was very dug in. As the others arrived, TB asked me, Sally and Philip to go through to his study. Both of them said they thought TB's position was more difficult than at any time before. The problem was answering the question what was TB for, given we all knew he was leaving? He was the proven election winner but now he was not standing again so what was he for, what was his purpose? And also why always facing us up to problems the whole time, when he wouldn't be the one dealing with the fallout? His note said the ideal way forward was that he work with GB for the handover after getting through his reforms. If we didn't win on the white paper without Tory support, it would be a big blow. He felt if we had to concede too much there was no point doing it.

His take was very down on GB, said they had a long chat yesterday and he was seeing him here tomorrow, but he was not hopeful of things improving. All the time he felt there was something that stopped him short of being a leader. GB just did not buy the analysis that New Labour won votes or that TB still had appeal in some quarters. 'He thinks the public see me as he does, and I did point out to him he was a some-what more biased observer.' He said he knew he was in difficulty but he felt they could still win people round on the white paper. I'm not sure about that. I said Ruth looked a bit shot to me. 'She'll be fine.' He also had problems on ID cards. TB said what GB did the whole time was put out arguments in private against what we were doing, and also against him, and then occasionally say something public by way of defence. But it would always be half-hearted and too late. We went round in circles, just the same old, same old stuff. Two hours of it, but writing this the following day, I cannot remember much.

He was wearing a very odd purple shirt with a criss-cross pattern that was too tight. He was surrounded by a pile of red boxes, which reminded me of the workload before. I felt neither in nor out. Not central, but expected to be. Not firing, but expected to be. Not on top of everything, but talked to as though I was. He was determined to go on a bit yet and would not be pushed out prematurely without his policies getting through. If he was – if GB came to office on the back of him being defeated over reforms – the Tories would be the only winners. If GB took over in those circumstances, we would lose the centre ground in a totally self-inflicted way. The party had still not got used to what needed to be done to win. GB was so desperate to be PM he was mistaking what he needed to do to bring it about. He kept asking TB to lash out at DC over this line or that. Wait a bit, see what he offers, set him challenges he won't be able to meet.

Sally felt a lot of his problems came from the party not being sure what his motives were, especially on schools. I think he was using this pre-meeting just to get a load of stuff off his chest, then everyone else was arriving for the broader meeting. Liz, Matthew T, John McTernan [director of political operations], DH and HC just back from Cuba, Matthew D, Ruth Turner, Ben W-P, Huw Evans, me, Sally and PG. It was all a bit flat. He said the best way is for him and GB to work together on reform and he has to try to make that happen. It kicked off a bit later when he was saying there was a bit missing here and I said it is the bit that says we have moved politics to the centre, the Tories are coming on our ground so we can move a bit left. He said that is so pea-brained it's not even worth considering. It may be, I said, but that is the argument that is gaining ground in the party, it is making him less relevant, he had to defeat it and that meant taking it on. There was no real oomph to the discussion. Lots of OK points but generally a bit dispiriting. Virtually everything came back to him and GB, and also the lack of operational capability. He then moved on to other stuff, more about forward policy, and I decided to go.

I was quite pleased to leave. I had not felt like I really wanted to be there, and I felt I was not firing and nor was he. We were not good for each other when we were like that, and we were sending out bad signals. Liz asked me if we had had a row in the earlier meeting. No, I said, but this was going round in circles, and he was putting too much pressure on me to sort GB. I couldn't do it without a plan agreed genuinely between them. Driving home, I had mixed feelings, but predominantly feeling the problem that I could only make this work if I was there, totally committed and central. I had always had to be on top of everything, or it didn't work. But when TB had gone through the foreign policy stuff earlier I had just not felt engaged. David S said when I saw him earlier that it was obviously important for me that I was doing big things and being recognised for the role I had, but he felt the dreams were showing frustration at same old, same old. Today was definitely a case of that.

Thursday 5 January

Bruce [Grocott] came round in the morning to see the diaries and have a chat. I wanted his take on whether and how I could do them without damaging the government, the party and my own reputation for saying it like it is. He skimread, punctuated by regular laughs but also 'ouch', and occasionally 'Oh God, I had forgotten that.' His overall assessment – brilliant, had to be done, but right to be worried. He agreed there was no rush so just get it all down on paper. He mainly read 1994 and he felt there was no problem with any of it, but later, including after reading about Neil going crazy at me on holiday, he said he felt there was some material that could only be published when we were out. Fiona was with us for some of the time, so they agreed loudly about education while I interspersed with jokes about election-losing strategies. They had a shared bogeyman in Adonis to go on about.

Bruce felt TB was in a really bad way, politically. On education – the MPs felt he just didn't get it. They felt he was pushing as hard and fast as he could towards a kind of covert selection. He was clear he should stay for a while and also that GB was really the only option. Bruce felt I should become an MP, get in the Cabinet ASAP, and think about the leadership. If not, he said, I must go to the Lords and get in the Cabinet that way. He said the Lords was Vauxhall conference not Premier League, 'but you're still on the pitch'. I said I am on the pitch now, but with a real sense of ambivalence. And 'Where there is doubt, there is no doubt.' I had real doubt. Not just about getting a seat, or going for the Cabinet, let alone even thinking about leadership.

I had doubt about everything right now. BG said he had seen a lot of political animals in his time and he knew nobody who had my mix of talents and felt sure I could make the jump easily, get and win and fall in love with a seat, and really go for it. 'You'd be a minister straight away. A big party voice, you'd have loads of MPs supporting you.' It was nice to see him. Such a constant voice. Bradders called to speak to him about a TB tribute to Merlyn Rees [former Labour Cabinet minister]. Another death. Bruce set off at lunchtime, as Mark arrived and we started on the second [Blair] term. Stephen Jones [rugby player] called – he was going to Llanelli and was worried about how to talk about Cardiff, whose coach got him, but then Stephen changed his mind. I said to be nice about them all, and be yourself.

Friday 6 January

Charlie Kennedy had finally confessed publicly to a drink problem and I was getting loads of bids on him, and on drink/politics. I turned them all down. I really felt for him, and dropped him a line, but it was hard to see how he would hold out. If I think about how hard it was to stop drinking when I did, when I was under no pressure to go back to work, I can't imagine doing it while in a job like his, and with that spotlight on him. I feared there was no chance they would keep him at the top. Mark and I worked on '01 diary then to [putative editor] Sue Freestone's with Mark and Richard [Stott]. We were going through stuff up to '96. Richard said he had never read anything like the account of my row with Neil in France, and there was a bit of a flare-up with Sue when I said I may drop the NK bit and she said you cannot do that. I said I will do what I want. Row-ette. Good laugh though, Richard stirring mischeviously.

To PG's. Peter M was in town and having dinner with PG and the kids but he didn't really want to see Fiona, because he knew she was so down on the whole TB scene. Sad. I chatted with PG and Georgia beforehand. PG's growing worry for GB was that PG couldn't see where votes were coming from, but he could see where they were being lost. DC was picking up the Liberal votes we thought would go to GB. Rory arrived then PM who said, 'My favourite boy' to R. I said you've not bothered with him for years. Still my favourite boy, he said. As ever

January '06: Charles Kennedy admits to drink problem

all TB–GB. PM funny ha ha re how Cameron was seen as TB successor by all his Rothschild holiday yacht friends in French West Indies, e.g. I asked them whether they preferred the most socialist member of the Cabinet or a nice charming young man, well educated, who wants to carry on building in the centre ground. But when we got serious he was in a way more up on GB than PG and I. He felt he was intelligent and driven enough to work it out. Perhaps PG and I had seen him too often of late, but we said there had not been much evidence so far.

He said GB was driven by two things – a burning desire to be PM and an absolute belief that TB and all close to him were conspiring to stop him. That was why he wanted me involved because he was trying to pull me over according to what he once said – TB without Peter M and AC has no strength. He said our role and duty was to rehabilitate GB, persuade him to do the things he needed to do to be in the centre. He wasn't convinced he really was a reformer though. He felt TB and he had broken down but something could be rebuilt. Meantime we had to change GB. PG was really pushing David M as a possible alternative. PM said there was no alternative at all. DM was not strong enough. Hilary Benn was not known. CC was not right for the public. It had to be a rehabilitated GB. He was scathing of the 'concession strategy', which is how he saw the TB–GB plan Philip and I had put together for the last election. 'Nonetheless, you seem to have ended up in the same place,' I said. Yes, but he felt it was demeaning for TB and the lack of strength that flowed from that was now a problem.

He was friendly, clearly quite enjoying himself in Brussels, gossipy and bitchy about colleagues and processes, and very funny in his usual self-parodying way. He and Gail seemed to think GB would step up to the mark. Having just transcribed the 2001 campaign, I was not so sure. It had been a nightmare and he had not shown leadership. PG was far too open about some of our discussions with TB. I worried what he said elsewhere. PM made the interesting observation that GB had never really been punished for the things he did that were wrong. He got away with it because he was not the main man. But now people were looking at him in a different way, and remembering things about him, and worrying about his leadership. But he was still the best option and we should probably work for it. PG saying what should AC and I do in these circumstances? He said probably what we were doing, given we had started out on this road.

Rory and I then left for dinner with Fiona at the Camden Brasserie. It was bad that Peter had felt she shouldn't be there, but probably right given what we had been talking about. She felt I should disengage from them, but that I couldn't. Said I put them before anything apart from the kids. She said she felt it was time for me to do something in my own right, nothing to do with any of them. Nice enough evening. But still tough and my head was still not right.

Saturday 7 January

I went out for a run in the afternoon, to try to chase away the dark clouds that were crowding in again. I was coming back via Little Venice and stopped to get a bottle of water from the shop near the canal. As I was paying, it came on the radio that Charles [Kennedy] had quit. Inevitable, I guess, but sad. It means Cameron will be the longest-serving leader come the next election. Watched *Schindler's List*. Brilliant. Really powerful. Burnley knocked out of the Cup by Derby [2–1]. JP called again about his council tax problems. He was due to see TB tomorrow. He asked how 'the patient' was. Meaning TB–GB. I said is it a patient or an illness. 'I don't know, but it's giving us all a fucking headache.'

Sunday 8 January

JP called, apologetic as ever about bothering me, but now seriously worried about his council tax issue. Basically he had misled people on it because he hadn't known the full facts, and had said what he thought to be true rather than what he knew. TB felt a minimalist statement was the best way to deal with it, and I sent over a draft. Not fully knowing or understanding the facts either, there were a few holes in it, but I said he must get it gone over by someone who knows. He sounded very down, said life at this level was shit, just dealing with rubbish like this all the time. He was even talking about jacking it in. Said he was definitely not standing next time. I wondered at one point, when he was asking about my own plans, whether he might not ask me to go for it. On TB–GB he said he was going to give it one more go. People in No. 10 were saying he was really offside at the moment but that was because nobody was managing him properly. He sounded down on both of them.

PG sent over the latest iteration of the note for forward TB–GB strategy and asked me to beef it up. Good note, setting out four phases – TB leadership/reform, transition, GB leadership, election. It had to be moulded into a coherent whole. A lot of this was about trust then operationalising a plan. We were due to have another meeting with them this week and I decided if nothing moved forward, I was not going to continue. Fiona was convinced I wanted back in. She didn't get my total ambivalence, or appreciate how hard I was finding this, how complex. Out for a run, then to see *Match Point*, which Fiona and Grace enjoyed, and I thought was totally dire. Dinner with Tessa and David, but I was avoiding political talk as much as I could. I was feeling very down about it all. PG called saying he had seen a new poll, GB ratings diving from 62 to 47, still reasonably high but vulnerable. TB was up, Cameron lifting the Tories but not massively, and he was polling ahead of his party as did, most of the time, TB. GB on a down definitely. Loads of people saying it. Brendan [Foster] had called for a natter, and he said he thought GB would struggle as PM, and not win an election. With a change of prism – TB heading to exit, GB arriving in No. 10 – people were starting to see both of them in a different light, and scoring TB up, GB down.

Monday 9 January

Another David S session with Fiona. I said we had made ten steps forward, nine steps back, and every setback sparked a plunge. He tried to get Fiona to talk about what it had been like for her when I was full on in No. 10, and it wasn't easy listening. She relived the start, in 1994, when she knew I would do it, and how I left early from holiday. How I had been uncaring when her dad died because I was so fixated about getting back to work. That felt harsh, but he interrupted and said I had to listen, and I had to hear. She said I could be impatient and intolerant. I set ridiculously high standards for myself, and expected them of everyone else, which could be tough. He said he had felt that my essay on humility showed a deep understanding of all of this, but I had a blind spot about admitting things could have been different, and meaning it. He said we both needed to move from acceptance to forgiveness.

Fiona said maybe we should both get out of politics / campaigns but if one in, or two, we both have to be able to do it all on our own terms. She said she found the way we did politics dehumanising, me disagreeing, saying politics basically good, she says basically bad. Him saying I have a strong sense of duty, that if asked to help I have to do it. Her saying I did not apply the same approach to helping her. He said at least when a man goes off with another woman, women kind of understand because they know it happens. But Fiona sees this as me having left her for a job, and since I came back, I have made it clear that I would rather be back with the job. But it wasn't as simple as that. I was getting back into longer runs but still not feeling great.

Tuesday 10 January

All morning going over Richard's suggested cuts. Run for an hour or so, bad idea because I still had some kind of virus and horrible skin blemishes. The *News of the World* asked for a guest column. PG called saying TB–GB seems sweetness and light after their various meetings. I was seeing TB tomorrow then both of them on Thursday. They had better have moved on, or else I am out. I was feeling more and more disengaged, yet also guilty at being so. Peter M sent me a text saying, 'Your/our duty is to rehabilitate GB for the public.' He'd called from Vienna yesterday but had barely begun the conversation when he got called back into his meeting. Mark B said I wonder if there is a page of any diary entry that does not have TB–GB at its heart. Anji called having seen Dickie Attenborough [actor, filmmaker and Labour peer], who wanted to help with an exit strategy. He knew them both, got on with them both and he was basically volunteering to help. I felt TB had to stop worrying about legacy, just do stuff and then go. He was doing the 'respect' agenda today, getting massive coverage and not bad though the sneerers would sneer.

There was a lot in it, the national parenting academy, action to deal with bad parenting and problem families, up to evictions, greater powers for community cops. He did a big speech in No. 10, a stack of interviews, a visit down to Swindon and a *Newsnight* special. He was buzzing with it later, said he could tell when out and about that this was the area where people felt they wanted us on their side, the low level abuse and anti-social behaviour. He said this was the stuff GB didn't get at the emotional level. But if we don't do this, Cameron will, and he will look like he means it. In fact, Cameron was out on much the same agenda, calling it 'Real Respect', and dismissing the TB stuff as gimmicky. At least today looked like there had been a bit of proper planning and co-ordination. They had sixteen different ministers out doing different parts of it all. The audience at the *Newsnight* special was tough, and he was finding it hard to hide contempt for some of them. Very much in 'I know I'm right' mode but he was sure he had public backing. Cameron came over as a bit Lib Demish on it. That was probably because the Lib Dems' leadership turmoil was going on, but in the long term I think it was the wrong move for him.

Wednesday 11 January

Interview with *The League* re Burnley. Calum doing his politics exam.
New schedule from Steve Loraine [triathlon coach]. To No. 10 for PST.
Mark Penn did a polling presentation to TB and a small pre-meeting.
His main point was that we are back into a two-horse party dynamic.
LDs down 5 and the split is falling the Tories' way. Cameron has persuaded people he is trying to move to the centre even if people are
still not sure of his party. TB ratings up to his best since the election,
GB favourability rating down from 61 to 46. The general mood of the
country was not bad. Views on Iraq were slightly better. Mood on the
economy was down. They had tested various attacks on DC and 'Not
sure what he believes' was the strongest, allied to the party as a whole
not changed. TB approval numbers had gone from 46/51 to 52/46.
Cameron favourability 45/24. Horse race neck and neck. TB strong on
terrorism and security issues, but we were dipping on the economy.

Trust was still the main negative. 'Time for a change' was not as
strong as I thought it would be, and would worry the Tories if they
were getting the same message. DC numbers were too good, though,
suggesting he could definitely drive a message of change if he got a
fair wind behind him. 'Securing Britain's Future' type messages were
the best for us. On the timing of TB going, 'after a few months' was still
top, 35 per cent, but 'stay the entire term' was up 6 at 27, and among
Labour supporters, it was 46, easily the highest. 'I'll leave you to tell
Gordon,' TB said. 'Happily,' I said. 'He will assume the other 54 want
him in tomorrow.' The discussion was OK, and teasing out the main
tactical questions on handling DC.

TB felt that the key was New Labour, that there was no point saying
DC wasn't really changing the Tories because he clearly was trying to
move to the centre ground, and we just looked stupid if we pretended
he wasn't. The response from us should be confident, it shows we have
won the arguments, and the question for the Tories is whether they
match the rhetoric and positioning with the policy changes needed to
make it real. He said he had not got the language right on this but the
key was to take New Labour to the next level. I said people don't see it
as vertical but horizontal, left and right. We need to be the ones giving
definition to a different sort of politics in which the linear boundaries
are less clear.

TB said it was clear DC was going to hug us on policy, make clear
he felt TB was not really Labour, once he went Labour would revert
to type and he – DC – would be the natural successor, a changed Tory

Party led by a right-of-centre moderniser following a changed Labour Party led by a left-of-centre moderniser. Then, like Bush, once in power they would go more right-wing. The question then was where did differentiation come from? TB's answer was to be patient, let them be the ones who panic and make mistakes. At the moment his party are letting him away with it because they think it is popular. But they will quickly tire of me too-ism, and they will want traditional Tory differentiation. It was a good discussion in some ways, but again the next steps were hanging there – what to do about the education white paper vote; and GB. TB had had a series of one on one sessions with GB and they seemed to be getting on fine at the moment. TB felt he was getting there. When he felt vulnerable, GB always reached out more. We were due for another meeting tomorrow, this time the original five added to by DA and Ed M, in No. 11 dining room. TB said he felt it would be better. Penn asked me if I was interested in working for Burson Marsteller [New York-based international PR company]. I said I would see him on his next trip.

Fiona told me NK was chairing the Compass event she was due to speak at, and she said he was doing something in *The Guardian* tomorrow and they would present it as Neil being critical of TB. I didn't want to discuss it. I had known for a while Neil was doing it, and of course as Fiona and Melissa [Benn] were the main speakers, it would get us embroiled in the TB v party, TB–GB stuff, just when I felt F and I were getting to a better place. She felt it was all about mutual respect and me not supporting her in her education campaigning, me saying I was happy to, but I was not going to go down the road of making life more difficult for TB and the government, because we had enough people doing that already. She said she felt we both had to be in this political world, or both out. I couldn't see the logic of that. Right in the middle, TB called, said he was surer than ever that the response to DC was to stay firm as New Labour, hold the centre ground.

Thursday 12 January

The *Guardian* splash, as expected, was on Neil being critical. I told Fiona I was sad he had crossed the Rubicon, that it had been to his credit and a strength to the party that he never publicly criticised TB, even when he disagreed, and the route from this to being like Frank Dobson or Peter Kilfoyle [Labour MP, critical of the government] was an easy one, especially as he would be showered with praise. I felt he had known enough about how tough it was not to do it, and of course there was the added element of it being attached to Fiona's education paper, and her event. I said I did not want to be thought as of crossing the same Rubicon as Neil, so it was probably better not to attend the event. That set off another great round of TB being more important than her, never supported her etc. This stuff just went on and on. I was currently doing 1997 diary editing and 2001 transcribing and it has been like this on and off for years.

Did a bit of speech work then into No. 10 as the Cabinet political meeting was ending. Saw CC, HA, Bruce, all said the mood was good. TB had squared GB to come in on the same script. PG had done a presentation and said the mood was better than for ages. But Bruce said it was like there was an elephant in the room not being discussed – the education white paper. HA said she really disagreed with Fiona's analysis. She said Neil wave-making was very much noticed. TB said to me he was surprised Neil had done it, as he had always tried to be supportive of him, whether over going to the Lords, or when he talked him up in the European Commission, the British Council, public statements, when in fact he sometimes felt Neil had left too many policy positions ambiguous, that he took a lot of the right steps forward needed at the time, but not all of them. He felt he could quickly become oppositionalist, which would be sad. PG felt the same.

TB–GB had a longish pre-meeting, just the two of them, while PG, the Eds and DA and I had a chat in No. 11. The mood was OK, but the Eds were still adopting slightly silly positions, Ed B for example thinking we should keep telling the public they were wrong if they thought DC had really changed. Ed M so did not get the crime and security agenda. He was totally on this notion that we made it worse the more we talked about it. Douglas seemed to me to have developed and come along a lot. He was far more confident of asserting his own view, not just echoing GB as the others tended to, and at one or two points he disagreed with GB, and his main point was pretty much the same as TB's – stay in the centre, let them try to come on, wait for them to press for the points of differentiation. In the meantime, we agreed TB should this weekend at the Policy Forum signal that GB will set out future challenges in a series of speeches and events. At least that gave a sense of them operating as a team.

As he and TB walked in and saw us there, GB said, 'Ah, like the start of the election all over again.' I said I hoped not. John, his son, was there, and Hannah the nanny. Nice little kid but very quiet. GB was much more friendly to TB and also listening more when we sat down to dinner, and less whingy. Ed B was the one pushing hardest for a 'Cameron is still a right-wing Tory' attack. TB said that may be right or wrong, but his instinct was that it was too much in contradiction to what the public were seeing and hearing and so we would look shrill and panicky. Far better to say they are in retreat because they have lost all the big arguments but what will they do policy-wise to meet the future challenges? Then we have to work to get the dividing lines on those, and on the policy prescriptions. The other thing we needed was GB to express what New Labour meant to him in his own terms, but there had to be a shared philosophical approach around the theme of the community delivering for the individual, empowerment etc.

I said we were missing tricks on DC. While we waited to get agreement between the two of them on topline approach, we did not hit DC hard enough on current points of vulnerability. We needed to have horses for courses, different people attacking on different lines. TB said DC strategy was hug us close on policy and turn it all into a beauty contest. I said it was a bit more sophisticated. It was to hug on policy but present TB as a passing aberration to be admired as political and strategic genius – but exceptional – and soon it would be back to old-fashioned politician GB. That made it easier to make it a beauty contest. So we had to stay in the centre ground together, but also we had to have a different GB out there, with TB in harmony. That was best done soon around education.

Salmon, salad, onion tart, fruit salad. GB kicked off, TB then the rest of us chipping in. We agreed – again – there had to be more stuff written down and circulated. On organisation, I said we need new people, fresh blood, we are all too samey and know each other too well. We need a short paper on the challenges, on the dividing lines we want to set, and on a multi-layered plan for DC. There were no volunteers when we talked about whether we should go back to daily meetings. My heart really sank at that one, and I said so, though I knew we would end up at that at some point. I said we needed a Jeremy Heywood [former senior civil servant]-type person in there for the transition, and we needed two or three either side who were working together on a daily basis. We need to find these people quickly. 'Your side will obviously have to wear white shirts,' I said, and they laughed, once the penny dropped. They were sitting in a row wearing identical white shirts with ties, and we were sitting there with a collection of tie-less casual gear. GB's shirt was covered in ink stains.

Ruth Kelly was getting into all sorts of bother over sex offenders working in schools, and it had the feel of something going wrong. I asked TB if it might be a reason for moving her on, 'or is that heresy?' Yes it is, he said. At the end I went through to No. 10 with TB to get some bottles signed for charity and he said he was really disappointed about Neil. He knew Neil had difficulties with him but they had always had an agreement that he could always have access to make whatever point he wished, but he would keep his arguments and criticisms private. I said I feared years of frustration were going to spill out. It was another bad straw in the wind. I said I was seeing Neil tomorrow because Burnley were playing at Cardiff. Eyebrows raised. He felt re GB that he was getting there but the flaw remained and he was alarmed at some of the nonsense Ed B in particular was talking. It was old left/right stuff, which did not take account of a changed mood, changed politics, in part by us. We had always been good defining political big picture and had to do that again now. TB off to do a NI thing. JoP seeing Martin McGuinness. Tell him he comes out well in my diaries, I said. So do you. Home, bit more work, another up and downer re me, work, in or out, never fucking ends. Call from Stephen Parkinson [former government lawyer] about a speech at his law firm re Hutton etc.

Saturday 14 January
Up at six today to run 10 miles – I was slowly getting back into the triathlon training groove with Steve's programme. Set off for Neil's with Calum. Rachel [Kinnock's daughter] and the kids were there. Neil off sneaking a fag somewhere. Glenys looking better. They'd had a great time in Tobago. I said I was surprised he went public with the attack on the white paper, because once you crossed the Rubicon it was hard to pull back. She said he didn't do interviews and would not speak out on other issues but he really felt it. Good chat with Neil on the way to the Cardiff–Burnley game, and on the way back – he was a lot more mellow than before. He went through why he felt the education WP was such a problem, he really felt TB was pushing the party too hard, but basically he was supportive of the strategy re DC. I told him without going into all the grisly detail about the TB–GB lunches and he was fine with that. Later when Glenys said TB should be clearer he wants GB to take over, Neil said what could be clearer than sitting in a room with him plotting the succession? They were due to have dinner with GB soon and he intended to say again, relax, chill out, be yourself as was without all the new-found angst.

He also bought my idea that TB was the key to the endorsement of him as successor, and the more they worked together the better. We just had to get back to that now. Neil very supportive generally and ditto Glenys when I explained to her what was going on. Later I told TB he should call him, say he understood he was seeing GB and be assured the transition plan was real. TB thought OK to do that. He had been worried Neil would think he was being heavied. The football was poor, and we lost 3–0. Sam Hamman [Cardiff owner] took Calum to the tunnel and dressing rooms. Calum came back, said Hamman was wacky. I did some media to promote the next round of fundraising I was doing for Burnley FC. Back home, watched the coverage of GB's speech on Britishness. It was OK, but felt a bit flimsy, cheesy even, the idea of a national day to celebrate British identity. The point about reclaiming the flag was important in terms of pushing back against the far right, but it didn't feel like a reform speech, it felt like he was looking around for new and fresh themes short of big reform messages. And inevitably, the hacks were on to the point about a Scottish MP leading the UK post-devolution, and how the speech was in part pre-empting that as a line of attack.

Sunday 15 January

Golf at Highgate with with David Mills, Andrew Cahn [British Airways executive, former civil servant] and a banker. I played not bad considering I had not played in ages. 2k swim in the afternoon. TB called as I was leaving the pool. He was trying to sort out the Ruth Kelly situation. It was becoming clear there were a lot more people with criminal records working in schools – including sex offenders – than we thought. He was thinking ahead to the reshuffle and I sensed he was thinking about her going for the first time. He said with GB it was better but though he felt yesterday's Britishness speech was OK, he felt they saw it as a substitute for New Labour. It was also too obviously about making the argument that it was OK to have a Scot in charge.

He felt what I had said to GB was good the other day but he could tell Ed B didn't buy it. He said he had been picking up more signs from people that they liked him as Chancellor, worried about him as PM. He said he felt the public liked his strength but they wanted strength allied to a feeling the strong person 'gets' them. They sense he doesn't get their lives. If they heard Balls at that dinner they'd understand why. He says, 'Why can't we make Cameron be more right-wing?' It doesn't work like that. I remembered, and passed on, an interesting point made by Neil yesterday: 'The centre is not an easy place. It is not a sum of different parts but has difficult choices at every stage.'

Monday 16 January

Slept in, tired after all the exercise yesterday and with a nasal nightmare. The chlorine just killed me but where else could I do the swim training? Grace was off school with a virus so I pottered around looking after her in the morning, while working on the *News of the World* column – Cameron v Gordon, Sven keeping on keeping on (after being entrapped by the *NotW* saying during the qualifying campaign that he would be willing to leave for Villa if England won the World Cup!) Then Parna called and said could I go in for lunch with TB and GB? Fucking hell. This was like every day at the moment. I saw him on his own first. He said GB's Britishness speech was a perfectly OK speech, but it is obvious he is trying to sound modern without actually pushing forward the reform agenda. He must stick with reform, and he must show he is up for doing the tough stuff. There is no point Gordon trying to do fluffy. I told him and later told GB what Neil had said – we need to make the argument that the centre is not an easy place but the place for tough decisions. TB said what do we want out of the meeting? I got PG in. We both felt they needed a work programme and new people. TB a bit down on GB again. I thought the Britishness speech was OK provided he now moved on to other areas.

GB arrived – nice mood, congratulations all around on the news that Sarah was pregnant again – he said he was so old he needed someone young for John to play with. There had been a definite downgrade in the catering at No. 11 this time – crap sandwiches, sausage rolls. As Ed M said – this is like a CLP dinner in Normanton [Ed Balls' constituency]. That triggered a fair amount of bonhomie as we swapped stories of bad food at CLP fundraisers. Everyone was of the view Ruth K was in trouble. TB and I had drawn up a note for him to speak to, and try to get some decisions. We agreed there had to be a TB–GB weekly meeting focused on making sure the four-stage strategy plan was unfolded. They wanted me to have a weekly meeting with key people to make sure it was on track. A grid group focused towards the election. Proper work done on policy dividing lines. The Tories were clearly hoping to turn small state v big state to an advantage, and we had to make that all about security. Identity cards was part of that. They were on the wrong side of the civil liberties divide.

We had to turn Cameron's strength into a weakness – he was good at PR. He was quick on gimmicks. That had to become a lack of seriousness. GB felt that Cameron was trying to present himself as a bit of a liberal, but with the view of moving back to the right if they won, and he felt his right wing would let him away with it for a while. The focus on the voluntary sector was designed to make him look modern, but it was about the state shedding responsibility for services. GB – 'The voluntary sector is not that great if you're about to get mugged.' He said the Tories cannot get to an 'on your side' position without losing their edge. They want to say Labour put money in but we will look after you personally, focus on the individual. They have to differentiate to the right. TB said the public are more likely to go for a traditional Tory Party more than traditional Labour Party. He thought Cameron was making a mistake in appearing to soften on law and order, and go big on the environment. Philip and I said he had to understand this was not about policy at this stage, it was about rebranding, and he was doing it perfectly well by his own lights.

Ed M said Cameron was recognising that the country was more progressive than the last time they had been in power, and he was trying to get the Tories to adapt. TB said yes, culturally there has been change, but don't underestimate how much they can still get from a traditional agenda. Douglas said this was what [Michael] Portillo [former Tory MP and Cabinet minister] had been trying to agitate for, hard-headed on the economy but socially liberal. GB: 'They think you should be able just to take drugs and have freedom without responsibility.' TB felt we had to move on state funding of parties, and limits to spending. He worried a modernised Tory Party would win back lost donors. He said we should get the Libs on board for it. We had a brief discussion on the Lib Dems. They were in a mess but we had to assume they would sort themselves out.

TB said maybe Cameron will hug us so close on policy they leave no gap at all in which case we have to redraw the dividing lines and force them into panic. Tory MPs will only put up with the fluffy stuff for so long. He said they're good but no better than us. He was adamant what Cameron really needed was to get into crime. Today Cameron went for crap cops. It was OK on one level but not sensible to have cops offside. If GB was out on crime, he would get respect with the cops, and the Tories would worry they did the wrong thing. The big coverage of GB's Britishness speech showed lots of interest in him and he had to go for it. TB banging on about crime – same old, same old. I said if you do this, Gordon, take it up as an issue where you think Cameron has mis-stepped, it will have impact. It could make DC look trivial and GB look strong on the message of securing Britain's future, which is where he has to be come an election – securing the future is a perfect way of allying change and continuity. We agreed to meet again on Thursday. It had been better than previous meetings. I went for a coffee downstairs with Bradders. He said I would never escape because I was the only one trusted by both.

Home, another heart-to-heart, Fiona feeling that me leaving would lead to real change, and it hasn't. I was back for the election, which was fine, but now back for the transition, and she could see what was happening with GB, that he was trying to make me feel indispensable, and then he would play on the guilt just like TB did. She said she felt she should get a job independent of me, have her own thing to do, get away from this dark cloud. She thought I was being too hard on her about the Compass event. PG thought I was being too soft. David Blunkett was round for dinner. He had lost weight, was feeling down clearly, he was doing a regular *Sun* column so could keep his voice out there, but basically he was wanting to know I thought he had a chance of another comeback. I said it was hard to see under TB now, and I could definitely ask GB if he wanted me to. He said if I could find out subtly, he'd appreciate that. I said my basic feeling about GB was that he would recognise you had real ability, the only thing would be whether he saw it as a risk.

He was also interested in doing more broadcasting. I said he had to decide first if he intended to stay as an MP, and then develop out from there. He still had the [Special Branch] cops who were a great help in terms of logistics and making his life work, but they would not be there for ever. He was not nearly as lively as he usually is, and the resignation saga had hit him really hard. He wasn't happy, I could tell. He and Fiona had a chat about her education campaign. He said that was the job he really wanted. It was a nice enough evening but after he left I realised Fiona was really angry that Philip had said he intended to 'punish her' for her Compass event. 'You lot are pathetic,' she said, and that was that.

Tuesday 17 January

Cathy Gilman [Leukaemia Research] came round for a chat about future events. She wanted me to get celebs in to do the triathlon. Fiona very frosty, and I wrote one of my angry emails but decided not to send. I was heading up to see Mum, and when we spoke by phone later, it just made it worse. It was becoming a dialogue of the deaf. She felt I refused to see things from her perspective. I felt the same that she couldn't see things from mine, and we went round in circles. I spoke to Grace and she said, 'Mum seems very sad.' That brought it home I had to do more to try and sort this. I gave Graeme [brother] a lift to Stansted, nice chat with him, but it meant I was not home till three.

Wednesday 18 January

Fiona was very nice when I woke up, apologised for overreacting yesterday, and we went for a walk with the dog. We went over the same old ground, and I could feel myself losing it, it was tipping point time. We were up in the little woody area near Kenwood House, she was saying we didn't seem able to meet each other's expectations any more, everything was such hard work, and I said I've tried and I've tried and what more can I do, and I felt a rage rising that was almost overwhelming, I knew I was lurching out of control, and I tried to walk away, but I knew she would take that badly, so I stayed and then I started punching myself in the face, four times, really hard, and I could see she went almost white, and I said this is driving me fucking crazy, and it has to stop, one way or the other. I said you've asked me to leave, and I had left. 'And now you are virtually back, and this is what it is doing to you. It is making you ill,' she said. 'I am not ill,' I said, but I knew I was.

This was fucking crazy stuff. I could feel my left eye swelling up. I leaned on a tree, I felt like crying but I held it back. I took a few deep breaths, I said listen, I have tried everything, I am seeing someone, I am on loads of medication, I am trying really hard. 'OK,' she said, 'but TB only has to call and you're off in there to help.' That is because he needs help, and he is running out of people who can give it to him. 'Why always you?' she said. Because that is the way it is, because I can. 'But you hate it?' No, not always, what I hate are all the conflicting pressures. 'It is making you ill again. You have to see that. And that is affecting all of us.' My face was hurting now, I had a headache, I was worried people had seen and heard what had gone on. We just about managed to stay civil on the walk back home but fuck this was grim, and tomorrow was her big event in Parliament and I was expected to go along and feel happy at a load of them basically slagging off the government, her and Neil included. I went upstairs to do some work, but I felt totally exhausted now. I sent her a message saying sorry for losing it, let's hope that was the high watermark of this particular wave of madness, and 'We'll work it out'.

Thursday 19 January

Fiona was doing a fair bit of media in advance of her event tonight. It was not going to be easy, because I didn't agree with some of the things she was saying, and I was bound to get drawn into it, and the media were enjoying that part of it, and it was getting a big build-up. I went to see David S and went through yesterday's flip-out. He said it sounded like we had managed to get things on to a calm level, but the underlying issues were all there, and so a storm just erupted, and then it was calm again. I said I guess so. He asked me what I had been thinking about when I was hitting myself, and I said I didn't know, I was out of control. Was I trying to hurt myself, really hurt myself? Yes. So it was self-harm? I guess so. Did you have any suicidal thoughts, then or later? I don't think so. I just felt in a total rage. He felt that F and I had a very intense relationship and it was almost like I was an appendage of her and she of me, so fear of loss is huge, like loss of limb, or loss of life. I said I felt like my head was in a vice, I was being pressurised from different angles by different people for different reasons.

He said I needed to try to understand why I allowed those pressures to build to such a state. Did I feel close to a breakdown? No, it was nothing like when I had a breakdown, though I could easily have done something really stupid. Did you feel violent towards Fiona? No, not at all. I felt angry, and I felt she was pushing the buttons she knew made me angry and pressured, but I could never hit her, I knew that, and also when I was hitting myself, and I saw her face, I realised the fear on there was as much for me as for herself. He had given us a book to read about forgiveness, and we had both tried to read it. Fiona was unclear what she had done that she had to be forgiven for. He laughed. 'Whereas you…' He said at the end, you know what, I think you're going to end up fine. You are two very strong people, you have been through a lot, but you are a strong couple and I think you will stay so. I said I hope so. It was a good session basically because I was in a better mood. He said just support her at her event tonight. Don't worry about what anyone else thinks, apart from her. Don't worry what the media say. Don't worry if people think it is odd or not odd that you are there. Just be there for her, that is all you need to think about. OK? OK.

I did a bit of work on the *News of the World* column, and then off to No. 10. Ruth Kelly just about surviving in the Commons. TB seemed a bit down and clearly he was dreading yet another session. He was in with GB for half an hour telling him he had to branch out, be more upfront about reforms etc. We – the Eds, DA, PG and I – had a bit of chat, mainly small talk as we waited. Ed Miliband was becoming a bit grander. Funny how 'MP' changes people sometimes. Again, we were a bit more structured and focused. TB said we needed to have third parties making the point that it could be a fatal mistake for DC to ape New Labour rather than reinvent Tories. They were vulnerable on law and order, and civil liberties. GB felt these needed to be part of bigger themes, globalisation, security, social change. Who could best empower people to meet the new challenges? What was a responsible society? He felt if TB were to set out big goals on child poverty, for example, which Cameron would want to match, then he – GB – would be able to show that only we could do the policy required.

He had moved to our side of the argument on how the ID cards issue could hurt them as social liberals in a party of social conservatives. We could do the same with regard to 'equipping you for the future'. A new deal for jobs flexibility. Either they have to support it or we say they have no response to the challenges of globalisation. Then they are the same old Tories. Laissez faire, can't make sense of global change that way. TB and GB were finally coming together in roughly the same place. Cameron was making a big thing of the voluntary sector but it cannot replace government. There has to be a role for government. Philip felt that Cameron would try to make himself the future, GB the past. But on security, people wanted strength and GB had to pitch himself as strength and security v weakness/flip-flop. Douglas thought Cameron was pitching himself first at professional middle-class people. He was reopening the door to a proper conversation. He would go liberal but then once the door was open he would go back to white van man. TB felt he would want to stay in the centre and 'We have to block them off'.

On education, GB felt we could get to investment as a dividing line, by setting the goal that state schoolkids get the same level of investment as private. That sounded a tough reach. GB felt we had to pin them down to accept details of our spending. I had another go at asking TB to hit private schools re charitable status.* Non-starter. TB said the

* Private schools were presumed to provide public benefit and therefore could automatically claim charitable status.

next phase has to be about them coming to terms with us and the next phase after that about their policy. They will shift whatever they need to shift but it will become a problem over time, not least because of his right wing. I said the key thing for GB is strength if allied to on your side. His strength has to be allied to the things people care about. He is strong on the economy, public services, but low-profile on law and order. That has to change. We also need to build a cohort of people willing to talk up GB as serious and strong, cf. DC. We should let Cameron hug us on policy, but then make sure the differentiation comes later, and he either looks redundant or right-wing. Looking ahead to conference, the idea has to be that Cameron talks about modernising his party. TB–GB did it. Their strategy rests on GB not changing and not going the New Labour route. If he stays in the centre it is hard for DC.

I ran home, saw Grace, then out with Fiona for her event. To Parliament. Big crowds, clips, being filmed. Jackie Ashley yacking. Neal Lawson [Compass] in his element, though constantly referred to as 'Mark' by NK. Neil went OTT in a very Neil-ish, witty way and was going to steal all the headlines. Fiona and Melissa both more measured and strong. F the one most on top of detail. Estelle [Morris] was excellent. Angela Eagle [former junior minister] came over as a bit self-satisfied. The NUT guy [Steve] Sinnott [general secretary] was not bad, audience very strong for the platform and it was getting loads of coverage. Audrey enjoyed it, smiling proudly and nodding along to everything Fiona said. Someone from the *Sunday Times* had been at the house earlier, which was a real pain, and when I saw they were at the event too, I supposed they were doing something about F, and possibly me, diverging from New Labour. There was too much interest in me being there, for example on the media brief it said both Sky and later *Newsnight* had been saying whether me clapping certain things that Fiona said was 'significant'. Fiona did well and she was clearly pleased I had been there, and I texted DS to say I was reporting in to my controller, to say I had carried out the mission as instructed.

I got driven down by Dennis Stevenson's driver to the Four Seasons near Basingstoke for another Anglo-French colloque. Fabulous place. Beautiful grounds and building and service. I arrived just in time for the main course – sitting with [Sir] John Holmes [UK Ambassador to France], Gerrard Errera [France's Ambassador to the UK], and Vicky Pryce [economist], wife of Chris Huhne [Lib Dem MP]. TB called later, said GB was making everything too complicated. He just had to show he was a reformer. Osborne was doing the after-dinner speech on how the Tories were changing. It was OK, and confirmed our assessment of their strategy. He was good on mood music but in Q&A very weak on detail and was given quite a hard time about Europe, though admittedly this was about as pro-European an audience as you could imagine. But they liked him and there was no doubt there were people moving to him. Ed Balls and I both asked pretty tough questions, trying to pin him on detail. I felt he was weak on where they would differ from us. I felt he was being too tactical, describing it all in terms of how to win votes from this group or that, for example saying we shouldn't talk too much about Europe because it is not what they want to hear in swing marginals, but these were French people, not swing voters. It was frustrating but he did OK overall, I would say.

They definitely saw themselves as being on repositioning and rebranding rather than needing to do big policy stuff at this stage. I had a nice chat with John H and Errera re old times. 'Quelles que soient les circonstances' [a phrase Chirac had used when ruling out military action in Iraq, which led the UK to harden the position] had really hit home. The French felt bruised by it, but I still couldn't see what other interpretation we should have put on it. It was basically Chirac saying there were no circumstances in which they were supporting a second resolution. Nice chat with Christine Ockrent [Belgian broadcaster, mainly in France]. Very bright and very sexy, in a very French way. [Lord] Chris Patten [former Governor of Hong Kong] seemed to want to have a chat about the old days. He was very nice about Neil and Glenys. He said she was by far the most effective MEP during his time there. It was quite a turnout for this kind of event. Michael Jay, David Willetts [shadow Education Secretary] – who looked quite quizzical when listening to Osborne I thought – Ed B, Douglas, [Lord] David Simon [businessman], Phil Stephens [*Financial Times*], Richard Lambert [former editor, *Financial Times*], Andrew Gowers [former editor, *Financial Times*], Eliza Manningham-Buller [director-general, MI5].

Friday 20 January

I didn't sleep well. My pulse rate was above my age – 60, about eight to ten higher than my average – and I should probably have rested but I took the bike out before breakfast. GB was the main event in the morning, so I got back for his speech, and he did well, no notes, big themes, much more impressive than Osborne on substance, but as I said to EB he needs better hair and clothes. I know it is irritating but this stuff matters once you get to the top. But he was very strong on substance, big picture and detail and I think went well. Then we were asked to split into four groups after hearing speeches on four different subjects, and I went for Islam. Really interesting. I was impressed by Sadiq Khan [Labour MP], who was good at setting out the issue from all sides, but had a basic message about inclusion. He had a nice manner too, cheeky chappy but with a bit of substance there. I lobbed in a question against faith schools but they came back on that as an equality issue for them re other religions. The French seemed a bit beleaguered post the riots and had no Muslims at all. But *Le Monde* editor was good, ditto one or two others.

Eliza MB was excellent on the work that needed to be done inside communities, and so was John Holmes. I thought Adair Turner [business-man, academic] was terrific on religion generally – really well informed and funny. He and I went for a run at lunchtime. So much for me not exercising today. Great scenery, down by a canal. We chatted re GB as we ran. He felt there were two GBs and we had seen the good one today, strong and commanding and able to put political thoughts into ideas and language everyone understood. Then there was the GB who had done him over on pensions, rude and paranoid and convinced he knew better than anyone else, and heaven help you if you dared to disagree.

I got back for the second session then my speech with a guy called Casanova. He was funnier than I was but I had a couple of good stories and hope I gave them proper assessment of the current political scene. I did a fair bit on Tory strategy, much of it based on what Osborne and DC had told me. Osborne was in full heckle mode. 'Eye-catching ini-tiatives with which I can be associated,' he shouted out, and a fair few laughed, remembering the TB note he was quoting from when we were on our major reconnection strategy before the last election. David Wil-letts told me earlier that by being sceptic on Europe they could keep the right quiet while they modernised elsewhere. He felt Cameron was serious about that. It was an OK event but I didn't feel I sparkled. Den-nis seemed OK with it. Back to London and to La Casalinga with Fiona and Grace. We were both tired, and drained, but I felt the week ended better. Things were always so much better if she and I were OK.

Saturday 21 January
Last night Rory watched the official Lions DVD and loved it. He thought Donncha O'Callaghan was the star. He felt Clive looked too much like

it was about him. Of course as we lost the Tests, the sales were not exactly going through the roof but I was glad he liked it. I went to the gym for a swim then TB called. He was joking re the media reports saying I was a rebel for having been at Fiona's education event. He said he totally understood I had to go and support Fiona, but he was glad I didn't speak. He felt Neil had been too emotional and as a result he went OTT, and it didn't help anyone. He also felt that Fiona's and my views were coloured by the fact we had the skill and commitment to help turn a school round, and had done so, especially Fiona. But lots don't, parents don't have the time or the commitment or the skills, and he felt if business was willing to help and get involved, why not, as they have a vested interest in schools producing well-educated kids too.

City academies were in the poorest areas and some did well, some did not. But overall standards had improved for those areas. Business partners could help a school drive standards. Self-governing trusts build on that and on foundation schools. He said we were being subjected to a huge welter of misinformation and we were not getting our argument out. I said Ruth and Adonis were not your best people to do this. It may be unfair, but AA hit the wrong buttons for a lot of people, and Ruth didn't command confidence in the way she needed to. He should sit down, write out the main arguments and then get them deployed properly. He needed GB, AJ, CC, this was going beyond just one department now. He said he had told GB this was the time to get out on it – now. Not as he did with the ninety-day detention issue when by the time he got out it was too late, both for turning opinion about the issue, and about his reputation.

He sounded quite chipper but he said if we hand this agenda to the Tories we will hand them the election. GB has to come out fighting on it. He was calm but also said he could see the party throwing it into their lap. Earlier the *Sunday Times* were chasing me about my new role with TB–GB, so that was why they had been stalking me, not because of Fiona's event. TB told me he had been having a recurring dream – John Smith comes back to life, and he just walks into the Cabinet room as though nothing has changed, says, 'Hullo, how've you all been getting on?' and makes it clear TB is sitting in his seat, and he had to move out and make way for John. TB is then standing there behind the chair and nobody is even noticing. We had a discussion about what it meant – probably anxiety re being too young for the job. I said you don't want to know about my dreams. At the moment, they involve a lot of death, and sometimes it's yours, caused by GB with an axe.

I took Calum to the train station – he was going to the Burnley game [v Preston, 2–0] – then left with Bruce and Tessa for [Lord Stratford, Labour MP and former minister] Tony Banks' funeral. Both were very exercised about the education debate. Tessa had heard Estelle on the radio this morning and thought she was devastating, as in devastatingly convincing and devastatingly bad for TB. Bruce just felt TB had to give in because he could see no way of getting this through our own people. Tessa said she had been at dinner with the Marrs [Andrew and wife Jackie] at [*Guardian* commentator] Polly Toynbee's last night, and said it was like work, she felt exhausted at the end because it was so hard to persuade people. Bruce was adamant it would have to be more give than take, tougher on selection and a bit more of LEA control. Tessa was clearly worried about TB. We arrived at the fantastic cemetery, enormous and beautifully kept, in east London.

JP arrived and straight away wanted a chat about education. He said he was planning to make a speech on it. He wanted to send me a speech he made ten years ago where he talked about modernising comprehensives, and his idea was to see how much progress we had made, but to say the solution was not what was being proposed. I put to him Bruce's idea of a draft Bill. He also agreed it was going to make sense for Ruth to move, make way for Alan Johnson, and give him the ability to change policy. He said TB was going into kamikaze mode on this. But it was a good chat and I think he was genuinely motivated and in wanting my help with his speech, he knew I would keep close to TB on it. Good turnout from Labour side – Margaret Beckett [Environment Secretary], [Lord] Chris Smith [former Cabinet minister], Harry Cohen [Labour MP], Dick Caborn, Diane Abbott [MP], John and Glenys [Baroness Thornton] Carr, Rodney Bickerstaffe [former trade union leader], Stephen Pound [MP]. Phil Webster was there. David Mellor [former minister] the only Tory I could spot. But the crematorium was packed and it was a great service.

Don Brind [former press officer] did the intro, then Margaret the main political speech, and she got through it but was in tears after. Then to Brian Davies of IFAW [International Fund for Animal Welfare] who was also close to tears. He had been with Tony when he died and spoke really movingly of their relationship and how Sally [widow] was going to take on the seal charity. Going to name new wing of animal sanctuary after him. He said Tony [Banks] had said if TB could escape the shadow of Iraq he will be one of the great PMs in history. Then the guy from the arts committee at the Commons on the changes Tony made to the Palace of Westminster and finally Mellor who was brilliant.

He started with the story of Rossini's funeral. A composer wrote a new anthem. At the end he asked another composer what he thought. 'It might have been better if you'd died and Rossini wrote the anthem.' He said Tony toyed with the idea of calling himself 'Lord Banks of the Thames'. He told the story of a Banks interview when Mellor was caught out with Antonia de Sancha.* 'Five times a night in a Chelsea shirt.' Banks said, 'I just don't believe this story, at all.' Good start, said Mellor. Then Banks added, 'Nobody ever scores five times wearing a Chelsea shirt.' He was hilarious about the stuff Banks used to say about Didier Drogba [Chelsea player]. 'He decided he was a donkey when he first saw him, and it didn't matter how many goals he scored, he was always a donkey after that.' He ended though with big points – he was so funny people saw him as a modern-day Max Miller [popular comedian of the 1940s and '50s]. But he was a serious campaigning force, and a brilliant MP. 'Also everyone says Tony would like us to enjoy it. Well, I can't. It is awful. It makes me angry he's done it, gone and died like this.' It was a brilliant speech and he was upset by the end too. Nice music too. Best crematorium service I've been been to.

At the wake I had a long chat with Tony Benn and Chris Mullin [MP and writer] about my diaries. I said I felt strongly I couldn't do them while GB is still there. 'You must, you must,' said Benn. Also I said I felt I had to take out a lot of the venom. 'No, no, no, venom is good.' Chris chimed in, 'They must be real, otherwise there is no point.' We all ended up doing little tributes, and in my mine I gave his reaction when Tony [Banks] was offered the sports minister's job – 'Fuck me!' – also how TB had found it impossible to bollock him when he said Hague would never be Prime Minister because the country didn't want to be ruled by a foetus. Out for dinner at Lebanese restaurant with the Goulds. Helping PG get people for his 'Red' charity dinner at home on 30 January. Nice evening, and I felt F and I were getting on better than for ages.

Sunday 22 January
[Lib Dem MP] Mark Oaten's resignation last night about a rent boy knocked me off the *Sunday Times* front page, said David Cracknell

---

* The then Secretary of State for National Heritage's exposed affair with an actress led to his resignation and divorce from his wife. *The Sun* published an allegation that the Chelsea supporter had made love to Ms de Sancha while wearing a replica team shirt.

[journalist], which was no bad thing as Fiona was due to be on the Marr programme. She handled it fine. She texted me to say Peter Oborne and Greg Dyke [former BBC director-general] were also there. She told Barney Jones [programme editor] there could not have been a worse green room for her. DM and Louise [wife] popped round. David had a few ideas on how TB could get in a better place on education and I urged him to send over a note. But Tessa saw TB later and called to say he was totally implacable, willing to go down rather than back down. I called TB and he was working on one of his big notes. He said Neil's intervention had been damaging, but it was an opportunity to re-make the case and he intended to do it and hit back. He said it had moved on from selection. It was about who had the power to decide if a school governed itself – the school or the LEA. He felt his ideas were evolutionary, but the critics were presenting them as revolutionary.

I said it was more that they disagreed with the changes on which he was building, and as they had been suspicious of those, they were even more suspicious now. He said the revolutionary bit was giving all schools freedoms that currently only some have. But those who had them did better. He said he had to get GB and JP to back him on this, publicly. I told him what JP had said at the funeral. He said I must get him in and get him on board. He is falling for the propaganda. I said I think he has thought it through. He was, as Tessa said, totally not for backing down. Convinced the improvements had more to do with the reforms than the investment, and also determined to get more businesses and sponsors out there talking up a new approach. When his note finally came through, there were pages on education, also about the planned white paper on community health, where he didn't seem to understand what DoH were trying to achieve, and how it fitted with other reforms, then his usual scream about Home Office stuff – not enough costing work done on ID cards, worried about the effectiveness of SOCA, worried about the slow pace of terrorist deportations.

Then there was a whole chunk on Iraq, more frustration, not least about lack of effective outreach to the Sunnis, and a worry about whether the unity government would be that at all, and then on Afghanistan, saying we were losing the propaganda war again. He called as I was still reading it. 'What do you think?' I said I was only halfway through, and I was hoping there would be a commercial break. He laughed, said he was feeling fired up and needed to get back on the front foot. He said read the Europe speech outline and call me back. He was back to wanting to make a big tour de force narrative speech on Europe, going right back to the beginning, non-entry, failed entry, eventual entry, how that had always distorted the view so that Europe was seen as something being done to us, not something we wanted. We had tried to change that but not wholly successfully. And the changes came too fast. Hence Euroscepticism, some of it reasonable, the media portrayal not, but the two have combined to present a difficult false choice – cooperation with Europe means betrayal. Failure to cooperate means isolation and impotence. He felt globalisation and enlargement were changing the debate and making it possible to win an argument about economic reform and a reformed European social model.

When I called him back, I said isn't this wishful thinking? He said everything is in flux. All countries are having to adapt to these changes, and it means new ideas and new alliances are possible. We have to do a better job of showing that Europe is a positive in people's lives. I said we have been saying that for yonks. But now, he said, we can point to the reform areas where this can have real meaning – economic reform, security, defence, energy. I couldn't really see it, but he felt there were new leaders and voices emerging which could gather around a new agenda and isolate the sceptics – [Nicolas] Sarkozy [French Minister of the Interior], Merkel, Zapatero. I'll say this for him, he is not lacking energy or confidence right now. But was there really that much he was saying on Europe that we hadn't said a thousand times?

Monday 23 January

TB out and about on schools, admitting it was a 'high-wire act'. There was zero sign of him backing down. Mark B finished inputting cuts to Volume 1. Volume 2 was now at 1,024 pages. Jesus. I was really going to have to think through a strategy for all this stuff. The side effects of the pills were a nightmare. Skin blemishes, tiredness – especially if I slept a lot – and my pulse was way too high.

Tuesday 24 January

Out to do a motivational speech for Labour campaigners in London, then to the party for a meeting. New poll in. State of the parties numbers were OK, but the Tories' 'certain to vote' numbers were moving up, better than ours.

Wednesday 25 January

Long run, then a swim, which sparked off the nose and the asthma again. Definitely stepping up regime. Swim sparked off nose nightmare. Watched TB at PMQs – again no sign of change coming, and the mood behind him didn't look good. This could be heading for a car crash.

Thursday 26 January

Simon Hughes [Lib Dem MP and leadership candidate] came out under pressure [from the press]. Loads of coverage for Galloway, who had won his libel case against the *Telegraph* saying he took money from Saddam, and was also being kicked off *Big Brother*. A session with DS, with Fiona. She felt things were loads better, and he felt it was probably because I had gone to her event and just been there, not as a force in my own right, but for her. He wanted her take on my mad explosion on the Heath, and it was weird, I had virtually forgotten it already. I was wincing as she described it and said how scared she was that I was totally losing my sanity. He read out an account I had written about a dream – this was from a while ago, I think – when I had walked into a room, and Fiona had been happy because I walked through all these other people, straight to her. He was back on to his 'appendage' point.

Out to a Morgan Stanley dinner where they were voting for great Brits. I met Seb [Coe] on arrival. Paps out in force. Lots of diarists wanting to speak to me, said no. Sally Morgan and John [Lyons, SM husband] there, nice chat with them. Also chatted to Jeremy Heywood and said he really needed to get back in there. 'I will if you will,' he said. 'No chance.' His wife seemed very sceptical. I told him he was one of the few both TB and GB respected and if he did the transition he could name his job thereafter. I was at a table with Alex Horne, FA finance director, and a TB lookalike polar explorer from Devon.

Good chat with Charles Dunstone [Carphone Warehouse founder] on the way in, who wanted to meet up to discuss possible work together. Robin Janvrin, nice as always, who said the Queen should be given the top award. Nice enough do. I voted for Seb who won the overall prize. Cameron was there to give a speech. There was a clear desire for him to do well, including a total blowjob intro from the Morgan Stanley guy. Clive Anderson [broadcaster] was compering and took the piss gently, which Cameron handled fine. I was trying to put myself in the shoes and eyes of the unpersuaded either way and try to gauge what impact he was making. I felt he was OK, but no more. It felt like a *Telegraph* editorial not a leadership speech. But I did notice quite a few appreciative nods and gestures at different tables when he wound up.

Friday 27 January

Neil had seen GB, he called last night and told Fiona that GB felt I was the only one who could persuade TB what a disaster it would be if we got the education vote through with the help of Tories. Then Martin Salter [Labour MP] called and they shared a little joke about Fiona saying all her days start with an argument with me about education policy. So it escalated from that, the call from Neil not helping either. DS had asked us to write a note in what we resented about each other. Good timing! I went to collect Mum from the station, who was down for three days. Sally Morgan called, said that she and Philip both had feedback from TB that he didn't think I should have gone to the Compass event.

Sunday 29 January

Blunkett on Marr suggesting that some kind of TB–GB deal was under way. I wondered if he was picking up on some of our conversation the other night. Cameron was out and about talking up TB so their strategy goes on. TB didn't call so maybe SM/PG were right, that he was more pissed off than he let on to me about the Compass event. The sense I had was that he was pissed off with Neil, fine about Fiona because he totally respected her on the issue, even if he disagreed, and understood why I had to go. We had another meeting on the GB front tomorrow, so I'd find out then. Having seen Jeremy on Thursday, and tried to persuade him to go back, I followed up with a call. I said he knew how bad they could be, but he knew how good they could be and at least they both knew and rated him. We were short of people both of them could or would talk to. Too much fell to me, and I wasn't there most of the time. I said he had hinted when we met for lunch he was thinking of a return and I just wanted to say if he was serious, now might be the right time. Long run, two hours, form coming back.

Monday 30 January

Cameron was making speech to Demos [think tank] with a clear pitch to be TB's natural successor in the centre ground. Ed Balls was sending me a series of agonised texts asking what the response should be. TB was on breakfast TV and had already put the best line, that those who started the big reforms – i.e. GB – should finish them. Ed had always felt we should have pushed back more aggressively on DC's pitch for the centre ground, but it was back to this issue of their wishful thinking. Just because we said he was the same old Tories didn't mean he was, and if we said it when the public saw and heard something different, there was a danger we looked silly. It was perfectly sensible strategy for Cameron to do what he was doing, especially with TB on his way out at some point in this parliament. But our reaction should not be to change tack, but to use it to show how we are dominating the arguments, and that is because we have won those arguments. Eventually DC will be forced onto policy positions he cannot match.

After the two steps forward at our last couple of TB–GB meetings, today was a few steps back. Sadly Douglas wasn't there. Liz Lloyd and Sue Nye were there, for their first experience of this particular variation of these meetings, and I think even they were shocked. It was back to the bad old days. PG, Liz and I saw TB for a pre-meeting and he was so not up for it, said he had had a bad meeting with him yesterday and he was fed up at the way he was making it so complicated. I said where has Sunday's vim and vigour gone? He said he drains me of it. As far as he was concerned it was simple – is GB New Labour or not? The problem was that GB thought an interview with *The Sun* after a whack from Trevor Kavanagh [*Sun* commentator] was enough to fix it. It wasn't. He had to show day in, day out he was totally New Labour. Both TB and GB were a bit sulky at the meeting itself, though GB was at least trying to help me and PG in our constant asking for ways to operationalise the outcome of our discussions. But today they could not agree on the smallest things. Instead of staying on strategy and systems, it degenerated into an extended discussion about the line to take on Cameron's speech today. Given that bird had flown, it was a waste of time. We were back to the same argument again – GB and Ed clearly felt we should be painting DC as right-wing but TB said it will just sound like carping. The food was shit again. Flat diluted orange juice. Sausage rolls and dead sandwiches. Ed B said it was like the food at a kids' party, but with no cake. Or singing, I said. Or any happiness at all. At least we could have a bit of a laugh, but this was grim. Ed M was pressing TB on what the plan was for education. It was the elephant in the room. TB said the votes would come if they fought this together. Not sure about that. I just wanted to be out of there right now. At the end GB took me back in and said only I could persuade him – one, that we could not risk getting the Education Bill through with Tory votes and two, that TB had to start going for the Tories much harder. I went home via a meeting at Al Jazeera. They were offering me a chat show. Not sure.

I went to see Tom Bostock [GP] later, filled him in on some of the DS stuff. He went off on one about women's lib, said Fiona saw TB as a surrogate but actually she was angry with me, and didn't want to admit it. Also, I was angry at myself for not standing up against Iraq policy. He said deep down I felt TB did the wrong thing and I did not use the influence I had to stop him. I said I love the way you put all your own views on to your patients! He said we were all better off in Victorian times, when people had proper respectful attitudes. I told him the DS analogy about Fiona seeing my old job almost as though it was another woman. I think a bit of competitive medical jealousy crept in. He said DS did not know me as well as he did, he still felt I should never have left, I should be back in there, accept I was unique in British political history, that is why they wanted me, that is why people still talked about me, and my place was there getting Tony Blair to do the right things not the wrong things. He said Fiona wants to hold the family together but she doesn't like what you did and she is more at home with all those wretched liberals who hate you. I said, 'Now, about my prescription...' and he laughed.

To PG's house for the Red [campaign to fight the AIDS epidemic in Africa] dinner. The house had been done out in red. I had a long chat with Mark Ferguson [businessman, son of Alex] who felt Cameron was on the march, making inroads well. He seemed to be buying DC's environment pitch. 'Do you believe it?' 'He has not given me a reason not to.' GB looked desperately pleased earlier when I told him DC's speech at the Morgan Stanley event was crap. Bobby Shriver [lawyer and activist] did the main speech plus one from some global fund guy. Nice enough do, though I was discombobulated re Bostock a bit.

Tuesday 31 January

With Calum to Brighton–Burnley. I was doing the Radio Lancs co-commentary. Dire match. 0–0 and not one shot on target. I felt I did OK though I didn't feel entirely fluent at times. It was also bloody cold. Good laugh with Calum on the way back. The radio news was leading on lost votes on the Religious Hatred Bill.* Lost by one after TB was told not to bother going over for the vote! I was booked to be doing *Start the Week* on Monday for AOL. I pulled out when I heard Clare Short was on. Bollocks to that. There was no point me going on and losing my rag. I was worried about the number of horrible, violent dreams I was having at the moment. The fucking depressions were mounting.

Wednesday 1 February

I worked a bit then Bobby Shriver and his team came round to try to get me involved more in the Red campaign and pick my brains. I did my best to give them a few ideas and insights, but I was conscious of these guys really giving their all and I was feeling unmotivated and detached. I did not sign up for more than a bit of advice, and I think they were hoping for a lot more than that. He was a bit loud for my taste. I missed PMQs where TB had a hard time from DC over yesterday's whipping fiasco on the Religious Hatred Bill. Dennis Skinner called, he said the Tories were clever, their tails were up, Cameron was not to be underestimated, he had played himself in well and was making an impact in there. He advised a windfall tax on oil and also said TB should give some indication of troops withdrawal before the local elections, because he was sure the Tories would do both. I asked him how he felt about DC v GB. He said, 'Worried.'

Thursday 2 February

Woke with a searing headache. Depressed. It got worse after seeing DS at 9. I couldn't put my finger on it but I was definitely back down the slide again. He suggested I up the dose of the anti-depressants. We went over lots of stuff – e.g. Iraq and was it actually the case, as Bostock said, that I could have stopped TB from doing it? Is that what I really thought? Did I actually believe GB when he said only I could persuade TB to change tack on education? And what did my demon think of that? Was it flattering, pleasing, did it make me want to go back? He said, 'I think your demon likes that.' I said what about me? He said you don't, but your demon is part of you, and it loves to hear that only

---

* The Bill, to make it an offence to incite hatred against a person on the grounds of his or her religion, was amended by the House of Lords, and the Commons failed to overturn the changes.

you can do things, because it gives you a reason when other parts tell you not to. He said what he heard from Fiona was a message that 'You care more about him – TB – than me.' I said it was totally different and if that was the case I would still be there. 'But you are,' he said. 'To all intents and purposes you are. How many times this week? How many dreams are about fights at work?' He paused, and said, 'Does she have a point?' I said maybe.

He said, 'What sort of relationship would you have with all these politicians if the power was not a factor?' I said you mean if we were all out of power, back in opposition. He said yes. I said probably I would maintain some kind of friendship with TB, but less likely GB. He said the ones I had stayed friendly with were TB, Tessa, Blunkett, JP a bit, plus my staff. Of the politicians, was it the same as with the staff? I said probably not. I asked him where he thought all this was going. I felt I had done a load of work, stirred a lot of stuff, but I was still on the pills and still getting depressed, and right now both mentally and physically, I felt shit. 'It is all going to be fine,' he said. 'Just hang in.' He said the higher dose will help after ten days. He was clear – and on this he totally disagreed with Bostock – that improving the situation with Fiona was by far the most important thing. He said he would worry for me if she wasn't around. I think she was really fed up at all my agonising.

Friday 3 February

Very depressed. I stayed in bed till half-ten then went out for a bike ride, but had no energy, came back, went back to bed. Mark arrived half-two and I got up and we worked through till half-five. But I was not feeling good. He asked if I was OK. I said not really, just the same old bollocks. 'Depression, ibid,' he said, which at least made me laugh. It was probably not helping that in the diary we were at the September 11 aftermath when things with Fiona were bad and there were all these references to how hopeless the Yanks were. I said at one point, I'm not even sure what I actually think about a lot of this stuff any more.

Saturday 4 February

The news was totally dominated by the Muslim protests about Danish cartoons depicting Muhammad.* It had been rumbling on but was now becoming very nasty.

Sunday 5 February

Up early to play golf with David Mills and [Sir] John Gieve [ex-Treasury civil servant, now deputy governor Bank of England]. I had a quick look at the papers before leaving, and it seemed clear to me GB and co had been at it. The *Sunday Telegraph* were running hard with the line that TB was leaving next year. *Sunday Times* on Neil telling TB to go sooner rather than later. Neil had told me that he had said that, and I assume he had told GB the same when they had dinner this week. Plus there was lots around about GB not being supportive on Iraq. TB called when I was playing and later when Fiona, Grace and I went to see *Walk The Line*, so I couldn't really talk till later, when we had a proper chat. He said he felt GB was playing the same games as before – things hadn't gone well last week and his instinct was not to weigh in with support but to cause trouble and try to push him over. He said GB was not really helping on the education reforms but allowing his people instead to say, 'Look, Gordon has to support this, but he doesn't really.'

They also believed DC was emulating Bush. He wasn't. He was emulating us from the right but for GB to admit that would be to admit we had been successful as NL [New Labour]. I told TB I was seeing GB tomorrow. He said he has to understand the deal is not that I go because he acquiesces. It is that he cooperates and helps me get through the agenda, which he just isn't at the moment. It is one thing occasionally to act because of a media problem when they spot he is being weak, and he says something. It is another to support the reforms. TB said if he was just going for the acquiescence route he had a problem. I asked him again if there should be a plan B. A long pause before he said I don't think so. Earlier I had driven back with Gieve, now enjoying a more leisurely life as Deputy Governor of Bank of England. He said GB had real strength and ability, and Balls was phenomenally clever, but where TB was different was in empathy and in listening. GB doesn't listen. He decides and then hits you round the head with his decision. TB can

---

* A Danish newspaper, *Jyllands-Posten*, had published editorial cartoons depicting Muhammad, regarded as the 'Holy Prophet' by Muslims, which attracted accusations of blasphemy. Supporters of the paper said publication was a legitimate exercise of free speech.

lead you to a decision. GB drags you. So Cameron, he said, might be the one who is felt to be filling the Blair gap that will be left.

He was not sure – nor was TB later – that GB could change. He was too set in his ways. But also he was not adapting. What change had he made? What adjustment? He hadn't learned from his time as Chancellor to be PM. John said GB had no idea what the difference in the jobs was. As Chancellor you can pretty much plan your year one year out. You put in the big dates and the big events. You can plan for them, build around them. Of course you are busy, but it is as nothing compared to being PM. As PM there are twenty or thirty things every day you're required to hit the right note on, decide on. Decide not to decide, be quizzed on. It is a totally different scale. He shared my fear that GB was constantly fed the grievance line and also that he personally didn't understand just how different it was, just how much harder, how many more decisions you had to make, and how much less time you had.

Monday 6 February
I did a two-hour run slowly after clocking a resting pulse rate of 49, which was more like it. The Sundays stuff on transition ran into today, with TB authority looking under pressure again, though the Danish cartoons ran big and I felt we were on the wrong side of the argument [the government supported the Danish government in resisting protests and pressure]. In at half-five to see GB at the Treasury. Ed B had flu so it was just the two of us and it was pretty much a defection pitch. He said I had to believe him when he said TB had no interest in cooperation and an orderly transition. I said I didn't believe that, and off he went. 'Why did he stop talking to me the day after the election? Why did he pick a fight with the party the day after the election? Why did he not discuss education with me or with you?' His basic take was that TB was on a personal agenda and couldn't care less about the consequences. Last week cost a billion on Afghanistan. 'A fucking billion.' He had his priorities on health which were costing a fortune and taking no account of what we needed for the election build-up.

He totally disagreed with the DC strategy. He was thinking about himself, wanting people to think DC had to ape TB to have any success.

The meeting was meant to be to discuss my scribbled note to EB during GB's colloque speech about changes I felt he could make to his style and to his operation. But it got straight away on to the old stuff and him raging at the TB operation – no modus operandi and no long-term strategy. He wanted to do things strategically but he got no No. 10 support and TB only focused on one or two things that he really wanted done. What on earth was he doing making another big speech on Europe? That was all about legacy, it has nothing to do with now. I kept trying to say there was more he could do himself. He needed a plan that laid out a speech and events programme for the next few months and into which TB and co bought. He said I was the only person who could persuade TB about anything. He was unlikely to listen to Neil any more and Neil went OTT which was a mistake. He doesn't listen to JP. The rest of the Cabinet are there to do what he wants. Cherie blows everything up in his mind. Peter M stirs. But he will listen to you.

He has to be persuaded he is wrong to think in the way he does – his basic position is 'I will do what I fucking well like for two years and then you can do what you fucking well like.... No, in fact his position is I will do what I fucking well like and then when I'm gone you'd better do the fucking things I want you to or else I'll tell everyone how useless it all is.' GB seemed to feel TB almost had a vested interest in failure which I didn't accept. I said I really don't think he wants you to fail. I think he wants you to succeed. He said he wants to be the great success, the only man who could tame the Labour Party, the only one who could win big. He doesn't want the rest of us to be able to succeed. And he will need money when he goes, and he will need to be doing and saying things we don't agree with to make it. I said I really didn't buy that.

I asked him what he wanted me to do. He wanted me to work with him and Ed and possibly PG 'if you think he can be discreet' in putting together a plan working back from the election – events, dividing lines, policy initiatives in security, globalisation, public services, technology, environment etc. He said he wanted me to give them the imagination to make the ideas cohere and persuade TB of the need to put a proper plan into action. He said he knew TB would not have been able to do what he has done without me, and he said he knew he needed me to help him too. I said, OK. He said, 'You are ambivalent, I can tell.' I said no. 'Are you sure?' He asked it twice. I said I was not ambivalent about him, but about me. I just didn't want to be drawn back in full-time to get my head back in a vice. I'd gone through a lot and I was only now just getting life and family back on track, it was not easy, and I was not going to risk it again. He said he understood that, and he would not pressure me more than he had to (John Gieve's description came into my mind) but 'There is nobody directing the traffic'.

He said what I showed at the election was that I was a great organising mind. The campaign was going nowhere till I went in and persuaded them all of a different tack. Now, because we won, TB was changing the story, he didn't accept things had been that bad, he won it, trust was not an issue at all, bullshit, bullshit. I said he was overstating things, both how much I changed things, and also what TB felt now. He said, 'You have to understand why I'm angry and frustrated. Tony is not doing the right thing but I am not in a position to bring about the change we need.' I said there is lots more he could do and I was happy to help in that. He basically wanted him, me and Ed to work up a TB-free plan and then get it implemented as a fait accompli. Someone came in to say TB was waiting for him but we had another ten minutes.

He went over his security and patriotism speech, full of newsy ideas he was pulling off. I said he had to accept TB had enormous qualities, including some he lacked, and it would do him no harm to make clear he realised that. Yes, he said, but he had qualities too, and it is those qualities that need to be front of mind when we are thinking of the election. He said, 'You and I have had our differences and it has been a roller coaster with a few low points as well as high but at least we both know the importance of long-term strategy and we can work together when we have to. I would like to work with you and we take decisions and implement them with a focus on what we have to do for the future.' Putting it all together it was as close to being a straight demand for defection as possible.

As we left Sue N gave him a BBC online cutting – TB saying we should spend as much on state kids as private schools. GB reacted in fury. We met his protection guy as we walked out to the lift and he said, 'What a bastard – I told him not to do that. You see why I get so angry and frustrated.' He was steaming, and when I left him to head back home, he said again, 'I fucking told him not to do that.' And off he went. Later he called to say, 'Forget the education stuff – it was nothing.' But he said it had not been a great meeting. He said you have to persuade him we need proper long-term strategy and a transitional plan. I got home, was having dinner with Grace when TB called. 'How was your meeting?' he said, tiredly. 'How was yours?' Weird, he said. I said I felt where he had a point was in saying you did things that didn't sufficiently take account of where things would be at the election. He said he could barely do more for him. He had made clear he was ready to go next year. He had totally endorsed him. He had said he would support him. He had agreed to make Douglas chairman, and put Balls in government even when EB talked to him like was a junior clerk, keep the likes of Dawn Primarolo [Paymaster General] and Nigel Griffiths.

He said it reminded him of dealing with the parties in Northern Ireland – every demand met leads to another one. I went over some of GB's complaints. He said, 'One thing you cannot accuse me of is being difficult to work with. Which one has that reputation? I have tried to do everything to make it work and even though I have huge doubts I am still trying to make it work. So please let's have none of this "six of one half a dozen of the other" – it's not.' I said GB felt I was only person who could persuade you to do the right thing. He said he felt that he was only approaching me out of fear, not because he really wanted to change. They just wouldn't see good in each other's motives at all. But how many days had this been the story and the narrative? Hence the call. No escape. Then after I got to bed, Ed Balls called because *The Guardian* had splashed on a story about me and PG going in to help GB image v Cameron. He was off in one of his panics, saying it would mean they would be talking about spin when we were trying to portray Cameron as spin and GB substance. They overreacted to these damn things. Then the idiotic Damian McBride [special advisor to GB] said it was all nonsense from start to finish. They lacked subtlety.

Tuesday 7 February
Looking forward to a day of diary work with MB and we managed to get three weeks down on paper but oddly GB called with a story he wanted me to place, said it needed 'someone of your flair'! Mmmm. He didn't mention *The Guardian*, or McBride's silly response last night, though I suspect that was why he called, to suss if I was pissed off. The story was a leaflet his team in Scotland had picked up, from DC to Liberals in the Dunfermline by-election, saying he was a liberal conservative and putting Iraq in a list of issues he now agreed with them on. TB's view was that GB wanted to go harder for Cameron but he didn't want to do it himself. I lined up Rebekah Wade and Phil Webster and they were keen enough. But then there was the usual nonsense – me fixing John Reid words, Sue Nye saying GB says get Reid words, GB then not knowing re Reid. It was never straightforward with these guys. Liz called for a chat and said they still were not cooperating at a practical level. Then TB called, and was really fed up with them. He said the reason GB wanted me involved today was he wanted 'our

people' to do the attack. 'I tell you, I'm happy to go along with this but they're fucking mad.'

GB had done a big security number today, tough on terror, on the back of Abu Hamza being jailed.* TB said why was he not saying all this when the going was tough? He says there is not forward strategy but there is – resolutely New Labour in pushing through reforms, don't give DC the space he wants, do the current reforms then future agenda. But what are these big ideas he says he needs to be PM to take forward? He doesn't have them. He's saying more money for education, a bit of constitutional stuff, environment, but what he doesn't have is a big new reform agenda. Fine, what he has is fine, but let's stop pretending the whole time. He said it is exactly what Clinton said had been the problem with Al Gore [Clinton's Vice-President] – he can't accept what we did was good so he misses the opportunity to say and do the obvious. He said he was willing to have the meeting again tomorrow but he wanted me and PG to be very firm, say we have to move this on to operational level, get moving work-wise, or else we were just wasting everyone's time. But as I said to Liz, I really didn't want to be sucked in any more.

Wednesday 8 February
The Times and *The Sun* both ran the DC leaflet OK though Abu Hamza was massive across the media. I watched PMQs at home with Mark, and DC led with his chin, going for TB on education flip-flop and TB lacerated him with the leaflet and a great end line – 'No wonder he's against identity cards.' So we were tails up but PG had sent over a note from recent groups and they were not good. A clear sense of the government weakened by defeat and division and TB authority waning. DC picking up though his party was not. He'd done an exercise getting people to write postcards to TB and GB and they were not good – TB go (with various degrees of friendliness) and to GB – smarten yourself up and be more human. And underpinning it, lack of delivery. Also racism was really picking up post the Muslim cartoon demos. Not a good scene. PG, JoP, LL [Liz Lloyd] and I were in for a TB pre-meeting before lunch with GB and team. TB read through the notes and said what he had was an authority problem. But he felt it would all be fine

---

* Militant Egyptian imam of a London mosque, sentenced to seven years' imprisonment for inciting violence.

February '06: 'It is like Clinton–Gore all over again' – TB

if only they worked together. I said GB was trying in his own way to do what he thought we wanted. TB said only in so far as it helps him, not the government as a whole, let alone TB's agenda.

I said we would never get perfection so in the absence of plan B let us try to make plan A work. TB said nobody could be trying as hard as he was but Liz was saying they had not even come back to her about the paper we went over on dividing lines etc. We were trying, they were not, he said. That was kind of borne out by the broader meeting. GB was back to his 'Where is the long-term agenda?' mantra and so we went round in more circles. We discussed the security agenda, how do we take forward today. TB doing his 'What shall I say on Friday?' act, just tactical, looking ahead to things he knew he was doing. He was often just looking out of window. Bad meeting. Ed Balls made a good point – the narrative was Blair to get through a few things then Brown take over. We were all making our similar points but for once TB agreed with Ed. Miliband was doing his usual line that the real attack had to be he was a right-winger, GB was saying it wasn't enough for the Tories to build an attack on flip-flopping unless they could make it seem unprincipled.

I was struck by the point that the public had not made up its mind re DC and he was still way ahead of his party so I felt we could do a lot more with the initial line of attack. PG said later GB relaxed when it was clear TB was listening to him. 'No wonder he wasn't relaxed today then.' Not a good meeting. Back to agreeing we need a paper and a modus operandi. I can't be bothered with this much more. Later I did *Newsnight* and was introduced as a Brown advisor which was weird and it was a crap discussion with Michael Gove [Tory MP]. Not at my best. Liz Lloyd called as I was on the way home. She was not sure what she was meant to do out of today and I couldn't blame her. Just muddle on, try to give the public sense of working togther even if that was frankly the goal not the reality. But as Fiona said about the way the *Newsnight* discussion was framed, it was almost as if GB was already doing the job. TB needed a few more wins.

Thursday 9 February

TB totally hammered DC yesterday but it didn't really come over that way. The press were definitely wanting to give Cameron the benefit of the doubt. Fiona and I at DS's with our resentment lists. No surprises.

Friday 10 February

Dunfermline by-election defeat a big shock.* Huge swing to the Lib Dems, and a lot of the hit was going to GB, who had been up there, it was his next door seat, and he had been trying to drive the strategy for it. To be frank, it was not great for either of them. TB had not been in touch as much as usual on his speech to spring conference in Blackpool today, which was OK – mainly security, strong on identity cards etc. – but it would be seen in the context of the by-election and how it affected his own future. He had sent a draft through last night and it was very defensive. He had a good section on what the party founders would think of what we were doing, which was fine, but also too defensive, and I repitched it. He was also starting to articulate the line about the Tories we had been discussing, that they were improving as an opposition, but at the expense of being a credible alternative government. The problem was draining authority, and there had been too many drip drips on that in recent weeks.

I left for Oxford, where I was doing a talk, when JP called wanting help with his speech, for the spring conference. I did a bit without much enthusiasm, on the theme of Cameron the chameleon. At Brasenose I was met by a young lecturer then met up with Vernon Bogdanor [academic constitutional expert], later joined by Robin Butler [former Cabinet Secretary]. Beautiful place. But boy they never stop talking. OK chat with Robin on his theory of [Bernard] Ingham [chief press secretary to Margaret Thatcher] v Campbell. That Bernard fed all evenly but I worked out we were in a jungle, we were monopoly suppliers and we needed to exploit our strength. He did a perfectly nice intro, said I had gripped the machine when it needed it, and that it was a myth I didn't work well with the civil service.

The audience was a mix of undergraduates, graduates and dons and I did my basic media management speech. We had to move venue to Exam Schools to accommodate interest and that was even without it having been advertised. Good questions – liked the one on whether we would expect ministers to resign for doing something wrong even if it was not in the media yet. I said I thought so, but it was one of those that had me thinking for a while. I was even nicer than usual about TB because Nicky Blair [TB son] was there, along with Rory and Georgia. TB had called earlier, aware I was going, to say Nicky wanted me to do the Labour club. Rory seemed to enjoy it, then he, Nicky and Georgia went off – it was funny to see how well they get on, and how they

---

* The by-election, caused by the death of Labour MP Rachel Squire, saw a 16.24 per cent swing from Labour and a majority of 1,800 for Lib Dem Willie Rennie.

February '06: Good to see next generation together

had all ended up here – while Fiona and I went back to the college for drinks, dinner and dessert.

It was all a bit weird, like moving to a different room for the port and cheese, fruit and what have you, and I could never quite manage this Oxbridge stuff, but Vernon was good company, incredibly knowledgeable and I felt generally onside. He spoke well of Cameron, who he had taught, said he was without doubt one of his cleverest students. He said he would not necessarily have seen him as a political leader, but he would have seen him as being capable of doing whatever he set his mind to. Also he felt that GB was a problem in England, and the devolution issue had made his Scottishness more relevant and more of a problem. He felt GB lacked the human skills that modern leadership needs, which he felt TB had, and was confident DC had too.

Sunday 12 February

I was booked to do the Adam Boulton programme, ostensibly on sport, but the papers were full of TB–GB transition, and they asked me to stay on and do a turn with [Lord] Michael Heseltine [former Tory Cabinet minister and Deputy Prime Minister] who pushed the line on TB being a spent force which was gaining a bit of currency. The GB lot were definitely trying to engender a sense for the chatterati that PG and I were helping him. There was an interesting aside in a *Sunday Times* piece on GB which had him joking about whether he had the right tie on, and 'You need to ask AC and PG.' I worked a bit on the diaries later including the time Peter said that GB always tried to divide and rule, telling PM TB was weak and relied on the AC–PM axis, but I was determined to be number one and so I destroyed PM. Charming.

Monday 13 February

CC had done an interview yesterday saying there was a dual premiership, not exactly helpful on the 'waning authority' front. GB had briefed up towards his big security speech today in advance of the big Commons vote on ID cards.* TB was in South Africa, and it had been

---

* After a great deal of public debate and concerns expressed by some politicians, human rights lawyers and others, the third reading of the Identity Cards Bill, creating national identity cards in the UK, was approved by the Commons.

announced he was cutting the trip short to get back for the vote. But then as the plane took off in Pretoria, it emerged it had a fault when the pilot noticed sparks and they had to stay there. The papers were full of TB–GB again and while on one level it was good that GB was branching out in different areas and being on the ID card agenda there was definitely a problem with TB's waning authority, and a grounded plane did not exactly help image and metaphor-wise. The authority issue is what Hezza had meant yesterday, that MPs and ministers would increasingly look to GB not TB.

TB called p.m., irritated at the plane malfunction. He said, 'What's going on?' I said how does it feel where you are? He said how it felt was that GB was over-cooking as ever. He felt there had been an operation in the last few weeks and this was the culmination of it, him stronger, me weaker. I said it probably felt worse inside than it looked outside, and don't forget, we had been pressing him to do this security agenda. TB felt though that it should be GB following, coming in behind, not leading out front. If it was the latter TB was enfeebled every time and then he would have to reassert himself. 'After all these years they still don't get me. I won't be pushed down by them. It has to be a two way thing.' I said the problem was they refused to acknowledge TB had been a success and it was a mistake. He sounded a bit hurt by it all and I judged from the line in the *Telegraph* today about PG and me being seen as the 'capitulation squad' that there was disquiet in parts of No. 10 even beyond what I knew.

TB said – and I assume meant to be passed on – that he was not going to be put upon and pushed out. There was a two-way thing here that had to be worked through properly. He was not having it if they thought they could just shunt him aside. But as I said to him there was something weirdly symbolic – he was stranded, his plane delayed while GB was posing with veterans in Downing Street and leading the fight on identity cards on the day of the vote. TB was back to his familiar complaint – that it was all one way. I asked if he wanted me to do anything. He said not yet, but he wanted to see me when he got back. Then minutes later GB called, he claimed he had called yesterday and left a message which I didn't get. He asked what I thought. I felt he was doing fine but he had to be careful at any hint he was doing it at TB's expense. He had to show the joins of teamwork. I said his next venture should be cultural, a talking point of some sort that is not just another policy issues, bit something richer. He said with DC around things were bound to be seen as personality driven but we needed to get to policy, he felt that we lost the by-election because of local issues but there was definitely a broader danger, a feeling that any protest was just an anti-government vote.

He was fine on things generally, denied any undermining of TB, even jokey in some ways. I mentioned half-heartedly the thing about him joking in one of the papers re 'Where are AC and PG to advise on my tie?' He denied saying it. He said the reason he'd called yesterday was because Marr asked him if I was back full-time, and helping him, and he claimed he said we spoke from time to time, but I was too busy doing other things to work full-time. He said to me he didn't think it helped either of us for it to be thought I was there full-time. It certainly fitted with my desire not to get more sucked in. It was an OK chat though, and I genuinely didn't think he was doing the high-profile stuff on ID cards as a way of doing in TB. As I said to TB, GB was in no-win ground here – do nothing and we say he is not there when the going gets tough; step in and we say he is exploiting TB's travails. I talked to Liz re the same. She said there was a lot of unease around because it all seemed to be one way and they were still not cooperating, for example GB speeches coming through too late to be commented upon. The vote passed fine, twenty Labour rebels, majority of thirty-one.

Tuesday 14 February

TB had a bit of time on his hands what with the grounded plane and the flight home, and he worked on one of his long notes, which he sent through in advance of our next round of TB–GB meetings. It was his usual run around all the policy areas that were troubling him, but the context was TB–GB and – very first point he made – the agreed aim of 'an orderly transition'. He was adamant that GB had to be seen as the fresh horse pulling the same carriage; or an entirely new carriage, signalling the end of New Labour with the end of TB. He was making the same points we had been making for ages – it meant genuine cooperation, not just expressions of mutual support. It meant the public feeling TB was genuine about wanting GB to succeed, and GB genuine about wanting to support TB. But it also meant he went when he chose to, with GB then setting out a forward agenda which TB supported. He was very open about the tensions that made it difficult – his lot believing GB would ditch NL; GB's lot worried TB would renege on a deal, and just stay. That could only be overcome by having teams on both sides who had a detailed plan and agreed modus operandi and we worked to an agreed strategy working back from a GB v DC election.

Then he went through it policy area by policy area, economy, globalisation, skills, science, SMEs [small and medium-sized enterprises], universities, creative industries. He wanted a new joint approach to win back lost support in the City, and to get the unions on to a more modern skills agenda. I said when he called it was like an economic mini manifesto. 'What can he disagree with?' 'He'll just wonder why you are doing it now.' He was also into setting out contours of the next spending review, and warning of the Tories avoiding big specifics and laying a 'tax and spend' trap. What we call investment they will want to label as waste. He had his usual rant about public services' main indicators all being good but the general sense of progress bad. Then he was into big policy stuff on health and education, criminal justice, next wave of constitutional change, more mayors etc., and again I couldn't see GB reacting that well to the idea of TB setting out plans that would take years to implement. Then foreign affairs, Europe, climate change, then finally a screed on party renewal.

I went to the gym and did an hour on the bike. I caught Ed Balls on breakfast TV on about a Private Member's Bill. Amazingly the presenters didn't ask him re TB–GB. GB speech and general support got OK coverage. There was way too much around about me and PG helping him. The *Times* leader did say though that despite me being seen as a cross between Rasputin and Goebbels I knew how to get things done. TB finally back on a scheduled flight, and called as he was heading in from the airport, when I was on my way in to see GB. He wanted to see me alone with Ed [Balls]. It was back to the doom and gloom. I actually felt things were not so bad, and as Ed said, we needed to get the reality to match the rhetoric and we would be in OK nick. GB said there were massive problems – the party was not capable of doing what was needed. I said wait till you see TB's next wave of ideas. He said the trust problem was still there. Competence of ministers is a problem. No drive or strategy in No. 10. The Tories dominating media more than we did. He said he was trying to do long-term challenges while TB was dealing with day to day issues directed to his legacy. I felt the two could be made to go alongside each other but he didn't.

He denied he had been pushing the dual premiership line – which seemingly CC never actually said – or writing TB out of the script. But he said the current position was not really tenable. I said it was provided both opted in to it – he backed TB on reform, TB backed him on future agenda and takeover. But the trust was still not easy to get. He said he no longer believed he would have a reshuffle because he needed to hold it over people who if ejected might vote against the government. He didn't believe TB wanted the same agenda as he did for the future. It wasn't a great discussion and yet again he had not produced a paper. Lots of joking about me advising him on his ties – though I actually did give him an assessment of the use of hands in speeches – when the other Ed [Miliband] and DA arrived. I went round to see TB who was with Liz L. He was jokey about the flight. He asked if I thought he should share his note with GB. I felt he should. There was a lot in it, and GB would probably feel too much, but at least it had the makings of a plan and a strategy. It was a serious piece of work and PG and I both felt yes, hand it over. Liz was not sure because she felt it handed GB too much. But we really had to get moving.

We went round and gave it to them. I said this is a note TB did while away and you guys should read it before he joins us. They sat reading it, pretty intent. GB laughed at the point where TB talked about more money for tax cuts or extra spending. When TB arrived he went to the end – dividing lines – and said that what went before wasn't sufficient to get us in the right place on that. Then lots of talk re tax, globalisation, security. TB had a different look today. He knew he didn't have the same power. Also clearly part of him resented this, having to negotiate on pretty much anything. But he still had the best arguments. How often had we been asking GB to come up with the kind of overview TB knocked off in South Africa. And on so many of the arguments he was right. Ditto on the best way to make this work for both of them. But even watching GB and team read it, it was clear they were suspicious, constantly seeing plans to block him off. On the big picture TB said people did not want more money for public services for the sake of it – they wanted to know it was working.

On globalisation we had to show people how our understanding benefited their lives. In the end it would be small state v empowerment. He slapped down Ed B a few times for comments he was making that TB found too simplistic or which he felt were signs of them deciding strategy according to what they wanted the Tories to be rather than what they were. He had been proved right re waiting a bit on Cameron, who was now finding it difficult to match policy to rhetoric. He felt GB was over-complicating things now. GB also wanted him to make speeches on state funding of the parties and child poverty. TB said he was up for both but on funding he wanted it to be part of a bigger package taking in Lords reform. He pointed out that if we were going for an elected element in Lords reform that would put the Tories right off it straight away. On child poverty he wanted to reframe this around three groups – comfortable, aspirant and 15 per cent poor. That produced agonising grimaces from the Eds etc. DA was the best at these meetings, for example on state funding just setting out why it needed to happen and what the vehicles might be.

GB said Lords reform was OK provided we're all clear it was camouflage. Then banging on re how bad the party was. TB said it was always like this, always had been and we should stop exaggerating. At one point GB produced his usual clutch of cuttings e.g. Andrew Rawnsley and Phil Stephens. Who briefed them? The same question Ed M asked as soon as he came in. I don't know and I don't care. Get above it. Stop over-obsessing and stop over-complicating. But their response to TB's note was not great.

TB said their analysis was so Shrumesque [US strategy advisor Bob Shrum]. TB also wanted delivery measurements on public service success which was going to be difficult too. So there was lots of good discussion but we were still not in great shape. TB said we cannot keep going in circles. He told GB to make any changes he wanted to make to the note and then put forward three people – his would be Liz, Matthew Taylor, and Ben W-P from No. 10 – who would meet to prepare our meetings. TB later referred to a period in opposition when he kept a diary. 'Diaries, huh!' snorted GB in my direction. As TB stood to leave, he said we had wasted enough time on this. We had to agree a plan for parliament, which led to an agreed strategy for the fourth term. If it is not real, it won't work and the people who can make it real are in this room, so I suggest we do it.

I set off up north for Burnley v Wolves. Peter M's mother died. I called and left a message. He texted a response. He would be hit hard by this. I drove north glad to be getting away from it for a bit. I was already in deeper than I really wanted to be. I was never going to have the same kind of relationship with GB as with TB, or indeed like the relationship I used to have with GB, added to which it was not clear to me he would really change. I checked in, then down to the match, not great, lost 1–0. I was doing the half-time presentations.

Wednesday 15 February

A long swim in a short pool. 200 lengths of the pool at the Oaks Hotel. I watched PMQs, then drove to Bolton for a meeting with Mike Forde

[Bolton performance director] who had asked me to help him plot out a strategy for Sam Allardyce [Bolton manager] to go for the England manager's job. We met in one of the boxes overlooking the ground. We agreed it had to be based on much more than the fact that Allardyce was English. 'There has to be more to this than a passport and a birth certificate,' was how he put it when we discussed for a bit. I'd always felt Sam suffered a bit for his rough, tough image, his style as a player, his accent, his looks, his size, he was easily caricatured as a big up and at 'em type, but in fact there was a lot more to him; and that was what had to come through. How he had studied new markets in targeting players for a club like Bolton; being ahead of the game on data and sports science; looking at sports other than football for ideas and thinking; also his ability to get average players to be good. Mike had heard me do the basic pitch on strategy, how to define it and then communicate it, and he felt that was what Sam needed for now.

It wasn't just about having good relations; more important was the message and how he put it over. The FA were far more media conscious than they ought to be, and Martin O'Neill [former Celtic manager] was seen as being one of the best at media. Sam was more in the say it like it is, not so subtle category. He had to show he was a match for anyone when it came to knowledge of the game, and above all how the game was changing. We also talked over some of the things the FA don't like about Sven – the circus, the scandal, the lack of clear internal communication, and turn to his advantage. They were worried that people would try to make something out of his son Craig being an agent, cause trouble for him like Jason had been used to cause trouble for Alex. He asked me to do him a note on the lines we had discussed, and I spent part of the afternoon on that, waiting for Rory and Alex to arrive. We had dinner at the ground with Eddie Davies [Bolton owner]. Fantastic food. I also had a chat with Phil Gartside [Bolton chairman]. I was sussing him out about Sam, who had told me Phil would only back him if he thought he was going to get it. Davies and Gartside both rated Sam, I sensed.

I had a chat with Alex about the GB situation. His view was that I should make clear I was willing to help but refuse to get involved in nastiness, and make clear that I wouldn't do anything to undermine TB. He couldn't see why GB couldn't just go with the flow, and realise that he would be in a stronger position if he let TB go out in his own way. He was a fan of Sam's, thought he was way better than his public profile, but said he enjoyed his drink, and also that Trevor Brooking [FA director of football development] was totally against. Bolton were playing

Marseille and Alex was watching Franck Ribery, Marseille winger, but decided by half-time that he was not good enough for United. It was a good game though, and always good to watch it with someone who really knew what was going on. It was also so much faster and more skilful than last night at Burnley. Alex set off for home before the end to miss the traffic. Rory and I hung around a bit, and we waited till Sam had done his after-match media then went to see him, Sammy Lee [Bolton assistant manager] and Tord Grip [England assistant manager]. Good chat.

Thursday 16 February

We stayed at the hotel at the stadium and I met Mike Forde for breakfast to go through an Objective Strategy Tactics template for Sam. My own sense was that Sam thought he probably wouldn't get it, but there was no harm being in the frame. In any event it was no bad thing to try and think through what he might need to get it. We worked up a short-term media plan for pre-shortlisting 27 February including him being the one to say it is not enough to be English then speech on big challenge of how the next generation comes through when we have all these foreign players coming in. We agreed he would brief Oliver Kay [*Times* football writer] on the English plus angle. Then a speech-type event on international trends. We saw Sam who signed up to it as an overall approach. He tended to bounce around a bit from point to point, but he was bright and listened. He definitely wanted me to help him. We left things vague re any financial arrangements, but did agree it was not sensible for people to think I was involved in helping him. But then when I spoke to Fiona she said she thought I had to stop being behind the scenes for all these different people, like I was embarrassed of what I did.

Rory went off to Burnley with Mike, while I drove over to Leeds for a lunch event I was doing, on leadership and strategy. They were mainly property and housing people and I sensed they were very down on JP. But I was also picking up more and more on GB not being friendly to business, and the idea that TB got them in a way GB doesn't. I lost it a bit with one blatant Tory who was trying to score anti-TB points on the terrorism stuff, but mainly they were OK. Several said they just couldn't understand why I didn't stand myself. I hated it when that happened because it got me thinking I should, and angst-ridden re why I didn't want to. It was a good session though. I drove back over to Burnley, where Rory had been spending time with Steve Cotterill and the players and we had a good laugh chatting over the various characters. He was definitely heading in a football direction, I would say, Oxford or no Oxford.

Friday 17 February

Out for a long run and then a haircut after taking Rory to the gym at the stadium. Then a drive through fantastic scenery to Gisburn to the medium secure psychiatric unit I was due to open. It was in the grounds of an established private hospital, and a really impressive new facility. A good chat with four of the medics who were filling me in on where their patients come from, and the kind of conditions they are treating, then up to the marquee for the opening. Maybe sixty people there. Magdy Ishak [orthopaedic surgeon], an Egyptian from Churchill [psychiatric clinics] plus a few suits. Interesting guy. Very pro-TB and also pro the whole choice agenda. He said we were the only government able to break consultants' monopoly which was holding up waiting lists. In his speech he said only Labour could do it and said I was brave enough to take on the intellectual aristocracy of the media and win. I did a speech re why Burnley and why I wanted to campaign on mental health. I paid tribute to them and whacked the media for their coverage of psychiatric issues. 'Do not be fazed by the fact that you will only get coverage if someone escapes and can be headlined as a psycho on the loose.' Having chatted to Madgy, I also talked a little about how TB was able to differentiate means and ends.

I was taken on a tour by an ex-Blackpool player, now head nurse. Sixteen beds. Some attempted murderers. Schizophrenics, bipolar disorder. One guy who thinks he can talk to planets. Violent in some cases. Some who had had no visitors at all. Art therapy was a big thing. Seemed good staff. Small astroturf exercise yard. Back to the hotel then to Turf Moor [Burnley stadium] for the fundraising dinner after Fiona arrived. David Dickinson [TV auctioneer] standing in for Phil Tufnell [cricketer]. John Parrott [snooker] was OK but a bit blue for some. Bill Beaumont arrived from Dublin, doing as a favour to me, given he was more Blackburn than Burnley. I did a Q&A with the various guests. The best was probably Geoff Thomas [former footballer] on his post-cancer cycling exploits, after which we raised 2.1k auctioning his cycling shirt. Then a chat with Steve Cotterill who broke down in tears telling the story of the Tom Smith funeral, the fourteen-year-old fan who had died of a brain tumour recently. He took the whole squad to the funeral of as way of showing their respects, but also giving the players a different perspective. I was pleased Fiona was there, sitting with Frank Teasdale [former chairman] and Jimmy McIlroy [club legend]. Good time, raised a fair bit of money too.

Saturday 18 February

Up and off to Liverpool v Manchester United. A fair bit of jocular banter on the way from the car to the entrance. Some not so jocular. 'Fuck off back to Burnley ... part-time Manc ... any pal of Fergie's is a cunt...' Nice chat with the guy on the reception who was a big Labour man. Saw Alex briefly. Lovely chat upstairs with Jimmy Armfield [former England captain turned media pundit], who has a real soft spot for Burnley. David Davies and Alex Horne [FA] both there and I was picking their brains about the runners and riders for the England job. Didn't get much of a sense that Sam was favourite. Sven was also there, as was Nancy [Dell'Olio], who said she wanted to have lunch. She was a total riot, and he was so quiet and calm alongside her, just smiling and nodding as she waved her arms around and generally created energy all over the shop. United were poor, Liverpool terrific [1–0]. Afterwards David Moores [Liverpool chairman] invited me into the boardroom. He was very pro-TB, he said, worried what happened when he went. Also said that he often cited me as a good example of someone able to let horrible press stuff wash off his back. John Motson [BBC commentator] was in his post-match zone, wandering around asking himself what he could have done better. He is such a pro.

Sunday 19 February

Up early and off with Rory to Birmingham for his 400m indoor race. 52.22, personal best. Fiona called as we were driving north to say there was loads more in the papers about the [Silvio] Berlusconi thing with David Mills, today's stuff focused on a letter to his accountant which seemed to suggest he helped Berlusconi lie.* He called me later and said

---

* Lawyer Mills had acted for the Italian Prime Minister in the early 1990s and was involved in setting up a number of offshore trusts. Subsequent allegations resulted in him being investigated for money laundering and tax irregularities, though the case was later settled without charge.

it was stupidly written but he didn't lie. I spoke to Tessa who sounded very down about it. David said he had to accept he had been an idiot but he had done nothing wrong. He said he felt wretched because he realised people would try to use it to damage Tessa and the government, and she was really upset and 'understandably very pissed off'.

TB called. He said that 'bizarrely', he felt great though things were a bit weird. Felt the TB–GB thing had gone a bit far. Also he felt GB was not dealing with the problem. He was strategising but not applying the right instincts and he felt it could backfire on him. 'I know this is self-serving in a way but his way back with the people he loses vis a vis me is through me. But he can't see it. So he does a military picture and thinks he has done defence. He thinks that just by saying he likes business it somehow deals with the fact that business thinks he doesn't like them. He does foreign affairs. But it doesn't carry. I've tried to tell him so many times but he doesn't listen.' I reported some of the conversations I'd had over the weekend with people saying they didn't like the idea of GB coming straight in. 'I know I have my critics,' he said, 'but one thing I am clear of is that left-of-centre governments should tilt a little bit rightwards the longer they're in. Right-wing governments should tilt a little bit leftwards.' Major had wanted to do that, but then he misread the mood on public service under-investment. 'But when I hear Ed Balls say the public want more spending and they have the polls to show it I want to blow my brains out.'

He said GB does not get middle-income people or business but he thinks he can do what he does with colleagues – bully them into understanding his point and backing it. It won't work. They don't think he has the right instincts. That is why policy was the key to this, getting on the same page on policy. He said what was infuriating him was this constant chatter that we were running out of steam, when we had a huge agenda right across the public services. There is no real rival agenda coming from the Tories, and if GB has a different approach, we have yet to see it. As for the Lib Dems, they are like an ineffectual pressure group. The TB–GB 'soap opera' is the real impediment, and the way to deal with it is through this policy agenda coming together under both of them, genuinely.

He was already talking about the next school reforms after this lot, which sounded a bit bonkers, but he said the reforms had to be seen as an ongoing process, not something with a cut-off date. He wanted to do a press conference for some of the best examples of schools reform around the country. He was also banging on about the need to do more in health with the private sector. He was gearing up for another big speech on social exclusion, and was keen on this new analysis that the division was no longer about working and middle class, but 1, ambitious middle class, 2, aspiring lower middle/working-class group and 3, a group shut out from society's mainstream, which he reckoned was a one in ten minority, but given so many were dysfunctional families, the policy implications were far greater than the numbers.

Monday 20 February

I was doing *Start the Week*. I liked DBC Pierre, whose novel [*Ludmila's Broken English*] was all a bit weird but he seemed an OK kind of bloke. Andy Marr was chairing and on the way in saying how sorry he was for David Mills. The papers were looking a bit grim on that front, with Berlusconi clearly going for him and distancing. Nick Broomfield, who had made the Eugene Terre'Blanche [South African white supremacist] film [*The Leader, His Driver and the Driver's Wife*], was as irritating in real life as on the screen, and the only one to have a rather pathetic pop, raising the Iraq dossier and the need to keep me on a leash with regard to the internet. I was quite pleased with myself that I didn't rise. I did say, having watched the film, that I felt squeamish about his clear fondness for the driver and ex-wife of Terre'Blanche whose views were repugnant. Linda Grant's book on Israel [*The People on the Street*] was OK and she seemed a nice sort, though very intense, pinning me down at the end to explain why she was so pessimistic. I enjoyed it well enough, and got decent feedback, but even 40 minutes didn't allow a really good discussion.

Home to do a bit of work, plus admin from last week, then a two-hour run, and in the evening dinner with Mark Penn. He was now CEO of Burson Marsteller as well as chairman of Penn Schoen [political polling firm] and running [Senator] Hillary Clinton's [second-term election] polling operation. He was a clever guy if a bit odd at times. I didn't see him as an obvious Bill and Hillary sort of person, but seemingly they swore by him. He was hard-working and detailed, and a good reader of data. He knew I didn't want a full-time job but wanted to know if I'd be interested in having the pick of their clients to advise on strategy. He was a bit of a name dropper, talked of clients as though he had led the campaigns not merely advised on them, and I wouldn't be surprised if he did the same when talking about his work with TB and us, though he did at least say we were nicer to deal with than most.

February '06: Chat with the Clintons' pollster

We ate at ZenW3 and he ate pretty large amounts as he chatted through the nature of the job and what I might do.

I'd discussed it with PG earlier and he felt I was best still continuing to avoid business as the main thing I did, because it was so easy to undermine reputation, especially if you had different clients in different sectors all around the world, and he felt I was rebuilding my reputation well by staying focused on other things which could not be identified merely as cashing in and making money. But I said to Penn that though I was not interested in taking on a major role, I was interested in the big strategic questions such as Islam, globalisation, reputation, crisis management, so there might be something in it, if he felt there were people he worked with who would want that kind of discussion. Needless to say, having talked work, then the US political scene, where he seemed confident HC was in a good place, we talked a lot about our situation. He said he liked working with us. There were similarities with the States, but differences too, like the scale and also the limits on funding made it feel smaller in a way, but it also meant you had to be more creative. He said he found TB and GB both impressive in different ways, but he felt GB did not have the same qualities as TB and it was a mistake not to see why TB's endorsement of him was so important.

Tuesday 21 February

Two-hour bike ride then round to see PG. He was feeling pretty down on the whole scene – that TB was losing his way and the public did not really have a clear idea why he was staying; that GB was in decline as a politician and they didn't see him as an attractive alternative; that DC was doing OK, not as good as we were at same stage, but not bad. PG was now moving from 'late transition to give GB honeymoon and then go' to early transition to give GB proper time to bed in. As to why TB should stay 'managing the transition for best benefit of country, government and party – in that order' was the best public line. PG felt in all the main discussions now, the people were being forgotten. They were in a different world to the one the politicians were in. He had played GB's security speech to focus groups and it did not connect – it was all seen as tactical, a ploy, part of taking over, not what he was really about. This was partly what Mark Penn had been saying, that he was trying to be something he wasn't and people sensed it instinctively, because he was not being true to his own instincts.

Philip also felt the GB team was basically just tolerating us as a way of helping them and stopping us, me in particular, going for GB, but they had their own operation and would just keep doing their own thing regardless. PG was used to me being very down about the situation. I was less used to him being so down. He was the one usually trying to draw me in, and make me feel more optimistic about being involved. But today it was roles reversed and I was having to try and make him feel it was still worth helping them. Without a plan B, we had to make plan A work. But maybe there was a plan C – stay out of it all and spark a free for all. PG felt a Reid a Miliband or a Johnson could emerge. The public would not see it as a GB shoo-in. I filled him on all the stuff I was doing with David S. He felt Fiona and I were getting on better, but he did say if we lost the education vote he was not coming to Scotland with us.

I had lunch with Liz Lloyd at Camden Brasserie. Parna was moving on. TB was down at Chequers. She said it was as bad as ever her trying to work with GB's people. There had been zero response to TB's note that we handed over. Then she was told by DA that GB had claimed TB said there was no need to do a written response. I was there when he said the opposite. She was told to deal with Spencer Livermore, who never returns her calls. Hopeless. Chatted away about me, what I was doing, she wanted me more involved but understood why I wouldn't want to be. She said the reality was GB barely spoke to TB, let alone his people, and I was the only 'TB person' he would deal with in anything like a civilised manner. It was nice to see her, but both my own life, and their operation, were feeling a bit wandery and lacking in clarity of direction.

Wednesday 22 February

Up early and out for a run over the Heath. I went in on the bus and popped round to see Parna, who had stuck up the 'Return of the Poisoner' cutting on her desk from today's *Mail*, their response to my whack at them on *Start the Week* attack. I met up with PG and went round to see TB who seemed pretty chirpy. He asked us what we thought. I said that three things were happening: he was being marked up by the chattering class because they were focusing on his departure, GB was being looked at more closely and not rising to it either with chatterers or with public, and DC was doing well but at a superficial level and it was too early to tell where it would end with him. But the TB–GB plan was not really working to mutual advantage because GB was incapable of doing both halves. He could only do what suited him and was incapable of saying New Labour as seen by TB had been a good or successful thing. So where did it leave us? It left us all feeling unsure we were doing the right thing. We were trying to put together a transition strategy but there was not in reality any cooperation coming the other way.

We had no plan B because there was no other candidate that people could gather around. So maybe we needed a plan C which was essentially continue to manage GB, help in so far as we could, and see what or who else emerged. TB said funnily enough he had moved to much the same view. PG said TB was down with the public because they were unsure what was going on at the moment. They felt uninvolved. But he was the only one with strength. They rejected GB's speech on security because it was seen as tactical, not really him, and also presumptuous, in that it was trying to depict him as the inevitable next PM. TB said that he was not addressing his problem which is that people don't trust his instincts. Also, they think he has been disloyal and most people are loyal in their own lives and so value loyalty. 'His disloyalty to me means they're just not sure about him.' He said GB and Ed B both think you can treat the public like a recalcitrant minister – you batter them into submission. You can't. You have to win their support. PG and I both felt if the public were shown a variety of possible contenders – Reid, Miliband, [Hilary] Benn, CC, Alan Johnson etc. – it might look very different. GB was not a shoo-in. His entire strategy had been to knock out everyone else so that we all joined in with the idea it was inevitable.

As TB said, most of the Cabinet were close to suicidal at the thought it would be him, but also virtually united in feeling it would be. GB was shrinking inwards at a time he should be growing outwards. Cameron was not top notch but he might be good enough. He felt the Tories could easily win an argument against the EB line that the country wanted more investment. They might, but only if they could be sure of real improvement, and the Tories will try and make waste stick and they will do it better than under Howard. 'You rate Cameron, don't you?' I said. 'I rate him more than you do. You must always strip out your own bias if you can. He is doing the things we would advise him to if we were on the other side; and he is avoiding doing the things we would advise him not to do.' I actually didn't feel DC was terrible, and agreed that he appeared to be trying to stick to a clear message. But I felt he was lightweight on policy and that would come through, and GB could play to his strengths. But only if he could connect better with people.

TB felt the GB security speech had been a good example of their 'battering' approach – 'He thinks if he just shouts out "IDENTITY CARDS" it will somehow just register that he gets crime and law and order and the broader security agenda. But people need to feel he gets it at an emotional level.' PG said the focus groups were straight on to it. TB was also fed up at the way they [GB's people] constantly moan about everyone else. And how they lack subtlety. But the problem, as ever, is that he is brilliant but impossible. Impossible but brilliant. He suggested I have a chat with Gus O'Donnell to see if there is any more we can do to improve modus operandi. I said it will only happen if GB wants to. The reality is he doesn't. But we also know if he wanted he could bring the show down, and this far he hasn't. He could easily stoke a bigger education rebellion if he wanted. TB was now thinking he should hold off the reshuffle till after the May elections. He said Scottish MPs were telling him GB et al totally fucked the Dunfermline by-election campaign. So on and on we went, pretty much the same view.

He asked me to hang around and go and see him later because he wanted a chat about Iraq and broader foreign policy stuff. He was frustrated at the media's inability to change the terms of debate. Any deaths in Iraq led immediately to the suggestions we should be out of there. Any sign of Taliban resurgency in Afghanistan and the question was, 'Why on earth are we there?' Anything bad said or done by a Muslim – it is obviously our fault for provoking them. I said that was inevitable in a way because people did not perceive either as unmitigated success, in the way Kosovo – eventually – or Sierra Leone had been. But, he said, in Iraq we are trying to help them build democracy, with the support of the government there, with a UN mandate, and our opponents are the extremists. Same story in Afghanistan. Yet so much of public opinion wants to blame us for the extremism, as though 9/11 never happened, as though all of this was somehow provoked by us. Story pre- and post-September 11, it is dangerous. He wanted me to think about the outlines of a big speech he could make revisiting the whole argument.

I said you are revisiting a whole lot of whole arguments right now. He said, 'We can't just take this stuff without fighting back.' He said Islamic extremism was now a worldwide thing, it could define foreign policy for the coming period, there was a link between all these things going on right now – from what was happening in Iraq and Afghanistan, and Iran, and Hamas, and the cartoons in Denmark. But because so much of our opinion buys the idea that we caused their grievance, they can fight hard, but we fight with hands tied behind our back. As ever, our opinion supports rather than challenges propaganda aimed at us. It is as though the Iraqi election never happened. He said he wanted an argument that was unapologetic about what we did, but set it in this bigger context. I said the Guantanamo stuff, and the stuff about prisoner abuse and soldier abuse more generally, didn't help. He accepted that, but said even with that we have to stand up and fight on this, and explain why the fight is so important. We will never win it if our basic posture if one of apology for intervening.

The media will hate it, he said, but he felt the public would understand especially if it is allied to another push on Israel–Palestine. But that, I said, is only going to happen if the Yanks up the ante and there is no sign of that. He said they can be made to do more to help the reformers in the Middle East. I said isn't this what Bush said he was going to do before? He said he wanted to do a speech that was strong on security, strong on multilateralism but strong on values, democracy, justice, human rights, dealing with global poverty. And that meant accepting reform of the major international structures and institutions because they were failing. I said it sounded to me like a massive thing he was suggesting, at a time when he had a lot of domestic problems too. He said he felt the timing for it was right. I felt if you added all of this to the agenda he was trying to push on public services as well, and Europe, and in the context of TB–GB getting worse not better, there was a lot of risk attached to this. But he was in bit between teeth mode, I could see that.

I met Bradders for a cup of tea, then met Gary Gibbon [*Channel 4 News* political editor] for a chat about a film he was making on DC, then a very nice lunch with Godric [Smith, former spokesperson for TB] to say farewell and also to go over speeches for his leaving do. We had a very good laugh reminiscing about some of the barmier times. Total good guy. Home for Grace's parents' evening. She was doing fine, they all said how bright she was, but concentration and effort could do with improvement. Then out with the boys to Chelsea v Barcelona as guests of Joe Hemani [businessman, Labour donor, AC friend] Fantastic second half. Sven and Nancy were sitting in front of us again. 'Are you stalking me?' I asked her. 'No, darling, you're stalking me!' Sven rolled his eyes and smiled. Had a chat with Dickie Attenborough who had seen TB recently and said he found him quite down. He said the GB thing had to be resolved. I know, I said, but how? Dickie had also been in touch with GB, but it was obvious that when people like him saw Gordon, he was perfectly capable of presenting himself as being cooperative, as well as being the big policy driver.

'He is so impressive when he is setting it all out, the state of the world economy, the things that need to be done,' he said, and of course he is, but what guys like this never see, and only get partially through the media, is the nightmare side of GB, and we had been seeing plenty of that recently. Dickie said if we felt it was a good idea for them to meet on neutral terroritory, he would be happy to host something. He said it was too important to lose a good government on the back of all these personality issues, if that is what it is. Joe Hemani had an interesting take. He said he was naturally to the left of TB in many ways, but he was very down on Gordon. Barca different class [won 2–1].

Thursday 23 February

Cathy Gilman [Leukaemia Research] collected me to go to a triathlon pitch at ING [banking and financial services corporation] in the City. Quite a dull bunch. I spoke OK but with few immediate sign-ups. Then we headed to Traindrun [triathlon store] to get fitted with new gear. Home for a long run, really motoring at the end, then watched the Marseille-Bolton return while working on TB's speech for Scotland. GB called just after the match started. GB: 'Hello it's Gordon.' AC: 'How are you?' GB: 'Why is Tony making a speech tomorrow setting out the long-term agenda for the country?' AC: 'I didn't know he was.' GB: 'That is what they're briefing. This is his Thatcher equivalent of "going on and on."' AC: 'I think he would have told me. I am working on the draft now. Where did you hear they were briefing that?' GB: 'From the press.' AC: 'They're winding you up.' GB: 'I'm not bothered re what he does but if it's back to silly games I'm not interested.' I said it was the Scottish conference, so he had to make a big speech, surely? Yes, he said, but not setting out a new agenda for the long term.

I asked him if he got the note I had done for him? Yes. 'And?' 'We should discuss it.' I had set out – again – how I felt he needed to change his overall mindset and his modus operandi, and also echoed TB's point that there was a difference in saying something to deal with a perceived problem in his image, and saying something because he really believed it. He was strong on the economy, but whenever he broadened out people sensed he was doing it for tactical reasons. I gave him a sanitised account of PG's account of how his security speech went, and even that was enough to send him into a bit of a spin. 'Of course I care about security.' I had so enjoyed the feeling of near exhilaration having been doing different things for a few days in the north last week. I said to

GB I would get hold of the latest version of the speech and make sure it was not as he feared. He calmed down a bit and we talked about the Chelsea match a bit, then he was just back to blame etc.

Friday 24 February

An hour on the bike at the gym. I did another note to GB, a stronger version of the last one, saying he urgently needs to reassess his strategic position and face a few uncomfortable truths. He was in danger of blowing it by failing to see the importance of recognising both what TB had achieved and how important it was that the transition was a genuine act of mutual support and solidarity. If he didn't change mindset and modus operandi he risked destroying himself. It was pretty tough and I decided not to send it until showing it to PG. Out to meet Nancy, who wanted to pick my brains about her Truce [peace through football] charity. She wanted help with access e.g. to GB, Bill C, she wanted me to be an ambassador for it.

She was such a livewire, a real flirt, very funny, though not always easy to understand. She was very open about Sven – he doesn't really enjoy her having such a profile, doing things independent of him. Her philosophy was that life was a challenge and love is the most important thing. She loved him and though he did bad things, one night's sex with Ulrika Jonsson [TV presenter] was not going to stop that. She was very tactile in that way Italian women have. She partly blamed herself for him going off. He was keen to be Man U manager. He liked working in England. But she wanted to stay in London. She was quizzing me about Diana stories. Nice enough time.

PG was up in Aviemore for TB's Scottish conference speech. I had been sending through new stuff via him but PG said he found him a bit stubborn. We did need to make it more people-focused though. He felt TB was a lot angrier than he let on. He felt a bit maligned and also the Scottish party and media always had this ability to get under his skin by making him feel like a foreigner flying in. He had quite a good insight about the media coverage of politics almost turning it into another branch of the entertainment industry, and I had worked on that last night to make it less about frustration for politicians than having an impact on the people they were there to serve, and tied it to the dangers of people inside politics sliding into a comfort zone without even realising it was happening. He had a good section on the Tories' and Lib Dems' policy incoherence, and on the SNP talking about anything apart from the one thing they really believed in – independence. He did touch on a lot of the policy areas from his last couple of notes, but not in the way GB had feared he would. It was a perfectly good speech, nothing more, and the bits of media I saw were going on the general message, with a bit of focus on poverty, and taking tough decisions.

Saturday 25 February

There was something in the *Telegraph* about me seeing Nancy for lunch, which I could do without. Off to Birmingham with Rory, then over to Coventry v Burnley. Paul Fletcher [former Burnley player working on new Coventry stadium] gave us a tour of the new stadium including the would-be casino. I had a chat with Geoffrey Robinson [Labour MP, Coventry director] who said he thought GB was doing very well, and would be an excellent PM. He also seemed to buy totally the line that TB had reneged on a stack of deals to go.

Sunday 26 February

Two-hour run. Tessa called, said the David [Mills] stuff was getting nastier and closer to her. She sounded OK but the sort of legal work David did was so complicated and I wondered if she knew everything. The *Mail on Sunday* ran a story saying I was calling for Kelly out and DM in at education. I got message to Ruth that it was not true. I wondered if that was coming from GB people, picking up on my body language at recent meetings. I had another go at the note to GB, toughened it even more, said he was simply not addressing his weaknesses etc. I wasn't sure about sending it. PG felt I should because it was true.

> This is designed to be helpful. I feel you need a significant re-assessment of your own strategic position and operation. I am not convinced you are getting or following the right advice. Without a change to strategy and modus operandi, I think you are in some trouble.
>
> The problems are these:
>
> • You are being looked at in a different way, because of the assumption that you will be next PM. But you do not appear to be rising to the challenge. You are broadening – i.e. addressing new issues, developing a profile – but not deepening – i.e. giving a richer and deeper sense of what you are about, which indicates what you would do as

PM. Where people do sense it, some seem to be anxious about what they feel. These feelings cannot be brushed aside. This is not about the media, though there are problems there too. It is about people and instinct.

- Qualities that were strengths when establishing yourself as the only leader in waiting, when in the main you were being closely watched by party adherents and the broader political class, are now becoming weaknesses with a wider audience. What internally was seen as legitimate ambition is seen as a pattern of disloyalty against a leader who, as I have said before and as happened to Clinton, will be marked up (evaluated positively) as the exit doors near. People think you care more about getting the job than what you would do with it. Politically, what was seen as a position slightly to the left of TB, and as sensible internal positioning, is seen as being old-fashioned and left-wing, and causing concern you will not be as New Labour as you say.
- Things in your operation that you could get away with at one removed from the top will not escape real scrutiny e.g. wayward and inaccurate briefing, undermining of colleagues, lack of subtlety in presentation. Some of these are things that could actually destroy you in No. 10. You cannot cut corners, mislead or have such a narrow range of operation. I know that was said about the TB operation. But that was because our opponents wanted it to be so. They did not actually, in reality, pin it because though we made mistakes, we were ultra careful almost all the time. Bold in strategy. Careful – usually – in presentation.

I think a lot of this flows from a mindset that simply has to change. You blame others for your situation. You think you were cheated back in '94 and on occasions since. It blinds you to some of the realities, not least how big the step up really is. This is not just about Tony but anyone and everyone. I hear you, Ed etc. constantly complaining about the weaknesses of others but rarely looking at yourselves and what you could do to improve your operation. This makes people doubt your leadership skills. You communicate unease and fear and divisiveness. You lash around at people who are trying their best in other jobs. This reinforces the idea that you are not a team player. Team leaders must also be team players. Too many of the team you would be expected to lead doubt that they should follow. I worry about who is going to be doing the main jobs around you. Perhaps you know but you have to be able to build a team of all talents.

So much of this would be resolved by you and TB working together properly. It seems impossible. I do not accept your basic take – that he is overwhelmingly a problem, that he is fundamentally untrustworthy or that he does not want you to succeed – in both senses of the word. But you make it so difficult. I see him trying to make things work between you, and you only seeing the things that prevent that from happening. Many leaders would have given up by now. I see the contempt with which some of your people view him, and I find it hard to think of any other leader who would accept that, let alone one so provenly successful.

You appear unable to see three basic truths which are overwhelmingly accepted by others at home and abroad. Until you do, I don't think you can progress to a different place strategically.

- Tony was the right man for the right time in '94.
- He has a phenomenal strategic mind and a strong record of leadership.
- His full endorsement of you, convincingly made, is essential to your defeating Cameron.

Until you see him as solution as well as problem you will thrash around in a strategic no man's land that will eventually become a wilderness. I think the above should even be openly expressed by you in a speech.

I sought to bring you together at the last election because it was the right thing for the party. I think it is still the right thing you take over.

But I won't be part of any plan that is divisive or seeks to undermine Tony's position. I am happy to continue trying to bring you together until he goes, at a time I thought we had agreed was about right.

And I seriously ask that you understand the sheer difference in scale between the two jobs.

The pressures are relentless. The media scrutiny is like nothing you have ever known and people you may think you can charm and cajole become a lot harder to keep on board. Understand that people like [Paul] Dacre [editor-in-chief, Mail group] says internally he talks you up as a way of undermining Blair because once Blair has gone, 'We've got them.' He has told Cameron he will be 'full square' behind him, whatever he does.

But above all you can't pull the wool over people's eyes. They work things out. They get to the point.

If they think you don't understand them and their lives, they will get it.

I have been alarmed by how negative people have been when I talk to them. Business is very down on you because it is now beginning to think what you will be like without TB there. The public are worrying that you don't have his basic belief in low tax, aspiration, tough on crime, and so on.

These are harsh things to say. But I feel you hear too much the politics of 'if only' a feeling that if only you were in charge, things would be so much easier and so different.

You need to broaden advice. You need to stop making your speeches so complicated. You need to soften your body language, stop emanating so much anger and hurt. You need to speak to people not at them. You need to listen to people for what they say, not for how you can win them to your view. You need to be more open and straightforward. You need to sort your media operation which will become a problem if you don't. You need to build bridges with colleagues. You need to understand that if TB is forced out, both of you will suffer. You need to learn the language of humility. You need to see good in others, not just those who follow you.

I am sorry to be so blunt. But the efforts currently being made are wasted. I have been equally blunt with Tony on many occasions. It has always been up to him whether he listens or not. You may feel you are in an impossible position. The way out is obvious. It involves both of you. But if it doesn't happen soon, and you don't start working properly together, I worry we are wasting our time. Feel free to ignore or to respond. But if the response begins, 'The problem is, the trouble is, if only Tony would this that or the other', you haven't heard.

After I told PG I regretted sending the note he wrote that he didn't think it was the wrong thing to do. It was honest and would probably strengthen my standing with GB. But we cannot rescue the situation, the more we try the worse it gets. Gordon is strong and there's a chance that all that anger and latent power may drive him towards success as leader. Right now TB needs to rise above it and heal the party.

I finally sent it and after the Man U v Wigan match [4–0 Football League Cup Final], GB called. I asked how he was. He said fine till he read through the note. 'What has changed in last few days?' I said nothing but I felt we were not being honest. Nobody was saying what they really thought because of the basic mistrust between them. I felt we were making no progress. He said he had done everything asked of him – speeches on the subjects asked to, in the way he was asked to, getting involved in education even though he felt TB had simply picked a fight with the party. He said it was wrong to say he hadn't engaged with TB. There had been a private exchange of letters. Yet again TB had broken his word. It was a character thing. Every time he secured his side of the deal he forgot the other side. The whole process recently had been about getting GB support through the difficult votes. Now he seemed to be OK on that so now it was back to it. He seemed to think that I was upset he had denied I had been advising him, based on his replies to Marr. I said it really didn't bother me. He said he thought it would have been bad for me.

He wanted to say that he was a friend of mine, had always been in contact etc. But on engagement, he felt TB was not even prepared to go to base 1, let alone to where we wanted him to be. By the end of the call, half an hour or so, I wished I had never sent the note. I said it was in part born of frustration that we were seeming to make such little progress – I spent ten years with my head in a vice and now it felt like it was going back on. He said, 'I can't give up. You sound like you're giving up. I can't and I won't. I won't let anything get in the way of us winning, but I need to know where people stand.' He said he felt I was basically Tony's friend and on his side, and so when I got frustrated like this, I went to a plague on all their houses position. I felt I wanted out but also said to him I had expertise and experience I should put to work for him. There were weaknesses there he needed to address. He said Philip was giving TB wrong info. 'I am getting polling and groups and I know what the weaknesses are. Your note just way overstates things but I can't move if he keeps breaking his word. He has done it again and again.' He said he hoped we would continue to talk, rather than send OTT notes. 'Keep in touch, regards to Fiona.'

Monday 27 February

Feeling down again. Out for a walk with Fiona who was convinced it was because 'those people' still had power over us and I was feeling frustrated and angry at my inability to move it on. Maybe. The computers and phone were also not working so that was annoying me too. To No. 10 for latest 'Group of death' – minus DA who, according to PG, was growing into the role and had said to him last night, 'GB can be a nightmare to work for but believe me, he really is trying.' I went in for a pre-meeting with TB and Liz. I said I'd pretty much given up because the mistrust was so bad I could not move things on. I sensed that TB thought I was moving over. PG told him I had been very honest and hard with him. The latest flare-up for GB was not being allowed to launch a constitutional report by Helena Kennedy as the backdrop

February '06: GB complains AC note 'way overstates things'

to his announcing a new constitutional committee. TB just felt there had been too much TB–GB stuff around last time and he didn't want another wave.

When I said that GB had said he kept every part of what they agreed last time, and TB hadn't, TB flared up, said it was fucking ridiculous, that no PM had ever done what he did. No PM would tolerate the way he treated him. No other Cabinet minister, not even JP, had ever hung up on him as GB did on Saturday, just slammed the phone down on him. There was no chance of these two going forward. We walked round to No. 11 having been told GB was ready. We walked in – Steve Richards [columnist, *The Independent*] was there so we trooped off again, back round to TB's office. TB then wanted to see DH and Tom Kelly [Prime Minister's official spokesman] and how they were handling the Tessa situation. TB was worried about Tessa personally, in that he knew it was affecting her, but suspected the whole thing was being deliberately whipped into frenzy mode. It helped the media in that it was all so complicated. That took a few minutes so we were late going round. Bad atmosphere. Better sandwiches. Nice fruit. Cheese. But generally, not good.

GB straight off said there is not much point agreeing anything if we then don't see it through. TB was very calm, kept his voice low volume. Denying there had been a 'on and on' briefing, saying he had discussed social exclusion ideas, denying he had sanctioned him with Helena's group a while back, also saying GB had not been upfront about what it meant. It became an exchange of old lines between the two of them and I could see one or both losing it. Then GB calmed down, went to a written response to the long TB strategy paper. GB went through it. TB said again we need agreed strategy, plan and modus operandi. I said there is so little trust I can't see how this is going to work. GB came back at the same point – we'd agreed something and it never happened. TB finally said, 'Sorry, I've had enough of this, I just can't be bothered with it. I am not prepared to be told I've done nothing when I'm the only Prime Minister in history to pre-announce I won't be fighting an election.' 'I never asked you to,' said GB. 'Not much you didn't.' 'I just want a forward plan for party and government.' He was steamed up and so was TB.

The next time GB got back to his claim that plans which had been agreed were not being seen through, TB said again, 'Right, I've had enough. Sorry, I suppose, but this is going nowhere.' 'Fair enough,' said GB. TB said, 'You and I are going to have to resolve this and it is becoming undignified to have this discussion in front of others. I have other things to do.' He got up and walked out. I indicated to Liz, who was getting up to follow him, that she should stay and she heard a milder version of what GB had been saying to me – he just needs clarity but TB keeps shifting. He was not as steamed up as before though he gave me a couple of the death stares, perhaps because of the note I sent him, or just because of how bad things now were with TB. He felt we were being complacent about erosion beneath the surface. I said – as I had to TB earlier – that it was like a failed marriage – they had their buzz points and when they were pressed, they didn't hear each other, just went off on the past. So as Ed said, when GB said the promise on the constitutional committee was not kept, he meant the earlier promises.

I said to GB it had not been a change of tack but the last TB–GB stuff went too far and he wanted to recalibrate. If there was trust it would be easy but there wasn't so it was impossible. They saw malign motives in each other's plans all the time. Maybe some of it was justified but not all. GB said I had reached a 'plague on all your houses', TB said similarly earlier that I was buying this idea that their problems were 'six of one, half a dozen of the other'. Not exactly. But I did feel TB had to let go a bit on what GB would be like in the job, stop thinking he could control it. GB had taken on some of the points from my note. But both still hurt I felt. TB hurt because he felt isolated and being done in. I said there was near hatred there between them. GB said he needed to know the truth. The party not in good shape. We were losing the initiative on key issues and we had to get it back. And now he went out. Liz, PG, the Eds and I carried on discussing, said we needed maybe the internal people who carried out the operation to be at the meetings rather than us and we do stuff from the outside.

It was really bad today. Quite dramatic. I said the only other time I could remember TB storming out of a meeting like that was when the NI peace process was doing his head in. Ed was to be fair trying to help I think. He said they should meet with all key people on both sides and indicate travel of direction, where to go and how to get there. But it was not a good scene. Far from it. Since Sunday I had been feeling a bit down and this wasn't helping. Fiona was convinced it was all about them and their ability to draw me in. I felt it was also in part a fin de siècle feeling. TB called after I went to bed. He said, 'Now you see what I face every time I'm with him one on one. Normally he moderates his behaviour if you and the others are around. I actually felt come the end it was totally undignified for the others to be hearing that. But I cannot have a situation where because I make a decision he can somehow go on strike or rant and rave like that. No other Cabinet minister would talk to me like that.' He said he always tried to put his own feelings of anger to one side and work out what was best.

He still felt probably it was best he took over but there is definitely a flaw there and he saw no sign of change. He said he appreciated the efforts I made at the weekend. He asked if the note I sent was as hard as Philip said. Harder than anything you've seen, I said. He said the problem was that none of his people were really honest with him, and they would be telling him you're wrong. He had nobody who gave it to him straight in that way that JoP AH and I did to him. He was now putting JoP, Liz or Ruth on their calls to make sure proper notes were taken. He said we should keep managing it. We couldn't let it go on the back burner because he was still looking to push him over. Ed M was going round stirring up MPs over the Education Bill. He said the line from GB people's was not that they supported it but that they had to do this 'to save Blair'. There was no way he was being supportive.

Earlier JoP had put two white flags out for me and PG. TB said he knew we were trying and we had to keep trying to make it work. But the reality was whatever you gave him he wanted more, moved to the next set of demands. His worry for the party was that psychologically he was incapable of accepting TB had done anything good. He would move from our current agenda on choice, reform, respect etc. and Cameron would just take it off the shelf and say, 'Look, have safe change with someone who is modelling himself on Blair.' I said he had to stop worrying what would happen after him. Both he and GB were wanting a fourth term but he would not be able to shape the agenda so much. The media temperature on Tessa and David was picking up, and I was getting lots of calls on that. TB seemed to be supportive and would see it as a load of nonsense but the press were definitely getting to frenzy mode a bit.

Tuesday 28 February

Long bike ride. Tessa called. She wanted to put out a statement explaining why the planned Gus O'Donnell statement on the David situation would take a bit of time. I advised against. I think she just has to let it take its course. Then David called having drafted a statement he wanted to put out. But it was over emotional. He was passionate in the way he talked about Tessa, strong on the evils of the press, adamant he was innocent. It was all very good, strong in so many ways, but too emotional, and I persuaded him not to put it out. I said it would take it straight to the top of the news and just bring more shit, more pressure. He agreed after a long chat, but he still did a doorstep saying he would speak out on Thursday – I had advised him not to commit to that given things were so fluid. I advised them both against these walking doorsteps. Just smile, get in the car and go. The media were outside the house in numbers and I know from experience it doesn't feel natural not to say anything when people are bombarding you with questions, but it all felt a bit messy.

Wednesday 1 March

First Tessa and then Margaret McDonagh called and asked would I go and see David Mills with Charlie Falconer [Lord Chancellor] to look at a statement David was doing and wanted to put out on the back of Gus O'Donnell, who was looking into Tory claims that somehow through David's behaviour she [Tessa] was in breach of the ministerial code. I was against, especially when I saw him, at Charlie's. He was trying to tell us the whole story but it was so complicated, so hard to follow and full of things that neither Charlie or I could fully understand. His big point was that he had been stupid but not criminal. In so far as he had made things up he had reasons, like trying to protect Tessa. He knew he had made mistakes but it was because he was so desperate for this not to damage Tessa. An Italian client gave him lots of money to invest. Some was left over that he took as a gift. But there was no deed of gift so it had to be taxed.

Charlie was very forensic. Both of us by the end said it sounded fine but it was hard to be sure because it was so complicated. All that mattered for now was for Tessa get through the statement by Gus and then find a way of separating David's business affairs off in the media mind. It was a different world – Gibraltar, Bahamas etc. Huge sums of money. Tax havens. Mortgage sign-offs. He had been dropped in it with the SFO [Serious Fraud Office] by an accountant. I kept remembering the conversation I had had with David S a while back about having felt suicidal and thought about driving off the road. I asked David if he ever felt it would push him that far. He said no chance of that. But he was going to find it all pretty hard. He was whacking back the wine by the end at a pretty alarming rate too. Worrying all round. Charlie was on good form as ever, so sharp. I reminded DM both Charlie and I had been through a few frenzies and you do get through. But after DM left, we discussed it and both felt even more confused than when he started. Tessa was dragged into it because of the possibility that their mortgage was paid off by the payment from Italy.

Thursday 2 March

Another big hit on the depression front. Bad place again. Usual stuff. Fiona felt every time things got better I let them slip because I always expected things to go wrong. Tessa and David frenzy was getting hotter. I also sensed talking to them both that they might be heading for a break up. David said he was feeling it was just putting too much pressure on them, and Tessa was so angry with him, he felt it was heading that way. Neither of them wanted that deep down, but I felt talking to Tessa as well this was going to have a very unhappy ending.

Friday 3 March

As I feared, Tessa called, and said they were going to separate. She was crying at times, but she said she had lost it with him, she was so angry because he had been so foolish. The thing had gone to a new level with a letter David had written which suggested he could rely on TB's support. I said she had to think where she wanted to be in a few years, not where she wanted to be with tomorrow's papers. She said it is not about that, she just felt this cannot go on like this. I said she should come round at half-two. I spoke to David as well, who was also in a state of real turmoil, but he too felt separation for now was advisable, not least as a way of helping her by heaping all the blame on him. He couldn't make out how on earth he had got to this. He felt he must have been mad in '04 and lost all judgement. I said he should come round and we would talk it through and then decide what to do. I had to go out for lunch with Magdy Ishak – the Christian Egyptian guy I had met at Gisburn. Pro-TB unsure re GB. He was picking my brains but I couldn't be sure to what end.

Back home, and I was talking to JoP about whether TB still robust re Tessa. He said yes. I warned him that it was possible they would announce their separation later today. He was shocked. But he said if that's where it's going, fine, but TB is certainly not pushing for it. I could hear David out in the street talking on his mobile, and I got him in. The *Sunday Times* had some leaked letter to do with the Inland

Revenue. Yet another complicated situation, though it didn't sound lethal. Tessa arrived, just very sad, David trying to express support but I could see they had reached the end of the road. David had to leave to go and get his car fixed, having smashed a wing mirror getting away from the hacks yesterday. They were with us from half-two till seven, Tessa staying longer than David and Jess [Mills, daughter], who came after a while. Tessa said she wanted space before going back to get bags and head to Charlie's. She said David was an antidote to her and that was why he was a life and soul and such fun but it was this wild part she couldn't live with for the moment. They were both very different people, I liked them both and it was sad it had come to this. The Berlusconi thing always had a bad feel to it, and it was the drip drip that got it closer and closer and it was obvious she just felt he had been so stupid and she couldn't bear being with him right now. So sad.

Fiona and I were due to go out for dinner at John Carr/Glenys Thornton's. The Hodges [Sir Henry, solicitor, and Margaret, Minister for Work] were there, Henry now a judge who sent a guy down for twenty-six years last week, and Andrew Graham [master of Balliol College, Oxford] and Peggotty [wife, academic]. Nice evening but Fiona got so angry in her conversation with Margaret H re schools. Henry noticed it. He asked her why she was so angry, and said she could not go through life being so angry, she had to resolve it. Did she want to be seen by others as an angry person, rather than someone who could adapt and make change? I think he realised the anger wasn't just about the issue, but about life more generally. She listened though, because later she said she liked Henry, and she didn't want people like him to think she was full of anger. Andrew Graham was very nice and made us feel better about Balliol [Rory Campbell's college]. There was lots of talk about Tessa and David, MH thinking Tessa would probably have to go, Fiona and I saying next to nothing, and certainly nothing about our discussion earlier.

Saturday 4 March

Up at 6.45 and off to Birmingham with Rory for AAAs [athletics]. I called Hilary Armstrong to make sure they set up a good reception for Tessa in the House on Monday. Charlie called, said she was devastated but being brave. He thought it was the right thing to do. Then Tessa came on, said she felt totally wretched but she knew this was the right thing to do, even if she could not really imagine life without him.

Peter M called, said he still felt she was not out of the woods. That the separation was a new factor and there was no way of knowing where it would go. I felt the reaction in Parliament was important and Tessa had a lot of friends and supporters in all parts. By the time we arrived at the National Indoor Arena, and the statement went out via David's lawyer, calls were coming in to do bids on it. TB's interview with Michael Parkinson on God had been running big on ITV with predictable howls of protest twisted by the BBC. All he said was that if you are Christian you trust in the judgement of God. But it was used to get all the anti-war people wound up. Through the day I was being chased by lots of papers trying to run the line I had forced the DM–Tessa separation by saying 'Job or marriage' – à la Robin Cook. Someone had let out that they came to see me on Friday and it was becoming a problem. How the hell do these things get out? Nobody apart from us knew.

Patrick Hennessy [*Sunday Telegraph*] claimed to have a quote from MPs. I said they were invented. It turned out to be anonymous. Charlie was looking after Tessa, and was still worried it would end in tears and departure from government. I spoke to her on and off through the day. She sounded very very down on a couple of calls, more focused on others. In the end I got Tim Barton [Labour press officer] to put out a line from me, Tessa and David been friends for many years, very sad but the first I heard of separation was from David on Friday. DM set off for US looking pretty down. He said he was fine. TB called as we arrived at the track. He said again we had to ensure the separation was not seen as tactical. Ben W-P was doing ring round re same. We got home by 9. Watched TB on Parky. Excellent. Interaction with Kevin Spacey good. Ed Victor called after a call from John Witherow [editor, *Sunday Times*] about David Cracknell [political editor] doing a story that I would not be doing diaries before GB leaves office. Another one presumably from GB people. Ed said I was like Zelig [eponymous character in Woody Allen film], people seeing me everywhere.

Sunday 5 March

I was speaking through the day to Charlie and Tessa. CF said the papers were ghastly but there was nothing new or overly damaging. It was just generally horrible. Later I had a read and they were pretty shit all round. There was stuff about me in the middle of most stories. There were made up quotes galore but of course they wanted me big in the story as a way of suggesting it was about political and media management, rather than helping a friend. Philip called earlier when I was out with Grace and the dog. He said had I seen Peter Dobbie's column in the *Mail on Sunday*? It had an account of my saying TB had a psychological problem about leaving. I had said something on those lines at the end of the meeting earlier in the week, after GB had left. So it must have been one of the Eds. PG wrote a short angry note to GB. I got hold of the paper and sent a longer angrier note. 'Blair's away with the fairies... and the men in white coats are coming.' The story attributed to a 'Blair crony' who is supposed to have said that Tony has a 'psychological problem' – that he cannot come to terms with giving up power. I explained to GB that after he left, I did use that phrase. I also knew they had lunch with the paper this week. I said I found his relationship with the Dacre papers distasteful. But this was beyond the pale.

'I have more than a decade's worth of experience of being told by you, [Charlie] Whelan [former GB spokesman], Ian Austin [MP, former GB advisor], Ed [Balls] and others that your team is not responsible for things in the press that I may have suspected them of briefing. In this case, there is no doubt at all. None. The idea that Liz or Philip would have done so, which will doubtless be the attempted claim, or broadcast my observations any wider in such a way that they reached the *Mail*, does not deserve a moment's consideration.'I said in my note to you last week that you needed to take a long hard look at your operation and the way you handled TB and others in the run-up to a transition. I have always been clear with you that I will help you in any way to become PM and win the next election – but I have been equally clear I would not cooperate with a strategy based upon divisiveness, not least because it is strategically and tactically inept. Nor can I operate if frank and private conversations are then regurgitated to journalists who exist to destroy us – you included, believe me.

'There may be fault on all sides. There usually is, in any difficult situation. But I think the lion's share, so far as malicious briefing to the press is concerned, falls in your area. I think Tony has tried harder than you give him credit for. I have tried as hard as I can given my own circumstances. Philip tries if anything even harder. But I am at a loss to understand what you or any member of your team thinks can be achieved by this kind of thing, and pretty much at a loss, if this is the way things are, to see a way forward.'

Ed Balls replied, saying he didn't know Dobbie, never read the paper, and said if they reacted as badly as this to every piece of anti-GB stuff in the press, there would be no end to it. He raised again the story about my and PG's supposed role in advising GB on image, ties and spin – they really did seem to think we briefed that. He was adamant this was coming from people determined to wreck the process we were trying to make work. He added for good measure that he thought my long note to GB was way over the top but he didn't want to have an argument about it. And he suggested that we were now finding reasons to make things not work. GB called later. He said he had spoken to the Eds and they denied having anything to do with it. He tried to claim it was work of people in No. 10 who didn't want the transition to work. PG had an email from someone saying the *MoS* team had been into lunch at the Treasury last week. I said there was no point us going on about who did, who might, who could have done, they just had to understand I felt there was a breach of trust there. He said there are people trying to do in the whole thing and we have to work together for it. In the end I couldn't be bothered and said let's simmer down and I'll see you on Wednesday. OK, he said, but we both want this to work.

Tessa called after returning home, fulminating about all the press still outside. I had written some lines for her in the Commons tomorrow. She had spoken to TB who had his 'How's the patient?' tone. She said he was totally supportive but you could never tell where it would end. She felt a good day tomorrow would see her through. But she was worried about David. She was coming for dinner but Jess and I persuaded her to stay in rather than go out in front of the hacks again, and instead Fiona went round with Grace. TB called as he was on his way back from Chequers. Said he had never felt more confident and yet all a bit weird. He was at a loss to know what to do re GB. He couldn't be bothered with all the madness. He said he really wanted Tessa to pull through. Grim all round if she doesn't. I went to the gym, did an hour in the bike and had a swim.

Monday 6 March

The papers were still rampant on Tessa. Phil Webster had a good, and broadly sympathetic piece on their relationship, Tessa the kind soft networker, David more abrasive and punchy, but she could forgive him virtually anything. David was now in the US, called a couple of times, sounded quite down, though so far the media hadn't found him. Tessa was due in the House later, and she called before leaving home. Carry only your handbag. Get someone ahead of you to organise the cameras on exit so it is not a mess. Smile, say hello and nothing else. Margaret

Beckett was superb defending her on the radio. I had briefed her but she went even further than what we'd discussed, said Tessa had a duty to see it through because we could not let ministers get hounded out by trial by ordeal. Glenda Jackson [actress turned Labour MP] was disgusting, personal and nasty, bitterness in every word. Tessa did fine. One or two nice Tories, as I expected there would be, Kitty Ussher [MP] good, Barry Sheerman [MP] comparing the ghastly modern media with *Good Night and Good Luck*, the brilliant film about Ed Murrow [US TV journalist]. The general feeling was that she did fine. Also the words was that the Commons standards guy was going to be fine. Mike Forde called in advance of Sam [Allardyce] seeing the FA tomorrow. His interview in *The Times* today came out fine, though there was a fair bit of talk of them wanting a foreign manager. I watched Wigan v Man U [1–2] while drafting an article on Tessa and Glenda and theme of bitterness.

Tuesday 7 March

I worked on a *Times* piece on Glenda and bitterness. It was pretty heavy and Danny Finkelstein [comment editor, *The Times*] was keen but Fiona was totally opposed. It specifically said she showed it was possible to campaign against the government without being bitter but she still felt it would give us a lot of problems locally, given Glenda was our MP. So I dropped it, pretty angrily. Ed Victor called, saying I seemed to be in every story at the moment. I said it wasn't deliberate. It was true though that I seemed to be all over the Labour stories right now. I worked on a speech for the event I was doing tomorrow, while watching Barcelona v Chelsea [1–1, Barcelona won 3–2 on aggregate].

Wednesday 8 March

I had a rest day on the exercise front, had really sore muscles after doing a long swim plus track drills yesterday. Out to Accenture for their women's day event. Well organised, good buzz. Claire Connor, England cricket captain, very nice and smart, grilling me on the Lions. Shirley Williams [former Labour MP and SDP MP, now Liberal Democrat peer] also speaking, still got it. Libby Purves [broadcaster and writer] was chairing the panel Q&A after I did the keynote speech, which went fine. Got them laughing, and then turned it to the need for positive discrimination to get more women in politics. I used the Margaret Beckett line on why it was so important Tessa toughed it out, and could see a lot of them nodding along. I really went for the media over their coverage of politics and that struck a chord too. Only Libby Purves seemed to be a bit iffy about Tessa. Shirley agreed on the media but she said to get more women in politics we had to have PR [proportional representation]. Talk about being on message.

She said she totally supported what I had said about the need for more women agenda and she sensed I really believed it, but it was the case I had been part responsible for macho politics because I had become so dominant in the era, and I was associated with a certain style that was very male. It was a good event though, and I hung around for an hour or so talking to people afterwards, several asking for work opportunities. I got a cab to see David S, him saying he thought I seemed quite chirpy, me saying I was still very up and down. We talked about the conflicted feelings I had about going back in the whole time, and why the GB/*MoS* row had angered me so much. He felt I was constantly torn between what I wanted to do, in a life of freedom, and what others wanted me to do. We also talked over the Glenda Jackson argument, which he felt again had hurt because it hit at a basic faultline. I had sacrificed another weekend to helping out the government, and individuals within it, and then it looked to Fiona like I wanted to prolong it by writing about it, and in a way that she felt I was being critical of any criticism, and so she took it personally. I felt I was really trying to change, but not getting that much in return.

Thursday 9 March

Fiona out to LBC, I went out to do interval training on the Heath. Tessa called because it looked like the press were getting into David's business partner, and she sounded very down again. DM was on the floor again, was worried this would lead to him just not getting work because of all the controversy. She asked me to have a chat with him, and he sounded pretty upset, raging at the way the *Mail* and *Mirror* were chasing this with a view to destruction of his livelihood. I said we had to get to a stage where we were able to say he was doing legit work with mainstream clients. Get through this and rebuild. It was all of a piece with the article for *The Times* I was doing. He was OK by the end but clearly worried. I was doing an event down in Hook, Hampshire, Four Seasons Hotel. The driver was a friend of Lawrence Dallaglio and Will Greenwood, and lots of the other rugby players. We had a laugh with me leaving notes for them in different parts of the car, mainly about the need for them to stop having anything to do with the *Mail*. Driver was very right-wing in a rugby club sort of way, but a nice guy, funny. I arrived, chilled a bit, then at the dinner I was seated with a guy from the Bank of England and Charles Prideaux from Merrill Lynch [financial advisors]. They were nice enough but it was all a bit public school for me. The issue with these events was whether I actually felt there was any purpose to them beyond a bit of entertainment for them, and a fee for me. So yesterday, I felt there was a broader purpose. This one, me telling a few funny stories then making a few serious points, it just felt a bit prostitutery really. Added to which there were a few rank Tories in there who, once the drink flowed, thought it would be fun to wind me up. Nice hotel though. I watched David Yelland [PR executive, former *Sun* editor] on the Andrew Neil show, who did a good job defending Tessa.

Friday 10 March

I didn't sleep that well, got up early and went for a long swim before the car arrived to take me back. The same driver – called 'Sketch' – and he had a copy of the *Mail* waiting for me on the back seat. He said he was driving Will Greenwood tonight so I got a thick felt pen and rewrote the headlines. I really liked the hotel, but had not enjoyed the event. I was also struck yet again by how down the business world was on the idea of GB as PM. They definitely had a sense that he would take things in a different direction. The mood about Tessa was just about OK, though damaging. I got back for a meeting with Ed Victor and Cathy Gilman. We had snapped up Mel Brooks [filmmaker], who was a friend of Ed's, as the first of our celeb events for the charity, and we were able to get access to one of [entertainment entrepreneur] Sally Greene's theatres. Should be great. Ed very excited about it, and in a good mood because his blood tests were good. I had redone the bitterness piece, Fiona was fine with it, and *The Times* were running it tomorrow, though they kept coming back asking me to put in more about my role. Off up north later with Calum to see Mum. Dinner at the local pub. She seemed on good form.

Saturday 11 March

I had my new bike with me and took it out for a spin. Fantastic, couple of hours on flat roads. Then we went to see Robert [Templeton, sick relative] before heading to Geoff Hoon's for lunch before the Derby–Burnley game. Calum was surprised to see the cops with machine guns as we arrived. Nice house in a fairly upmarket area near the M1. Showing us some of his record collection, generally being affable. He was a very warm sort of bloke, and seemed to take the rough with the smooth pretty well. He was joking a bit about how much I still seemed to cop it for all the anger over Iraq. I certainly felt at times I was next in line after TB. We had lunch with him and a mate called Robert. Small talk and football mainly but Geoff was very good with Calum. Dire match, really bad [Derby 3, Burnley 0]. Back to Geoff's to collect the car then head home, and out to Siobhan Kenny [former No. 10 colleague] wedding anniversary party. Fiona was not well so I went with Grace and Tessa.

Tessa pretty down but glad to be getting out among people who were all nice and supportive. We gave her a lift back home and had a great chat with Jessie, who totally got the picture. Tessa was raging about the press, me saying we should have dealt with them when we had the chance. Thatcher gave them a real sense of their own power, and she exploited it to her advantage, then with Major they continued with the same sense of power but against him, and with us they had gone with the flow when the honeymoon was in full flow, but now they were back to the status quo ante and worse, and in part we had colluded with that. I said how many times had we argued about this? Part of the problem was that TB always felt he could persuade people to be reasonable and persuade people to his way, but some of these guys were beyond any kind of reason now, it was all hate.

Sunday 12 March

Fiona and I both seemed to have a bit of flu. She stayed in bed, I took the dog out, and then went to do an interview with Jon Sopel [BBC] on the press. It was OK but I always felt there was never enough time for these kinds of discussions. I got back home and just lay in front of the telly watching sport and reading a bit, and feeling shit. TB called, clearly pumped up, and off on one. It was amazing how a day down at Chequers, even if he was working, seemed to re-energise him. He was thinking beyond the education vote this week, and saying we had to use it for the next big steps forward, possibly his press conference, maybe a speech at the end of the week. The Tessa situation was just the latest in a long line of stories that the media could gorge on as a way of saying there was nothing else. We had to show the something else, and we had to show we had momentum in a way the Tories do not. They wanted to say the entire story of the government was TB–GB division, ministers involved in a succession of scandals, and nothing happening on the things people really cared about. The only upside, he felt from meetings with MPs last week, was that they realised there was a problem, and for once they were willing to engage rather than just whinge.

DC was being taken more seriously, but he still felt we could dominate the policy agenda. I felt he was overstating the PLP support for the reform agenda, and the feelings around the education vote were still fluid, but as ever his argument was more reform not less, more New Labour not less. He wanted on the back of the vote to have a big push with new partners and sponsors and local authorities signing up for reform. He sounded if anything like he wanted to go even faster and further in health, but I said I think he underestimated the opposition there will be to his stuff on expansion of the independent sector, and the whole choice agenda. He said he didn't underestimate it all, he knew there would be opposition, but it was the only way to get the improvements people wanted, and keep cutting waiting times. He felt that if we could show we can win these difficult arguments in education, we have to do the same in health. He was also setting a lot of store by the public health plans later in the spring.

He was into the same public/private argument on pensions, saying we were fucked unless we could get a better balance between the state and private provision. He said the weak thing to do was to say, OK, we hear you, you don't like the difficult things, you want it all to be easy so we will slow down. But he reckoned if he could get JP and GB motoring in the same direction – and he said he was thinking of asking Neil to take on some kind of role too – then he reckoned we could get the party more on board for the general thrust. I was worried that if all we did was talk about this urgent need for more and more reform, there would be no capacity to communicate – and have accepted – the idea that we had actually delivered.

I was in agreement that the only way for delivery to be heard was when attached to plans for the future, but if all people heard was the need for more reform in schools, more reform in health, crime, anti-social behaviour, how did that sit with a record we wanted to be able to defend? We had to do both, but I worried he was going to over tilt the balance. I said he was taking an over optimistic view of the way the party was feeling about the way the education debate had gone. When his note came through later, he was if anything even more fired up. He had also added in the need for a whole series of speeches on Iraq, on foreign policy more generally, and in particular finding ways to push back on the idea that the West somehow caused the terrorist threat. He wanted a country by country analysis. And he was obsessed with this idea of generating more attention for moderate voices within Islam, who were becoming more and more marginalised.

Tuesday 14 March

I was working on diaries and exercising lots but feeling very down again for some reason. David Davies [FA] came round. He was planning to leave by the summer and was looking to set up different business opportunities, including possibly with me. Crisis management. Sports legal work which was a huge and growing area. He felt he might end up doing something with Sven. Sven just couldn't understand our press, and the way it worked. He was getting lots of job offers, but he felt the Nancy relationship might be tested by a move. It was nice to see DD, I liked and rated him, but again it all gave me a sense of purposeless-ness. I warned him he risked feeling the same going from full-on, to a mix. He asked me how long it took me to settle into a rhythm I was happy with. I said I am still looking for it. Josh Lewsey was dropped after the thrashing by France [31–6]. Ronan O'Gara called inviting me to the Ireland match. And I got an approach from Unicef about playing in their big charity match organised in part by Robbie Williams. One for the kids to vote on, I think.

Wednesday 15 March

I was working at home most of the day, following news on the Education Bill, watching *Channel 4 News* when up popped Jack Dromey [deputy general secretary, Transport and General Workers' Union]. Quite a moment. The media had been running stories about past loans worth £3.5 million from three party supporters who were nominated for life peerages. Classic bad funding story. But Dromey, party treasurer, was on saying he knew nothing about it, and he was full of that indignation he does quite well. It felt like a big bad moment, and my immediate thought was that he would not have done it unprompted. If GB was involved, it was all out war really. I knew nothing about the issue, but I knew enough about the politics of it to know it was a bad moment. He said neither he nor Jeremy Beecham [NEC chairman] were aware of the loans until they read about them in the press. He said there would be a party investigation and there would also be an Electoral Commission investigation. It was very hard to imagine he was doing all this solo. I called JoP who told me GB had threatened this if he didn't get his way on something else. It was a pretty dire state of affairs. We got through the second reading [Education Bill] with Tory votes but it was not a good time. Fifty-two Labour rebels, his third worst rebellion, but the first time he had needed Tory votes to get through.

Steve Cotterill called in the middle of it all asking if I could help nudge Fergie about getting Phil Bardsley [Man U footballer, on loan to Royal Antwerp] on loan. Out for dinner with Mick Hucknall [singer-songwriter] and Gabriela [partner]. Nobu. Nice enough place and both were very good fun. Fiona was late because she was doing an event at Keats House. We didn't really discuss the education vote but she was basically now arguing for PR too. M and G were moving to Paris. She had something very special about her, definitely a good match. Fiona hadn't seen the Dromey stuff, but realised immediately it was a big hit. It was also the fact he was Harriet's [Harman, former Solicitor General] husband, so she would be dragged into it. The hacks who were calling me were all assuming it was a GB operation, but I stayed out of that for now. Dromey was saying the investigation would include interviewing TB if need be. It was bizarre stuff. By the time we got home it was all over the news, and had a bad bad feeling to it. The timing as well, just hours before the vote, could not have been worse. Done for maximum damage at the worst possible time, with the vote today and TB's monthly press conference tomorrow. *The Guardian* were saying the loans scheme was dreamt up by Michael Levy [TB's personal envoy to the Middle East] and Matt Carter. The business guys who had made the loans seemed to be asking for their nominations to be withdrawn as well.

Thursday 16 March
So much for TB's great plans to push on with the next waves of reform on the back of the vote. He tried, to be fair, pushing on reform, and some of them ran with it, including his line that we could do with yet another Clause 4 revision, but it was perfectly obvious where the media interest was going to be and at the end of his remarks he announced a number of changes in the area of party funding and appointments, including trying to broaden it to other parties. He said he didn't know a single leader who didn't hate fundraising but they all had to do it.

And donations should not be a bar to honours. But it was less about the issue in a way than the politics of it, and he looked a bit vulnerable. He said he was aware of the loans but there was no connection to peerage nominations. Also it looked like the sums involved were way more than £3.5 million, as much as £13–14 million. Alan Milburn called – bizarrely, as I was in diary mid-sentence about an argument he was having with GB in '02 – and he said he had never known such anger in the PLP; he felt they were really going for him now. He also felt that TB lacked a proper explanation as to why Dromey didn't know, and it was not clear what the party was expected to say-think. It was not a happy state of affairs.

The other 'same old, same old' from the bits I was transcribing today, JoP had said that a 44-page GB letter on foundation hospitals was a 'declaration of war' and now he was saying exactly the same about this. I pointed it out. He said, 'No, this really is.' He said he half-expected a horse head to appear in TB's car. Mafia-style tactics. He said we couldn't put up with this any longer. It had to be resolved but how? I was getting lots of media bids, said no on the advice of No. 10 but later discovered TB wanted me to do some. The Dimbleby programme [*Jonathan Dimbleby on Sunday*] was chasing me for Sunday but then came back and said Howard wouldn't do it with me so could Fiona do it instead? Later to David S and it was not good. I had been down for several days. He felt the Dromey thing would be pressing all sorts of buttons. TB called en route to Sedgefield [constituency], and echoed JoP's 'declaration of war' line. He was on a mobile so we didn't talk much, but said we should talk over the weekend and 'discuss how it is all becoming impossible'. I told him what was going on four years ago, much the same stuff. 'No,' he said. 'This is very different.'

Friday 17 March

Steve Bell [*Guardian* cartoonist] at his cruel best/worst, TB naked on all fours – bald patch growing, he would hate that – begging the Queen to 'Strip me of powers and horsewhip me, Ma'am,' and Her Maj saying, 'What's in it for one?' Down again. It wasn't helping that David was asking me to record these moods. But this was really not good and this black mood seemed to be lasting longer and longer. Pat McF and Sally M both called early on, felt things were really bad but also that the mood on GB was moving a bit too. Sally said a lot of the MPs felt quite scared by what was going on, because if it was the case that

GB was behind this – and most assumed so – then it really was war between them. The problem was that there were people there who just didn't care what happened. I had lunch with Calum and Mark B, back to do some work, but I was in bed by half-seven. I chatted to Fiona, said I just couldn't seem to lift my head at the moment, and sleep was the only escape.

Saturday 18 March

Heart-to-heart with Fiona. She said she couldn't understand how the political scene could affect me so deeply. David S had said that he thought I felt a sense of something I had helped create being dismantled, and I saw her as part of it. I don't know. I had felt for a while the medication was getting me to a better place, but these dark clouds were coming in more and more often, with smaller and smaller gaps. Tessa came round in advance of her trip to India and Australia. I sensed that the after-shock was setting in a bit. She had aged a bit, and she looked really sad, which was all the more striking because she was usually one of those you would look to for constant chirpiness. She said she had felt really well supported politically, and had had some wonderful reactions from people of all parties, and also from parts of the media. But ultimately she just didn't know where things were going to end. At least though she was through the immediate political storm and could hopefully get a bit of space to settle the personal stuff.

TB called from Chequers. He sounded low as well. He said things were as bad as they'd ever been with GB. On Wednesday, as he had been dealing with the education vote, he was due to have a meeting with GB and John Hutton on pensions. GB asked for a private meeting first. He thought it would be to beat him up on pensions again. But it wasn't that. He said he had had many ugly conversations with him in the past but this was the ugliest yet, full of real menace. 'It was the first time the mask just fell totally.' He told him that the loans issue was not going to go away and that he was minded to call for an NEC inquiry. TB said, 'What on earth are you saying? Are you saying that as you can't bring me down on education you will try on this?' GB: 'You've done far worse to me.' He asked him several times and said the threats just kept coming – 'There are questions I know you can't answer' for example. TB said what he hated was the cowardice. GB made the threat to do it himself but then instead got Dromey to do it. The idea Dromey did it solo is absurd. He said too that GB was saying,

'It's time to end the deception and lies' re funding. And the last thing he had been asking for was a peerage for [Sir] Ronnie Cohen [business, Labour supporter].

I said, 'What are you going to do?' He said he didn't know but what PG and I had to know was that he could not go along with the current plans. It would be utter hypocrisy to endorse him as PM. What he saw on Wednesday was like something out of the Mafia. It was simply unacceptable. He won't stop it. So Monday's meeting was off but he wanted me to think about how he went forward. He said it was basically an assassination attempt. Yet in the PLP there was no real desire for a coup. I said the only way was to get from a position of GB endorsement, which is where he was now, to one where he did not interfere or endorse any one candidate. As we were speaking I got a text from Balls asking if I got his texts of yesterday and Thursday. I said yes but I feel there is not much I can do and I've had enough of it all. 'So have I but if you quit now it is a disaster for the party,' he said. TB said GB had just raged at him, all the old stuff about betrayal, but with these threats in and out of the conversation. I was off to Stoke v Burnley, Bardsley and Andy Gray [player] making their debuts. Poor game [1–0]. And still feeling like shit when I got home.

Sunday 19 March

Fiona doing Dimbleby, Howard having refused to do with me. The papers were pretty dire for TB on the loans front. There was nothing that much new but the sheer volume just drowned out anything else. TB was absolutely clear GB put Dromey up to it. And of course while TB had all this to deal with, GB had the Budget coming up and could project himself as the man with the big policy and the big ideas and TB was just this guy drowning in scandal, unable to get the party focused on a forward agenda, unable even to do a reshuffle, which was still being talked about but without much sign it was actually happening. Grimsville. Quite a lot of bad stuff re Iraq around as well. I went out for a long bike ride and for once left my phone at home.

Monday 20 March

James Stewart [family friend] round for a chat for his dissertation then into No. 10. Pretty gloomy atmosphere. TB was seeing staff who were leaving for some farewell pictures. I popped in to see Ruth Turner [head of government relations]* who had been dragged into the papers over the peerages nominations. She seemed fairly relaxed, and I told her at least the public will think there are decent looking women in the office if they keep using pictures of her. We had a good laugh, but generally the mood around the place was not good. PG and I went in to see TB, then we were joined by Liz, Ruth, JoP, DH and MT. TB very down [about peerages row] and I felt the best thing was to try to cheer him up a bit, for example PG and I both saying this had not cut through to the public in the way he might think. 'Yeah right,' he said, chin on hand. OK, I said, well if you won't fall for that one – we have been through worse. The question was how do we get out from under? All those who had made loans were being named today and they were hoping to put pressure on the Tories to do the same. But the media had no interest in the Tories really. Then Charlie [Falconer] was doing new moves on fundraising laws. But how the hell were these loans going to be repaid?

TB looked a lot more worried than last week. He was hanging on every hopeful word. We were saying keep the focus on policy and rise above this. He felt the reason this was so bad was that it brought to a head the destabilisation that had been going on for so long. GB had been destabilising so much that he now had a lot of MPs saying, 'This is all so destabilising so let's get it over with.' He agreed we had to make more of the fundamental democratic point that he had been elected for a term. Also that he now had the toughness, resilience and experience to go through shit to deliver and so he would take the pain for gain for the party. I asked what would happen if he told GB he would not endorse him. PG looked horrified, said that was what they feared, the ultimate betrayal after all the others. TB said he didn't intend to do that but he did find it very hard to recommend him. How could he when he had seen so much, and he felt that he was not psychologically suited to the pressures of the job.

My point was would it liberate him, TB, to feel he was not the whole time tip-toeing around on eggshells, or feeling he was not being true to himself? DH said that all their conversations with the media were stymied because the narrative for the parliament was basically when is he going and what will GB be like when he takes over? 'That is what I am worried about,' said TB. DH said TB had to have a rationale to explain

---

* Turner was to be interviewd several times in a police investigation into any connection between political donations and the award of peerages. She was subsequently found innocent of any wrongdoing.

why he still there and what he was for. There was no real explanation out there so people felt it was either legacy or power for the sake of it. I had not seen TB so down for a long while. He said he hated it when it was about 'this stuff' – funding, integrity. He wished they could just wish away the need to raise money, but you can't, and of course the way politics is seen these days, there is no way we could just palm it all off on to state funding. He said he still had things he felt needed done and he didn't think GB would do them. He was due to see him later but said he now wanted a notetaker at all meetings with him. Pretty pass chapter God knows how many. He said if people knew the reality of how he behaved they would be appalled.

JoP and Ruth stated in terms they felt we would be grossly irresponsible to help him become PM. TB said give me a better idea. JoP said, 'Anyone.' A lot of angst around. On leaving a while later, I went for a pee and there was TB standing there. 'What you reckon?' he said, 'How bad?' I said, 'How bad do you think?' 'Pretty bad,' he said. 'Has a nasty feel to it.' I said, 'Just keep going, get your head above the noise, and work out the best time to go.' Plan A was effectively dead. It was impossible to see them working together on an agreed plan given recent events. He just had to let things happen, and not try to over influence the outcome if GB got it. Interestingly, when I got back home, I was working on the diaries at a stage where in '02 TB was saying two terms was all you get and at the time he had been thinking he would definitely go before the '05 election. And now here he was, still not sure when he was going, conscious he had committed to GB, but riddled with doubt. The team from Mind [mental health charity] came round to persuade me to do their awards in October. Nice bunch of people. I definitely wanted to do more on that front.

Tuesday 21 March
Off first thing to meet Jamie Rubin at their new house and drive down to Queenwood Golf Club in Surrey. Height of luxury. Debenture scheme around quarter of a million dollars then five grand a year. Caddies, club cleaners, shoe polishers, really OTT and luxurious, lots of banker wanker types. I had a bad first hole and then hit a run of pars, got ahead and stayed there, beat him 3 and 2, despite my usual mid-course collapse. We had a couple of great caddies, and mine was telling me the whole place was a bit feudal. It was a fantastic course and having a caddy who knows it definitely improves things, probably worth half a dozen

shots at least. There was a no mobile phone rule but they turned a blind eye, and could tell two of the calls were from TB, who had a big foreign affairs speech tonight. Jamie was quizzing about GB, and the extent to which we thought he was involved in the funding stuff. One of the caddies dropped in that he thought Gordon was a good No. 2, and he wouldn't hack it at the top. It was definitely an opinion that was out there. Jamie said he was enjoying the Sky show but the figures were low, and he worried they might not keep it. He didn't seem to mind too much. I don't think he had quite the love for telly that Christiane [Amanpour, journalist wife] did.

The main news was the NEC meeting on funding which was being put over as a big hit on TB, making clear he was required to take all funding decisions to them. Jeremy Beecham was clear it was not as bad as the media made out. Dromey was looking a bit ridiculous. Charles Clarke had a pop too. David Mills was back from the US and I went out for dinner with him and Jessie with Grace and her pal Nina. He seemed to have recovered a lot of his mojo. Jessie was fantastic, saying it was all going to be fine. He had been given better news on the prosecution front, expert opinion saying they didn't feel he could be done, and it would become clear the whole thing was political. He was more confident than last time I saw him. Then I got a load of calls when it emerged the cops were getting involved in the peerages issues, based on a fucking complaint by the SNP. This was getting ridiculous.

TB's speech at the Foreign Policy Centre seemed to go OK, most of the focus on what he was saying about how to tackle terrorism, but also as per our discussion last weekend, his big theme about the need to fight back against the idea that setbacks in Iraq and Afghanistan were reasons to withdraw. 'Not a clash between civilisations – a clash about civilisation.' I liked his line about 'we' including many Muslims, but the fact he was having to make it was a sign of how far away we were from the right perception on this. I watched it in full and felt he was on form, in terms of the substance, but I could tell he was worried. He didn't look as confident as usual. At least he was still doing these big speeches, and this one drew back to his Chicago speech in 1999 and his US Congress speech in 2003. And he trailed this one as being very much a chapter in a series. He was well into the whole faith stuff, quoting from the Koran, giving his analysis of it, albeit saying he could not be an expert. It was a rich speech but it felt quite defensive in parts, like he was pleading with people to see the issue as he did.

Wednesday 22 March

Budget day. Seemed to go down OK. GB the usual message machine. Started with all the facts and figures and got a big cheer when he said, 'The only government in history entering a tenth consecutive year of economic growth.' We'd gone from seventh of seven in the G7 for GDP per head, to second behind only America. Presented himself as Mr Investment and Improvement in public services, Tories just for tax cuts for the rich, and with some terrific figures to back it up. Also strong on the environment. Good on child poverty and childcare. Extra cash for sport and the Olympics. Military. Africa, a lot of his usual priorities. Big finale on extra money for schools. TB clearly out of the script a bit. I'm not sure he even got a mention though he did his usual name check for loads of ministers on stuff they would be rolling out in the coming days. I didn't think Cameron was that great in response though the clips on the TV bulletins were not bad, using the line I had first heard from Osborne about Gordon being an analogue politician in a digital age.

A bit of a row with Fiona because she said PG and I relished GB not doing well, which was a misrepresentation. I was perfectly happy he did well, but wished to God the TB thing could get sorted. Then to David S, and he had a bit of a new theory, that Fiona didn't like in me the things others found the most attractive – the fact I was a bit wild and dangerous. Then to Parna's farewell with Kate [Garvey] at the Soho House. Anji [Hunter] was there and we chatted about the TB situation. He had discussed with her the idea of a date and only he, GB she and Sue know it. She said the GB lot think the whole thing with me and Philip was just to get through the education vote. She felt TB now had to get his mind focused on an exit strategy. [CB aide] Angela Goodchild's boyfriend came over and said I should go for Parliament and be the bridge between the TB–GB generation and the 'not-ready Milibands'. He said people liked fighters and they knew I could fight. Home half ten. I had a long chat with Alex who had decided to pull out of the Unicef Soccer Aid event because of the fly-on-the-wall media element, and also because of some of the agents who were involved. I was still in two minds about whether to do it, whether it didn't look a bit showbiz and winky wanky woo, but the kids all thought go for it.

Thursday 23 March

GB got a very good press for the Budget. A call from Endemol re Soccer Aid. I wanted to pin down the extent to which it was a genuine charity thing. They said they were taking 580k and everything had to be paid out of that, but millions would get raised if it went as big as they expected to. They were disappointed about Alex dropping out as Rest of the World manager but were now going for Ruud Gullit [Dutch manager, former player]. Good chat really and I felt it should be OK. Lift with Rory to Euston. Val Amos and John Hutton were in the same carriage. There had been a political Cabinet this morning. Val said it had not been great. The TB–GB body language and the broader atmosphere really poor. She was worried about the future. She was asking me who I thought GB would keep. She said she would love me to go to the Lords just to get up nose of the establishment. John Woodcock [special advisor] up for a chat, told me Hutton one of the three or four who just didn't care because he had no intention of serving under Gordon. They felt the Dromey attack had been a response to GB saying he would retaliate if he didn't get his way on pensions. Pretty bad scene all round.

Then Hutton came up for a chat. He too said Cabinet had been pretty dire. People were looking both ways all the time, not sure where power lay. TB came across as being unsure of what he was trying to do or achieve. JP was OK, he said, though TB told me yesterday that he was asking him to name a date as the best way forward. John H said the last couple of weeks had felt as bad as anything he could remember. Really bad. Problem was people knew this was an act of war – 'I can't get you on education so I will get you on sleaze. It had that feeling to it.' Said also he was unclear what the GB agenda forward really was. Cameron was poor though which was a hope. Arrived half-six. To the Lowry, worked on the speech for tomorrow.

Friday 24 March

Up early, tough gym bike session, bit of '02 diary work, avoiding the newspapers but caught a few headlines on NHS cash crisis. TB was heading off to Australia via Brussels and was clearly worried about being away so long in the current atmosphere. I got a cab out to Man City ground, and the event I was doing, organised by Dennis Tueart [ex-player, now director] very lively, full of himself but at least in charge. Also he had the balls to tell me at end it went well but I spoke too long. Fair enough. The event was Grant Thornton accountants. Did my usual strategy spiel plus a run down of the budget and how the main themes were same as ever. Q&A OK, very friendly. What was interesting was that there just wasn't the frenzy out and about re TB that there was in the media. So when Danny Finkelstein called asking me to do a short comment as part of a spread on the question 'Should TB go?', I was happy to do so. No, was the answer, and there was a fundamental democratic point. Elected less than a year ago to serve term. Media attention span and intellectual depth of a gnat so after Tessa and education, now this. It would also be politically stupid. If a successful, winning, by historic standards popular leader was kicked out by a mix of ejected, dejected and rejected pandering to media frenzy, the lasting beneficiary would be vacuous opposition leader. So it was bollocks from start to finish. Did a bit of work and then got driven to Burnley for the game against Norwich [2–0]. Stopped to see Frank Teasdale for a chat and a cup of tea. Nice chat with Delia [Smith, Norwich major shareholder] at the match. She was so Labour, and said her mum was desperate for me to get a seat, and thought I should take over from TB. Clive Holt [director] was bending my ear about GB again, said he was not a PM.

Saturday 25 March

Long swim at the new pool in Swiss Cottage, which was OK though the lanes were too narrow. Then walked Molly before going into town to meet Grace, Glenys, Rachel, kids etc. Nice lunch then to see *Mary Poppins*. Neil collected us afterwards and off to Ealing. Mainly small talk till towards the end when Neil took me aside, said he had read my piece about the way TB was being treated. I said things were very difficult. He said TB deserved better than to go out on something like this. Both he and Glenys thought we had sorted things out, but I told them they were worse than ever. He said all he has left now is surprise and should just be thinking about that. Not now, but thinking of it. He looked sad, said he would have a good legacy whatever but the mood was bad and he needed to think about his own reputation. It was interesting how reluctant some were to believe GB would have had anything to do with Dromey's Channel 4 move. Neil seemed a bit more open to the idea.

Sunday 26 March

The Milibands round for breakfast and a walk. David M very much on the 'Things are terrible' end of the market. He felt the loans thing was just the accumulation of the out of touch elite problem. The Tessa situation didn't help on that front either, he felt. We spent a lot of our time defending situations that to most people just seemed from another world. He felt TB was not really on top of his game at all. Cabinet this week had been desultory, and a dire mood. He was worried things were not going to get better. He felt he should be looking to announce around conference that it was his last one. That wasn't the universal view, mind you. He said that when GB said at Cabinet it was his tenth budget, CC said, 'Better get ready for two more.' DM was not sure where it was going to end but he was not confident. I still felt the Tories were not cutting it despite a media lift. I went for a run and ended up doing almost three hours down my old canal marathon training routes. Nipple bleed and thigh chafe but at least I did it. TB had done a radio interview in Australia saying it was maybe a mistake to have pre-announced that he would not fight a fourth term. Latest frenzy spark. It would be seen by most people as an admission of weakness/waning authority, and by GB as a signal he was still staying.

Monday 27 March

Christ, that was a first. Jack Dromey in a dream, phoning me and asking me how to deal with TB trying to force him out. Tube to London Bridge. Absolutely vile. How do people do this every day? Muscles sore after yesterday's run. Fellow passengers saying, 'Can you tell Tony how awful it is on the train for me, please?' I had a good meeting with Keith Blackmore [*Times*] on doing pieces on the Unicef match and the Mel Brooks LRF event. I called JoP who said it was TB himself on the plane out who started this whole frenzy about a departure date. He just didn't shut it down. That, plus the Aussie radio journo who just said, 'Mistake?' and TB fell into it. Minor frenzy time, and taking away a bit from the speech to the Aussie Parliament, which was the second in his foreign policy series. I don't know why he still did those little chats on the plane. They only ever ended in trouble. JoP said TB had specifically said to them don't let him go down the plane. I suppose the fact it was a world-record-setting long flight, nineteen hours or somesuch, meant they felt they had to. But no point.

Anyway it meant next to no coverage for his speech and loads for the latest blah re him and GB. Cameron was piling in, saying he was causing uncertainty. It hadn't helped that TB said he had a date in mind. He got some coverage for the speech, mainly on his defence of the US, and his worry they would walk away from allies because of all the anti-Americanism around the world, but he didn't really get his bigger message about the need for multilateralism across. The TV pictures were OK, and he seemed to go down well with the Aussie parliamentarians, said they were important to building a global alliance for our values. Home. Fiona's latest idea for doing interesting new stuff together – we go to choose a carpet! She said, 'What about that time you called Alex and he said he couldn't speak because he was buying curtains with Cathy? If he can do it, so can you!' But she would decide anyway so what was the point?

Tuesday 28 March

I was working with Mark a.m. and we got three weeks done, almost into 2003, then helped Calum with his French. Tessa came round, back from the Commonwealth Games in Oz. She was raving about the Games but also said our sports model was getting good play with the Aussie politicians. She had seen TB when out there and told him he had to just get through this, that she was no longer convinced GB would get it because so many people thought he was not right for it. She even felt things could work out that the party felt TB was the only person who could defeat Cameron. Clive Woodward called on the way to Burnley v Southampton [1–1] and said stuff about him going back to the RFU was wide of the mark, all got up out of not much, but he felt things at Saints not going great, and relegation still possible. Gym bike. Council strikes. French riots. TB was now in New Zealand, and attracting a fair few anti-war protesters. And he was also being accused of being too close to the Yanks on climate change, and whatever replaces Kyoto [Protocol, international treaty on climate change].

Wednesday 29 March

Long session with David S. Not great because we went through why I was down now, why the explosion happened last week, all a bit tramlines-ish. I was saying maybe when I was down I should disappear for a day or two. He felt it was far better to be open and honest and confront it all. I was worried though at what was being stirred up, and also the impact on the kids at these mood swings. It was a good chat, I felt better after. I ran to Run And Become to get new running shoes. The billboards were all blaring 'Yard to quiz Blair' [on cash for honours]. Fucking ridiculous. Then at St Pancras, where I went to get train tickets for Saturday, I bumped into Matt Carter [now working with Mark Penn]. The loans situation was becoming ludicrous. The police had put

John Yates, deputy assistant commissioner, in charge, and they were really going to make the most of it. Matt said he had no idea where it was all going, but he felt very sorry for TB. How could parties function though if you have a full on police investigation based on a punt by some SNP MP?* Then Milburn called, he felt things were really not good, as did Matt. But these things can turn round again.

I ran home and worked on a piece about how ridiculous it was to have a deputy assistant commissioner chasing down a case like this. The police were so fond of chasing publicity these days. Out to a Cap Gemini [technology services company] event. [Michael] Portillo the MC and host. Good crowd. I liked the chief executive, Mark, and a guy called Tom, board member who said he was solid Labour. Mark seemed pretty onside too, said he was married to a Lib Dem. There were a couple of women from TfL at top table, who briefed me on how the Oyster card had come into being. It was a good event, and included a tour of Kensington Palace with a Dutch guide speaking flawless English. Portillo was very nice about me and TB. He told the story of the Labour MP who went for a haircut, and refused to take out his headphones. Then he died in the barber's chair, the barber removed the headphones to hear what he was listening to and it was AC voice saying, 'Breathe in, breathe out.' He was good on our professionalism and also emphasised that he believed we actually believed in everything we did, and it annoyed him when TB's sincerity was questioned.

I did my usual strategy/leadership spiel and I felt they were hanging on every word. It was odd how sometimes these kind of talks clicked, and other times less so. Good Q&A, nothing too difficult. Again, quite a few on why I didn't stand for office, and Portillo shouted out, 'He's had real power!' Nice evening compared to most of those kind of things. Michael said he had moved on from politics. He basically saw himself as a journalist now, he didn't want to spend his fifties wondering if he was going to be Foreign Secretary. Seemed to agree with my take that Cameron was good without being top drawer. He said when he wound up at the end of the evening that he hoped I did not go back for the Tories' sake but he really felt the government missed me. JoP called, said he felt my cops article was madness because they would think No. 10 put me up to it. TB in Jakarta now, doing stuff on terrorism

---

* The Metropolitan Police inquiry was initiated after the MP Angus McNeil complained that four wealthy businessmen who had loaned the Labour Party a total of £5 million had been nominated for peerages by Blair.

cooperation, but fair to say most of the media noise about his trip had been about his departure.

Thursday 30 March

Mark B round most of the day and finally we reached 2003. A lot of Iraq and pretty major league depression. Bike ride later, last exercise before Sunday's race. The frenzy was calming a bit but TB's return from his travels would doubtless re-spark it. Today he got a moderately rough ride from schoolkids in Indonesia, at a school twinned with one in Keighley, which underlined how far he had to go in moving perceptions as he wanted to, about how East viewed West and vice versa. The thrust of several of the questions – echoed later by some of the politicians – was the need to get out of Iraq; plus there was a lot of scepticism about commitment to MEPP. The President had a bit of a pop too, and there were more Iraq protests pretty much wherever TB went. The anti-Americanism he had talked about in Oz was on full show. He also had a meeting with moderate Islamic leaders and they were pretty tough too.

Friday 31 March

Guardian splash on a 'Blairite' saying GB deliberately didn't do old people council tax rebate because he was trying to damage us at the local elections. Usual anonymous crap but it would spark things off again. Watched *Shameless* with Grace. Godric had sent the DVD, saying it was the best TV ever. Certainly funny but also pretty depressing about the reality of some lives. Written by Paul Abbott, from Burnley.

Saturday 1 April

The Addison Lee driver taking me to the station said I should persuade TB to stay and fight another term. He said GB was not in the same league, and there were no other leaders out there. Respected. Clever. Didn't believe he would lie e.g. re Iraq. And said re me that I was 'bloody brilliant' at my job, 'You were light years ahead of press and Tories and they hate you for it.' Nice start to the day! I read *Le Monde* on the train up, which had a good piece on how French people demand change at every election and baulk when the change happens. *Guardian* April Fool almost took me in – Cameron doing podcast with Chris Martin. Byline anagram of April Fool. David Mills called. He said there were snappers at Shipston, and both he and Tessa were being followed wherever they went. Not nice, but I said if it bothers you stay in and if it doesn't just carry on as though they are not there. I was picked up and off to David Blunkett's place in Beeley [Derbyshire] before Sheffield Wednesday v Burnley. He had lost a lot of weight. He said he was hoping to do a book after conference. He was going through notes now. We had a good laugh going over different episodes we had come across where we fell out!

He felt he would get blown away by me and TB when we did our books, so he wanted me to keep him au fait with timings. I told him how worried I was about doing damage, especially to GB. He agreed sometimes he got obsessed and obsessive, and felt that maybe the blindness [GB blind in his left eye] contributed. I said, 'I'm not blind and I'm obsessed and obsessive,' and he let out one of his huge, head-back laughs. We had lunch while I talked to Alastair [son] who was at the local council and thinking of being a cop. DB seemed a bit sad. He was still too wrapped up in it all, though who was I to say that? He said he intended to stay to see what GB was like. He was still not sure what he would do. Nor was he sure it's absolutely certain GB would make it. He was constantly on about the past and a bit about current events. We drove in together to a truly dire match – 0–0 – then got driven back. Another driver telling me TB should stay and I needed to go back. Fiona was out at the ballet with Carrie [Dickinson, friend.] I watched Barca v Real [1–1] then bed.

Sunday 2 April

Off at 6.45 to Kingston for the 16-mile race. LRF stand, race OK. Second lap pretty windy. Fairly uneventful, but I ran OK. I went at the end to see Richard and Penny [Stott]. He was powering through the diaries, loving it, said the TB–GB stuff was Shakespearean. I said it gets worse not better. He and Ed Victor were both constantly saying, having read parts of the diary, that every time they read in the press today that I was back helping him, they found it either madly loyal or just mad. I was getting a fair few calls re the TB–GB stuff in the Sundays which I hadn't seen but which was presumably pretty dire. TB called as I was driving back. He sounded quite chipper. He said he had actually felt good to be over there rather than here. Said he got amazing reception everywhere, 'though, boy do we have a problem with the Muslim world'. He said our press were totally ridiculous at first but after they saw how the Aussie media were covering the speech – seriously and straight – they got into a better mode. Re GB, he had spoken to him this morning. He was still wanting to work with him and do the transition but he wasn't really interested. He just wanted him out. He was tempted to let people know he had given him a date – summer '07.

Ashok Kumar [Labour MP] was basically out saying why didn't they sit down and agree a date and then get on with it? That is what we've done, and yet it looks like I'm just dicking him around. He felt now he just had to get on with the job. Focus on health, keep going on public services, and NI. JP was important as a kind of guarantor of the whole thing. He still wanted it to work but they were dumping on James Purnell [creative industries and tourism minister] today in the *MoS* which they use a lot more than they let on. He wanted to see me later in the week. He said in NZ they were still talking about my trip with the Lions! Tessa and David came round for dinner. DM was not his usual self, clearly finding it hard not having his own London base. Tessa was convinced she was being followed because the media were willing to pay big money for a picture of them together to say the separation was all a scam. She said she just didn't know what she felt right now, or where it would end. She was pressing very hard for me to go back because she said there was no political or strategic direction at the centre. She felt TB was not sure what to do but there was a growing feeling GB was problem not solution. The mood was bad pre-local elections.

Monday 3 April

TB had sent over another of his long notes, called and asked if I had read it. I had. What did I think? Then before I answered he asked if I could go in later. I said I was seeing him tomorrow anyway. Ah, OK. 'So what do you think?' I think you're getting very frustrated and you're starting to think even longer term, as though you are thinking beyond when you're gone. 'What do you mean?' 'It is as though you are trying to take responsibility for the fourth term.' 'But if we don't do the right things now, there won't be one.' But he had, for example, talked about having updates of the five-year plans. 'What's wrong with that?' 'Nothing, if you basically want to signal to Gordon you're thinking in a fresh five-year cycle.' But look at pensions, he said. That has implications for long after both of us are gone, but we need to decide it now. He had also set out a whole list of big domestic speeches he wanted done. Again, fine, nothing wrong with it. But it felt like he was trying to create a whole new programme of government. He said he wanted to have a series of domestic speeches to match the foreign policy speeches he had just done.

I said his foreign policy speeches were fine, but he was kidding himself if he felt he had moved the dial with them. But he had a whole list of speeches he wanted to make – on tax and spend, Big state v empowerment, next steps of democratic renewal, public services, energy, civil liberties. I caught the news later and there was such a difference between the TB with that big agenda and loads to do, and the TB on the news, all a bit fragile, totally into another soap wave. Stories like GB being excluded from local elections launch, though inaccurate, were just peddled away. TB was launching SOCA [Serious Organised Crime Agency], but it all felt like it was submerged in all the crap, and he ended up being asked about it, said it was all just politics being portrayed as soap opera, and he said – not very convincingly – that he assumed the story about him and GB falling out over the local elections campaign was an April Fool. Adair Turner was also setting out a few home truths on his pensions report, but that too was seen as part of the No. 10/No. 11 riftology. The Condi [Condoleezza Rice, US Secretary of State] and Jack [Straw] show moved from Blackburn to Baghdad, a bit cloying.*

Tuesday 4 April

The Times ran a poll headlined 'Voters tell Blair it's time to go', though the figures were not nearly as bleak as that suggested. Interestingly Labour voters in particular wanted him to stay on. Peter M called from Brussels as I returned from a bike ride. He said did I think it was time to do less exercising of my body and more exercising my mind about the current political situation? He felt things were very bad though not critical let alone terminal. But TB had somehow to get above the soap and let the press go hang themselves. He had to be the policy PM again. The public were totally bored by the soap. They could not care less about most of what the political traffic was, who up, who down. They wanted a government on their side taking the right decisions and also not wasting their money. He felt it was true that GB had overreached but not true that TB was firmly back in the riding seat. He felt I should go back to

---

* The UK Foreign Secretary had struck up a good relationship with his American opposite number and had personally guided her on a tour of the north-west despite having attracted criticism for a joint tour of Alabama, branded 'a folly' by the opposition. They were now on a joint visit to Baghdad.

do what he did after I left in 2003. Steer things. Give strategic direction because that is what is currently missing. TB was not being seen as the PM in the same way as before. He has to regain that strength and drive and it may mean I have to go back in some form, not announced but not denied either. DH won't like it, he said, but there we are.

I said I was not interested in anything that involved dealing with the press. He felt the model was the way he did it when I left. In once a week, do notes etc. and get people in there to do my bidding. I wasn't convinced it would work. He was able to operate like that, but I wasn't. If I did something, and had responsibility for it, I had to be full on. At the moment I was taking responsibility for trying to get TB and GB broadly on the same page, it was taking up too much time and energy and was not going terribly well. He said he felt if I was in there more often, and with a clear role understood by all, it would be easier. Not so sure.

In for lunch with Paul Smith, a former *Mirror* colleague who was looking after a business guy called John Lewis, who ran a science park up on the old ICI site in Runcorn. The idea was that I become a kind of evangelist for science and the need for public sector investment, by them getting the RDAs [Regional Development Agencies] all to have me at their conferences and put the case for more science. I said I would have to watch out on the commercial conflict side. He was pro-TB, dubious re GB. David Sainsbury [science minister] was clearly popular with the science community generally. From there to Downing Street to see TB. He was in with Liz and Vic [Victoria Gould, diary secretary]. He looked a bit tired, and was joking about how he makes all the big decisions now – so he was seeing Liz and Vic to decide whether he should go up to the flat at 5 or 6, and whether he should eat dinner on his own or with Cherie. They left and he put his feet up on the chair. He said he actually felt great in himself but there was no doubt there had been a bit of a flap here when he was away. He said the loans issue had really taken his assessment of GB a lot lower.

He felt he simply lacked the neccessary leadership qualities. Maybe he had been naïve and too willing to forget. He had no doubt, for example, that they had been involved in doing in Peter M first time around over the mortgage. But he felt the loans business was beyond the pale. He really found it hard to respect them after that one. So what to do? He was seeing GB and JP tonight and felt he should agree to an assumed departure date of around July '07. JP would have to become the guarantor of that and meanwhile he had to be able to get on and do the changes needed. He would make clear he was not looking for an alternative to GB. But there had to be an understanding that while he is still PM, he has the final say, for example on pensions. I said was he not worried that the minute GB had a date, he put it out there, and he became even more lame duck? Yes, but he couldn't see a way around that. He was also still not sure when he would do a reshuffle but he knew he had to and again it had to be his not a compromise. He said he couldn't be bothered with everything becoming a great big discussion like it was part of a deal. It just wasn't on to keep going in that way. He had pensions and energy in particular that he wanted to get through and he had to be able to.

The reality was when GB did not get his way on what he wanted to set out on the Constitution he went on another round of destabilisation. He had even said to JP he intended to raise the loans issue and then Dromey happened. Beyond the pale. He felt he could manage him and work with him up to a point but 'without any warmth and affection', and that is hard for me, he said, because I like to get on with the people I'm working with. He also said he felt public services would be in a better place in eighteen months and so would Iraq. I said you've been saying that for three years. 'That's true and it worries me, I confess,' he said. He had seen Jack and Condi last night after their visit to Baghdad. Things were definitely on the edge there but the insurgency had died down a bit. It was going to be hard though.

I asked if he actually wanted to stay for another term. No, he said. I'm clear about that though I do think I am doing the job better and am better qualified to do it than anyone else. He said he would jump at the chance of running the UN but the general rule was no P5 [Security Council permanent members] country and France and Russia would probably veto him anyway. He had been asked to run Davos [World Economic Forum] and seemed moderately interested in that. He felt his own operation was not as bad as Peter M felt. JoP also raised me going back to chair and drive strategy meetings but TB wasn't desperate yet. He said he actually felt good and on top of things. He was ready to make an argument about the media. There were parallels with sport – Mourinho, Wenger, Alex constantly going from from zero to hero, hero to zero. Neither position was right. It was all about impact journalism. Has to change.

The thing he said he couldn't be sure about was where the public were. Are they just fed up with us? I felt they were perhaps fed up with the soap but he had to get his head above that somehow, really make clear he was not interested in the soap stuff, he was only interested in what he did that had an impact on their lives. I reminded him in early '03 he had come back from the Christmas break clear he was going to sack GB but had to wait for Iraq. He had forgotten that, as had I till doing the diary last week. He said Cabinet were getting into a different place. They all knew GB's position with the public was eroding as the scrutiny toughened. CC and JR were vehement. He had told GB his route to rehabilitation with the public was working with him together, that they were getting a really bad impression from the sense he was undermining TB and being disloyal. But GB was so determined to get the job that he couldn't see that.

Wednesday 5 April
TB and GB did the local elections launch which seemed to go OK, helped by GB in advance retreating partially in his opposition to the [Adair] Turner plans on pensions, though he was still holding out against a 2p tax rise to fund the shortfall if they were to be relinked with earnings. After all that, I was mainly working at home, out for a run and a swim, then later out to the opera. For once I quite enjoyed it, though there was some major league staring going on. It was weird how in some places – e.g. football matches – people seemed unsurprised to see me, but opera and ballet, the weirdest stares. At least F and I had a good laugh about it. Bird flu in Fife, a swan.

Thursday 6 April
Bird flu was the latest frenzy. I finished writing Athens and Kent speeches, sent my police article to the *Mirror*, as *The Times* seemed to be stalling. David S was mainly going through dreams – he said the central themes all seemed to relate to uncertainty about direction of travel, and also belonging. Nothing new there. TB was doing a few bits and bobs of media and the mood was not quite so bad. He was then off to NI to kickstart the process but all overshadowed by the murder of Denis Donaldson, the IRA guy who had been exposed as a Special Branch and MI5 informant. It was tricky stuff but he and Bertie [Ahern] put out words saying they were satisfied it wasn't the work of the IRA, which meant they were pointing to getting the [Northern Ireland] Assembly [suspended since 2002 after power-sharing government failure] back up again.

Off to Maidstone for a Business Link event with Kent County Council

Learning and Skills council. Fair few local media there so knocked them off then into the event. The Council leader was a nice guy. Very pragmatic. Big on modern apprenticeships. He said he liked TB for the same reason he liked Thatcher – he did what he thought was right whatever the personal consequences. He was trying the same kind of leadership at a lower level – shutting forty primary schools, libraries, making the case for change in the long term. It sounded like a lot of tough stuff. He said he wouldn't die in the ditch for grammar schools but was adamant cooperation was working well. He would be happy with all schools as comprehensives provided there was a grammar stream within. It was a fairly Tory audience, I would say, but went OK. Moderately hostile Q&A at times but a lot of support for the anti-media line and no push back re TB. Resistance to GB was clear though.

Friday 7 April

Up before 6 and the Addison Lee driver was a really nice guy. Ethiopian. Been here sixteen years, joined by wife and daughter four years ago. He had studied in Bulgaria then during cross from socialism he came here and claimed asylum. He had done two degrees but was addicted to mini-cabbing. He was incredibly well informed re politics. Knew more about me than was entirely healthy. Aged forty-five. One of those wise souls who reflected and spoke in very simple terms. He felt I should go into Parliament and even go for the top job. TB a phenomenal leader. GB has something lacking and people sense it. Call it charisma or whatever but it is not quite right. Good man, clever man, he said, but you will lose something when Blair goes. He felt a lot of the attacks on us were born of jealousy, a point I made to DS yesterday, that people resented others who were successful. The driver said he formed an impression I was a strong person and had strong beliefs. Enemies were politically motivated and also jealous. He thought there was something of that in the Lions frenzy, which he had also followed.

He was very big on family. He said if you are worried about your family in the slightest, do not go back. Have a nice life with them, he said. But their gain is politics' loss. He said maybe I should think about doing a big international job. He said he didn't feel I had a public problem at all but a problem with the UK media that 'always has to focus on the 1 per cent bad not the 99 per cent good'. Nice chat, lovely man, hilarious on why he was addicted to mini-cabbing – just feels comfortable with it, everything else would be such a challenge. Good chat and

I liked the fact he shared my analysis, that if you just kept going you came through. Good bloke. Bird flu raging in the papers.

Off to Athens, siting on the flight out next to Nicole Vettise of JP Morgan who was going out to make a presentation. Chatted away re things, job, running, usual stuff. Did several TV and print interviews. Usual stuff. The speech and Q&A was fine, though went on for hours. Talked to the Israeli Ambassador at dinner and then a couple of New Democracy ministers, and the former Greek Commissioner in Brussels who said she always found GB a nightmare to deal with because he was so rude. Lots of senior editors. Organisers pleased, but the general mood was quite depressed re the state of Greece. They were amazed there was talk of pushing out TB. After the dinner a woman called Pandora was taking me round for little chats with smaller groups, and there was so much knowledge about our politics it was ridiculous. I sensed they preferred to talk about that than their own.

Saturday 8 April

Up at half-three for a flight to Amsterdam, then change for Manchester and get a cab to Burnley. I used the club gym, then met PG off the train, and took him for lunch at the club. He loved all the old-fashioned boardroom stuff, and meeting the QPR top brass. Both sides were poor but we won 1–0. I was sitting next to Ian Dowie [Crystal Palace manager] who was scouting us. I had noticed he came here fairly often and he said he still lived in Bolton. Very Labour. He felt TB's success was to get people to feel you could be successful and Labour. Off to Carlisle, staying at a Colditz-style hotel before heading up for a few days in Scotland.

Sunday 9 April

Set off for Scotland, beautiful house in a beautiful area. En route we went to the Glencoe Inn, ignoring the 'No hawkers or Campbells' sign, assuming it to be a tourist thing.* But the manager snapped, 'Can you not read?' I said I ignored it. He said yes, you're good at ignoring good advice. We got served though, and people were friendly enough. David Mills without Tessa, Lindsay [Nicholson], Mark [Johansen, Lindsay's husband] and Hope [Merritt, Lindsay's daughter] up. The Italian election

---

* In 1689, Campbell-led government troops massacred thirty-eight MacDonalds at Glencoe in the aftermath of the Jacobite uprising.

April '06: Old clan enmities surface in Glencoe   293

was close. [Romano] Prodi claims victory. Berlusconi pushing it to the end. Lots of walks. Golf on the Wednesday. Lots of somewhat godly moments especially out on the bike in the rain.

I don't know if it was the scenery or what, but I was also feeling strong sensations of closeness to, and succession from, Dad. I even found myself popping in to the lovely little church at Ardgour. Beautiful cemetery. The house had a good collection of Glencoe books which I was reading. PG was making running jokes about the Campbells being untrustworthy. Then we went to the Glencoe Museum, and a guy who worked there came over and he said, 'You do know the Campbells were the scapegoats ... there were lots of others involved in the massacre and the Campbells were used by the government as scapegoats.' Then he laughed and said, 'Nothing new there then!'

Sunday 16 April
The day before we left for home I went for a long walk with Gail and I proposed the idea of doing edited highlights of the diaries, but with stuff that was bad for GB left out, and I would admit so. It was the only way I could see that would allow me to do something in the time-frame they wanted, but without damaging him if he was still around. She had read parts of them and realised how sensitive it all was. She was still keen on three not four volumes, and her immediate reaction to a sanitised version was to dismiss the idea out of hand but when I put the arguments she was won round, and PG felt it was doable too. Everyone will be having their say when TB goes and I should be in there. And as long as I was honest in saying I had edited them with a deliberate desire not to damage GB, but with the assurance one day they would all be published, I felt I was as good a compromise as we could get. If I was expected to do the full works immediately, I knew that I couldn't.

I called Ed Victor who also, at first, felt it was a non-starter but then warmed to it. Really nice little break, in quite the most beautiful part of the world. Although Fort William was not the nicest town in the world, the surrounding area was as good as you'll get anywhere. I didn't have much to do with TB or GB while away, apart from feeding in a few comments on his NHS speech which seemed to go fine though the money problems were growing – at least questions about where it was all going. I had a couple of chats with Charlie Kennedy, who was definitely needing help on the drink front, and asking me how I had managed to go from all to nothing. He was still really sharp politically though, and could see the TB–GB thing ending in tears sooner than we thought. Mum hit eighty, called her and she sounded as fit as ever.

Wednesday 19 April

I pottered around for a while and then went off on a run. I was only planning on an hour but got into it and ended up doing three hours. In for a meeting with TB, JoP and PG. TB said he was full of beans and he seemed it. He was now fixed on a strategy that was basically do the job, work hard, be seen to work hard and above all face up to the difficult choices. Stop all talk of the leadership, legacy and succession. Work collegiately, try to build relations with GB but not preferentially, at the expense of others. The most important thing was policy. He was worried about the police loans investigation because it made people so nervous around the place. He felt the whole thing was an outrage, which it was, and 'Yates of the Yard', as he clearly loved to be called, was lapping it up. He said it was hard to check what was really happening because there was not much leadership there and also the Met was so unlikely to stay quiet if we made any inquiries.

He felt it was an outrage that Des Smith had been arrested as a result of newspaper entrapment. Smith was a headteacher who had been taped saying it was possible to get honours for sponsoring academies. Next thing he is being arrested as part of so-called cash for honours. TB said, 'Top civil servants, High Court judges, captains of industry get their Ks automatically but not someone who is from a tough background, runs schools well…' I had only been vaguely aware of the story which when I checked it out sounded like a classic newspaper sting, and the guy being very loose with words. But there is no doubt there was a scent of blood in the air on the honours scene and if they came knocking at TB's door, it would be meltdown time.

On the general scene he felt DC was perfectly serviceable but frustrated because he had the wrong target. TB gave him nowhere to go. GB would maybe give him more space. He felt DC was very bright, and could definitely be made into something. The problems were a lack of depth and maybe he didn't work hard enough. But he didn't feel the Tories had to change as fundamentally as we did to go from opposition to government. They just had to ensure sensible policy, whereas we had had to show real fundamental change. He was very down on GB, felt he was not coming up with the ideas, needed to get the big picture, also that the proposals he had finally produced on pensions were hopeless

– lift state pension a bit, cut credit over time, lots of fiddly changes but end up with a system that would lead to less saving, poorer pensioners and less spent as proportion of GDP than before. Added to which Turner would reject it. 'Where are the politics in all that?' PG made the point TB was not visible enough. I made the point he was not putting out big picture message and context enough.

He agreed he needed to do more in depth and also talk less politically. I felt he was on good form though. The problem was the public were quite down on us at the moment. It wasn't even anything specific, just a whole series of things building up to a pretty shitty mood. He felt the local elections, which were not going to be great, will be the time at which the GB lot may make a move. He didn't think they would do it at conference. He had clearly hardened his GB view even further. He said we had to make it hard for Cameron by forcing him to face difficult policy decisions, and confuse him. GB would give him a far easier strategic picture.

Friday 21 April

The next few days were fairly quiet. I was trying to work out exactly how to do diary extracts as discussed with Gail. Met Ed V to go over it. He had warmed to it, having realised how much stuff there was to choose from. Politics was fairly quiet apart from Cameron's Norway trip. He certainly does good pictures, him being hauled around by huskies, and it was pretty bold to say he was going to turn the Tory Party green. I said to TB it was one of those pictures that would connect and resonate, and we had to use it quickly to get him to policy positions that caused him problems. The party had put out quite a funny cartoon video on Cameron as a chameleon, but this showed quite a lot of his confidence. GB was at the UN talking about climate change and would be pissed off that Cameron was getting more coverage for a picture than he did for a big speech on the need for a 'global solution to a global challenge'.

On our side, the most testing thing at the moment was the constant reporting of NHS cash problems, even rumblings of a nurses' strike, and then, a total disaster for the local elections, courtesy of the Home Office, almost a thousand foreigners in jail who should have been deported had been let out, among them rapists and murderers and paedophiles. They dated back to 1999, but only a hundred or so had been located since release and only twenty of them had been deported. Grim. I was working on various speeches for the future plus sorting out the details

April '06: TB has 'hardened view' re GB

for Soccer Aid, which I had decided to do. Matthew Freud hooked me into doing a turn at the Russian Economic Forum. He roped in a good list – me, PG, Will Whitehorn [Virgin Group director], Simon Lewis [Vodafone executive] and a Russian woman who was very good. But the event was clearly B list as we barely got 100 of the delegates there, and it was a bit of a waste of time. An annoying story out of the Electoral Commission when they published party payments related to the last campaign, including 500k for Mark Penn, 140 plus for PG and 47 for me. Plus loads of rubbish about how much we spent on things like Star Trek uniforms, with no context. It was totally ridiculous how much power we gave away to these new bodies who basically saw it as their job to damage us.

There was also a bit of coverage on Cherie's hairdresser being more expensive than [Michael Howard's wife] Sandra Howard's! But all the issues were dire at the moment – not winning argument on health, crime. Local elections tough. TB was doing a fair bit of local campaigning and actually felt the mood was not so bad. But he underestimated how much of that was a celeb thing, and also how well the party organised visits when he was involved. On the diaries I was well into Iraq 2003 now, and surprised how much doubt I was expressing. TB was not expressing doubt even at low moments. Jack Dromey was up and about again, saying people round TB used loopholes in the law to exploit the loans issues and hide them as donations. So much for the theory he would have regretted landing as big a blow as he did with his C4 interview. One or two ministers were out and about saying that MPs should not use the local elections to make a move against TB, which however well-intentioned, did two things: put in mind the idea that they might; and signal that we were worried about the results.

Wednesday 26 April
I was in a cab en route Eurostar for Paris, to do an event for John Holmes and heard on the radio that JP had admitted to an affair with a secretary.* I got hold of the *Mirror* at St Pancras. Tracey Temple. Total news to me. This, plus Charles Clarke trying to get on top of the ongoing disaster of the 1,000-plus freed foreigners, and Patricia [Hewitt] about to get slow handclapped at a nurses' conference meant inevitably the media

---

* The Deputy Prime Minister admitted he'd had an affair with Tracey Temple, which had ended 'some time ago' and which he deeply regretted.

were dubbing it Black Wednesday. Totally OTT but it did, as Penny Holmes [wife of Sir John] said, feel a bit like last days of Major. I was met by Tom Fletcher [UK diplomat] and then did *Le Figaro* followed by TV with a gorgeous French reporter. Lots of current stuff, TB–GB, also trying to get me going on the lack of leadership in France. They failed though I did make the point that Brits found it hard to see how even minor reforms could cause such such chaos and mayhem in France. The Embassy view was that Dominique de Villepin [Prime Minister] was finished. Chirac had still not announced he was definitely going.

Sarkozy and Ségolène Royal [French National Assembly member] were still the big thing. She was getting huge poll numbers just by being different. She said very little, no real policy. A bit Cameronesque. John said the other socialists totally hated her. John was not sure what his next move would be. Maybe Brussels, maybe NY. Delhi attractive because India was so interesting but Penny was worried about her mum's health, and being so far away. I tried to sus out if he had any interest in going back to No. 10. He was really not keen, which was a shame. He had been so good [as principal private secretary to the Prime Minister] in the early days and he would be brilliant in the transition. I went out for a run with Tom. Bizarre moment when we were stopped by a woman who just stood in front of us, said I am really sorry but I can't miss this opportunity… She was from Worcester and wanted to lobby me for an honour for her sister. I was not running well, and I was almost late for my own speech and was suffering that after-exercise sweating as I did it. It went fine though, usual mix of stories, strategy, analysis. Excellent Q&A from a good audience, lots of ambassadors and media.

Christine Ockrent asking about whether TB might change his mind and stay. Mick [Hucknall] and Gabriela were there and said afterwards it was ridiculous I was doing that stuff as a talk rather than doing it all in practice. 'The thing is you understand all this, you get it, you should be doing it,' said Mick. He had a point. Went fine. Usual message. Q&A good. Not bad turnout of ambassadors and UK media. Same jokes. Same stuff. Mick and Gabriela who was really enthused by the whole thing. Then to the dinner, with Catherine Colonna [former Chirac spokeswoman, now minister] and Jérôme Bonnafont [current Chirac spokesman]. John said Jérôme was more relaxed than he had ever seen him. He was quite open on who he saw as good bets and he said Ségolène was not to be underestimated.

Catherine said she had seen a lot of Douglas [Alexander, Europe minister], he was a good guy, works very hard, she sensed he was a little more anti-European than TB. They were all fascinated by the TB–GB stuff. As with the media, they imagined it to be better than it actually was. Fabulous food, John a good host, really nice to reminisce with Catherine, though I sensed she was glad to be away from the Chirac grind. It was all too easy to pick up the sense of malaise about French politics though. I was staying in the Stuart room, the main guest room, with that lovely view out over the garden. I caught the late news at home, and the foreign prisoners issues was getting worse for CC, as it appeared almost 300 more were let out even after he had first been told of the scale of the problem.

Thursday 27 April

The Embassy had sorted the English papers for me. I wished they hadn't. Dire all round. JP bad. Pat bad. CC bad, and today it came out that some of those released had already re-offended. The Tories were whacking in all sorts of embarrassing questions to keep the JP/Tracey Temple thing going, and our own side were starting to report back that the 'laughing stock' point was hitting us. Off with John for breakfast with Jean-François Copé, who was government spokesman plus budget minister. Fresh and bright and close friend of de Villepin. He had never been close to Sarkozy but he said NS was one of those politicians who was more interested in people who didn't support than those who did. He was keeping powder dry and would say that it depended on the ideas. His spokesman job meant he was never off TV so his profile ratings were rising. French media are obsessive about polls and while Sarkozy and Royal were up there, the press would keep promoting them. It was a little bizarre but Chirac was barely mentioned. Copé said that Sarkozy and de Villepin were really at each other. Sarkozy had done him in even though the reform he was pushing was the kind of thing he will have to do. He said the situation was 'much tougher than Blair–Brown'. John and I pushed back a little on that.

I liked him. He was very canny and smart, and open. He said they had remodeled their communications following his visit to No. 10, but they still felt they were behind us. I recalled the meetings I used to have with Claude Chirac, who seemed perplexed that our media was far more anarchic in terms of content, but also somehow easier to organise. In the car with John he felt the most interesting thing was that Copé was signalling his own ambition, maybe the time after next. Train back, then home for a pretty tough exercise regime, road bike and swim. Dinner then head for Brighton. TB called. 'Well?' he said. I said of the three CC was the worst for the public. It just went too close to a lot of concerns. Pat H was just dealing with a difficult situation, probably making the right decisions but not handling the politics too well. JP is politics as soap opera, it will get the most attention but probably have the least impact. He sounded a lot more worried about JP than I thought he would. He said the first he knew was the other day. JP was not saying much. But it all added to a credibility problem.

The combination of general malaise and specific issues meant the locals were now going to be bad. Had to keep going. He felt GB would probably have a push post next week. He said maybe I should do the live coverage. 'It's not going to be easy.' He asked if I had spoken to JP. I said I had texted Joan [Hammell, Prescott PA] to say I was happy to help, and had had a couple of chats with her, but he was clearly pretty embarrassed about the whole thing. I was surprised he hadn't called me before it broke, but I can only imagine the embarrassment he was feeling. TB said he was very philosophical about his own position. He knew what he was trying to do and he was just going to do as much of it as he could. If it all ended, so be it. He knew he was trying to do his best for the country and there was not much more to it than that. I arrived at the Grand Brighton Hotel 11 p.m.

Friday 28 April
Up early for a run on the seafront then to BIBA [British Insurance Brokers' Association] event. Very well organised, good crowd. I focused mainly on crisis management, then OK Q&A. Mainly Tory, I would say, but a very nice man came up at the end, said he was Labour, and I was one of his heroes because I survived demonisation. On the train I got a message to call JP. The train north was too noisy so I waited till I got to Newcastle. Brendan picked me up and I called JP from the car. He was very down, said he was thinking of jacking it all in. He felt his credibility had been shot and that was the one thing he had, particularly in the party and also with TB and GB on the handover. He was worried about the weekend. Lots of people were being approached and asked about affairs. Lots of harassment of relatives and so on. I've been daft and will pay a price but I don't see why all these people have to. The press is out of control. He said TB was very loyal, maybe to a fault.

Re CC and Pat H he thought these were policy situations that would resolve themselves. He couldn't see such a resolution for himself. I said don't do anything rash. Things could look very different in a few days. They could also look very different out of the centre to you being in the eye of the storm. He said he would do nothing rash and would tell me before deciding anything. He said Pauline [wife] had gone from hurt to angry to confused and back again. But she did not want him to quit, did not want him driven out. She was clearly up for trying to make things work. I said that was really important. Her support means something. I said just accept that some people will be laughing at you, some will think you're a silly old fool, but most won't care as much as you think. You have a thick skin. Use it. He sounded close to the floor though.

I had a coffee with Brendan [Foster] who was on his usual top notch thinking form. He was even more down on media coverage and issues than ever. I was staying at the Malmaison, which I didn't much like. The gloomy look was deliberate but not my thing. Luiz Felipe Scolari later pulled out of the England manager job, citing media pressure, so I made that part of the speech I was intending to make anyway, about how the modern media was changing the nature of democracy and decision-making, and not always for the best. The event was the Royal Institution of Chartered Surveyors, black tie, hot and crowded, good people on my table, Prof David Fleming of Northumbria University, nice bloke, really proud of running the 'biggest design school', and a very nice woman called Maggie Pavlou who was lobbying me to get TB to do the North East Chamber of Commerce.

Saturday 29 April

Very little sleep, then up at half five to get the 6 a.m. train south. The media still wall-to-wall re JP and CC in particular, and there was worse to come because Tracey Temple was doing a big number with the *Mail on Sunday*. Charles was coming under a fair bit of criticism for the way he was handling his situation. Home to collect Fiona, making a rare trip to a football match, then off to Chelsea v Man U. Breakfast with Joe Hemani. Chat with Paddy Crerand [former United player, MUTV commentator] who felt the wheels were coming off a bit. I went down to see Alex in the tunnel before the match, and also briefly met Mourinho. They were both just standing at the doors of their respective dressing rooms watching the players come back from the warm-up. 'What is happening to MY government?' was AF's opening gambit when he saw me. He said fuck me, it all looks shambolic. TB – he said he felt sorry for him but couldn't understand for example why Hewitt was still there. As for John and the secretary... that was the trouble with this scandal-type situations. They just submerged all other impressions if you weren't careful.

It was the usual celeb-y Stamford Bridge crowd around where Joe sat. Angus Deayton [actor and broadcaster] – who was also going to be involved in Soccer Aid – Richard Wilson [actor], Tim Lovejoy [TV presenter], the *Soccer AM* guy. Rudd Gullit was there too so I chatted to him about the Soccer Aid thing. Fiona was people-watching mainly, and couldn't believe how many posh types seemed to be there. Quite a lot of Eurotrash with sunspecs. David Mellor was behind us moaning about everything, very funny. He said he supported Chelsea but hated the club. United not great. Lost 3–0. JP called later when we were taking Grace to the theatre. He and Pauline had had a proper chat. They were definitely staying together. She was trying to make it work. She was making conditions. The *MoS* stuff did not so far sound lethal. The scene was pretty dire though and going to make bad local elections even worse. He went through some of the things being rebutted. He admitted it was all self-inflicted though Max Clifford [controversial publicity agent] and cheques for Tracey Temple were not going to help.

Theatre to see *Woman in Black*. Nice old theatre. Grace and her friends enjoyed it. Wandering around at the interval, nobody mentioned JP. The media were going pretty wild though and once the *MoS* dropped I started getting bids. I said no, but then David Hill called and asked me to do media so Matthew T was briefing me. Tracey Temple seemed to be doing the usual 'He used and abused me' line, and as ever it was the little details that did the most damage, like them having sex in his office, also after the Iraq memorial at St Paul's, and another time in a hotel when Pauline was downstairs. JP called as I was getting to bed, said he had now seen 'all fucking nine pages of it', and while some is true, loads is not. As Max Clifford knew though, once the big thing was true – they had an affair – the little things were harder to deny. Like David Mellor, who never wore a Chelsea shirt.

Sunday 30 April

Did a tour of the Beeb, including Radio 5, and *Broadcasting House* [BBC radio show], then Adam Boulton, clips for ITV. I was pretty robust defending JP in general and saying this was all the about modern media culture. Peter M called and said he thought I was making a terrible mistake. 'JP is a disgrace and every time we defend him our own credibility is hit,' he said. I felt nonetheless that there was a point to be made about the way things that really mattered got next to no coverage, things like this got tons and the result was an impoverished political debate. Others thought I was on great form. Particularly the line about the *Mail* being a national poison. Wayne Rooney having got injured at Chelsea I also said that the country was more interested in Rooney's foot than any part of JP's anatomy. The *MoS* inevitably had Tracey Temple on camera and released some of that to keep it going. It was all pretty low life stuff. I got very spiky with Boulton suggesting not taking lectures from JP on morality. All the old No. 10 lot were supportive but maybe Peter M was right. Maybe I was better just to stay out of this kind of thing.

TB called. He said he was feeling a bit beleaguered but we just had to get through it. He was planning to have the reshuffle immediately after local elections but he felt the GB lot would make a move so he had to be careful. He felt results were clearly going to be worse and though people would recognise the dire circumstances, it would not stop the focus moving to him and his future. He had been planning with JP's agreement to cut his departmental stuff anyway. He also wanted to move Jack [Straw] to Leader of House and move CC to FCO. He felt he had one last throw of the dice – a clear timetable with different steps, but he was reluctant. JP called again and he put me on to Pauline. She said she was veering between angry and resigned. 'But I am determined to see it through. I am well aware there is nothing dafter than an old man. People say I'm not political but I'm very proud of what John has achieved and I've been part of that so I am not going to throw it away. I am going to make it work.'

She said she was getting up in the night to read the papers over and over. I advised her to stop. But she felt it was the best way to deal with it. JP came back on, and I said you are very lucky to have her, so don't fuck it up again. Re TB, he said he strongly felt he should give GB a timetable. He was also asking, 'Why is he so determined to do all these changes now, is this the right time?' which is pretty much the GB line. When I fed that back when TB called later, he said GB and JP have been around, but the younger ones need to know that in the end it is about difficult decisions and breaking eggs to make omelettes. He felt that Patricia probably made the right decisions but couldn't explain them well. CC definitely made mistakes in his handling, the latest thing being how he didn't tell TB when he knew about over a thousand foreign prisoners who had been released without being considered for deportation. Tricky times for sure. He felt very philosophical about it all but definitely Thursday was going to be hellish and there was likely to be a move against him. Reshuffle immediately and the offering of a time-table was probably his last card.

Monday 1 May

Out leafleting [for local elections] in the rain early on. Not many people up. One old woman giving me a hard time, but generally not bad. I was not doing media today and I was thinking a lot about Peter M saying my defence of JP damaged my own reputation too. I asked Fiona what she thought, and she said that on the one hand people liked the fact I was loyal and that meant standing up for people in bad times as well as good. On the other hand, it risked sending a message that you would defend absolutely anything they did. Vernon Bogdanor [academic] sent an email which went even further than Peter – he said he thought I should not be defending CC either. He felt TB risked real damage to his legacy unless we signalled major change for the last period of his premiership. We went out to George [Mackie] and [political journalist] Catherine's farm [MacLeod, family friends] at Nazeing. Fiona had finally had a big fallout with Janey, who had been looking after Grace's pony, and so it had been moved here. Much nicer, and also a good excuse to go and see them. Catherine was such a solid citizen on the political front. She was having a bit of a crisis of her own though, and thinking she needed to get out of journalism.

Tuesday 2 May

Out to the gym, and as I was walking across the road, three guys all shouting, 'You wanker, you fucking tosspot.' There was definitely not a great mood around.

Wednesday 3 May

TB felt PMQs and CC's statement went as well as they could have done in the circumstances but he was convinced the locals now were going to be even worse than we thought. He and GB were out today trying to rescue the campaign, and saying don't let nine days of bad headlines wipe out nine years of progress. He was sounding a bit beleaguered. I told him Vera Doyle [No. 10 messenger] had just called me to say would I go back because he needed help, was running out of friends. Time was he would have laughed but I could sense him taking it in. He said it was going to be bad and he really only had two immediate things he could do. Reshuffle, and timetable. He was still reluctant to lay out a timetable. On the reshuffle he asked me to think about David M for FCO. He said to show a new team he had to make changes at the top. Was it crazy to think of David for FCO? I felt instinctively it was too big a step. Also David was probably thinking family a lot at the moment. Agreed to sleep on it. DM called me almost immediately afterwards. Serendipity? He said if I was involved in the discussions, and able to put in a word, he would like education. Not transport or NI. He didn't think TB should reshuffle for the sake of it, though. He thought far more important was what direction did he want to go?

Thursday 4 May

PG called to point out that the weather just like 1 May '97. That was about the only similarity. The mood very different. Fiona had let the local party use our place as the committee rooms so I spent most of the day calling to urge people to vote. The feedback wasn't too bad but as the teller papers came in, too many were not tallying with our list of promises. The general picture round London in particular was bad. We finished at ten, I helped Calum prepare for his French oral, watched a bit of the TV coverage and then bed. Not going to be good, especially in London and the south.

Friday 5 May

Fiona woke me up with the single word, disaster. The Tories had gained over 300 seats, we had lost around the same. Lost seventeen councils. Definitely our worst showing in any election under TB. The results were especially bad in London but Mark [Bennett, a local councillor] increased his vote and we won Lambeth. Camden dire. Out of London the Tories were not doing well, so it was not as good as they might have hoped. But the dynamic was bad for us. TB was straight on to the reshuffle but the GB people were moving against him. There were going to be endless interviews saying the need was for renewal, also making comparisons with Thatcher going out in a messy, disorderly way. TB had had very few meaningful conversations with GB so it was hard to get a handle on it. Andrew Smith [Labour MP] was out calling for a timetable. John McFall was on much the same kick. Compass were out making the wrong noises for TB. So the reshuffle though dramatic did not exactly buy space.

There was quite a lot of shock at Jack S leaving the FCO, and even more at Margaret B replacing him. Jack replaced Geoff Hoon as Commons Leader, and he was now doing Europe. Charles Clarke resigned after refusing a move anywhere else. John Reid took over as Home Secretary, and he was not far off double figures in terms of positions held. JP stayed but with some of his responsibilities gone 'at his request'. Alan Johnson to education, Ruth Kelly communities and local government plus women, David M to DEFRA [Environment, Food and Rural Affairs]. Loads and loads of moves but still all the talk was about when he would go and what was the direction etc? It was a tough reshuffle in some ways, sackings and demotions, also in Reid and Johnson and David M a message that he was promoting his own people and unstated was the notion that these could be leadership potential. There was certainly little talk of orderly transition right now, other than from the GB people out reminding people how Maggie had ended, and there was apparently talk of a letter doing the rounds for MPs to sign, urging the setting out of a departure timetable. It was becoming a pretty miserable existence.

Saturday 6 May

Mum down for the weekend. Out to the stables with Grace. Out to the Blackburns' [David and Janice, art curator]. Brian and Anne Lapping [producers, broadcasters]. Mel Clore [Sotheby's] and husband. All very alarmed at the idea of GB taking over apart from David. Mel thought maybe the country wanted an anti-charismatic figure. David thought he would go with real fireworks. But not the universal TB must go. Indeed, NotW poll had 25 per cent saying stay another term. But the media prism was all about him being finished.

Sunday 7 May

I played at Stamford Bridge for Cystic Fibrosis Trust v MPs though loads didn't turn up because of the reshuffle or because they didn't want to be seen enjoying themselves. Pathetic. Enjoyed the match, played 60 of 80 minutes at left back and once I got used to the pace it was OK. Could be a struggle to last 90 but that was what I wanted for Soccer Aid. GB was on Marr and was pretty clear where he was heading. There was nothing you could take as a 'time for Tony to go' clip, but the mood, tone and body language was all pointing there. And he had plenty of people out being more direct on his behalf.

Monday 8 May

I did a bit of work then watched TB's press conference, followed by Sven announcing the England squad. Both did pretty well though TB got next to nothing but leadership, transition etc. He was robust about not giving a date for departure, saying it would not, as people claimed, bring an end to all the nonsense, and that it risked paralysing the government. He looked OK, but it was not a great place to be, and of course the hacks were being fed plenty of 'Why doesn't he just fuck off?' from elsewhere. I had to leave for a meeting with [Lord] John Browne [CEO, BP oil and gas company] at his house in Cheyne Walk. Small talk re TB–GB. He wanted me to have a think about what he could do to help BP distance itself from Exxon. He felt they were all damaged by them. Their antics gave them all a bad name. Top Exxon man on $400 million. Also part of the subtext was that I sensed Browne was hoping to stay beyond his tenure, and was thinking of how to draw up a long-term plan.

I went to Calum's Monday night football group at Gospel Oak. I needed to start playing a bit more if I was doing this Soccer Aid thing. Peter Riddell [*Times*] called me to say the Tories had an eight point lead in their latest poll, which was our worst in years. And the feedback from the PLP was that though there was support for TB, a lot of people were pressing on when he would go, and he was pushed into saying his successor would have 'ample time'.

Tuesday 9 May

Woke up very down. Coverage out of TB's press conference was almost wholly negative. The post-locals, post-reshuffle frenzy was still raging. GB was out now claiming they had never discussed a date. Jesus. He had asked for it so many times. I got loads of bids but in the end only did Pat Kenny [RTE] as a favour. I was working on '03, when GB was trying to bounce TB on the Euro while Iraq was raging. Gym then Ben W-P came to see me to discuss what was going on and how to get out of it. He said Damian McNasty, as he called him – McBride – ran a briefing operation against TB the whole time now. The PLP was an example. Party press office briefed it went OK. Counter briefing was immediate.

They basically felt GB had waited a long time and it was his turn, simple as that. He had to go soon or else they could not renew. He said it was a full on operation, non-stop, and because the rhythm of our meetings had slowed, there was nothing to stop them doing it. I asked if TB had yet said, 'Fuck it,' as in 'Right, I will go.' He said no but he was getting close to saying, 'Fuck it I won't endorse him.'

TB was fed up at the constant claim – played back at yesterday's press conference and PLP – that he had not given any indication when he was going. I drafted a letter to *The Times*, for my, his and JoP's eyes and not to be sent – 'Sir, To the small number of MPs pressing for public confirmation of private discussions about a prime ministerial handover between TB and GB, could I put their minds at rest. The timetable has been made clear by TB to GB. I was there.' As PG said these lies entirely depended on us and others staying totally stumm. It was unbelievable that he still did it and he would get caught out big time if he got the top job. I couldn't give Ben much of a steer other than to say be more expansive, spread the range of tone and content and also maybe play them at their own game a bit. Above all try to rise above it.

Neil K had asked to see me and we went for dinner at Luigi's. He was late because he had been at CC's farewell. He said Charles made a very nice speech about duty. Neil felt TB made the wrong decision but also that CC was right to turn down other jobs, though FCO would have been hard to refuse. We got to the point fairly quickly. He basically felt the game was up. He had seen TB after the election and told him he should go when it was least expected. But the pressures were building and forces gathering in a way that cut his room for manoeuvre. But he felt something had changed and it was not going to change back. It was unfair and he deserved better but it was just the way it was. It was a smell, a feel, and it was not going to get better. I said – so you're saying he should bow to a collection of the media, GB's strand of disloyalty which had grown recently and a bunch of malcontent has-beens and never-will-bes.

I explained to him some of the GB shenanigans going on in recent days which, if as explained to me by TB, were bad as ever. GB was seriously expecting us to believe he had nothing to do with what Andrew Smith, John McFall and others were saying or that his new 'renewal' buzzword was not a coded threat, like the comparison he made with Thatcher and how we would show the world we could do it in a civilised way. I told Neil about some of the stuff in my diaries where GB had behaved monstrously, like the period I was doing today when he tried to bounce him on the euro and on the second Wanless review* at the height of Iraq. Neil said he knew GB and his people did things they shouldn't and he also thought TB's people did, though he knew GB's lot were worse.

I said I thought TB was amazingly charitable still even to be thinking of backing GB. Told him re the Balls–*MoS* episode. He said the way we were going, the next election was lost. He also knew that GB did not have the full deck of political skills. As the evening wore on it all became a bit NK telling old tales of political skulduggery. Then we discussed Fiona and whether she should become an MP. He felt only for a totally Labour seat. I said part of me resented me being got out of the game and I had to watch if she then got back in. But he felt I would just be so proud of her, especially if I could come to terms with my own role. He said we were very lucky with our partners, and that Fiona had put up with a lot. Added to which, when TB did move on, maybe I would be able to move on too, and decide properly what I wanted to do.

Wednesday 10 May

David S. I was feeling very down again. The political scene was really getting me down and I felt powerless to do much about it. Lunch at an Italian restaurant in Seymour Street with Nancy D'O. Pressing me to get involved with Truce. She was not wanting to be in Germany for the whole World Cup tournament because very few of the wives could sustain a conversation for long. She was very down on GB. Desperate for TB to stay. Felt I should go back. Then to the Landmark Hotel for a meeting with Cathy Gilman about a south of France LRF fundraiser. Then to Gail's plus Ed V, RS and Sue Freestone to discuss where we were on the book, particularly the compilation version. Not clear re what exactly, me still ambivalent re GB, Ed and Gail for short, rest of us for long. Then home by 6.

TB called as I was walking in. 'Hellooooo,' he said, usual jokey self. But he admitted in the last day or two he had not felt good in himself because it was so hard to see a way out of this. Either he was forced out in some way, in which case he felt the public would just take a settled view that the party had something wrong with it, and even people who didn't much care for him would think it was no way to treat someone

---

* Sir Derek Wanless had in 2002 carried out a review of the future funding of the NHS at the behest of Gordon Brown.

who had won three elections. Or he would soldier on but it would be hard to get things done and it would be a miserable sort of existence. As for GB he had clearly taken the decision to go for it but, as ever, short of the final push that actually challenged him directly. He said what he hated most was the mendacity. 'I'm the one that's supposed to be deceitful, but this guy goes out and tells barefaced lies, like we have never discussed a timetable. I'm the one supposed to use the press to undermine people. This guy has a whole operation dedicated to doing just that.'

I said what do you do then? He said the worst thing was that it was hard to know. He felt he had something still to offer. He also felt GB would not beat Cameron unless he changed his ways and there was little sign of that. He felt sure that he was going to lose the Murdoch press and that was a big card to chuck away. But the reality was they didn't believe he was a reformer. He had done too much to put together his coalition on the left. He said Murdoch himself had become personally very supportive, but he could easily see them backing Cameron. Cameron didn't have to do that much now. It was all falling for him. Labour divided. Reform blocked. Polls moving in his favour. He would need to do more than so far, but not a massive amount more. And what was GB on about? Buzzwords. Complex arguments that he didn't make simple.

TB felt he still had to try to make it work but it was going to be hard. They had a better meeting today. But no matter how many times TB told him he was going GB didn't believe it, or at the least he wanted more. I said to TB I found the whole thing really depressing but he had to think about his own exit not being a dragged kicking and screaming situation. I said I would do whatever I could to help. But I knew it was limited. That was what was depressing me I think. I watched *Newsnight* with Calum. Some fucking rubbish about JP that had every word and frame slanted against him. Free hit for the Tories on their A-list of candidates. Then a BBC2 programme on spin, media manipulation, usual fucking junk. I had loads of media people phoning me at the moment and was so glad not to have to speak to them.

Thursday 11 May

Bike early. Then a long chat with Fiona. I said I was sure I would get through all this, but it was taking so much longer than I thought. Something had to give at some point. David S was convinced all this stuff was helping me, and there were times I felt that too. I also knew how hard things had been for her, and I wanted to put that right, but having walked away in 2003, I couldn't fully walk away while I saw it all falling apart. Bob Wilson [former Arsenal goalkeeper, broadcaster, AC friend] called about a guy dying who wanted a tour of Downing Street for his last wish, so I got on to trying to fix that. Workwise though I wasn't not really motoring. The TB situation had calmed a bit but still not great.

Friday 12 May

I ran with Molly to Regent's Park and breakfast with PG at the Honest Sausage. He felt things were pretty much up for TB and there was a case for trying to get him to conference and then out. He couldn't see a way back up whereas if he went then he would still go out on a high. I said that was not much more than a year into a supposed full term. Sure, he said, but if he was just going to limp on like this. But these periods have a habit of passing, I said. 'And then they don't,' he said. He agreed it was an outrage he was being forced out by a mix of GB, the left and the media but we all seemed to be moving to that view that he couldn't really get it back sufficiently either to enjoy it or to achieve what he wanted. I couldn't remember TB having sounded more down than when we spoke at the weekend. And there was clearly still no Plan B, and the reshuffle had not really created one. PG said he didn't think GB would ask him to work for him and he didn't think he would want to. He thought he would ask for me but that I should not get too sucked in. Back to work with MB. OK run but not feeling great.

Saturday 13 May

First day of Soccer Aid training. We had to meet up at the Conrad Hotel, get to know everyone, and get briefed on what lay ahead. The usual mix of OTT TV security men claiming to be ex-SAS and pretty-ish production assistants fussing around over everyone. I was on the Rest of the World team and the first team-mate I met was Ben Johnson [former sprinter] then Sergei Fedorov [ice hockey]. Sergei was one cool guy, light shades, very smartly dressed in a cool casual kind of way, every inch a top sportsman. Next to arrive were Eddie Irvine [motor racing] and Brian McFadden [singer] and the conversation quickly turned to which countries had the best looking women in the world. Brian said there might be a bit of tension between Eddie and Robbie Williams

[England captain] because they had shared a girlfriend, and there was a bit of rivalry.

David Campese [Australian rugby player] arrived and was quickly into his very negative analysis of Clive W. He said he had been looking forward to seeing me as soon as he saw my name on the list, 'so I could slate you about that Tour. What a debacle.' Running theme time. He said the problem with Clive is that he thinks he is the game and it all revolves around him. Harsh, I said. I felt he was someone who had good ideas, good principles, but I didn't buy this idea that he took all the credit for England winning the World Cup. 'So why did he write a book called *Winning!?*' Because he was the coach and they did win it. He told the story of Martin Johnson [World Cup winning captain] at Sydney telling Clive it was all under control and Clive was angry he couldn't get in to talk to players. Bullshit, I said. I could tell this was going to be testy. He was very Aussie. Ben Johnson suddenly piped up, 'Am I the only black guy in this team?' And then he said, 'It's too cold here. I hate running in the cold.'

Craig Doyle [broadcaster], Paddy Kielty [broadcaster, comedian] and Gordon Ramsay [chef, Rest of the World captain] were already there. Long journey out to Fulham training ground on the team bus. The production values were going to be high, that much was obvious. Dozens and dozens of TV people waiting for us. There was loads of hanging around and then shots staged of us coming off the bus to be met by Ruud Gullit and Ramsay. We were all taken off to do pictures and interviews, and then a briefing after breakfast. Ruud and Gus Poyet [former Chelsea player] who was his assistant manager were stressing that it had to be fun. If we had fun, we would play well. We would have half a dozen pro footballers at any one time on the field and even though some were getting on, we would learn more from them on the day if we started learning now. But the most important thing was enjoying it. Enjoy it, and you have a chance. Get tense, and you don't. Fulham's training ground was not exactly Carrington, but the pitches were good quality, the dressing rooms OK if a bit on the small side, and there was a ton of kit for us, not quite on the Lions scale, but not far off, and all with names plastered all over it.

We had to fill in a few questionnaires etc. and then out to the pitch. Warm-up with Gus, including choosing our own warm-up exercises from a choice he gave us. Then six v two inside a box, and if you went seven passes without getting the ball you had to do press ups. Then passing and shooting drills. Lots of stretching. I was doing OK once

I got my breathing sorted. I worked out I was easily the oldest there. Ben J and Campese were really struggling with the ball, just lacking in basic skill. Sergei and Brian were really good. Eddie was laid back and quite dirty. I enjoyed it though and felt OK at the end if a bit stiff. But they had ice baths, massage, physio, proper set-up. Met up with Terry Venables [former player and manager], who was managing the England team here, and he, Gullit and I, later joined by Ramsay, had a bit of a political chat. Terry raised TB and the general situation. He said the press was totally ridiculous, TB was top quality, it was obvious to anyone with a brain, and you would be mad to get rid of him. He said he never understood why he had committed to going before the election. 'He would beat Cameron, I reckon.'

Gullit said he loved England, had had some amazing times here, but he felt the press was the worst thing about this country. He said it was OK to be passionate, and to want the best from the people who represented you, whether in sport, or politics, or anything else. But actually they wanted the worst, and they wanted people to think the worst was the norm. The England team had been doing similar to us and then we all met up, and had a bit of a laugh, usual football-type banter, but the truth was this was quite an interesting mix of people, and once we started getting involved with the real footballers, it was going to be interesting. I took an instant liking to Gullit and Poyet. I had met them before, Ruud at matches, Gus when he played in another charity game I was involved in, and they both had infectious enthusiasm. We had physios from Arsenal, Palace and the David Beckham Academy and they were all saying my body would be in pieces after my triathlon next weekend so I needed to be careful. They were basically saying it would be sensible to pull out of it, but I had committed for Cathy and we had built quite a team on the back of it, so that was not going to work. Eddie Irvine and Patrick Kielty seemed to be seeing who could eat the most sausage sandwiches.

Sunday 14 May

The papers were full of TB–GB again but with less than the usual venom. The *Sunday Telegraph* had a story on the divisions between the 'capitulators' so-called – like me and PG – and the 'ultras' who wanted him to keep going and keep GB out for ages. I made my own way to training as I had a speech to work on, and I arrived at the training ground just before the rest of the team. Campese took a knock yesterday which meant no training today. Alessandro Nivola [actor] arrived. I didn't know much about him but then realised he was the guy who had been starring in the football film that I saw being made with Steve MacManaman [former England international] in Madrid not long ago. We had lunch together and in between times we were watching England train. They seemed to be taking it much more seriously than we had been yesterday. It looked like proper pro training sessions. Their celebs seemed to have generally better ball skills, especially Ben Shephard [broadcaster]. It also made a difference that their pros were already with them. Even so, I could feel our confidence starting to wilt just watching them.

Gullit and Gus Poyet were so much more laid back, constantly just saying it was about having a good time, whereas Venables and his support team were really looking like this mattered. Gus said it would take a couple of days to work a few basic things out, so in the meantime just go with the flow. They were probably just trying to work out what positions to play us and how to link to our main players when they arrived. Our training was delayed endlessly while England finished, not just the training but then all the stuff they had to do afterwards, interviews and the like. We went out the back and then in the dressing room just doing kick-ups and messing about.

Ben Johnson was definitely looking a bit out of it. Sergei was the most skilful. Training – warm up, then a tag game supposed to show tactical awareness but none of us could really work it out. Five-a-side. Patrick in goal, me, Alessandro, Eddie and Craig. I thought we would get marmalised v Adam Bartlett (Newcastle United goalkeeping coach) Ramsay, McFadden, Federov and Ben. But we did OK. Gus reckoned we were all better than yesterday. 17 minutes flat-out and it was tough. Also did a chasing game. Take the ball 30 yards out and run with it towards goal with someone five yards behind you. My five yards behind me partner was Ben Johnson. Fast or what. Then penalties. My first went so far right it was ridiculous. Then I changed to my left foot and did fine. Good free kick. Interviews, photos, messing about then up chatting to some of the England players after physio as I'd had a bad knock on the knee. Gazza [Paul Gascoigne] looking too thin. Bradley Walsh [actor and comedian] a laugh. Dean Lennox Kelly from *Shameless* ditto. Photos then head home.

TB called, said he felt we just had to draw a line, stop even thinking and talking about the GB scene, get on with doing what we could do. If we could get the new Cabinet doing well, MPs would calm down. Maybe, I said, but a lot depended on how GB reacted. The problem was that the media tramlines were so well laid, they knew where to go to keep the same old same old stuff going. It would only stop if GB did something bold and dramatic to stop it, and he would only do that if it suited his purposes. TB felt that a part of him would be worrying he had pushed things too far, but I was not so sure. There were people around him who positively loved to see TB so discomfited. As ever, TB was hopeful that by focusing on a big policy agenda he could get above the noise. The next steps on law and order and civil liberties this week, we had a new government of national unity in Iraq hopefully about to be formed, and he was talking about doing another visit there on the back of it, and he had his big CBI speech. He also felt he had got to a realistic and reasonable position on pensions.

He'd sent over an outline of the CBI speech, which was all about maximising strengths for Britain to do well in the era of globalisation, and how to meet challenges from China, India etc. Do we stay open or closed, meet the challenges or retreat? Answer, open, outward-looking, reform, and then he was into his usual script on skills, education, lifelong learning, science, reform of energy policy, push on renewables, signal his support on nuclear. Also, Hugo Chavez [President of Venezuela] was spending part of the week in the UK, as guest of Ken Livingstone [Labour Mayor of London]. He said it would get a lot of coverage, and be used as part of the backdrop to his CBI speech, so he needed to embrace it, defend the New Labour approach on the economy. When I went upstairs, a lot of this was in his note for the week ahead, but it also had one of his scattergun 'This is what is bothering me' lists, going from mobile phone theft, and the impact on violent crime figures, his feeling the data we had on the NHS was confusing, worries about JP, also whether we were using Pat McF properly, and whether Ruth Kelly's ultra Catholicism was a problem on anything to do with gay rights.

Wednesday 17 May

Jack Straw had done an interview talking about how there needed to be a calm handover, and that any timing could be agreed by TB and GB, without need for it being public. If only. TB was out basically pre-empting the energy review by saying nuclear energy was back on the agenda 'with a vengeance', and though he provoked the usual howls from the green groups, the argument was strong, and fitted with his overall agenda as he set it out over the weekend, namely if we were to stop dependence on foreign gas we had to go for a new generation of our own nuclear power stations. A session with David S, feeling on a better keel. Then to No. 10. I went to the toilet and bumped into TB. 'Ah, you're still allowed in this part of the building are you?' 'Yes,' he said, 'just a couple of hours a day, but it's very generous of him.' I had missed PMQs because I was heading for lunch with Jo Sheldon [former colleague, journalist turned PR] at the National Portrait Gallery. He said it had gone a lot better and he felt DC was getting too cocky again. I went round to see the press team then back for the main meeting. Matthew Taylor, fresh from a 1.30 half-marathon, had done an OK note of future challenges and narrative. It was a perfectly good piece of work, took in some of the note I sent to JoP on the need for a more open and reflective speaking style. But the discussion around the Cabinet table quickly became a bit rambling and anecdotal. TB was a bit too close to the 'initiatives with which I can be associated' kind of mode. He was stressing some of the difficult long-term things but in a context of not being really clear where GB might be on it. He felt he still had to try to get on with GB but it was not easy. The nuclear speech had gone well but as Sally said he was looking a bit manic, looking like he was running out of time and a bit desperate. I wasn't concentrating part of the time, felt unable really to shape it. I said that I felt he was doing the right thing – focus on long-term challenges, keep going, don't get sucked into the soap the whole time. What we missed was the narrative that made it best for him to be doing all this – and for me that was experience, plus independence from having to face re-election, so a help to a successor.

He did seem to be making a bit of progress setting dividing lines v DC. He was very worried about the NHS financing situation and felt Patricia was seeing it too much as an accountant rather than a politician and that was because she was trying to impress GB, possibly with a view to becoming his Chancellor. Ben W-P said they hardly saw the Health people who were in and out of No. 11 the whole time. CR told me earlier that Harriet [Harman] was almost contemptuous of the No. 10 people and at one point openly scoffed at something TB had said. The possibility of HH becoming deputy leader was being pushed again. TB said that though the nonsense had calmed a bit, there was still active stuff going on in the PLP. PG said that for all the fuss, a consensus had settled – that neither public nor party wanted him out now. They looked to him to sort it, repair the divisions, and prepare for a dignified exit. They wanted things done in the meantime. Tories were now on the line of 'government paralysed'. That theme played big on the news following some hapless, hopeless civil servant saying at a select committee that he didn't have the faintest idea how many illegal immigrants were here. JR was trying to sort it but how often did the Home Office give us these kind of problems?

I felt pretty down about the meeting. This was not a strong set of horses pulling in a clear direction, and TB seemed distracted. Home, then to the James Purnell–Chris Bryant [Labour MP] fundraiser at the Arts Club. I sat with Rosie Winterton [MP] and Sara Latham. Rosie was clearly feeling maybe JP had reached the end of the road. 'What a silly old fool, falling for that one!' She definitely felt that he should give up Dorneywood [country home for senior minister]. Maybe that he needed to know honestly from TB what he wanted him to do. JP had done his first Questions in the Commons since the whole story broke today and by all accounts it was laughing stock time, though not as bad as some had feared. I said the problem was the area he had always reserved for credibility had been eroded now. He was not seen as the vital presence he once was. But once you stripped away layers of authority, it became more and more difficult. She also felt re TB that the governing style had become odd and disjointed. Several of them said it needed me back there but I don't think so. Arsenal v Barcelona in Paris so lacerated James in my speech for not being there. I did some decent jokes on football, my 'professional debut' in Soccer Aid – the media build-up was already getting noticed – and then a big number on how I felt anger and bewilderment at the way our own people gave ammunition to our critics the whole time. How tough government always is. How this is a good country and a good government and we have to say it because the media won't. Nice enough time. I did the raffle and the auction, and announced that Arsenal had lost [2–1]. Home late.

Thursday 18 May
I was picking up on a briefing operation by GB that TB should be given 'months not weeks' to indicate his departure. On the one hand, it might be a good sign, that they wanted to calm things down. On the other, it was a bit patronising and underlined a sense of TB weakness. JP called, he said he had discussed the chat I had with Rosie, wanted me to meet up with him next week. He sounded very down, and I wondered if he was indeed thinking of jacking it all in. I was also talking to Endemol who were doing all the telly for Soccer Aid, and wanted me to try to fix a visit for both teams to see TB in No. 10. MB and I had a good session on the diaries, into July and then September 2003, including the

final days and also that remarkable meeting with Bill C, when he was advising me and PG. If I had not kept a diary, I am not sure how much of it I would have remembered at all. Things were quietening down a bit on the political front but still not brill for TB.

Friday 19 May

A lot of Iraq in the news, with the new government being formed hopefully, and the context here whether TB and GWB would then be able to withdraw troops. I was working on and off on the diaries in between trying to help Calum with his French revision. I was trying to get rested for tomorrow's triathlon but instead was up late to watch *Calendar Girls* with Grace after we had a row about her watching that wretched *Big Brother* the whole time. Mum was back from Poland.

Saturday 20 May

Cathy Gilman was round first thing and we set off for Blenheim. The Soccer Aid guys had said it was mad doing a triathlon, added to which I woke up with a bad throat, but hey ho. The event was very well organised, in a beautiful setting, the grounds of the Palace, but the weather was not ideal, a bit cold and drizzly. Also, it was clear from the swim that the Channel 4 team were going to be following me the whole way. The swim went fine but the transition was a nightmare, a 400m run uphill. Then a telly cameraman got a pole in my spokes as I was doing the transition. Worse, I forgot my asthma inhaler and the bike stage was really tough. The run not so bad. At least I got through it and didn't feel like I was too knackered. I hung around for a bit then got a lift back with a very nice Kosovan driver, who said it made him mad the way people attacked TB, that without him he and his family would still be suffering.

Got home, Neil, Glenys, Johanna and Camilla [granddaughters] there for dinner. Nice chat. No angst, or at least less than has happened in the past. The kids were having a great time, it was amazing how Grace and Camilla just slotted straight back in where they left off, though we were all a bit worried about Molly who was kept in at the vet's for the weekend because of continuing pain. I was also worried about Donald [brother] who was laid-off for two weeks [from his job at Glasgow University security department]. He sounded very down for the last three days. A car came around half ten and took me back to the team hotel. Some of them in the bar but I went straight to bed. I could feel a cold coming on.

Sunday 21 May

I slept really badly, woke at half-two and I never got back to sleep. I had a bath at 5 a.m. and then did a bit of work before going to get drugs for my cold. Back to the hotel and waited for the others. Some of the celebs were starting to get a bit grumpy about all the hanging around. But the training was a lot better now that we had some real players with us. Gianfranco Zola [former Chelsea player] was terrific, not just the skill, but the ability he had to explain how to do simple things better. Dunga [Brazil] was also very patient with us. There was already talk of needing reinforcements, as we already had Eddie Irvine, Campese and Ramsay with injuries. There was to be a penalty shoot-out today and Ruud and Venables – or probably Endemol [media production company]– wanted us to have a 50k bet on it. I downplayed the cold as much as I could, and we did lots of very gentle running and stretching exercies then a few partner skills exercises. I was with Dunga most of the time. Different class ditto Zola. Good having them there and they were both of the Gullit–Poyet view that we had to enjoy ourselves.

Zola said if people tell you football is serious, tell them to go away. It is fun, fun with dedication but still fun. Dunga watched the England training session and said they were too serious, that it was being done for the coach not the players. Gus saying we want to win but not at the expense of fun. We were definitely having the better time. I was feeling a bit ropy but glad I trained today. Zola was definitely taking it seriously. Gordon was being treated for the tear. Ruud was dropping a few hints that if he had to pull out, I would be captain. 'At least you know a thing or two about leadership,' he said at one point as Ramsay was limping around. Then in the penalty shoot-out I was the last of the five to take it so maybe that was a sign of trust. Robbie Williams was their fifth. Gus theory was the TV people wanted it to be a Robbie triumph but with help of Brian, Alessandro, Ben and Sergei, we did it. We all went mental as if we'd won the whole thing.

There was a fair bit of spice already, for example when Ben Johnson false started, running in before the whistle, Ben Shephard said, loud enough for people to hear, 'Once a cheat always a cheat,' and it kicked off with Brian and Craig.* I had a very funny chat with Eddie Irvine who told me he had never heard of me. When we first met, he said he thought I was a cricketer because he was vaguely aware of a cricketer with my name and also because 'You're not very athletic but you do look quite sporty'. Of all of them, he was the one most in his own world. Ben seemed to be coming out of himself a bit. We were mixing more and more with the [ex-Tottenham Hotspur] England team players. Jamie Redknapp such a nice bloke. He reminded me in some ways of Stephen Jones, very enthusiastic, relentlessly upbeat and inquisitive. Les Ferdinand [former England international] a real gent. They all seemed to know about my Burnley madness, and had loads of stories about playing there. Venables was a really good laugh, and had been trying to wind me up throughout the whole penalty shoot out. It had definitely been a bit of a mistake doing the triathlon, and the cold was getting worse. Later I went home to see Calum and do some French and I ended up staying and getting an early night because I felt so crap.

Monday 22 May

Cab out early to get to the hotel to meet up with the rest of the squad. Campese was going off on one about our press, also starting to get into me for being 'English not Scottish', having checked out I had been born in England. He was a classic Aussie wind-up merchant. *The Sun* and the *Mirror* were running huge ads for Soccer Aid which looked pretty good, and I was starting to do a few columns on it, for *The Times* initially though the tabloids were on to me too. There was still a lot of simmering anger towards Ben Shephard for his jibe at Ben Johnson. The TV people were loving the spice developing though. We had two new players today. Michael Greco, actor ex of *EastEnders*, now a pro poker player. I chatted to him about Rory who was getting more and more into poker. Also Peter Schmeichel [Danish goalkeeper, ex-Man United]. He was very friendly and very bright when it came to politics. It turned out he went to my show at the Bridgewater Hall [Manchester], the one I did with Mick Hucknall, and he said he really enjoyed it. He felt whatever walk of life we're in, we had a duty to understand politics because it affected everything.

---

* The Canadian Johnson won the 100m sprint final at the 1988 Seoul Olympics, breaking his own world record. A blood test revealed the presence of the banned substance stanozolo and he was disqualified. He later admitted using steroids and his record times were rescinded.

He felt TB was really good, we had really modernised, but would not get the credit we deserved. He had no time for GB. He felt Cameron would win, not necessarily because he deserved to, but because we were stale. We chatted about Helle. I said I was confident she would be Denmark PM one day. He said no chance, because Danish Labour is too left-wing and run by the unions and they had never faced up to the need for modernisation as we did. He thought Helle would be a great Ambassador for Denmark but she will never be elected. The media label 'Gucci Helle' was also hurting, he said. Training was OK, then an OK five-a-side. It made such a difference having Schmeichel behind us who could order us around. Good mood and we definitely had the better team spirit. Eddie was badly injured. Gordon Ramsay still not fit. Zola kept saying we were getting better every day. Not sure yet.

We were due to have a match against Scotland's Euro '96 squad on Wednesday and we went to the teamroom for Ruud to tell us who was playing. I was in the starting eleven at left-back. Kielty – Doyle, Marcel Desailly [France], Lothar Matthäus [Germany], AC – Nivola, Sergei, Dunga, Campese – Zola and McFadden, subs Ben, Grecko, David Ginola [France]. I texted the boys to say I would be making my international debut with three World Cup winners, Desailly, Matthäus and Dunga.

Desailly was so laid back, but also a great encourager. Matthäus was exactly what I imagined him to be, tough, focused, definitely wanted to win. Another long politics chat with Peter Schmeichel on the bus back to the hotel. Re TB he said he couldn't understand why he keeps taking it. I said because he was worried about what comes next for the party. He ended up coming back to NW3 for dinner. We chatted a fair bit about Alex. He liked him well enough, though they had had some bad moments, and he said he was not someone who really understood goalkeeping, which is why he had made a few bad calls. But he clearly respected him. Peter's son Kasper was making good progress, definitely wanted to be a pro. His daughter was doing a GCSE tomorrow. They felt both Danish and English. We got a car back to the hotel, and a few of them were still up drinking. Good bunch. Good laugh. Why the fuck can't I sleep?

TB was in Iraq. He did a press conference with [Nuri] al-Maliki [Prime Minister] and the sense was pretty positive, though he couldn't give much by way of departure dates for troops, but at least he and Maliki were able to talk up democracy, progress, and a plan going forward. Of course he couldn't go anywhere apart from the Green Zone, so it wasn't easy to get a full picture. There was still a lot of sporadic violence going on and a fair few murders, shootings and bombings today.

Tuesday 23 May

The first nice day at training weather-wise. Eddie Irvine had done a bunk which was a bit odd, just decided to up and go because there was no way he was going to get in the team. Brian very pissed off – again. Training good fun. Lots of ball skills and a good five-a-side. I felt things were coming together especially with Schmeichel, Zola and Dunga who were really getting us organised. We practiced set pieces. Schmeichel said he thought I had natural nudging skills, as in knocking people off their stride as they went for the ball. I called Pete Boyle [Manchester United songwriter] to get him working on some songs for us. After training, I heard that Gavin Henson might be coming. Ruud asked me what I thought. I said he was a bit of a loner, but he had a bit of a following. It depended what they wanted. I said in terms of adding to team spirit and being an entertainer, there were half a dozen of the Lions guys who would be better – Ronan, Alfie [Gareth Thomas], Stephen Jones, BOD.

Later I got a snotty email from Henson's agent saying he heard I had spat my dummy out and threatened to walk out if Gavin came in, which was nonsense. Later we spoke on the phone and I said while Gavin would not be top of my list it was up to the programme and the coaches not me. The agent was now trying to smarm his way back in. But I think the reaction had underlined what I meant when I said he tended to bring angst with him. Meanwhile I was chasing ROG and Alfie. Both were dead keen but not totally clear if they could do it because of their rugby commitments. I was also sorting the No. 10 visit and trying to sort out one or two issues re [former Argentinian star Diego] Maradona's arrival. Even the top players were so excited at the idea he was coming, though it was not exactly clear when or how. I was beginning to enjoy the whole thing a lot more though. Very good fun to see these guys at work close up, and also such a range of characters. We all headed out by bus to Craven Cottage for England v England Legends. England were good, probably better than us. I think their celebs were stronger than ours.

Home for a bit of revision with Calum, then back to meet the Scottish Legends we would be playing before going out to do ITV2 after the Ant and Dec bit on the match. Lots of hanging around again. The highlight of the day was earlier when Dunga was sitting on a bench, and rolled a load of socks into a ball, and then doing the most amazing skills with them. He said as a child they could not afford balls and they played with old socks, and that is why so many Brazilians had such amazing close control. If you can keep a ball made up of socks in the air, a perfectly formed leather ball is easy. Zola was constantly going round us all telling us we were getting better and better. Campese was starting to get on people's nerves with his constant moaning. Henson's agent was saying Gavin was keen to speak to me and make up. He was clearly desperate to get into the Soccer Aid thing. But I had already asked ROG, Alfie and Stephen J, and so were they. Alfie was looking the most likely. I was back in the news for the wrong reasons again, with the story of the Hutton Report Cherie and I had signed as an auction prize at the Purnell–Bryant fundraiser. It wasn't the first time, but this time it felt like it might have legs. Tory MPs were raising it and asking for an apology from Labour.

Wednesday 24 May

Pete Boyle came on with the first songs for our team, which I started to pass around. Did a bit of revision with Calum then we set off for the hotel in Chelsea where the Scotland Legends were gathering, Calum loving watching the players just mill around. He said sorry, Dad, but I will have to support Scotland. Nice chat with Gary Macallister [former Scottish international]. His wife had died recently and he was with his two young kids, now basically a house dad. Ruud was in the lobby as we arrived. He and Gus had just had meeting with Venables. Said it was un-be-liev-able. Terry really kicking up, because Ruud had wanted to change the format to have more pros and fewer celebs. It was definitely the case that they had better celebs and we had better pros. But Terry went off on one saying we were deliberately pretending to be shit and messing around! I said I would go in and tell him, no, Terry, we really are shit. Desailly was really nice with Calum. He spotted his French revision book, and spent a bit of time going over some of it. Alfie called as I was about to do an interview. He was on for it. Brilliant. On his way immediately. I said I hadn't heard him so excited since he talked to TB in NZ.

He said he couldn't believe it – playing with Maradona and those guys at Old Trafford. Fucking hell! It was interesting how these guys, who had played at the top level in their own sports, nonetheless got such a buzz from being involved in a football match. Also the publicity machine had really been cranking up. ITV were doing tons every day and that was driving quite a lot of paper traffic too. The buzz was it was going to be a sell-out, and even the warm-up games were getting

OK crowds. We set off on the coach, arrived into the dressing room at Craven Cottage, and Ruud gave me the captain's armband, without really saying much at all. I couldn't believe it. 'Are you sure?' 'Yes.' Gus said to me football is about skill and intelligence. 'You have intelligence and you can lead.' Christ, it was the first real match since I was at university and I was leading out Zola, Dunga, Matthäus. My shirt was hanging up in the dressing room between Matthäus and Desailly, which was ridiculous. We went out for the warm-up but one of the phsyios said we were going to end up with more injuries because we were not taking as much care as England had done.

The Scots Legends were really friendly, and even though they were long retired, the basic message was that they were desperate for us to win in the game against England. Both Bryan Gunn and Ally McCoist [both former internationals] said so in terms – anything we do today it to help you beat those bastards at Old Trafford. Seeing them line up, they looked a lot fitter than the Legends team England had played yesterday. On to pitch, then toss coin, we got the kick-off and end, off we went. They tore us apart in the first ten minutes. Desailly was talking to me the whole time, telling me where to be, what to do, and I settled into a rhythm OK but it was tough. They were taking it seriously and we were 6–1 down at half-time. At half-time, Ruud said OK, this is the first time we have played together, there are good signs, just get a little tighter, all will be fine. The second half was so much better.

David Ginola arrived just before the break and he came on and made a massive difference. We won the half 2–0. I did OK compared with the first half. A couple of bad passes but defending better, and at least I managed to get through it. It had rained most of the time and there were some deeply unflattering photos doing the rounds later of my body-clinging wet T-shirt look. All in all it was not as bad as the scoreline, and McCoist said as we came off, all you need to do is stay close to one of the pros and offload every time. If you have Desailly and Matthäus at the back, Maradona pulling strings, Zola and Ginola up front, you'll win. I swapped shirts with Colin Hendry [former international], who was another one desperate for us to win. The thing with England ran deep. Shower, a bit of physio, then on to the bus and off to No. 10 [Soccer Aid reception]. Alfie was calling the whole time … I'm just leaving home now … I've arrived at the airport … I'm on the plane … I'll be there by six. He really was like a big kid.

It was a bit weird going back to No. 10 in these circumstances, all kitted out and in the team bus. There were cameras all over it, and it was nice to see everyone but the event was badly organised which really annoyed me. Also TB seemed low, and there was not quite the same magic. Thabo Mbeki [President of South Africa] was in there for a meeting, and we had a nice chat. He said it was good to see me helping Unicef. I said I'll be honest, I would do anything to play football with these guys. He said he had found TB quite low as well. It was unusual for others to notice it, as usually TB managed to lift himself when he had official meetings. 'Keep doing your stuff,' he said. 'He needs you.' The players seemed to enjoy the trip. Schmeichel was taking hundreds of photos. Jamie Redknapp was constantly quizzing me re what everything was, who did what where. Les Ferdinand and John Barnes [former England international] asked if they were allowed to lobby him about bringing down the top rate of tax. Robbie Williams said he found TB a lot more personable than he thought he would be.

The Unicef lady made a speech, which went on a bit too long, then TB did a nice little speech, with a few jokes at my expense, and a suggestion that he hoped for the sake of the legs of our opponents I was left on the bench, but the whole thing around him didn't feel quite right. Maybe I was overthinking things, but it didn't have that everything under control feel that I was used to when seeing him at events, and he had the slightly scared look he sometimes got when he felt something bad could happen any second. I had a little chat with him, and he said he wanted to resurrect the GB meetings. He knew he was a nightmare but short of a Plan B, we were going to have to make Plan A work. He said he was beginning to get the measure of Cameron, who was just a bit too cocky. Confident good, cocky bad. He said the Iraq trip was good, but they had to make sure this really was a unity government and didn't replace one form of sectarianism with another. He was off to see Bush tomorrow.

It was nice to see Vera Doyle and Glen Baxter [messengers] but I could tell people were worried about TB. Back on to the bus, back to the hotel, change then out to Chelsea FC for dinner. Lots of bun throwing. Gus was briefing us on the ongoing discussions on the format and everyone was convinced it was all rigged against us. Robbie said to me we would end up with goalie plus four pros. He felt Ruud was just as bad as Terry in terms of trying to rig things to suit their sides. He said it was best we stay out of it and leave it to the TV people. I was meanwhile getting inundated with people wanting tickets for Old Trafford. PG had been with Calum to watch the Scottish Legends and he said he thought I was OK, a lot better than he expected. Richard [Stott] on the other hand was sending me lots of 'Stick to the day job' messages. There was a quiz – lots of this being done for the telly – and again we were complaining about it being rigged against us, because the Rest of the World questions were so much harder. So for example, we got, 'What was number one in the year Robbie was born?' They got, 'What makes you a cockney?' But we won 27–26 and went even madder than when we won the penalty shoot-out.

I walked back then we stayed up late chatting in the bar. I decided not to go on the clubbing trip with Sergei and Brian and their girlfriends. Brian was with Delta Goodrem [Australian singer, cancer survivor] really nice. Sergei's girlfriend was a Moscow interior designer. Campese had got himself a Lions jacket so he could take the piss out of me and Alfie, who was meanwhile so chuffed to be there, and telling everyone he was a lot more fun, and a lot better at football, than Gav! He said, 'He is gonna go fucking crazy when he knows I am here.' When we reached midnight, as it was my birthday tomorrow, Brian M got the whole bar singing happy birthday at midnight. McCoist came down for a few drinks. I didn't get to bed till half-one, which for me was late. I had to watch it. I was also drinking more than usual – and without Fiona, which I think was a first – so I had to watch that too. And I had to watch some of the women who were hanging around. Row about me and CB signing the Hutton Report for a party fundraiser was rumbling on – Fiona had been on Sky about something else and they raised it and she said CB should apologise! It was raised with TB at PMQs, though not by Cameron, and he just said no offence meant.

Thursday 25 May

Happy birthday. Another bad night on the sleep front. Out early for a coffee, a bit of work and then off to the training ground. I sat with David Ginola who was totally not like I was led to expect. Yes, he was very French and with all the mannerisms, but he took the piss out of himself, he was warm, friendly, very funny. He was clever too. He said he was seeing Sarkozy next week. Desailly was singing little songs to himself. I also noticed he had a Champions League theme ringtone. Out to the training ground and birthday surprise as we had breakfast when they brought a cake in, and all sang 'Happy Birthday'. I did a little speech in several languages. They were a terrific bunch really. Light training. Alfie and I were laughing our heads off as we ran behind Schmeichel, Desailly and Dunga in their tracksuits. 'This is fucking fantasy-land,' he said. Later, Ginola took me to one side, and showed me how to mark a winger, what you could get away with in terms of shirt-pulling, slowing the body etc. He said there were lots of little tricks and it was important I learned them if I was playing left back. The telly people wanted me to do a series of interviews through the day.

Ruud had asked me to get hold of the bagpipes for when we got to Manchester. England were doing really hardcore training again, and we stood on the balcony jeering them. It was definitely turning into England as serious v us as having a laugh. Schmeichel – 'A day not laughed is a day not lived.' Brian Macfadden saying, 'Why do the English make it so easy to hate them?' Then Ruud called us to a meeting, having asked all the telly people to leave. No cameras, no microphones. It all felt cloak and dagger and dramatic. He said that he wanted to know how much we wanted to win. If we were only concerned about winning he would make tough decisions. I guessed he was asking if he wanted us to pick the team entirely on merit, or make sure we all got a game. The general feeling was win but not at all costs. Also he said in the second half the only way we could do rolling subs would be to come off injured so we would need to be clever on that front. There was a bit of a discussion then Ben suddenly stirred, and shouted out, 'Hey guys – mind over matter. Let's go there and win.' The whole place fell about, as he had slept through Ruud's entire talk.

There were a few hangovers around the place today. At lunch, more birthday stuff, then on the bus back more political chat with Ginola and Schmeichel. Ginola found it a bit odd that I was even doing this, rather than still being in No. 10. We were sorting out numbers. Ruud had said he would probably start me left midfield but Campese wanted No. 11 so I went for 49. May as well make something of being the oldest there. In the afternoon I was resting, working a bit on Pete Boyle's songs, then waiting for family and friends to arrive. I had a long chat with Gazza, about booze, fame, the press. He was a lovely guy, but there was a sadness there that he hid in all the never-ending larking around. I had noticed in training that he was easily the most naturally talented player but he was always on the edge. He didn't seem to be drinking that much, but he said he just never knew when he would fall off the edge and go on a total bender and then anything could happen. Also he knew people loved him, and that was great, but usually it meant they just wanted to have a good time with him, and that was not always for the best.

Jamie Redknapp and John Barnes said they worried about Gazza a lot. He had a heart of gold, but there was something tragic about him.

They threw a little party for me downstairs. Another 'Happy Birthday' moment with Gus and the same cake. Kasper Schmeichel was a good kid. I was telling him about Ginola's lessons on how to be dirty and get away with it, and he gave me a few more, despite Ruud's wife's quizzical looks. Ruud was very anti-war. All about oil, he said. Ditto Ginola though he said he was not left-wing. He said the problem with France was too much democracy. Out to the pub, playing silly pub games. Then did ITV2 and PG said I sounded a bit loutish. Need to watch it, I really do. Alfie was pissed after a day on the lash with Nike. Great mood though. Delta Goodrem agreed to sign up as a name-change ambassador for LRF. Back to the hotel bar and Matthäus was beginning to open up, much more friendly. Once Maradona arrived, we would have four World Cup winners. 'How can we lose? Who can England have unless they get Bobby Charlton to play?'

I didn't sense the international players thought much of England on the international scene, though they loved our football culture. Matthäus felt we would be OK because he and Marcel would pick it up. The closer we got to it, the more they wanted to win. He said he didn't really know why we were so bad in the first half at Fulham but we will be so much better. Zola was telling me about the anaerobic side of things, and assured me everyone got that terrible feeling after a few minutes, where you were gasping for breath and felt off the pace. He said you have to go through it. Then it's fine. Relax and keep going. It is all about the mental side. Get through it and then comes the second wind. Lothar felt I had been responsible for two of the six goals, when I let [Darren] Jackson [former Scottish international] past too easily. He told me what I should have done to stop him. Basically bring him down. 'Two yellow cards?' 'Depends how you do it.' It was all a bit unreal, sitting there on my birthday with some of the best footballers of all time, getting lessons in how to foul, and them asking me about international politics.

Friday 26 May

Still not sleeping. Downstairs to get a Burnley shirt signed by everyone. I was chatting with Matthäus' agent Florian Krumrey, who is also [Chelsea and Germany player] Michael Ballack's agent and who was wanting help to position Ballack marketing-wise in the UK. He was worried he would not have the broader appeal in UK. These guys are brands now, and that is how they see themselves and talk about themselves.

On the bus out to training Ginola and I now into major league banter the whole time. Also lots of political and near philosophical discussion, for example about integration of races, about fame and what it did to people – he thought some celebs got arrogant for example, but wondered if the arrogance helped them be a success, or they became arrogant because of it. The *Mirror* asked me to do player portraits 'like we do for Cup Finals'. At the training ground, Brian Macfadden went in and cut up all the England socks, which was good for a laugh but of course meant they would try to do something similar, so we had to have a full-time guard on our dressing room.

Eventually Gazza put tuna in Gullit's coffee. Gazza was like a big kid with a massive great smile and everything was a laugh. Breakfast then a good easy session to warm up, ending with playing eight-a-side. I was now on the left wing with Matthäus and Desailly directing me the whole time from the back, and Ginola in front. I had to pinch myself to think I was on the same team as these guys, who kept telling me I was getting better with every session. Even though some of that would be the bullshit of camaraderie I felt I was doing a lot better. In any event I was loving every minute. It was going to be amazing. The team spirit was great. Nobody disliked anyone. Campese was an acquired taste but I had acquired it. Ben was always a bit out of it but funny. Zola a legend in every sense. Alfie was an inspired choice – people took to him instantly, in a way they wouldn't have done with Gavin, and he was a very good centre back. Then Brian got another injury. Both his thighs had gone. He was totally gutted.

Desailly was very patient in explaining why he called out the instructions he did. 'It is quite a simple game once you understand it.' He was getting into the media now and wanting to make his own films etc. Gazza and Jamie Redknapp were probably the friendliest of the England guys. Always yacking away. Jamie was constantly trying to get me to do stuff for *Icon*, his lifestyle magazine. We had the idea of a touring Rest of the World team, going to different countries. Would be great fun. Back to the hotel, rest, then get the team suits, as tonight was the big pre-match TV show when the line-ups got announced and also, after all the toing and froing, when Maradona arrived. Robbie Williams came over. We agreed that if we need to get an extra player, we'd have to do it. Too many injuries already. Then Campese disappeared because his daughter was not well. Dwindling. Gordon was looking better though and determined to play.

Left at seven for the TV studio. Lots of hanging around. Chat to Ant and Dec. Desailly was never off his phone. Worse than me. So cool and relaxed though. Schmeichel was really getting into the idea that we were being discriminated against, and the whole thing was being set up for an England win. We were all on this gigantic set, and to be fair the production was good. It was a good programme, and Ant and Dec were very good at this kind of stuff. Off to Stansted Airport, plane up to Manchester, Diego sitting up front. And on the bus, I started up one of the songs we had penned for Maradona ... Diego, whoa-oa, Diego, whooooo o – he plays for the rest of the world ... and England play like girls. His family was loving it. Him too. He was like a child reacting to it all. Then the chant got louder and louder, he and his family and friends at the front of the bus stood to clap and cheer and sing along. He grabbed a home video camera and asked his pal to film it. I've seen the way women swoon over Ginola. But now he is swooning over Maradona. He says, 'You see when I see him sitting there. I am no longer a former professional footballer. I am a child who wants to touch him, get his autograph, hear him speak. I love this man. I have played with many great players. If I play with him tomorrow, it is a dream for me.'

Later, Maradona sees him and says, 'Ah David Ginola, how are you?' And Ginola is like a kid, saying he can't believe Maradona remembers his name. It was the same when we all first met Maradona in the ITV studios on Friday night. Marcel Desailly, French World Cup winner, a highly intelligent man, said to me, 'If Maradona says "Hi Marcel", I will faint.' We started singing another Diego song in the Lowry reception, and the England guys took it badly. 'Diego, whoa-oh, Deigo, whoa-oh-oh-oh ... he's quality, poor class, he'll put you on your ass.' Really spicing up. I think they felt Maradona was a bit of an ace to play. It was amazing to see the impact he had, not just on the celebs, but on the pros.

Ginola, for example, is off again as we watch Diego shake hands with the hotel staff. He said, 'We are all professional footballers but we see him and it is a different league. He is on his own with Pele. He made people dream. All ages, he made them dream. He made it so beautiful. When he was fat and useless ça faisait mal au coeur [it hurt the heart].'Zola said much the same. No matter how big we think we are in the game, there is only one Maradona. He is different to everyone, we all feel it. Alfie said to me, 'I will never forget this. I fucking owe you for getting me into this, butt ... but you're still a fucking posh boy.' Bed at 3. Knackered but excited.

Saturday 27 May

Couldn't sleep. I was literally doing that thing you do when you're a kid, imagining a last-minute corner it's 2–2, and I head the winner, and the place goes crazy. Then imagining Ruud would spot I hadn't slept and so he would say sorry, but I've changed my mind. I went down for breakfast, and it was so early I was the only one there. Got myself a coffee and hung around. Then Richard Willmott [Maradona friend and assistant] arrives and he can't sleep either, jetlagged. He is quite political and we sit and talk politics for a bit and then he gets a text from Diego. He can't sleep either, and he fancies heading up to Old Trafford. He hasn't kicked a ball for a few days. He needs to practise. And then he says, 'Do you want to come with us?' And I'm like, 'What, have a training session, me and Diego? Yeah, I can do that.' So I go and get my boots, and I come back down and we get into a mini-bus and we're off. He looks tired, but he's smiling and he is chatting away in Spanish, me in English. There are a few stewards, but the place is virtually deserted. Maradona walks down the tunnel in the corner of the ground, whistling. He gets to the pitchside barrier. He raises his arms, says, 'Wow' and a huge smile lights up the stadium. 'Show me the dressing room.'

We go into the away dressing room where the kit man is laying out our strips for the match. I look at the time. Nine hours to go. He is the only one who has decided he needs to practise. His shirt is in the corner next to Brian McFadden's. He undresses, rummages through a kit bag and pulls out an undersized shirt and oversized shorts. He looks in pretty good shape. There are a few more pounds around the middle than in his heyday but there is none of that fat that once made him so overweight that David Ginola said it 'pained my heart to see him, the greatest player of all time, being stared at like a freak'. He is used to being stared at and as we go out, everyone is staring. Word has spread. There are maybe fifty people in the stadium in total. But they are an expectant crowd. The pitch has not yet been cut and the ground staff want to limit the damage to it. So I hear the most extraordinary sentence imaginable coming out of the mouth of the guy in charge. 'Only Maradona and Alastair allowed on the pitch. Everyone else stay here.' I am almost embarrassed to walk on with him. He is very short, a bit stiff, and with a fair few scars on the legs, he walks on, and I follow. He walks slowly, looking around each stand in turn.

He breathes in deeply, fills his lungs, and then let's out a sound that is a mix between a war cry and a child's exclamation of glee. 'Whoooooooaaaar-eeee-yaaaaa.' Then he laughs and he turns to me and says – at least I think he says – I am imagining the game, visualising how it will be, imagining how I will play. I speak fluent French. Never have I so wished I spoke Spanish too as he talks to me and I struggle to understand, as I talk to him, and he struggles to understand. For that reason, I cannot vouch for the accuracy of my quotes, though I think I have the sentiment. The main one is that he loves football. Not just loves it like I love football, but loves it like a man loves a woman or a child loves a parent. It makes him happy. It fulfils him. It gives him joy because he knows he can give joy to others. Then he stops again, looks around again, breathes deep again, then grimaces a little. He seems worried about his knee, points to it. I ask him if he is OK. He smiles and nods, says he is always OK on the football pitch.

By now we are at the far end of the pitch. We still haven't seen a ball, other than those he signed so patiently for Ken Shepherd [football agent, ITV fixer] in the dressing room. So we walk a little more. He 'realise' – I think that meant visualise – a little more, and he beams joy again. He asks how many people will be there. 70,000. More maybe. He nods the nod that says he loves it here now, but he will love it even more when he runs out to a full crowd calling his name or booing him. He says he doesn't mind being booed. I said they will boo him tonight. 'Hand of God and all that.' 'Hand of God! My best goal.' And he laughs. Then he started singing the 'Diego' tune we had been singing on the team bus, and ever since. Thumbs up. He likes it. Now someone has found some balls, they're in the far corner of the pitch, we jog slowly towards them. A Soccer Aid crew has arrived, so I decide to play it straight. Nothing fancy. I pass the ball to Maradona. I'll repeat that. So I pass the ball to Maradona. He lets it hit the side of his boot. It rolls up his left leg, over the tattoo of Fidel Castro – he told me he was his political hero – he lets it go as high as the thigh, flicks it away from himself with his body, then hits a volley towards the net.

I have the other ball now and I play it into him, too slowly. He runs towards it, gently, flicks it up with his left foot, then starts to head it in the air again and again. Eventually he lets the ball settle on his head. It sits there as his neck moves a few millimetres this way and that to keep the balance. Then he is still. Then flicks his head forward and the ball lands on his neck before he lets it roll down his back and thigh and then flicks it towards me. I trap it, then pass it back. He runs a little, using only the outside of his boot to move the ball along, then crosses it back to me from forty yards. It is in the air and I can see it is spinning. I think, 'Don't mess it up. Just bring it down and play it back.' I do, and breathe deeply. Now he wants to shoot. We have four balls. He hits one into the corner of the net, then runs off in celebration. I don't just mean like a kid who is pretending to score at Old Trafford. I mean like Diego Maradona when he was winning World Cup medals. He raises his eyes to the sky and screams his own name and a few words I didn't understand. I think he was simply saying, 'Diego has scored a goal.'

He did it half a dozen times. He was visualising again. There had been one or two worries he would just show up, showboat, inhale a bit of adulation, and go home. But he was the only player who wanted to train on the day of the match, and I was just there for company. Talk about dreamland. I kept thinking how jealous Ginola and Desailly were going to be, never mind Alfie. He gives me a lecture on visualisation. He wants to win, he says. OK, he says, it is not all professionals, and it is a game for charity and kids not medals, but it is a big event. Big TV build-up, big crowd, great stadium, great players. I want to help you win. Thanks, Diego. That was on a par with the moment when Ruud Gullit told me I would be playing in the space just behind you, and I should think mainly of getting the ball to you.

He's bored with just hitting the back of the net now. He wants something more challenging. He announces he will try to hit the crossbar from 25 yards. The first ball goes a little over, the next a little under. The next hits it, but only fleetingly on the underside. He's not happy. But then he hits one bang in the middle, and he turns away, runs a few yards, raises his arms and screams at the sky, 'Diego, Diego, Die-goooooooooh.' Then another one. Miss. Miss. Hit. Miss. Hit. Hit. Miss. Now he wants to hit the angle of the post and the bar. He curls it left to right. Bang. Bullseye. Celebration time. A couple of his friends have joined us and now they too are hitting the ball at the bar. I have a go. Miss. Miss. Miss. Not embarrassingly so, but enough to make me watch rather than try again.

As we leave the pitch of course everyone is asking for pictures and signatures, as has happened to him every day of his adult life. He stops, does the pictures, signs the autographs, and then we head back to the dressing room. He enjoyed it. He says he feels good. He thinks tonight will be great. He gets undressed and sits there naked, just thinking for a while as around him people lay out more kits and memorabilia to be signed. I have the Rest of the world shirt I wore against England. I have the Scotland shirt Colin Hendry gave me. I have a '60s retro Burnley shirt all my team mates and the England players have signed. I worry I might be pushing it given all the other stuff he is signing. But he signs one, two, three. Then he sees my boots, and signs them too, then my shorts, then my spare shirt. The smile never leaves his face. Shower time, and again I'm thinking that as this whole surreal week nears its end, things seem to get more surreal by the day. I think of Dad, and I wonder what on earth he would think if he knew I was now in the showers at Old Trafford with Diego Maradona. He'd probably have said, 'I always knew you'd go places.' But I doubt the Old Trafford showers was what he had in mind.

Diego gets dried, dressed, puts on the shades and then off we go, back into the cars, and back to the hotel in time for the team lunch. The other players cannot believe what I have been doing. The professionals every bit as much as the non-pros are wide-eyed. At first they think I am winding them up. But then Maradona arrives and confirms the terrible truth. In a team full of greats, he took the oldest, least experienced, least skilful member and gave him the footballing experience of a lifetime. Lunch, team talk, then a bit of banter with all the songs Pete Boyle and I had written which we have put on flipcharts around the place. I get Pete to come in and get them all singing a few of them. Ruud had written on a big board, 'A day not laughed is a day not lived.' Big smiley face underneath. I put up the new Diego words and Pete led the singing. He said later it was one of the most awesome experiences of his life. Soon we're on the team bus. Maradona arrives last. He sits next to me, taps me on the leg and does a pumped up grimace that says, 'I am really up for this.' Gianfranco Zola is over the way. He speaks Spanish and acts as translator. Diego really wants to win tonight. He has only played at Old Trafford once, for Barcelona and though they won the tie, they lost the leg. He doesn't like grounds where he never won.

A song goes up on the bus and though he doesn't know the words, he picks up the tunes and joins in.

> We have joy we have fun
> We'll put Robbie on his bum
> Then we'll make Gazza cry
> When big Alfie scores a try …
>
> Then to Winter wonderland…
> Eng-er-land
> Are scared to play us
> 'Cos we've got
> Looothar Matthäus

Desailly
Ginola
We're in a Maradona wonderland.

And the one we'd written for Ramsay:

> Swear swear, forever on TV
> He is the greatest chef Ramsay
> Though his thigh has a tear
> We swear that he'll be there
> And David G's got the greatest hair.

A big crowd greets the bus. Some boo, some cheer, but he goes over to both sets to shake a few hands, then into the dressing room. He sits quietly for a while, then undresses and slowly, methodically puts his kit on. It is clear there is a ritual to it. Finally, slowly, he laces his boots, never taking his eyes off them, oblivious to all the noise around him. Everyone is really excited, especially the celebs I guess, but the pros are really up for this too. We got out for a warm-up, and I fall over backwards, catching myself in a hole in the turf. I went right over on my ankle, and was desperately looking round to make sure none of the coaches saw me, because to be honest I should probably have come off. I spent the rest of the warm-up just running it off. Then I was knocking a ball around with Desailly and Ginola. I had latched on to Marcel as the one to calm me down, and Ginola the one to fire me up. Quite a sight to see the ground filling up. 'Do you miss it?' I ask Peter Schmeichel. 'How wouldn't you miss this?' he says.

Minutes from kick-off, Ruud Gullit calls us into a circle, hands piled on each other, in an act of pre-match team bonding. Maradona hangs on every word, then let's out a loud roar to get the dressing room going. Then a set of bagpipes is brought in. I blow them up and launch into Scotland The Brave. The entire squad are clapping along. We had kept the cameras out to make it a genuine moment for the team. But how I wish I had film to show the kids Maradona, Zola and Ginola dancing around a physio table shouting, 'Bravo, bravo' as I played the pipes. Peter Schmeichel's camera got the only record of it. Then we are out.

Minutes later, we are in the tunnel. Desailly is in front of me. Maradona is behind me. Desailly tells him he should do his tradition, which is to be last on to the field. Maradona nods and runs to the back. As we walk on, I tell Desailly I feel really nervous, like close to hyper. He says, 'Just do what I do, follow me.' So I do, including touching the turf and crossing myself! Then we walk out, and I see Fiona and the kids, and Philip and family, and the Bridges, and it feels so bloody weird. Packed Old Trafford, lining up with some of the greatest players who have ever lived.

I was next to Diego and Alfie as we were in the official line-up, introduced to Bobby Charlton and David Gill. Then suddenly I realised I had forgotten to put in shin pads. I borrowed them from John Barnes, who was a sub for the first half and owed me one because I had landed him some extra tickets. I knew I would almost certainly only be doing one half, as Ruud would want to give everyone a go, and I was a lot worse than in training. Partly it was the noise. I had got so used to Desailly and Matthäus telling me what to do, and now I couldn't hear a thing. Also having been training as left back and now moving up to left midfield I kept going too deep. I did one or two OK passes. Did a quite good bodycheck on Les Ferdinand, and the ref – Collina, the bald guy – said, 'Next one yellow.' 'Nice one Al,' said Les. I think I felt it more than he did. I also had a weird moment where somehow, though in open play, I ended up BEHIND Schmeichel. 'What the fuck are you doing there?' he said after saving a shot coming my way. Then as he cleared it, he said, 'You are the second player ever to do that to me... the first was Eric Cantona. Now get to where you are meant to be.'

It all just whizzed by in whirr of emotion, adrenalin, noise. The pros took control on both sides. Gazza was fantastic. At one point he was running at me and I just thought, wow, the skill. It was like the ball was part of him. More than once I had to pinch myself. I had Desailly directing me from defence, Lothar Matthäus from midfield, and Maradona coming back to get the ball from me. I said to the boys afterwards – even though Rory's first words were, 'Dad, you were so out of your depth it was embarrassing' – that it was right up there in the greatest days of my life.

My best stuff was defensive, harassing Damian Lewis [actor], shirt pulling Bradley Walsh, body checking Ferdinand. I had one good headed clearance. Best thing was a headed clearance. We went two down but fought back OK and got into it more as the half closed. Desailly talking to me as we went off about positioning. He felt I did OK. Ditto Matthäus but then Ruud said he had to make some tough decisions and me, Craig, Gordon and Lothar – we were coming off.

Ben had to play. He wanted Zola and Ginola on obviously. And Paddy Kielty for Schmeichel. I was down a bit but fine. I was desperate for us to win and it was great to watch the second half as we dominated. Ginola got injured, off for Gullit. Then Poyet on too. Zola on fire though he missed a chance later. 2–1 a good result in the end. Could have been worse. Great mood now and people just hugging each other. Jonathan Wilkes [TV presenter] the best non-pro by a mile. Our best were Greco and Nivola probably. I didn't do as well as I had hoped but it was a great experience overall. Medals from Bobby Charlton, Desailly saying they shouldn't be doing this because it was not about medals but kids. I said it was because this was nearest England would get to winning a Cup this year. Hugh Dulles [Scottish linesman] and Pierluigi Collina [referee] laughing at that. Hugh said he had loved the pipes. We did a lap of honour, the teams together. On for ages and then in. Ruud nice about everyone. Desailly kicking things in the showers because we lost. All getting shirts signed etc., including the pros. Matthäus: 'You sign shirt for me!' Ginola had joined the club nagging me to get back into politics. He said, 'Tu es le personnage complet – politique, parle des langues, lit des livres intéressants, fait des tas de choses intéressantes, ça inspire, tout ça.'* Sam Allardyce and Andy Townsend [player turned pundit] had been doing the live commentary for telly. Sam said, 'You didn't make TOO big a fool of yourself.' Andy said his best line on commentary was when Clive Tyldesley [commentator] said I had chosen No. 49 because that was my age, and Andy said, 'He's looking a lot older today.' But the mood was great. Kids loving it. Telly people happy at ratings. Unicef thrilled at profile and at money raised. Down through the dressing rooms and the tunnel, out to the bus. Big crowds still. All kids on to the back. Bit of singing. Ginola back to say hello. Hector [Mackie, family friend] with Desailly. Calum talking to Alfie. Loving it. Arrived at the Lowry party. Gazza was brilliant with the kids, gave Calum his training top. Jamie and Alfie great with them too. And Desailly talking in French to Calum and Grace.

Schmeichel was interesting on England and sport. He said if you get two million people out to welcome a cricket team and celebrate them for beating one country at cricket what will it be like if England ever again win a World Cup? But he felt it was unlikely. Our media made it harder. He noticed it when United players were with England. They didn't play with confidence. It was all nerves. We talked about family life too, and he had an interesting take on my situation. He said having

* 'You are the most complete person – political, speaks languages, reads interesting books, makes interesting things, inspires everything.'

met the family, I should make them the focus of all my choices. He said they were very special, and in the end though politics was important, family was more important.

I was up till gone three. Maradona was well pissed, but wandering round balancing a glass on his head. He said he was happy he played all ninety minutes, and happy he scored. But he said to me, 'Still no win here. Sad.' I also learned he is a massive rugby fan and he asked me if I thought Alfie would get him a signed Welsh rugby shirt. When I ask Alfie he thinks I am taking the piss. When Maradona says no, he would like one, Alfie looks like he wants to faint. 'Diego fucking Maradona wants a signed fucking Wales shirt. My life is complete!' What a day, what a week. Crazy really just how much I enjoyed it.

Sunday 28 May

Breakfast with Richard Willmott, thanked him for the Diego session. I had been writing about it for the diary late last night, and offered a piece to Keith Blackmore, who loved it. 'You jammy bastard!' Ken Shepherd had taken some photos on his phone in the dressing room, and the Soccer Aid team had some too so we sorted those. My ankle was in a right mess. I should probably not have played after the pre-match trip, but I was glad I did. Some of the papers taking the piss out of my performance, helped by a deeply unflattering picture of me – looking highly unathletic – and Damian Lewis looking like he was running rings round me. Packed, then got the team bus out to the airport, though some had already made their own way off. Maradona looked exhausted. Partly playing the whole game as hard as he had, partly because he had partied as hard as he did. He was still going strong when I had gone to bed. He signed a history of Boca Juniors [Argentine club] for me. There was still a fantastic mood around the place. Gus Poyet laughing as ever. He said I told you it would be fun.

Lots of farewells, first at Manchester Airport, then at London. It really had been a fantastic experience. It had been a bit weird on many levels, and the visit to No. 10 halfway through perhaps underlined there was never going to be an escape from that. But on the other hand, as I told Ros Philipps [TV producer], who had been brilliant from start to finish on the whole project, if I hadn't been known for what I was known for – working with TB and politics – then there is no way I would have been asked. So swings and roundabouts. I wasn't daft enough to think it mattered in terms of life purpose – though the Unicef profile and fundraising wasn't to be sniffed at – or that I had a new career as a celeb footballer (not with my 50th year underway especially), but for the first time I felt maybe I can carve out some kind of proper balance. It was also interesting how many of those old players, though they had all stayed involved in some shape or form in the game, whether coaching, media, commercial, or just living off their fame, had gone through a similar kind of experience to mine when they had stopped playing.

It was like with the Lions. High-level sport and high-level politics had a lot of differences, but similarities too, and one of them was the difficulty of dealing with leaving it. Ginola said to me he had loved every minute. He was gutted when he had to go off injured. Because getting it back, even for a moment or two, just reminded you why you loved it. My problem with the political side of things right now is that the more I got sucked in, the more I knew why I had left. Yet I could see no other form of existence that would give me real purpose and meaning. And belonging I guess. The belonging you felt with a sports team was real, but it was transitory. I thought that when we were all swapping numbers and emails at the airport. Some would stay in touch. There was a chance some would become friends. But there was a chance that some of us would never meet again. When I said goodbye to Maradona, I told him that yesterday morning had been one of the greatest experiences of my life, and if I never met him again, I could guarantee I would mention it to someone, somewhere, every day for the rest of my life.*

I got home, was exhausted, and fell asleep. JP called, waking me up. He had watched the match, and we talked about that for a fair while. The *Mail on Sunday* had done him over, publishing a load of pictures of him playing croquet at Dorneywood! I hadn't really seen the press, but did realise how bad it was. These grace and favour houses were a disaster area. Croquet toffs! 'I know, I know,' he said. He had been thinking of going and he thought maybe TB was pushing in that direction. I said he had to stay or go, but not do the in between stuff. If you are in, you are in. If you are out, you are out. If he gave up the house, it was like trying to admit you had done something wrong but not give up the job. It wouldn't wash, and next they would be on to the car, then the next thing. He was really down, he said he was ashamed his career was ending this way. He knew he had brought it on himself, he had no excuses, it was just daft.

He said his credibility in the party and with TB meant a lot to him

---

* He has!

and he knew he had lost a lot of credibility and knew he wouldn't get it back. What advice? I said be clear. Stay or go, don't do the halfway thing. He seemed OK re that but he read it as me very much saying stay. He said he was desperate to speak to me yesterday when he had heard about the croquet stuff because he felt so bad he was thinking of throwing in the towel. 'I didn't want to bother you because I knew you had the football!' Sweet, in a way. But I said he should not have worried about the football. I was worried for him, but also he needed to be there if he was going to continue to act as a stabiliser between TB and GB any more. It might be that the credibility hit was an issue on that front too, but even so he could often be assisting GB, when GB went over the top, JP did at least call him out on it. But he sounded down. I called Rosie Winterton and said she needed to keep an eye on him.

Monday 29 May

Fantastic show for the Maradona piece in *The Times*. Out to the stables. Regaling George [Mackie] with stories of the match. As he had played sport at a top level [a former Scotland rugby international] he loved all the stories about their professionalism, especially Maradona and his visualisation. On the political scene he felt the JP situation was really bad and he should go graciously. I felt there was a more serious general problem; that there was just a tone and a taste to the government that was all about scandal and division, and the policy issues that were front of mind at the moment – crime, asylum, immigration, tax, NHS, transport – were in there almost as secondary, and the public would get the feeling the government had stopped being about them, the people, and were more focused on themselves and surviving their own mistakes. It wasn't a good mix. But my sense from TB was that though he thought JP had been daft, he wanted him to stay.

Tuesday 30 May

I was working on a piece for *Icon*, Jamie Redknapp's magazine, then doing a BP strategy paper for John Browne, when JP called again. He was still getting hammered on the croquet and the papers were full of 'What does he actually do?' and why did he get to keep Dorneywood etc? He said he had decided to tough it out. He was buggered if he was going to be forced out by a mix of press and e.g. Peter M, who had said yesterday that he thought JP would do 'what was right for the party'.

Pretty clear signal there. Other MPs were piling in, including – to my surprise – Stephen Pound [Ealing North MP]. It was looking a bit shaky for him. Also, as I said to him, the croquet took it to a different place, namely laughing stock, and that was hard to pull back from. In fact the affair did the first stages of that, but there was always a bit more understanding for politicians and affairs than maybe we thought. But croquet! It just took it to a place people would not expect him to be. He knew all that but was determined to make a go of it, do his committee work, carry on with his role on the environment, drugs, standing in for TB. But he did feel Dorneywood was a major problem. And now with the photos it had lost the one thing it had going for it – privacy and the ability to relax a bit.

He used it for team meetings and the like but why would anyone want to go there if they thought it was just going to be on the front pages? He was the named resident of the place. Like Chequers it was run as a trust, and there had to be a named resident appointed by the PM. I had been suggesting that we turn it into a government hospitality place for visiting heads of state and other dignitaries. He was up for that but he was not sure it was doable. What was sure was that he was going to get done in by salami-slicing and that was what I felt he needed to avoid. He was pretty clear about the damage he had done to himself. I said he had to work out how to go out with more than this as his contribution. It was hard to see at the moment and there is no doubt they are after him big style, but he just has to keep going for now. He asked where I thought Tony was. I said I had not discussed but I think he would be thinking we just had to decide and see it through. I said I would try to find out. We chatted then about what his plans were for the coming days. I called TB who was out walking in the Tuscan rain. First he wanted to hear all about the football, and he sounded very jealous and excited about it all.

He loved the Maradona stuff. I said he should do the next one. He was very flattering and supportive about the position I had got myself into. 'You have actually managed your transition well. I thought that when you came in the other day. Everyone knew you were part of our operation. But you were genuinely part of theirs too. It said to me you have found a decent balance.' I said I hoped so. Then he was straight on to asking me to do more for him; more in the party and also get back into regular GB talks. He said that he would give it a go, though he knew it was pretty hopeless. The truth was that GB had not really cooperated from day 1. He just wasn't big enough to be able to accept he was a

No. 2, and so had been at it to greater or lesser degrees the whole time. He looked at some of his people, like Harriet at the moment – he really found it hard to imagine she had known nothing about Jack Dromey going nuclear, and it was clear GB was lining her up as deputy leader. 'Part of me wonders why we are even trying to help him, but I guess we have to. And I need you to help me with him.'

'And what about your other current personnel problem?' I asked. JP's strongest argument was that if they managed to engineer a deputy leadership election, they would then press for one for the leadership too, and that a lot of the people going for him were really going for Tony. TB said he would support JP in whatever he decided but he felt I should perhaps try to persuade him that the best course of action would be to resign as DPM, and stay as deputy leader of the party, and focus on the revival and regeneration of the party. He would also then have a place in the transition. TB would meanwhile appoint a DPM – probably Jack [Straw] – and we would not need a deputy leadership election. I said JP would see that as pretty much a total humiliation. He felt we were maybe just at that stage that all governments get to, but he still felt however weakened he had decisions to take and he just had to keep going. It was not so bad that he couldn't do the job. The one thing he knew was that he hadn't handled GB well but it was too late now to resolve as maybe he should have done a long time ago.

I could hear the pouring rain in Tuscany while it was a beautiful day here. He asked me to try to see JP today. TB's basic view was that it was irrecoverable for JP, also that hanging on to him was damaging him too. But he was clear he did not want to push him. He would rather I had the conversation before he did. In an ideal world, he felt they should both end where they began – TB as the great crusading moderniser, JP as the party traditionalist able to tell the party why they needed the TB approach to win and govern well. I arranged dinner at the Camden Brasserie. Then TB called again later, said he felt that there was a big difference between the two of them. He still had a lot he wanted to get done and the ability to get it done. He feared JP was so damaged that he lacked clout politically and now our enemies could run the line that he was staying around just so that he could have a title and a big house. There had always been part of him that was status conscious and it had damaged him. But it played badly into out-of-touchness. 'It is not exactly what the founding fathers had in mind, croquet lawns for the masses.' Indeed not, but he was right, JP valued his status.

TB said both of them had to get to a place in the public mind where when they went people say well whatever their faults, they got a lot done. JP was more likely to do that if he finds a new narrative now, which is about him reconnecting the government to the party in the run-up to the transition. He can still be in Cabinet maybe as ex-officio, travel, be TB's eyes and ears around the country. TB also felt GB was directing some of the destabilisation around JP so that people would start to think, let's get the whole thing over in one go. Jamie Redknapp called for a chat about the Icon piece, and we had a bit of a reminisce, and then he was asking me what I was up to today, and I said trying to sort TB and JP. 'At least it's not Gordon then this time! Go on, mate, sort 'em out!' It really was like the old days with calls back and forth between TB and JP. Neither seemed fully to grasp how bad things were for John. TB wanted me to get him to a position of staying deputy leader while giving up DPM. But when we met at the Camden Brasserie, first alone, then with Joan [Hammell] and then Fiona, he was a long way from that. He was really just focused on the Dorneywood issue.

His own analysis was that there was no real way back with the public, who would have their minds made up one way or the other. But he could get back in with the party if he was out there campaigning and travelling. But he was determined to keep his job of re-organising Cabinet committees, making them less about departmental compromises and more about expertly reaching the right decision, e.g. on waste, rather than just split the distance between DTI and DEFRA, he wants to have experts come along and then make a real decision, the right one. He still felt he was best placed to do that, and to stand in for TB etc. He had gone round in circles on Dorneywood but now he felt that he had no gain from it. The best thing used to be that he could get away from it all there. That had now gone.

The whole evening the main discussion was houses, cars, avoiding the press. It was if he had lost sight of policy. I said, based on what TB said to me, that they needed to get to where they began when finally it is over – TB as the relentless moderniser who even in the fag-end days with all the grief got things done. And JP the man who could persuade the party it was the right thing to do. He was up for that but didn't grasp the logic – it meant do a party not government job. As soon as I even floated it, he said without a place in Cabinet he had no authority at all. I said he could be TB's eyes and ears around the country, his stand-in, his fixer. He wasn't biting. I had another go but with the same response. He sussed it right off. The only issue he raised when Fiona came was Dorneywood and of course her view – fresh from a Labour general council meeting saying TB must go – was that the problem was deeper, it was about TB, Iraq, all the rubbish, the scandals, CB's hairdresser, freebies and so on. JP had a draft press release re giving up Dorneywood which he intended to give to Mike White [*Guardian*] in an interview tomorrow. Joan and I were both against.

The decision was stay or go in the job. If he stayed, don't get salami-sliced out of it all. He could stop going there without making a big deal of it. He just needed to stay out of the papers for a while. He said he was ashamed where it was all ending. Joan said his judgement about Tracey Temple was awful, that she had warned him but he wasn't having it. They were able to laugh about it but when Fiona spoke to Pauline later she felt she sounded a lot more down than last time. JP felt she had been great but it was still tough for her. I said he mustn't do Dorneywood without TB's agreement and my instinct was that though TB initially favoured giving it up, he would be against making it a big deal. I said the croquet pictures had taken it to a near comic realm and it was damaging. Jamie Redknapp called back later, having reflected on the conversation. 'Hey Al, tell me this. When did it become illegal to play croquet? I've read it all now, and I don't understand the fuss. Tell them to get stuffed.' Interesting take.

Others – including PG, and a lot of the women MPs according to Rosie and Tessa – felt he was now a figure of fun but also damaged in parts of the party because it chimed with a bit of a suspicion of misogyny; added to which he set such store by the party and he was now doing damage to the party. I felt he didn't really get it. He said GB was pushing him to get more work to do. But TB felt GB was also at it vis a vis JP. If there was a deputy leadership election there would be pressure to go the whole hog and TB face a challenge too. JP said he could hardly complain if Harriet went for it. He said he and I had always been right about her. When she did her number the other day on telly about the need for next deputy leader to be a woman she called Pauline and said it wasn't meant to destabilise me. She also said, 'The party treasurer [husband Jack Dromey] is right behind you.'

I was a bit angry with Fiona because having said to me earlier she thought JP should go, and knowing I was sounding him out on being deputy leader without being DPM, she said she thought he should tough it out. Earlier I had a session with David S. He could see I was up about the week and he went over the reasons as he saw them – interesting, centre of attention but surrounded by others, making a difference to the event, a cause, new and interesting people, family involved and loving it. Spot on really. So he said I had to think how I could built a life that generated that kind of balance. I couldn't reject all the things I cared about, even when they were in conflict. I cared about politics. About Labour. About elections. About the team we had built. But I cared a lot about the family. I cared about sport. I cared about myself and my own life. I had to balance them somehow better than I had done in the past. Rory was not well.

Wednesday 31 May

JP called first thing to say he was definitely giving up Dorneywood. He had told TB and TB was fine with it. I said what about anything else? No, he said. I'm staying on. Fair enough. I said TB had been clear with me from the off that he would support you. He did not want to push you out. He wanted me to be the one to float the idea about being deputy leader but not DPM, because he didn't want you to feel he – TB – was pushing him out. If you'd gone for it, fine. But you didn't, so fine. I said there were plenty of people trying to do him in, and he knew that, but TB was not among them, and nor was I. He said he appreciated that. He knew this was not perfect, but he felt he had to give something to show he got why people were pissed off. I said the important thing now was to do the job and show that is what motivated you. Just keep your head down and get on with it. I set off for the airport for a trip to Aberdeen.

The Soccer Aid thing had definitely cut through with a different section of the public. I normally had mainly political people coming up to talk. But loads today about the football, including the guy at security who was asking me about Maradona. I was definitely on for doing my 'mention Maradona every day'. I was working on the speech for tonight in the lounge where I was last with CW in the Lions build-up. Arrived, driven to the Marcliffe, one of my favourite hotels with that fabulous landscape painting in the foyer, went for a really good run on the disused railway line, then back to wait for Donald [brother] to arrive. I was doing an oil company conference, also meeting up with Anne Begg [Labour MP] and Fiona Stalker [BBC]. Friendly audience. The speech was fine and so was the Q&A. Enjoyed it OK then back for a dinner with a small group of them, dominated by MD attacking us over Iraq as a folly etc. Stayed for a while then sat chatting with Donald. Didn't seem so bad. David S had mentioned a new drug he might try out for the schizophrenia so I wanted to talk it through.

Thursday 1 June

By amazing coincidence Cathy [Gilman] sent me an email asking if I was going to be anywhere near Aberdeen in the next two weeks to promote one of three VisitScotland Great Trail triathlons. So we organised the *Press and Journal*, *Daily Record*, BBC, North Sound, PA. Easy enough though broadcasters did me on JP giving up Dorneywood and me broadly defending him was leading the news by the time we got into the car and set off. I tried to buy the painting in the foyer, but the owner said it was a gift from his wife! Donald was on OK form. We drove south via seeing Sheena and Alex [Downie, relatives], then to get Donald's blood tests done, and later to Aunt Jean's [Caldwell, aunt]. If Uncle Jim had been alive, it would have been her golden anniversary so nice to be there. She also felt Donald was in better shape. Got back to his flat to find his lodger had done a runner. He left a note and a month's rent. Donald worried he was hinting at topping himself.

Friday 2 June

Donald drove me to the airport. I worked a bit on the plane, but by the time I landed the political soap moved on post-JP giving up Dorneywood to Alan Johnson in a *GMTV* interview saying he would be interested in going for the deputy leadership. The Tories were still getting an easy ride. Worked a bit with Calum on his revision, then to the Roundhouse Studio with Fiona – *Foolish Young Man*, really tough and challenging on the problems of young homeless, drugs, sex, racism etc. I was interviewed by BBC documentary on way out. Out to La Casalinga for dinner. Feeling OK, but tired. GB off to Germany, and seeing Merkel, so all playing into the Leader-in-Waiting theme. One of the German papers called him 'charming as a bulldog', but the overall message was that she was meeting our next PM, which was adding a bit to the fin de siècle feel re TB.

Saturday 3 June

Working with Calum on politics, out on the bike, then David Miliband round. He was really on the full moan about everything – what is TB for, where is the strategy, what is his plan? He said he couldn't see a way forward right now, it had to come from TB. GB didn't need to do that much. I felt DM should be getting more into the bigger debates, and also we needed to broaden the people taking on DC, who was getting away with murder. Out to Balliol later for Andrew Graham's jazz evening. Even there lots of people had seen the football. More Maradona stories. The main jazzman was a big Labour man and during the break, he sought me out, said he wanted to thank me for everything I'd done and 'never let the bastards get you down'. Met the guy who would be Rory's philosophy tutor, and his very nice Japanese-American girlfriend. John Browne really keen on my BP note according to Nick Butler. He had already got Anji [Hunter, now at BP] working on a sports ambassadors scheme. Alan Rusbridger [*Guardian* editor] was there telling me how brilliantly Cameron was doing. 'He hasn't put a foot wrong.' I said that is because you guys don't want to trip him.

Nice chat with Adam Swift, ex-William Ellis School now politics tutor and his social worker wife Jo. A couple of New Zealanders who wanted to talk about the Lions tour. Nick Macpherson, now permanent secretary at HMT [Treasury], was quite indiscreet I thought, in front of others, saying it now felt like the last days of Major. TB–GB showed on pensions they could do it when they had to but it was all so slow and painful. He felt that since Balls and I were not in there full-time there was a real lack of maturity in the operations. Felt I should get back in and 'get a grip, as you used to say!' I was talking to another of Rory's would-be tutors about the same thing, and he said he got the sense we were no longer doing the basics very well. Andrew Graham a lovely guy, but I never felt totally at home in these Oxbridge/establishment-type events. I had a feeling Rory was going to have much the same relationship with Oxford as I had with Cambridge, though at least he knew a bit more about that kind of world than I did before going. Georgia [Gould] popped round and was regaling everyone with her own Soccer Aid stories, and laughing hysterically about me falling over and then looking around in the hope nobody saw.

Sunday 4 June

TB on, sighing heavily, saying it really was like swimming through crap the whole time now. Dorneywood had just become a symbol of something deeper. Decay, end of era, all that stuff. 'You have America about to talk to Iran for the first time in a quarter of a century, and our media goes on about a fucking country house.' The other problem of course was that the Tories were getting a lift, partly out of us, partly because Cameron was doing and saying a lot of the right things. He was successfully reframing the way people looked at them, which was the first step towards getting them to see them differently too. I told TB what Rusbridger had said, but that just set him off on how the left always helped the right, whereas the right never helped the left. I also told him of David M's general gloom and pessimism, and he said these younger ones needed to step up more. He then went into a far more upbeat assessment, said there was a big programme and we were still dominating the policy agenda, there was a long time to an election, and the Tories were avoiding policy choices and we still had time to force them into making them.

By any stretch of the imagination, a government that had stayed ahead for as long as we had, in a country like ours, with a media like ours, was a bit of a miracle. But we had reached that point where 'time for a change' was starting to kick in. That was opening the door to Cameron, but that didn't mean they were ready for him to walk through it. We had to block them off, and the key to that was policy, and the transition. He recognised it was a moment of potential danger, because as we had seen in America, Germany with Schroeder to Merkel, Italy, the incumbent could fall quickly. We had become the norm as a party of government. But it could change fast. He felt he was getting the measure of Cameron, that he was good at the soft stuff, less good at the hard stuff, and that played into our narrative of facing up to the tough choices that we had to make for the long term, whether on public services at home, or Iraq or climate change, or whatever. Cameron wanted people to think he was a centrist. Heir to Blair. But the tough policy choices would come.

I said I hope you're right. It might be he doesn't need to do much other than positioning, if we get defined much more by division and scandal. That is why the GB thing is so important to resolve, even though we knew how difficult it was. If he was not going to try to find a different successor, we just had to make it work. TB said he was worried about getting the balance right – he had been elected for a term, and even though he had been clear he would not stand next time, he couldn't go too early. But he accepted he needed to give GB, or anyone else if they emerged, time to settle in before an election. He said he was getting more and more frustrated that he kept having to press the Home Office, Health, Education, to keep their feet on the accelerator. If you didn't badger them the whole time… He had a whole raft of stuff he was talking to John Reid about today. He felt JR would get on top of it, but it was not an easy scene.

On the courts, prisons, asylum, drugs, bail breaches, he said he was still banging on about the same things. JR had given the Home Office a going over and was demanding new plans on pretty much all of it. He said he felt more confident about Iraq, his visit was good, and he could at least see a timetable of sorts for security getting transferred to the Iraqis. He was back on to wanting a proper job done on our media though, possibly by bringing Iraqis here to be out and about, putting a different perspective. I went for a run, then had a chat with Philip. He had been talking to TB too, and said he had found him a bit ground down and lacking in energy. I felt the opposite in a way. He started out like that but by the end of it he was beginning to sound a bit like his old self. We kept coming back to the same problem though, namely GB, and the reality is Cameron had changed the dynamic a bit. PG said if you were going to design a candidate to beat Cameron, it was TB not GB.

Monday 5 June

Working flat-out on finishing the last part of the 2003 diary, up to resignation. Mark B said it was like reading a thriller. I laughed, said it didn't feel like it. World Cup [in Germany] frenzy was mounting. GB was out again on his Britishness theme, saying immigrants who came here should learn English, and British history. A call out of the blue from Ginola. He said he was telling his local mayor about the football. 'I had no idea you were so important! The mayor asks if you will come out!'

Tuesday 6 June

John Browne and Nick Butler came round. JB said he loved the paper, which was exactly what he hoped for, a fresh set of eyes looking at problems on which they had become a bit stuck. I had gone over the environmental stuff, but also given them new ideas on how to broaden and deepen profile in new areas, and get him in particular into a more obvious and strategic thought leadership role. I had given them food for thought and now they needed to translate it into what needed to be done. He said they would need to translate it into BP-speak and present it internally as having been their idea. He was very frank that it was probably better to keep any role I had in this between them, as I was still, to some people, 'radioactive'. It was a good meeting if a bit circuitous at times. He was an interesting guy, very smart. We were avoiding talking about payment though. Calum had wanted to go to the Grand Prix at the weekend so I sorted tickets and had to collect them from F1 HQ, and ran there. I recognised one of the guys in there – he used to work for [José María] Aznar [Prime Minister of Spain], now working on F1 rights.

Wednesday 7 June

Rory had not been well ever since Soccer Aid really, and we got the blood tests back and he had glandular fever. Nightmare timing with his exams about to start. I had a session with David S but we talked mainly about Donald and trying to get him on to the new drugs programme. I spent most of the afternoon helping Calum with his revision. Jack S seemed to be on manoeuvres, expressing an interest in taking over from JP, and also saying TB would go well before the election.

Thursday 8 June

Rory's first exam and he was totally washed out, really weak. I cancelled the TB meeting and decided just to stay off with the kids. I was also meant to be doing some media but cancelled it all, though the BBC still sent a car.

Friday 9 June

To a pensions conference at ExCel. It was the usual anti-politics, anti-government, anti-all regulation spiel from the guy before me and I hit back pretty hard. He said afterwards he was 'proud to have been Alastair Campbelled'. TB called after the Germany game [v Costa Rica, 4–2]. He had been in France, and said Chirac had been really friendly, he seemed to want to get to a better place. On the general scene, PG felt he was still too focused on reform but it had become a mantra. Just saying reform was not a narrative. GB still grim.

The party had asked me to do a regular World Cup blog and the feedback was there had been a massive response to my first one, which had been a moderately amusing swipe at women columnists suddenly getting interested in football, and at Marr and two-way TV pontificators. The party press and website people were really happy. Not so some of the sisters. Harriet Harman called Peter Watt [general secretary] to say the blog should be taken off the website. He told her not to be ridiculous, and called me to say if I wanted to have a pop at her fine. GB did a piece backing the next generation of nuclear power stations, which was again being seen in the context of sorting things with TB, but also him now taking responsibility for decisions that would be part of his not TB's time.

Saturday 10 June

Rory was in a real state, really not well, and later Fiona took him to the hospital, Calum and I having set off for the British Grand Prix. I did a couple of broadcast interviews on the World Cup blog, including with Nicky Campbell [Radio 5 Live] but I could tell they were not taking the idea that it was sexist too seriously. I was pretty blown away by the scale of the operation at the Grand Prix, to think that the whole circus travelled the world like that, though I still couldn't get into it as a spectacle. We watched the warm-ups from the pitlane, then met Jackie Stewart [former F1 world champion]for a chat, friendly as ever, very warm re TB [neighbour at Chequers]. He was not terribly fond of Bernie Ecclestone [CEO, Formula One] and Max Mosley [president, FIA, the sport's governing body], said they needed help, Bernie in particular, on how to manage themselves in public. Chat with Fred Goodwin [CEO], as RBS was one of the big sponsors, wearing the branded gear. Not warm. Nice chat with Frank Williams [founder, Williams racing team] who was trying to explain to me why the sport got people the way it did, but in the end said, 'I guess if you haven't got it by your age, you never will.' I said but isn't it all about the engineering, which people can't see in the way they can see a man pass a ball, or take a free kick? 'Yes, but if you study the engineering, you can imagine.' And then you wrap up your interest in the characters of the sport.

Peter Hain [Northern Ireland Secretary] was there, and he was trying to persuade me too. He was a total fan. I got doorstepped by a couple of the broadcasters, just asking me what I was doing there, and what I thought of it all. Tried to be upbeat without pretending it was my thing. It was not easy to talk politics as there were so many people buzzing around, but I had a little chat with Peter Hain who said he felt the politics scene was much worse than TB believed. TB–GB a permanent faultline, and it meant people were unsure what their instincts were. He said since I left there had been no message co-ordination, and no real organisation. TB still showed the odd spark but at times it felt like we were marking time. Lunch at the Brooklands suite with Alan Donnelly [former Labour MEP] who was still very close to Ecclestone and co. Frank Williams sorted us a tour of the garage. I watched the England [v Paraguay, 1–0] match in the Williams motorhome then later

Argentina v Ivory Coast [2–1]. England OK at the start but wilted in heat. Argentina fantastic.

Sunday 11 June

Up earlyish and within an hour we were at Silverstone. To Williams for a little party for Jackie's birthday. We watched the race from Brooklands, in Donnelly's suite. Peter Hain was very nice to Calum and later took him to the podium for the presentation. Dick Caborn there, upbeat and happy as ever, said he would soon be longest-serving sports minister. Good bloke. Solid. Keith Vaz, Jeff Rooker, Richard Burden [Labour MPs] there too, all emphasising just how important F1 was to manufacturing. No Tories that I saw. Williams told me he was right-wing but his friends in politics were left. We watched the race itself from a balcony with Hain and Jonathan Prescott [JP son]. It was a pretty impressive spectacle at the start but dull after a while, and I just couldn't get into it. Lunch at Williams chatting with Jackie S and some of his pals. A fair bit of 'We backed TB but have doubts re Labour and GB'. I liked Jackie's sons including Paul, ex-driver and cancer survivor.

The *Sunday Times* did a big number on the blog, but the party people seemed happy enough and asked me to do another one on how England have to get better, how Scots feel watching England and then saying Bernie Ecclestone would actually have a knighthood equivalent in any other country in the world, given what he had done for the sport and for UK industry. That is one thing I had not realised until this weekend, just how many top-end jobs were involved in the sport, and the sheer scale of it. Alex called, having a bit of a go at Sven. 'He said to me "This could be my last chance to win the World Cup." Like it is all about him. I said it's not the last chance for the players.' I watched Rio Ferdinand's World Cup wind-ups show on TV. Hilarious. Best telly for ages. Just a series of brilliant practical jokes, the best involving Becks getting kidnapped by a taxi driver, and David James [footballer] being suckered into thinking a load of kids' paintings were modern art.

TB sent through another long note, and asked me to have a think about it before he sent it around the team. It was all the same stuff, really, but at least he was really trying to think it through. He was worried that we were getting trapped inside our own bubble, and not seeing the broader perspective. But in the end, all he had was this idea that because he was taking on the tough decisions for the long term on all the really hard issues, that gave him purpose and people appreciated that. But the 'Why him?' question didn't have such a clear answer given we all knew he was going. His answer to that was that he could take a lot of the shit and the strain, then have a point at which the change comes and the party and government get a new lease of life. Cameron's strategy will be to say that with TB goes New Labour, and that helps him cement the centre as his natural ground. He said whether GB sees it or not, we have to help stop him from falling into the trap.

'The tragedy is that because he doesn't want to see any good in me or in New Labour, he cannot see that he needs both to get himself in the right place to take on Cameron. He just wants to see Cameron as a right-wing, over-privileged Tory toff, which he might be, but it is not how the public are seeing him. They are seeing him as bright and new, and GB will be old and tired by comparison.' He said it was obvious from Cameron's public statements what he was trying to do – talk me up as a reformer as a way of saying the reform has to go on, and GB is not that man. And of course GB won't be able to resist being as different to me as he can possibly be. He said he wanted me to have another go at getting GB and EB into agreeing that we shape a new approach to the Tories which is less about attacking them in traditional ways than getting them into difficult policy choices, and expose Cameron for ducking the big issues.

At least GB had done the nuclear power thing in the end. Tories nowhere. ID cards – deep down DC probably wants to do it, but he prefers to exploit our difficulties. And Europe? What was his line? We had to force them into real policy positions, expose the way they were running away from them, make them come out. He talked the talk on family friendly stuff, but where was the policy? Pensions? They exploited our difficulties but where was their plan? He also felt they were vulnerable on health, because they oppose the measures for change, and just try to turn it into local campaigns for more spending. I asked him if he thought he had been using PMQs strategically enough? No, he said. But he was getting there. I reminded him of the way we eventually got to big lines of attack on all of DC's predecessors and we needed to start defining the best one for him. He felt it was in the area of being good at the showy stuff but weak on real decisions.

Monday 12 June

Looking after Rory, who really wasn't well. I just stayed in with him and worked on the diary as we watched various football matches. I did another party blog on Rio's wind-ups, which was brilliant TV. Jamie and Louise [Redknapp] came round for dinner. Hummer car. Pringle top. She was really sweet and bright as well. The kids really took to Jamie, who was such a warm and open guy. They had good insights on all sorts of things, especially fame and how it changed people. He didn't like the whole Ingerland flag thing because of the hint of BNP racism attached to it. They were not massive Posh and Becks fans, I sensed. He said he always loved playing with Gazza because you could just give him the ball and watch it happen. Bryan Robson said Gazza was the best player he ever played with. He thought Keane – who retired today, – probabably had too big an ego to be a manager. Venables a good man manager. Glenn Hoddle [former England player and manager] strange. He really did rely on that woman, Eileen Drewery [faith healer and counsellor to Hoddle]. He said he went to see her because he thought if it helped him get in the team, great. Ray Parlour [Middlesbrough, ex-Arsenal and England] went and asked her for a short back and sides – didn't get picked.

They were quizzing re Bush, couldn't see how TB could possibly get on with him. Both liked TB. Nice couple. Of all of the England guys last week, he seemed the one who had most sorted himself in terms of adapting to a new life. But he said he loved Soccer Aid because it just reminded him what a great life playing football had given him. These guys at the World Cup now, he said, they will be amazed how quickly it flies by, and before they know it, they are retiring and joining all the rest of us fighting to find a little space that still wants us in the game somewhere.

Tuesday 13 June

Major major drama because Fiona thought she had lost her platinum ring at the pool. It turned up later but not before major drama time, tears galore, it was a metaphor for her life, blah di blah. I don't suppose I was much help as I never really understood the attachment to something like a ring, but we did have a good laugh when finally we tracked it down. Worked on diary in front of the football, Togo v S Korea [2–1], three great goals, France v Switzerland [0–0] – poor – and average Brazil v Croatia [1–0]. Hay fever kicking in so I didn't exercise. TB was fairly low-profile at the moment but PG had been doing some groups and was convinced there was quite serious erosion.

Wednesday 14 June

I did a new blog on the fact that TB's standing ovation after his GMB [trade union] Blackpool conference Q&A got no coverage whatever apart from short piece in *The Guardian*. The opposite reaction would have led the news. Rory was still not great and Mr Kidd [teacher] was wondering whether he could even do his politics exam. To the tennis at Queen's with Calum. People were still talking about the blog on women commenators and columnists getting into football, Alice Thompson [*Daily Telegraph*] the latest columnist to have a pop today, *The Guardian* having had another go yesterday. The tennis was OK, Calum enjoyed it, but it was not among my favourite spectator sports and there was a fairly high ratio of wankers in the crowd. We went to watch Tim Henman [England No. 1] train. I liked his style. He saw me and gave me a little wave, then clocked me again on court in his match v Jamie Delgado [GB Davis Cup player]. Calum was very sweet, said, 'I think you've spurred him on.' We watched Rafa Nadal [Spain], then Lleyton Hewitt [Australia], who Calum loved, warm up and match. Nice time with Calum.

Thursday 15 June

DS. He felt I was a lot lighter, less bound up in TB. He was back on to his theme that I saw Fiona as an extension of myself. Donald was finally getting the go-ahead to transfer to clozapine [medication]. Trip to Haselmere for the Association of Colleges [non-profit further education organisation] awayday. I had done a speech for them around eighteen months ago, and this was much more about trying to help them review their own strategy, and find a way of auditing their own progress. It seemed to go OK, fairly lively Q&A. A guy from Burnley who was very down because he felt they were still seen as the Cinderella of the sector. They were down on the Lib Dems, quite down on us and I didn't like the sense that they were saying Tories resurgent. They set up England v Trinidad in a separate room. It took them a while to get the message I didn't want conversation while watching football. England were dire but won 2–0. I did a blog on that plus the poor repertoire of England fans' songs. Home to watch later match. Felt it was an OK event though. Another little TB–GB flare-up with someone briefing that the next spending review was being downgraded, was not nearly as important as TB had signified and that maybe it would be Stephen Timms [Treasury chief secretary] not GB who presented it.

Friday 16 June

TB called, asking me to go in at the weekend to see him, maybe for dinner, PG, PM and Sally re strategy. He was really worrying how the mood was developing that we were in dog days and the Tories were finally a credible alternative. Pat McF called and said he thought he, PG and I should meet to discuss Cameron strategy. I stayed in with Rory and we watched Argentina v Serbia-Montenegro. Argentina awesome. 6–0. Holland beat Ivory Coast 2–1. Then to the Hurlingham Club in Fulham for the Teach First awards. Impressive set-up. Great scheme. Simple and yet already having such a positive effect for the students getting into teaching, and for the kids and for the schools.

I was at a table with teachers who were either now going into business after two years, or some staying, one as an assistant head. Great quote from one of the pupils of an award-winner which I used in my own speech. 'I am so proud she's my teacher and I'm going to make her proud with my GCSE results.' Did my usual jokes and banter then a really serious uplifting thing about education and about the amazing work they did. Went well. Enjoyed it. Still hated a lot of the small talk at dos like this, but I liked being able to absorb the feel of an audience and then adapt pre-prepared remarks into something much more spontaneous.

17–18 June

Loads of football all weekend. Tessa called to say there were still reverberations about my first blog. Christ, I still had the capacity to make waves without really intending to. She said the PLP women's group was talking about making an official complaint. Also the DCMS select committee was thinking of calling me. This was getting out of hand. She said it was fine that I was still neuralgic but for some reason this had taken the neuralgia to a place it normally didn't go, namely the party. I said our line should be never lose a sense of humour or a sense of perspective. I was also getting conflicting signals because the party people trying to generate a new interest in their internet stuff were loving the fuss, and loving the extra traffic to something that was not essentially political. Sunday Grace was at the stables so I drove her out and also took the bike and went for a longish ride, and stayed for lunch. George and Catherine had the *Mail on Sunday* there. GB had had the top *MoS* team in to watch the England match with him. That is dire. I was almost tempted to do a blog on it. Tessa felt I should only do it if I wanted to use the football blog to create another great wave of party fallout for a second week running. So don't. But given how they had denied briefing that story a few weeks back, and how they claimed the *MoS* were always doing him in, and Balls saying he didn't even know them, and there they were all buddy buddy with GB, it was pretty awful stuff really. Tessa said she was currently finding politics really dispiriting. She was really not sure if she wanted to be in a GB government, maybe get out and get life with David sorted. She was very down. She said even her party members were pissed off at the moment. Football – Argentina still best. Brazil struggled to beat Oz. France better but South Korea pegged them back. Their fans the best so far. Ghana strong. England looking poor relations. Hay fever dire.

Monday 19 June

Breakfast meeting with Nick Butler. Starting to talk detail of a possible role with BP. Maybe a day a week. Specifically wanting me to work on JB profile. Anji quite alarmed seemingly, presumably thinks me taking over her job there, which I would certainly not want to do. Nick also wanting me to think how to announce me and when. Met up with Steve Norris [former Tory MP, twice losing Tory candidate for London mayorality] to discuss a crisis management session in September. All straightforward. Home to do bit of work and football. Wrote a new blog on weekend matches, exhuberant South Korean fans being amazing v France [1–1]. Brazil not firing [v Australia 2–0]. Also had a revisit of the women football commentators issue to make clear I was not saying they know nothing. Plus I had a little dig at Michael Meacher [Labour MP], who was saying yesterday we would lose the next election.

Later in to see Liz and listen to TB on 606 [Radio Five football phone-in]. He did OK though a bit too much glottal stopping and modified accent. They clearly weeded out all the angry callers and though Adrian Chiles [broadcaster] was funny it was probably a bit too soft. Peter M and I name-checked by Chiles and he mentioned the Maradona match. I waited for TB to get back from White City, and we went up to the flat and we were straight into the age-old discussion. He felt in himself we were doing the right thing. But GB made it impossible to have a cooperative strategy. We agreed finally that he was going to have to park the GB issue. Peter M and I felt at some point he would have to move from endorsement to neutrality. Peter was the most scathing of GB, as expected. He said TB owed it to the country and the party to stay for several reasons – he was best placed to argue for difficult reforms. He had to make sure the party did not go backwards to old election-losing policies and postures. We agreed there was a lack of fight and a lack of operation. His note of a while back on a narrative on securing Britain's and the party's future was fine as a basis but nobody ever heard it. We had to operationalise.

I said we did not do nearly enough on record, general progress as a bridge to future policy. Truth be told I was bored with hearing all this. I said from a slight distance I just got angry. So many mistakes. Not enough fight. So few politicians able to make an argument convincingly. So little cohesion. Too many of our politicians commentators not fighters. No attack on the Tories at all. What was clear was that the GB scene hadn't changed at all. TB said he came in today again and just said he wanted his 'proposals'. TB ended up saying he was fed up with it. 'What more can I do? I've made clear I'm going. I've given him a date and he still goes round saying I haven't. Every concession they take as weakness and keep piling on the pressure.' Ruth, Liz and PG were the others there, later we were joined by Sally. PG came closest to saying he should think about going earlier but couched it in terms of 'If you have another year of being shredded you may as well go. You're fucked if you don't fight, so you have to fight.' The problem at the moment was any defence of TB was seen as sectarian, so much had they pummelled into him. Also most junior ministers were looking to GB as the holder of the keys to their future so they took no risks.

Peter, with one of his little glances and me and Philip, said by saying he would leave TB had disempowered a lot of his own supporters – 'as I believe I warned at the time'. We were there several hours, started in the lounge, ate in the kitchen, back to the lounge. There till half-ten, quarter to eleven. By the end of it he was saying he was going to fight, not putting up with it any longer, just taking blows and not fighting back. I felt TB's whole posture was born of ambivalence. He had got himself into a position of supporting GB but actually had real doubts for party and country. He could see nobody else though. When I railed at the lack of leadership being shown by others, and the lack of support for TB when under fire, Ruth pointed out so many of them were looking to GB and therefore worried. I said name someone. She said even James Purnell. I said ask James who GB fears more, me or him.

TB said think back to when Neil was leader. A lot of us thought we were not going to win but we didn't want to rock the boat. It is just how the Labour Party is. Now we have the situation where virtually everyone is signed up to GB being leader and PM and virtually everyone who really knows him thinks it is not a great idea. But we can't find a better one. I think he had been hoping that getting me and Peter in the same room we would have come up with something better than we had. It was not a success. I gave PG a lift home and he said, 'It is all starting to feel too ragged to repair.' Ruth was clearly anxious about the peerages inquiry. She had been interviewed by the cops, and it was clear they were going for it as hard as they could. She felt they would reach a point of saying that the law was widely if inadvertently broken. No bribery but not going to look good. TB more hopeful on that front. But at times tonight he looked really down, beaten almost.

Tuesday 20 June

Off early to meet Jamie Rubin and head to Queenwood [Surrey golf club], Jamie Redknapp having wanted to set up a golf match. Jamie Rubin seemed fairly relaxed about losing his Sky show. It was maybe just too much of a leap to go from their usual rolling news to something so foreign policy-based and a bit highbrow. We met up with David Mills and the other Jamie [Redknapp], who was deadly serious about his golf. Such a fantastic course. Good caddies. Started with a birdie, a few pars and the usual mid-course collapse. Lost by 2. Most of the talk as we went round sport. DM quizzing Redknapp re football. He wanted me to get more involved with his mag. I played OK considering I had played so little, and the others – Redders and David especially – played so much. Tessa called from the Sweden v England match, asking if I wanted my name to go forward for the Sport England job. Felt I wouldn't get it though because of the baggage, and I was also beginning to get more into the peripatetic life. Home to watch loads of football. England looked like they might click but then lost it a bit. 2–2. The pull-out of some of the forces in Iraq began, but all overshadowed by more violence, including the pretty gruesome slaughter of a couple of young American soldiers.

Wednesday 21 June

I got a message to call Stott. Bombshell, Bad news, he said. Cancer. Pancreas. Prognosis not good. He was almost apologetic about it, as he would have to get out of the book project, said it was too important to have me hanging around. I said let's wait and see what happens. We don't need to decide anything yet, and I would like him to stay involved if he could. I felt devastated for him and Penny, they were so much a couple. He sounded stoical though a bit choked at times. As Fiona said, I owed him so much and he seemed so happy the last time we saw him. I mentioned it to Gail and Ed but said I would rather not make a change unless I really had to. It was frankly not obvious who else if anyone could do as good a job as Richard. He had been such a part of our life at key moments, but the way he was talking it sounded like it was a matter of months. I went for a long swim, then watched a dull 0–0 draw between Argentina and Holland.

GB committing to retaining our nuclear deterrent at Mansion House. It was presented as news. It would be news if he wasn't. Some of the usual suspects on the left were out attacking him, and again it was being seen as totally in the context of him being next PM, and at times being treated like he already was. He was also however pushing back on some of the soft left calls for a shift in a new direction on reform, which was exactly what TB wanted, though likely he was doing it because of the audience, City and business types, rather than to be of help.

Thursday 22 June

Clare Short having a go at GB over his stance on Trident, and saying it was all about making sure he had TB supporters behind him when he went for the top job, but she felt this changed things. On verra. Off early with Calum. Met Cathy at Luton Airport, heading to Monaco for her LRF south of France fundraiser among the ex-pats. My first Easy-jet–Luton experience. Not as bad as I expected going out. Picked up at Nice, down the motorway to Monaco. Staying at Hotel Mirabeau which was nice enough. Out for a run around the port. Big showjumping event going on. Plus a yacht show. All very glitzy and naff. Real major wealth all over the place. Calum and I had a little wander, then to the dinner with main sponsors at the Pacific restaurant. OK crowd, albeit a bit right-wing. One Tory Scot who had had too much to drink even before we started. Once I got him off politics, he was quizzing me about my *Times* sports column, which he really liked, and also the piece on Maradona. I'd say of all the people that I'd met that I get asked about, there was a chance of Diego getting up there with Mandela, Clinton, Diana, Queen! People were fascinated by him.

They had got a decent turnout and some decent money. There were a couple of guys from Merrill Lynch, one of whom had a skin-tight vest over a vast belly. Not a good look. I was sounding out views re our politics, and picked up a lot of anti-GB sentiment, but no warmth for Cameron, and definitely the feeling that he didn't really do the big decision stuff. One of the women there got very pissed, going on at me about how she didn't think it was physically possible to maintain sexual relations for four decades with the same person, which is why people had lovers.

Friday 23 June

I had a swim, finished working on the speech, then off to the Café de Paris. I was warned by the organisers not to make any jokes about the Monaco royal family. The guy in charge of the event was actually worried he would be kicked out if I did. I told him the story of when I had been arrested there years ago for busking, and did a runner from the nick, and escaped on a motorbike. Even that, he said, might be a bit dodgy. 'They would probably come and re-arrest you!' I didn't know that much about Monaco till this trip. Basically owned by three families, including [reigning monach] Prince Albert's. Nothing happened without them knowing. Everything was covered by CCTV, he said. The opposition party was invented to get them in the Council of Europe. Good venue. I did an interview with *Riviera Times*, mingled, then lunch with a selection of business men. All men. One was a member of Cameron's Leader's Group, which he said was basically funding. Pretty right-wing bunch. The speech went fine, ditto the Q&A, not the anti stuff I thought might happen given it was such a Tory audience. Cathy seemed happy enough, felt it would have raised good money now and in the future through the contacts made.

I went back to collect Calum and then we met up with Alex [Ferguson], who was out on holiday, with Cathy, her sister Bridget and husband John, and a couple of friends from Aberdeen. We met at the Fairmont for a drink. It was a bit gaudy and casinoesque for me but they've been going for years. He said he was a bit alarmed yesterday by a call from Mark [son] who had been to see both GB and Cameron when Al Gore was over. He said the set-up at No. 11 wasn't impressive. Cameron was. Alex was worried we were losing it. He was worried we were losing the plot on crime. On the football front, he was confident of getting Michael Carrick [Tottenham Hotspur player]. He had been out to newly knighted [British businessman] Philip Green's yacht to discuss because Green saw himself as a bit of a transfer kingmaker. He was after Carrick, Senna from Villareal [Spain] and Mascherano [Argentinian player].

Not sure what going to happen with Ruud van Nistelrooy [Man U player]. Very self-centred. The last straw was when he told [Cristiano] Ronaldo he had found a new dad in Carlos [AF's assistant] – just after Ronaldo's dad, who was an alcoholic, had died. Carlos asked him to show respect and he said he didn't respect anyone there. He later apologied but CR was not having it. Alex sent van Nistelrooy home when he heard about it later. He was not sure what he was going to do with him. Out to a very nice restaurant. Lots of plastic surgery around. France 2–0 v Togo. Good time though and felt OK about things. I was talking to Alex about how Gazza had been when he texted saying could he call. We both, and Calum, spoke to him. Clearly in a bit of a bad way. Not watching the match because he said he was better than some of the players there. Also how much he was missing Soccer Aid etc. He kept repeating himself as well, and sounded a bit paranoid. Alex said he was the one player he wished he had landed.

Saturday 24 June

Grim journey back. Nice airport totally chaotic. Queueing to join to queues. Then once we got on the plane waiting for a few British pissheads who went missing after checking in their bags, and finally came on laughing their heads off. Totally without shame. I worked on the Egypt speech on the plane, then home in time for Germany 2, Sweden 0 and then a fantastic match between Argentina and Mexico, 2–1 after extra time. Absolutely breathtaking stuff. Got an invitation from the genealogy programme, *Who Do You Think You Are?*, which looked more interesting than most.

Sunday 25 June

Off early for Hackney, Victoria Park, LRF 10k. Bit sluggish still. 47 minutes. That is shit. I was finding it harder to lose weight, even with all the exercise. Did *London Tonight* and LBC, and got asked about Jonathan Ross asking Cameron if he ever wanked thinking of Thatcher! England 1, Ecuador 0. Poor stuff though. They really had no chance. My hay fever was a nightmare. I could barely breathe at times.

Tuesday 27 June

Charles Clarke on the rampage, whacking JR for slagging off the [Home

Office] department so much, and by implication TB for getting rid of him [CC]. He also said TB had lost his sense of purpose and direction. It was pretty damning, quite personal, and another bad sign. I was doing a piece of work for John Browne then lunch with Rory. Brazil v Ghana [3–0]. Later missed Spain losing to France [1–3], because I was speaking at the British Egyptian Society. I got a lift in with Magdy Ishak and his wife Rita, an anaesthetist – very livewire – in a chauffeur-driven Bentley. There was me thinking he was a doctor, and he was basically a mega-wealthy businessman. The audience seemed to be made up mainly of lots of Egyptian private sector medics. At my table there was an ENT specialist who diagnosed polyps just hearing me speak. Plus a psychiatrist who was asking me about my breakdown. Magdy constantly quizzing me on my life and future and wanting me to join boards.

[Baroness] Liz Symons [Labour peer] chair of the society. Did she always sound as posh as this? She was very much on the board circuit, mainly in the Gulf. Some amazing belly dancers, including one with breasts going in opposite directions. Preceded by an Egyptian Nobel Prize winner, physician. He did a really naïve 'We should spend war money on education' and I did my speech about difficult choices, got into some of the foreign policy stuff, MEPP via North Ireland. Went OK. Loads of pictures and all that. Home lateish. Watched Spain v France highlights. Chatted with Margaret Beckett earlier, who was doing some interviews and wanted to discuss how to handle Charles' attack. She was pretty stunned to have been given the Foreign Secretary's position, would have plenty to say on that, but also wanted a bit of help re the [party] direction question. I sensed she was a bit worried about TB, though thrilled to be where she was.

Wednesday 28 June

I went to see Bostock about the polyps. He threw a bit of a wobbly because I said I came on the back of some Egyptian guy telling me to. He was in a really strange mood. 'Why are you letting an Egyptian you don't know interfere?' Well, he heard me speak and he just said to me, straight out, you need an operation for polyps! So I've come to check. There was a pigeon outside driving him a bit crazy. He was raging about TB. Not just Iraq this time, but also he had ruined the NHS with his constant interfering. Then he was back on with his 'I shouldn't have left' shtick, things had gone downhill because at least I could curb TB's worst traits 'though you failed on Iraq'. Eventually I said, 'What about the polyps?' and he had a look, and said he would refer me. Margaret's interview in *The Times* came out fine, though it did play into the 'smooth transition' line. I did a long blog on *The Guardian*, not even covering the attack by Ken Clarke on Cameron's stance on the Human Rights Act.* I got the feeling Rusbridger had totally fallen for DC. In for lunch with Sarkozy's people in No. 10. Something very weird happened on the way in – a cop in a car stuck in traffic saying, 'Thanks for making a complaint about me.' 'What are you talking about?' 'Lamb's Conduit Street,' he said, had a big moan, then drove off. I told Special Branch at No. 10 to check it out, if someone claiming to be me had made a complaint. The Sarkozy meeting was a bit odd. JoP in chair, me, Sally, PG, Steve Morris [head of strategic communications]. Four of them, the chief of staff very ENArque [Ecole Nationale d'Adminstration, where many of French political elite are educated]. All very hierarchical, calling each other 'vous'. A bit ponderous. Not sure about things. They were confident it would be Sarkozy v Royal but clearly worried about [Jean-Marie] Le Pen [president, French National Front]. I didn't feel they had it really. I asked what the slogan would be if there was a campaign tomorrow. They all looked at each other. Biggest issue was 'probably security or the economy'. I didn't much take to them. But TB was clear Ségolène Royal would be even worse than [Lionel] Jospin [former Prime Minister]. The question was whether Sarkozy could deliver on the direction of reform he had promised. We ate in the small dining room. I said he was seen as a divisive figure. Also trimming a bit on reform. PG and I both said bits and pieces strategies, scratching round for this section that section of the electorate, didn't work. You had to have a clear message and strategy and see it through. They seemed glad enough for the chance to talk, but I was glad to get out. JoP seemed on very good form, which is important when TB is dipping as he seems to be. Also the CC attack seemed to have faded quickly. Liz S told me yesterday Neil had said Charles should have waited, kept his powder dry, till he did real damage. Doing it so soon after leaving risked looking like pique.

Thursday 29 June

Difficult session with David Sturgeon. Feeling stuck in the tramlines. Had an event at the Royal Opera House, for Alliance Bernstein [investment

---

* Clarke described Cameron's plan to replace the Human Rights Act with a British Bill of Rights as 'xenophobic and legal nonsense'.

management firm], loads of Yanks, mainly men, pensions experts. Usual spiel, OK Q&A, one total bore whose question went on and on and and on, but all fine. I got a nice present for Fiona on the way home, a three-part pendant, but we agreed to give it to Zoe [Richardson, Rory girlfriend] for all she did for Rory when he was ill. We were out for dinner with her and her parents, Heinz and Jenny. Very nice couple. Zoe's sister Eva a real laugh too. He is an architect, big in the sustainability world, fascinating about some of the new ideas becoming mainstream.

Friday 30 June

Really grinding out long bike rides and swims for the triathlon training, though hay fever and usual post-swim nasal flare-ups were a real problem. Two by-elections overnight, one bad for us – Blaenau Gwent – and bad for the Tories in Bromley and Chiselhurst, almost losing to the Libs. I was finding myself only really following the World Cup though, trying to avoid the news as much as I could. I took Grace and her pals to the stables and while they were riding, took the bike out around the lanes, just killing time before Germany v Argentina [1–1], Germany won 4–2 on penalties and then Italy Ukraine [3–0].

Saturday 1 July

Early swim at the lido. World Cup street party preparations and then the do itself kept things ticking to 4 p.m. when Rory and I went to Philip's to watch the England Portugal game. TB called at 3, said he had a feeling Portugal would win. He said things were pretty much as before but he was now just determined to get on with it. 'If I get a year, fine. If they throw me out, there you go, but it will be a pretty extraordinary thing to do. Three wins and then out.' I said imagine how Churchill felt. He said that whenever he got out and about around the country things were not so bad but the party and media Westminster bubble prism was a nightmare. GB was not changing. 'I have to chase him for meetings not the other way round. And all he ever does is say how terrible things are, but takes no responsibility for the fact that his people feed so much of that feeling. He was forever telling us not to do law and order and now wants to do more. I thought his handling of the Trident issue was clumsy. And all this stuff about his great passion for England at the World Cup is just embarrassing.'

TB sounded a lot brighter than of late, though he said he was really worried about Afghanistan, and the military were asking for more support. He was saying again that he thought I should be doing more telly not less because I did it better than virtually everyone, especially when it came to defending him and the general approach of the government. He felt CC made a bad mistake, that serious people would mark him down about it, because it came over as being about him and his role, but dressed up as an attack on lack of direction. I said yes, but he was making the point that we have been making too. You can't deny there is a problem with direction at the moment. He said the problem is you can count on the fingers of one hand the really serious people we have. People who are serious about winning. The right have most of the serious people. On the left we have people who want to agonise about what they believe. We know what we believe. The question is do you have what it takes to win. He said Ruth Kelly had impressed him since leaving Education. Jack was diddling at the moment and he worried even Charlie was a bit, whacking the donors for example. 'Serious people would stand up and defend them.' As for the Tories, they were just doing the obvious.

England were poor in the first half, Rooney sent off, Ronaldo's little wink to the bench night make life difficult when both got back to United, then a good back to the wall job before defeat on penalties [3–1 after 0–0 draw]. I did a blog for the party pointing out England had some of the best players but they never gelled into the best team. One or two spotted the possible resonance to us. I was whacking Alan Shearer [England international turned pundit] for saying England players didn't do the cynical stuff. It's true Ronaldo did wind up Rooney but Rooney had already stamped on [Ricardo] Carvalho's knackers, which seemed quite cynical to me. Home to watch France v Brazil, and updated the piece to say [Zinedine] Zidane [Real Madrid and France star] had given a masterclass. I hadn't been aware till he called me late on that JP was in more trouble. The papers were making something out of him visiting [American entrepreneur] Philip Anschutz's ranch, the guy who owns the Millennium Dome and wants to get one of the first mega-casinos there. JP said he had been there to talk about a film about [William] Wilberforce, which didn't sound terribly convincing. The Tories were pressing the parliamentary standards people to get into it.

Monday 3 July
I worked on a piece for *The Times* on the BBC coverage of the World Cup, which I felt was way too focused on England, and looking at

everything through a narrow prism. I was especially provoked by Alan Hansen [Scots player turned pundit] in the *Telegraph* now saying that only a handful of Portuguese, French, German or Italians would get into England's first choice eleven. It was rubbish. I broadened it into something a bit more thematic, about how our addiction to hype and the need for ever stronger opinions focused on the prism that was already set actually hampered proper analysis. Out for a long run then lunch with Richard Wallace [editor] and Conor Hanna [deputy] of the *Mirror* who wanted me to do more for them, including regular Page 6 [comment] pieces. I got the sense they had the plot re TB and GB, but their staff were getting the GB line fed in the whole time. Wallace said at one point, 'I am well aware of the skills of the former – TB – and the gaps of the latter.' But he asked rather innocently, 'Why can't they just get on?' I wish we had the answer. A lot of things would get easier. They kept in touch with Piers, who was now seemingly going big in the US as a Simon Cowell figure on a NBC talent show. [Sir] John Reith [UK General, NATO deputy Supreme Allied Commander for Europe], who I remember as a top guy and very smart and sensible, had gone public with the demand on NATO to provide more helicopters for Afghanistan forces. Afghanistan getting very tricky again.

Tuesday 4 July

I finished the piece for *The Times* on BBC coverage. It would probably lead to the loss of friends in high-ish places but so what in the end? There was such a narrow nationalism to the coverage, and I had started to watch on German telly which yes, focused on Germany more than anyone else, but without that one-eyed bias to it all. I'd also decided to go to Germany after all. Cathy came round to work on a spreadsheet for invites for the Mel Brooks dinner, and we were also sorting a Delta Goodrem dinner. Then to the airport and off to Munich, leafing through the whole diary transcript to see if the shorter version might be a runner. The mood around Munich was fantastic, and after a few hours I called the *Mirror* and offered a piece on how the World Cup really was part of the rebirth of a new Germany. Cab to the Hotel Sofitel. They had real pride in their team and their country, but they also had a greater sense of internationalism than we seemed to manage. It was also noticeable how even in bars and taxis, when I spoke German, so many would reply in near perfect English. Italy v Germany amazing match. 0–0 after full time, Italy winning 2–0 after extra time. Germans plunged into immediate gloom, but seemed to lift fairly quickly. I didn't see any violence or even major anger at all.

Wednesday 5 July

Finished the *Mirror* piece, then met Florian [Michael Ballack agent] for breakfast. He was very open and honest about the whole Ballack operation. Two poles of power, a lawyer in Luxembourg who did all the deals, transfer-wise. Peter Olsson, a Swede sports marketing guy who had built up and sold a company. Florian was both part of his Performers agency but also ran his own company, Inside Out. Florian said Ballack was a pretty typical footballer, but aware of his own strengths and weaknesses. He felt that what I could bring was knowledge of UK media, plus strategy, but predicted – rightly – that what Olsson would think I was useful for was bringing in new corporate sponsors. I said that was not really my thing. After tidying up bits and pieces I went down to Olsson's office. Two huge steel painting-type things with quotes from Muhammad Ali and Mandela. He went through his company at length. I went through the concept of strategy, and how it might be applied to using profile to attract a different kind of sponsor but I was not sure he got it. I suspect Florian was more my kind of guy and wanted to do business in other ways.

Olsson was a big talker and it was pretty obvious Florian didn't like him much. There were clearly a lot of politics in the situation. Olsson suggested we meet MB once he gets to London and we try to make something work. But I sensed he didn't quite get what I was saying, namely do the strategic profile building first, before going aggressively for the big sponsor contracts. We left it that I would send over ideas on media and other activity. I had lunch with Florian and his sister and a friend from RTL Television. Florian seemed to think it went fine but I felt he would believe it when he saw it re seeing Ballack. I sensed that he wanted to do something a bit different and more imaginative, whereas the others just saw a big money high-profile move with the prospect of more big money deals attached to it.

Gazza called from California, clearly the worse for wear. He was rambling, paranoid, talking about fixing meetings with TB and the Pope, and all a bit sad. He said he needed help because he had fallen over pissed and he thought he had broken his rib. But he and his girlfriend were angry that they had not got an X-ray quickly and they wouldn't give him pain killers because he was drunk. They sent him away. He was rambling on incoherently. He kept putting me on to Courtney, telling her who I was, what I did, who I knew, how I was going to sort him out, how they were going to meet TB. All very sad, but I did manage to persuade her to take him back to the hospital. I called Alex about it who said after our Monaco chat he had spoken to him the next day and he was totally incoherent. On Rooney and Ronaldo, which was still getting the full hype, he was confident they'd be fine. He claimed all the talk about Ronaldo going to Madrid was coming from Ronaldo's girlfriend. She was ten years older than him, he was besotted with her and putting it around that he was going there.

I did a new Labour blog based on the *Times*–BBC piece, players of the tournament and the *Mirror* piece re Germany. Then a long run before heading out to the ground. Fantastic stadium. Would have rocked with England v Brazil, but it was France–Portugal and though the atmosphere was OK, it wasn't awesome. I met up with Florian and his friends. The whole thing was a strangely passionless affair. I became mesmerised by two women in front of us who just talked, talked, the whole time, make-up, shoes, shopping, holidays, food, barely watching the game at all, even the Zidane penalty which turned out to be the winner [1–0]. I talked to them at half-time and it turned out they were married to McDonald's people, and had tickets as part of the sponsors' packages, both American, didn't really get football, so just saw it as a holiday. Quite sad to think of all the Portuguese who had been scrabbling for tickets outside.

Ronaldo was booed the whole game, mainly by England fans who had got tickets on the assumption they would be there, but soon pretty much everyone was joining in. Lilian Thuram [France, Man of the Match] was terrific. Once they got the lead, the French just closed it down, and it was all pretty dull. Afterwards up with Florian to see Didi Hamann [German international], who was moving to Manchester City. He seemed pretty bright, quite political. Boris Becker [former tennis champion] was doing the rounds, still a big draw. We went into the city centre and hung around the Marienplatz but it was fairly flat. More England fans than French, I would say. Bed by 2.

Thursday 6 July

Having got here and got into it a bit, I was keen to get to the final now and hopefully get tickets for the boys too. Put out some feelers and Dick Caborn came back with a contact in Fifa for three tickets for a grand or so. Then Rory and Fiona at home were sorting flights all day. There was nothing to Berlin at all, so we sorted Koln-Bonn by air then train. Sorting hotels was tricky too, but I had been talking to Peter Torry [UK Ambassador] about the stuff I was writing on Germany, and he suggested we stay at the Residence, which was brilliant. I had a nice quiet day pretty much to myself, doing a bit of work at the hotel then going for a long run around Munich in the heat. Beautiful place. Clean, well run, nice people, for example at the train station where I was struggling to make sense of the train booking system and put the guy on to Fiona on the end of the line, and he sorted it in flawless English.

I worked on a paper on Ballack for Florian on the flight back to London, then met up with Fiona and we headed to La Casalinga. The boys really excited about going to the final. Tessa called, said the costs of the Olympics were going to rise, and we needed to make sure people understood the regeneration side of the deal, that it was not just a sports festival. It was the same old story of most past Games, but there was a danger if things really spiraled that we would lose a lot of the goodwill. She and TB were doing a 'one year on from winning the bid' event and so needed to use it to set the context and expectations. She was full of it though, really excited, sure it was going to be good.

Friday 7 July

Out early to a restaurant in Old Compton Street to meet Nick Butler. He said John B really liked the paper I had done, and the note on his recent speech, but he was worried that if my involvement came out now it would look like I was hired in as crisis PR. I sensed they were quite thin-skinned and paranoid as organisations go, sure for example the Yanks were digging into them – they probably were. I said it was best we say nothing till the autumn and if anything leaks we simply say have I have advised informally for a while. The other issue was Anji. She had successfully made the transition from No. 10 to BP. She liked what she did. She didn't want to go further up and have more hassle. The board people liked her. But she was bound to be thinking, why was I being brought in to overshadow her again? I said I didn't really see her as a corporate status type of person, in any event I was due to see her at Wimbledon today so would sort out any issues. I sensed they got some but not all of this. The important thing was to get them fixed on a strategic line and hold them to it. But they sounded, and Anji later confirmed, a bit prone to rabbit in the headlights when a few bad press cuttings came along.

We agreed I'd do a note on JB forward programme. Also get a head of press. Fair enough meeting. He went through his possible successors. Bob Dudley [CEO of TNK-BP] in Moscow, John's favourite. Tony Hayward [BP chief executive of exploration and production] (a big Tory according to Nick) current favourite. It was clearly a highly political set-up. Out with Calum to Wimbledon and up to the BP Suite. Npower boss. Lots of BP people. I liked Anji's immediate boss. Other guests included Adam Ingram [Labour MP/armed forces minister], and Maureen [wife], Adam Boulton, Simon Heffer [journalist] and [wife] Diane. Calum said afterwards he thought both Adam and Simon were good blokes. Adam Ingram was off on one re GB, said he was just like this awful glowering presence hanging over the whole government. Maureen chipped in, said it was like Tony had a smile and a bit of optimism and he cast it around and then this great big cloud came over, and it was Gordon. I think Adam was finding it quite tough that Des Browne [Defence Secretary] used to be his PPS, and was now his boss.

A lot of talk re JP, and it really was hard to get beyond the laughing stock point, especially with non-political people. The punch had been replaced by the secretary as the go-to JP point of conversation for outsiders. The papers were already starting up on the 'Who's in charge for the summer?' stories, and TB's holiday would doubtless get even more coverage because of the JP situation. There was talk of Jacqui Smith [government chief whip] and Hazel Blears [party chair] also being around so it wasn't all about JP. I had a long chat with Anji, explained how the thing with BP/JB had come up, assured her I had no desire for a job, let alone one that ate into what she did. She said she'd tried to discuss my project with JB but she felt he was putting it on the back burner. I told her I had told Nick that if ever they felt I was too neuralgic, just say so, it really doesn't bother me. I know I am neuralgic in some quarters and I am really not bothered about bad press, but if they are, they just need to say so.

I explained how it all came about, and then how I had suggested her way back when. I had enough self-awareness to know that if I suddenly ended up in a big corporate, it would need a bit of handling, but also the truth is I didn't want to do that, or indeed anything else right now, on a full-time basis. So if she had any worries, she knew she just had to say. It was not going to be a problem. She seemed fine, though clearly she felt a lot of the things I was suggesting to JB came out of her brief. I assured her it was basically just me advising JB re getting his and the company's profile in a slightly different place. Lunch went on longer than planned because of rain, but then we watched the men's Wimbledon semi-finals while I did a whimsical piece for *The Observer* on Europe and the World Cup and would euro membership have helped England? I had got it done by the time we got home.

I had a good session with the new German Ambassador [Wolfgang Ischinger] who wanted to have lunch. I raised the Ballack situation with him, and he was keen to get to know him. [Roger] Federer was awesome against [Jonas] Bjorkman. Total massacre. [Rafael] Nadal v [Marcos] Baghdatis was closer but still a straight sets win. To Gospel Oak Primary School for a farewell. All the talk was World Cup. I was still getting asked about Soccer Aid. It was amazing how jealous blokes were at the the thought of me playing with those guys. I finished the *Observer* piece, then started on a piece for the *Mirror* on who the best fans were. The World Cup seemed to have revived a few journalistic instincts in me.

Saturday 8 July

I did an hour on the bike then did the usual, setting out way too early and giving the boys a big laugh at my expense all day. Cab, train to Gatwick, check in – with three hours to spare. I worked on the *Mirror* piece on fans which was fine if a bit long. The boys were on good form and the whole day we had a good laugh. Calum really taking the piss out of me and himself. TB called as we were waiting. On good form. He said he felt good at the moment. I said the World Cup had given him a bit of space to breathe. Also people were starting to question a bit more deeply whether it was very sensible to push him out. He had lots coming up, the energy review, gripping the Home Office stuff etc. He was worried about JP. It had gone from being colic to a bit serious because JP was a laughing stock. He said he was just lacking in basic credibility. He was telling me about a conversation they had the other day, where JP was talking about a discussion on an issue as though it was a person. Re GB, no better, no worse. But he really couldn't see why GB didn't see the damage he was doing to himself. Just losing the plot in some ways.

Nice chat, lots about the football, including him – he had seen the *Times* piece – saying was it wise to whack Gary Lineker et al? He was singing the praises of Jacqui Smith and Ruth Kelly. We got to Cologne pretty much on time. The hotel was next to the station, right by the cathedral. We had dinner at a little café with terrace and a really nice grown-up chat about all sorts of things. Then down to the Fan Fest zone [multinational fans' area for non-ticket holders] for Germany v Portugal and the third/fourth place play-off. The boys gobsmacked when I got totally chatted up by a young German-US girl, Veronica! One to dine out on for a while. Calum said something really sweet. 'Do you realise after tomorrow we'll be able to tell our grandchildren we went to a World Cup final? Thanks, Dad.' I told them the story of the 1966 World Cup final, which I watched in Longtown Police Station because Dad had been driving us halfway to meet our Uncle who was then taking us on up through Scotland. No mobiles, no way of sorting out things when arrangement didn't work out, Dad had to get back to work, and so left us at the cop shop while they tried to find out where Uncle Ian was.

Sunday 9 July

Up at 5, hadn't really slept. Out for a run down the Rhein. Fabulous at that time of morning. Big TB piece in *Bild am Sonntag*. The Germans were getting a great press globally. I sent a note to Tessa on how we needed to start planning now for the broader messaging out of the Olympics. It was hard to see how much of the German success was planned, and how much accidental, but it was strong, palpable. I offered a piece to *The Times* on the value of these great sporting events, how we now need to get the World Cup after the Olympics and maybe TB post-office could lead it. Back home the JP stuff was kicking off again and some of it related to stuff I had been writing on the party blog which was being picked up and spun by the Tories. I got the boys up after my run, breakfast and then head off on the train. Spacious, comfortable! Bang on time. Great fun with the boys and they were getting on so well at the moment. We arrived and after struggling to find a cab we got a train out to the Intercontinental where our tickets were waiting. Amazing mood around the place and got loads of colour for the *Times* piece. Couple of Italian Brits almost begging for tickets. The boys feeling a bit bad I think that we had tickets.

Off to the residence to see Peter Torry. Not as grand as Paris but a lovely garden, and the usual Home Counties feel. The boys watched Federer while I talked to Peter about TB–GB and also Merkel. He felt she was in quite a lot of trouble. Business was losing it with her because she was so focused on consensus that they saw it as a lack of drive and not doing the things she said she would. Also health reform just stuttered. But she was impressive, and resilient. It would take time to see what sort of Chancellor she was going to be. He shared my assessment that the World Cup had gone well for them, despite the obvious of them not winning it. It really had felt like a new page being turned in history, especially the way young Germans had projected themselves. I'd liked Peter when he was in Madrid, he was bright, a good bloke, picking my brains on all sorts of things but above all re the TB situation. He was another serious person who didn't think GB had all that was needed.

He said he couldn't put his finger on it but the GB–Merkel meeting had not been that great. They both have the work ethic, and say a lot of the same things, but he felt GB was trying too hard. And of course they all get the same kind of briefings from their people in London, and they are full of stuff about the TB–GBs, and no matter which way you cut it, they see someone who has not been terribly loyal, and they make a judgement about that. He said the feedback he got afterwards, though it was not always easy to get a real sense of what Merkel thought was 'a bit underwhelmed'. We set off in a police car for the ground, got driven into the VIP bit which cut out a load of hassle, but then had to find our way back out and back in to where our seats were. Loads of big political figures around so the security heavy. We found our seats, behind one of the goals at the back of the ground, and four blokes came and said hello – Burnley fans who were tying up their flag at the back of the stand.

The atmosphere was OK but a bit flat for a final, as I said in update on the fans for the *Mirror*. The corporate thing had gone too far. There was a German bloke behind us who kept saying he was bored out of his mind. France took the lead with a Zidane penalty. Marco Materazzi equalised for Italy with a header from a corner. Tight and defensive match, [Fabio] Cannavaro was awesome. Extra time, amazing save by [Gianluigi] Buffon from Zidane, felt like a game-changer. Then Zidane sent off and we had no idea why, everyone having to text home and Fiona asking, 'What is the point of going if you can't see what happens?!' It turned out it was a head butt into Materazzi's chest, seen by the fourth official and he was off. What a way to end his career. Alex texted from the other side of the ground to say Zidane must be off his head. The talk was it was an insult by Materrazzi. The atmosphere finally picked up and Italy's every touch was booed, but it was clear it was going to penalties.

Italy scored all five, only [David] Trezeguet missed for France, and [Fabio] Grosso hit the winner and the Italians went wild. But even at the end it was not so awesome. I think they just about deserved it, but it was not quite the heartstopping stuff we hoped for. As the Italians celebrated I filed a couple of ads to the *Mirror* and that all worked fine. Back to the Residence and a drink with Torry, chatting over various things. He was clearly of the view Merkel was 'on probation'. Said the business people at their box were absolutely down on her. Up till around half one.

Monday 10 July

I ran for an hour or so down by the lake near the Residence. Stunning scenery. But my running was not good at the moment. Breakfast then began a long day's travel. I finished the *Times* piece. I was enjoying reading the German papers, used TB in *Bild am Sonntag* in the stuff I was doing today. I reckon if I came out for a bit my German would come back. It hadn't been dreadful, though the majority definitely spoke English in a way they didn't used to. I did an end of the tournament last blog, and got a nice note from Andrew Saxton and Paul Simpson at the party who said the blog had driven loads of traffic to the party site. We got the train back to Cologne, loads of Brits around the place, late lunch, then fly home. Really enjoyed the boys' company. News-wise, a bit of setback for the Home Office reform scene, with JR announcing they were not going ahead with merger of police forces.[*]

Tuesday 11 July

I spent the morning dealing with a bit of a work backlog, then cycled in to see Bradders. I had a copy of *Bild* for him, to add to his signed TB article collection. He was raging at the way *Today* programme and [John] Humphrys were treating the Prescott story. He had a copy of the *Metro* to show me, where David Ginola said I knew the game inside out. Nice! I sent him an email thanking him. 'I love you,' he said. Top bloke. I kept the cutting to put on the fridge later to show the boys. Out at half-five with Grace and Anna [Sirius, friend] to Braintree where some programme called *Only Fools on Horses* was being recorded, a kind of celeb-y showjumping thing which Ros from Soccer Aid had invited us to. They made it quite exciting and Endemol certainly don't cut corners and do stuff properly. I had a nice chat with Robert Smith [showjumper] about his dad [Harvey, former showjumper; AC's father was his vet] and

---

[*] Previous Home Secretary Charles Clarke had planned to merge the forces throughout England and Wales.

the time I was their interpreter in Nice. He said his mum often recalled my busking times, when I went out with her and [showjumper] David Broome's wife near Nice and got the pipes and the hat out. He said I ought to get into UK equestrianism because 'it is still being run by all the old farts he [Harvey] couldn't stand'. Grace and Anna loved it all, but I found the whole celeb TV thing so ludicrous, though without it I would never have had the Soccer Aid thing, I guess. There was clearly no end as yet to this kind of telly though. Maybe there never would be.

Wednesday 12 July

Charles Clarke out having another whack, this time about JR's reversing his plans on merging police forces, which he was linking to fighting terrorism, and also the lack of direction point. I had a long session with David S. I had enjoyed Germany, but I was down again. Things still not right. He was grilling me on the circumstances in which I had a drink, said watch it because it can creep up. He felt it was possible that drink was replacing politics as my interest receded. I was feeling bad at not being there but also relieved at not being there. Then as I got back home, took Grace to Anna Sher [theatre school] and then started to get a string of calls asking me to do interviews on the fact that Michael Levy had been arrested [cash-for-honours investigation]. Jesus. I spoke to JoP who said TB and Michael were both like rabbits in the headlights. Why wouldn't they be? This was fucking ridiculous. Some SNP MP calls in the police based on next to nothing and before you know it people are getting hauled in by these attention-seeking cops. Politics was going to become impossible at this rate.

As PG said though, if Levy is charged TB gets guilt by association and people will think he has to go and there may be nothing anyone can do to stop it. I wanted to go up and say, 'Why is this only happening to our people?' I thought of all the funding scandals under Thatcher and since, and how nobody batted an eyelid. It was all part of this notion that the Tories in power was the natural order of things. Added to which, the cops had become much more focused on their own media profile, and a desire to get popularity. This guy Yates was really loving himself as a media high-profile case figure, leaving no stone unturned, no fear or favour, and of course the media were giving him big licks as a way of cheering him on. I wondered about going up on it and also about saying this could lead to elected cops one day.

Meanwhile the chapter closed on another ludicrous cops thing. I had totally forgotten but a while back the Welsh cops had written saying they were investigating complaints that TB may have said racially improper comments about the Welsh and they may need to interview me. It came out of something in Lance Price's book, when he swore at 'the fucking Welsh'. When the cops first asked me, I had said if they did interview me was it OK if I brought a camera crew? Today I got a letter from north Wales cops saying they were taking no further action re TB's fucking Welsh remarks. This was the same chief constable who said they had to learn to focus on priorities. Long chat with Richard [Stott] who was still ploughing on with editing the diaries. His chemo starts Monday. Out for dinner with Grace and Calum. I was only really happy with the kids at the moment. Nothing else got near.

Thursday 13 July

Fiona and I went on a little boat trip to Greenwich. I couldn't bear reading the papers and all the Levy coverage, which was wall-to-wall. An over-the-top cheeky chappie Cockney as tour guide on the boat from the Tower down to the National Maritime Museum. The best stuff was on Nelson, including a sketch of Trafalgar battle and a necklace with a dog sent by Nelson to his daughter Horatia who wrote to him saying he promised to get her a dog! I was glad we went and we had a nice enough time but then an instant depressive crash on the way back. Literally couldn't function. I went to bed for an hour before meeting the *Who Do You Think You Are?* research team. I tried my best to be enthused, but it felt like a whole lot of work, and for what? It was just drawing me further into this media celebrity shit. I liked the programme, which had a lot more to it than most, and I know Mum would like it if they went away and dug into the family history, but was it really where I should be right now? Or was it just the sudden depressive mood dragging me down about everything?

I had been invited to the *Superman* premiere – again, more celeb bollocks – and didn't feel like going, but had sorted tickets for Rory and co, so decided to go. Loads and loads of media on the way in, some wanting interviews, but I decided against. The film was OK but really not my scene. There was an after-party at the High Court, and it was quite strange to see all these places that for me still resonated mainly of Hutton and Iraq now being the scene of a party. Roger Alton [editor, *Observer*] was very up on TB, down on GB, said Cameron was really working them. I had a nice chat with Kevin Spacey. He said he so loved being an honorary Brit. He was easily the best thing in the film. But he said the Old Vic remained his main passion for now. GB was setting out spending but it was far less of a big deal than TB had been wanting, and the message one of toughness and restraint on pay and spending. John McDonnell [Labour MP] was putting it out that he would challenge GB for the leadership whenever TB went. Cameron was also copping it, his own MPs saying they were worried he made up policy on the hoof. We had to do a better job of forcing him into the tough policy areas, because if his own people were starting to worry, he could be made more vulnerable.

Friday 14 July

Nice day at the Test match against Pakistan at Lord's, with PG and his mates at PepsiCo. Bumped into Dickie Bird [former umpire] who said I should 'git thasel a seat and tek ovver from Tony'. Beautiful day. Nice way to spend it. Picked up a few sponsorship leads for LRF. Walker's crisps the biggest Pepsi brand but learned they had loads of others. Quaker e.g. Also Robinsons [fruit squash] was owned by Britvic and the guy said he was constantly amazed by how the Wimbledon connection helped drive up sales. Later out for dinner with Rory at his usual casino. He was keen for me to understand better why his poker playing was a good thing! He said it was like chess for clever people. And he took money from people who weren't clever.

Sunday 16 July

Rory and Zoe off to France to see the Tour de France mountain stages. I set off for the London Bikeathon. Did a few interviews with Geoff Thomas [LRF] after we came in together. Then to [joint party of] Illtyd [Harrington, Labour politician] and [Fiona's brother] Gavin [Millar QC]. The papers were shit all round, home and abroad. Middle East out of control. TB out at the G8 in St Petersburg, and set off another little GB firework when he said he hoped to be at next year's G8 too. Putin made a barbed reference re Michael Levy, which was getting our lot excited. He was asked about the UK criticisms on human rights, and replied by saying there were also issues of corruption to discuss, and then he made clear he was talking about Michael. Putin was definitely redefining his approach to diplomacy. It meant TB got asked about it at his press conference with Bush, which would doubtless have amused Putin.

He had a load of digs at the Americans as well. Bush having said he hoped one day Russians would have the same freedoms as Americans, Putin said he just hoped they don't have the same kind of democracy as Iraq, and then he had a blast at [Dick] Cheney [US Vice-President] for good measure.

Monday 17 July

I had been overdoing the exercise front, and went to see Mel Cash [sports physio] who told me I had one calf smaller than the other. He said if I didn't do more stretching I could end up with all sorts of problems. To Lord's for what should have been really exciting last day but petered out to nothingness, but there was a wonderful sports photography stall and I bought some fantastic pictures of Lance [Armstrong], Tiger Woods [golfer] and Maradona. Brendan [Foster] was down for some meetings, including with TB, on how to boost sports participation. He broadly agreed with my general analysis re the media, including the Beeb. Calum was playing PG at tennis so I went along to watch. Philip had been at a meeting on party renewal earlier and said they were all a bit shot. G8 struggling to get agreement on how to handle Israel–Hezbollah.* The fissures with Putin were becoming harder and harder to manage, and he was looking like he didn't much care. TB and Kofi Annan [United Nations Secretary-General] were calling for an international force to go into the south of Lebanon.

Tuesday 18 July

A nice G8 mini-frenzy for the media to gorge on, with Bush and TB talking at the summit without realising their microphones were still on. 'Yo Blair!' That is going to enter the language pretty quickly, I fear. Added to which they had 'President says "shit" [re Hezbollah–Israel] shock'. And all the stuff about exchanged gifts, and Tony joking he knitted Bush's jumper, amid all the serious stuff. It was funny in a way, but came over as a bit weird. First good run for ages. Long swim later at men's pond. John Reid saying we would need a massive prison building programme, prison population soaring.

---

* Lebanon Islamist militant group Hezbollah fired rockets at Israeli border towns, prompting retaliation by the Israel Defence Forces and escalation into full-blown military conflict.

Wednesday 19 July

I did a long interview with the BBC for a film they were making about how to win power from opposition. I don't know whether it was all the diary stuff, or what I was doing with David S, but I felt myself being much more reflective, and starting to harden some views of how we did things, but also challenging others. I just felt I was being a bit more considered, measured, still not erring in saying anything that might be seen as doing in TB but definitely more considered. I liked Susan Gill who did the interview, who was thoughtful and reflective as well, and she said none of the others, especially [Michael] Howard, were really allowing themselves genuine reflection, so at times it felt like they were trapped in the mindset of then, but hadn't allowed themselves to work out why they lost. I felt we had done a lot of the strategic stuff right, but some of it we could have done better. And I think I was beginning to appreciate much more that for all the hard work and the fight in us, we had also had a lot of luck, not least in our opponents and the difficulties of their politics. That is why Cameron might be different, though the jury was still out, including with his own people. But I sensed the reason they were making the programme was because of the feeling Cameron might be the next to come from opposition, after GB came in via government.

Thursday 20 July

David S with Fiona. We went over the Maritime Museum visit and my total crash, which I just couldn't explain. Fiona was saying she was happy to put everything in the past behind us but I couldn't let go because of the emotional bond to the whole TB project. It was a bit rough and we were both down by the end of it. She said she felt I was a better person than him, with real morals and values and ability but for some reason I allowed myself to be seen as an appendage. Boris Johnson [shadow education minister] was putting it around that I had said at the cricket that TB would go in just over a year, and I was getting a few calls on that. It was pure stirring, and I put out a short statement and left it at that. Off to golf at Swinley with David Mills, Jamie Rubin and Clive Tyldesley. Took a call from Neil Wallis [deputy editor, *News of the World*]. He said TB should try to regain some of the moral high ground on the peerage probe by volunteering to be interviewed, making clear his view that there are none so mighty that they should not be interviewed etc. I put it in through JoP who said they were thinking on the same lines.

Friday 21 July

Observer photographer round first thing to do triathlon pictures, so out for a swim, then run, then bike pictures. Then did a piece for *The Sun* on how terrorist groups were becoming more and more sophisticated at the PR game, and using the media landscape of democracies to their advantage. Cameron was getting fair licks for his speech on the need to think beyond mere money and into well-being. It was counter-intuitive for a Tory, the thing about an increase in quality time being as important in its own way as tax cuts. He was definitely sticking to his positioning / talking point approach rather than just doing nuts and bolts policy. More grief for JP, the parliamentary standards saying he should have declared his visits to the American ranch, whether he discussed Dome and casinos or not. And even though it said the department, not he, kept the Stetson and cowboy boots that the American guy gave him, it all added to the general sense of out-of-touchery, and what the hell was he doing there?

Saturday 22 July

JP called first thing. The report from the standards guy [Sir Philip Mawer, Parliamentary Commissioner] had not been great. JP said he was being hammered, and was due on Marr tomorrow, and wanted to go over the best way to deal with it. He sounded pretty down but said TB was still supportive. I agreed that if he went now it would quickly move to TB. So best to stay and try to get up a message about politics not being about all this rubbish. The problem was he kept focusing on the rubbish, going over in detail about his visit to the ranch of this guy Anschutz. I hadn't really followed it all closely, but the more he tried to explain the detail the more I said he needed to get his head out of the detail and into a message about himself and why he is in politics. I suggested that as a main message – part of modern politics is this constant battle of two agendas, the serious stuff we want to do, and all the rubbish we have to deal with which gets all the attention. It fitted with what he thought and thinks, but he sounded a bit shot.

I did a long run then off to Anji's wedding to Adam Boulton. A hot day, though it turned to light rain a bit later and there was a surreal moment when an anti-war demo wandered by. I sat with [Baroness] Cathy Ashton [parliamentary under-secretary, constitutional affairs] and Peter Kellner [husband, pollster]. Neil and Glenys directly in front. TB with Liz [Lloyd] and Richard [husband] in front of them. Mick Hucknall and Gabriela. Tessa and Charlie/Mariana [Falconer]. Loads of family. Anji looking nervous as I'd ever seen her. The kids of both did readings and music. Really hot. Nice hymns. I could vaguely hear drums of the anti-war march. Loads of Sky people. Media people. I walked down to the reception with Ronnie Grierson [businessman] and [General Sir] Mike Jackson. Grierson one of those non-stop networkers, but sharp, picking my brains on US and UK politics, and asking to meet up for lunch; Jackson reminiscing about some of our contretemps during Kosovo, but a good laugh as ever. Reporters asking, 'Where is Cherie?' as we walked over. I chatted to Jonathan and Sarah [Helm, wife of JoP] who was still bending our ear about Iraq, and she said she was doing a piece for the *Standard* slagging off TB about the Middle East. 'Can't you get a grip of her?' I asked JoP. 'At least I could get her to come to the wedding!' Fair point.

Good chat with Peter M, but he was more worried about TB than ever. We looked over, TB was standing surrounded by a little gaggle of people, and Peter said, 'Look at him, he looks petrified. Even with people who in the main support him, he is losing his nerve.' Cab home with Tessa, who got very emotional. She said Matt [son] and Jessie get a lot of strength from knowing they can always rely on me to be supportive but she is not always there, and now that the thing with David was such a mess… She said she was still so angry with him. She just felt he had been too cavalier and without regard to the consequences for her. I got home and then we drove down to Shipston-on-Stour to see David [Mills]. He was on good form. New puppy. Up in arms about the Israelis and Lebanon.

Sunday 23 July

Swim first thing. Watched [Open Championship] golf most of the day. Tiger was awesome and wept for his dad at the end. Good show for the triathlon piece in *The Observer*. Tessa constantly trying to get me engaged on the political front but I was feeling more and more divorced from it. I felt bad for TB but for the rest – JP had been daft, GB just wasn't right, JR was overdoing things and trying to do too much at once, MB seemed to be finding the FCO hard, and there was a feeling David M, as Tim Allan put it, was lacking the neccessary *cojones* to get in there. So if things carried on as they are, that little fucker Cameron and all his ghastly people were in. Yet I couldn't feel motivated to help stop it, other than in my own way. No. 10 called asking if I could go to a TB dinner with Tessa, Milburn, Charlie, JR and Sally next week. The media were loving the open mic chat between TB and GWB – Yo Blair – not great, going to be obsessed over it for a while yet.

Monday 24 July

Fifty-minute run from Shipston to Ilmington and back. I got a message from Nick Butler about the late edition of the *FT*, saying John Browne was definitely going to be leaving. He said Peter Sutherland [BP non-executive chairman] had bullied the press office into saying it and he was fed up with it. I spoke to Phil Webster to pass on to business desk that he was clear he would stay on if people at the company wanted him to. Back to spinning I guess but there we are. It was clear that it was going to turn a bit nasty. Later in the day it was going to be obvious John would have to make clear at the results meeting tomorrow that he was going. We headed back into London and I headed for a meeting with LRF and London Triathlon. Good bunch. Lots of partnership potential. Up to Gail's for meeting with her, Richard, looking a lot thinner and so both more and less healthy, Susan Sandon [senior executive] and Caroline Gascoigne, who was an editor. She had read all of Volume 1 and most of 2. She said she was riveted.

RS said third volume was even more riveting. He was now strongly of the view that the single volume, largely cleansed of the bad GB stuff, was not a runner, that if we did that and then later produced a truthful version showing TB, my and others' massive doubts re GB, that would lead to my reputation being shredded. We went around on that for a while. I swung one way and the other on it. Then a good discussion of the format and how it might look, a few process issues and away we went. A good meeting even if we had not resolved the main issues. Gail was clearly wanting something out there as soon as TB went. In a way so did I, but not at any expense. Also how would things be affected if I worked for GB in the campaign? Richard and the others, having read it all, could not believe I was even thinking about it, but as Gail said, 'Listen, he will end up with Gordon, let's just accept it.' All tricky.

Caroline said that she thought some of the most interesting stuff was about what went on in my head re myself and my own feelings about my role. Richard and Penny gave me a lift home, and we chewed it over a bit. Neither of us were sure. I still felt that provided I was totally honest about it not being a full and frank version, that might work. 'Being honest about being dishonest?' said RS. 'Being honest that it is a partial account, being honest about the reasons, and undertaking to publish the whole thing later.' Another bad report – this time from the Lords – on funding, with their Appointments Commission saying it was blindingly obvious the loans should have been declared in the same way as donations. They aimed it at both main parties, but the coverage was mainly pointed at us, because of the cops' involvement.

Tuesday 25 July

Two-hour bike ride up through Cockfosters, out to Potters Bar and beyond. John Browne made a statement that he would go by the end of 2008. Meanwhile, FirstGroup [transport] were also pushing me to do stuff for them. I spoke to Tim [Allan] as it might be more up his street. PG took Georgia to her first focus groups, up in Edgware. He called me afterwards and said she was in a state of shock. They were the worst he had ever done. Nothing good to say about the government. Absolutely dire for TB. Not much better for GB. And they were really warming to Cameron. Georgia came on, said she was really shocked. 'Oh my God, it was horrible. If you listened to them, the government has done nothing, Tony is awful, the country is awful, and anything is better so we might as well give Cameron a go.' 'Welcome to our world… but remember we won three elections.' But PG said it really had been grim. Normally there would be voices of reason and context, who would say, 'Hold on, let's be reasonable, life isn't that bad,' but there was nobody, nothing. He said Georgia was almost white as a sheet when they walked out.

There seemed to be a bit of new thing going on in the PLP too, to get TB to commit to this being his last conference and say so in terms. Four UN observers were killed by an Israeli bomb in Lebanon – Chinese, a Finn, an Austrian, a Canadian – which was grim, and TB was really starting to get hit on it all. It was too nuanced a position to be resisting a ceasefire, even if he had good arguments, and everyone knew deep down that a line about 'the utmost restraint' to the Israelis meant carry on crushing Hezbollah as they see fit. It was unfair that TB seemed to take so much of the heat on this, but in a way people didn't expect anything else from the Americans and the Israelis. Sally was really worried about his position in the PLP right now.

Wednesday 26 July

PG was having a do for No. 10 people tonight and had felt Fiona shouldn't go because of all the rows over education, and because the kids wanted to go, that set us up for a bit of a rage day. PG was being a bit silly but hey. Added to which I was seeing TB for dinner, so I decided not to go to Philip's as well but Rory persuaded me I should. We were first there. I took them the hilarious over-stylised portrait that Keith Vaz [Labour MP] had had done of me. TB came a bit later and made a beeline for me and Rory. 'I hear you're one of my remaining support-ers,' he said to Rory, who urged him to fight another election. Chatted a bit but then Liz Lloyd pointed out to him that I was with him for din-ner so he should mingle a bit more. JoP confident the cops peerages thing would be OK, that they'd got themselves into a bad place and because Ian Blair [Commissioner, Metropolitan Police] lacked leader-ship, they didn't know how to get out of it. I left earlyish and headed for No. 10. Charlie and Tessa were in the waiting room so we had a bit of a pre-meeting. Tessa was not sure we could be totally frank in front of Alan Milburn because he was hedging his bets regarding his own position. I felt we could.

Charlie was strongly of the view nobody could stop GB. He and Tessa both felt TB's position had weakened further. Tessa in particular felt that Lebanon was doing real damage, because of the sense TB always gave of wanting to side automatically with the Israelis. I felt – and later told TB – that I couldn't see how things were going to get much bet-ter for him. He was being shredded on the international front because of Bush. He was shredded on the domestic front because of GB and a sense that even his own ministers weren't really motoring. He was shredded party and public-wise re JP. I felt he should worry less about the state of the party afterwards, whether GB was New Labour or not, and worry more about his own exit plan. All he had left was surprise and the ability to shape the mood around his departure. Once we all assembled upstairs – Ruth T and later Sally the final guests – TB asked us all what we thought. It was pretty gloomy, so much so that by the end of the first round he was making jokes to Vera, who was serving up the food, to get the removals men lined up. 'How many vans can you get in the L-shaped road?' 'Now don't you be listening to all these doomsters,' she said. But she said to me afterwards she felt things were not so good.

TB went through his own strategy – basically to take all the shit and on policy show that we were the only people with the ideas for the future, that whether it was Cameron to the right or GB to the left they were not coming forward with an alternative policy agenda. Where Cameron has ideas, they're ours, where he has his own, they're bad. So on energy, we have big a forward agenda, he has turbines. Get on to policy the whole time and we're strong, they are weak. The problem with that was that it was a bit same old same old and it lacked the reason for longevity, the purpose of staying. Tessa was best on that, saying that we had to show a bit of fight, that he had been elected just over a year ago and we would get hammered if he went amid some kind of deal with GB, about whom so many had so many doubts. True, said TB, the public would say they had to decide who PM was. He said on policy he had never known the machine in better shape. JR was doing well despite all the flak. I said I had heard him say the same about a succession of Home Secretaries, but they all went, and he ended up complaining the system wasn't responsive enough. How was it going to get better?

Charlie asked what at best he could achieve say with another year, or two? Alan was saying CC and AJ were both likely to go for the leadership – didn't mention himself – but TB said they didn't stand a chance against Gordon. The tragedy was that he had most of what it took – the range, intellect, political skills – but he lacked the extra bit, the character and personality parts of the package. He was alarming in his assessment of Cameron. He felt he did have it, that my line that he couldn't do policy was fine up to a point, but he didn't really need that much at the moment. He had been impressed by him so far, much more than he had expected to be, and he felt he could rise to it. Maybe GB could but he wasn't so sure. He was in a good mood, and there were a few laughs along the way, e.g. his description of JP describing a discussion as though it was a human being. 'The discussion came in and we had the discussion and then it went out again.' He was also still able to self-mock and what have you and when he went through the current problems was his usual optimistic self.

On Lebanon, he was off to see Bush this weekend and was confident we would get a ceasefire and his role within it would be clear. Sally went on for ages about how damaged he was because of his stance on this. She said it is as if you have a blind spot, or you want to provoke the party. No, he said, but the easy thing to say is not necessarily the right thing to do. On peerages and the cops he said he was more confident than a few weeks ago, and he felt most serious people thought the whole thing was politics pure and simple, and the cops had been foolish to get caught up in it. On GB he felt he just had to keep managing it. What was interesting was that the party and the PLP were getting more and more worried about GB's ability to deliver electorally. He was very worried about JP, knew it was doing enormous damage but said that if he forced him out, JP would quickly move to a position of saying there should be a leadership election and change too. So while he accepted all that everyone was saying about what a liability he was, he said there was no easy answer.

Tessa felt the JP problem was chronic and had to be settled before the holiday. Milburn said the media would shred him during the summer if he was 'in charge'. Charlie felt they were exaggerating. TB said he knew it was a problem but there was no easy way of dealing with it. And as we both knew, when we gently raised the idea of JP going of his own accord to help the party, he gave short shrift. He said the problem was JP was not sensitive enough to how the public would feel about him having sex with a subordinate civil servant in his office. He underestimated how bad that was for most people. But having said he could stay, and then feeling that in the situation with Anschutz he had been stupid but certainly not corrupt or even wrong, what was the misdemeanour now? Charlie seemed to blow hot and cold on how bad things were. Tessa felt they were bad but the only thing was for TB to fight.

TB said he was really disappointed at the lack of leadership being shown by the next generation, including David M. He had spoken to him over the weekend and he sensed someone trapped in the headlights. What he didn't realise was that if he was out there with an agenda and ideas it made him more electable but also more unsackable if GB saw him as a rival. Tessa felt DM lost the will when he had the press into him over the adoption.* But nobody was really putting head above parapet. That included GB. Where were these new ideas? TB said Steve Richards [journalist] had been up with him in Nottingham for his public health speech and asked why he didn't let GB set out new ideas. That was clearly the GB line, that he was prevented. TB said he would love it if he had new ideas. He was very keen on the new generation of people and ideas for conference. But I felt that it only worked if GB was also signed up for it, otherwise it looks divisive and anti-GB. TB felt there could be something worked out on the lines of stability at the top and the next generation coming through. TB very funny on his upcoming trip. 'I start with Bush. Then I move on to Rupert [Murdoch]. And then it's Arnie [Schwarzenegger, actor, Governor of California].' Sally – 'is there any chance you could be seen with someone vaguely progressive?'

---

* David Miliband and his American wife, Louise, had travelled to the United States in December 2004 to adopt a baby boy. They were present at the birth of Isaac James Miliband on 13 December.

We did agree that he should, if he was staying, simply ignore the stuff about departure at conference. Charlie felt TB would have taken a very heavy message. Tessa that he was lonely, said it was almost poignant the way he so clearly was looking to me for my opinion on everything. She had suggested I go back full-time, but for all sorts of reasons I wasn't sure that was a runner. All were still raging re the GB press operation. All clearly feeling if GB didn't shape up, we would lose the election. TB wanting them, plus Alan actively involved, to work on the development of New Labour support in terms of people, ideas and organisation. Tessa gave me a lift home. As we left, he kept slapping me on the back, telling me how well I looked, what a great kid Rory was, how was Calum, how was Grace? Tessa was still clear that it was not time to get back with David. Too raw, too sore, too angry. Re me, she felt it would be great for TB and government if I went back, but felt there would be real problems with Fiona and also that the kids were loving having me around, and that mattered.

Thursday 27 July

Fiona was cross with Philip, but he pointed out that she cannot have it both ways, expect to be able to operate as a free agent attacking the government and No. 10, and then be invited along to events. We had to sort it out though. PG was the last person either of us should be falling out with. I worked on a piece for *The Indy* on Graeme Obree [racing cyclist] then lunch with Calum. There was a very odd incident in the afternoon when a photographer appeared in the skylight in the house opposite appearing to point his camera in our direction. I took Grace to the stables and bike to Triandrun. Nice time at both. Lunch with George and Catherine and Hector [Mackie] who had come off for 20 minutes for Stevenage against Spurs in a friendly the other night. He seemed pretty hopeful he could make it.

Friday 28 July

TB off to the US. I was watching the cricket on Sky, England doing well v Pakistan, and channel hopping during the adverts. His plane arriving in Maryland on Sky. How many times had I been there at those moments, as all the blather started to get filed from the back and at the front everyone getting fussed about what now. And there I was, sitting on the sofa, channel hopping between cricket and, whenever Grace came in, showjumping. TB was getting a lot of flak for his stance on Lebanon. I knew why he was holding firm, but he was paying a price when he didn't have that much capital left. I caught his press conference with Bush, which GWB started with a joke about them being so close now that TB told him when the microphones were on. The substance was all Israel–Lebanon, TB much more fluent than Bush, also more balanced than Bush, who saw it very much as being only about Hezbollah, whereas TB was a bit more nuanced, but it would still look to the ones giving him grief here that he was totally on the US and Israeli lines. Where he was good was setting the context of the broader strategy of terrorists more generally, but it was a complicated point in a story that had, for most of those asking the questions and listening to them, fairly simple contours.

They couldn't really see what was so hard about calling for an immediate ceasefire. He took it back to 9/11, and was strong in terms of his grip on the issues, 'the global ideology' etc., but their position would be so much easier if the previous military campaigns had gone as planned. TB was heading on to California, doing more business and techy stuff. And as if the optics in the White House were not great, one of his hosts down there was Murdoch. And another was George Shultz [former US Secretary of State]. Earlier PG sent me over a poll which showed a sharp dip in people's assessment of the US–UK relationship. Most, by around two to one, felt we were too close, and fewer saw the benefits. There was also a worrying message about his idea of the international force, because the support for any kind of intervention anywhere had fallen pretty hard. Also, on the Israel–Lebanon fight, most sided with Lebanon.

Saturday 29 July

Calum's birthday, did his presents first thing, then I headed up north for the triathlon tomorrow. The England cricket team were in the same hotel and I ended up having a drink with Geoff Boycott [former England cricketer turned pundit], who was full of the usual stuff, right-wing on politics, nostalgic on cricket, but I sensed able to laugh at himself more than he let on. I put in a call to TB after first Sally re the PLP, then PG re some polling he had seen, called me about just how badly his stance on Lebanon was going down. It wasn't helped of course by the fact he had to stand next to Bush, both saying the same thing, or that the issue was so complicated, but he was definitely heading for more problems on it. By the time he called back, I was getting calls about Jack [Straw] having what was taken as a pop when he did one of his constituency meetings, and said that the Israelis were at risk of destabilising the whole of Lebanon and beyond. TB said he had been as balanced and measured as he could be, but said it would achieve nothing just to slag off the Israelis. Whatever solution they got to, they would need to agree it, and there was no point making that harder to achieve for the sake of a few easy headlines. I said I appreciated all that but be aware you have a lot of voices ranging against.

Jack gave the clear impression that he felt the Israeli actions were far worse, and said ten times as many Lebanese had been killed. He also leaned on [Foreign Office Minister] Kim Howells' words that it was impossible to understand why they were using the tactics they were. TB said the last Cabinet had been pretty tough, in that several of them spoke out against the Israelis and urged him not to get too close to Bush on it, but in the end he had to shape what he thought was the right strategy, which was building the alliances needed to sort something for the long term as well as addressing the short term. He said he was aware of the feeling, but he was pretty unbudgeable. Addded to which, just as he felt Charles had been diddling on the Home Office because he was no longer there, he felt Jack was doing a bit of the same as he was no longer at the FCO. Probably true, I said, but he might have a point.

I got to bed early to try and get some sleep before the triathlon tomorrow, but there was a rash of calls later on about a poll the press were getting excited about – TB's ratings the lowest they had ever been. The Lebanon thing was becoming something of a tipping point. One of the papers said he had fallen more over this than over Iraq. It was IPSOS Mori, more than 2,000 people, done over four days and not easy to dismiss, especially as it would get such play. 23 per cent satisfied, 67 not. Even a majority of Labour supporters were not satisfied with him. On the general scene, the Tories had a four point lead, but as it happened DC's ratings had dipped too. There was just a lot of grunginess out there, but the Lebanon situation really had cut through. People just couldn't understand why he was so reluctant just to say, outright from the off, there should be a ceasefire.

Sunday 30 July

The poll stuff was being wrapped up into a general story about TB being more and more under attack from within over Lebanon. Jack's thing was going quite big, and also it turned out Hilary Benn had been saying much the same, so to some of the Sundays it was 'Cabinet revolt' time. The *Telegraph* had all the usuals, plus David M and Bruce [Grocott], saying he had to take a tougher line with the Israelis. So TB was out having to defend the basic position again, with much the same messages, including that 'Hezbollah is largely to blame for the conflict', as he was going around various tech places, and also making a speech to Murdoch's executives in Pebble Beach, where his main message seemed to be that left/right divides were no longer what they were, and no longer the answer to political challenges. Then Condi Rice, Bush having made a big thing of her going back to the region when he did his press conference with TB, called off her planned trip to Beirut after the Israelis bombed a village, killing more than fifty people.

The other issue that has been bubbling away under it all, with Margaret B critical, was the Americans using Prestwick Airport as a refuelling stop. Bush had apologised but it turned out they were still using it, including for the planes packed with more bombs. I didn't do badly in the triathlon. The water in Salford docks didn't look great, but the swim was fine. I got round the whole thing in 2 hours 44. Not bad, a bit down on what I had trained for. The swim around 32, bike maybe 1.15 to 1.20, run 51. I lost a lot in the transitions.

Monday 31 July

Having got Rupert out of the way, now TB was seeing Arnie, though at least John Browne was there to add a bit of gravitas. Added to which the message out of it was a commitment to fighting global warming together, which at least gained some distance with the Republican right. They were talking about the UK and California doing a deal which created a joint market and shared approach to greenhouse gas emissions.

Tuesday 1 August

Fifty-minute run then drive to East Midlands Airport to collect Graeme [brother] and Mikey [nephew] flying in from Poland. Home later and out to Neil and Glenys's. I was pleased Rachel was there because I wasn't up for engaging too much on the political front at all, and I ended up playing football v Grace, Camilla and Johanna [Stephen Kinnock's daughters] On the occasions we did get near politics, and especially on the Middle East, it was tough. Neil giving a long list of people who in his eyes didn't understand foreign policy. Most of our MPs. Virtually every ambassador. He was off on one. Also he and Glenys both had a pop at Hillary Clinton, saying her only reason for now whacking Israel was 'because she wants to be elected'. But though it was unspoken, I think a lot of the anger was for TB, and his being too close to the Americans over this, having been too close over Iraq, where often enough Neil had stood on my side of the argument, but much less so tonight.

It was a nice enough evening though, but largely because the girls made sure we talked of very little politics. TB was speaking at the World Affairs Council in Los Angeles. They had sent me a draft, but by the time I saw it and did comments, it was almost certainly too late. Grim backdrop though, not just Lebanon but overnight more British troops killed both in Iraq and Afghanistan. But he said that the main argument of his speech was planned before Lebanon blew up, and he believed it was still right. His big thing was the 'arc of extremism' using religion, that it was war, but a totally new and unconventional war requiring new ways of fighting it, including 'an arc of moderation and conciliation'. His problem in communicating it right now, especially with the deaths of the British guys overnight, and the way the Israelis were operating, was that it all looked like very conventional war. But it was clear in virtually everything he said on this trip, and as I said in the note, that he was sounding more and more frustrated at the sense of losing the argument that we created this, rather than we are responding to it. Hence the focus again on 9/11. It was important, and accurate, but it sounded a little like he was fighting past battles while the new ones moved on.

Wednesday 2 August

Did a mile-long swim then met Fiona at DS's. Pretty grim session. She had just about reached the end. She felt that until the TB thing was done and dusted it would always be an impediment to improvement. I felt I had tried my best, done lots that I was asked to, but it made no difference. I felt the whole thing was part of an incessant battering of me, and it instilled a feeling of failure. Really heavy session. Worst yet, David still saying he felt a lot there and we both wanted to salvage. Lunch with Roger Alton and Kamal Ahmed [*Observer*] at Clerkenwell Kitchen. Liked them both but I was probably too open both about myself, and also on the general situation, including TB–GB. They both felt GB was a goner against Cameron (as had Rachel last night, who said that while Cameron was deeply irritating to people like us, she found a lot of her middle of the road friends warming to him). Roger was good on

TB's resilience, felt that conversely as he got a worse press, he had the sense of him doing the job better – a point TB made often enough too.

I did a few miles on the bike then to the track for very hard session with Terry [triathlon coach]. Earlier popped in to see Keith at Runner's Need. He was so appalled how much weight I had put on that he measured me. I was really piling on weight. Out for dinner with Audrey at Café Med. Very good laugh. Then to collect Rory from Heathrow, who had decided to come home early from his Greek holiday, still not feeling well. Seemed fine about it. News still all Middle East. TB back from States after his Bush, Arnie, Rupert trip, and really getting hammered still. The French were enjoying his discomfiture. PG called from a plane about to take off in the States as I was going to bed, having had a hysterical Gail on, prostrate having fallen in a street and waiting for an ambulance. Broken and dislocated ankle. Tried to contact her. Eventually got Georgia who was on top of it.

Thursday 3 August

Last exercise day before Sunday. Cycled to Rachel's because Grace had left her phone there. TB back from the States, did his monthly press conference, much the same stuff, much the same answers, but heavy pressure, added to by a leaked note from William Patey [outgoing UK Ambassador to Iraq] that things were grim, and civil war likelier than successful transition to democracy.

Sunday 6 August

A couple of days up north, seeing Mum, back and off early for the London triathlon. Got there early and had ages to hang around. Good atmosphere, but I was maybe more tense than last time. I was doing stuff with *Grandstand* [BBC TV] at every stage – Craig Doyle the interviewer – and later signed him up to do it for us next year. Swim not bad, did fine going out, a bit wandered coming back. Transition long. First bike lap OK, second a lot windier. Grace had found herself a good spot with Mikey and was cheerleading really loudly, but by the run I was a bit knackered and finished in 2.50 overall. I was a bit disappointed but hadn't realised just how hot it had been until I saw how many were in a bad state. Home and out for dinner at Café Med. Signed up a couple of guys at next table, who had been with their French girlfriends since lunch at same table, to do the triathlon for charity. Home and TB called. He had delayed his holiday to try to do the final stages of a new UNSCR [United Nations Security Council Resolution]. He said the US visit had gone well, despite everything said here. Bush had sent regards, asking how I was, and what I was doing. I said I wished I knew. He wanted my view on whether he could go away Tuesday, even if final agreement was not secured. I said go.

People know he had delayed the holiday and by now it was all down to detailed negotiations and he had to show he was on top of that. Also Bush, Chirac and Merkel were all away at holiday places and it was better he saw it through. He said that he missed me a lot, felt there was something lacking in the strategic advice. I said do you want me to come back? I certainly want to see you more, he said, and get your input in a more structured way. I said we need to think of a modus operandi, but I felt full-time return was not on. We agreed next summer was probably the best time to go, but it must not become a given. Whenever he goes, there should be an element of surprise. He had Reid and Hutton out today defending him and it had made a difference. Re GB, he said if he had any sense he would be out there saying he backed TB, and people would clock it and say, 'That's leadership,' but even today GB was saying he didn't think it would help. Good chat, sounded a bit down, quite reflective, isolated. But felt he had made a difference on the UNSCR scene, and though he knew how much flak he was taking for his stance on Lebanon, he said he was not prepared to make arguments that he didn't think were true.

Monday 7 August to end of holiday
Off on holiday. OK journey and getting on fine with Fiona. The Milibands arrived Tuesday. Isaac sweet and very noisy. They were good to have around and we avoided too much political talk. The Middle East was a nightmare though and there was still no UNSCR by the time TB left for Barbados, the family having gone out a week earlier. He called a couple of times, and said he may as well have stayed at home for all the time he as spending on the phone. No let up on the political pressure – Jim Sheridan [Labour MP] quit as a [Defence] PPS, and Ann Keen [GB's PPS] was one of the voices out calling for a recall of Parliament. He was really pissed off when leading Muslims, including some of our MPs, and the main UK Muslim organisations, produced a joint letter really going for him over Lebanon, Iraq, foreign policy more generally, and totally playing into the idea that 'We caused it', as opposed to 'We have to deal with it'. 'It is like 9/11 never happened,' he said.

But he was becoming a bit tin-eared on it. The problem really was that in his tone, he had just sounded throughout like he was siding with Israel, and although people who were really into it could understand why, it was easy to caricature his position and that is what was happening. Sally was worried the Lebanon scene would be the death of him. Jimmy Carter [former US President] also had a really strong go at him, basically said he was about the only one who could have got Bush to restrain himself a bit and he totally failed. And he was another one basically feeding the message that we created the chaos.

Inevitably, lots of talk in France re TB–GB and David M seemed pretty down on both. He was working out his own position but without much clarity. We both wondered whether Alan Johnson felt he might have a go for the top job, but I remember Alan telling me when I did a fundraiser for him that he just couldn't see it. Peter Hain was motoring on the deputy leadership front. He felt JP was a disaster area, it was tragedy it was all ending for him like this, and though he understood why TB had to stand up for him, he felt it had damaged TB too. 'What about you?' I asked him a couple of times. Rory had noticed with DM that he spent a lot of time asking questions rather than putting forward opinions. He was definitely working out his own position. He was clearly thinking about it, but unsure of the route, and aware of the 'unmoveable object' aspect to GB. He felt he had to be a bit apart from both of them. But he had some interesting ideas and felt he could he could articulate future change better than GB.

Thursday, massive story in the UK was a huge terror alert which led to shutdown of flights and huge disruption. A plot uncovered to blow up ten planes at once. DM had been called by JP and Douglas A who had been airlifted off Mull because they couldn't tell him over the phone. John Reid thankfully still home and led the way on it, though once he started chairing COBRA meetings, it all played a bit too much into the JP soap opera. I don't know what we can do to stop this annual nonsense about 'Who's in charge?' when the honest answer is that TB is.

Puyméras [village in south-eastern France] much the same. Stayed in more. But Gail was now unable to come at all because of her ankle. I was mainly swimming because I had a bit of a mental block on the running and also going through Volume 1 of the diaries. David and Louise were both reading it and said they felt it was virtually impossible to do because the GB stuff was so bad. Unrelenting. DM laughing out loud at some of the portrayals, for example Robin Cook when he was doing PMQs. David also felt for me there was a danger of cutting off future options by being so open and honest about people. Added to which he thought it was not great for me to be mulling about the past the whole time. Louise said they were an incredible read, but how on earth could I be helping Gordon when I knew what I knew? Papers full of terror and the start of the football season.

Out for a long walk with DM the second time they came over, and I said he needed to reframe the way he projected himself. Too much analysis not enough solution, and it made people feel he was over-calculating. He had not seized enough of the opportunities the DEFRA brief gave him to pitch himself against DC given his seeming conversion to greenery.

Loads of kids around at one point which all got a bit noisy for me, but as Fiona said, it was brilliant that our kids all wanted to be with us the whole time, and that their friends felt so at home with us too. Exam results all fine. The kids were missing PG. He definitely added something to our holidays and it was a real bummer that they had been grounded by Gail's ankle. I spoke to her a couple of times, not least to keep her up to speed on thinking about the diaries, and she sounded very down. She may not be able to walk properly for months. We took in a couple of Marseille games, kept in touch with Ginola but didn't get it together to go down to his place in the south. Fiona worked out 28 August was the 26th anniversary of our first meeting, at the [Mirror Group journalism] training scheme in Devon. We had been getting on a lot better, and it brought home just how much we had going for each other. She is a fantastic mum to all the kids, and their friends all adore her too, because she is so chilled with them. I knew what a nightmare I could be, had been in the past, almost certainly would be in the future, but sitting thinking that we have had more than half of our life together, more than a quarter of a century, and all we have got through together, it would be a complete act of fucking madness to screw it up and lose it.

I had some good chats with the kids about it all too. I felt they had such different takes on the whole thing about me and work, and the impact on them. Every time we were talking big politics, as when David was around, I sensed Rory liked it, and liked that I was still part of it. He told anyone who would listen that Tony should fight another election, and I should go back. Calum was much more reflective about it, really into the politics of it, but also, if we were out just the two of us, asking about what making decisions was like, and also asking about the effect on Fiona. And Grace seemed OK with it either way. She had known nothing else. Fiona was actually moving towards becoming an

MP herself, she said she could not see herself doing anywhere outside London and the polls for Hampstead were not great right now.

TB, PG and I had been writing each other notes about conference and beyond, and TB shaping them into one of his compendium notes which he sent round the day we were heading home. He called when I got back and asked for PG and me to go to Chequers on Thursday. PG was pretty strong with him, in terms of telling him that the dip in his standing, and the move towards DC, were real. Also he had a real problem in the way that the terrorism arguments were getting bound up both with perceived foreign policy failings, and also immigration. Immigration was growing more and more salient, and not just in the usual groups. And he said the link to Bush, bad enough over Iraq, was even worse on Lebanon, and had hit him harder than he perhaps wanted to admit. TB said he knew it was bad, but he was sure he had taken the only sensible realistic approach that he could.

Mid-term, third-term, all knowing he was not going to be around much longer. Media worse than ever. GB still at it. Centres of power and authority shifting. In some ways, I said, we ought to be grateful things aren't worse. But the reality was we kept coming back to the same issues, without true resolution. We had pretty much tried everything. His big worry for the party was that too many were calling for change without knowing why. GB's lot, it was obvious. Others because they saw the dip in the polls. But we had had dips before and seen them off. But also there were calls for a new direction, without any real sense of what or why. He was even more down on the party than usual, not least because since the NEC took back fundraising, they have raised next to nothing, and the trade unions were making clear that without a new direction, there would be no more money. As ever, his answer was all about showing strength, spelling out home truths, and focusing on policy. There was probably no other way, but PG and I were both worried it was not working. For strength read stubbornness and refusal to listen; for home truths read arrogance; for focusing on policy, yes fine, but you keep saying you need new policy so where have you been for ten years.

We had some fairly testy exchanges, PG and I playing devil's advocate in a way to try to get him to a stronger position but one that was a bit more willing to accept some of the critique. His absolute fear was that without even realising it was happening, the party was going to slip backwards, dump New Labour, revert to type, play the Tories' game of being a traditional left-of-centre party which, he was convinced, would give DC victory on a plate. GB was too clever to go the whole way, but he was already part of the way there, and there were plenty people pushing him to go further. He said we should get the party to feel confident from DC feeling he had to imitate, instead of which they were using it to say we had to change. 'It is playing their game for them.'

We had done a few sections for his conference speech but he wanted to refocus it, on modern policy messages, going back to core NL themes on the economy, business, crime, reform and investment, welfare, but applied to the modern age, and he wanted us to think of how best to frame the argument re immigration. 'People know we need it, but they don't think what we have is working. It has to be managed. It cannot be uncontrolled.' He said people were more nuanced and open on this than we think. 'He hasn't been to a focus group,' was PG's reply to that. He was more seized of PG's point that foreign policy and immigration were becoming entangled to some extent. They both lent themselves to easy counter narratives. Just stop being so close to the Americans. Just stop people coming in. Simple. But not. With massive consequences and difficult to do.

He said PG was absolutely right that the fall in the polls was driven in part by the feeling that the 'war on terror' wasn't working, and that immigration was part of the failure. It was also all getting mixed up with worries about the flows from Eastern Europe, and all the pressures on public services, especially in the south, but they would spread. We couldn't just say suck it up, but we did need to give a context. That was back to explaining the downsides as well as the upsides of globalisation which, I said, we have never done well. Part of this was mood, he said. It is not that long ago London was feeling great because we got the Olympics, and everyone was saying it was because of modernity and diversity, and now these are negatives. We can turn it around, he said, but we need a real strategy for it. He was very seized of just how grim the media was, and not just the usual haters.

We had a discussion the night before the Chequers meeting about whether 'war on terror', even though it was totally part of the language because of Bush, was really the right way for us to frame this. It was partly about the point TB had made in the States about it not being conventional war, yet the optics of action looking conventional. He agreed it was misleading. But he said all of the different aspects we were up against – whether the kind of plots recently foiled, or 7 July, the Madrid bombings, or the fight against democracy in Iraq, or the fight to drive the Taliban back in Afghanistan, or Iran supporting terrorism, it was all in the same space – an ideological battle, a common ideology, and driven by a hatred of the West and especially of Israel which too many of our own people echoed. That is why we have to keep showing we understand the centrality of the Palestine issue, and doing what we can to push it in the right direction. Bloody hard. But impossible if we just do the easy, obvious, join in the anti-Israel chorus. As he went on, I said, please, I know we have to do all this, but this cannot be a foreign policy speech. No, he said, but we have to educate about the link to domestic.

What he called 'the grievance case' – that our involvement in Iraq and Afghanistan caused this – is a form of madness. We had UN backing for Afghanistan, 9/11 was real. We tried negotiation with Iran and Syria. And what do they do? Support the terrorism. So we were really back to keep making the case. He felt we had to stop the talk of dates and departure, and challenge the party to say if there is to be a new direction, what is it? They will come back to the basic policy positions we have. If there are others with a different direction, let them be clear what it is. He also felt the reason it had been so important that people like JR and Hutton had been defending TB as well as they had was because if we allowed people to say TB = NL, that it starts and finishes with him, then we are dead. We have to bring on a new generation of New Labour voices. He felt the Tories were vulnerable to attack, and so are the Lib Dems and we were missing tricks in not going for them.

Wednesday 29 August

TB called late 29th. Said the first week had been all work and the *Mail* bothering them everywhere they went. Last nine days a great rest. But in no doubt we were in for a difficult phase. Said the party seemed intent on making a mess of things. He'd spoken to GB and it was 'grisly'. Not interested in a policy debate, just wants a transition ASAP. He sounded pretty down. Didn't yet know what the message for conference would be as it was too early to tell exactly where the mood would be. Agreed to meet tomorrow at Chequers.

Thursday 30 August

Drove down to Chequers with PG and Sally. Agreed that things were really bad now, worse than ever, and we had to agree the exit strategy. Agreed best to hold fire for a while, get proper assessment of the mood, let the carping and criticising develop, and then try to set the pre-conference tone. However, as we were driving down, TB was doing an interview with *The Times*, which would have as the topline him refusing to say any more re departure. It was misreading the mood and going to over provoke. I could tell he was nervous about it by the number of times he mentioned it when we got there. Sal and PG were trying to persuade me to go to the Lords but I was half feeling I wanted right out of it all, and I certainly didn't want to go to the Lords. They liked it for different reasons but when I said, 'Come on, can you really see me in there?' Sally did say, 'No, you're probably right.' But she said if he was going to tough it out much longer, I would have to get more active, and he would have to start listening more.

We arrived, nice sunny day, security tighter than ever, TB out on the steps in sleeveless running vest and sports gear. He had been working out. He asked me to go upstairs while he ran a bath. He said his most recent conversations with GB had been terrible, and he was clearly going for a big push. In the last two days he hadn't even returned calls. It was embarrassing, he said, calling the switchboard and asking if the Chancellor had been found yet. When we joined the others, he slightly misread what we were saying about an exit strategy as a combined call on him to go sooner than he had been planning. In fact we were saying he should create space but also take by surprise, possibly by saying at conference he would be gone by spring and in the meantime there was clearly going to have to be a contest. Time and again he was giving what he saw as evidence of GB's unreasonableness. He felt on NI [Northern Ireland], MEPP and pensions, plus the health and education reforms embedding, he had a very good reason to be there for another year say, but not beyond. That too, he felt, should be reasonable, but was not necessarily seen as such by others.

JoP was being pretty jihadic re GB, said we were all mad if we thought he was the right man to take over. Where I felt he had a point was that TB's cred would take another hit if he was visibly forced out but then also backing GB. And the party was going to be in a very bad way by the end of this. He felt GB was panicking, that he knew Cameron was making inroads, that if too much exposure fell on him, the desire and demand for a contest would open, and there would be trouble ahead for him. PG was convinced there had to be a contest. Sally and Liz, despite both knowing his weaknesses, felt David Miliband may have to be the man, or AJ, anyone but GB. It was all incredibly depressing. CB came out and to add to the end of an era feeling, TB said we should all have our picture taken together, which we did. A group of spads and No. 10

staff then came down by bus for a reception. TB asked us to stay and talk to them a bit. All a bit down. There was definitely the feel of things coming to a pretty bad end. I asked TB if he was enjoying the job at all. He said he felt there were things he had to do, but the honest answer was No. However much he conceded, GB wanted more. He didn't just want to force him out, he wanted to see him humiliated too.

Saturday 2 September

A bit like the old days in that Saturday morning was a stack of conference calls, including with TB and Peter M. TB called from Balmoral. He said he was at a loss really to know how to resolve the next stages. Felt pretty sure now GB was going to go for it. He knew *The Times* had not come out right. The only question was whether he did need to add via briefing that it was his last conference. Andrew Smith was out on the airwaves saying it was debilitating and destabilising and had to be brought to an end. There was no way he was doing that without GB's knowledge, I suspected. After a conference call with PM, Ben and Liz, Peter M came on again to bemoan the operation, said nothing had been written down, they had drifted into doing *The Times* without thinking it through. GB was running a thought-through campaign and No. 10 people were running around like headless chickens. We had to work through everything in a systematic way, as he and I would have done. But it wasn't happening. Just a series of random calls.

Sunday 3 September

Jamie Redknapp sorted tickets for Brazil v Argentina [Emirates Stadium] so I took Calum. It was so nice to get away and not be talking about politics. Out for dinner with Philip, Gail etc. Gail's first outing for ages. She and Fiona pressing us on how bad things had been at Chequers, both having said bad.

Monday 4 September

Took Grace to the stables then drove to Stapleford Park, where I was doing an after-dinner speech. Simon Clegg [CEO, British Olympic Association] was the other speaker. I liked him, and he had a great fact – Team GB's last five Golds at Athens – the four man rowing team, Chris Hoy in the 1km time trial, Kelly Holmes's two, plus the 4 x 1 relay, a total of 13 mins 2 seconds of endeavour. Combined winning margin 0.545 seconds. Brilliant. Nice do, well organised etc. But getting asked about all the old stories all the time was just reminding me I was not where probably I ought to be, and therefore feeling pretty hopeless about it, not least because the TB stuff was clearly heading into full on frenzy mode.

Tuesday 5 September

I enjoyed crisis management session with a big tech company, which Steve Norris had sorted. But the meltdown in Westminster was well advanced, with a letter from MPs to TB asking him to go gathering pace, and another one doing the rounds about him at least setting timetable. The talk was that Sion Simon and Chris Bryant [Labour MPs] were driving it but they wouldn't be flying solo. The mobile reception was crap and at one point I looked down and saw half a dozen missed calls, four of them from PG. Later I spoke to TB, who was up in York making a speech, who said it was absolutely grisly. He said he had no doubt GB was behind most if not all of it and it was a peculiarly brutal form of negotiation. TB felt he was banking on his basic decency, that he – TB – would still want to do the right and least damaging thing. He asked what advice I had. I felt he had to try to rise above it, resolve with GB if he could, but it is now unthinkable there should not be a meaningful contest. I was being inundated with media calls, refusing them all.

Feeling neither in nor out. Kevin Spacey called out of the blue, basically asking what the hell was going on? He said most Americans looked at TB and couldn't understand why he got so much grief. Alan Milburn called, saying TB was going to have to be clearer about his plans. On the other hand, he felt that GB was destroying himself. Tessa called from China suggesting I go out and state the obvious, which is that we were in danger of destroying ourselves. Nightmare time. It felt like the election was being lost day by day. David M was out on the media and did an OK job calming it down, but just saying that he thought a year was 'reasonable', even that added to the sense that everything and everyone was focused on TB's departure.

Wednesday 6 September

Session with David S. Dreams chaotic and confused. Things getting out of hand on the political front, adding to the depression. Tom Watson [defence under-secretary] having written to TB urging him to resign and end the speculation, and having resigned as a minister, the sense of decay was setting in. That too was adding to my depression. Letters to TB from MPs, plus a handful of PPSs, were building the pressure, but also shifting a bit towards – finally – where was GB in all this? TB had no doubt at all he was orchestrating it as a way of putting on pressure to negotiate TB's earlier departure and the terms on which he stayed. Alan Milburn called, said it was like something out of *The Sopranos*. I wanted to go out and do media, hit the message that these people were unlearning all the lessons of recent years and handing the election on a plate to Cameron, but JoP and DH were both a bit hesitant. The feeling was of mild panic and not knowing what to do. They were getting out more measured voices but the damage being done was severe.

I met Kate G for a chat, mix of how awful it was and her life etc., then Liz and PG, at the Trafalgar Hotel. Philip was keen for us to get a written strategy down, as too much was happening in a state of flux. TB had seen GB twice. She said the first meeting was awful, the second less so. Liz wanted to know what we thought of the next steps. I still felt TB had to try to rise above as best he could, not concede too much, build other voices to create space pre-conference. Then he needed to make a speech only he could make – on how we did what we did, how to win the next election too – but make clear he won't be there beyond this conference. I felt there might be a case for saying he was going sooner. Also I was beginning to think for his own credibility he should distance himself from being so tied in to GB position, but that may not be possible. I felt recent events showed once more GB's lack of genuine leadership, and also that the public just would not take as credible a TB endorsement of GB when they felt he was at least in some ways responsible for his downfall. All very grim.

Did the LRF triathlon and marathon awards. Really nice event and as a couple of the winners weren't there, I used Grace and Sissy [Bridge] to collect a couple as a way of showing there were survivors too. Nice to see Lindsay who was looking really well. The doctor who looked after both Sissy and Ellie [Lindsay's daughter], though, had his own son struck down with it on holiday, aged fourteen. A guy there really pressing me to try to do an Ironman [long-distance triathlon]. Just don't know. I got home and took a closer look at all the Tom Watson stuff. Full on, even harsher in a way than the news had been reporting it. No longer in the interests of the party or the government for him to stay. He was being described as a Blairite, but the argument and the messaging had GB all over it.

Thursday 7 September

Papers pretty grisly for TB, and talk of as many as a hundred MPs ready to back calls on him to go. Far too much on the ins and outs of his two meetings with GB yesterday. It was almost like watching a particularly tough NI crisis session. G and C back to school. I was reading up on Mel Brooks, ahead of the LRF event. PG sent me over the tough note I had sent to GB a while back, having marked up key sections and commented alongside, 'If only he had done this.' Spoke to TB later who said in one particularly surreal moment, GB had suggested that TB needed to do more to make introductions to other leaders. 'He basically tells me I have ruined his life and so now I am supposed to tootle around the world saying here is my pal, be nice to him.' TB was having to concede, to make clear this would be his last conference. He also apologised to the public for the feuding in the party. The last few days had been truly dreadful. I went out for a run, stacks of media bids as I went, ignored them all. I hadn't even got as far as the corner of the road when I was stopped by a delivery driver who said I must be glad I'm out. He said it was awful for the party and awful for the country, and a terrible way to treat 'someone we have elected'. He said GB was no more electable than Neil, and drove off, tooting his horn. Then by the time I got to the Heath, Alex called. Awful for the party, he said, just as the van driver had. And awful for Britain. What a shower, what a mess. He said he was down to do a couple of party events in the coming weeks but he was pulling out, said he was not going to do things for people who treated TB like this. He said he felt sure GB could have stopped all this earlier if he had wanted to; then off on one about who the fuck did these people think they were, Watson, Bryant etc?

Then Brendan Foster was another one calling to say all this was terrible, these people were total pygmies pumped up with their own importance because they knew they could get on the telly if they played into this idea that he had to go. He said to pass on a message saying he hoped to see TB go out on the steps of No. 10, say, 'Fuck the lot of you,' then walk back inside and make clear he had no intention of leaving any time soon. At least it raised a laugh with TB when I told him. 'It is tempting, but might be seen as somewhat provocative in the circumstances.' It was all very depressing, and probably the worst possible time to come off the medication, but having felt OK over most of the summer, and having nagged David S that I didn't really want to become stuck on medication, he had agreed we give it a try. GB went out today to say it was up to TB when to go, but even if the words on paper could just about have been taken as supportive, the tone and the context came over as more menacing.

TB then did his 'This will be my last conference' line on a school visit in London. He was looking pretty down, though I guess they were the clips the broadcasters took. It was done now, he was another step closer to the exit door, and I couldn't help feeling in a bizarre sort of way the public were thinking it was better for him but worse for the party. One or two, like Graham Stringer and Doug Henderson [Labour MPs] were still on saying he needed to go further. But I think for the public, he had probably gone far enough. GB did a clip up in Scotland, saying all a matter for TB, and Peter M was out saying Labour had had its 'moment of madness' – that one again! – and now needed to get on with governing. Slept p.m. then out to a Standard Life event at the House of Lords. Norman Blackwell [Tory peer, former advisor to Thatcher and Major] was hosting it. The speech went OK but I did a Q&A which got a bit out of hand, and all they really wanted to hear about was Labour meltdown.

Friday 8 September

Things were turning a bit against GB now, as people focused a bit more on what had happened, and how. There was definitely the beginnings of a backlash and the talk starting of who else might emerge now TB had clarified a bit on timings. I was due to have lunch with Ed Victor but TB called me in for a meeting, him, JoP, PG and Sally. Just as I was arriving I got a call from Sue Nye to say GB wanted to speak to me. I had a cup of tea first with Liz who said that despite it all TB was now back into GB cooperation mode. Charles Clarke had done an interview attacking GB who realised he got himself into a bad place. Over lunch, with DH, Ruth, Ben and MD also there, lots of anecdotage about the last few days, which really had felt like close to meltdown, and there were real feelings against GB. I briefly saw Gus [O'Donnell] who said he felt GB would realise he had really mishandled things. He dreaded what Cabinet meetings would be like. There was just too much bitterness around. Too much nastiness. He felt TB had been reasonable but GB couldn't cope with more delay, couldn't hold back.

In the smaller meeting, outside on the terrace, we went over things, trying to work back from TB's exit. His current thinking was to go after the Scots and Welsh elections, but announce before. Then the contest after. At the moment he felt GB was OK with that. He was still of the view he could not be seen to do anything that stopped GB or got a contest going. And on balance, despite everything, he saw nobody who would so obviously be better, or who was ready. So despite it all it was best to try to help him get it. If someone emerged or made things different, we would see, but he doubted it would happen. He also felt that on current showing GB did not have a prayer against Cameron. Our only hope was that he would become a different person once he got the top job. Maybe, once he was released from the burning ambition, and the desire to see him off, and he was gone, GB would grow into it. But it was all a bit unlikely.

TB had seen David M last night to discuss conference but he didn't think DM had it in him to go for it. He thought JR might wield the knife at some point, just because he felt so strongly GB was wrong for it, and if that happened it was possible DM would come in. I had spoken to Louise last night and said I felt David had to rethink, and at least decide in himself whether he felt he might go for it, because it could all be happening sooner than we think. If he reached a view that GB was in danger of being unelectable, then he had to think about going for it. PG was emphasising the need to build on the new tone of yesterday. He felt actually that for all it had been humiliating on one level, the public saw a side of TB yesterday that they knew they would miss. Certainly that is what I had picked up anecdotally. Reasonable people felt those out to kill him were being deeply unreasonable. It gave him an opportunity to get back on the side of the people.

We went through ideas for his Progress [Labour pressure group] speech – a new leader will face new challenges. Labour of today not the same as '94 because world so different. Need to become more reflective, go over lessons of leadership, try to show why we have the right ideas and can therefore be more confident. We covered a lot of ground and actually the mood was good. He said there was a part of him that felt liberated by what had happened. He knew in his own mind when he was going and we could work back. He also was clear what he wanted to do – embed NHS reforms, build a critical mass on trust schools, keep NI moving forward, another go at Palestine, pensions, energy and so forth. I felt he needed to zone in on one or two, not look like he was rushing around. But he was on much better form. The office felt more relaxed though a lot of them would need to start going for jobs and so on. He still felt GB was not right for the top job yet felt it probably had to be.

He also had to disabuse himself of the notion there would not be a debate on policy. He should engage on it, use it for dividing lines with the Tories and so on. Nice meeting. A lot better than a week ago. He was now settled in his own mind on a departure date and if he could survive that long he could push his own agenda. The Tom Watson brigade would feel on the one hand they had achieved what they set out to, in that TB was now more clearly on the way out. But in truth they had been expecting him to go much sooner, and those who had quit would be straight back in government. All madness really. A spasm that went wrong. GB had a lot of recovering to do. But TB knew his own authority was badly dented too.

I got home to collect Calum and head north [to Burnley]. Neil called urging me to speak to GB. GB was trying to reach me and sensed I was not wanting to talk. Neil said his own feeling was that TB had not deserved any of this but also that GB was not directly behind it in the way that we thought. He felt both were damaged by recent events and both needed support. GB called as I was halfway up the motorway to Mum's. Small talk and jokey chat about football. He was in no doubt about the damage done. He was doing an interview with Marr tomorrow and he was looking for advice. On recent events he described it as a series of happenings that just got totally out of hand. He denied fuelling it, said this was not in his interest. He felt trust as ever had been the problem. But he now recognised we were damaged, both of them, and had to put it together.

He was angling to get me to commit to support him and also work for him. He was also admitting there had been problems in the past. And he was making clear he wanted to branch out in terms of the people he had around him. I said I felt the last few days had been especially humiliating for TB, and I sensed the public mood would become harsher on him – GB – quite quickly if he was identified as having caused all this. I said people would find it hard to believe Andrew Smith, Watson, all the rest, were operating off their own back. But anyway, we are where we are. TB has said he is going. I told him about the chat we had had about him, where TB was clear he had doubts, but ultimately he saw nobody else and he would help him. It was a fairly tense, quite spiky conversation. I felt he was worried that I was totally buying the line he had orchestrated the whole thing. I did say to him that in the end I was driven by a desire for TB to go when he wanted, and go out well, and for Labour to win the next election, and if he was leader, I would help him. He said we had the same interests and we must not let recent days get in the way of that. But fuck me, I said, what a mess, and what a way to go about it all.

Saturday 9 September

David M called. I had said to Louise I felt he should seriously think about being ready to stand but David felt there was no way he would get it and it might all just be very divisive. He felt TB had to accept a lot of the responsibility for recent events even if he didn't deserve to be treated like this. He agreed it was potentially election-losing stuff. To the match. Terrible. Lost 2–1 v Colchester. Did MUTV interview for Alex twenty years tribute programme.

Sunday 10 September

GB called again. He felt *Marr* had been OK. But he said we were in a hole and we had to get out of it. He had talked to TB yesterday about ways of working together on a possible policy process for the next phase. He claimed he had not been pushing TB, that last week was not acrimonious. He felt TB's *Times* interview was a mistake, as did I, but he said he had been willing to go out and say it should be up to TB alone when he goes. He was not involved in the way people were saying, the thing just took on a momentum of its own. 'Come on Gordon, you could have stopped it.' 'I don't think I could.' He also knew he had to reach out to people. He felt that Charles had gone OTT with his attacks on his psychology but even with him, he had said on Marr he was willing to bring in critics as well as supporters. He said he was not asking me for support for the leadership right now but he did I hope I could influence people to stop behaving divisively.

He said we have had ours ups and downs. Sometimes he had felt aggrieved at things I had said and done. Sometimes I had felt aggrieved at his making Tony's and my life more difficult. But he felt there had always been mutual respect between us and I commanded a lot of respect from the politicians, and none of that had been changed by anything. He was asking me to help him put things into a better place. I said I felt the last few days had damaged him, Tony and the party. To recover we had to think short-term – up to conference. Medium term – leadership election/transition. And longer-term – the election v the Tories. He said he still felt he was the best person after TB to take on Cameron. He intended to make his conference speech more personal and he hoped I would help with that. He felt his passion for education and his real belief in the power of community, and his experience on the economy, these were all strengths against DC. But he knew he had weaknesses as well as strengths and he knew I could help with both.

So he hoped I could see beyond the badness of recent days, and see a role for myself helping him. He knew recent events were bad but we had time. He wanted me to try to get Alan Milburn, Steve Byers and even Peter to help in all this. He had said in the interview anyone who wanted to stand should stand but he didn't feel that a Brown v 'I am a true Blairite' contest would help anyone. He sounded a mix of firm and also slightly pleading. He said whatever happens I want you to phone me if you think I'm doing something wrong, or missing something. I want to keep a diaolgue going. I want your help in getting to a better place. I said he felt he could be more expansive about how he saw future challenges, also stuff from his own background.

Alex called. He had been calling regularly. I asked what he thought of me getting involved with GB. He said don't do it. You are so allied to Tony and you've clearly got doubts. He had doubts too re GB, felt he would now forever be known as the No. 2 who knifed the No. 1 and it was probably best if he made way for someone else, just stepped aside. It is not going to happen, I said, he will be there, it is virtually certain, and I feel if it is him v Cameron, I have to help him if I can. We had a chat about Roy Keane. He felt he had what it took in so many ways but he had demons in there and they would come out. He was actually someone who didn't like people that much unless they met his own standards. He said he was pleased with Carrick so far. Sounded quite chirpy but said he felt really bad for TB, and felt that GB was trying to have his cake and eat it if he was pushing him out and then expecting me to help him.

Monday 11 September

TB in Beirut, hounded by protesters pretty much everywhere he went, and several ministers apparently refused to see him. The Iraqi Parliament Speaker also made a point of leaving town for the day. TB looked pretty beleaguered on the clips I saw, though making all the usual points with the usual vigour. He had been willing to meet the Hezbollah guys who were in the Cabinet, but they refused. The rhetoric against him was pretty heavy. He got a better reception in Israel and the West Bank, though there was a bit of a demo in Ramallah. He sent through his TUC speech for me to have a look at and when he called later, he said, 'At least today will help prepare me for tomorrow.'Dinner at Magdy Ishak's. Bunch of Tories really. He had been pressing me to join a private equity firm board as a non-exec. Really not my thing.

Tuesday 12 September

Really wrestling with the diaries decision now. Tricky as hell. I was due to see Nick Butler but he cancelled last minute. I suspected the BP thing would disappear. Then to party HQ to do a pep talk for the press team. PG and I tried our best – usual stuff re creativity and strategy etc. but it was a depleted group and the energy felt a bit low. Think we got them better directed. Clearly all felt we needed a contest. I was pushing the idea of conference being where we put it all together. TB wasn't far wrong about his reception at the TUC. The speech wasn't a bad speech, very much part of his 'educate about globalisation' mindset, good on Labour record and values, but a bit flat, probably too foreign policy focused, and anyway the way it was set up the reaction was going to be the main story, with a staged walk out by Bob Crow [general secretary, Rail, Maritime and Transport Union] et al, a bit of heckling on his stuff on schools, again when he hit back at the idea that Bush was more dangerous than Islamic terrorism, and protests outside and inside about Iraq and Afghanistan.

GB put out something attacking the people who walked out when they had the chance to ask questions, but it all felt a bit forced. Added to which he did an interview talking about how Tony was his friend, always had been, always would be, and again it just felt inauthentic. I said to TB at least you can be sure it will be your last leader's speech to the TUC. That ought to make you feel a bit happier about the future. 'Definitely a bit of a relief.' He said he actually at one point almost got a fit of the giggles when he looked out, was listing all the things we had done for working people, and all he could see was a load of big blokes waving 'Blair out' placards, 'Time to go', with the 'o' in 'go' just a great big spattering of blood. 'They don't like me much, do they?'

Wednesday 13 September

Lunch with Endemol. Desperate for me to get involved in some way maybe on a political programme. Then to the Wolseley to interview Mel Brooks for the *Times* piece to promote the LRF event. Really liked him. Not just the obvious – funny – but empathetic and sharp as hell. A pretty brutal piece in *The Economist* on our travails, and turning much more towards GB and raising doubts about what he would be like as PM. The idea that Tom Watson's trip to GB's home in Fife was all about taking a present for Fraser [GB's young son] was all adding to the farce really. But hidden in the piece was the message, and one I had been worrying about, that DC might just be one of those guys who gets lucky.

Thursday 14 September

Spoke at a sports sponsorship seminar. Quite interesting, and got into a good barney about the growing role of alcohol in sports sponsorship, and said I felt one day it would go the same way as smoking. It didn't go down well but led to a good discussion. GB had done a Sky interview and was talking about the little girl he and Sarah lost, and looked close to tears at one point. TB said Cabinet had been 'a bit weird. Everyone knows the plates have shifted but nobody really knew whether they were meant to be the same, different, or indifferent. It was all quite odd really.'

Friday 15 September

Down to Wentworth all day to watch the golf. Major staring going on. Mum down for the weekend.

Saturday 16 September

Long run. Mum and Audrey shopping. Tessa's party. Mainly talking to Matthew [Mills], who is such a laugh. Then to La Casalinga. Doing very little work. TB asking me to start motoring on his conference speech.

Sunday 17 September

TB called as I was out on the bike going to see Grace at the stables. He was getting down to rewrite the conference speech and was basically on the theme on being there for the people. How we lose touch when we cease to be there addressing their concerns. He felt the real problem recently was that people were looking inward not outward and it was all leading to us losing touch. He wanted the in-touch line to run through the speech. I said the big problem with that, which maybe had to be addressed head on, was that on Iraq – the reason why some felt he was being kicked out of the door – people felt he had not listened. He said listening and leadership were not always the same thing. In the end we are elected to make the big decisions and many will be unpopular but that is what we have to do.

He wanted me to work on that section in particular. He called again later to reiterate the point about being there for the people. Once they think we are more interested in the party than them, the public, we are in trouble. On GB he knew he had said a lot of the right things this week, but it underlined the basic problem. He knew he had fucked up in letting the meltdown go too far, and his way of rescuing his own position, he thought, was to say how much he liked and admired TB. 'People aren't daft. The ones in the know know, and the ones not in the know aren't daft, they work it out.' Similarly, he said, they had obviously decided GB needed a strategy to make himself look more human, and it just doesn't work like that.

A good meeting with Ed Victor. We had decided on yes to the single volume, and yes to editing to protect GB, and yes to being honest about doing so. It meant I would be in the mix after TB went, it would probably make the first one do way better than subsequent ones, but I felt much more comfortable doing it this way. It had taken us a long while to get here, Ed had enjoyed labeling me his most complicated client but to varying degrees all of us, me, him, Richard, Gail and her team, felt OK about where it was heading. Ed wanted to try to use it to renegotiate the money side of things.

Monday 18 September

I was out for lunch with some of the Random House team, and a guy came over, said he was a pro boxer, certainly looked like it, and he said, 'I love other fighters and you are a fighter.' He had a bottle of wine with him and gave it to me, said it was all he had as a gift because he didn't know he would see me there today. Then he came up with a great line on TB. 'Everyone is asking when he's going – I say why?' David Mellor was also in the restaurant, and I had a little chat with him. Then over to Notting Hill where I was doing a Q&A with Freud staff as a favour to PG and Matthew. I enjoyed it, good crowd, though I could not believe how many of the women smoked.

Tuesday 19 September

Golf all day. Over to see Jamie Rubin and down to Queenwood. Tessa told me she had seen Andy Marr who told her – presumably based on something GB said when he was in there last week – that he was 100 per cent sure GB would ask me to work for him. Had certainly got close but I was not sure how I would react if he went the whole hog, given I had been clear I wouldn't go back full-time for TB. Added to which though I just about managed to keep reasonable relations with some of GB's people, mainly the Eds, and actually had come to see a much better side to Ed B, others like McBride were beyond the pale for me. GB called when I was out on the course, and we arranged to speak later. I was on form, actually had a little run where I went par, birdie, par, birdie, but then collapsed. It was me and Jamie against David and Matthew Mills, with them giving us shots, and we won 2 and 1. David and Matt seemed to me to be longing for Tessa to get out of it all, though she was probably locked in for the Olympics. There was definitely case for a generational shift, but I don't think the David M generation was up for it, mainly because GB seemed to have it all locked up.

Wednesday 20 September

Up early. Meeting Martin Gilbert and Moir Lockheid [executives] at Euston to go over FirstGroup problems. Agreed to a bigger picture plan, also Tim Allan to do hands on stuff. Lunch with Brendan and his colleagues prior to their meeting with Tessa and Dick re the Great Run plan. Brendan going on about how awful the *Panorama* on Sam Allardyce had been, all innuendo no evidence. I decided to do a piece on it. Brendan another one who was really down on GB, saying he would find it harder to call on people for support, and also once TB was gone, they would realise what they had lost. Ed Victor saying to me that I should be trying to find another leadership contender. Gail came back with a fairly generous offer based on early single volume.

Bruce came round pm. He felt TB was now totally weakened and should go soon. He said at Cabinet people now basically looked towards GB not him. That was not what PG said, having done his polling presentation to a group of ministers this morning. Bruce felt everyone had to shut up and make it happen for GB. He said he really felt I should go in there and help him. He said it is duty time again. 'I know you have your doubts, and I know you are sorting out a new life, but he is going to need a lot of help.' I said I was very ambivalent. Told him why. As he knew, TB could always at least motivate and was good to work with. He also let me get on and build my own team, and get them motivated too. GB was very different. He had a culture around him I didn't like.

We were all grown up and we knew politics was tough, and we know politicians sometimes have to be devious and all the rest. But

I never felt in TB's inner circle that we didn't have a basic trust and a basic commitment to being truthful with each other. I never sensed that with GB's team. There were just too many times where it all boiled down to 'It wasn't me, guv.' The Tom Watson thing was just the latest. Did they seriously think we were supposed to think that was all just some kind of random osmosis, and then all of a sudden Tom is driving hundreds of miles for the urgent task of giving some books and a jig-saw to Fraser? We were laughing about it, and I love Bruce to bits, but he knew what I meant. 'Ali, my old son, that is all spot on, no doubt. But here is the thing – do we want a Tory Prime Minister, or a Labour Prime Minister?' As ever, he knew how to get me. PG sent me through the note I had sent to GB several months earlier warning of the way tougher scrutiny was exposing his weaknesses and he needed to act to deal with it. If he had, he could have been in a very different position. But Bruce clear I should work for GB or go into the Lords on the back of TB resignation.

Thursday 21 September

Out for a run then to see PG and go over a few things. He felt I could do the single diary early but not then work for GB. He felt GB had really damaged himself because he had been involved and it meant working to help him would be working to damage TB. He felt we were best placed giving really strong honest advice to GB. Truth was most people who knew him now felt he was the wrong person. But if we sought to help TB now that was the best posture for us throughout it. He said TB was actually rising in the polls again. GB could be in trouble if he fucked up at conference. I sent through note to JoP on the core argument, felt there had to be more to it than TB's thing about being there for people. Also, given the build-up, he could really afford for once to be more personal.

Friday 22 September

Richard was having second thoughts about the single volume. He felt there was a real integrity issue. He was also emerging as ever more angry about GB. Having just read the diaries, and then followed recent events, he said he just could not see why I was thinking of protecting his reputation. 'If I were you, I'd be tempted to put the whole thing out there now, and watch him get destroyed.' I said but that is because you have always been a proper journalist in a way that I stopped being a long time ago. PG sent me through a polling graph – echoed in *The Guardian* today – showing that GB had dived since the so-called coup attempt. The public saw him very differently and he was going to have to work very hard to rebuild, as we had both warned him. PG kept referring back to that note I sent GB. He said he had it on his wall, and every day GB was paying the price for not doing the things we advised him to.

Long drive up with Rory to the hotel in Wakefield. Spoke to Alex. Asking re TB and how he is. Still very down on GB. PG sent me a new poll on possible leadership contenders. GB big dip since the Tom Watson fiasco. Really not in good shape. Spike downwards. Chatted to Rory re my various dilemnas on timing of books and can I work for GB etc? He has a very good take. Basically felt best to do as complete books. Can only work for GB if nothing published. Didn't like the idea of a sanitised version. TB called after sending through a new draft. 'True believer' as top line. Still very focused on facing out not in. Said GB still messing about. Felt challenges important and needs to be tough and rigorous.

Saturday 23 September

Out for a run round a little country park then gym. JP called. 'So you're back in the game then?' he said about the *Mirror* piece. I said not really but I felt it needed saying that we were not operating as we should be. He said he imagined I felt really down. I said I hadn't enjoyed the last couple of weeks but felt it could be put back together. All depended as ever on TB–GB willingness. He said he had had it out with GB. He said there was no way he wasn't involved in it all. He had Balls etc. winding him in the wrong direction to do the wrong things.

JP was angry at a piece in the *Mirror* saying the party didn't want him to do his usual closing speech. He felt he had to. He was planning to say he had been proud to have been part of it, when we unite we are strong etc. Signal his last too. But he was with me in feeling we had to keep off the agenda of future leadership. He said he felt a bit down about things and knew he was in a different position himself. I said we need to have a good GB speech, not least re TB, TB has to be at his best, Clinton will be great, plus we need some decent speeches from some of the younger ones and JP wind up. The whole thing has to be about reconnecting with the public. He said TB–GB had both been at it, and he sensed they knew it had to stop. They were laying lines for war if not careful. Need to shut it down. He said he felt we had a shared agenda and he wanted to meet tonight to get a feel for how to make the week go better.

Off to Zoe's halls of residence then to Burnley 2, Southampton 3. Great match. To Manchester and up to see TB in his suite at the Radisson. He was in an odd frame of mind, and so was I. He said he couldn't quite get the atmospherics on the speech, and I was basically just finding it really hard to get my head into being there, and in these circumstances. As ever he was obsessing about the core argument. He wanted me to come up with a phrase that was the today global equivalent of economic efficiency and social justice. In the area of inter-connectedness. How threats were now global. He could tell I was not up for it, but he said, 'I need your best mind on this. This speech has to work, has to be good.' He was about to see GB. He said he was still of the view he could help GB become leader but he needed a proper strategy, and he felt we were the best people to help him get it, though he couldn't see it. He was getting bad advice and taking the worst bits. And even after all the ups and downs of recent weeks, where he knew he had been hit too, he was still pushing on him, trying to force him out early.

We worked on the speech for a bit, partly message, then the first half line by line, but I was finding it hard to get the will and the drive that I knew I needed if I was going to add anything by way of real value. I was definitely moving to this being the last. I saw GB briefly and we had the usual chat about football, and then he said he would like to meet up later, 'if you have time.' He and TB had a short meeting, I saw TB afterwards, he said the mood was not great. He felt GB was panicking, he didn't really know what to do. Still playing the old tunes. We then had several attempts trying to rewrite different parts of the speech. He was doing most of the writing himself, I was honing and rewriting, and there was lots of decent stuff but it was not yet hanging together as a speech. As ever, he kept having to pop out for various conference functions, and he said he was getting a terrific reception around the place. He said there was a lot of warmth and emotion and again we had to decide how much of that to play into. I didn't feel I was contributing much. I did a section for the opening and for the end, but I wasn't enjoying myself. I was also resisting any efforts to get me to get out and about. Even coming into the hotel, I had felt I really didn't want to get caught up in the whole circus that was building.

Sunday 24 September

More of the same. Did a bit of speech work. I felt we were coming at it the wrong way round. We were honing and polishing sections, without being clear what the bigger framework was that we were trying to shape and play into. The only decent section I did was on 'the core vote is the country', and a bit on aspiration and compassion being reconciled, and social justice and economic efficiency between partners and drivers of progress. It was getting there, better than yesterday. TB did a new delivery section which was a lot stronger and we had a neat passage on how we had unbanned things that should never have been banned, and banned things which should never have been allowed. Around the office everyone was talking about GB, and it was all getting tedious to listen to. Margaret McDonagh wandered in at one point and said she wouldn't be surprised if people started chanting, 'Four more years'. The general mood around TB did seem to be OK, but he was getting totally fixated on the idea that the speech had to be one of his best.

We had a lot of words now, but no speech. So I spent part of the morning trying to discard stuff we didn't really need, and hoping if we got it slimmed down we would get nearer to seeing wood for trees, and having the core argument to drive through. Two good sessions with TB. We had a chat about how to address the GB issue in the speech. He was going to say something nice about JP at the top, but we had to decide whether, when he went into 'This is the last conference speech I'll do', he talked about GB in that context. In the end I drafted two or three different ways of doing it, and the one that worked best was the one where he just talked him up as he always had done – a big figure, a big part of New Labour, a big part of our success, and leave the audience to take a pretty clear message. Over dinner CB was in a spiky mood, definitely had me as one of the people to blame for letting GB force him to make the statement he had made, constantly having a go at GB and saying there as lots left in TB yet. She overheard us having a chat about the GB section, and asked straight out, 'You're not endorsing him in the speech, are you?' and he did one his little 'shush' shakes of the head.

We did a bit more after dinner, then I met Tessa and Peter M for a little chat, which was dispiriting because like so many other chats around the place it was all so internalising. We were running the line in interviews, agreed for TB's *Marr* interview, that we were facing out not in, out to the public not in to the party, and so no discussion of the leadership issues. But of course all around the place that is really what people were talking about. On the few occasions I ventured downstairs, or out to get a bit of fresh air, it really wasn't a great atmosphere. I was getting pounced on by hacks and snappers and to be honest I didn't really have anything to say. I was there to help on the speech and that was about it. Andrew Marr had done a documentary on GB, and most of the office watched it, and told us it was pretty soft-soap stuff. But TB was still saying despite everything – though not in front of CB – that it had to be GB. Nobody else had the reach. The weekend polls were not good for GB though. He had definitely taken a hit on the coup stuff.

Monday 25 September

Call from JP to see him later. TB working on speech. I did him a little note saying that if he did the 'GB big part of past success' section, that could act as a pivot to stuff on future challenges, almost as him passing the baton, but saying the challenges were different and greater and here is my advice on what we need to do to deal with them. It made it much more reflective and he went for it, and we did a fairly big rewrite through the day. I had a long chat with Bruce when TB had to go out, and I was being much more open about GB and his failings. Frank Luntz [US commentator and strategist] was busy hyping his *Newsnight* focus groups which showed GB in a state of collapse with swing voters. Luntz was convinced that John Reid was the one we should go for. The public felt he got their concerns in a way GB didn't. TB doing most of the speech himself, just polishing and honing lines and working on the central arguments, once we got the basic shape sorted, and he was happy with the opening, the ending, and the tricky bits, I didn't feel I was contributing much but he was fulsome, said it made a big difference just having me there, keeping the thing going in the right direction, and keeping people calm.

I saw JP in his suite before GB's speech. He was looking tired and fed up. He said that he felt there was nothing much more to do to bind TB–GB together. It all ran too deep. GB WAS involved in the plot to push him out. And TB feels bitter and angry. I don't blame him. It was terrible and he rightly feels put-upon. But I think he has had it in some ways. He can't do all this policy review stuff. It just undermines his successor. He was really down on the whole show. Then he was asking me whether he should say sorry (about the affair) on Thursday, and how. I felt he had to be careful not to go OTT, not to have it all about that, and lose the opportunity for a bigger political message. Then up for another session with TB, and we were coming and going on it all day, but it was pretty much done, provided there was no major panic. GB's speech was OK but not one of his best. He did a little bit of mea culpa, regrets we've had a few, but in the sense of badness on both sides. Needless to say he went OTT re how great TB was, and set a lot of the future challenge stuff in the context of TB having been right about the big things, and lessons learned from the way he did it.

He also did some good personal stuff, big section on his parents which Mum said she loved when I spoke to her later, but as a whole it didn't really set the heather on fire, and his seeming determination to name-check just about every member of the Cabinet always got in the way, but it seemed to even more so this time. I didn't feel his Britishness section worked either. He was trying to be tough on immigration but also have a big outward-going message and it felt a bit muddled. But he ended well, and when he framed it as 'I relish the chance to take on Cameron', the message was pretty clear and it felt OK to most people in there. Then Bloomberg put out a line from a reporter claiming Cherie had said, 'That's a lie' on hearing GB say the line in his speech that it was a 'privilege to work with the most successful ever Labour leader and Labour PM'. She denied it but it was all too believable, the story was round and about and unstoppable. Totally taking over. I went to the gym later and bumped into GB who had been for a swim. Small talk re keeping fit. He said the Cherie thing really pained him. Then he said, 'The ultras won't stop' – Milburn, Peter M etc.

TB was now clearly of the view that he lacked the temperament for leadership, that he allowed problems to crowd in and therefore didn't lead out of trouble. He was still adamant he would help him but it wasn't clear how or whether it would work. DH and team were doing their best to calm things down re Cherie but it was a total frenzy and was going to dominate coverage entirely. DH and HC were keeping Cherie in the hotel but TB and I thought it was a bit daft and we needed to get her out there. She did a denial. I did Channel 4 and gave Jon Snow a bit of a duffing up over the way the media did politics, which most people thought was OK but Fiona said I looked so angry it was bad. Worked till maybe 1 but TB really was doing the main stuff himself now.

Tuesday 26 September
Up early. TB had done a new ending and was happier with it. I added in 'head and heart' as resonance to the '94 speech. We were also joking

around about the CB GB situation. Bruce and David Bradshaw were having a laugh about the old Les Dawson joke – 'My wife's run off with the bloke next door. I do miss him.' Then when we were going through everything – TB, JoP, Liz, Bruce, Bradders, we worked up a line around the idea that at least TB had never had that worry about CB, and we had a decent icebreaking joke at last. 'At least I don't have to worry about her running off with the bloke next door.' Cherie was fine with it, GB less so when we ran it by them later. The other issues still to resolve were how to thank JP and GB. I put in a line about TB taking New Labour to the country, JP to the party, which worked fine. He had gone for the more positive line re GB. The only discussion was whether it looked like an endorsement if he did it like that, in the context of him saying this was his last speech as leader. The office was split but in the end we agreed to keep it as it was. The rest was all tinkering and sharpening.

We had it done by 11, earlier than ever I think. Autocue rehearsal, a few changes but not many. It felt strong and was also going to be very emotional. Weird feeling it would be his last but I was glad in a way. I was glad Rory was with me and we all trooped over together, and he and I sat with Georgia. Loads of people from the '94 period as well as today's team in the same block. A few in tears. Good atmosphere. The joke at the start worked really well. He was into it easily and though the policy section flagged a little he was on great form. A few 'Don't go' banners etc. The best lines worked really well, including the attack on Cameron, and the ending was superb. They loved the line about 'If we can't beat this lot we don't deserve to be in politics'. And though he had been worried about the section on 'People think I hate the party, but what I really hate is losing', that went down a storm too. It flew by, couldn't have gone much better, got the right mix of record, forward plan, big challenge, and also good strong politics. Cameron won't have liked it much. Good videos either side of the speech.

I did a round of media. Fairly chilled apart from having a go at ITV for being *Heat* magazine and losing it later with [Peter] Allen and [Jane] Garvey on Five Live. I just hated the way they tried to drag everything down to the trivial. I was tired and bad-tempered though and probably should not have bothered doing media. But generally I was pushing the lines he was a class act, party liked him, GB would grow into it, Labour was well placed. Later Paxman and Mark Austin [ITV newsreader], both also fine. After the event a few parties. One in Kate's room but smoke awful. Office party. TB said thanks for help but I said it was all his work. Yes but it doesn't half help having you there. He felt it was good GB was asking me for help and even though there was a growing thing in the media – why on earth were they getting rid of TB, and why on earth had TB never got rid of GB?, TB said, 'He is still head and shoulders above the rest.'

I went to Les Hinton's party. I was chatting to him when GB and Sarah came in. GB said, 'Great speech, could see your handiwork.' I said it was all his own. He said, 'You're talking to me. I know the score.' Then he took me aside and said to me again I had to get back and get properly involved. This was no longer about him. It was about the party and how we stopped a rot. I was conscious of e.g. JR people and journos watching us. He said there were too many people not wanting to pull back. It wasn't the place to say the fault was on his side. I didn't say much. He said please come and see me. I can explain how to get you involved.

I had a chat with Jack Straw who seemed fine re TB but Sally said he had been getting closer to GB. I did the rounds a bit with Rory, Georgia and Nicky [Blair]. It was brilliant how the kids got on, then I left them to it and went to help David M with his speech. But I was feeling tired, drained, flat. I left him with Bradders and went to be bed.

Wednesday 27 September

TB got a great press, only the *Mail* and *Express* failing to shift out of their ruts. Generally people felt it was possibly his best yet. But the other strong line emerging was the idea that his speech had been head and shoulders above GB's or anyone else. GB was having a bad week. I went up to the office, where people were sitting round just gassing. There was too much negativity around. I told them of when Alan Clark called me once when we were in opposition and saying that we had it in the bag because they hated each other more than they hated us. There was too much doing in of colleagues around. To be fair to TB, even though he had no doubt GB was involved in the shenanigans of a few weeks ago, he was still willing to help him. But lots of others were just hoping he failed now. TB also knew GB had to listen. He needed a strategy that was inclusive and policy based. He still felt he could just fix the politics and get straight in without a contest. There would almost certainly be a contest, and probably in the end it would be better for him if there was.

At 9.30 I went to see JP re his speech. I made a joke about him not clapping enough yesterday and he said he clapped more than ever but he was also taking notes to see where he could echo TB. Usual chaos in his room with phones ringing, JP shouting, staff running round. He was adamant he had to do some kind of apology, and I advised him to refer back to TB's speech, e.g. TB said thank you, I want to say sorry. Also make clear it was his last conference as deputy leader, but do so amid an achievement section. The apology section could be very powerful and he went for it. Over to the hall and did a few interviews, then in with Rory and Georgia for the environment debate. Q&A then DM speech but it didn't really fly at all. I was waiting for a message from Sara Latham re Bill [Clinton]'s arrival. I went backstage to where I was due to meet him and there, sitting in the dark on his own, was GB. He was clearly intending to gatecrash the TB BC meeting. He asked if I was seeing him. I said yes, his people had asked me to be there when he arrived. TB must have known it was to give him a briefing on the current scene.

He then returned to last night's discussion at the News Corp do. He said things could slip away quickly if we weren't careful. He was clear that a 'Brown v ultra Blairite' contest would be a disaster. 'They would have to present me as anti-Blair, anti-reform and if no great ideological divide was there it would all come down to personality and character assassination. It would help nobody.' But don't you fear the idea of an anointment without a real debate, I asked him? He clearly didn't want the contest. Or the debate other than on his own terms. He clearly felt Peter would be a problem. Ditto Milburn and Byers. Ditto Reid who he felt was the one most likely to have a go. East Scotland v West Scotland. He asked me again to 'get involved'. In what way? Come and see me and we can talk about it. One or two people were wandering by, e.g. Polly Toynbee who had been chairing a debate session. I was conscious of people wondering whether there was some kind of growing involvement. It was going to be hard to say no, because of the duty-responsibility gene, but part of me just wanted out.

I said he had been badly damaged by the suspicion of disloyalty and he had to work at getting it back. He clearly thought it could be fixed by making out he was inclusive, but he needed a much bigger message and strategy. He didn't look up to it to me. Tired and jowelly, and offering real negative vibes the whole time. We talked for ten minutes or so. He was very nice about my involvement in the speech but not about the speech I noticed. He said the issue now was the future of the party at the election which was a bigger issue than him alone.

Off to wait for Bill. The entourage seemed bigger than usual. Into a side room and on the way out we chatted briefly. He was looking a bit tired but managed to get up for the speech needless to say. He asked how the mood was. I said it was all a bit weird because TB was on the way out, there had been a little bit of buyer's remorse yesterday, people wondering why it was all happening, but it was probably inevitable. He asked if anyone else was coming through, and I said not really. We were chatting about Ireland when TB and GB arrived. GB saw him first and said, 'Thanks for coming,' as if he was coming to see him. He said the same to the BC staff. The three of them had a five minute chat then GB had to go to the platform. All felt a bit weird. I asked Doug Band [BC advisor] if he was OK on the politics. He said he was well briefed. I was sitting with JoP watching the speech. Not his best but still bloody good and with some great lines – time for a change, you bet. You are the agents of change. DNA almost all of us identical. Success of govt. Ubuntu – African word meaning I am what I am because of who we all are. Good message.

Rory thought the speech was even better than TB's. Georgia loyal as ever, said TB best by a mile. Great seeing how well she, R and Nicky got on. Real sense of new generation. Did a couple of interviews then over to the hotel for lunch. I briefly took Rory in to say cheerio to TB and introduced him to Clinton. TB said, 'Rory is one of my last men standing, thinks I should be fighting on,' and Bill just laughed and said, 'Always good to fight on.' I was really glad to get away though. I chatted to Rory on the way back about my continuing dilemma re working for GB and timing of diaries. He said what was interesting about being there with me was seeing how clearly the big guys all seemed to look to me for support but also, he felt with TB and GB especially, a kind of validation. He said he thought I should do it, but on my own terms, which is kind of where I was heading.

Thursday 28 September

Into the West End to meet Nick Butler. The BP situation was pretty grim. He was head down in the detail, edgy, not focusing on the big picture at all. John had lost power within the company to Peter Sutherland. Nick was also going to be leaving to run an energy group but also stay on in some capacity to help JB. He said John had not wanted to be seen with me, that he was worried about the implications, of the fuss people would make if they knew I was around and helping him, and it was pretty obvious it was a very political company and there would definitely be people up for causing trouble over it. We met at a café in Greek Street, various people stopping as they walked by, and several mentioned TB's speech. Overwhelmingly positive reaction. Nick was alarmed at the slide for John. We chatted away for an hour or so, also on the way GB was coming to be seen as more of a risk in business circles whereas Cameron was seen as pretty harmless. Home, long run on the Heath then to see David S with the whole family. He had wanted to get their take, but also explain a bit about depression and make sure they understood it was not about them.

They all did well. Rory saying we had politics that had bound us closely in the past, but now we just argued about it. They could tell I was struggling to develop a new life, but they all said in different ways we were good parents and they knew how front of mind they always were in our judgements. Grace said there is no way they will ever split up. Calum and Rory both thought once TB was out of the job, I would find it easier, and David made a little joke about what Gordon would say about that. They seemed to like him and I felt a lot better that at least they knew who this guy was that I was going to see. GB called earlier, asking me to see him next week. I discussed with PG who felt I should take a lead from TB. He said they knew that I had more or less opted out from GB after the *MoS* briefing saga. He had stuck with it a bit longer but the coup attempt was something of a last straw. Alex called. The commando son of a friend from Aberdeen, Gordon Campbell, had been killed in a military training exercise. Alex close to tears, and wanted me to sort a TB letter, which I did.

Friday 29 September

I wrote a long letter for Rory before his leaving for university. For some reason I had agreed to do a lot of radio, did that, then went for a massage to sort my back. TB called later. Had a good chat. He said GB was clearly hoping just to be swept along, no contest, but it was not clear how it would now resolve itself. The unions would ballot and that was likely to show a desire for someone else. He said JR went down well at conference though contrary to reports TB did not lead but followed the standing ovation. I told him about the Frank Luntz thing – he was obsessed with the idea that the public would go for JR. TB said he had no doubt which speech would have gone down better with the public. JR's. I asked what Bill had said to him over lunch re the situation. 'It is him and Gore all over again.' BC said he had taken Gore aside during his campaign against Bush and said to him that he had learned a lot from him, for example about how the internet was changing politics, and changing the world, also about issues like climate change. Now listen to me about something I know about, Al – winning!' He said Gore had always felt he had to do it in his own way, on his own terms, and GB was probably going to do the same, and given we had won three times, it would be a mistake not to apply a lot of well-applied lessons.

TB felt he could see a clear strategy for GB to win but wasn't sure he would or could take it. He felt GB needed new and better people around him. He felt that even though some of TB's own people were so angry with GB, we had to try and make it work, and having all said the focus must be on the country not the party, now we had to show that was the case. Not going to be easy though. We had to make sure everyone understood that if even after all that had happened, there was just this obsession on speculation about when he went, and all the ins and outs with GB, we would make no progress. They actually had a shared interest in getting that all behind them, but even if GB saw that, it didn't mean his people or TB's people would, I said. I said I had been a bit alarmed about the atmosphere around the place when I went out and about in Manchester. There was always an element that was about gossip and in-fighting but it seemed much more prevalent.

It struck me that all those who had caused trouble over the letters to him, and the Watsons etc. who resigned, had actually only ever known winning really, and I felt there was a sense almost that they took for granted, TB goes, GB in, we win again. He said he intended to sit down with GB, and just hammer out the policy areas they would work on together, and be seen to. 'If you're speaking to him, make sure he understands it is in his interests every bit as much as mine.' He was also planning to put together new teams of people to meet across different policy areas, chaired by him, with GB on all of them, staffed by No. 10 and HMT. All the modern economy areas – he thought we were not where we needed to be on biosciences, the creative industries for example, but also next wave of public service reform, security, welfare, foreign, energy, public health. I said it sounded like he was trying to write GB's manifesto for him. He said he knew what they needed to do in the time he had left and he was determined to do it.

He also wanted to address party reform with him, but I felt on that GB was bound to want to have his own ideas. He was worried about Health, but for the Queen's Speech was focused on the Home Office agenda, which was pretty massive. He said he felt the party got the ID card argument more than we realised, but I think he may have been taking too much out of the fact that it came in his speech when he was on a roll, and getting applauded for pretty much anything. He was confident JR would grip it all, but the scale of the issues he had on his plate was pretty alarming, crime, terrorism, ID cards, asylum, immigration, and TB was talking again about taking another look at the Human Rights Act. His other big thing was Palestine. He said we are not going to make progress in the way we need to on everything else unless we make progress on that. Later off with Grace, Sissy and Nina to Newcastle for the Great North Run. I asked Rory to read letter I'd sent him before leaving. We were going to miss him a lot.

Saturday 30 September

Beautiful sunny day. The quayside looking terrific. Breakfast then down to the start for 11 and a while hanging around but watched some good races, both the elite and the mass participation races for kids. I got Sissy into Grace's race so they could run together and leave early as they had to get back to London. Fabulous atmosphere, bigger crowds than ever. Quite an amazing thing that Brendan has built here. They did their race, I got them up to the station and off then went back to the hotel to do a bit of work before the official dinner at the Baltic [arts centre], where Brendan had asked me to say a few words. I gave him my opening line – privatise BBC and nationalise BUPA [main sponsor] and for a second he fell for it.

Much the same crowd as usual. Nice chat with Nic Bideau [athletics coach, husband of athlete Sonia O'Sullivan]. Good guy. Looking after Craig Mottram [athlete] who struck me as a decent all-round Aussie. Mottram was doing the race tomorrow with Sonia O'Sullivan, both dressed in Sunderland shirts. James Cracknell [champion rower] and his missus. Steve Cram and Alison Curbishley [athletes]. Sue Barker [former tennis champion]. Dick and Margaret Caborn. David Moorcroft [athlete]. Really good crowd, good event as ever, and I said to Brendan did he ever think this whole thing would become as big as it had? He was incredibly modest about it considering just what a phenomenon it had become.

Sunday 1 October

I did a down-the-line interview for Andrew Marr, partly the run and the charity, partly the conferences and I got in a whack at DC's Webcameron [series of online videos], his latest PR wheeze. Fiona called and said I needed to get a bigger LRF running shirt because the one I was wearing on the telly was too tight. She also said it was too obvious that I found it hard to say anything positive about GB. It was hard to get the balance though, between talking up the conference as the point at which things came together, talking up TB both legacy and what was still to do, while also pointing to a GB era. Out to the start by car. Usual hanging around but it was a lovely sunny day, and a nice atmosphere all around the place. Did a few interviews at the start, then met a guy from Workington who used to weigh 44 stone, got into running, now 14. I thought he was winding me up until he showed me the pictures. I ran with the same pacer as last time. I started too fast, suffered a bit in the middle, and finished in 1.52, which was a fall of ten minutes over three years. My running is definitely going to pot a bit with all the cycling and swimming. I still felt I was overtaking more people of my age and shape than being overtaken, but I definitely felt it was harder than before. Helen [Mitchinson, Brendan Foster PA] got me on to one of the first helicopters out so I could get into town, back to the hotel and watch Burnley hammer Norwich 4–1 on Sky. Train home, knackered but glad I had gone. Picked up by Fiona and the kids and off to Marine Ices [ice cream parlour].

Monday 2 October

Legs really sore when I woke up, despite the crap time. GB called to fix a meeting tomorrow. My heart sank a bit when Switch said, 'I have the Chancellor for you.' I spoke to PG who sent me over a long note, really detailed and thoughtful and later I went over to talk it through with him, and we ended up having one of those long chats where we really tried to get to the bottom of stuff and work it through. The great thing about Philip was that though he was always thinking things from the party's perspective, and knew that meant helping, he was also the only one who really knew how bad things got from time to time, and so was thinking about my perspective too. His note was several pages, brilliant stuff, and I told him I was very grateful and lucky to have him as a friend. His starting point was that even after all the fuss and the nonsense, what last week showed was that TB remains the pre-eminent politician of our age. But he was going. Fact. There had been some thought that conference might produce a future election contest by proxy. But David M and AJ faded. John Reid shone but not brightly enough for people to see him as a challenger.

So GB was 'damaged but the winner'. And the best thing about TB's speech, we ageed when we talked about it later, was that it had been essentially healing. It may have left some people thinking 'Why the hell is he leaving?' but the over-riding sense was it is time to go, we have had our difficulties, but now let's move on together. So that created both 'the need and the opportunity' to drain the poison and help GB. BUT – this was his main point for me – it cannot be unconditional. We know GB as well as anyone. We have known him for years, worked with him well, worked with him badly. And we know he has to change. His strategy, his political approach, his attitude to TB, to his staff and personnel, to people. The thing about you, PG said, is that you can only work well with people if you feel you are driving things and if you like the teams you are with. That doesn't mean you are all buddy buddies like we are. But you have to feel you enjoy their company because you enjoy their input and their intelligence. And there are some people in the GB circle who are never going to give you that. So don't work with them and don't let him give them influence. GB also needs to know you will always be honest with him, and he also needs to know you will walk if he doesn't work as agreed.

They know post the *MoS* saga that if they fuck you over, you will stand up to them, and leave them be if it is the only option. They have to know that is real and can happen happen. So all support has to be conditional on real change. He was totally of the view that GB was actually in a bigger mess than people realised, emotionally ill at ease, low in confidence, at times he could seem insincere, inauthentic and so deeply unattractive. He felt that people had been overly dismissive of the Frank Luntz research because it was 'a brash Yank coming over and telling us what was happening', but it was spot on. The public have always bought GB as a good Chancellor. But they don't automatically see the step up. Even if they think TB got stuff wrong, or if they are angry about Iraq, they think he can do the job and what last week showed is they are right. He said if there was a leadership election now with a credible alternative, and the party listened to the public, GB would almost certainly lose. So – bottom line – his honest assessment was, and he knew I shared it, was that the chances of GB winning a majority v DC are slim.

Not all his fault. Far from it. Time for change mood. It is a big thing in our system to ask the people to elect a fourth-term government. He said in his note, 'This is a democratic impulse, one that is hard to shift.' And the problem was that even if DC was not TB or Thatcher, he was an acceptable alternative and if we stood back and analysed what he was doing, he was doing it well. Second problem was that DC was strengthening where he needed to and GB was weakening where he needed not to – the south. But the other problem, created by the soap opera, was that it was almost as if the purpose of the third term had been lost, other than as an answer to the question about whether we could win a fourth? This is the message we had tried to get going at conference but it didn't work, because the soap shit was too strong. But what we both knew was that we could both make a difference, both to help TB finish well, and to help GB make the changes he needed to make to get there. So we should frame this and set it out for him. The note I did a while back is a starting point.

We need to be much clearer that if he does not take a more collegiate approach, especially with TB, he will fail. Added to which, if he doesn't do that, we can't help him. I said I had been pretty clear, when he had made a couple of rather clumsy efforts to get me right over, that I would never dump on TB, or help him at TB's expense. In fact some felt I had already done that but TB was not among them. We also had to do him a note being really brutal about the need to stop being so tactical. All that stuff about loving England, Arctic Monkeys, heaping praise on TB. Nobody bought it. Hopeless. All tactical. The strategy he needs is one that answers the question 'How can I win back London and the south? How do I become the party of change? He has to be bold and brave and decisive.'

The personal motivation was harder to work out. PG, who knows me better than most, reckons that even though it is true that I don't really care what the world thinks of me, I do have a need for fairly constant external validation from people who matter to me. Fiona and the kids for sure. Family and friends more broadly. But also within the party and politics more generally. So the reason I feel bad about turning my back on all of this is because I think I can make a difference, which I can, but I also need to know that others think that I can. He said what I needed was to shift from a reliance on external validation to a reliance on internal confidence and self-belief. He said I should ask myself, 'If the world knew nothing about me, what would be left of me?' Good question. So, 'If you are driven to work for GB because it validates you, makes you feel that you're still important and still belong then I think you should be cautious. If, however, you are doing it from a position of inner strength it is much more likely to work.'

He said this was the area that gave him real doubts about me working with GB. He felt if I went in for the wrong reasons, I would end up with major head problems. We agreed, there was a danger I got sucked back rather than stepped forward on my own terms. There were issues with the book. Big issues with Fiona, whose interests had to be paramount. Issues with the media, who would love it if I went back and became a target all over again. So in summary, his view was – good for GB if you do it, lots of risk for yourself. And the only way to proceed was to be aware and make sure he understood all of that. And agreed you do it all on your own terms. Conditional. Nothing that overwhelms. 'You are advising him, not saving him.' He also felt I should go to the Lords, but I felt that was as much about him as me. It was a very good talk though. I felt better and clearer about it. It clarified where I had basically been heading. I knew it was not going to be unalloyed fun. But it was important, and if I could get the balance right, it ought to be OK.

David S felt it was all bound up in this thing about the conflict between self and service, Fiona that I couldn't bear to be away from it, Rory that it was very hard to walk away from something you helped to build, and that even though GB could be difficult, you would rather have him there than DC and the Tories back in. It was a mix of stuff, I guess, but the point was I was not soaring into it with joyous heart Then again, how much of that was down to the general malaise I was feeling a lot of the time, having finally decided to try and sort the depression once and for all?

Off to Oxford with Rory. He was totally in control of his own space, seemed pretty chilled and confident about it, liked his room fine, looking out on to quite a nice view, trees and a lawn. It felt like quite a big moment though, and I was going to miss him a hell of a lot. The best thing about life of late had been spending so much time with the kids. We said goodbye at the college gate then a journey home with spirits raised by Grace being very funny in the back of the car then a brilliant Radio 4 interview with Michael Palin [comedian and actor] on his Monty Python diaries. Long chat with Richard S when I got home. He had hardened his view against the single volume, but I had pretty much decided. I went out with Calum to his Monday night football. We were on opposite sides and my team lost 12–1. I could barely run. Cameron was getting quite a good run at his party conference, he and Osborne staying on modernising message, playing down tax cuts, saying they had to stop obsessing about Europe and pushing his 'There is such thing as society' line as a way of differentiating from Maggie.

October '06: Cameron makes a shift from Thatcher

Tuesday 3 October

Feeling pretty down, and despite having cleared my head yesterday, feeling a bit anxious about where the GB thing was heading. I got the bus in, reading on the way, straight to the Treasury, up to the dowdy waiting room, looking out over the park and really trying to decide if I wanted to be there. And if not, where? I was pretty clear what I was intending to say, including that he had to stop the blame game, had to stop being a victim, had to change his personnel and his modus operandi and start to understand what leading a team meant. He came in, quite jolly, bouncy, energetic, and the first few minutes was all football, and his excitement at having persuaded Rangers' Trinidadian Marvin Andrews to go to Raith Rovers for a grand a week. He asked about Burnley, about Fergie, about Fiona and the kids, almost as if he didn't really want to get into the politics. Eventually I said, so, what are your plans? 'Well, we cannot have another month like the last one.' I said given we got through conference intact, and TB did well, you could argue our position overall strengthened. I said your position was weakened but recoverable. He said what CB and others were doing and saying was unforgiveable.

He was angry at all the things people had said about him, but he was also clear about a way forward. I felt the anger was over done and getting in the way. He said for example Monday was always the worst time to speak to TB because over the weekend Cherie would be in one ear and Peter in the other. I said he overestimated all of that. I had witnessed many times, including in Manchester, TB resisting all manner of noises urging him against GB. I drafted the section on GB in his conference speech, but TB was the one who strengthened it and made it more powerful and more personal. I had been there when CB had been making clear she didn't think he should endorse him, now or in the future, and he batted it off. Likewise I was there when TB told the staff to stop all the bitching and the chats in the bars slagging off GB. And I asked him if he ever did the same with his people? I said he had to understand most people, and not without some reason, be honest, did not accept GB had not been part of the general undermining recently.

He said it suited No. 10 to think it was a conspiracy rather than a broad-based uprising urging him to go. I said look where we are now though. People wishing he wasn't going. He had to rise higher than this. If he didn't get his head above all this shit, it would drown him. He said he had good opportunities coming up – a number of serious reports, Pre-Budget Report, Budget. He felt his way back was through substance v style. I said I agreed but the style dividing line must be seen as DC not TB. If you try to define yourself against TB, we all lose. He said it had to be about getting back on to the big issues and he had a number of ideas on that front. Went through them. Sounded OK if a bit same old same old. He was worried at the way TB was changing tack on his future policy process. At the start the idea was four committees, two chaired by each. Now he had six, all to be chaired by TB. I felt he had a point on that, and I said I had said as much to TB, that it looked too much like he was trying to direct the policy process long beyond his departure. But I said he would still be advised to go along with it, because the more they were seen to do policy development together, the better.

Even if he changed tack on some of it later, it didn't matter. I was trying to emphasise that he needed TB as much as TB needed him, not just to get there but also in terms of what happened when he did. But I could sense resistance in the body language. When I raised it with TB, he had said one of the problems they had was colleagues not knowing what direction he would go in and this was the process by which he could signal clearly he was staying on the modernising path. GB felt though that a virtually explicit 'bind him in' strategy simply sent out the message he was a risk who didn't believe it at all. I felt he had a point there too, but again TB felt the doubts were real and this was the way for him to answer them so that he didn't then have a leadership free for all. On the leadership election GB was still clear he didn't feel the party would benefit from one. If it was him v arch Blairite, it would all be division or personality attack. Him v Reid would be two Scots, two old politicians, East v West Scotland. Not sure it was the best advert. He had seen JR recently and wasn't sure what he was up to. Clearly he had a big job to do, and he recognised he had ability. But even that was said somewhat through gritted teeth. Milburn and Byers were the two he saw as totally irreconcilable.

He seemed fairly unfazed about Cameron, felt he was good at show but would be weak on policy. Their conference was not breaking through as planned. He wanted me specifically to get TB off the process he had set out in his new committee structure and on to something more collegiate and less TB driven. 'It would be absurd for him to be writing the next manifesto when he is not going to be there,' he said. He felt they should do a series of speeches where GB was more new Labour than expected – e.g. on education reform, and TB was more progressive than expected – e.g. did a speech on child poverty or the values of the UN. That was fine in so far as it went but as ever did not really add up to a strategy. I told him PG and I had had a long discussion about him, and that we felt if we had a role to play it must be to give him real honesty about what we thought about what he did and said. I was fairly straightforward about some of his problems and went through them. It was a lot harder to be brutally frank though, because whereas TB usually welcomed it, GB did seem to take it more personally.

At one point I said he should get someone to write down all the attacks made against him and work out how each could be portrayed as part of a strength. He laughed, saying, 'Including some of your attacks.' Let's not go there, I said. He was keen for me to 'get to know Ed Balls and Ed Miliband better'. I said I knew them well, I had known them for years. Yes, but I don't think you rate them as you should. They are really good. We discussed DM who had faded a bit at conference. He asked straight out if I thought he was leadership material. I said possibly, probably even, but not yet, and not on what we saw last week. He felt Ed M was more charismatic and had 'a better touch with people'. Twice, three times, he said he really wanted me to try to develop good relations with the Eds. I said I can work with anyone, provided they are straight with me and provided there is no bullshit and we all know what we are trying to do.

He asked me what I wanted to do with my life. I said I didn't know, and to be honest I was struggling at times to find the answer. I admitted I felt ambivalent about politics, that there was a time when I went into No. 10, or here, and felt, 'This is where I belong,' but I didn't feel that the same way. It had been the same at Manchester and you end up feeling a bit of a heel, so many would love to be where I was, doing what I was doing, but it didn't feel as it should. I had to take care of myself. I had loyalty to the party, and if he was leader, I would want to help, but not on any terms, and I am more conscious than I used to be of the risks I run in terms of my own health and happiness, and the family.

I felt if I had gone for a seat a while back, I could have done all sorts of things differently, but then I wouldn't have done what I did with TB, with him, with others, the campaigns. So it was a question of choices. Lots of people seemed to think they knew what I needed to do with my life, but they were not me. He said he knew we had had bad times as well as good, he knew I sometimes had doubts, but he felt we were not that far apart politically, and he knew I was someone who could make change happen, and he needed people like that, because there are not many of them. So, he said, I hope we can work something out. It was ninety minutes or so and at the end we walked out to the lift. He said he wanted to keep in touch and he hoped I could speak to TB before they met tomorrow. I said I would. I was feeling pretty depressed anyway because Rory had left home and I was feeling a big void. This put me down further, to be honest. I thought about popping into No. 10 but couldn't face it. I got the bus home and worked on Richard's '94–'97 cuts. Then to the gym with Calum.

Wednesday 4 October

Bit of work then off to Heathrow. I called TB on his way back from Spain and briefed him on GB. There wasn't much give there. He was adamant it was in GB's interest that he was seen to be part of this poli-cy-making process that had agreed plans for the long term. He felt the position had moved so that colleagues needed more assurance before they would back him without a proper contest. They were both right but the basic lack of trust remained an issue. I said that at least GB realised he was in a different position and was up for a different kind of dialogue. Flight to Budapest. Nice feel to the city. Conference was a B2B human resources event. Nice enough crowd. But definitely a big anti-GB thing developing. A good question on why we didn't present the creative tension side of their relationship. Bog-standard speech went OK, Q&A not bad. I was fairly candid but felt I was at best on 7 out of 10 form. Out for a drink with Mick Hucknall and Gabriela. Nice time. Very down on GB as well. Everyone basically thinking what next. PG was texting me endlessly saying DC made a breakthrough conference speech. It was a tough mood at the moment.

Thursday 5 October

Up and out to airport. I had enjoyed the little trip away. Things had been getting too crowded in on the political front. I liked the feel of Hungary, though I had little sense of the political upheaval that was going on.[*] Back for an interview with the *Independent on Sunday* on mental health. Seemed to go OK. I watched DC's speech of yesterday. PG had got me a bit alarmed by saying he felt it was a real breakthrough speech. I didn't

---

[*] A private speech by Prime Minister Ferenc Gyurcsány confessing that his Socialist Party had lied to win the election earlier in the year became generally known, causing widespread anti-government protests.

October '06: PG sees Cameron speech as 'breakthrough moment'

feel that. It was OK but not great. I didn't think it would really push him through. Lot of platitudes nicely delivered. Short on policy. It was still not clear what his plan was for how he handled TB and then GB. The event as a whole seemed to have been OK for them but I didn't see it as the big moment Philip seemed to see.

It was a perfectly good line – TB's priorities in three words – education, education, education, DC's in three letters, NHS – but it didn't really amount to a strategy, just because he focused on health more than anything else. In so far as there was a strategy, it was about driving a message of change and dragging them into the modern world. There were some sections though that almost felt like a lift from some of our earlier speeches – people's priorities our priorities right at the top, also the confident restating of the centre ground, being clear there were some of our changes they were accepting, making another pitch for the environment.

Friday 6 October
Out early. Train to Chester and then to Carden Park Hotel for a speech. Nice enough bunch. Not as down on GB as the Budapest lot. Substance v style definitely had traction. Train back then quiz night at William Ellis.

Saturday 7 October
Working on future speeches, one on mental health, another on how to differentiate between crisis and frenzy. Rory back for the day. Met him in the park and ran back. He said he had noticed how often at Oxford they were told they were brightest and best. Watching loads of football including amazing Scotland [European Championship qualifier] win v France [1–0].

Sunday 8 October
The *Independent on Sunday* piece came out fine, I think. They were billing it as part of a big new focus on mental health and mental illness so I felt it might turn into something decent. I also felt so much better having it out there, rather than having to pretend, which is how I had felt a lot in the past, pretend things were fine when they weren't. Anyway it got a pretty good response, a bit of pick-up elsewhere, nice reactions going around the place. TB on later asking if I had taken my

pills. He said he wanted to restart the him, me, GB, PG meetings. I went for a long run out in Essex, and then later we went to see *The Queen*. It was perfectly entertaining, I guess, though I couldn't quite work out why it was becoming such a big thing. It was quite odd being in there watching it, and having been spotted sitting down. Grace was funny, at one point whispered quite loudly, 'Why are they doing you as a yob?' and the people around us all laughed. In so far as I could work out why it was such a success, it was partly the story, partly the audacity of Helen Mirren portraying the Queen as she did, but also that she and TB were done as rounded characters, not caricatures. The rest of us – CB, Philip, me, Robin Janvrin – we were definitely more in the caricature category.

I was also a bit iffy about these instant history films which mixed real footage and totally invented dialogue and events, though I guess Shakespeare did plenty of that in his time! Quite a few funny comments on the way out, including one old woman who I would have guessed as a total monarchist and who said, 'You should have killed them off when you had the chance.' I called Janvrin later to see if he had seen it. He had, had much the same reaction as me. Also, they couldn't resist making out the whole thing had been about tension between No. 10 and the Palace, whereas actually it was amazing how well we had all managed to work together.

Monday 9 October
Quite a lot of follow-up to the mental health piece, almost all of it positive, and the charities were on in force, not just Mind but others. I was working on the mental health speech again for tomorrow's Mental Health Media Awards, and feeling good about getting it all out there and trying to shape a campaign around it. I think Fiona was a bit worried about it, but David S felt if I felt I should, I should.

Tuesday 10 October
Both direct and via Mind, I'd had a blitz of media bids about the *Indy* piece and the speech tonight to the awards audience, and so all day on and off I was doing interviews, fairly basic stuff, depression, the breakdown, the stigma, need for change. *GMTV*, John Stapleton [presenter] really good. Then Sky down the line, Eamonn Holmes [presenter] good but a last question from his co-presenter dredging up me and GB/

psychological flaws.* The producer later aplologised, said they hadn't expected it, but truth be told I had, it was bound to come up at some point, and I just batted it off. Then to the Beeb. 5 Live with Victoria Derbyshire. Totally positive phone-in. Sophie Raworth for the lunchtime news. We had a nice chat about running and I think I got her signed up to do a marathon for LRF. To the City then for a meeting with Martin Gilbert and Tim [Allan] about FirstGroup. Out for a run later, and then out to the Mental Health Media event. Good atmosphere, nice crowd. Really good feedback from the piece and from the interviews, and there was definitely a feeling of an issue on the move if we could get more people out there talking about it.

Paul Abbott [Burnley-born writer] made a terrific speech and was really nice about me in it. David S and his wife were there at my invitation and he said he felt it was really good I was able to be open, and to use it for public good, and he encouraged me to do more. The speech went fine, a mix of the personal and how it could be used for the political. Rosie Winterton there as [health] minister, very funny, said she always knew I was potty, but never realised I was quite so potty as that. Polls showing if anything we had had a bigger conference bounce than the Tories. And GB was out making a big foreign policy speech, and pitching himself as strong on security.

Wednesday 11 October

I had an hour with David S. He felt last night was good, for me and for the issue. He had liked the session with the kids as well, and felt even more sure than he had been that the big thing, whatever I did politically, was to sort myself with the family. That was the most important thing. Out for a run then an interview with Jeremy Vine. Nice guy. Good interview. I really sensed he got it, maybe had it himself. Lunch with Bradders, then met Natascha [McElhone, actress and friend] for a cup of tea and a natter. She was worried about me having the occasional drink. Also felt I had to watch being dragged into celebrity life. She was supportive on the idea of the mental health campaigning though, said that I had definitely moved the dial already and could do more.

The media follow-up inevitably was getting a bit nastier, a really snide piece in the *Telegraph* on how depression was the new must-have

---

* AC denied having used this phrase in a January 1998 briefing about tensions between Brown and Blair given to Andrew Rawnsley of *The Observer*.

celebrity disease. Matthew Parris apparently had a dig. The *Mail* of course. The *Standard*. All the usual tossers but it was definitely worth doing, and the charities were ecstatic. I worried LRF would be pissed off, but I felt the mental health space was one where I could make a lot more difference. The fundraising thing was not really my strength in the same way that I could do campaigns and comms. Put a call into Cathy Gilman though, just to check it out. She had certainly noticed it all, and said fine so long as I wasn't dumping them, and got me to agree to get involved in the next [Ian] Botham [former cricketer, charities supporter] walk.

Thursday 12 October

Met PG at the Honest Sausage. We felt we had probably got to the right place re GB and how we worked with him. He had done himself a new little life plan – more work with Freud's for financial security. Involvement at the LSE for ideas. Politics via the Lords and TB–GB, plus with me, and family. He said if he could keep all those four strong, he was fine. We also talked about maybe helping Helle in Denmark. GB had another big speech, the Donald Dewar [former Labour inaugural First Minister of Scotland] memorial lecture, and was focused on social policy, and especially the role of parenting, the need for fathers to do more with sons. Fairly basic stuff, and maybe a bit of a contrast with DC, who recently had been more speech by talking point than hard edged policy.

Friday 13 October

Crap run, crap bike ride, asthma shit. 3.30 meeting at Gail's. Gail, Susan Sandon, Caroline Gascoigne, Stott, Mark B. Pretty much on track now. Single volume ruthlessly focusing on half a dozen key themes and building other stuff around it. Meeting with group lawyer, who set out problems – libel, Official Secrets Act, confidence. It was not an ideal outcome but we were getting there. RS more on board for the idea I think though also saying still must have GB strand in there. It cannot be totally sanitised. Long chat with Alex. TB's letter to his pal whose son had died in military training had arrived. It clearly meant a lot to them. AF said he couldn't even think about it without getting close to tears. He wasn't sure about Steve McClaren [England team manager] – great coach, but felt he was too focused on media and seeing himself as a clever manipulator. TB was having to deal with the fallout from

[General Sir Richard] Dannatt [Chief of General Staff] doing a piece in the *Mail* attacking policy on Iraq and saying we were endangering lives. If it had been during a Tory government he would have been torn apart but needless to say he was being feted for it. There was no way he would be sacked but he ought to be.

Saturday 14 October

Up and off with Calum to Burnley v Hull. Went M6 route, and bizarrely saw seven of our players on the drive in from the motorway to the ground. Jon Harley and John Spicer in a Range Rover. Frank Sinclair at a cashpoint when we stopped for petrol. John McGreal at a garage shop. Michael Duff with personalised plates, M600DUF. Kyle Lafferty and Chris McCann in a cab. We started really well, two early goals, finished that way. Then drove down to Oxford to meet up with Fiona and see Rory.

Sunday 15 October

Went for a run. Lunch with Rory and Zoe. He seems fine and settled. Some great people watching outside the college. He seemed to know a lot of who was who and what was what already. Then to Kevin Spacey's for dinner. Sinead [Cusack, actor] called earlier about him being solipsistic. He was a bit. He was basically wanting advice on the best way to go about reshaping a board. David Liddiment there. Good row with him about the BBC now he on the new board thing [BBC Trust]. A few arts financing and charity law guys. One woman who I think was a producer. We kept coming back to the need for a written plan that he oversaw and drove through. He had not even met the whole of the old board yet. Good bunch of people though and Spacey was dead serious about his role here.

Monday 16 October

Botham walk, Oxford and Cambridge, much tougher than I thought. Train down with Cathy. Drama on arrival because the police had pulled out of giving it proper support. I sensed a bit of a stitch up. Sarah Botham [daughter] pretty good, and got it sorted. Nice day. Botham friendly and on form, but my God he really does pound it out. We did the first stint in Oxford then longer at Cambridge. Helicopter in between where I seized up a bit. Nice crowds around, and he was good with them. Nasser Hussein [former England cricketer] joined us in Oxford. He and Ian good banter. I did bits and bobs of telly and radio en route. Interviewed Ian for *Times* Ashes guide on the way. Chopper back after we visited Addenbrooke's Hospital. Nice bunch. Enjoyed it.

Tuesday 17 October

Golf with Jamie [Rubin] at Queenwood. In pain yet played better than for ages, having been dire on the practice range. Gary Lineker was also out there warming up, and there was definitely a chill, so he had clearly seen the *Times* piece. A very curt nod when he saw me, then back to hitting balls, and after I hit a particularly bad shank, he turned and said very quietly. 'Good to see your golf is as bad as your TV reviews.' Not happy. I said come on, it was a fair point, the coverage was one-eyed. But he wasn't having it. Glad I had seen him though, and we had a bit of a chat about leukaemia stuff. I ended up playing really well for me, and hammered Jamie. Mainly chatting US politics, and what he might do. He had felt TB's position had strengthened and couldn't see why he was being forced out. But he did remind me, as always, that 'I told you so' about the neocons [ideological right-wing Republicans] being a disaster for us. We had lunch, a really nice chat – he felt don't get too drawn in by GB – then home to prepare for the Kingsley Napley [law firm] lecture, which I was doing partly as a favour to Stephen Parkinson, who had been such a help during Hutton. It went fine though by the end my back was in real pain. Stephen really happy with how it went.

Wednesday 18 October

Back pain dire. Foot swollen. I did a bit of work on the David Frost tribute speech and the *Times* piece on Botham. Breakfast with David Davies, who wanted to explain his new plans. A kind of consultancy portfolio I guess. He was also mulling over maybe doing a book. I felt it was probably a mistake for him because there would be so much pressure to do all the inside Sven kiss and tell stuff, frenzy galore but he would be damaged. He had always managed to keep his own credibility intact through all the madness and he shouldn't risk that. He was convinced I should go to the Lords. I said I was convinced I shouldn't. The veil issue was really taking off, an LEA [local education authority] in Yorkshire having suspended a teaching assistant who refused to remove hers, Jack [Straw] having said he always asks women who come to his surgery to let him see their face, and now TB had piled in too, saying it was a source of separation and in general sources of separation were bad not good.* But it was totally taking off as a talking point, and was leading to some tricky stuff. I totally missed TB's press conference yesterday, where the veil thing came up, and PMQs today, which was maybe a sign of moving away from it all.

I went to see Ron Marx [osteopath] about my back, which helped a bit, but by the evening I could hardly walk. I was out at a tribute dinner for David Frost at the Mansion House where a few of us had been asked to make little speeches. I had a nice chat with [Lord] David Owen [former Labour Foreign Secretary and co-founder of Social Democratic Party]. I always felt he wished he had stayed in the Labour Party, that he would have been a big part of the scene still if he had. He had mixed views about TB though, could see the strengths and achievements and the way he matched progressive values to pragmatic politics, but bought into the idea that a long time in politics and leadership drives you mad in the end. He was following my mental health stuff, and said it needed to happen. It was sitting next to his wife Debbie [literary agent] at the dinner itself, who was nice, warm, and interesting on the subject of agent–client relationships, plus Rolf Harris [comedian] on the other side who despite it being a tribute to Frost made an incredibly self-centred speech.

My little speech went down OK, some corny DF stories, OK without being brilliant. Debbie said David had always been annoyed that he couldn't really do after-dinner speeches as well as lectures and policy speeches. Rory Bremner [impressionist and comedian] tried out his gags on me and Debbie. Very funny. Mary Parkinson [wife of Michael] really friendly, yet again urging me to get on to telly more. James Whitaker [*Daily Mirror* royal reporter] was there, and said Penny Russell-Smith [Buckingham Palace press official] had said the portrayal of me in *The Queen* was a real travesty. James was in hysterics, recalling all the conversations we used to have about how we needed to get rid of the royals, him defending them to the hilt, 'and now they're telling me you saved them, and that film is a total travesty of your good character!' Good night all in all. I had been sounding out a few random people about Cameron though, and I couldn't help thinking the majority who had switched to us under TB could easily switch back.

---

* Straw's remark fuelled a debate, with some arguing that Muslim women should not wear veils in the UK and others calling for the veils to be banned.

Thursday 19 October

In to see Tim at Portland [Communications] offices for a meeting with Moir Lockhead [FirstGroup]. Tim had definitely grown, and had a very good way with these business guys. Moir clearly up for it and agreed we would have a go next Tuesday at putting together a proper plan. I did a Q&A with Tim's team which was fine. Audrey called during a *Channel 4 News* about some report on the Cancer United campaign I did. Ian Gibson [Labour MP] had pulled out on learning it was funded by Roche [Pharmaceuticals]. I was more pissed off that there was no quote about LRF. I spoke to them after the report and later *The Guardian* were chasing. All a bit wanky, but I don't know how we can get the cancer research done in the way it needs to be if there is this unmoveable negative about any involvement with pharma companies. I did an OK swim because it was all the back could bear.

Friday 20 October

Working on cuts for the single volume then out to Camden to get Rory birthday presents then home to work on speeches. Clare Short resigned the whip, after Jacqui Smith [chief whip] had warned her about urging people to vote against Labour candidates. I am not sure it carries that much weight. But I guess it does add another bit of the fin de siècle feel to things. It is pretty clear a lot of it is about TB so far as she is concerned. Her explanation was expectable but strong stuff. Rory home later. Seemed buzzing and happy.

Saturday 21 October

Took a stack of diary material and worked on it on the train down. It was a FirstGroup train (Great Western) and there had been some pretty ferocious double booking. Texted Tim to say my first experience of First since we got involved was not great. Cam and I grabbed a couple of reserved seats from Reading and thankfully nobody claimed them. Marianna Falconer on the train on way to see a friend in Devon. Not really possible to talk because the train was so crowded. She did say Charlie spent seven hours in a car trying to get to Manchester yesterday and didn't make it in time for his speech slot. Arrived, met by Geoff Lakeman [former *Daily Mirror* colleague] and Sam [son]. The kids were all doing really well on the musical front. Lunch at a quayside pub then up to the match. Not a bad game [v Plymouth Argyle] but ended 0–0. Lively start to journey home as a load of Burnley fans staying down in Teignmouth for the weekend piled on after us. They were friendly enough but a bit all over me. Nice time with Calum though. The train back was late, but we made it for La Casalinga for 10, dinner with Rory and Zoe.

Sunday 22 October

Took Grace to the stables, and did a long bike ride. My back seemed to have cleared up but now my fucking calf had gone. I kept thinking I would just ride if off but it got worse and by the time I was home it was like a brick. Back to watch Man U beat Liverpool [2–0]. The Milibands and the cousins round for Rory birthday. Then Real Madrid v Barca. Great game [2–0]. DM and I not really engaging much on the political front. Part of me really wanting away from it. David seemed pretty concerned about things. Worried that GB just wasn't getting himself into the right place. Douglas, according to PG, was very down on GB at the moment. There was a also a bit of a ding dong going on about whether and what limits could be put on Romanian and Bulgarian immigrants, which had become a Reid v Beckett thing, and it looked like JR would get his way, and at least some kind of limits in place.

Monday 23 October

Good poll for GB in *The Times*, showing he was way of ahead of DC with swing voters in terms of who they saw as PM material. Meeting at Kalendar [restaurant] with Nick Keller [businessman, Beyond Sport] who wanted to get me involved in a social enterprise using sport for social good. He had a lot of contacts, a lot of good ideas and it felt like quite a good thing to do. Then then into No. 10. PG, JoP, Liz plus TB. Interestingly Vic [Gould] felt it best to hide me and PG away while he was seeing Jack S re Lords reform, which JS was trying to get him to commit to it being more elected. TB on good and jovial form. He was very funny about my depression, 'Ah Mr Campbell, do come in, how are we today, now come and lie down on the couch and we'll get to the bottom of all this...' He was laughing, but Liz ticked him off, said he should be more sympathetic. I said don't worry, it's probably the only way he can cope with knowing he is probably the main cause! He said that in his earlier meeting with GB he had asked, 'Why is Campbell going on about depression?' It was as though it was some kind of hit on him, bloody hell, that I was talking about being depressed as a way of sending him a signal that I didn't really want to be involved.

As for the main strategy discussion with TB and co, he said the new structures had to work, they didn't bypass existing policy-making. But GB's greater role in the Cabinet committees had to be understood and the machine needed to know the changes mattered. He felt GB was being cooperative without being enthusiastic. He was still worrying mainly re NHS and also ID cards. He wanted Pat McFadden brought in much more centrally to help drive the process in terms of the detailed work out of them all. But when I asked if these groups had agreed memberships yet, he admitted, 'Er, no, not yet.' He said they would have to resolve all that soon. He also wanted a programme of outside visits for these different groups, so they were not just reading, but also going out and about to test their own analyses. And he said he was clear with GB that both for the PBR [pre-Budget report] and the Budget itself, there had to be far more involved Cabinet sessions. He said the way to think of the whole process was to see us as generating our own think tank. It did beg the question what the policy unit, the strategy unit, the delivery unit were all doing, but he felt this was a way of making better use of all the different functions they already had. He said he hadn't been impressed by the first papers that had been done. It was all too standard. We needed new and fresher thinking right across the piece.

I asked JoP if TB was right that GB was engaging OK on it, and he just laughed. We had quite a good discussion on how to handle the Tories. There were mixed views about whether DC had really cut it at their conference. PG felt he had. Liz thought he had. The polls though had not really shifted for them, though PG felt that was because we had been in a dire place and got back to somewhere half-decent and sensible. But he felt DC was doing enough. TB was still of the view that we had to pin them as trying to face all ways, and therefore being unable to decide the big policy areas. Not being able to do the policy because there was one message for the country – we have changed – and another for the party – don't worry, we don't need to do much. So you could get them on shifty but also take it to weak leadership. That felt a bit weak to me, that we needed to be able to make them more of a threat to jobs, living standards. Osborne had done quite a good job, again reading the New Labour, GB mid-'90s rule book, on discipline, rigour, no false promises. But at some point they were going to have to show more.

Mood wise, it was a good meeting. A lot of the pre-conference angst had faded. But substance-wise, I felt it was still a struggle, and I wasn't convinced just having a few more policy committees with him and GB at the same table would drive much by way of change. TB PG and I all had worries re the deputy leadership contest. JoP felt it didn't matter. He asked if my diaries would record me as being pro or against the Iraq policy. I said basically pro with the occasional wobble. TB said to be fair, Ali and Sal were never the biggest fans of the war in Iraq. I said I had just about convinced myself because it had been my job to support it – ah, the Nuremberg excuse, said Pat McF who had joined us by now. Truth be told I wasn't entirely sure what I thought. TB said Rory had said to Nicky, 'My dad said your dad was crap at PMQs' last week.' TB said it was great to see the kids as they were – 'so much smarter than we were at that age'. Rory told me Nicky had defended TB even though TB himself agreed he was crap last week.

I knocked over a drink at one point, and TB was off into more jokes about my depression, me saying how all last week I'd been saying what an understanding employer he had been, and if ever people wanted proof that I lied on his behalf, that was it. Liz said she was shocked at the way he took the piss out of me admitting I was regularly depressed and suicidal! At the end he asked me and JoP to stay back, and we had a little chat about Iraq and Afghanistan. So many of the problems he had would dissipate if they could get both to a better position. JoP said they were both long-haul situations. TB said the only possible strategy in Iraq had to be building Iraqi capability. He felt there must be things we were not doing that we could be doing to boost that, whether personnel and training, equipment. On Afghanistan he was worried the comms effort was going backwards again and asked me to take a look at whether they needed to install a whole new approach as per during previous crisis times.

I went for a chat with the press team, who seemed OK and then was about to leave when I got a message to go and see TB out on the terrace and we had a little wander round the garden. On the forward process on policy with the six groups, I said the only diminishing thing for GB was that it looked like he was being boxed in and having TB set the future for him. His answer was that if GB reacted properly this was his strategic salvation. He had to understand that TB was having to fight off the Reids and the Huttons etc. from insisting GB was properly challenged. He was having to tell them he would be fine. But the only thing that mattered on that was policy decisions. John Hutton not surprisingly felt unpersuaded GB would take the New Labour route on welfare reform when he had been resisting a lot of change. GB had been saying to TB there had to be a more radical approach to Incapacity Benefit reform but when it came to 'What?' It was basically the stuff he had been blocking. TB said he had been constantly complaining about the policy process but TB really believed it was key to GB being able to beat DC. TB said if a traditional agenda was put to the country we may as well wave bye bye.

GB was not perfect but if he could just grow into it he might be the best option still. But unless he got his act together, it might be too late and you could not rule out someone would challenge. I felt his basic strategy was still right but if GB wouldn't buy in properly it was important he think about his own exit. His current thinking seemed to be summer not spring. If so he had a small number of major opportunities to connect and carry a message. I felt he needed to be more reflective and more open and considered about strategic choices. He needed to talk in a more reflective big picture way, take people into his confidence about how it worked, pressures, different points of view, how you decide in the end. There was a strong story to tell about a country changing but it wasn't currently being told properly. He conceded Iraq was a major problem now. Bush was not handling it well. He had fallen into a trap in allowing the Vietnam comparison to be made. He wanted to get to see him soon, to get him more engaged in a more thorough international strategy – with MEPP at the heart of it. I felt I had heard this bit so many times before, and I wasn't convinced the US could or would move in the way he wanted.

There had been a fresh spate of rumours [Donald] Rumsfeld [US Defense Secretary] would go but he was still there. The policy was getting hammered media wise and we didn't have much of a message about how we intended to get through it. He still said though that this was going to be judged in a much longer historical sweep, not a few years. But was that just his way of avoiding the weight of the current judgement. He said it always lifted his spirits when I went in and he wished I would go in more, because the team liked it too. He then asked me, more seriously than before, if the depression had always been as I had described it. I said only when it was bad, but I was more conscious of it because I was seeing someone very often. I still hadn't told him of my current diary plans. I was worrying more and more about how impossible it was to do a single volume that didn't at least allude to the GB problems. Home, then a long run.

October '06: TB still thinking GB could grow into PM job

Tuesday 24 October

A.m. pottering and diaries, preparing for the Mel Brooks event, then three hours at FirstGroup with Tim and team. It seemed to go OK though not really my scene. What a thought to be a bus executive. Good bunch and Moir led them fine. Tim asked me again to be chairman of Portland, but I wasn't sure it was for me. To Ed Victor's to do a *Jewish Chronicle* interview and pix re Brooks. Then chat about where we were on diaries including the need to tie in documentaries for the time of publication. I agreed to speak to Stuart Prebble [TV executive]. Ed said he had bumped into George Osborne who said they were looking forward to my diaries because they would then have even more ideas and tactics to steal from us. TB seeing the Iraqi deputy PM [Salam al-Zaubai], who seemed quite confident that there would be more control by Iraqis soon.

Wednesday 25 October

Good meeting with Stuart Prebble on the possibilities for a TV version of the diaries. I took him through where I was and he felt it would make for several hours for the UK with other possibilities elsewhere. I was doing stacks of media to promote the Mel Brooks event because because tickets were not flying as expected from the piece in *The Times*. Ed and I did a joint thing for the *Jewish Chronicle*, which was a laugh, and they fixed for me to do the *Evening Standard* Thursday. To Lord's cricket ground and speaking at a dinner in the Long Room. Fantastic venue, really special.

Thursday 26 October

Had a session with Justin Coulter, podiatrist, to see if he could sort all these injuries that kept happening. His approach was to study the way you ran, and he discovered all sorts of imbalances, but also that I had seriously flat feet, and he wanted to see me again but he thought I would probably end up needing fitted orthotics. Nice guy, really knew his stuff. Out later for an event for LRF for Durrants media monitoring who were doing some stuff pro bono for the charity. I was doing a lot of public speaking at the moment, both paid and unpaid, and it was very hit and miss whether I enjoyed it or not. The driver who took me to the dinner said he 'had that George Osborne in the back of the cab the other day'. He said GO was a lot nicer than he had expected, and he was 'pretty cocky about beating you lot'. He – the cabbie – said he was basically Labour, but he felt that watching Labour at the moment was like watching a slow motion car crash. 'Everyone knows your new man is not right but it's going to happen, isn't it?' A bit alarming really.

Friday 27 October

Early flight up to Edinburgh, to do an event for Edinburgh University Politics Society, which I was doing as a favour for Nigel Bennett [lawyer] whose daughter was studying there. Donald [brother] collected me at the airport, off to the Sheraton to meet Simone, president of the politics society, and then Olivia, Nigel's daughter. Both really nice, and very bright, politically switched on. Good crowd at the event, and although I had prepared a speech mixing politics, media, culture, a bit of life and times, I ad-libbed a fair bit and could tell they were into it. Very engaged and the Q&A much more enjoyable than most. It baffled me why the media were so determined to pretend young people were not up to much. This lot were top. There was just the one question on Iraq and even that was not so hostile. I felt a lot of them were buying into my basic argument about the media, and the negative impact on politics and also on people's lives. As Donald said, who was not that into politics, there was something really quite innocent and quite inspiring about a lot of them, and how they felt they could change the world.

We went off to see Auntie Mattie [AC mother's sister], then a swim, and then I was out to a black tie event for 500 plus chartered accountants. Sounded grim but in fact they were OK and the top table was really quite a lively bunch. I managed to sneak out reasonably early to watch the end of the Burnley v Preston match [3–2] which annoyingly had been moved to tonight for TV, after I had already signed up for this event. They basically wanted a straight, funny after dinner speech, but I also did quite a strong defence of politics and of TB, and it seemed to go down OK.

Saturday 28 October

Lift with Donald to the airport, flew back, working on the single volume edit on the flight back. Rory home for the weekend again.

Sunday 29 October

Bike ride then out to the stables. Beautiful sunny day. As the papers filled with trailers of the Stern Review [Economics of Climate Change] and all the global warming warnings, TB called later as I was watching West Ham v Blackburn. He sounded OK but the GB scene sounded the same as ever. Everything too hard. Things they should be able to decide easily just weren't. At Cabinet he had been fine but then in the meeting with TB afterwards anything but. He asked where I thought things were. I felt the same as where they'd been for a while though with the US mid-terms shortly Iraq was really bad at the moment. Even he sounded a bit down about it, said though that the only thing now was long-term and strength. He asked me about my diaries and whether I had decided when, how, what etc? I said if I published the lot it would not be good for GB. He said he also felt it was important for me – and for him – that I didn't do any kicking over the traces type of thing. I said it would not be like that in that there would be no hindsight at all, other than maybe an introduction. But I had actually felt in recent weeks, whatever the reality about how the public saw him, that I got stronger with the public by staying loyal and not joining in the distancing.

He said Gale [Booth, CB's mum] had said to him that she had seen me talking about him and the government on telly after conference and 'nobody does it better'. He said he still thought I should get a regular column and regular TV but I just didn't want to be tied to having to do stuff on the media other than when I wanted to or there was a clear need. I said re the book/books I was going to have to get my head straight on timings and tactics. It was tricky but there would be nothing at all while he was still PM, and even after he had gone he had nothing to worry about compared with others! I said he actually came over as being pretty normal and sane – 'unlike myself.' He said he felt I hadn't been popping in to No. 10 quite as much as before. I said it was just that before I had been doing strategy and also transition, but since not engaging with GB so much things were a bit different.

Monday 30 October
Stott came round to discuss where we were on things. He said he tried to put himself in my position, which he found hard because he really found a lot of the GB stuff gobsmacking and if it was him, he would have taken his bat and ball away a long time ago. But he understood the pressures and he knew I felt torn between loyalty to Labour, and a sense of integrity about the book. He felt it was important to be truthful but to be truthful meant to be disloyal in some form, because you could not realistically tell the story without at least some sense of the driving

TB–GB narrative, and how hard it got at times. But he, and also Fiona who had now read most of the last volume, felt there was so much in it for a very very rich book, that it would be a shame not to do something close to when TB went, but both of them felt the GB thing could not be ignored. Richard flicked randomly through about ten pages in different periods, and on seven of them there was some sort of TB–GB thing going on. 'It is all pervasive, even in the good times,' he said. I felt we just had to get on cutting and chopping and see what we ended with.

Tuesday 31 October

Working at home all day, catching up on loads of stuff I had pushed to one side. Dealing with a lot of the follow-ups to the mental health stuff. Out later to Luton v Burnley, yet another great away night at Luton. Two goals for Andy Gray, good win [2–0], good turnout for a Tuesday night, and one of those funny moments of instant singing when one of the corner flags broke and immediately the away end started up 'Shit ground, no flags'.

Wednesday 1 November

See David S. Mainly about drink, both the history, and today. He worried I was slipping back into acceptance of some kind of 'normal relationship' with it, while feeling that once you had had an abnormal relationship with booze, a 'normal' one was difficult. Part of the issue though, I think, was a desire for normality, the idea that I didn't constantly have to feel different, or explain or justify, and could just say 'One or two drinks'. It never went beyond that, and it made me wonder if in fact at the time of the breakdown it had not been so much about drink, as all the other things going on, and the drink was a symptom not cause. But then when he asked me to go over how I used to be, how I used to drink, that fell away really. He was right I had to watch it. Even though I had my own little rules – never daytime, never without Fiona there, never reach a point of even the beginnings of feeling drunk – over the summer it had got a bit too regular and was maybe not the best way to be when I was trying to get to the bottom of the depression. His big thing was that when I was fine, it was fine, but something could happen and set me back and if I was thinking it was normal, and OK, it could easily slide into something else. Best to knock on the head again.

November '06: AC discussing booze with psychiatrist

I was actually feeling angry with myself. Going as long as I did without a drink of any sort, thirteen years, was actually one of the things I was proudest of, and the time I slid off the wagon I hadn't even meant to, it was almost accidental, stupid.

Lunch with Ronnie Grierson [banker, businessman] at his house. His friend Vernon Jordan [businessman, civil rights activist], who was a big player in the Clinton transition team, joined us for the first part. Very impressive guy. Tall, funny, came from a really tough background in Atlanta, and built himself up to become one of the best connected political and business guys around. Very close to BC and we talked a bit about how he had advised him as an insider/outsider, sometimes there all the time, sometimes not, but always on tap. He said he was not sure he could have done the thing I did, full on in, and now the halfway house, that it was a balance that he had always found easier by not being there all the time, but having BC know he could call on him any time. Like a lot of Americans, he was fascinated by how TB had gone from being so close to BC to GWB, and whether it was purely a matter of statecraft, and thinking that is how it had to be, or whether there was something genuinely personal there. I said don't be too shocked, but there is!

He asked me if I still considered myself to be in politics, which was a good question. The answer was yes and no, in that I felt myself dragged in all the time, but I didn't have that full on motivation. In which case carry on doing it as you're doing it. He was still, despite banking, a big figure in civil rights and constantly trying to get more black people into top jobs, and felt we had a long way to go on that front. He had just seen *The Queen* and thought it was wonderful. The three of us then swapped notes on various Diana meetings. He said he would never do a book of his political and business life. When I said I was doing diaries he said the only word of counsel I have – don't use it to settle scores. Don't cut off relationships. Grierson mentioned how the diaries became quite famous during the Hutton Inquiry and Jordan was fascinated by what had happened when I had been asked to provide my diaries to the Hutton Inquiry and especially about the way my relationship developed with Jonathan Sumption [QC] when he came down to where we were on holiday in France to give legal advice. He seemed especially interested in how I, as a control freak, managed to give way to someone else's advice and authority. He also talked a bit about how he helped BC through the Lewinsky time, including getting her work after she left.

Grierson eighty-five. Very lively mind still. He had worked for Harold Wilson, when he ran the old Industrial Reorganisation Corporation, and Thatcher. He felt DC was doing OK, but he had met GB recently and felt in private he was nothing like the public image, and he felt if he could be more in public as he was in private, he would do better. The issue with that was there were very different GBs in private and I could tell he had had the full-on charm and intelligence. He was interesting on TB legacy, felt that the reaction to conference showed that there was still respect for him, an understanding there was something special there, and that would come through when he was gone.

I got home to discover there had been a row going on in the Commons about the Speaker saying TB cannot be asked about GB in relation to succession. It was a classic case of Michael [Martin] trying to be helpful but in the process helping the Tories not us. Cameron had asked TB if he still backed GB to succeed him, yes or no, obviously trying to stir and get into the mix of all the recent stuff, and Michael just slapped him down, but DC then challenged it and it all got a bit messy. It was pretty clear what they were up to, trying to set up GB v DC as one he relished and which played to their benefit. To the Roundhouse dinner for the new board, which Fiona had been helping. Peter Stothard [editor, the *Times Literary Supplement*] saying as well as being keen to read the diaries from No. 10, he would love to read a diary from me about how my perspective changed as time elapsed and I became more distant from events. 'And that', I said, 'takes up much of the time I spend talking to my psychiatrist.' I think he thought I was joking.

Thursday 2 November

Train up to Stockport, then over for the Burnley business lunch. Big Sam [Allardyce] had already done his thing and gone. Mike Forde and Humphrey Walters the other speakers. I also had a meeting to discuss a school project up there, then drove back with Humphrey. He was yet another one – his wife even more so – who liked TB but couldn't bear GB, and felt we would lose if he took over. Interesting history lesson on the origin of leadership – a ship showing the lead, like ice breakers in Canada, and lead was an Anglo Saxon word for way ahead. Also, bankrupt – Italians who reneged on a deal had their benches broken for them. Banco rupto. Learn something every day.

Friday 3 November

Another day, another speech, and quite an unusual audience. A few hundred people there, all in the business of writing stings [short musical phrases, often for advertising] and telly promos. A whole industry of it. Great news on leaving – Ed had flogged a hundred tickets for ten grand for the Mel event. But we were still only half full. Then to see *An Inconvenient Truth* [documentary on dangers of global warming] with Fiona. Al Gore did it really well, stunning, and all the more baffling that he had never been able to communicate so well before. My God how different might things have been for all of us if he had beaten Bush, and if he had shown a bit more of what we saw tonight, and less of the wooden, slightly tentative Gore we saw in the campaign – and if he had used Bill properly – I am sure he could have done it. The film was one of those that needed to be seen far and wide, though as we filed out, I suspected most of the people in there were converts being preached to. But it was a fantastic piece of work, and so simple. Steve Morris sent me Lord Hutton's article in a law journal on the media coverage of the inquiry. I got the impression he was quite shocked by it. Needless to say it got next to no coverage – had it said anything bad about us it certainly would have done.

Saturday 4 November

Fiona had now read the last volume. She said it was riveting, and there were times she was reading it when she virtually forgot that it was about us, and that she knew what happened. She said it brought back a lot of bad memories, and she was sorry if I hadn't felt supported during the last period in particular, she apologised for how hard she must have seemed at times, but said she wanted me to understand she was trying her best in terrible circumstances. She was definitely moving to the view that there was so much that was not about GB that I could do the single volume OK. She felt that though my resignation was the obvious cut-off point, I should include some of the stuff that happened after we left and maybe even up to the election. But looking at the mountain of words RS and I were cutting through, I felt leaving No. 10 was the best cut-off point, and I could do all the later stuff way down the track. I drove up to Burnley v Ipswich with Calum and Mike Lownes [neighbour, Ipswich fan]. 1–0, last-minute winner. Good laugh and Mike knew the planning and property world inside out and so had some good ideas for the speech I was planning for BCSC [British Council of Shopping Centres].

Monday 6 November

Walk and lunch with FM. Just plugging away on the diaries now. Political scene fairly quiet. Iraq bad in the run-up to US mid-terms, which looked like being dire for Bush. TB at his monthly press conference saying he was against the death penalty for Saddam and asked the Iraqis to rethink.

Tuesday 7 November

Podiatrist. Not in good shape. He said I had done quite a lot of damage and it would take a while to fix and definitely needed handmade orthotics. He felt both running and cycling not advisable for a while till we fixed it. Fuck. TB called having spoken to Alex to congratulate him on twenty years in the job. Then by one of those bizarre little quirks I accidentally spoke to Alex when I called Paul Allen, who was up in Manchester at the BCSC event I was due to be speaking at, and AF answered. Sounded on good form and we arranged to have lunch tomorrow, but later United lost 1–0 at Southend [League Cup].

Wednesday 8 November

Bush was hammered in the mid-terms. Rumsfeld went. Enfin. Even by the usual standards of mid-term upset, it felt like quite a moment. Democrats controlling House and Senate, and with a majority of governorships and state legislatures now too. According to the pundits in the States, they seemed to think the anger at Bush was as much about housing and also the handling of the Katrina hurricane as about Iraq, but it was Iraq that was getting a lot of the play here, with TB thrown in the mix. Up to Manchester for the BCSC event then met Alex for lunch at Stock, in the old stock exchange. He was disappointed about Southend but a part of him was relieved because it meant he didn't have to be fighting on all fronts. He said he wasn't sure he had the squad he needed to be doing that. He said Park Ji-sung was the best off-the-ball player he's ever had, absolutely raving about him. He had a new two-year contract in the offing, and was working on a big pension too. They would have to pay him 9 million if they sacked him.

He was raving about *The Queen*, and wanted to hear all about what actually happened re Diana. His jaw dropped when I told him of the time one of the Palace people said, 'So, the die is cast,' and also at some of the messages that came back from Balmoral about making sure the

November '06: Rumsfeld goes after Bush mid-terms hammering

boys walked with the coffin. The rest of it talking about TB and GB. He had not liked the way GB had been operating of late, felt that whole thing about 'It's a matter for Tony when he goes' was menacing, not nice, all he needed to say was he is doing a great job, but he wanted it left hanging there. I said there was a lot worse than that going on. He seemed genuinely shocked that GB was constantly asking TB just to go. He felt it would store up problems. He had OK advice on the diaries. He felt it was OK to hold back on GB if I was open about what I was doing. And he felt that whatever doubts I had about helping GB, I had to do it, because he sounded like he was going to need a lot of support. Good news as I left, a message from Cathy that the Mel event had sold out.

Thursday 9 November

Justin now saying don't run or bike for weeks not days. Real major pain in the arse. Up to see Mum. Nice to see her looking really well, totally on top of the world. Off to Leicester for a property event at Walkers Stadium. Ed called as I was driving, said Alex and I should think about doing a book on winning in sport and politics. Leicester looking a lot smarter than when we lived there. I was staying at the Holiday Inn at the stadium, working away on the diaries then over to check the venue. Peter Wheeler [former rugby player] was MC. Nice bloke and dead keen to swap notes about the Lions. I'm afraid for guys like him there was no getting away from seeing it as a total disaster. Speech seemed to go well, basically just played for laughs. Then I had to do the awards and I did a big number on the way towns and cities were being steadily transformed. A few women admirers at end, including one who was very forward and asked me to change my plans and stay over. Right out like that. Drove home and didn't get back till almost three because of an accident on the M1 and a huge diversion.

Friday 10 November

To see Mel Cash [physio] re the foot. I arrived early so went for a coffee, and a nice old guy from Huddersfield said hello, said he remembered an article from Lord [James] Hanson [Yorkshire industrialist] defending me and saying I was a good thing and he wondered if it was a Huddersfield connection. Yorkshire, maybe, I said. His son had died in the States and he was one of those bereaved parents who loved to talk about the child but who looked sad the whole time, a real pain in there even when he was smiling. Really nice chat though, said he would never get over it, and he didn't actually want to, because every time he felt a stab of pain he felt a point of connection. He was also very perceptive on politics, and gave a very good analysis of why he felt Cameron was not up to it, that the things he was good at – making headlines, looking confident, exploiting problems – were ultimately not leadership. Mel worked legs and foot and agreed with Justin that I needed major rest. It was all a bit depressing but he felt micro traumas had become major, and if I didn't rest up properly, I would do lasting damage.

Home then out to a bizarre event at the Café Royal. Five hundred lawyers, bankers and accountants all in the business recovery profession, and it was a lunchtime black-tie piss-up, which reminded me a bit of old style Fleet Street. One or two wankers but OK. Got home and GB's office had called asking us to a dinner with him and Sarah. Out to do a party meeting for Jim Dowd [Lewisham West MP]. Seemed to go OK. I was tired though, doing too many events and speeches without a real sense of purpose. Lots of people suggesting I get a seat again. I had never felt less like it. TB was seeing Helen Clark [New Zealand Prime Minister] and Eliza Manningham-Buller having talked about as many as 1,600 British Muslims under surveillance, and dozens of plots foiled, he was out with the usual messages on that. The problem was people were looking for security answers but they were only part of it. The stuff of the mind was harder, and he was struggling to find the right way to address all that. David Sainsbury stepped down as science minister, and said it was nothing to do with the fact that he had been seen by the cops over the loans investigation.

Saturday 11 November

Off to Cardiff with Calum, chatting and working on the train. Met by Neil at the station and off to the ground. Lunch with Peter Risdale [Cardiff FC chairman], later Sam Hamman [former chairman]. Quite a lot of banter with Cardiff fans, not all of it pleasant. We lost 1–0, not a great game. Drove back with Neil and Glenys. I was not really engaging on the political front. Neil agreed GB was a hard sell at the moment. Glenys was very fond of him though, clearly felt he was going to be good, great even, and that once he was there, free of TB shadow, he would emerge as something special. I kind of wanted to believe that too, but I wasn't totally convinced. The news still dominated by US elections fallout, party loans in the Sundays, and Iraq big time again.

Sunday 12 November

Home most of the day working on diaries and watching loads of football. Rory home. Later out with the Goulds. Delighted in showing PG the lead letter on the *Metro* problem page – I want to shag Alastair Campbell. He then sat loudly reading the reply from the agony aunt that this was OK if it was a harmless fantasy, less so if it was consuming all thought or even that you imagined it to be real. Funny. Bit of a scene in the restaurant with a really nasty-looking woman staring over the whole time, and Grace was getting unsettled by it. Eventually we had words. Nice evening out though, managed to stay off politics in the main, loads of sport, family, usual stuff, and PG being manic.

Monday 13 November

Out to play golf at Wisley [Woking] with Jamie Redknapp. Nice time but I played absolutely shit, and it can't just have been the various physio ailments. Jamie a top bloke, very funny, always the same temperament, mildly obsessed with his golf. Seemed genuinely to have found a good balance in his life post-playing, mixing media, business, family.

Tuesday 14 Novemnber

JP called, having been asked by Alan Yentob [BBC executive] to come tomorrow to the Mel Brooks event, and he was getting worried about being drawn into the BBC licence fee debate. I assured him it was me who had suggested he come, purely as a social thing for him and Pauline. They were standard tickets and he could make a donation to LRF for at least face value. It showed how sensitive he was to anything right now. In to meet Liz Lloyd for a chat. She said not to let on but TB was a bit down at the moment. We chatted for a bit, and I admitted my heart tended to sink now whenever I was involved. She said the policy review situation was going reasonably well, but it was still difficult to get GB engaged or on the same page. We were walking down to the Cabinet room and I bumped into TB as he came out of giving evidence by video to the Iraq Study Group [bipartisan panel to assess state of Iraq War] headed by Jim Baker [former US Secretary of State]. He hoped the administration would not be too alarmed at it, had basically pushed his position on the importance of MEPP, and attempting to engage Iran and Syria.

TB said he just emphasised again and again that the way the US was perceived with regard to Iraq would not change until the world felt a real step change in their approach to Israel–Palestine. He felt that Baker was definitely in the same place as him, but he wasn't sure what the balance of opinion was around Bush right now. He was bemoaning the BBC coverage of last night's Mansion House speech. They were determined to show it as going back on existing policy, and distancing from Bush, cuddling up to Iran and Syria. He said it was impossible to say anything without it being reduced to a cartoon, but the reality was there was going to have to be some kind of dialogue with Iran or else the Middle East never got resolved, but he had been very clear about the conditions. Through to his room, much banter about the 'I want to shag Alastair Campbell' *Metro* headline. He said things were fine – apart from Iraq and the loans police inquiry. I said they sounded like quite big 'aparts from'. On Iraq he felt the Baker-Hamilton inquiry did at least give us a chance to forge a new direction and he felt the inquiry would echo what we were pressing for.

On loans he felt it was difficult. They would feel under massive pressure to come after him because of the media. And though he knew he had done nothing wrong, and though he felt they would find it very hard to go at JoP or Ruth, he worried about Michael [Levy], simply because they would feel they had to go for him hard. He didn't think he would ever have offered honours for money, and he said, the only two he ever really pressed for were [Sir] David Garrard [property developer] and [Sir] Victor Blank [chairman, Lloyds TSB] who wasn't even a donor and didn't get there in the end anyway. He said his own relations with ML were fine but Michael would not be human if he was not trying to make sure he was not the only one in the frame. I told him of my chat with Len Duvall [London Assembly member and Metropolitan Police Authority] who had told me on Friday night that [Metropolitan Police Assistant Commissioner John] Yates was not pursuing a vendetta but kept being given leads and also that 'Michael keeps putting Tony in the frame'. I said there had to be some sense of fightback because this was being dripped out the whole time, millions of quids worth of bad publicity and it was damaging. In the end, he said the CPS [Crown Prosecution Service] had to make a judgement and the question was whether they resisted media pressure and based it on fact.

The decision would be made by a QC who would not want to recommend a prosecution if a conviction was not likely. I passed on what Len said about Yates not being a bad bloke, not having a political agenda, feeling between a rock and a hard place, but TB was as unconvinced as I was. He said there was no way all this leaking was not from the police. He had sent a message through to them saying he would rather be interviewed to get it cleared up and out of the way but he was not sure when or if it would happen yet. It would be grim and grisly when it did. Clearly this was going to rumble on for months. We chatted re GB. He said it was still TB doing the chasing on the policy process but other ministers really were engaging, and it was producing better quality work. He felt JR might still run, and he said it was interesting as he went around the place that he met lots of people saying they felt JR should go for it. I told him of some of my recent speech experiences, and other outings, and the difficulty in selling GB. He said the problem was people knew he was strong but were not sure about his instincts. And strength allied to the wrong instincts was not great for him.

Added to which he made people feel depressed. He started laughing, said it really isn't good for a PM to make the people feel depressed. Be honest, he said, we can sit here and have a perfectly good chat, and enjoy company and conversation even if we are having to address serious things. And even if it is sometimes a nightmare, we can always start the day with a spring in the step and end it feeling we did something to move things forward a bit. 'If that door opened now, and it was GB, we would know it was him before he even came on through, we'd feel it, and we'd be depressed. Go on, admit it.' He was laughing, and then went into, 'Sorry, I shouldn't be making jokes about depression, not with you being on the pills and everything … How are you? … Blah blah' … laughing.

Liz came in to ask what the hilarity was all about. 'He's taking the piss out of my madness again, Miss.' He had a point though. There was something about GB that pulled you down a bit mood-wise, and that was a worry for me right now. TB asked about the diaries again. I said I would sanitise to protect GB. Most people came through as they are, he would not be shocked by any of the portrayals. It was not perfect for anyone but probably the least imperfect for him. He was clearly still motoring, or trying to, on policy. We worked on his Queen's Speech for a bit and then he had to go off to a round of NI talks. I wandered round the building to say hello, then home.

Wednesday 15 November

Saw DS first thing. Back on the theme of forgiveness. Forgive the person, don't forget the thing. I had been going through the diaries where I had been feeling real pressure from Fiona to quit, and it kind of made sense.

Forgive the person, not the thing. Good meeting with Ed, Prebble and Nigel Bennett on a possible TV series re the diaries, though the size of this whole project and the work needed was dawning even more. I felt at least I could trust them. I worked at home, then watched the Queen's Speech debate with Calum. TB really went at DC on the claim that nothing had been delivered, and that he had 'promised so much and delivered so little' – harsh – and then seemed to endorse GB by saying it would be a flyweight against heavyweight and a great clunking fist was coming his way. I felt DC was in danger of getting himself on the wrong side of the argument on terrorism, crime, anti-social behaviour. I understood why he wanted to set himself a different stall, but there was definitely a risk there.

TB was stronger on defending the record and explaining the need for a tough approach to security than on some of the bigger messages he was trying to get over. But as a final QS, nobody could say it didn't have a lot in it. Eight Home Office Bills. I set off for the Criterion Theatre for the Mel Brooks event. Mel was sitting in the second row when I arrived, looking tired but saying he would be up for it. Alan Yentob, who was doing the interview, had done a good job getting people and clips together, and intended to use a series of film clips to punctuate the interview. Mel signed a few cards, ran through a few lines with Alan then off to his hotel to change. The pre-reception was OK, right mix of celebs and non, paying and non. Total sell out, and the mood really good. I went out to introduce the whole thing, talked a bit about why I got involved with the charity, then Ed on to talk about his own experience as a survivor, then Alan took over. Mel was excellent. It drifted a little in the middle but Alan had great clips, Mel told some hilarious stories and then a Q&A which could have gone on all night.

All in all a good do. JP and Pauline came in the end, and JP asked a question on the difference between UK and US humour. Good answer – he said everyone in the world loved *Monty Python* but would it have worked if they had been Americans? He thought not. He said he liked *Borat* but later told me he hadn't seen it! Lovely feeling to have hundreds of people leaving, all chatting away happily, and a real buzz about the whole thing. The charity ecstatic. He got a standing ovation and seemed really moved, and of course the connection back to Anne Bancroft [Brooks's actress wife] having died, he was quite emotional by the end of it. Then he, Ed, Cathy, us, the Yentobs, Sally Greene, to the Wolseley for dinner. Mel really loved the evening I think, going on about how nice the people were, how much love he felt in there, and so on. His son Max quite intense re foreign affairs. Alan lobbying re licence fee, RPI [Retail Price Index] plus one.

Thursday 16 November

TB got an OK press for the QS but it is amazing how quickly it all passes these days. Time was the Queen's Speech would dominate for days, but it was almost like, well that was a big day now on to something else. Pm, speech to the Publican conference. Jim Naughtie [broadcaster] chairing. Bit of a dull crowd and I wasn't feeling on form. Emma Freud [broadcaster] lobbying me to do a Comic Relief version of *The Apprentice*. Sounded like hell. TB got a bit verballed doing an interview with Al-Jazeera TV into provoking a sudden rash of calls asking me to comment on TB saying Iraq was a disaster. When I checked it out, it was pretty obvious the words had been put in his mouth but it would run a bit.

Friday 17 November

To the gym to do some weights, then a swim but it was amazing how much I was missing the running. Into a bit of a dip. I went to see *Borat* with Fiona, Calum and Tessa. Yeah, funny, but not as great as billed. Tessa back for dinner, telling us about her plans to use the Olympic Games to drive youth participation. She was still unclear about what she would do when TB went. Matthew was quite down and thinking of giving up the pro golf. Jessie was close to a proper management contract. She was very down on GB, felt we were sleepwalking to disaster, we all felt we knew it and we all felt there was nothing much we could do to stop it. I was definitely heading into a dip.

Saturday 18 November

West Brom v Burnley with Calum. Worked on my Deutsche Bank speech in the car park. Got hammered [3–0], two defeats in a row. GB in Iraq, TB in Islamabad. Looked reasonably well co-ordinated, both committing future funding, and GB meeting troops on his first trip there.

Sunday 19 November

Long swim p.m., otherwise all day on and off going through the cut version of diaries. Richard had savaged the GFA [Good Friday Agreement] stuff, which I would need to review.

Monday 20 November
Long swim at Swiss Cottage. Met Noreena Hertz [economist] to go over her plan to raise cash and awareness for carers and nurses, including getting Premiership footballers to give a week's wages. Doubtful!! But she had loads of energy and drive. Felt it was maybe a bit scattergun though. Said she should work out what she might be able to achieve, also get herself a policy team.

Tuesday 21 November
To Berlin. Adlon hotel. Big political comms conference. At the dinner, all Germans, good crowd, very bright, massive interest in our scene. A bit ashamed that we spoke almost entirely in English, but when I switched to German, my brain slipped into French. The dinner was at Freshfields law firm a few yards from where the Wall had been. I had spoken to Joe Haines [former *Daily Mirror* columnist] earlier about his letter in *The Times* on party funding. He had a good line on DC – deep down he's very shallow – which someone once said of George W. It could definitely resonate re DC. Not run for weeks now. Swim and weights.

Wednesday 22 November
Breakfast then through to the speech, which went fine. Hans-Dietrich Genscher [former German foreign minister and Vice-Chancellor] was there, and I made a gag about him not wearing the yellow jumper he always wore when I was a journalist, which went down well. He spoke well about the new world order and the need for more not less international cooperation. He felt TB had all the right insights but had gone awry because of Iraq. I did a basic strategy speech but set out the need to be more strategic, worry less about the day to day media. I did a few interviews on the back of it, and their media was so much more serious than ours. It made it a lot easier to put forward an argument. The guy from *Der Tagesspiegel* interviewed me in the car out to the airport, and felt if we could somehow match the energy of our politics with the media reasonableness of theirs, we would have a good balance.

Thursday 23 November

I had been resisting Emma Freud's blandishments re Comic Relief but then she and a producer came round, just as Grace and her pals were getting back from school. Emma was laden with sweets and chocolate, and chatted them up to come in and persuade me, which of course they did. The idea was a team of blokes against a team of women having to do various fundraising tasks set by [Sir] Alan Sugar. Piers Morgan was up for it and their dream scenario was the women beat the men and there is some kind of shoot-out involving me and him. 'You have to fall out. It is part of the deal.' It did sound a lot of fun, even if too celeb-y, but the one thing Emma was very very good at was selling you an idea as being worth doing because it was for charity. To be fair the whole Comic Relief thing was a phenomenon and if I was doing telly it may as well be this. So I said no about five times until eventually between them she and Grace got me to say yes. We had a bit of a reminisce too, as an interview with Emma about a shock issue I did for the *Mirror* on the environment was my first ever 'proper telly interview', for a kid's show she was doing. Off to Calum parents' evening, best yet. Gym. Beginning to hate doing weights.

Friday 24 November

Dick Caborn on, pressing me to get more involved and be less gloomy about the prospects. It must be great to have that irrepressible optimism he has. I can get it sometimes, but not sustained. I called Piers about the Comic Relief thing. He was even more bumptious now that he was making it big in the States. 'I think you'll find my diaries will outsell yours... I think you'll find I am reaching levels of fame most cannot even dare to dream of...' We agreed though that we would have to play it for laughs and that meant being deeply unpleasant to each other. 'At least it will come naturally,' he said.

Saturday 25 November

Depressed big time. To Cambridge to watch Rory run for Oxford v Cambridge seconds. He wasn't feeling great, ran badly and was very low afterwards. I felt sad that I couldn't lift him. Burnley lost at home to Birmingham [1–2]. Working on an intro to the diaries and agonising about GB again, and whether I could really face going in there on anything like a regular basis. Interesting *Telegraph* poll saying Scots and

English both wanted Scotland to be independent. It didn't feel right but it was an interesting take, which needless to say they pushed as TB being a threat to the Union.

Monday 27 November

TB getting a lot of coverage for a planned official apology about slavery. One of those symbolic but important moments, I guess. It seemed to be going fine according to what I heard on the radio driving out to Watford via Copthall to get new golf clubs. Home feeling a bit better but not much. Media dominated by Russian spy [Alexander Litvinenko] killed by radiation poisoning. Putin in the dock. Also starting to think about the Comic Relief event, which was clearly going to be a bigger commitment than I first imagined.

Tuesday 28 November

Meeting with Peter Watt and Marianna Trian [Labour officials] at Victoria Street. Discussing leadership elections. Picking my brains on how it would work and how we use it to try to get message trained on the Tories. They seemed down on GB, not sure he was changing much or getting the need to. Also agreed with me there was not much to commend a deputy leadership election. We agreed GB had to use it as a test bed for a different approach to the public in a general election campaign. CRE [Campaign for Racial Equality] event quite good. Chairing session on the media. Pretty packed. Simon Israel of *C4 News*, Tim Toulmin [director, Press Complaints Commission] and the editor of *Peterborough Evening Telegraph*. Went fine. Generally down on telly in particular. A funny moment when a guy asked me to talk about 'Your time as Prime Minister'. Questions OK and there was definitely an opening there for starting a different kind of debate about the way the media had changed for the worse, and the need for politics to take a different tack on it, more challenging.

I did a French TV interview on strategy, then off to City Airport, and was airborne before I realised I had left my glasses and the speech at the airport. Jotted a few notes from memory, thinking it would probably be better not to have a set speech anyway. Staying at The Westin in Dublin. Presidential suite, nice, and a really good gym. I was doing an event with Brian Keenan [former Beirut hostage] and we did some snaps for an *Irish Independent* piece. I did the pre-dinner speech, then a Q&A afterwards which was lively but pretty positive. There was definitely a desire here to have a more positive portrayal of TB than in the UK. New Ambassador David Reddaway was there and he felt it was a good exposition of the whole Blair story. He said the FCO were not that wild re GB coming in as PM. Good evening. Enjoyed it. Nice chat with Joe Lennon [Bertie Ahern ex-spokesman], now working in health, on the times we were working together. He felt TB was different class, and we were mad to be losing him. TB meanwhile gearing up for a speech announcing a massive expansion of academies, with the usual responses around the place.

More sad news for GB, their son Fraser diagnosed with cystic fibrosis. Spoke to TB briefly before he set off for Riga for the NATO summit, where even though it was more about Afghanistan than Iraq, the lines were in the same place – us and the Americans and one or two others trying to get more input from the others. The Europeans apart from us and the Dutch were pretty much opposed to getting more involved in the south, he said. It was going to be testy. And he said he was going to be trying to get them to understand the need to take energy issues more seriously. It was something for NATO to think about given Putin getting much tougher. He would hate seeing them all meet up in Latvia. There was a bit of play here for a state department analyst who was out saying Bush totally ignored TB, we had no influence, the special relationship was all bollocks, and we had been used. I actually thought it might have gone worse than it did, but perhaps people sensed it was as much about internal US politicking.

Saturday 2 December

Rory back. Calum and I off with Mike Lownes to Ipswich v Burnley and one of those days when I am convinced fans can affect the outcome. A really loud, rousing, rolling chant going on and on and on through various waves of play, ending in us taking the lead in the 87th minute, then their fans getting up for it and they equalised in the last minute. Annoying but good game, good day out.

Sunday 3 December

Swim. Do *The Sunday Edition* with Andrew Rawnsley and Andrea Catherwood [Irish TV presenter] for ITV about Cameron one year on. Found myself defending GB OK and really going for the DC as style not substance attack. Steven Norris did a good job defending him and also

Cameron's interview pretty good. He managed to sound passionate defending his strategic positions. Out p.m. to skating with Lindsay – Ellie would have been eighteen now. TB sent through a note on a speech he was making this week on Islam, social integration, terrorism, and he asked me to work on it. His main message was that if people come here, they are welcome, but they must integrate. I read through some of the stuff JR, Ruth Kelly, Jack S had been saying, and also in this context GB's Britishness arguments were useful too. I worked on it a bit and sent through a couple of OK passages, including on how Cameron had changed the tone and how it was hard to imagine the Tories playing the race card as before.

Monday 4 December
Golf all day. David Mills and I v Jamies R and R [Rubin and Redknapp]. They beat us on the 18th after I hooked my drive. Very annoying, but I was playing better. Lift back with David and chatted to Tessa on the phone. We both felt it was best if she went the same time as TB, but she was locked into the Olympics, and would not be giving that up lightly.

Tuesday 5 December
Up early to see Ashes disaster unfold in Oz [Australia won by six wickets]. Work and potter at home. Berwin Leighton Paisner law firm dinner, off-the-cuff standard speech. The host was a big TB fan, but I was also finding the hostility to GB abating a bit.

Thursday 7 December
Bitty day. Paul Moore [executive] at Paddington re FirstGroup – ideas for them getting involved in sport, charity events, deepening profile for Moir. Over to the Roundhouse for meeting with Paul Abbott who wanted to pick my brains about the FCO for new series he was writing. He was also doing a film on the BNP. All very bitty. I was constantly feeling like I was having my brains picked but in the context of existential drift. Later out to the ballet, trying to get into it because I knew Fiona wanted us to enjoy it, but it was so not my thing, couldn't stand the crowd and the staring, and said to Fiona why do you expect me to enjoy it when I know you wouldn't enjoy going to football? She said Rory and I were like grumpy old men.

Bumped into Amanda Levete [architect, friend] and she said she was like me, also preferred football to ballet and the only way to enjoy it was to imagine the dancers were playing football. It helped, a bit. TB was in the States, and felt that the Baker study group was opening up a bit of space for a different kind of foreign policy debate there. He felt Baker was on much the same lines as he was re MEPP more broadly and would want to use it to shift things. I was chatting with Piers Morgan about the charity thing next week where he was clearly up for me and him creating major fallout for telly purposes. Prebble was motoring with the BBC re the documentary idea on the diaries.

Friday 8 December

Breakfast with the German Ambassador [Wolfgang Ischinger]. The main line of inquiry GB and whether he would change much when he became PM, who he was close to, who he listened to, whether I would be involved. Their sense was that GB was more sceptic than TB, but I said it had not always been so, and I felt he would take to Merkel in a big way. He said Merkel loved talking to TB, really liked picking his brains. She was not gossipy but she liked to hoover other people's impressions of other leaders. They had all been saddened to watch the way the Schroeder relationship went. There was a time when they felt it was really leading to somewhere new and interesting, when TB's Third Way and GS's 'Neue Mitte' [New Centre] looked like they might merge into something really significant.

They thought GS was making a deliberate choice to go with TB not Chirac as a way of signalling real change but one or two issues – above all Iraq – meant he went back. He said Merkel felt GB, on their brief meeting, had a good analytical mind but it was too soon to say if there was likely to be any real warmth there. Nice guy, very smart. TB was out doing his big speech on integration, which was getting a lot of play, seemed to go OK, but it was coming under a lot of attack from the Muslim Council [mosques umbrella body]. It was so hard to get the balance right on this stuff.

Saturday 9 December

Up to Coventry v Burnley, met up with Paul Fletcher, then Geoffrey Robinson swept us up to the boardroom. He said GB is a very lucky politician, because he is not nearly as damaged as TB by Iraq. I was trying to tease out if he saw why there was so much concern out there about GB taking over, but he said he picked up overwhelmingly positive noises from the party and the public. He didn't seem to buy my line about there being a lot of worries out there about him. We had lunch in the boardroom, then popped down to see Steve Cotterill, pre-match a bit manic as ever. We lost to a very dodgy penalty, then set off for David Mills' place in the Cotswolds, though got lost a couple of times en route. Tessa seemed quite down for her. We were all trying to persuade her that maybe it was time to make a break when TB did, but I think she found the thought quite scary. So much of her identity was wrapped up in being MP for where she was MP, now the Games. I think she was in for the long haul, and maybe still fancied a shot at the deputy leadership.

Sunday 10 December

Golf lesson with Matthew. Fantastic player but he said it was so hard to make it as a pro, and even just getting the sponsorship to keep going was tough. We stayed for lunch then headed home in time for Chelsea v Arsenal [1–1]. I was starting to drop behind schedule on the book, and having spent so much time worrying about the GB angle, it was dawning on me there were all sorts of other areas where I was going to have to clear a lot of hoops with the vetting process – I remembered some of the sensitivities about anything to do with the royals, then there was a lot of the foreign policy stuff, and the spooks.

Monday 11 December

Lunch with Piers Morgan to discuss tactics for Comic Relief. He wanted to meet at The Ivy 'so we get noticed'. He had become an even greater – and funnier, to be fair – caricature of himself, having bounced back and thanks to his involvement with some Simon Cowell programme I had never seen, he was 'big in the States, baby', so 'thanks for getting me driven out of town!' The Comic Relief people were clearly chuffed they had got us to agree to do it together and had been told to expect fireworks, 'so we better give them what they want'. We had no idea yet what the plan was, other than it was five men v five women. Karren Brady [businesswoman] was on the women's team and she had successfully wound him up to think it was a swimming gala and he had been calling Emma to say there was no way was he doing that, and no way was he stripping. Cheryl Cole was on the women's team as well, and possibly Jo Brand and Maureen Lipman, and someone called Trinny from something called *Trinny and Susannah*. There was a whole celeb thing out there that I barely knew, but which he clearly knew inside out.

We swapped notes on what we had been able to pick up, and he felt it was going to be about which celebs we could pull in to do stuff. I said it was going to be a business challenge and we would have to do a start-up of some kind. They wanted me and him falling out and arguing and generally being macho and over the top. He got his way in terms of us being seen in there and noticed, and there was a succession of people coming over to say hello. Waheed [Alli]. Sally Greene. Michael Parkinson had the best line: 'Ah, the devil has lunch with Beelzebub.' Jimmy Carr wandered by – 'No words, there are no words'. Piers had definitely fallen on his feet though, and he said that the show having gone big in the US, Cowell now wanted him to do one in the UK. I reminded him of the first time when we met when I said I wanted to change the world and he said he wanted to be rich and famous. On his published diaries, he admitted he had not really kept a diary, but had recreated it with notes and schedules and papers and all the rest. He was funny about mine. 'Be funny. Don't settle scores too much or be bitter. Make a lot of the access.' I said he seemed to think I was going to rewrite them like he had. 'Well aren't you?'

He said he had got massive mileage out of saying he had fifty-odd meetings with TB, but people overlook the length of the time-frame and it just sounds like a lot more than it is. 'It's a total con job then really?' I said. 'Totally,' he said, then out came that loud laugh. There was something quite admirable about his 'What you see is what you get' approach. He was loving the fame, made no bones about his desire and need for it, and he never turned off the tap, just playing out the whole time. He was doing a fair few speeches and said his absolute banker story was the time I totally stitched him up when I gave a Clinton article he had asked for for the *Mirror* to *The Sun*, and when he called to go berserk at me, I just said, 'Piers, I did it for peace.' He can laugh at himself though, which is a good sign, and he is not a big grudge holder from what I can see. He was also absolutely clear that he saw the Comic Relief *Apprentice* thing as 'a bloody good opportunity to promote myself back here having made it so big in the States!' A bit of a dip for the Tories in the polls, and one of them showing slippage to UKIP. Cameron could still have real problems with his right if he is not careful.

Podiatrist. A lot better. Could get back into light running soon. Alex called after Steve Cotterill asked me to speak to him about maybe getting Giuseppe Rossi on loan. He said he still felt it was on for United to win the Premier League.

Terrible dream. Neil telling me he totally disapproved of me doing a diary, and saying he would organise protests against me wherever I promoted it. Snotty text from Sue Nye after I approached her to ask about GB doing something on the tax front for Comic Relief which we could do in the programme. Car collected me around 4.40 and off to some studio just off the A40 out west, towards Hangar Lane. I had a slight feeling of dread about the whole thing. Some of the other 'celebs' – God is this what it was all becoming? – were already there, Karren Brady quite grand but friendly, Cheryl Cole very cute and smiley, Jo Brand and Maureen Lipman hilarious, clearly as bemused to be there as I was, and hoping I think to take comfort in forming a bit of a Labour group. Trinny was quite a strange creature, very loud and nervy, and I was still a bit unsure what she did. Piers was being very Piers, loud, deliberately obnoxious, winding up Cheryl about 'Cashley Cole' [Ashley Cole, footballer husband of Cheryl who left Arsenal for rivals Chelsea] being a traitor to Arsenal. Ross Kemp quite edgy, and later he told me that he and Rebekah had basically split up.

Rupert Everett was very strange, clearly didn't really understand what was going on. Well, none of us did really, but he really seemed to know nothing. Just said his agent had said it was something to do with a charity and it ought to be fun, but he was dreading it whatever it was. The reality TV element was clear from the word go in that they didn't even want to brief us without us being made up and wired for sound. Richard Curtis [screenwriter, producer, partner of Emma Freud] came in and did a little speech saying how great it was going to be, how Comic Relief did amazing work for charities and causes around the world and this was going to be one of the big-ticket items for this year. He did a little welcome of us all as individuals and was very nice about Labour and what we had done for Africa, and debt and development, and went way over the top about my role in all that. So anyway now we knew 'the teams' – me, Piers, Ross, Rupert Everett and Danny Baker [radio presenter]. Against Karren Brady, Cheryl Cole, Jo Brand,

Maureen Lipman, Trinny. Richard said they could not have imagined a better line-up.

We all looked a bit nervous. We were driven round to the reception area, more hanging around and then in through a tunnel, all on camera. First Cheryl then me and so on till we were all in there, just forced to make small talk really. People's personalities were on show quickly. Piers rude and abrasive but funny. Me rude to him but trying to get on with the others. Ross quite actor-ish, not quite deciding yet whether to be himself or play the character people thought him to be. Danny Baker wisecracking. Rupert Everett looking genuinely quite disturbed. Jo Brand and Maureen Lipman taking the piss out of everything, including themselves. Karren Brady very focused and clear. Trinny hyper and didn't strike me as very nice. Eventually we were told to go through to the boardroom, and there was Alan Sugar with Nick Hewer and Margaret Mountford [both *Apprentice* assistants to Lord Sugar], and we all sat down, in total silence. Piers broke the silence. 'Get on with it then.'

Sugar went round us all one by one in a very pisstakey way, embarrassingly so with Ross, constant mentions of Rebekah and when he did Everett, he pretended not to know who he was, making him out to be a bit B league. He got stuck into me on honours, suggested I ought to get nicked, said I was known as a great salesman and my most recent work was with TB selling honours for cash for the party. Libel alert! He was into Piers on anything. After a bit of faffing around, we finally got told what the task was. We were going to have to set up and run a fairground, in the same space, in competition with each other. Sugar was very rude to everyone, which was obviously all part of the shtick and I didn't take it terribly seriously but in no time the producers were apologising to us. Piers had decided just to be obnoxious with everyone, and take the piss out of Sugar. So we were going to have a few days to set things up, and we had to sell a hundred tickets and basically just make as much cash out of different rides and attractions as we could.

We were driven to the Radisson Mayfair hotel, and I got told off for calling Alison [Blackshaw, PA] to make some calls because we weren't allowed to use anything but our own resources. I called Annie Robinson [TV presenter and journalist] and Mick Hucknall and got them lined up to do something for us. To the hotel and we had a little team room where we sat down to work out strategy. Rupert seemed to be in a total panic. We'd been told to pick a team leader and Piers said, 'Go on then, I suppose it has to be you,' to which Danny said, 'Well, as long as it isn't you,' and so I was unanimously chosen. But Rupert looked to me like he was genuinely on the edge. Piers said we had Philip Green lined up on our side, but later I learned he was basically playing both teams off against each other.

The first big test was to negotiate who got what rides, and we met to negotiate. We both wanted the dodgems but we conceded so long as we could pick the next three. Went for hoopla, coconut shy and ferris wheel. Karren was tough but Trinny was even tougher and certainly more irritating. I felt from the word go we would lose because they really cared and were much harder nosed on money. Piers was all talk and scattergun, and I was saying the key was making good telly and not blowing good contacts for other charities just because it was Comic Relief. 'Are you getting excuses in early?' Yes. A discussion about whether to do food, Piers arguing it was a massive distraction, but Danny and Ross arguing we had to do food and we could charge shedloads provided we got the right people there. Karren and I did most of the negotiating for the rides and the general feeling was that we got the best deal. But the first big issue was trying to work out what to do about Rupert. He just wasn't there really, said nothing, kept looking around himself, and of course Piers couldn't resist winding him up, asking him for Madonna's number, saying why didn't he have all the Hollywood A Listers on speed dial?

I was right out of my comfort zone, and didn't sleep well. I had to do a little interview about the basic strategy we had decided and also talk about how I intended to deal with Rupert. Piers was fit to kill him already, said he is obviously useless and we would be better off without him. I asked Rupert if there was anything we could do to make it more bearable. He said he had no idea there were going to be cameras everywhere. I said, 'But it is a TV programme.' Yes, he said, but this is really not what he expected. Piers said, 'Do you want us to write your lines for you?' I could see those two coming to blows.

Thursday 14 December

Out to Millennium Bridge at the Tate for some photos. Calling lots of people trying to get them involved but it was tough, and all the tougher for the fact the cameras were there the whole bloody time. Meanwhile Rupert had done a runner, just upped and gone, so we were a man down. I got a call from Alan Sugar to get hold of Tim Campbell, young whizzkid who had been in the last real *Apprentice*. So I did and he sounded like he would be a good addition so we got him in as a sub, and before long he was getting a bit of order into things. It was going to be murder this though. Piers had got this idea of getting a busload of rich bankers flush with their bonuses who would all come down and give us tens of thousands. He said he knew someone at Goldman Sachs who would sort it, and we spent ages chasing them and the other banks, but getting nowhere. Back for a review of where we were. Ross and Danny focusing on food. Interlude when the women's team's chef came to wrong room. We kidnapped him, then Trinny came down in what seemed like genuine hysterics, and stabbed me in the back with a pen, then drew it right down my back. Fucking mad stuff. She was close to tears, like it really mattered. I suppose this is how this reality TV stuff works. We really kidnapped the chef. She really got angry!

Nick Keller was helping out with gifts and sports names. I left with Danny for the BBC to get Chris Evans on board, then managed to get away for a couple of hours for the school play. I was suddenly feeling totally exhausted, and even though ultimately it was only a telly programme, I already felt we were running out of time. I went back later via Matthew Freud's party. Sabrina Guinness [TV producer] a help. Ben Goldsmith [financier] nice guy, said he would bring rich friends. Usual Freud-type party. Celebs and business. Mick and Gaby. Tessa with Jessie. Natascha McElhone, both of us stunned the other was there. Karren and co were also in there hoovering up celebs. I had a chat with George Osborne who said he felt they could see a very clear strategy now, and that TB's departure was an importart part of it. They didn't feel GB was rising to the challenge, but fading from it.

Nice enough party if I could have concentrated without all this *Apprentice* nonsense going on. Cameron was leaving around the same time and we were filmed going out as I was trying to get him to come down to the fairground and support us. He said he would only do so to back the other team so I lost. I felt he had grown a bit in terms of presence. He definitely had presence around the place, seemed if anything even more confident. Philip Green had definitely defected to the girls' team. Karren told me that Trinny had been genuinely upset by the fight over the chef. This is fucking madness. Also we were getting hit because of their strict rules on donations. We couldn't just get pledges and fat cheques, the people had to come to the fairground and give it over then. Back in the real world, TB had finally been interviewed by the cops [re cash for honours]. Big, bad moment. I got tons of bids through the day to talk about it but decided not to. Piers going on about it endlessly. TB meanwhile off to Brussels.

Friday 15 December

Another walk-out possibility, with Ross threatening to leave. He felt the rules were making it impossible and the whole thing was becoming ridiculous. I did another little lecture about how the important thing was that there was a good telly programme at the end of it and the rest was for the birds. But it was all getting quite stressful. Tim Campbell was a great help, calm and focused and keeping us in order. Funny moment – and by now you really do forget there are cameras filming you – of me trying and failing to use a stapler. Piers still going on about his Goldman Sachs bus. Tim and Danny sorting the food. Out to Norwood with Piers and Ross for [pillory] stocks. In the back of the car trying to sort all the tickets and get order into all the various promises we thought we had. The stocks place was amazing, a treasure trove of stuff for film sets. Piers wanted the electric chair and the noose as well.

Drive to BHS to get stuff from Green. Now totally wilting. Piers said, 'Take Red Bull, it is amazing.' I did, and it worked, got some new energy from somewhere. To Nick Keller's to collect a load of stuff he had been gathering and then down to the site. Good banter with Piers and passers-by now. Margaret M helpful. To the fairground. I don't know if it was the Red Bull or the fact it was almost over, but I felt a lot better suddenly. Sorting out our special attractions. We were definitely winning on the quirky stuff, like people paying to pelt us in the stocks and also we'd got Tracey Emin painting coconuts as breasts. We had [John] Rankin [photographer] raking it in by doing portraits. Mick Hucknall brilliant on the hoopla, really hamming it up. Martin Offiah, Kyran Bracken and Kenny Logan [sports stars] all out for us running stalls. Yentob good too. But we were definitely losing out in terms of the cash coming in through their celebs. Cheryl had called in the Chelsea lot, so Ashley Cole and John Terry suddenly arrived throwing their cash about.

We then went into kidnap mode again, kidnapped someone from Take That, tried to kidnap Cheryl. Apologised to Trinny for the chef incident which apparently was still bugging her. Michael Winner [film director] meant to be doing Mystic Michael. Was hopeless. Annie Robinson fantastic fun, really got into it, and paid for me to have my picture taken with her friend who fancied me. Stocks and Tracey Emin our best stuff. Got Terry and Cole to do Annie in stocks. Piers and I were the most popular stock victims by far but hilariously Tessa felt she couldn't throw anything at me in case it hurt! Sugar arrived. Piers pestering and annoying him as much as he could. Chris Evans good. Nice atmosphere. We did OK towards the end. Karren worked a masterstroke by putting everything down as food to get the bonus. Tim and Danny exhausted but brilliant. I worked up a line to take – 'We won the fair but lost the finance' – and our team going around reciting the mantra. Simon Cowell backing the girls not us. We had loads of gifts left at the end and quite nice to give stuff like a flight to Miami to a total stranger. I was so glad it was all over though. It had had something like the rhythm of a party conference, total nightmare, came together, then gone.

We got a lift home with an exhausted Maureen Lipman and her Scottish bloke. She said she had not really enjoyed it, as she and Jo felt the others were so different. One or two of the papers trying to get GB into the loans cops inquiry, but it was running as 'Blairites smear GB' type thing, so that it was hard to know if it was real or just a daft McBride/Whelan-type story gone wrong, full of moral indignation at the idea GB would have known, and linking it to TB trying to get peerages for Ronnie Cohen [businessman] and Wilf Stevenson [director of Smith Institute]. They were also running that Michael was to be seen for a third time by the cops because his statements contradicted TB when he was interviewed. The whole cops' operation on this was a disgrace, giving a running commentary. TB off to Turkey to see Erdogan, and Piers having a lot of fun with the story that the government had stopped the Serious Fraud Office [alleged corruption] inquiry into BAE for fear of pissing off the Saudis. The line was 'national and international security' but it was basically economic, with a huge contract at risk. Messy, but [Lord Peter] Goldsmith [Attorney General] was out saying a prosecution would not succeed.

Saturday 16 December

A few hours' sleep, then a car to the studios. Neck sore because of so much time in the stocks. Neck massage from Emma. Jo B there, then dribs and drabs arrival. Loads of tired banter. Piers still abusing Ashley Cole. Trinny so loud. Hanging round then over to the boardroom lots of larking around while being told to be quiet. Told Tim to be businessman first showbiz second. In and kicked off fairly quickly. Piers at it. Sugar said we won creatively but they were better business people and they really did the money. On the figures they trounced us. We won on the rides but that it turned out was in part because Karren had put everything down as food. They were well ahead on food, us on rides and them massively on ticket sales. They won and went out celebrating, all really happy. We then had to go out, go to a café and discuss why we lost, blah. Ross Kemp easily the most recognised everywhere we went. Interesting though how often you can go into a place with a camera and it is treated as a commonplace.

Agreed we would all stick together, but Margaret had told me last night I would have to take two back in if we lost, so Sugar had a choice of three to fire one. I said not Tim, as he had done brilliantly for us, definitely me and Piers because they had told us it was going to come down to one of us for the chop, and we may as well play the whole thing for laughs, so Danny the third. When we got back to the board-room again Piers and I agreed it could not be Danny and it was down to me or him. Sugar basically said I was crap but fired Piers for being offensive to everyone. Piers and I had a pre-arranged bitch at each other. When Sugar said he was fired I turned and said, 'Again?' and we heard a great laugh all over the place [Morgan had been fired from editorship of the *Daily Mirror*]. All a real hoot and Piers hammed it up well. Sugar apologised off camera for all the rudeness. I said I really didn't mind. Without it they wouldn't have had a real programme. Emma was delirious. She said they had been looking at the rushes and it would make fantastic telly. I was totally shagged out. Funny how something that didn't ultimately matter very much could drain you so much. Mum was down having nice time. TB off on his travels heading towards Middle East.

Sunday 17 December

Still not sleeping. Also waking the whole time thinking why didn't we do this that and the other? We could have got Bill Gates, Ecclestone, Bill C. Could have done a Mick H turn. Should have had billboards saying the dodgems weren't safe. The papers full of TB and the cops and it all smelled bad for JoP, Ruth and McTernan as well as Levy. Outrage. Politics will become impossible at this rate. Cops out of control. Media out of control. Liz pointed me to Iain Dale's blog on all the papers who published stories based on info gained illegally. The *Mail* followed by *Sunday People* top of league. Took Mum to station, watched the next stage of cricket disaster in Oz then to West Ham v Man U with Rory. First we watched Chelsea on TV score three amazing goals to beat Everton so Alex was very deflated as he came through to see us before the match and give us tickets. Had been hoping Everton would have done bet-ter. I was sitting behind Bobby Charlton, friendly as ever, but it was a poor match and United really never showed. Chelsea win and United loss [0–1] meant all the momentum was back with Chelsea. Piers sent a very nice message saying he was with his mum and she was incredulous because he had told her we were now best friends. And he said, 'Thanks for making it tolerable and amusing amid a sea of luvvie nonsense.' TB in Iraq, also heading to Israel and Ramallah.

Monday 18 December

Out for breakfast with Noreena Hertz about the footballers/nurses project. She was too scattergun, needed support and also to go club by club and build a network of leaders in the clubs. I could probably help her easily enough but I was not sure the driving idea – show we care for nurses by foootballers giving them money – really added much. It could be tough. I was a bit unsettled by Natascha, who had said to me she thought I should just not do diaries, full stop, because it was too much the obvious expectable thing to do. I called Alex to bounce the Noreena/nurses thing off him and he thought it might be a runner because it would be good for football. He agreed to speak to Gary Neville [club captain] about it on Wednesday. He reckoned that if we could get a few big clubs involed it would go fine. Re yesterday he was really furious. The Chelsea result definitely hit them mentally. Also he felt Chelsea was a real working team now. His team didn't really turn up yesterday though. He said it is a horrible feeling, because there is no apparent reason but they don't get going as you know they can. He felt Mourinho was becoming a loose cannon. His attack on Andy Johnson [Everton player] diving the latest.

Alex said the whole intimidation thing was 'real Latin and Russian influence – absolutely anything goes. No sense of fair play or decency.'

Karren called for a natter, said she was missing the *Apprentice* scene. I must admit I wasn't though it was weird how much I kept thinking to myself, shit, I wish we had done that, why didn't we think of that? Testy exchange of emails with Sue Nye. Me saying I felt they missed a trick, that GB having got involved on the tax and charitable giving side would have been good. I also said I would have preferred 'no' to no reply, and said they had a bad reputation for being a bit one-way traffic – reaching out when they needed people, not the other way round. She replied saying they were doing other stuff. Also she couldn't believe that I suggested Gavyn [Davies, her husband, former BBC chairman] do the stocks. She felt we had always been able to be professional despite the rows between me and the BBC but she was shocked and upset by this. I said fair enough, maybe she had a point and it was insensitive, but I thought it might have reflected OK on both of us if he had done it, him pelting me, me pelting him.

I called JoP, who was in the Middle East with TB. The weekend press had been grim, more stuff pointing at him and others. Then today's story saying that they were now investigating destruction of emails. He still sounded fairly chirpy despite it all. He wanted me to check out whether one of the reporters breaking stories in *The Times* was related to one of the coppers investigating, which was a rumour doing the rounds. Both felt it was all an outrage but equally becoming clearer they were determined to get someone, probably Michael Levy. Spoke briefly to TB who asked me to take a look at his speech in the UAE later in the week. He was flying all over the place, Egypt, Israel, West Bank, and wanted to do a big number in Dubai on the bigger questions, especially on MEPP and also the 'generational battle' around extreme Islam. He was becoming a stuck record on it, but said it was the argument that had to be won, and people were already slipping back.

Tuesday 19 December

Breakfast with Ed, Gail and Susan, trying to get a fix on timing for publication. Various scenarios. Lunch with Carolyn Dailey [businessman]. Trinny there. How weird, go my whole life without meeting her and now she pops up like that. Still smarting I thought.

Wednesday 20 December

TB's speech went fine, but Iraq's deputy PM had a pop in New York, said Bush had stopped TB from agreeing to a timetable for troop withdrawal, and had 'brainwashed' him, so it was hard to get above it – Iraq not going as planned, TB Bush poodle. He was back pushing his line about Iran and Syria, how there was a chance to involve them properly if they gave up their bad ways. He had rewritten the Palestine section and he came over as pretty frustrated, so I guessed the meetings had not been brilliant.

Thursday 21 December

I was working upstairs and got a rather bizarre email from someone in Liverpool, who said he shared my name, and he had a horrible feeling he was getting my emails, and he 'was seeing things I know I shouldn't be seeing'. At first I thought it was a crank, but then he mentioned stuff to do with TB, and transition to GB, and TB's speeches, and it dawned that he was actually getting all my emails. I called Simon Lewis [Vodafone] who checked it out, and it turned out there had been some kind of cock-up. I spoke a couple of times to this poor guy, who seemed fine by the end of it, said he just couldn't believe all this stuff coming into his inbox. I said to Simon, who was flapping about things from my perspective, and getting me sorted with all sorts of special access to 24/7 service and so on, that they needed to take care of the guy too, who sounded spooked by the whole thing. It kind of didn't bear thinking about what he could have done with the back and forth stuff on GB, transition etc. It was a real fiasco for Vodafone and I think from the volume and level of calls they put in they were worried one of us would go public. Out for dinner with the Goulds, PG enjoying my discomfiture because he was normally the one leaving computers on trains and leaving papers lying around for anyone to read.

Friday 22 December

Off at the crack of dawn to Chequers, thinking it would probably be the last time with TB as PM. Really foggy. Arrived, parked up, Gale and Leo up and about, nice chat with them, Leo very sweet. Gale looking tired and said everyone was looking forward to a bit of a break 'though I don't suppose Tony will get one'. We sat and had a cup of coffee while Leo pottered around us, and ended up having quite a reflective chat. She asked how Fiona was, I said fine, but I realised it had not been easy for her, I hadn't always handled it well, because I was so focused and the thing was all so-consuming, and at the end it had all been a bit grisly. So now she was hoping I was out, so was I to be honest, most of the time, but it was never going to happen. 'So I see,' she said, indicating that there was the Christmas tree in the corner, and I was down for a meeting with TB. We had a natter about the time right back at the start, when she came down to France with them and TB talked me into doing the job. She said she remembered being on a drive, we were taking her to the airport, Tony and I, and she said she knew Tony was going to talk me into it, and she knew I was a bit worried, and she could tell the whole time she was there that Fiona had been hoping I'd say no.

She had been worried too, but she felt TB was made for it, and it was always going to happen. But she said these things were always difficult for families, and especially for wives, and she hated some of the things that had happened to Cherie, the nastiness and the media being so vile. I said I hadn't always handled that well either, and I felt sometimes I should have been more supportive of Cherie. She said Fiona had done a great job for her [as advisor], but it had never been easy. We moaned a bit about how Labour always got treated worse than the Tories. So Norma Major had written a book about this place – Chequers – can you imagine the fuss if Cherie had done that, even if all for charity? It was like the Tories were meant to be in power, we were 'little interlopers', she said. 'But we have got through it,' and she said the kids were all fine, as were mine, and so 'all's well that ends' kind of thing. I said she was such a fixture, it was a bit like Audrey with our kids, she had always been there when I was flying around the place, then when Fiona came in too, and it all got a bit crazy at times, but yeah, I guess we have got through.

One of the [Royal Navy] Wrens [security staff] came in and said TB was looking for me, so I went off to his little lounge, bumped into CB in her pyjamas, who was warmish but not warm, looked a bit startled to see me, did a kind of 'What you doing here?' kind of look, but then was perfectly friendly as I went to the table where all the papers were laid out, and turned them all over to the sports pages, and said, 'Rule 1, don't bother reading the papers.' TB came out, seemed very chirpy, we went back into his study, he said his trip had gone well, he was totally seized of all the arguments, determined to keep pushing on MEPP, now and after he'd gone, because without it getting to a better place, nothing else really improved fundamentally either. We chatted about the Yanks. He felt GWB was a good man trying to do the right thing but the capability of their system weak. He agreed Rumsfeld had been a disaster in charge of the aftermath. He had another big decisionn to come. US siting ICBMs in Europe and were assuming after Trident we would not. But actually there was a good reason to have them.

So far only GB, JP, MB and Des Browne were in on the discussion and he said it was JP who got the point that with 'the nutters' like Korea we might actually want to press the US to site here. But GB was not so keen. TB said the police investigation was more and more of an outrage the longer it went on. Stuff was just leaking out all over the place, and they were creating a momentum for themselves that in the end if nothing happened, they would look ridiculous. He said his own interview had been fine, almost two hours, a couple of cops who seemed a little bit embarrassed to be there. Yates himself didn't do it. They seemed to be going through a fairly set pattern of questions, and a lot of if was about Michael and what he did, how he operated, but he said the only thing that had worried him was something that apparently came from them investigating [Sir] Christopher Evans [businessman] and a line in his diary that talked about a kind of price list. He said it was certainly not a great moment, two cops coming into his office, and the atmosphere around the place awful, and of course the media loving it once the news broke, and being the first serving PM to be interviewed by the police was not a nice thing to have on your CV. But he still felt it would in the end probably go nowhere and 'certainly it shouldn't'.

Politics was becoming impossible. How can you run parties and campaigns without some kind of resources, and how can we raise funds when the general mood is so anti-political, and there is zero chance of the public backing more public funding for parties? He said he was even angrier for Ruth and Jonathan than he was for himself. They were bearing up considering, but it was horrible to have to go through all this. Awful. It wasn't long before we were on to GB. He felt the new policy process teams had been of some benefit, but no, GB was still not really engaging with it. He reckoned GB might have another go against him in January. At one point TB asked straight out, 'If he comes at me again, do I survive?' I said I think he would still be a bit worried about the way the last coup played out. Yes, TB was weakened, and yes GB was more established as the only contender, but he was weakened, especially with the public, and he wasn't daft, he would know that. Yes, he said, but do not think for one second the ambition to get me out as soon as he can has gone.

He said his current plan was to announce in May that he would be gone by July. He still felt there might be some kind of contest, though perhaps not immediately. It might be that GB settled in, but then people felt he was not hacking it. So, slim chance of a contest to succeed TB – I couldn't see that at all right now – and perhaps less slim some kind of challenge down the track. He still felt GB would benefit from some kind of contest in any event, and also I felt there was a danger we had a change of leadership but no real debate about whether anything else needed to change. There was still very little sign of what GB would do differently, and I was worried his instincts would lead him to define himself against TB, rather than DC. I told TB about the little chats I had had with Cameron and Osborne, and even putting to one side the fact they would be wanting me to think they were confident, and wanting me to think they rated TB, they could not have been clearer that they felt TB was a threat to them and GB was an opportunity.

TB said he still had an instinct something might happen to stop GB from being there at the next election. He said he too had been picking up much more favourable assessments of JR, and also 'David Miliband is definitely starting to get restless… that generation can see this thing slipping away if we are not careful.' The problem was that throughout the Cabinet, the PLP and the party, he said, everyone was persuaded of two deeply contradictory things: 'One, GB would get it. Two, he couldn't win against Cameron.' Jacqui Smith [Redditch] was clear it was her seat gone, and yet she had to sit there and watch us sleepwalk towards it for the lack of obvious alternative people or strategy. It was not about being Scottish, he said, any more than with Neil it had all been about Welshness. These were reasons that people gave for something deeper that they felt. And what the people we won over worried was that deep down GB didn't really get them. He felt that for all the trust stuff thrown at TB, and the hatred over Iraq, or the anger about tuition fees, or any of the rest of it, in fact 'people at least felt I am sincere, that anything I fight for it is because I really believe it'.

They doubted GB's instincts. They had a respect for him – though a lot of that was because we talked him up so much – but there was not the same 'liking' that he had been able to engender in people, and what last September did, with the sense that it had gone from media talk to something more organised to unseat him, was give them something to articulate it. Even people who respect him thought there was something odd about it, and when he came out in public around that time, he looked so shifty because people knew he was up to no good. There was a darker side there, known to people in the know, but which was suddenly more widely visible. But it is not even about ambition. It is a feeling a certain sort of person has – 'and I have always had an instinct for who and where they are' – that he does not get them or the modern world. He was being very open and almost philosophical about it. He said the truth is that I contracted a lot of power to someone who is very intelligent, very driven and very flawed. He said he had been determined not to make Thatcher's mistake and try to pick a successor in own mould. But maybe in standing back a bit he was making a bigger mistake, and giving party and country the wrong man.

We have always managed to keep the Tories where we want them, because we staked our ground and would not be budged from it, and because the alternative PMs they brought forward did not offer an attractive alternative. DC can be that attractive alternative, and even if he is not great, he is good enough. People can see him in the job.

Politically he is going to pick New Labour off the shelf if GB gives him the room, and GB is already starting to, because he has tried to pretend to the Murdoch lot he will be unremittingly New Labour and to the Compass lot he will be more left-wing, that once I am gone, we will be real Labour again. This is the problem in the difference between operating at Chancellor level, and PM/leader. He thinks you can reconcile everyone by creating different arguments for different constituencies, but you can't. You have to confront difficult choices and the reason I have always been comfortable in my political skin is because I believe in the New Labour positioning and the policy positions that leads to.

So even the most left-wing trade unionist or activist might sometimes take a look and think, fucking Blair, might as well have a Tory, but then it is so easy to push back on that – hold on pal, who did the minimum wage, who did Sure Start, who did the schools and hospitals, spending as well as reform? And all because of this driving belief in a different approach that understood what you needed to do to win, and the instincts of the British people to make it happen. 'It has never been a compromise for me, because I believe it.' GB has bought too much into this idea that the soft left put out the whole time, oh yeah we had to do all this New Labour stuff to win, but now we have shown we can win, we can go back to being a more traditional Labour Party. So he says that to the party and something else to the public, and they work it out. That is why, he said, he felt I – AC – had to get involved with him and make sure he understood all that, because the advice he will be getting elsewhere will be pushing him left not centre, and you're right, he will want people to be saying, 'he is not Blair,' when what he needs them to be saying is, 'There is more to him than Cameron, that Tory lightweight.'

He said DC definitely had confidence, but he had felt a little bit of fear there when he did his 'clunking fist' line, and said when it came to the fight, DC would be carried out of the ring, 'but, you know what, I am no so sure'. He was definitely totally resigned to going now, resigned to it – more or less – being GB, and maybe it was because it was Christmas, I don't know, but he seemed more settled generally. He asked about my current thinking on diaries. Still not settled, but maybe a short version out in May as he was announcing departure, take the agenda, be part of the original voices setting the tone for when he went. Then three one-hour films to go with it. I said there had to be tricky stuff in there, including about him, for it to be authentic, but he would come out seven out of ten or higher, way better than anyone else. He seemed

OK on it. 'I'd certainly rather have you out there on it than most of the so-called experts on me.'

I asked him if he was doing resignation honours. 'What, you want a knighthood, or a peerage?' Neither, I said. Jonathan and I were both clear on that. In fact, he didn't seem to realise that outgoing PMs do resignation honours at all. He said he probably wouldn't bother, or maybe he would just do a few for people nobody had ever heard of. Of course the police inquiry didn't exactly help, but he seemed genuinely not to have given it any thought, and not intending to. On what he would do after he left, he said he would have Africa and global warming as issues he would keep trying to push on. But his two chosen projects were probably going to be inter-faith dialogue, maybe a foundation on that, and governance, especially for governments of developing countries. He had this idea of maybe him, a John Browne, a Mervyn King [Governor of the Bank of England] type taking teams to different countries advising on governance, business and infrastructure. He felt I could get involved in that maybe. He felt we had a pretty unique set of skills and now experience in the core team and it would be good to keep it intact to some extent.

He said he felt I had got myself to a good place, personally and reputationally, but he still felt I was lacking purpose. I told him that Fiona was still basically pretty negative about the whole experience. He seemed really saddened by it, said it was in some ways the worst thing about politics at this level, that friendships got tested and families torn apart, but he felt she and I were still strong together and he felt one day she would have a different take on it, that it was all still too raw. He felt deep down I would have preferred had I been there the whole way through, beginning to end. Part of me, yes, part of me, no. He said in some ways he was looking forward to going, having more freedom and time. He might live abroad for a while just to get his bearings again, and think. He said there are three groups of people who want to deny him leaving when he wants. The media would like to see me kicked out ASAP because they want a new story and a new set of characters to play with. The Tories want me out ASAP because they think I bring Cameron down a few notches. GB wants me out because he is impatient. I said I felt we were sleepwalking to car crash.

He agreed but also said I should not use the book and any publicity around it to damage GB. GB respects you, he said, fears you, and it is important to keep that. If you really go for him, you will lose influence with him. I said I have been clear with GB, I will help him, but not if it means playing divisive games vis a vis TB, and only if I can engage on my terms. It almost certainly will be him and therefore I won't do anything that could be thought to be helping the Tories to do him in. I told him Stott's assessment, that the TB–GB story was a faultine which he never dealt with, and which ultimately would bring us down. He said maybe. He had thought long and hard and the reason it had been such a constant faultline was it was a constant dilemma, almost from the off. Sometimes, even now, he feels he should have dealt with it, then immediately I think, no it was impossible and the consequences could have been even worse. We'll never know. We didn't do it. So we are where we are. 'I felt I managed it just about as well as possible, but the one thing we know about GB is he is a real force. If I had put him out he would have used it to even greater damage. He would not have just disappeared.'

Probably true, I said, but the story of the government is we could have been 20 per cent, 30 per cent, 50 per cent better if we had somehow managed to work together better than we had. We had been in there, just nattering, for ages, three hours or so, and eventually CB came in, much friendlier, and said she had an idea for the night Comic Relief went out. She would pelt Piers in the stocks. 'Ah progress,' I said. 'I thought you were going to suggest pelting me.' TB asked me a bit about *The Apprentice*, and how much I hated it. He was amused by it all but said he could never, ever do something like that. He said I hope your book makes clear that at least we had a lot of laughs. He asked if I wanted to stay for lunch but I had to get back and so we walked out to the car. 'You're right we could have been a better government. But we have been better than most. We have a record I would be happy to put against most other governments. The country is a lot better, more open and confident, public services are way better. We count on the world stage. But definitely, yes, we have been held back by division and ego and all the usual stuff and maybe politics is always like that.

I said I can remember at the start, when I drove through France and I was thinking OK, I will do it, and I was visualising ahead, and trying to see how it would go, and one of the things I said to myself, having covered Thatcher and Lawson, Thatcher and Howe, Major and Lamont, Neil and John [Smith], wouldn't it be amazing if he and GB, me and Peter would just be rock-solid as a team, defy gravity, just keep on winning. I really thought we could do that. 'Well, we didn't,' he said, 'but we did a hell of a lot of stuff.' He felt he was leaving when he still had a lot to give, but GB effectively made it impossible. He was back to saying he would not have done a third term if GB had worked properly with him. 'Come on Tony, you're talking to me...' A lot to think about as I drove back.

It had definitely felt like one of those end of chapter conversations, he was much mellower than usual, had clearly been thinking a lot and was now just getting himself in the right shape for the last lap and then go.

I told Gail and Ed V that TB seemed to be up for the idea of me doing something, like edited highlights of edited highlights, even while he was still there, though perhaps it might be unrealistic in terms of the content, and also I wasn't sure if we had time to get it all through the vetting process. I got the other AC from Liverpool to do me a note on what happened yesterday with Vodafone. I was worried that having successfully appeased me, and apologised to the hilt, they were not doing enough to make sure he was OK about things from his perspective. Once they realised it was me they were dealing with, they just ignored him, and the truth is he was the one more likely to create a fuss. I mentioned it to Gail, who thought I should really kick up a fuss and threaten them with MI5, the works. Not sure I could be bothered. Helena [Kennedy] and Iain Hutchinson [surgeon husband] party. Jim Naughtie very down on GB. He felt he hadn't changed at all and that indicated an inability to do so. He was amazed how tolerant we all were. Joan Bakewell [broadcaster] also there though and she had met him recently in her arts role and she really liked him, said she thought he would be a terrific PM.

Saturday 23 December

Calum got offers from Manchester, Leeds and Nottingham universities. Off to Burnley v Derby. Only just made the kick-off, because the traffic was so dire. Good game, though 0–0.

Christmas breaker

Got to the end of the Stott cut version of Volume 4. Amazing what we were losing. Having another crise about whether it was the right thing to do. Really not sure. But definitely felt GB a problem. Out to get Fiona's Christmas present, which had been a stroke of luck, part inspired by Amanda Levete at the ballet a while back. She had said to enjoy the ballet she imagined they were footballers running around a pitch, and out on the bike the other day, I went past a gallery in Hampstead and there in the window was a sculpture of a footballer as a ballet dancer! Had to be. I went in and ordered it and today went to collect it. They told me Thierry Henry had also been taking a look but I beat him to it.

Christmas went fine. Barnsley v Burnley crap game [1–0]. To the

Kinnocks on the 27th. I had been meaning to chat about plans for the diaries but it was not the right time. Bill Keegan [journalist] and family were there so it was not easy. I was mainly chatting to Helle about her situation, which was improved. She definitely had a bit of steel and resilience. I had been keeping in touch periodically with Peter Schmeichel who was telling me she was done for, but I sensed she could still do it. Dinner at the Milibands on the 28th. David even more down on GB than before. He felt he wasn't developing or growing. They had had a real argument about the Climate Change Bill.

Despite it all, though, David said he didn't see the circumstances that would open up the leadership for him. GB has it stitched up. Why would he set himself up for a big hit? But he felt GB was not really getting the scale of what was needed on the environment, and on political strategy more generally, he was in much the same place as TB had been at Chequers – feeling GB knew it was coming but was unsure what he would do with it. David was definitely changing though. He was enjoying the brief, was definitely expanding his arguments and the political space. He also seemed much more calculating in his language though, something Louise also pointed out once or twice. They were all very down on the Iraq situation and he felt TB's recent speeches didn't really grasp how bad things were.

Saturday 30 December

Saddam executed 3 a.m., for crimes against humanity. Pictures in a noose and then wrapped in a shroud. He looked pretty calm on the gallows, but then footage emerged of him being jeered and abused and even countries which had argued for the killing were saying it was going over the top. Alex called, said he had put the Noreena idea to the dressing room and Gary Neville was resistant. I kind of understood why. He said they would make donation instead. Alex sixty-five tomorrow. Still going for Owen Hargreaves [Bayern Munich player]. Felt Chelsea were finally being stretched by other teams for 90 minutes. Re wealth of players – [Robbie] Fowler [Liverpool] probably the richest. Neville building a village! Rooney and Ronaldo running the dressing room.

Sunday 31 December

Off to David Mills's place for New Year. Very quiet but perfectly nice time. Odd situation with Tessa on the phone to him from Ireland as midnight struck. He was still thinking they'd be back together one day, but it was all far from certain. He was on good form though. Andrew Knight [journalist, director News Corp] came round and after a bit of chat re Murdoch days – and him telling me James was even more ruthless than his father – I was probably a bit too loose about the diaries. I was going over some of the dilemmas, especially re GB and how to do a book that was truthful but did not damage him, but also how much of private conversations with people like Clinton could really be published. I was also worried that some of the exchanges with Neil were just so heavy, did I really want to put all that out there. In a way GB was the easiest because I had settled that one in my own mind.

Monday 1 January 2007

Burnley's game against Stoke was off. So we stayed down and later went to Andrew Knight's beautiful house set in hundreds of acres. Clearly pretty loaded, lovely pool and so I had a swim with Grace and Nina. Nice chat with Andrew and his wife Marita. She shared the Natascha view re the diaries, felt it would be really cool for everyone to know they were there, but never publish them. She was quizzing me about GB. 'Why do people not like him?' she said. 'I have met people who have really quite violent reactions but he seems to me to be OK, nothing like as bad as people say.' I found myself defending GB more than I expected to in these circumstances. The news was still dominated by the ramifications of Saddam's hanging.

Tuesday 2 January

Fiona really enjoyed her birthday, and we had got on pretty well over the break. I went overboard on the presents front this year. I was doing schoolwork with Calum, then all out to the Camden Brasserie, in between working on a piece for *The Times* on the film of Gillian Slovo's book [*Red Dust*] about the South African Truth and Reconcilliation Commission. Out for a run but I was still not right.

Wednesday 3 January

Out with Grace to the stables. Nice chat with Catherine MacLeod who felt my diary strategy sounded fine. She was really sticking up for Fiona in terms of her right to have felt I allowed our lives to be overtaken by the TB scene, but also said she would have worried for TB had I not been there when I was. Anji called for a natter. She said Sue Nye had been really shocked to the core at my suggestion that Gavyn Davies should have come to the Comic Relief fair. Sue had said they basically felt it showed a side of me that was not prepared to stop at anything once I got into a competitive situation, and of course that had resonance for what had happened over Kelly and Hutton, because then too Gavyn felt I had shown I would stop at nothing. I suppose it had been a bit insensitive, and I was probably kidding myself in saying I had seen it as a way of maybe making up a bit with Gavyn by inviting him. But they felt it was just a sign of me wanting everything on my own terms, and as I knew GD had loads of money, I just saw him as another rich bloke we could get to help us in a silly TV show.

I had actually not really seen or had any contact with Gavyn since Hutton, and I suppose I underestimated how much he felt I had ruined his life, given the Beeb was his dream job.* But I said to Anji, having just done the diaries, I still cannot see how they think I should have reacted differently, and their handling of it was woeful. 'Listen, darling,' she said, 'none of that means it was anything but odd that you asked Sue if Gavyn would like to come to a fairground and have you throw tomatoes at him in the stocks.' 'He could have thrown them at me!' She said she was relieved to hear I agreed that even doing the Comic Relief thing was 'borderline dangerous'. Be careful about this telly stuff, she said. 'Piers is Piers and you do not want to be seen as Piers.' I said the charity stuff was the tip of the iceberg. I told her some of the crazier offers I was getting, including the one of being made into a black man and exposing racism.

TB sent a note through, not quite as compendious as usual. His main point though that with opponents inside and outside wanting to show he had run out of steam, it had to be contradicted by reality, all focused on policy, leading to policy review outcomes in the spring. NHS, trust schools, energy, pensions, welfare to work, all the Home Office stuff. But it all felt like he was just trying too hard to set up a process that outlived him.

---

* Davies had resigned as chairman in the wake of the Hutton Report, which had criticised the BBC.

Thursday 4 January

David S. Asking me a lot re how I felt about Saddam's death. Cetainly no release or feeling of it being a new phase because the media just using every part of it – the insults filmed on mobiles in particular – to make it all seem terrible. Also on the diaries, current plan was really losing me sleep. Didn't feel right. Even had Arsene Wenger telling me not to do it – in a dream! Saw Stuart Prebble who had read both short Volume 1 and long Volume 1 and felt like slitting his wrists because it meant losing so much. He felt there was a real risk of the baby going out with the bathwater. Really conflicted. Fiona thinking I should do a totally different kind of book, narrative not diary. Long chat with Ed later too, said I didn't feel we'd reached the right decision. He felt we had. I couldn't see the point in enforced delay of so long for reams of stuff nothing to do with GB. Another day working on them and agonising. Not like me in some ways. Too many tough calls attached to them. Worked on it. Longish run later, first in ages.

Tuesday 9 January

Meeting at Susan Sandon's house, to go through cuts page by page, and also talk about the cover. Sort of edging to the right decisions, probably. More US troops going to Iraq. TB post-holiday media flurry on climate change offsetting etc. Also big noise around Ruth Kelly admitting her son had moved to a private school because of 'significant learning difficulties'. TB sympathetic, but not easy. He was also finally out on Saddam, saying what happened re his death was wrong and it would have been better had he faced trial, but also restating basic justification for the action in Iraq.

Wednesday 10 January

Nice lunch with Annie Robinson and her friend Di Donovan. Lots of reminiscence re [Robert] Maxwell [late Mirror Group proprietor] times. I admitted to her I had been falling off the wagon a bit and she was giving me a bit of a talking-to. But she was very up on how I should see my life, felt it was all OK and going to get better. She felt she and I had emerged as the big stars of that era from the *Mirror* because 'we stuck our heads above parapets and we dared to break out of the mould'. She was happy RS was doing the diaries, felt it would give him real purpose to fight the illness. Di a total star, funny, said she was like a lovestruck teenage groupie!

Thursday 11 January
All day working on cuts. Met Ed and Nigel Bennett to go over the Prebble project. Chatted to Syd [Young] about all the various dilemmas, and felt more comfortable afterwards. He felt the approach on GB should be 'chronicle the past without jeopardising the future'.

Monday 15 January
All day at Stotts' finalising our cuts. Hard going but we got there.

Tuesday 16 January
I missed TB's office meeting because I was off to Scotland to launch the Great Edinburgh Run with Brendan Foster, Andy Kerr [MSP] and Liz McColgan [former athlete]. The driver taking me to City Airport was a former ballet dancer fascinating about the sacrifices they had to make, said a handful made a good living but a lot of even top dancers were barely on more than a grand a week. Met by Donald at Edinburgh, then up to the castle. The launch went fine, nice atmosphere, me playing the bagpipes on the ramparts as the clock struck one, nice chat with Gavin and Scott Hastings [former Scotland rugby players]. Brendan absolutely raging about how unfairly TB was being treated. Some programme called *The Trial of Tony Blair* had just been on C4, a drama based on the idea of him being tried for war crimes, and Brendan was livid about it. Andy Kerr said it was not worth worrying about. It was 'total horseshit'. Brendan happy with the way the launch went, then I was off to see Jack McConnell [First Minister] with his two main people. He said things were in not bad shape, and that overall he was winning the argument on remaining in the Union. But the SNP were up for a fight and confident they could win the argument on independence.

It helped that Salmond was a bit flaky, he felt, and prone to run away from arguments. I said that is not how he came across to me. There was a big job to be done in making sure people really knew what separation meant. He felt if the SNP could define it as all being about 'independence', they had a head's start. We had to define it as separation. But they had a lot more money and would definitely be able to mount a campaign. TB had included 'Scotland' in his list of weekend worries, and had asked me to check in with Jack to make sure they felt they had a campaign in place. This was one area where both TB and GB wanted the same outcome. TB did not want to go out on the back of a bad vote, GB wanted and needed a better base, and would also cop the blame if Scotland turned against us.

Jack felt the more input from TB, GB and Reid and the other UK politicians who could help the better. He was not blessed with deep talent in his own team, but still felt they should be OK, but they needed help with personnel and the basics, like storyline development. I was with him an hour or so, and he felt broadly on top of things. A very old-style civil service building, but he looked and sounded the part and his private office seemed OK. There was definitely a lot of nervousness around the place though. TB press conference today, a lot of it was about Scotland, because of the 300th anniversary of the Union, and the SNP out making the case for a referendum, TB saying even raising the question caused uncertainty and instability. But the other news out of it was him saying 'Of course' when he was asked whether he would be at the Brussels summit late June, which set off another round of 'So when does he go?'

Thursday 18 January

Lunch with Noreena Hertz to go over her project. Gary Neville had called and she was pleased re that. The 'big thing' in the media was a race row arising out of *Celebrity Big Brother* and I had a long series of email exchanges with Tim Hincks [Endemol] about it. They had been trying to persuade me to do it, which was obviously a non-starter, but I said they were making me realise how right I was. The whole thing was horrible. His argument was it held a mirror to life, and raised issues normally swept under carpet, me saying low-life dumbing down, symbol of the modern media's epic, historic awfulness. *Big Brother* was even dominating the coverage of GB's visit to India, because the Indians were talking about making a formal diplomatic complaint about the Bollywood actress in the series [Shilpa Shetty] being racially bullied by Jade Goody. It was fucking ridiculous that this is what politics and diplomacy has become. Both TB and GB having to deal with this, and Tim telling me it was all about the media shining a torch on real issues. There was something odd about the whole thing, and what it said about us as a country, that everyone seemed to be talking about this fucking programme. I think other countries must think there is something weird about us.

Friday 19 January

Caroline Gascgoine round to do picture research for the book. As she went over the timetable – really tight – I thought it best to put a call into Gus O'Donnell. 'God, it's terrible, isn't it?' he said. He assumed I was calling about Ruth [Turner] being arrested, but I hadn't known. 'What is terrible?' 'Haven't you heard. I assumed TB would have called you and that's why you're calling. Ruth got arrested this morning.' Fucking hell. This was getting ridiculous. I said don't tell me anything I am not supposed to know. He said it was bound to be all over the news before long, because that seemed to be the way of it. He assumed TB had called me. I called around later, including TB, and it turned out the police arrived half-six in the morning, did that thing where they stood with her while she got ready to leave, common criminal stuff, and then hauled her in for a few hours, then briefed it was about the honours and, for good measure, 'suspicion of conspiring to pervert the course of justice'.

TB asked if I thought he should put out something defending her? Definitely. Four arrested now, said Gus, and the mood around it getting nastier. I said to Gus, I don't want to add to your problems but I am doing a book/diaries and I want to do the first instalment around the time TB goes, so I need to get stuff into the system soonish. He said Sue Gray [Cabinet Office] would be my main port of call. I said how did it work? 'Basically from what I know, people submit their books, we ask them to take lots out and usually we get ignored.' I said I had already taken lots out myself because I was determined if GB took over, I was not going to let the Tories use me to damage him. He said as these things did take up a lot of time and work for his people, it was important it was proper vetting and not us just presenting them with a take it or leave it fait accompli. I said I had discussed with TB and he was broadly happy with the approach I had taken. 'And GB?' he asked. 'I have not discussed and I don't imagine he will be happy, but I am very sensitive to his needs, overly so say the publishers.'

The Ruth situation was fucking grim. I gave her a call later. She said they just turned up while she was in bed, stayed with her while she got herself sorted. She said she totally hated being the centre of attention and an embarrassment like this, but she was sure she had done nothing wrong. It was horrible though, for her, for TB, and no doubt there were others they would be doing the same to as the days went on. The SNP guy who started the whole thing off, Angus MacNeil, was out crowing that 'water was now lapping around Blair's neck'.* The whole thing was Kafkaesque.

Saturday 20 January

I called TB and we started with our usual 'Everything is great' joking around. He said yesterday's arrest was an outrage – 'both the fact of, and the manner of.' All they had was something in Christopher Evans' diary that may or may not involve ML and what was annoying them about Ruth was that she was refusing to change her story to suit theirs. He was clearly feeling the whole thing was now unpredictable, and that 'celebrity cops' was a new problem – this nonsense about investigating Jade Goody over racism the latest. Christ knows how many police hours have gone into Serious Crimes honours probe 'a political issue made a criminal investigation'. Generally, he felt on top of his game but, he said, the media allow no sense of a narrative other than trivia and crisis and GB 'is now just ploughing his own furrow'. It was clear there was next to no proper contact or discussion. He felt GB was still barking up wrong trees, like national identity/Britishness, next steps for the Constitution, but he was refusing to come together with TB over the policy agenda he was trying to set that would connect with the public. And he still feared he would be going back on New Labour if he could. So all in all, not great.

But he said other things were going better. Sinn Fein had moved in the right direction on policing and courts, things were reasonably calm, and he reckoned with a few more next steps, they were on for power-sharing [in Northern Ireland Assembly] back up by March. He was also convinced the US were finally going to do something bold on MEPP – I'll believe that when I see it – and on the domestic front, he said the presentation he had on the NHS showed we were getting through the problems and the changes were coming good. He admitted

---

* In 2006, several candidates for peerages nominated by Tony Blair were rejected by the House of Lords Appointments Commission. Suspicions that donations to the Labour Party by the men had influenced their nominations led to Scottish National Party MP MacNeil making complains to the Metropolitan Police.

life felt pretty shitty most of the time, and things like yesterday brought it home how it affected people all around him, but he still felt he had a lot to give. Also that it would be plain wrong to go before even getting halfway through the parliament. We joked about him doing an Alex [Ferguson] and changing his mind. He said maybe when we bring forward the policy stuff in the spring, and it is clear GB rejects a lot of it he should go out and say, 'OK, I've had thirteen years of this nonsense, all because we didn't have a contest thirteen years ago – so let's have one now.' Then we were off on one about what parts of the *Celebrity Big Brother* format we could use to generate more interest in the vote.

Sunday 21 January

Out for a run, then out to Geoffrey [former *Daily Mirror* political journalist] and Margit Goodman 60th wedding anniversary. Fiona telling Neil about the book. He was not keen. Michael Foot, on the other hand, told me if I had kept a daily record, as everyone said, 'you have not just the right, but the duty, dear boy, the duty to publish. This is history.' He was speaking so loudly and I could see Fiona and Neil at the other end looking down, and both shaking their head, albeit with a smile! Met up with Rory and off to Arsenal v Man U at the Emirates. United one up then two down last minute. Great stadium but atmosphere not great. Too many United tourists. Back then out to the Roundhouse for a Jim Capaldi [drummer and singer] tribute, as Fiona friendly with his widow. Nice do.

Monday 22 January

Waiting for latest book version to come back. Seeing Stuart [Prebble] and Judith [Dawson, documentary-maker] to go over a few ground rules. Caught a bit of the news at the gym. Shit for TB on most fronts.

Tuesday 23 January

In to LRF to sign thousands of letters for the City Challenge [charity cycling event]. Chat to Cathy about her exasperation at the conservatism of trustees. Asked me to approach Ed and Tony Ball. Both said yes, Ed very enthusiastically so. Ran back, got latest version back from RS/RH. 355k words, now going for last cuts. Not doing much else.

Wednesday 24 January

David S. Pleased that I had not touched the booze since I last saw him. Keen for me at some point to go away, totally on my own, for a month, with no contact with the outside world, and just see what happened. 'Can I read?' Yes. 'Can I write?' Yes. 'Can I go out and buy things I need?' Better to get them beforehand. 'What is the purpose?' To see what happens when you strip everything down to the bare essentials. He felt I found the idea scary because I needed other people, but he thought something like this was needed to get to the bottom of the depression. 'Things would bubble up, and you would find themes and patterns and make sense of it. Maybe.' Maybe, I said. He looked a bit tired and down himself. Can't be easy listening to people drone on about their problems all day. He told me of a fire victim who took ten years to work out what to do next. By comparison, he felt I was doing OK.

To Dover House for a Scottish campaign meeting. Douglas, PG, PH, Sue Nye, Ed M, Spencer, Matthew Doyle, Paul Sinclair [Scottish Labour special advisor]. The polling suggested things were a lot worse than Jack led me to believe last week. Jack was beaten by Salmond on every rating bar conceit and weakness. The MSPs were seen as second raters, and the public had little sense of what they did. The feeling was that anyone who was any good went to London and forgot about Scotland. So that damaged GB, JR etc., but not Salmond because they felt at least he went there as a Scot, stayed as a Scot and caused trouble all the time. Douglas said the question was how do we use TB and GB? We were probably OK driving down their numbers but how do we get up ours? I felt a real lack of energy in this gathering. We were all saying what we had said for years. PG drilling down on the numbers. DA asking questions, setting out problems, but then wanting other people to lead to decisions. Me saying we need big strategic arguments which we then hammer home. Peter Hyman saying we need big bold policy moves, double devolution, even a referendum on the same day.

The GB people seemed to be there almost as spectators, though thankfully Sue was perfectly friendly after our recent spat. I felt uneasy about the whole thing, though. I had a quick lunch with Liz, who said the mood around the place was not great, and then in to see JoP who was a bit down about things. He felt what was happening to Ruth was dreadful and the political fallout obviously bad. The cops kept coming back because they could find nothing. He felt the longer it went on the more confident he was it would lead nowhere, but it was not a nice thing to have in the background the whole time. I went through to No. 11, having been invited to one of GB's little dinners. I was met by Sarah, friendly enough, mainly small talk. Shriti Vadera [investment banker] trying very hard to be friendly. Stuart Rose [CEO Marks & Spencer]. Duncan Bannatyne [Scottish entrepreneur] and his wife, John Hutton and Heather Rogers [permanent secretary to Alan Milburn]. Andy Hornby from HBOS. Matthew D'Ancona [journalist, *The Spectator*]. Some bloke who made TV programmes whose name I didn't get, and who knew all about *The Apprentice*, including how it ended (on which we had been sworn to secrecy). Nick Klein from Citibank, who had just signed up Noreena for a board place. Noreena who had called me just before I came in after her visit to Man U where she got Gary Neville signed up.

GB arrived. He had a button in him that was pressed whenever he saw me and made him say something about football. 'So no Burnley tonight?' Then into a chat re reality TV and talent shows. He said he actually liked the talent shows, that they were a great way for people who had talent but who would otherwise have no way of getting known and making a success of themselves. He said he thought Simon Cowell was an impressive guy, me raging at the way he set the shows up so he ended up owning virtually all aspects of everything. I said it was a classic case of where he felt he had to say he liked these things, because clearly the public did, but come on, deep down, you hate it as much as I do. He did say it had been surreal to be in India and having to do interviews about *Big Brother* and a diplomatic incident. Through to dinner, and I was next to Joanna Bannatyne and John Hutton's girlfriend. JB said her mum has leukaemia and because of my LRF work she won't have a word said against me or TB. She asked me what Bush was really like, and I was halfway through the answer, when literally my chair collapsed. In slow motion.

One leg just gave way. I could feel it going, and then as it went, I tried to rescue myself and grab on to the table, but it just crashed. I grabbed her leg on the way and almost pulled her down with me. The whole thing was out of some awful farce. GB, sitting opposite, jumped up, ran round asking if I was OK, and I was laughing now, saying, 'Ladies and gentlemen, Gordon has had his revenge for all the things I have done to help Tony stay in the job,' and at least he was laughing about it. I could feel a fucking great lump on my hip where I landed. GB said, 'Put in a claim to the Treasury.' Sarah was off getting me a new chair, which I tested gingerly. 'You wouldn't do it twice, would you?' It certainly got the mood a bit lighter. Heather said John [Hutton] was just waiting and watching. It was an odd time. GB clearly didn't see him as being one of his closest colleagues, but the fact he was there tonight showed he wanted to keep him on board if he could. But it was impossible to know which GB was real, the one being nice and charming at an event like this, or the one whose people were working the whole time on the press and doing in anyone who might be viewed as a threat, and plenty more who would never be a threat.

Fiona was sitting next to GB and they seemed to be chatting away OK. She also had a chat later with Sarah who said she has never been in the No. 11 flat and not seen CB for months. It was quite an odd evening, and not just for the chair incident. Fiona said that GB had been very warm, like his old self, but clearly intent on me being in there to help him, and also trying to persuade her that she should think about getting a seat. Anji was in No. 10 and she said they could hear all the hilarity and she realised it was something to do with me because they could hear me through the ceiling! It was the first time Fiona had been back in there at all since we left. TB was getting grief for missing the Iraq debate in the Commons.

Thursday 25 January

Stayed up late last night to finish the latest edit so out for a run early this morning, first OK run for ages. Then got a cab in for the TB strategy meeting. I briefed them on the Scotland meeting and we agreed he needed to get up there and really start to land blows on Salmond. He had to be seen to campaign and win an argument, and really show he knew there was a fight on. He was suspicious of DA on this, felt he was analysing not leading and they were all talking Jack down because he was an easy target to blame if things went wrong. He was also not sure of GB's game, felt it was self-evident that they both had a lot to lose from doing badly in Scotland, but he was not clear yet that GB was really focused on it. We went round in circles a bit but concluded he needed to spend a fair bit of time up there. On the general scene he said there was lots he was doing that he felt needed doing but the media line was 'What's the point of you being there, you have no authority whatsoever?' Also in response to Matthew Taylor saying why not dovetail with GB more, TB said because their line to the media the whole time is that there is stasis, nothing will happen until TB goes.

We agreed it was far better that he just leave GB to do his own thing and he concentrate on his. I was also again trying to get him to start being much more expansive about the nature of the job, ups and downs and so on, what it was really like and he had to be a bit less frenetic, more focused. Ruth was looking really calm considering. It was a fairly tired discussion but I felt he was in a better frame of mind than a week or so ago. After they all went out he kept me back and said he felt fine and energised but he had the media trying to kill him off, the police thing was just like a horrible dark cloud and he had GB next door just wanting him to go. We agreed more had to be made of the democratic point that he won an election and had things to do. He had to get out more, not worry about the day to day judgements, start to talk up the country city by city, step by step, and also talk more about the challenge of leadership so that people know what mattered and what didn't and were able to make a more rounded judgement.

He was generally in good form. He felt on reform, as some CBI bods had told him yesterday, things would go back if he left. Also on NI and Iraq he felt he had the chance to push through more. He had decided he had been worrying too much about what comes after. He said he was being inundated with offers to do things after and for all the shit here the brand abroad was enormous. Lunch with Danny Finkelstein at Simpson's in the Strand. He seemed to think a general News Corp deal on the book was a strong runner. Nice chat with him. He loved idea of a piece on all the crazy TV programmes I'd been offered. Black pudding and steak and kidney pie, like the old days with Alan Clark.

He said the article I wrote during the Tory leadership campaign was seminal and had a massive impact on Osborne and Cameron. They read the message – on the need to go to the centre and mean it and be tough about it and understand it is a hard choice not an easy one – and they decided to do that and probably lose but at least brand it. Instead they won. 'It's down to you,' he said, laughing. He felt they were struggling a bit to 'find an encore', but they were totally convinced they could win against GB whereas TB not, even after Iraq and everything else. He also said that he felt DC and GO both had a real equilibrium and it meant he would be more confident they would not automatically go down the traditional Leader/Treasury route of fallout, let alone let it go to TB–GB proportions. To BP at the IoD [Institute of Directors] for speech and Q&A for their quarterly review. Then to Hill and Knowlton [PR consultants] for LRF partnership launch. Nice do. Signed up a fair few people.

Friday 26 January

To Chelsea to meet Delta Goodrem. We had talked about doing something for LRF and after a chat around options we agreed she would front part of Alternative Hair Show, which had become the hair industry's biggest fundraiser. She would be perfect. We agreed a launch via interview with me, do other stuff later as patron etc. We talked about her illness, her recovery. She would be absolutely brilliant. Cathy very pleased. Nice to see her and yack re Soccer Aid. She said Brian [McFadden, boyfriend, AC team-mate in Soccer Aid] still talks about Maradona too!

Saturday 27 January

Loads of FA Cup. Long bike ride, then getting all the diaries ready for first Sue Gray meeting. TB in Davos, but he was getting wall-to-wall shite press. Home Office stuff, a lot of it, judges piling in now, loans rumbling on, but generally just wall-to-wall noise and blah.

Sunday 28 January

Took Grace out to the stables, and had a really interesting chat with George and Catherine about whether we can ever change others or we can only change ourselves. I was moving to the latter. Fiona and I definitely wanting to change each other but where we were getting on better it was when we accepted each other as we are. And then there was the whole GB situation. Catherine felt GB was incapable of change, not because he was GB, but because we all reach an age where are just set as what we are, and he was 'very, very set'. Big day on the NI scene, with a Sinn Fein special conference voting to accept policing. It was one of the big pieces of the jigsaw slotting into place, fantastic news, but what was incredible about the news coverage was that TB barely even figured, not even mentioned in one of the reports I saw. There was a real mood not to give him credit for anything at all right now. Gerry Adams [leader, Sinn Fein] spoke well, the mood music from the DUP [Democratic Unionist Party] was OK, and Hugh Orde [chief constable, Police Service of Northern Ireland] spoke well too.

Monday 29 January

Into town, to the Goring Hotel to meet Seb [Coe]. Most of the talk was running at first, trying to pick his brains about how I got over the mental block on running, and also what I could do to stop getting so many niggles. He said stretch, reps and strides. 'Don't plod. Plodding is death!' He still looked in amazing shape, bang on 11 stone. I was 16. Diet, he said. You can run all you want but if you don't eat well... I do eat well. Well, you can't be eating that well. Then we had a long chat about knees, and how to stay flexible round the knees, and suddenly he started laughing, pointed out Ben Brogan [journalist] at the other side of the room, who was watching us, and said, 'He is probably having a little guess about all the things we might be talking about – politics, Olympics, business – and we are sitting here like two old men worrying how long our knees will last.' He seemed OK about 2012, but felt it would be better if ministers did more to work on and emphasise benefits across the board – health, crime, community etc. – and left costs issue to them.

He was also desperate to develop a better relationship with GB. He said TB had been great, always accessible, easy to work with, always got the point and was yes, no, no messing about. But getting to GB seems impossible. He said he wasn't sure where GB was on the Games. I suggested he write him a very personal note, and set out how he thinks his goal and strategies for a successful Games can fit with and help GB's – Britishness, community, regeneration, economic confidence. I said GB was bound to feel that in so far as the delivery of the Games had a government political profile, it would be TB, Tessa, but GB would also see the obvious benefits if he did manage to be around in 2012. So I thought it would be possible to get him to a better place. As Chancellor, he would just be sitting there thinking of the ways it could end up over-running on costs, because that is what happens. We had to get him to start thinking of it more as a PM in waiting. I said I would have a word with him, and I tried to persuade him GB was a genuine sports fan. I said I would also explain that even though Seb had been a Tory MP, he was not really the kind of Tory GB hated!

I really liked Seb, and we always had a good laugh talking about some of the battle stories from when on opposing sides in the TB–Hague period, but he was also, given he was a genuine sports legend in my eyes, someone who had a real modesty about his sporting achievements, and had moved on to this amazing place where he was now central to delivering the Games. He said he felt like a round peg in a round hole. Off to the Cabinet Office, bumped into [Sir] David Omand and [Sir] Richard Mottram [senior civil servants], a reminder that the mandarin class just kept on keeping on. Sue Gray lovely as ever, but she was looking a bit tired and careworn, so I apolgised for adding to her workload. We chatted re TB. She said she was appalled at what was happening to him – the media was vile, his party didn't appreciate him, and above all the police investigation was a total disgrace. She had seen him last week and he looked exhausted, beaten up. I gave her the manuscript, and talked her over the strategy. Edited highlights of my whole time with TB. Focus on key themes and key moments. Protecting GB as best I could. I said we had cuts millions of words, mainly for length, but we needed more. So don't worry about telling me there is stuff you want to go. But it has to be realistic, authentic, to be credible.

She said she really hadn't enjoyed dealing with Lance Price over his book. Blunkett and [Clare] Short had been tricky as well. I asked if she thought a May deadline was unrealistic. She thought not and she agreed it could be better for TB if I was out with something even before he went. It was rather sweet the way she said, 'It would be nice if there was one nice book out there about him, because no doubt there will be plenty of others trying to paint a horrible picture.' She said she found it really strange that there was all this media hatred and all the grief in the party which had made him say he was going. She said most people round the place loved working with us, and part of that was because TB was actually just a nice guy, and good at the job, and he had people like you and the other key people around him who were just easy to work with. She said Gus had pretty much delegated this to her, she would only involve him if there were really difficult areas we couldn't agree on, but it ought to be fairly straightforward. She asked if there was much on the royals. Fair bit. Mmm, that can sometimes be tricky. Spooks? Fair bit. Ditto.

Anyway, at least we now had a process under way. I went off for a swim at the Oasis, before going to the Gielgud Theatre for *Frost/Nixon*. David and Carina [Frost] had invited me and Fiona and I was really looking forward to it, not just seeing the play, but seeing it with him. Loads of hacks and snappers there, met by the producer then David and Carina and Fiona arrived, and we were taken up to a little room for a drink, then taken to our seats. David loving the buzz as people suddenly realised he was there and then as he sat down, the couple in front of us barely able to contain themselves. The play itself was brilliant, and at times David appeared to be mumbling the words to himself. Frank Langella as Nixon reminded me of [Robert] Maxwell. He was played quite sympathetically. Michael Sheen as David was a bit more lightweight but the whole thing was superbly put together and gripping at the end when Nixon confessed and apologised. It was also such a fantastic thrill for David to have this rebooting of his reputation as one of the great interviewers. Partly because he had become a bit softer with age – though he could still be lethal when he wanted to be – and partly because he was so much part of the great and the good, and also because of some of the softer fluffier stuff he did now, he was not seen as quite the cutting-edge figure he once was. But this was like a new lease for the old Frost, and he totally loved it.

We waited for everyone to leave at the end then went backstage to see Langella and Sheen. Nice blokes, both pretty exhausted. Then to The Ivy with David and Carina. Reliving the whole episode. Filled him in on book strategy. He thought OK. Amazing response from Random House team. Earlier, out on a bike ride, I was up at Golders Green, and cycling past the crematorium, big crowd outside as a coffin arrived, and I started to think who could it be, so many people, and by the time I was at Whetstone Pond, I had the idea for a novel… Literally it had just popped into my head, that the guy who died was a psychiatrist, and these hundreds of people were people he had helped, and his family was gobsmacked. So it would be a story about the patients and the shrink. I had two or three character ideas and stopped to scribble them. And I had a lot of stuff now from the sessions with David S that I could use, added to which he could help me on the detail. It felt like one of those moments, a real creative buzz, and I headed home and started making notes, then started to write.

Tuesday 30 January
Rewrite intro for the diaries. Brief Random House on the Sue Gray chat. Also discuss longlist of possible titles. The Blair Years seemed the simplest. Roundhouse for lunch with Calum. Then the Comic Relief team came round for final final filming. Ended up having quite an interesting chat re the way TV was going. They felt this drive to reality, personality, jeopardy TV was set and irreversible and said something about what British people wanted. I felt it was reversible but only if we accepted and challenged the extent of dumbing down at the cultural level. In to see TB. Just the two of us for a while. He said he felt fine but the police investigation was a nightmare. They seem to have found nothing that would lead to a successful prosecution so they just keep coming back for more, and they have made so much of the whole thing they obviously feel they can't let it drop.

He said both when they interviewed Ruth, and with John McTernan, the main thing seemed to be try to get them to change the story. I said I know they are difficult to take on but we should probably have had a strategy to get them on the back foot. To have the whole thing started on the back of a political challenge. He felt Yates was just part of that modern era thing where people felt the media profile was important. The media were being fed constantly on this thing. He felt on substance, policy and positioning he was fine but could not get clear of all this. If Michael Levy was charged it was really grim all round. It was probably too late to get a proper comms strategy around the whole thing. No. 10 and the party had been playing by the old UK rules whereas it seemed for the cops, it was much more the American way. Maybe we were heading that way too, where police and courts stuff became much more about PR. But it was pretty hideous. In the meeting of the wider group, it was all a bit tired and they felt a bit beleaguered.

We were talking about his National Policy Forum speech for the weekend. Their plan was to link it into a survey on the marginals but it all sounded a bit processy. They said they couldn't get coverage for speeches without a device. Liz said it was worse than ever, the days when the idea of the PM making a big speech equals news was gone, there had to be something newsy and different. TB and I were both saying we have always had to go through these periods and this was a particularly bad one but we had to get some confidence and resilience back in the system. We agreed we needed a basic outward-looking NL speech for the weekend. PG and I wanting him to focus higher up, big message and big causes. NI, WTO [World Trade Organization], climate change kind of thing. Show that anything worthwhile was always difficult and all only possible because of the building of different coalitions of support for different arguments and campaigns. TB could get a lot by showing just how resilient he was. Northern Ireland was an example. Maybe there was a case for taking what had happened on policing at the SF conference, and then doing a bigger picture message about all the setbacks on the way, and it was the same for everything we did that was worthwhile, nothing easy, always tough, always people trying to screw you over.

Pat said the message should be a new warning to the party not to go for the comfort zone, because that is where it felt like it was heading. TB agreed with that, felt that the party was beginning to slip back a bit in all sorts of ways and he wanted to arrest it. There was a real problem though in the way the media were just trying to make him irrelevant.

Still felt lots we could do. Bertie A was due in and I had a little chat with him. He was chuffed about the policing thing, felt the power-sharing ought to fall into place now. He asked how I was doing, and I said fine, but I was worried about TB. 'Cheer him up,' I said. 'Christ, it's normally the other way round,' he said. Michael Levy re-arrested. Fucking dire.

Wednesday 31 January

David S. He felt I was doing OK. I told him about my novel idea about the shrink's funeral and said I might need to pick his brains. He said, 'Should I be worried that you are writing about a psychiatrist's funeral?' I said the basic theme was going to be how patients, and their families, come to rely on these shrinks, yet we never really know what is going on in their lives. We talked a bit about his, including, he said, that for long periods he'd had daily therapy, and most did. He asked me why I wanted to write it, and I said I don't know, but it had been one of those moments where I felt alive again, that I saw something, it kicked something off in my head, and I felt a real energy out of it. I also felt if I was going to get more into the mental health side of things of the public angle, speaking and campaigning, this could be useful. He asked what Fiona thought. I said I hadn't told her. I was not going to tell anyone, just do it, and see if I liked it and if it was any good.

Over to see Philip with Calum at the Honest Sausage, but there were a couple of women with the zappiest, most out of control dogs and it became unbearable. PG felt yesterday TB had looked a bit shot, that even when he was trying to lift people, he looked like he knew he wasn't having the right effect. The police thing was bad enough, but the whole mood around him was so bad. Later to see Paul Moore at FirstGroup, and discussion about the sports event we had been talking about. They had come up with First Monster challenge, a biathlon around Loch Ness after heats round the country, loads of staff involved. Good idea. Liked it. Paul and I then saw Moir to go over a few issues for his board meeting tomorrow.

Thursday 1 February

To First. Paul presented his strategy paper, I spoke in support and all seemed to go OK. There was definitely a bit of scepticism about what I was doing there, and what I could add, but fairly easily broken down once we got on to broader strategy, and the signal from Moir and Martin

Gilbert was clear, that he wanted a different way of doing things. Not really my thing but I liked Moir, Martin and Paul and happy to help. All called me during the day to say they were grateful. As I came out, I turned on the phone and had lots and lots of messages, mainly bids about the news – which was news to me – that TB had been re-interviewed by the cops last Friday. Yates had apparently insisted on a news blackout, and on nobody mentioning to anyone else, because they didn't want Levy to know the line of questioning. It was absolutely clear to me it was being spun against TB the whole time but he still didn't want me to go out there, or to have a strategy for pushing back. Osborne was out for the Tories getting as close as ever to saying TB ought to go, saying it was not entirely clear why he was hanging on. Then Cameron something similar. Lib Dems wittering on about Watergate.

The SNP guy was out again, loving it, and also trying to make out that because the police had successfully operated a news blackout, it showed it was a lie that they had been leaking about the inquiry. Yeah right. It partly explained I guess why TB had been so low, and the fact he didn't even raise with me in the pre-meeting showed he had taken seriously all the 'nobody must be told' stuff. It turned out hardly anyone knew and so now it was out, the press office were being accused of having misled people about what he did on the day he went to Davos. All grim all round. Then as I was in the cab heading back, GB called. Small talk re the dinner the other night, jokes about chairs, how well Fiona seemed. Then he said the situation in the party was terrible. 'It is clear you are going to have to get involved in planning for the next election in a big way.' Heart sank a little, then a lot. Even with TB, I had been feeling low about the extent to which I was still unable to get out from under. He said would I come in and talk about it? I said I would. I didn't mention book, or how I felt about it.

He didn't mention TB's situation which thanks to the cops was pretty awful at the moment. Meanwhile the first signs of a shift in the PLP mood – that this police thing was so damaging something had to give. That was chief among TB's concerns when I called him at Myrobella [constituency home] later. He had done a speech to 2,000 sports college people and got a standing ovation – not that anyone would know it from the media. I said I had made the mistake of watching the news a bit today which was truly awful, and I didn't believe he could just keep taking these hits without anyone fighting back. There had been a few voices saying how appalling this was – meaning the cops' handling of it – but it was dwarfed by the noise about TB, the optics were awful and all surrounded by political voices saying how awful they were. The overall effect was absolutely dire. He said he genuinely didn't know what to do. He now felt Yates saw this almost as a battle between the two of them. I said the problem was he had taken the hits and so much damage was done. He had to fight back better than this. This was death by a thousand cuts, and today's was a big one.

He had the *Today* programme interview on the NHS tomorrow, meant to be on health, but this would dominate. I said why not say you can say nothing but at least put out the line that this is going on too long and the running commentary is damaging. He said he would think about it but it is tricky. He was appalled at the smearing of JoP and Ruth, as over a story about the destruction of emails which never existed. He still felt the CPS would struggle to say there was a case here, but the aim of the media frenzy was a lowering of the bar. That was what they hoped for – make the CPS feel they had to charge someone for something, otherwise what was all this about? He felt on the stuff he was doing – like NI, Iraq and Afghanistan, the public service stuff he was doing today, he was in good shape, but he was finding it hard to get above this. 'You were worried about me today were you?' He said when I first heard, I was appalled, then when I watched the news I felt sick, and I really felt we had missed a trick from the word go, because the whole thing was set on their terms, and they had successfully managed to get everyone on the back foot, and you looking like you had something to hide. I said it may be too late to revise strategy, but you cannot take this stuff lying down.

Friday 2 February

TB called early, before his *Today* programme interview with Humphrys. They had been doing a whole load of stuff on health, and that was meant to be the focus, but it was all going to be cops, and why don't you just fuck off? I said the health thing is useful, because you have to keep talking up the two agendas – what you do day to day, and what you have to deal with day to day. Go through your diary for yesterday, talk about the school sports stuff, Northern Ireland, all the different meetings he had done. And the democratic point about him being elected. We talked a bit about how to handle if JH raised the Ecclestone affair and 'I am a straight kind of guy', and when it came to it, TB said, 'I am not going to beg for my character,' which came over strongly.* I hadn't listened to *Today* for yonks but tuned in, and given how tough the wicket is, he did fine really, definitely got over what mattered to him, but there was just so much in the ether about it now, so every time he felt like JH might move on, he had another quote from another Labour bod, or another obvious point about how it doesn't look good, and he clearly enjoyed saying, 'Nobody says you're a straight kind of guy any more.' He called after, I said I thought it was fine, but the narrative was set and they were not budging off it – time for him to go, GB could do it, this cops thing is the last straw, so what is the point of hanging around?

Peter M had emerged as my latest big worry re the book. The effect of protecting GB means it risks being very unfair to him. A lot of the Peter M bad stuff relates to GB and so if the GB factor is less visible... Fiona felt the same. She thought that a basic mutual respect came through, but there were so many incidents where Peter was just tricksy or flouncy, and without GB in there on the same basis it lacked context. Again, maybe if I was just open about it – said the book risked being unfair, but defend him generally when doing media. The truth is I had been so fixated on GB and the possible impact there, I hadn't thought about this nearly enough. Richard, who likes Peter and has done ever since he used to do his column for *The People* [edited by RS], thought it was not as bad as I feared, and agreed with Fiona that the respect thing, and the basic friendship being strong, was clear enough. But when I flicked through at random, I found in no time half a dozen bits that I know would drive him up the wall. I had a chat with Jonathan, said the TB cops thing explained a bit why the meeting the other day was so unfocused, but I felt they really had to sharpen up on strategy, both generally and re the cops.

Peter M called. We were due to meet later. He felt on the cops, as I did, that we needed to push back. He was convinced GB was behind some of the voices coming out saying the whole thing was a mess and something had to give. Meeting with Les Hinton. He had pretty much accepted I would go with Gail for the diaries but still hoped I could do a big deal with them on interviews / serial etc. I took him through

---

* In 1997, prior to Labour's landslide election victory, Formula One boss Ecclestone donated £1 million to the party. It became public the following November when the government announced proposals to exempt Formula One for a tobacco sponsorship ban. In the wake of the resulting controversy, Blair went on TV and commented, 'I think most people who have dealt with me think I am a pretty straight kind of guy, and I am.'

the basic approach, including going for sooner not later, protecting GB, a film attached to it. He said he and they were very excited about it. Obviously he said he would prefer if I went the whole hog and did HarperCollins but he understood because of the friendship with Gail. We stumbled towards a plan that was basically, kick off with an interview in the Saturday *Times*, big hit of the book for next day's *Sunday Times*, a week of blah, with maybe a podcast and also occasional interview, then part 2 a week later, then the book out, then maybe a third extract, and with the TV series to go straight away. I told him Ed had overdone the 'no GB thing' with Witherow. GB was a big presence in the book. But I was clear that I was taking out any parts that I felt the Tories could use to damage him.

I felt back on track mentally, and found myself in spare moments scribbling notes about the novel. And I felt if I was so concerned to protect GB, it must mean in part because I think I should help him more generally. Pat McF called about something unrelated, I told him of the GB call, and I asked what he thought of it he said, 'I imagine you would rather eat your own organs but I hope you do it.' At 5.45 up to see TB in the flat, Peter M and Ben W-P already there. TB said what he could gather from all the various interviews was that they were desperately trying to get Michael for something, anything. Ruth had been under real pressure to change her story. He said there was no question of him or anyone in office facing charges. The only question they seemed to keep coming back to was something Christopher Evans had said. He said based on what he knew of the law, he was not convinced the CPS would buy it as a viable prosecution, but clearly we were living in crazy times. Peter and I were both of the view they should have been making sure people were aware of how Yates was handling all this. There was an obvious danger the CPS would do the wrong thing because of the frenzy.

We talked about his speech for tomorrow and he said maybe he should get up and say he apologised for Iraq, he was basically a war criminal and now an ordinary criminal too. At that moment, I spotted a 'Statesman of the Decade' award that was on the side, and got up to pick it up, put it my bag, said, 'I don't think you'll be needing this any more.' He was a bit more upbeat than the other day, but genuinely worried, I could tell. He asked me if I thought he could tough it through. I did but I felt this was more grim than most of the periods he had toughed out. But Peter said it was important we keep emhasising strengths. If TB had not been there when Bush wobbled at the WTO, the wrong decisions would have been taken. He is a key voice on climate change. He is still one of the voices other leaders look to for what he thinks and what he says. And he is still the one with the clearest domestic agenda. Meanwhile, he said, the Treasury was showing they are just tactical, blocking things for the sake of it, the [David] Freud welfare report [on welfare to work system] the latest.

He was scathing about GB on the issue of US ICBM sitings. The US happy to give us one rather than Poland or Czech Republic. GB coming up with some nonsense that we would have to give agreement on how they were to be used. Also on Home Office re-organisation, GB knew the proposals are right, but is blocking for now because he wants to be able to do it in his first hundred days. He was on a very Peterish roll now, went off on one about the No. 10 operation being amateurland. 'You need more muscle, more muscularity.' He left after an hour or so then had to go off to a dinner or something. Then Kate and Anji arrived to see TB for a drink. So off we went over the same old story again. He said his big worry was the PLP. A message was taking root that he had no purpose, did nothing. He felt Neil was out there as well, pushing the same negative message.

Saturday 3 February

Run, bike, then to QPR 3, Burnley 1. Saw Steve Cotterill after the match and he was pretty down about things. Alex had a good win at Spurs. Jonny Wilkinson made an amazing return for England. He really is something special.

Sunday 4 February

Sunday Telegraph did a big number on TB–CB buying another house, and the whole piece, pictures of the houses, big figures bandied around, loads about what his future earnings might be, again just another thing to make everything look sleazy, and also emphasise he was heading for the exit. I did a bit of work at home then later we went out to see *Dreamgirls*. We had dinner with Tessa and David, who seemed to be getting on OK, though things were still raw and tense. Tessa was pretty sure she was being followed part of the time. Dinner was fine, largely because we mainly avoided political talk. There was a bit of blowback against Yates but it still made my blood boil the damage this must be doing. Did a note to TB re his Liaison Committee tomorrow. Had to use it to show scale of grasp on foreign policy, and scale of remaining ambition on domestic.

Monday 5 February

Going through the whole first diary manuscript. Amazing how much we had cut. I guess we'd done the right stuff but the power and intensity lost in a way. Constant drip drip of stories from the police probe, all presumably designed to put pressure on CPS to bring charges. Long swim. Also football later at Gospel Oak. Tired legs. All fine. TB was on the back foot for the Liaison Committee – 'Another of your little inventions to help us communicate directly to people!' he had called it last night – but he did OK considering. A lot on foreign policy, Iran the top line, not ruling out military action, lots on the special relationship, and on the domestic stuff he did OK, in that he was on top of the detail and also full of ideas for the future. But what a scene right now. The heavy media did it on Iran, most of the others on 'overshadowed' (cliché No. 3,287) or 'shrugged off questions about...' – take in all the old stories re the cops inquiry.

Tuesday 6 February

The Times splashed on JoP to be interviewed again and linking him to conspiracy, talking about three areas where charges were possible. It was unbelievable the way this was being cranked up now. I finalised my speech for tonight then into No. 10 and TB strategy meeting. TB looked tired and drawn and the meeting felt tired. Re Scotland PG reported on what sounded like a mess. John McTernan was up there helping but he had the cops thing hanging around him too, and he was being done in. GB was not really engaged. TB said we had to have someone who was our person in there [Scotland] and making a difference. On the police issue he said there was a limit to what could be done. Fine there could be a sense out there that they had overreached and were behaving improperly but in the end it was all going to be down to the CPS and outcome. CPS had made clear they would not be pushed around by the media coverage, but this had been some long-running frenzy now. Also TB remained confident that within a month it would be behind us. But it was hellish hard to get through. He said all we could do was get through it, there was no easy way.

PG and I argued though that there had to be much more effort put into getting people up and about with voices pro-TB that both supported him through this specifically but more importantly played into legacy. TB said the most important thing was that he was seen to be making decisions still on issues that mattered. Truth was there were a number of decisions on issues recently – pensions, endowments, welfare, gay adoption and Catholic agencies not being exempt – that probably would not have happened without him. It would be better if there was some kind of GB tie-in but for now it looked very difficult. He was just doing his own thing again, he was pretty much invisible, seemingly planning away for when it came. TB felt GB underestimated the backlash if there was no election, no contest and no real debate about what the change meant. He said, 'What is this great new agenda? Independence for the NHS? How long did that last? Some bollocks about a written Constitution. And then what?' TB wanted work done promoting the idea that for all the shit that swilled around, we were still the only real political argument in town. He said Cameron is having to follow and his only hope is that GB vacates New Labour and goes backwards.

Apart from that little fizz of energy at the end, it wasn't a good meeting. Philip and I kept suggesting ideas for new ways of getting support out there and it was all too difficult. No real energy. Sal and I stayed back for a bit and he said he was totally sure this perversion of the course of justice would go nowhere. It was all horrible for Jonathan and Ruth but he did not think there was any chance of them being done, and that even with ML it was less than 50/50. It all depended on whether the CPS were influenced or not by the frenzy and the noise. Sally said to me afterwards she had spoken to Charlie F yesterday and he was less sure about all of it. The whole thing was a bloody nightmare. I ran home, sluggish as hell. Virtually everyone was overtaking me, but I got a couple of good thoughts on the novel. Thinking ahead to how to deal with GB Thursday. Part of me felt I should help. Large part felt not.

Wednesday 7 February

David S. Over the same old ground. I was not making that much progress with the American book he had asked me to read. At some of these sessions, we just chatted really, like two friends who meet up for a natter. Other times he zones in on something specific. We talked about the GB meeting, and my ambivalence. He clearly felt it wouldn't be great to go back full-time but he said there was a part of me that wanted to be involved, or a duty bit there that pulled on me hard, or else I wouldn't even think about it. I was due to see Sue Gray, and I called to check it was still on. She had not finished the whole thing but felt there were bits, for example the Diana death week, that were 'very, very difficult', just because it was all so close in on the royals. She said the royals were often the most difficult with these government books, and she felt it not impossible they would ask the government to injunct. I reported back to Gail et al and I felt less sanguine about the whole thing, that maybe it would end in a legal mess that I really didn't want.

Then to a meeting at Gail's with her team, RS, MB. We covered a lot of ground. Title and jacket. I later spoke to Nick Danziger [photographer] and he was fine re front cover. I stressed the need for legal precedents re previous books. RS had lots, like Joe Haines's book directly quoting the Queen. We agreed May was not likely so we would go for 4 June with the first *Sunday Times* extract a fortnight before. But I had been set back by Sue G. Gail said they would now be viewing me as an outsider. Home for dinner, Fiona saying don't worry but it was hard not to. I really didn't want this to become any more of a blah than it had to, and there were enough worries there re GB, PM, Neil, friendships, without a great thing about the royals feeling I shouldn't write about meetings on Diana at all. Moir called to get my input into First's acquisition of Laidlaw [yellow school buses company] in the States which was going to be a huge deal. I felt they rather overdid the union fears but he needed reassurance. England booed off after losing to Spain at Old Trafford [0–1]. Better news on the loans front, the media saying Des Smith was no longer a suspect. But Ruth and Michael still on bail.

Thursday 8 February

Slept badly, always a bad sign. Heavy snow overnight, and so the schools were shut. RS and I worked on the front cover blurb and biog. I was also doing bits of Comic Relief PR stuff. Cab into SW1. Really good chat with the driver on football. Saw GB at 11.30 for over an hour, just the two of us. More football. Him quizzing about Alex. Telling me about the shoestring operation at Raith Rovers, how desperate Scottish football was, the ins and outs at Rangers. We got on to sports strategy pre the Olympics, and I suggested he develop a proper relationship with Coe, said he was a really good guy, he was not remotely hostile, and he was easy to work with. The line Rebekah had once used about GB about 'barbed wire and flashing lights going off if you raised something he didn't like' came to mind. He said Coe would knife us one day. He is a Tory. He feeds the Tories. He will turn against us. I said that was ridiculous. He had been a Tory MP. He was a progressive, left-leaning Conservative. But his time as an MP was an interlude in a life devoted to sport, to which he was totally dedicated and at which he was brilliant. He really ought to give him a go.

He glowered and then smiled and then we moved on. He asked me what I was up to and whether I would come back in some form and get involved in a more structured way before the election. I said I was very ambivalent, and I didn't think the ambivalence would go. I had felt close to losing my life in a way, not in a death kind of way, though there had been moments, but just that I had lost any control over it, and I had felt events slipped beyond me, and mentally, and family-wise, I had paid a price, and so had they. I felt I had just about got my life back, but it had been a slow, hard haul, and although I felt reasonably confident about the future, I could easily slide back. I had felt for the last bit in the job, and a lot of the time since, like my head was in a vice and I had just about got it out. I hated most of the media. I had kept in touch with very few of the politicians with whom I used to spend so much time. He probed a bit on what I was up to. I had been planning on telling him about the book but in the end decided it would just complicate things. So I decided also to be clear and said, in terms, I didn't rule out helping him but I was not ready to commit to anything big. I didn't want a job. I didn't want a title.

I didn't want to feel I had to come in and get on top of everything because that way lay the past, and it was not where I wanted to go. He said I was politically committed so it must be in me that I wanted to stop the Tories and really get the party back up to what it could be again. He said we had to get away from Labour just being a campaigning machine, and set out great goals and great causes and that's where I could make a big difference. He said I think you get frustrated because you are defined as the media man, the spin man, but the one thing I have always known is you see politics as big causes and big challenges, and you did a lot to drive those but now you can do more. I said that is all well and good, but be honest, you want me because of what I can do on strategy, on comms, on driving message, on writing for you, big speeches, big themes, big message, and you need to understand I have cut just about all links with the media, there are journalists I used to see and speak to every day I have not spoken to since I left, and I felt behind the times already with all the new media stuff.

He kept coming back at me though, said he knew I believed in these things – education, opportunity, kids getting a real chance, all kids – and we had to get people back on our side. I said if I came back there was a chance it would be bad for him – spin and all that. He said I could do much much more than that. He felt that TB got so used to me doing what I did, and became so reliant, that I stayed on the media side of things longer than I should have done. I should have moved out of the media earlier than I did. I should have got a seat, maybe been sports minister allied to some big party role that allowed me to run the big campaigns. That is how I see this, he said. Not coming back to do what you did, but coming to help Labour regain purpose, big goals, big challenges. He felt I could help shape these goals and causes and then help meet them.

We didn't talk much about TB. I said I felt very very sad at the way it was ending for him, that he had started out adored by party, media and public, and how was being pushed out by the party, reviled by the media, the public better but absorbing all this stuff day after day, and the cops thing as a horrible nightmare swilling all over it. He said I know you don't believe me on this, because I know what Tony says, but I said to Tony we too should agree a secret deal on timings and I should be out there supporting you on everyrhing, working together and then retain some surprise about departure. I said no, you're right, that is very different to his version. He said TB had not wanted him to get more involved in certain things. He had still not met Bush, for example. Surely it made sense, if TB was saying he thought I should take over, that he set up that kind of thing, as he did with Merkel to be fair. He felt TB had fucked up this last phase of his leadership. We have all made mistakes but at least we can learn from them, he said.

He was pretty mellow most of the time. When he talked of the challenges and the goals and the changing face of the world he was pretty compelling. But I was still putting up barriers, he could sense it, and kept coming back to try to break them down. At one point he said that for a time, given the mood, maybe politics has to be taken out of the political process. I said what, so that we can have six fucking ministers, including TB, seeing bloody Shilpa Shetty from *Big Brother* yesterday (when she thanked TB for support re 'what I had to go through' on the TV show). GB agreed that had been tacky but there is no doubt we had to reframe how we connected. But some of the big organisations and causes had shown it can still be done. There was a lot of energy out there that we were not tapping into to.

We talked about DC. I said I felt he was very vulnerable and he was in a strong position to damage him, but it was vital he did not define himself against TB but always against DC. GB said analysing that vulnerability was an area where I could help. His worry was that Cameron would not be expected to produce too much. The media were desperate to give him a lift. He felt the party was in poor shape. The deputy leadership contest was dire. I asked if he didn't feel he needed a debate and a challenge himself. He said if the deputy leadership people had any sense they would challenge him – 'Don't suggest that' – but he was still of the view better get in quick and then start to do things. He sounded me out on David M. I said a lot of people wanted him to go for it, but I didn't think he would. It was a very friendly, almost warm conversation. I said I really didn't want a big job but I would try to help in other ways. He said let's talk in another month or so, and he laughed, and I knew what his laugh meant, and he knew I knew. He was basically saying he would wear me down. He said he was seeing the Pope [Benedict XVI] at the weekend, and he would ask him for guidance for me! Sue Nye showed me out, really over-the-top friendly. Ran home.

It had been fine seeing him, and we were perfectly friendly. I also did want him to do well, even if I doubted his capability in certain ways. Still far too much blaming and 'The problem is...' I also felt it was almost certainly best for me that I try to make a break. But he was very compelling when talking about the big challenges, and very effectively pulling on strings, when saying I was too political and too young and too able just to walk away from it all, and let the Tories roll back in.

Friday 9 February

Conference call at home re the book with the publishing lawyer, Martin Soames. A lot of stuff to get through. Going to have a lot of different pulls and pressures. Going to have to operate a bit double agent-y at times. I wanted to do the book but I also genuinely wanted it to be OK for TB and with not too much fallout with friends, colleagues, media blah etc. I suppose I was kidding myself if I thought it could be done quietly. He went through some of the precedents that might help us on the legal front. Although the Sue call had spooked me a bit, I suppose on the bright side she had felt with most of the government stuff there had been fewer big issues than she had expected. To Marylebone school to talk to the politics class as a favour to Florence [Bridge, neighbour] Did how to win elections, how to elect leaders, and a Q&A. Nice crowd. Only one knew who Major was. None had heard of Michael Foot and they only knew Neil because he came up in their last lesson. All knew

Thatcher. Most quite liked TB. GB jury out. One of them really liked Cameron.

GB got a fair bit of play for seeing the Pope, another PM-in-waiting thing, even inviting him to visit UK, and he had also done an interview setting out some of the stuff we talked about re sport in schools, and he was talking up going for the World Cup after the Olympics. I sent him a reminder to get hold of Seb and develop a relationship. I worried the World Cup thing was a way of avoiding getting too drawn into the Olympics. Cameron was feeling a bit of heat, the papers full of stories about him taking drugs at school. Tories closing ranks, our lot not really going for it, him talking vaguely about everyone having done stuff they regret when young.

Monday 12 February

David M in *The Times*, pretty clear message re GB – saying we would only win a fourth term with bold Labour, not old Labour. Quite a lot of resonances in there – TB's 'at our best when at our boldest' v GB 'at our best when Labour'. Better meeting with Sue Gray. She was less alarmed on second reading about the Diana stuff, but said it would all have to go to the Palace. She said she was also surprised about just how personal the conversations with TB were at times and she wondered if Jonathan shouldn't read it to get his take. I was fine with that. I would also be sending to TB at some point. She said she thought TB came over well in the main, but there were lots of little lines and observations that might cause him problems and difficulties. I could tell she had enjoyed reading it, and she did say that most of the books she had to deal with could be a real chore, but this had not been difficult to read at all. I asked if it was worth me putting in calls with the people I knew at the Palace, and she felt maybe let her pave the way. She did think they would be very sensitive, just because it was so detailed and I had been there at the centre of the planning.

I was so glad she was in charge of this though. She was definitely coming at it from a friendly, helpful perspective, not difficult. 'Do you really want people to know you swear so much? Even in your diary?' she said. 'I don't think people will be terribly surprised by that.' She said a lot would have to go to SIS [Secret Intelligence Service], FCO, MoD, but I felt at least we had a process under way and she was the perfect person to be in charge of it. Lunch with Dennis Stevenson [chairman, HBOS], who was swapping notes on depression and talking about stuff we could do together. He was pressing me to go into business, felt I had the right kind of mind for it. He was worried about GB taking over. I sent TB an exchange of emails I had had with Vernon Bogdanor about the cops probe, and whether there were any constitutional issues worth getting into the debate about it. He called for a natter. He felt better, said he was really motoring, just accepted now that it was very hard to get any positive traction via the media. But he said when out and about he had found the mood pretty good.

He said he appreciated the way I had been around a bit more, that it gave confidence to people, and they needed it right now because this police thing had really dragged everyone down. JoP was amazingly resilient and upbeat, but it was a very hard thing to live with. I filled him in on my meeting with GB. He felt partly it was him acknowledging my ability but also he would be trying to neutralise me on the diaries. He asked where I had left it. I said happy to help, but not with a big role. He said he would keep grinding me down, and he felt in the end I would and should do it. 'Look, we know the doubts, but if he does it, we have to do what we can to make him work.' I filled him in on the Sue Gray meeting and again he seemed quite chilled about that. I said if he wanted to read it, he could at any time. Vernon sent me back an excellent piece he had done for a US magazine, making clear he really felt TB on foreign policy had been excellent. Nice dinner with Mick [Hucknall] and Gabriela at Casalinga. Going over baby name. They wanted True. I was pro Reggie, his dad's name. Nice time. Really like both of them. So much more to him than just a performer, or the serial shagger of the past. Bright, political. Home to a message from Lindsay. She has breast cancer. Jesus. How much does one woman have to take?

Tuesday 13 February

A long meeting at home with the RH team including lawyer plus RS. I felt we were getting there. JoP and I in an email exchange with Jonathan saying TB now saying he had never agreed to pre-departure publication. Hopefully JoP reading it would make him see it was not as daft as it sounds but who knows? Sue had said there was talk of new rules were being brought in post-Chris Meyer and Lance Price books to stop civil servants doing diaries, which was what happened in the US. Long chat with Alex. Chuffed about Darren [son] getting the manager's job at Peterborough. I told him about possible problems on the book. He thought take a hard line because of all I had done for them.

Lindsay news not good, though she sounded remarkably upbeat, and then more bad health news, Mark Neale [university friend] had had a skateboard accident and the X-ray showed up three aneurysms, and he was straight in for a big operation.

Wednesday 14 February

Up at 7 and off to Leeds with Calum to check out the university. He quite liked it but I sensed he was a bit sensitive when some of the teachers spotted me and came over to make a bit of a fuss. We had a good day though. Sue Gray called and said she had sent relevant sections to the spooks, and would let me know what came back. She said she was not sure whether we could commit to a definite date by which it would be done but we were fine to announce there would definitely be a book. Just hold fire on the date in case things get slowed down. Independently of me raising it, she also said she felt that Peter M got a bit of a hard time because you had a sense of him causing grief but without the GB context it was not balanced. Good reading, I said! I was still not sure how to handle that. She said she laughed out loud at the account of me and Peter sort of having a fight over whether TB should wear a tie. She said every page has something totally arresting!

Thursday 15 February

David S. He felt the novel idea was a good thing. He felt it showed that what we had been working on was getting me to think differently. I went over some of the characters I was developing – the Kosovan rape victim, fire survivor, alcoholic – and he had interesting ideas about how to develop them. We also had a good chat on the whole TB–GB scene. He felt as long as I was going in with my eyes open, it was fine. To First for a two-hour meeting with them and Portland on various things that would flow from the Laidlaw deal. Lunch with David North [ex-civil servant, now at Tesco] at ZenW3. David M came round later. He was really worried about GB and what he wasn't doing. Charles Clarke and Tessa and others were putting it round – like Frank Field [former welfare reform minister] in print – that DM should go for it. He felt there was a lot of worry among MPs that GB was not going to cut it. DM said he was not pushing himself forward but it was clearly on his mind.

I felt if he wasn't going for it himself, he had ideas that would or could be the right strategy to put forward for GB but he was not really in contact with him. I said he should go direct to GB and try to help him get a plan which currently he didn't have. He seemed a bit anxious about it all, in that he felt the pressure from others to do it, but knew that the clunking great fist might come down more against him than against DC. I felt he either had to go for it, or try to engage with GB. He said what he couldn't decide was whether in a way the whole Blair–Brown era was over, but he felt our approach needed a big change in ideas and style of politics which GB doesn't really get. I could tell he was really conflicted, kept saying he had not any intention of running but then giving the arguments why GB not well placed to win. Why was he doing nothing, saying nothing? GB's stance was indeed a bit odd right now, even taking into account the idea that he might be holding things back so that he could start with a bang.

Friday 16 February

Meeting with Bernard Edwards [businessman] on a dinner I was doing for his firm. Interesting take – more jihadic even than me about the media, felt they did real damage to our standing in the world. Lawyer and diary team p.m. Got through it all. Noreena pushing to involve me in her nurses film, and wanted to come to Burnley. Some horrible shootings and killings in south London, three in two weeks, TB and JR both out on it, and Cameron trying to make it about broader social issues. Our lot criticised him, but he was totally taking a leaf out of the way TB had handled the Bulger killing when he was shadow home affairs.* Cameron using it to get onto the Tory agenda of two-parent families, parental responsibility etc.

Saturday 17 February

Went up with Calum to see Wolves v Burnley, lost 2–1, then over to Mum's. Philip called, told me he thought Jonathan was very twitchy about the book. Mum on good form, but I wish she wouldn't say coloured when she means black. We had an argument about it but I gave up.

---

* Two-year-old James Bulger was murdered in 1993 by two ten-year-old boys who were subsequently convicted. Blair initially blamed the killing on a general breakdown in society under the Tories, but later admitted this conclusion was 'flawed'.

Sunday 18 February

Over to Burnley, puncture en route. Staying at Barry [chairman, Burnley FC] and Sonia Kilby's very nice house in Ribchester. Not giving any indication Steve Cotterill was in trouble but can't be great given results.

Monday 19 February

Nice run, some incredible hills. Misty but fabulous. Gail called having seen JoP last night, and he was clearly not too happy about the book and felt TB wouldn't be either. She said he thought it wasn't that good for TB and that it was certainly not possible to do while he was there. He felt that the swearing, his and my lasciviousness but above all confidences with other leaders were a real problem for the future and what he intended to do. I also had a chat with [Sir Richard] Dearlove [former chief of SIS/MI6]. He said he felt it must he harder for me to adapt to a new life because despite everyone knowning how central I had been to TB, the whole spin thing, and politics, meant that I was not seen as a legitimate figure whereas people like him, and mandarins no matter how useless, could slot into a certain post-government life. I told him about the book, said it was with the spooks and so he might want to take a look. I did a visit to [headteacher] Julie Bradley's school, St Leonard's [Burnley]. Good visit, she and the teachers doing some fantastic stuff, but boy do they have problems? Some really tough social challenges. Virtual apartheid too, in that there are white schools and non-white and if the schools try to integrate, parents turn up to take the kids out.

Popped in to see Steve C at Turf Moor. Full on about the job. Going over every match of the season virtually, with a photographic memory. Totally obsessed and obsessive. Really felt it. He said he was determined to be up there with the Fergusons and Wengers but wonder if he has to learn to channel the intensity. He was coming over for dinner at the Kilbys but first going to a game to watch a player. Nice enough evening but Steve really cannot talk about anything but football. I like the intensity, the obsessiveness, but the others kept trying to talk about something else, and back it came to football.

Tuesday 20 February

Over to Manchester with Calum. Meeting Simon Andrews at Malmaison about the Man U Players' Programme. Nice guy, ex-player who never quite made it. Now with St James' Place but half his time on the

PP, trying to help United players with advice on money, agents, life-style, media. He wanted me maybe to do a series of sessions with them about dealing with the media. We talked a bit about other stuff I might do. He felt start as a one-off and then develop into an advisory role. Over to the University, and even more than at Leeds, I sensed people making a bit of a fuss because it was me, and it was annoying Calum, I could tell. Odd to think that in a few months both the boys will be away, though Rory seemed to be around at home most weekends. Back over to Burnley for the match against Leicester. We played well, totally dominated and then lost to an own goal. I felt for Steve, who looked gutted. Another one for him to add to his fine margins file. Home by 2. Rory in Lille, United fans teargassed.

Wednesday 21 February

Caroline G round to go through pictures for book. Left for Earl's Court Confex Exhibition [business and strategy products]. Whole place just a mass of exhibition stands. Accoustics not good but went fine. Then in to see JoP who had read book and had real concerns. He felt on timing that to do it before TB left office, in any form, was a disaster. He had marked with red pen alongside all the bits that worried him, and there was a lot of red. Swearing. Personal. Private. Especially chats with foreign leaders. He said TB was still going to be dealing with them after he had gone. And some of them would still be in power. So would Bush expect to have private chats published verbatim? Also Bill C may be favourably presented overall but it is still a very close-in portrayal and with a lot of personal conversations. I felt he was over-reacting and only seeing the negative, but agreed to take it on board. Earlier I had seen David S and said I was pretty settled now that this was the point of departure in a way. Using the past to set down a marker for the future. Not going back full-time to politics, use this for new directions. He thought that best too. But Jonathan was the one most strongly against publication. He felt a lot would be easier if we agreed to post-TB. But even then a lot would still be difficult.

I saw TB briefly before he headed to the Commons where he was announcing the first troops to leave Iraq, 2,000 by the end of the summer. It should have been a good moment in a way, but it came as the Americans were having to send in thousands more because of the chaos in and around Baghdad. So the news was as much about that, and about the US being OK with our draw-down. TB said the UK troops in the south would now mainly be training the Iraqis, securing the border with Iran and keeping support routes flowing. He was also pressed a bit on having a full inquiry, but stuck to the need to get the job done and learn lessons in due course. Back later for a political strategy meeting and it felt a bit tired and all the same questions – how do we drive the narrative, how to deal with GB, what media to do, it was all so tactical really. I was tired of it. Pat said re the Iraq troops statement that our side had been strangely becalmed.

TB felt a lot of the backbenchers were now being totally wound up re the idea that GB could not do or say anything while he was still there. The meeting wound up and TB ushered everyone out, saying let me have a word with my author. He was doing his 'eeh oop' northern accent, being jokey and friendly but there was a bit of steel in the eye. We went round the garden and he said, 'Are you sure you are not committing posthumous suicide for both of us with this book of yours?' I said it was rounded, broadly positive but the power and impact came from the reality and the authenticity. If you took out all the JoP red pen bits there wouldn't be a book worth publishing. I was pretty determined to do it and to make it work, and I was sure I could. We can't just worry about *Daily Mail* headlines. They will present the worst possible case anyway. But it will be a big thing with me out there driving the narrative and one of the few authentic voices who knows you better than anyone able to project a positive case. But it only works if it is real. I said people who have read it say it humanises him and it humanises politics.

We strolled round for 20 mins or so and he did undertake to have a proper look. But I felt we had gone several steps back. Then to see Sue Gray who was altogether more positive. The spooks had not come back yet. She was saying there had to be good reason for omissions, they couldn't just rule out everything. She seemed better than before and felt we could get others in better place if we delayed til departure. I said I still want to make a full announcement 1 March. Maybe trade delay for lots of content. The meeting with SG was good, less so with the other two. TB quite steely. He referred at one point, albeit jokily, to my 'nest egg'. I pointed out I had turned down a much more lucrative deal with HarperCollins/News Corp because I was determined to retain control. PG's view was that the book as edited was strong but the TB portrait was skewed by a lack of GB. I left No. 10 feeling pretty down about it all. Losing the will to live a bit. Worried it was going to end in a mess. Michael Cockerell [journalist, filmmaker] programme last night [*Blair: The Inside Story*] getting limited play. Generally negative though.

Thursday 22 February

Michael Meacher throwing his hat in the leadership ring, but unlikely to get nominations. I chatted with Richard S, filled him in on the various chats of yesterday and he felt less bad about it than I did. Lunch with Fiona at Kalendar who felt the same, that TB would come round and see the potential benefits, JoP probably just looking for the worst because they were all a bit bunkered just now. Conference call with the RH team and we agreed we probably have to concede to them on timing and wait for the TB view. I was surprised to see Jeremy Greenstock so outspoken, but he had had his book banned by the FCO.

Friday 23 February

Early out to City Airport. Bought Gandhi's autobiography [*The Story of My Experiments with Truth*] and read it on the plane to Edinburgh. Yesterday I had done a line for a charity about regrets, saying my main regret in life was not reading enough books at university and I intended to make up for it. Gandhi pretty compelling, Pooterish style. But fascinating not just the obvious and the spiritual but e.g. his forced child marriage at thirteen, chronic shyness, his detailing of his sex life and his battles with lust, the account of his radicalisation in South Africa. The Edinburgh event, mainly lawyers in the audience, was well organised and there was a terrific atmosphere. Nick Davies [investigative journalist] compering. I had a nice chat with Margo MacDonald [SNP politician]. Good do. I spoke OK, mainly off the cuff, had a good few digs at Salmond, defended TB, told a few funny lawyer stories. Did the speech then awards and off. I was getting recognised and approached when out and about more than usual, which was odd as I was very low-profile at the moment. At the airport, a whole gaggle of people coming over, some talking about Scotland, some Labour, some sport.

Saturday 24 February

Stables then Colchester v Burnley. PG spoke to TB and said he was in a better place than JoP re the book. He said he had started reading it and though he had loads of work to do, he had found it enthralling and brilliant, couldn't put it down, but, 'Was it good for him and the record?' Philip said he was not hostile. I had been hoping he would get into it and he seemed to be. Colchester was a trip back in time. Ramshackle old terraces. Corrugated iron entrances. I met up with Alastair

February '07: TB less hostile after reading

McQueen [former *Mirror* colleague] and we had a reminisce. Poor game, 0–0, but quite liked the ground and the atmosphere. Only about 4,000 in there but more noise and passion than a lot of bigger grounds. Home via collecting Grace at the stables then to Melissa Benn's 50th at Lemonia. Nita Clarke [TB political advisor] was pressing me to go back. I told her a little about GB approaching me and she was insistent I had to, that it would be such a powerful signal that he wanted New Labour people and strong people around him. Good chat with Tony Benn on diaries. He was pressing me on the Queen, and whether the royals were being difficult. He said he would check on CD Rom how many references he had made to me in his diaries, but he said, 'I think they will all be positive!' He said he was always grateful to me for the time I let him into a lobby briefing when they were still all supposed to be a great mystery. He met Gandhi when he was six because his father was Secretary of State for India at the time. He remembered that he spoke to him, if not what he said, but we agreed that one of the things about having diaries and going back on them is that you can easily confuse memory and recollection. All his marbles still there, bright as a button. Nice speeches by him, Melissa, Stephen [Benn, son] and Melissa's husband Paul.

Sunday 25 February

Dreadful cold, felt like shit, watched loads of football and worked on the sofa, Inverness v Celtic and then Chelsea v Arsenal [2–1] in the Carling Cup Final. Spoke to TB later. He had read a fair bit, said he found it incredible, and a sign of how much energy I had, that I managed to do that level of detail on a daily basis. He thought it was compelling, an amazing read, a reminder of things even he had forgotten. He had forgotten the tortuous route to changing devolution policy. The balloon going up on the decision to send Euan to the London Oratory. Some of the big moments which seemed big at the time and now we had forgotten. The agonies of big speeches and reshuffles.

He was much more positive than JoP though. Also, more relaxed about CB than I thought he would be. More chilled generally. He said he could see why JoP felt some stuff very difficult but he felt it would be easier after he had gone. He said when it was all published it would be a truly extraordinary historic document. 'When on earth did you have the time?' He said he hadn't got to Iraq yet, but in general he seemed to get the picture much better, and could see both the screaming headlines but also the deeper point I had been driving at. He was a lot happier than I feared he would be from what PG and Gail had said, and from JoP.

Monday 26 February

Trying to pin everyone down to a publication date. Still feeling rough, finished Gandhi autobiography and started on Camus' *L'Etranger*. Reading books not papers definitely a better use of time. TB asked me to send Sally M a copy of the diaries.

Tuesday 27 February

Meeting with Sue Gray and we just about agreed date. Assuming TB was going mid-June maybe get serial started while he is still there, and then publish the book as he goes. Then TV. Ed had told Stuart that they could go to TV the same day as the book was in the shops, but I felt there should be a gap. Tea in the park with Bradders who said JoP had wound up Hilary C and they were really worried about some of the stuff I quoted TB as saying. Then Liz Lloyd, who said she was worried for me. This was my first really big project and I would want to get it right and there were now all these people trying to stop me.

To lunch with Rebekah Wade. Chatted re her situation. After the fight with Ross they tried to get back but it didn't work.* Now living alone in Chelsea. OKish. Thirty-eight. Been an editor for eight years. Tired but still enjoying. She was with TB before he called me at the weekend, and said he had been saying to her what a great read it was. I was probably a bit too open about the GB sanitisation, and I sensed there would be a game on to find out the kind of stuff that I had cut. She was very down on GB but so were a lot of people at the moment. She was on generally good form. She felt TB really hated GB but differently to how he was hated by GB. I said I wasn't so sure about that. He found him maddening, frustrating, difficult, impossible, but I had never heard TB say he hated him, and even now he still tried to make it work. She was a bit closer to the JP view that there was a load of guilt in there. Home and a long round of calls to keep everyone sweet and in the loop re timing. Then JoP sent me an email saying TB definitely didn't want anything published pre-resignation, including serial. All

---

* In 2005, Wade had been arrested following an alleged assault on her husband. She was released without charge and the couple subsequently separated.

a bit nightmarish. Watched Cockerell part 2 which included the line about us suggesting 'My fellow Americans' as TB's opening line in a speech.

Wednesday 28 February

Out filming with Stuart's team all day. I liked Louise [Osman], who was directing, but it was all almost like acting at points. I wasn't feeling great, but had to get back and out for speech at the House of Lords event. As often recently I felt totally strong on all the main arguments apart from when asked about GB, and I could feel myself getting defensive, and very much putting a line to take. As with all lines to take though, which I repeated often, I was never sure how much it was a line to take and how much I believed it. So when I said I felt GB when he got there would surprise people, because he would finally be the main man, he would be free of all the nonsense that had dragged both of them down at times, and do his own thing, I was sort of persuaded, but then in the car on the way home, I thought about it, and I really wasn't sure. [Lord] Nick Lyell [Tory peer] had been the host of the do, nice old-fashioned Tory. He did a rather good line drawing of me while I spoke, and presented it to me at the end. Home late, tired and knackered, still feeling ill.

Thursday 1 March

Judy Lewis [TV team] collected me and we drove over to Crouch End, where they had rented a house to do some filming. Just writing in the diary mainly, in different positions, different clothes, different parts of the house. All a bit odd, but I just had to get into it. Gail was on wanting me to go to all manner of sales things once the date was out. I broke off at lunch to go to [*Times* journalist] Danny McGrory's funeral. It was in the same church as Ellie's funeral, and was absolutely heaving. Loads of old faces from the past. I didn't feel much empathy with [*Times* editor] Robert Thompson's speech about how marvellous journalists are though. Fantastic crowd though and nice to be with Fiona and meet up with some real blasts from the past, including a lot of the old guys who worked with Bob [FM's journalist father]. Liz Gill [McGrory's ex-wife] looked pretty distraught. The kids were strong when speaking but it is always so awful. Back for filming and we were at it till late. Cameron having a pop at TB for being too subservient to Bush.

Friday 2 March

In early to see TB. Sally had read book and she liked it. That seemed to have made him a lot more mellow about it. He hadn't read that much more since the weekend but he felt generally OK. He was worried a bit about the royals, CB, Peter M, and the whole 'Attaboy' bit re Bush.[*] I was trying to get him to agree to the start of the serial before he went and the book as he went. He said fine but later JoP came back and said he didn't want anything done while still in office. He said whatever TB said to me, he was saying something different when I left. TB was in remarkably good form, definitely over the wobble around the time of the cops seeing him. He said David Miliband had done a brilliant presentation on climate change at Cabinet yesterday. He could sense people watching him in a different light. It wasn't just that he was so on top of the detail, but he had real passion, and a real ability to explain it, and especially set it as a huge challenge in which we could play a leadership role. He felt it was moving, that if David stood he would get at least half the Cabinet. The point was that people were looking over a cliff and now realised there was a signpost giving the option of a different direction.

He felt David M was thinking about it. He hadn't talked to him, felt he shouldn't. If he did stand he would stay neutral. I said I had spoken to David, and he was right that he was thinking about it, but I don't think in the end he will do it, because he thinks GB has it stitched up. TB said GB showed not a sign of changing. That he had tried to give him the right strategy but he wasn't taking it. He was diddling around on issues but not staking out solid New Labour ground. I said what the full diaries showed was that Sally, Peter and I were at him early on about GB operating against him. He refused to accept it. Then when he did, his argument was that he was so brilliant that we couldn't do without him. Then, for example during the '01 campaign he realised he was neither loyal nor brilliant but by then he had persuaded himself he could make it work, or that he had to manage it. By the time he felt he might sack him he was effectively unsackable.

TB said he sometimes felt that he shared his premiership with two crazies constantly in the corners of the room, GB and the press. He really never imagined when he and GB started out that it would end so badly

---

[*] In March 2003, Blair and President Bush were discussing Iraq and when Blair said that despite difficulties caused by the UK's support of the US's planned invasion he was 'fighting on all fronts', Bush replied, 'Attaboy!'

between them. They were like brothers and because he doesn't have that bitter side, 'because in the end I am only ruthless when I really have to be,' he never really imagined GB would be quite so bitter, so destabilising. He felt that even though I had removed so much from the book that was bad for GB, it was still there as a shadow and the story that came over was of a very small number of people who kept the show on the road in the midst of a lot of madness and badness. He agreed I shouldn't put back any of the bad GB stuff, but it did need to be out there one day, not least because their narrative of six of one, half a dozen of the other was so compelling in a way.

They were totally involved in the plot last autumn [when some junior ministers resigned over TB's refusal to supply a departure date]. They had tried to knock him over several times. It was tragic really. He said it may be that when he gets here there will be a release and he will improve but he was not confident. He said he had not yet worked out the details of the departure. Probably after the European Council. I had a chat with Liz then JoP joking about how they kept being given different outcomes of my meetings with TB. I saw David Hill to go over where we were on things, and agreed I would call GB on Wednesday and tell him what was happening. Bit of work and then off to Oxford for a talk to the Labour Club students. Met Rory and his mates then Georgia and out to Porters restaurant. Good bunch. Did 25 minutes speech without notes, usual stuff re politics media Labour-Tory. Good Q&A. Fairly New Labour bunch, though there was one very funny Trot who was very pissed, and they had a very old style flag, forward to socialism. The general mood was that GB ought to have a leadership challenge, and a debate.

Sunday 4 March

Quiet time. Fretting about my chest getting worse. Booked to see Bostock [GP]. I had a kip p.m. then as I was leaving for the Football League dinner TB called. He had read more. He felt that it got darker and darker as clearly the depressive side of my mind took over from the optimist who started out with him. He felt it was an amazing document and would be trawled over for years. He said when he did a book he would not need 'much more than this, plus a few papers'. He totally got what I was saying about it being an opportunity, even though there would be a lot of bad headlines out of it. He said because it was so important it was important we got it right. He felt the c word was not good in any circumstances. He felt I had to really think about Bush, how he would feel at seeing verbatim stuff spilled out like that, and also watch out for getting dragged into US politics over it.

He also had loads of minor points and I said you are beginning to sound like a copy-editor. He felt that the GB portrayal was so obviously limited, and the overall impression was therefore skewed, but even with all of that, he felt like a dark shadow across the place. 'So all the bad stuff? You have that in the same level of detail?' Yes. 'God, no wonder he is worried.' He said GB was hiding away at the moment, just not engaging on the policy process. He saw little sign of positive change and meanwhile DC would not need to do that much. TB said he advised him against the really tough (public sector) pay awards but he was still on his tough kick. He needs to be more subtle. He was also now looking to mess around on Europe.

PG sent me an interesting note and suggested something I had already been mulling, namely not do a serialisation. It was funny how sometimes we got to the same point at the same time. My worry was losing control of how it was presented, the stories chosen to lead on, all that stuff, and also people thinking it was all about money. The Football League dinner at Grosvenor House Hotel was fine but I was still not feeling great. [Lord] Brian Mawhinney [former Tory minister, chairman Football League] did a bit of a going through the motions speech. He sought me out afterwards and suggested we meet up to discuss me doing something in football. Burnley won 'Kit of the year' and we went into exaggerated wild cheering!

Monday 5 March

Filming with Random House first thing for marketing. But the sleepless nights were really building. I was dreaming about the book the whole time, and things going wrong all over the place. I definitely had doubts which were getting stronger. Was it the right thing full stop? I could just about be OK with that one. But PG was adamant I shouldn't serialise and even though that was a lot of money down the drain, I had definitely moved on that. Cherie was apparently reading it now too, which might complicate things. Liz liked it but felt there was too much foreign and still lots that could be used against TB. I was wondering when and how to tell GB. He was bound to see it as a hostile act even though I had probably bent over too far for it not to be. To see Bostock. He had noticed I had put on weight. He was in a very spiky mood, very down on TB. Put me on antibiotics.

Home to work then off to Cambridge with Fiona. Richard Dearlove had become the Master at Pembroke and had talked me into doing a talk for their students. He said they had originally intended to open it more broadly but there had been massive interest and so it was Pembroke only. He and Rosalind [wife] had a nice modern house inside an old city centre college. [William the Younger] Pitt's statue there and we had a little tour of his rooms. Prime Minister at twenty-one and then there for nineteen years. Amazing. Massive drinker, apparently. Richard seemed like a round peg in a round hole. I'm not sure I would fancy all that stultifying academic world though. Really not my scene, though when he talked over some of the other Masters around the place there really was an old boys' club still operating. He and I chatted over old times, the ups and downs at Hutton. I think he had found the whole thing pretty difficult.

He was as appalled as I was about the police inquiry going for TB. He had some of the same over the Shayler business.* The speech went OK, democracy, media, role of politics, some fairly bright questions, not hostile, and he seemed pleased enough. The dinner was yet more Oxbridgology, but fairly relaxed once it got going. Richard was sitting next to a Persian expert, Charles something or other, quite effete, very posh, and I heard him saying, 'I thought Campbell did a predictably competent job for you there!' One of the students who had been invited was reckoned to be a physics genius. There was a guy I had met at Tim Allan's wedding who was an expert in markets, and another guy who had been a Lib Dem candidate and who was meant to be the world's leading expert on 'the history of the book'. The general mood quite down on GB. Rosalind and RD both felt he would lose to DC. We stayed overnight, nice place, though I was really being ground down by this chest thing.

Tuesday 6 March
Cameron getting quite big licks for a speech on Europe, same old same old in one way, need to reconnect, need to redefine, all the stuff everyone has been saying for ages, but the whole focus on 'a new EU' felt like a bit of a moment, even if he was stealing clothes on the language

---

* A former MI5 officer, David Shayler, had alleged that MI6 had been involved in a failed assassination attempt on Libyan leader Colonel Gaddafi, carried out in 1996 without ministerial approval. Sir Richard subsequently denied the allegation.

again. Breakfast with RD, chatted away about the general scene and his new life, and also why I had not liked the place when I was a student. He said things were changing but very slowly, and the thing is on the academic front, there really is excellence there and that is what drives them more than feeling they have to make social change. Train to town. I was trying to collate all the various suggestions and demands for cuts that had come in from around the place, via Sue, Jonathan, others.

I was arguing for some, conceding on others but making sure I held the line that even if cut now, they could go in the full versions whenever I did that. Sue was pretty clear I would have to go through the same process again. I was also now looking for additions to match cuts. I got driven up to Birmingham and ploughed through it all again. I was speaking at the National Housing Federation, just rattled off a speech off the cuff, stayed for the starter and then home. Chest still not right. TB doing a big number on the arts, who were worried the Olympics would see them starved as the focus shifted to sport.

Wednesday 7 March
Early out to City for the flight up to Dundee for the Scottish Institute for Enterprise [entrepreneurship in universities] event. The other speakers were on the same plane. Jacqueline Gold [businesswoman] and a little entourage, Caroline Plumb [FreshMinds research consultancy] nice enough, plus the guy who started Egg [internet bank]. I was on a bit of a Steinbeck kick and was reading *The Wayward Bus*, and really into it and the guy next to me on the plane kept trying to talk. Dundee was looking nice. I went for a run with one of the interns along the Tay. Two thousand students there for the event. Interesting chat with someone called BJ Cunningham telling me how the whole fashion marketing world works, and why fashion editors wield such enormous power. He said whole shows are entirely tailored to them. He was accompanied by a girl from Keighley who had invented fridges for Africa. The event as a whole really good and some terrific ideas some already in practice. Just before I spoke Sue Gray called asking could I delay the press release. I said it was difficult. Her issue was that TB had not responded to PASC on memoirs and they were worried this would get it back in lights and put them under pressure. I said it would be really difficult and also I was running out of messing around tokens with the publishers.

JoP said it was Gus pushing for this new approach on memoirs, including the idea that people shouldn't keep diaries let alone publish

March '07: Struggling to pin down publication date announcement

them. It would not cover me but it would look like it was a response. Worse though, if I announced after this change was announced, it would look like I was putting up two fingers to him. Not ideal. Toed and froed. Eventually, after I got to St Andrew's Bay hotel, I spoke to TB as the Man U v Lille [Champions League] match was ending. He really didn't sound that bothered. He said Cherie was not keen in principle but did feel the content was not as bad as she thought it might be. He blew hot and cold. He could see why it was a problem but he also saw 'advantages'. He said he worried about how I came over, said he was less worried about 'people thinking you're a bit of a nutter' than the fact I was seen by most people in the party and the government as the ultimate team player and this might erode that. On the cops probe, he felt they came out worse from recent days and his current hunch was that nobody would be charged.

The pressure was still being piled on though. Ruth was bearing up really well considering. JoP appeared to be able to compartmentalise. Michael had started to fight back publicly, said he was being smeared, and the whole thing was about putting pressure on the CPS. It was clearly going to rumble on a while yet. But the legal side was getting messier and messier, injunctions succeeding and failing and even I couldn't quite work out who was wanting the injunction and who wasn't. GB same as. Good chat and he seemed on top of things and focused, and he was definitely moving to greater acceptance of going. The COSLA [Convention of Scottish Local Authorities] dinner was OK, and I picked up a few vibes for my speech there tomorrow. Quite a nice bunch. Devolution was clearly impacting in unintended as well as intended ways. I caught the end of the Man U game [won 1–0] then Celtic extra time [1–0 to AC Milan]. I called GB and left message to say the book was happening but I would not harm him as PM. Big news on the Lords, with the HoC voting for a largely and then fully elected Lords. I'll believe it when I see it.

Thursday 8 March

I spoke to Sue Gray first thing, agreed and then implemented changes to the press release to de-hype it a bit. Then a long chat with Gail and Susan Sandon to finalise and then away it went. To the gym briefly before going down to do the COSLA speech, which went well. I felt on real form on the speaking front at the moment. I was barely relying even on notes, and had started to develop a little device whereby I looked at a couple of friendly, inquisitive faces and if I was getting to the end of a point, I imagined them asking a question and then talked straight at them. There were one or two critics of TB but I stood up for him, and used some of the framing of the arguments I would use for the book, about how very few people in public life would withstand the scrutiny we get, and that what the diary showed is that in the end it is just a team of human beings doing their best to do what they believe in. A guy called Sam Campbell got a good laugh when he started his question by saying he and I had got a bad press since 13 February 1692 [Glencoe massacre]. My main message was the need just to keep on keeping on, and always see the big picture of others. But the devolution debate had definitely shifted things up here, and there was a different feel to it.

The press release was already causing a bit of a stir and I had a stack of messages on it. I spoke to Phil Webster, and later Mike White, trying to emphasise I was not in it for the money, I felt this was an important part of the TB legacy debate that would follow his departure, and I also laid it on about making sure there was no big problem for GB. GB called as I was waiting for the plane at the airport. He said he was reassured by my call and he was grateful for the decision I had taken to present them as I was. He said he was still hopeful of persuading me to work for him in some way. I said I was sure I would end up doing something. He said he had known this book idea was in the offing, he had not raised it – though I know he had raised it with others, e.g. Gus – because he didn't want to put me under added pressure. But he said he felt it was important that I, and others, did not see this as a memoir that signals the end of an era. 'It should be the end of the Tony chapter, and the start of something new.' He was still sure I could help him. I said I wanted him to make sure his people were relaxed about the book, and just stayed out of it. It was a good chat and I felt better about things. Then Jonathan sent me an email saying someone had clearly spoken to Peter M about content and he was 'off the planet'. Also he later sent me a funny email, word for word the same as he had sent in advance of publication of the 2002 WMD dossier, which had set off a great hoo-ha when we had to give all our emails to the Hutton Inquiry, saying, 'What is the *Standard* splash likely to say?' In fact, we had both seen it, and it was '£1m wages of spin'.

The copy was not that bad, but I suppose it was inevitable they would go on money, but at least the line that I was protecting GB came through and they seemed to buy it OK. Gail was pressing me to say now that I would not do a serial, I discussed with Ed who said don't move yet.

'This is eye of hurricane time,' he said, which I thought was a bit over dramatic, but he made the point that amid the swirl of the fuss we just needed to let it swirl and then make judgements. He said he had had the *Mail* and the *Telegraph* on with big numbers, though he did say the *Mail* woman said she assumed I would rather boil in oil than do the *Mail*. I chatted to RS too. He was still pressing for more GB and JP. I flew down, off the plane, straight out and all over the place billboards and front pages with 'Spin chief's £1m secret diaries'. Another message from JoP to say I needed to calm down Peter M. I was definitely moving towards not serialising it as a way of showing it was not about the money and also because I didn't want one newspaper to decide 'what the story was'. Cameron showing a bit of steel, and on his own message too, sacking one of his defence team [Patrick Mercer] who said that being called a 'black bastard' was OK in the forces.

Friday 9 March

I was going through the whole of the original again just to rebalance foreign v domestic, also to offset some of the cuts we had been making. In the press coverage to lots of focus on a million quid, which they all just took from the *Standard* I guess and assumed to be true, but it was all fairly straight. Very little of the really adverse comment I expected. Stuart and Judith Dawson came round to talk about the TV programmes. I emphasised I wanted it on the heavy end of the market. OK meeting and they are basically trustworthy. I was generally feeling better now it was out in the open but it would lead to problems with people pressing on TB and others to get it either delayed or watered down. Out for dinner with Tessa and Matthew at Strada near her very nice new house in Highgate. Mainly chatting to Matthew about sport. Tessa said there was a lot of anxiety in the govt re the book. Gus was very worried about it. She said she had defended me but it was going to get tricky.

JoP sent me an email saying Peter M going crazy about it. Anji sent a text saying why the rush? They would be pressing TB. PG had his doubts re the private chat stuff but was acting a bit as honest broker. He also sent me an interesting US poll, TB ratings there down a bit but still way higher than most American let alone foreign leaders. High 60s in the main. But way higher with Republicans than Democrats. He was in Brussels for a summit on renewable energy, Merkel in the chair, which seemed to get a lot more than outcomes on wind and solar. TB now pointing to the G8 for the next big steps.

Saturday 10 March

Breakfast with Ed at Honest Sausage. He felt the announcement had gone OK. We had to decide whether to do serial or not. I said I felt money said yes, integrity and control said no. I said how does that make you feel? 'Well, 15 per cent of a big number is a big number,' he said, then laughed. He said it was important I was comfortable with whatever I decided and he knew this troubled me. I said partly it was about being locked in to a deal where future books were also committed for future serial. You just don't know what will happen meantime. Even keeping a semblance of control of the announcement yesterday, look how hard that has been. So do I want to lock myself into something that has me beholden for years, through all the volumes? He totally got it, and said well, we don't need to decide finally today. And don't forget we can always do serial when we do the volumes. I said sure, but this is the one where there will be the biggest interest. He felt he should first try to establish what the different groups would offer. *Mirror–Guardian* were bidding. *Guardian–Observer. Telegraph. Mail. Times–Sun. ST.* We agreed he would get the bids in and see, but I felt I was definitely moving to non-serialisation. I felt maybe instead I could write a long piece all about why and how I did them, problems and judgements in editing, academic project etc., but also say why I was not serialising, including the fact that I didn't like being beholden, and also that part of my argument was that the media has become a problem for democratic politics, so why am I taking all that dough from Murdoch or whoever? PG and Gail were really pressing. Gail felt the focus on the money in the coverage meant it was best to say quickly that I wouldn't be doing it. TB funnily enough felt a serial might be worth doing so that we could at least get some control over what the main take on it all was. Need to decide fairly soon. The headline money deal was big, but I did think, given how many books were involved and how many years I would be having to deal with all this, RH were getting a pretty good deal here. I was watching loads of sport with Calum, two Six Nations matches, Man U at Middlesbrough then Real Madrid at Barca.

Sunday 11 March

Took Grace to the stables. PG sent me a text saying TB was being got at about the book and getting nervous. Gail called to reiterate that we were just going through inevitable turbulence and had to keep calm. I was. I was about to go out on the bike when TB called. He said he had been quite taken aback by the violence of the reaction. By who? He said the problem was, as Peter said, it would be like a box of firecrackers going off in any and every direction and we would not be able to predict it. That was why TB disagreed with me about the serial, felt it might be the only way to get control. He agreed that once it was all out in a few years' time it would be an amazing record but for now it was just difficult. I said I had moved through the pain barrier with the media, and I think so had he, that we couldn't let our judgements be dictated by worries about what papers like the *Mail* or the *Telegraph* did with a book that contained so many angles and stories. This was in part about a historical judgement that over time would be good. He was not saying don't do it, or delay it, but that was where it would probably head. He said he himself was in two minds. He saw both sides. I said I did understand all the objections but I still felt it was doable, and a good thing to do, if we held our nerve.

I said it would be around for ages and it was a cross for me to bear – joke. You bear it so well, he said. He felt the reason people were so worried was that actually for all the shit the press said about me being a liar, people reckoned you were a very honest sort of bloke so you would be telling the truth and in a very well-written way. He said when it came to doing his own book whenever that was it would be a real help. 'Will you send me the whole thing?' He was then off to talk to Michael Levy. He said the papers today, filled with briefing from the cops, were a disgrace. Leaking the whole time to put pressure on the CPS. Total outrage. MPs are actually starting to see the whole thing as political, and really quite wrong. Nice enough chat and he was on good form. He said CB didn't want in the stuff about pregnancies and he was a bit worried about Carole [Caplin, former 'lifestyle' advisor to CB] (who had a big whack at me in the *Mail* today). But I didn't feel he was saying No. Maybe saying delay. On verra. He felt I should call Peter 'and prepare to be on the receiving end of a real volley'. But Peter was not answering my calls and was also ignoring texts until later when he said, 'Sorry for being a wimp but I will sit this one out.' I said better to be informed that agitate in ignorance. He said precisely, so I will call when I have remembered I am not the sitting-out type.

David Miliband called later for a chat. TB had told me he intended to talk to him tomorrow, not press him but maybe check it out. He said the party was beginning to realise GB was just too big a risk. David was still not going for it but he was sussing out what I thought about where everything was. GB was out trailing that he was going to be pushing a much more green message, which was seen as taking on DC, but it might also have been with David M in mind. Then Tessa called asking me if she could help get the book through the processes. She said she hoped it captured the truth which is that for years not only did I protect Tony but I held the whole show together. People got to know with a straight yes or no what the score was. She was going to impress on TB that it was important for him it was an honest book etc. Sally was also acting as something of an honest broker though for her troubles she was getting calls from CB raging at her, clearly much more hostile to the whole thing than TB had indicated. CB would be having emotion clash with reason.

Monday 12 March

Pressure mounting over the book. Email from JoP saying TB says you agreed to delay to September. Not so but I was getting used to his shifting ground and the story changing. He said Gus was appalled by it and telling TB the chats with other leaders would be a real problem. First decent run for ages. Rory back home, disappointed re the weekend run at Busa [British Universities and Colleges]. Train to Brussels for the Random House big bash, where I was to be a surprise speaker. Bringing back Kosovo memories, and all those trips on the train, not least because I was working on that section. I had made the point to JoP that if stuff comes out more has to go back in. I was working on a long article about the background which was also helping me to clear my mind. I did a bit of work on the novel too. Ed called, and when I said what about we wait till the autumn, he said, 'You are the 900lb gorilla in this – you sit where you want. September not a problem.' Charlotte Bush [Random House] met me at the station, and I was telling her about a film idea I had been working on, about a dad who takes his son to university and then just decides to stay, just doesn't go home again, basically becomes a student again, totally embarrasses the son, marriage collapses, blah di blah.

Then Natascha called for a chat and I filled her in too, she said she would be a lecturer love interest for the dad. I locked myself away working on the book before going for dinner with the RH sales people. Nice bunch. They wanted to hear about *The Apprentice*. A bit of a discussion about interview strategy. They were lively and engaged though and would really go for it I think. Filling me in on how the sales thing all works. Trish who sells to WH Smith's and Waterstones. Olly who does the supermarkets. Rob their boss. International sales guy. Gail joined us later. Nice Oz woman who wanted me to go out there. Irish sales guy keen. I said there was definitely an Irish-only version to be done too. Plus Europe. US. Media. Etc. etc. Could do this for ever I guess. Had to be careful. Charlotte good fun and professional. Susan S busy rehearsing for her presentation tomorrow. Perfectionist. Nice enough evening at La Quincaillerie. I talked to Gail about the pressure coming in. Inevitable, I guess. Turbulence ahead. Bed by 1.

Tuesday 13 March

Staying at the Sheraton. Last here to interview Hicham el Gerrouj [Moroccan runner]. Breakfast with Gail and Georgia, who was really nice about the Oxford do, said the feedback was it was their best event ever. She had talked to JoP and said she would leave it to me to sort date with them. Nothing could happen without me so September was maybe OK. I just felt we were being stalled and stalled and needed to make decision and see it through. Once GB was in there would be a different sort of pressure coming on. Gus would be wanting to push back. PG honest broker. JoP hates all this but that's his job. I felt I could manage it. I did half an hour in the gym, then down to the event. A little film, me and TB on the plane on election night 1997, my pager going with seats falling to us second by second, a scene in my office, Peter Stothard saying I was the electricity around the place, intro by Susan, then on. Did one gag, then just talked about the diaries, why I did them, what they were, what they were seen as, and then Q&A. Was TB OK with it? I said he was 'fine'. GB? 'Fine – ish.' Regrets? Is it true I said it was my pension? No. What was motive in doing? Mechanics of roll-out etc. Gail and Susan thrilled, said it was perfectly pitched and so on.

More email exchanges on way down to Lyon. JoP – I told him to tell CB not to shout at Sally when it is me she should shout at. He said that was his fault because he told her not to call me to avoid a fight. And so on. I guess what today showed – not least with the *Apprentice* publicity now building – is that I was becoming more my own man. I was better than most at writing, at speaking, at knowing how to pitch to an audience. The RH lot were all thinking this was bestseller time.

Sitting in shorts in the sun at Lyon Airport writing this. Feeling pretty free. Mentally better. My head is not in the vice. I am enjoying the moment more. If we can get through the next period, it should be OK. I flew to Nice in a near-empty plane so was able to work on book in peace. Stuart sent through a dire BBC draft release which had about as much enthusiasm as a rotten banana. I was met by David Mellor and a driver in a black Range Rover. He filled me in on Three Delta [internet systems company], who had 4 billion of assets from the Qataris, and the guy who had asked me out to speak had gone from nowhere to big in rapid time. It was nice to talk to David M both about old times – I always reminded him of his role as my lunchtime drinking buddy the day before I cracked up – and also current. He had no time for DC at all. He felt he couldn't hack it, didn't know what he stood for, just fancied being PM without knowing why, but in common with many others at the do, he was dubious about GB.

The event in Cannes was MIPIM, a huge real estate conference. I had vaguely heard of it but had no idea just how big it was, or how gawdy and tacky. Hotels dressed up as countries. Guys in dark suits and shades all over the place. Big willy contests all over the shop to do with the size of yachts and the size of the party. We arrived at the yacht I was speaking on. Elegant, for sure. One of the biggest. Shag pile. Bar. Dining rooms up and down. Band rehearsing for the evening. Mainly fairly classless nouveaux, some of them very wealthy, a few young bucks. Paul Taylor the [Three Delta] boss, married to a beautiful Grenadan woman I had met at Chelsea and at Tony Banks' funeral. Stunning. She said she was the only Labour person there. Actually I found another, Rachel Mortimer, coincidentally a friend from university of Caroline Plumb. David was clearly seen as a mover and shaker though he didn't seem to do details on deals.

I worked a bit in a very comfortable cabin then to the drinks do before dinner. About thirty people, a mix of their staff, bankers, lawyers etc. I was sitting with Mrs Taylor, second marriage, forty-two and looked about thirty. He was all in black, crucifix, pointed Armani shoes, low-key but flash at the same time. I spoke for about half an hour, with a lot of backwards and forwards banter with David. I found myself defending Israel and Bush against his tirades. Drinks afterwards and then I got press-ganged into going off with them to the Martinez [hotel]. We got driven there, I took one look at the zoo of humanity and decided to go back. As Rachel said, I would have been a 'twat-magnet' – brilliant word. Loved it and started to find ways to use it. I headed back and was in bed by 2ish. They were quite a nice crowd on the boat but the whole thing was such a display of conspicuous wealth, big willy exhibitionism, testosterone-charged men, literally thousands of them. Something obscene about it when you see it en masse. Earlier, TB, GB and David M had done a big number on the Climate Change Bill. A bit of GB/DM speculation around again.

Wednesday 14 March

I went for a run with Rachel, and was filling her in on the novel, and also the idea of 'good must come from bad' as a driving theme. Alex and Les Dalgado [AF lawyer] were guests of another company, aAim [property investment], and I was invited over there for lunch. I got a call from Jean-François Copé. He wanted me to speak at a conference in Paris. I couldn't do it but it was a good chance to discuss the French elections. The papers were currently full of Chirac announcing he was not going for a third term. [François] Bayrou emerging [as presidential candidate]. Royal 'minable' [useless] but Sarkozy was having to adapt and it was not clear he knew how. Good to chat. He was aware of diaries via the French media. It had definitely connected and a lot of people were asking me about the when what how who etc? I could not believe the scene down at the MIPIM main event. Alex arrived and on to another big yacht, hired by his mate Stuart Le Gassick [businessman]. He was on great form and between us we kept a mix of high flyers entertained mixing chat between politics and sport.

Alex having a go at me for our failure to do something about the media when we had the chance, said we should have legislated to deal with them. He said Darren Fletcher [footballer] had been in a car crash this morning and the press knew in minutes. Cops, almost certainly, I said. Les a nice guy, very dry humour, able to peg Alex down a bit. Alex in and out watching Cheltenham and winning every race. Nice afternoon then back to the yacht, for another speech/talk. I didn't feel as on form as yesterday but it was OK. A major mover and shaker from Qatar was asking me to be a non-exec. He said he wanted to take on the media with me. Full of it, how he had done this and done that and the Qataris were wonderful and how he was going to fight a tax probe and on and on and on, manic almost, how I was amazing and had achieved more than most would in a lifetime and I had been one of the most powerful people in the world (!) and 'You know about power and we know the richest people in the world, and we ought to be able to do something' and here is my card.

It was definitely one of the more interesting speaking gigs I had done of late. I don't think I had ever seen so much major league wealth, or at least the appearance of it, so packed up and intense in one place. It was pretty ugly. I guess there was good in there somewhere but it really was so not my scene. Several of them telling me I should get involved, e.g. Stuart Le Gassick telling me how much United players were investing, but they needed brainy people to help. An American guy telling me how what they did all worked and how they were now getting into PFI [private finance initiative]. Bed at 1.30 but loud music till three so not much sleep. Big [Labour MPs] Trident revolt at home and it was seen as much as a hit on GB as TB. Almost 100 MPs voted for a delay on renewal, and they needed the Tories to get it through.

Thursday 15 March

Up at 6, late-night revellers still wandering around, off to the airport and home by lunchtime. In to see Sally who went through the first half-page by page. Said CB had really lost it with her as though it was her fault I was doing a book. She said she was finding it hard to get TB to focus on the future. We met at her in-laws' flat. She said reading it the second time around she felt less sanguine than the first. She felt it was more *Peyton Place* [US soap opera]. Cabinet barely there. GB just about OK but of course some of them were desperate for him to fail which was daft. She said it was a different and narrower perspective, more about me-TB than she expected. Sue Gray texted as I was there to cancel the meeting tomorrow. I wondered if they were deliberately dicking around now, with Gus so opposed. She insisted not but we were going to lose almost a week. RS was cutting my inserts and also agitating for more GB. GB bombing in the polls at the moment.

I bumped into Andrew Adonis in Lower Regent Street. He said everyone was desperate to find themselves in the index! There was certainly a lot of interest but I just wanted to get it done with. He said GB had called him in – don't tell Fiona, he said, as she is no doubt thinking GB will reverse all the education reforms – and he was warmth itself, really keen to work with him, understood the importance of reform etc. etc. AA said he was surprised how comfortable he felt doing the job. He felt able, was making a difference and enjoying it. Met Bradders for a coffee, then off to do *Richard & Judy* with Trinny to promote the Comic Relief thing. She was manic as ever, but she said on screen that she ended up liking me.

I got home to see Comic Relief which was, to be fair, a good laugh. They did quite a good job in disguising just how useless we had been, and it did make for good TV which I had always thought was the best way to make money for CR. The kids loved it and we didn't come out too bad overall. A big focus on me beating Karren at the rides negotiation. Loads on the Trinny fight. The fair itself was a bit thrown away really given all that went into it. My favourite bit was Cheryl asking Trinny if she had OCD. To be fair, it was not that well edited and maybe they could have used two hours. But at least it was not the reputation-shattering disaster area I had feared when I had been lying in the hotel unable to sleep and wondering what the fuck I was doing it for.

Friday 16 March

I did a long run out to Stoke Newington, but I was heading into a despond I feared. Later out with Grace and her friend Abi, Fiona and Zoe, to Comic Relief at TV Centre. The figures for last night were good – 6.6 up to 7.1 million, 30 per cent share. Tonight up to 11 million, 50 per cent share. They were now trying to sign me up for a big Sport Relief challenge. Lots of good response to last night's *Apprentice*, and looking forward to the finale tonight, when we had the firing. Nobody had blabbed, but most people assumed it would be me or Piers for the chop. The whole thing was producing a different kind of response from a lot of people. Warmer I guess, but it was hard to take seriously. Grace was having a good time wandering round green rooms and dressing rooms. Catherine Tate was really nice, did Grace her own 'Am I Bovvered?' Her scene with TB one of the best of the evening, but the star for me was Ricky Gervais doing a fake Africa film with, eventually, Jamie Oliver, Bob Geldof and Bono. There was a touch of genius to it. Emma Freud took us into the studio where we watched the boardroom scene and Piers' sacking. All's well that ends. Lots of suggestions he and I should do a TV double act. Funny how things work out. There had been some pretty brutal editing. Ross K, Jo Brand, Maureen Lipman were sidelined really. Lots of Sugar and clearly he had pressed for more and more. But it all seemed to go fine, and Grace was loving it, and taking all the credit for me having done it at all.

Saturday 17 March

Off early to Preston with Calum. Doing French coursework on French presidential powers, me reading a new book on Claude Chirac [JC daughter]. Poor match and we never looked like scoring. Lost 2–0. Getting closer and closer to the drop zone. Huge police escort for the

Burnley fans back to the station. What a waste of money it all causes. Slept on way back. Calum really working now and got a fantastic letter from Mr Kidd [teacher] re his recent politics work. Rory home, and out for dinner with his friend Jamie, but I was heading into a slump.

Sunday 18 March

Woke up depressed, and it stayed all day. Went out to the stables with Grace to try to get away from things, but it was still there. Feeling sick and empty, and dying inside. Couldn't run. Couldn't think. Talk. I went out, ostensibly for a run, but sat and just tried to chase it away. Wrote a bit. Needed to use all this in the novel. I have two depressives, maybe more, needed to make sure I found a way of using all this shit. Good out of bad. But why does it just fall on like that? Is it the pressures of the book coming in? Dunno. But really low, as bad as it has been for a while. A car came by, slowed down, looked at me as if to say was I OK, did I need help? I did a little wave, and they went on. I walked back, but felt so fucking empty. People think I matter, but I think I don't. TB ticking over but the polls are moving in the wrong direction and Cameron is ticking a lot of boxes and getting away with far too much. Also, *Sunday Telegraph* had the chief prosecutor of the ICC [International Criminal Court] saying one day TB and Bush could face war crimes charges. It ran less than I thought it would when I first heard it.

Monday 19 March

Major depression day 2. Apart from when talking to Calum, unable to lift myself at all. Sleeping on and off. Not getting any work done. Went out for a walk but felt like shit. Rory off to Portugal for warm weather training. Watched Man U v Boro in the Cup, might as well have been watching the walls. I was getting calls on the Budget, both from GB re speech and TB re strategy, and finding myself just not calling back. GB was out doing a decent job of saying he wanted to keep on reforming the public services, and seemed to be echoing the TB language on personalisation, but there were a few of the mandarin class, including Andrew Turnbull, making waves, AT calling him a ruthless Stalinist.

Tuesday 20 March

As bad as it gets.

Wednesday 21 March

Day 4 of feeling complete and total shit. Waking on empty. Falling asleep on empty. Empty in between. Tearful. Edgy. Seeing DS for first time in a while. I talked him through recent days. France. Book. Comic Relief. The suddenness of this one. Not the usual build-up at all. Normally I feel it coming. This was like an instant hit. Now feeling tired the whole time. Feeling dead inside. He said he felt it was a feeling from way back but I couldn't remember the last depression let alone the first. He said normally these things do go back to childhood or trauma or both. He felt it was a tension within me about what sort of person I am and what sort of person I want to be. The conflict between public and private, duty and desire, fame and anonymity, work and freedom not to. Also he felt deep down I probably hated the wealth of France and the glamour side of Comic Relief, being both part of it and separate from it. Definitely there was something about belonging or not belonging in all this. He felt we should really work at trying to get it worked out, where these dead feelings came from. Another discussion about medication.

I got a car over to Fulham, to meet Delta Goodrem, Cathy, Tony Rizzo [hairdresser and fundraiser] and team to go over Alternative Hair Day. Working out a few lines to work on with Delta for *The Observer*. Cathy thrilled at her involvement. She'd be good for this and agreed she would sing on the night at the Albert Hall. To town, to meet Mike Forde at the Trafalgar. Big Sam thinking of moving on. Getting into school sports issue. I said make sure he knows what he is on about, don't just bullshit and mouth off based on what the papers say. We talked about money in the game. Loads of squad players now a million-plus a year and not really contributing much at all. Madness. But at top end getting worse. Bolton players 'sub-elite', top guys at top clubs earning unimaginable money.

I missed the Budget. To TB strategy meeting. GB 2p basic rate tax cut from 22 to 20 next year the top line from his Budget. But 10p rate scrapped so he was getting hit on give with one hand take with the other. His big figures on growth – best in G7 countries – and inflation were good. He had his usual big numbers for schools and other public services, a cut in corporation tax, also did a big number on the need for more for intelligence and the military which was another PM-in-waiting move. Overall TB felt it was a good New Labour budget but Sally was saying people over 38k worse off. 'Say goodbye to swathes of the south-east,' she said. TB said the general problem was GB had been pursuing a differentiation strategy when he needed more continuity.

Apart from TB nobody effectively defended the record of the government and GB's lot had been presenting the record as poor so what did they expect? He needed to get to a sense of there being continuity before people would hear him on change. PG was more pessimistic, felt that there was such disgruntlement and revising down of opinion around GB that he could not do the change candidate thing at all. JoP felt it was classic Gore-Clinton, GB did not want to acknowledge success of the past because he wanted to say the future was better. So the record went by default. PG was clearly of the view we had to press for another candidate. TB was pretty clear at the moment that GB was home and dry but PG felt GB just would not shift people back. DC was not doing great though. I felt that with the right approach and the right strategy, and genuinely doing continuity as well as change, GB could beat DC and also that people were being too negative. TB said when he was out with the media and public he pushed only the positive. But we had to face the truth. Sally was even more down on GB than usual.

JoP said GB had not spoken to him for twelve years and was now only beginning to do so re NI. Sally and I were arguing that TB should be going after G8 [heads of government] rather than European Council. He seemed to be moving there too but also argued that it was important to get something done with Sarkozy. He had a deal to cut on the Constitution and he wanted to do it. Not a great meeting. To see Sue Gray who had [Sir John] Scarlett [head of British Secret Intelligence Service] comments. Basically he would prefer not to be in it! That was a nonstarter. Sue also saying the royals would be really difficult, echoed by JoP later. I was slightly losing the will to live on it. Maybe I should just have done an ordinary book. Out to *The Sound of Music*. Really good production. Backstage to see Lesley Garrett [soprano] and her GP husband. Really nice. She sang 'Happy Birthday' to Ines Nebi [Grace's friend]. Home, still very down.

Thursday 22 March
Into town for a Dick Caborn meeting on a Wembley fundraiser for the party. Eight or so people, Dick firing off in all directions. Aiming for a million out of it. Would be tough though. Didn't feel I was on top of my game at all. Did a script for the event for briefing purposes. There was a fair bit of interest in the fact that the Beeb were doing a deal with me for the film of the diaries, given the history between us.

Friday 23 March

Fiona off to Devon. I finished the latest edit, then into No. 10 for lunch with TB, Liz and later JoP who had just endured several hours with the cops. It was truly dreadful what was happening to them. Sue had told me there was a chance CR [Catherine Rimmer] would be questioned because of something written into a briefing note for God's sake. They seemed to have moved from any criminality in the arrangements to conspiracy to pervert the course of justice which of course could be taken as anything. JoP was amazingly chilled given how awful it was. He said his strong impression was that they were just reading accusation and denial into the record. On the book, TB started with a long 'Well?' that didn't bode too well. He said issues were timing and content. I said they always had been. He felt September. I argued a new PM trumps any book big time. But at conference it could indeed become a problem. He and JoP both felt serialise. Liz agreed with me on the timing, felt I should be out there on my own terms, and defending him as he went, and the book was a good platform for it, in part because so real.

I wondered if she was just saying what she thought I wanted to hear. I had told her about my dive and she felt it was all to do with having this stuff swill around me again. We had a chat with TB on his own future – do a foundation, make money giving advice to companies and governments, plus the speech circuit etc., in order to do pro bono stuff on governance in Africa especially. He said he wanted to get people like me, Charlie, Michael Barber [former head of Downing Street Delivery Unit] involved. Another little chat about the book before I left. He said he still saw the chance of it being a positive. The problem was it was a diary. People, whatever they said, basically saw me as honest and so it would be seen as definitive. It only showed one perspective but it was an important one. His concern was – as Robin Janvrin had said – that 'once close advisors do this, you have a problem'. Also all the key people were worried that I should be the self-selecting author of the 'first draft of TB history' so people like Peter, Anji, Jonathan were all bound to have concerns and worries.

I said there will be dozens and dozens of books about his time as PM, eventually hundreds. This was about making sure in the first mix he had a guaranteed pro voice out there with a real and authentic platform. He said again he was worried about GWB, e.g. if it became a big bad thing over there, showing him totally gung-ho re Iraq. He said there was a view that it was a betrayal so though this was irritating, I had to understand the concerns. But these were points of principle I thought we had dealt with. I also said the royals should not get too worked up and it would look bad if they tried to suppress. JoP to be fair was pressing for decisions on my behalf. TB said he wanted the weekend to take another look, and see what everyone else was saying. I briefed Gail who sounded less pissed off than I was. To Alloro's to see Steve Norris, Paul Smith [ex-*Mirror* colleague, PR man], John Lewis [businessman] to discuss the Heath scientific park at Runcorn and a series of AC SN events. Rebekah Wade was there with a group of people from Ladbrokes and also someone called Charlie who I reckon from the body language was a new bloke.

24–25 March

Mainly spent watching football. Scotland winning v Georgia in last minute. England dire 0–0 in Israel. Media endlessly engaged re Woolmer death.* Feeling very down now and doing no work. Sunday Fiona spoke to Gail at Neil and Glenys's wedding anniversary while I went to *Mr Bean* – not funny – premiere with Grace. What was happening was people were getting at TB and his initial views were being unsettled. I was getting unsettled too. Was it the right thing to do? Was I doing it for the wrong reasons? Where would it end? Maybe the answer to the questions DS was posing was to become 'ordinary', get out of the public eye totally, fade away. But how realistic or possible was it, or desirable? I was reading a lot more, which was good, but not really engaged beyond that. Fiona was away in Devon part of the weekend at a school governors' conference, so Audrey came round to look after me. The problem was I was neither very down nor remotely up, just a kind of nothing in between.

Monday 26 March

Stuart and Judith round. Briefed them on where we were. Judith had produced a first draft for episode one. I didn't like it. Too much of the titillating stuff, not enough of the serious. It also brought home how few words you get even for an hour of telly, compared with the printed

---

* International cricket coach Bob Woolmer died suddenly in Jamaica at the age of fifty-eight just hours after his team, Pakistan, was unexpectedly eliminated from the World Cup by Ireland. Jamaican police launched a murder investigation but later concluded he had died of natural causes.

word. Stuart P came round later to assure me he would grip it. I said the reason I wanted to do it with him was because he shared my basic media analysis and we should be challenging the down-market dive not going with flow. Bike ride and later football. Still overweight. Asked by *Cosmo* to do male centerfold! Must be joking. Breakthrough time in Northern Ireland, Adams and Ian Paisley [leader, DUP] together to announce power-sharing from 8 May. Quite a moment to see them together, both saying the right things, even if the body language looked a bit awkward. Reading another Henning Mankell Kurt Wallander novel. Did a bit of work but not much. Feeling like a flat battery and even the NI stuff didn't really lift me. Another troubled night, tossing and turning about the book, GB, Diana and the royals, generally uneasy, catastrophising, imagining the worst, and thinking a lot about death.

Tuesday 27 March

Really struggling to get going. Stuck on every level. In to HMT, having agreed to do a Q&A with [head of media relations] Anne Shevas's staff from Customs and Inland Revenue. I bumped into Jeremy Heywood who was in there for a meeting. Brief chat. Both agreeing NI was amazing yesterday and we were both surprised TB was not more attached to it. Core speech, Q&A OK, questions more political than I expected, plus one twat asking if today was a good day to bury bad news. Cab to Paddington for a First meeting, a presentation by Rod Connors [marketing agent] on the Monster Challenge. It went down really well and was ticked off more easily than we expected. Walked home, bit of work, run and drift. Bad polls in Scotland. SNP looking like they might do it.

Wednesday 28 March

I took Fiona with me to see DS. This has been a long, bad run now. The good news was I had managed to stay more or less civil with her, but it was really hard for her to live with this when the gaps between the plunges seemed to get so narrow. The bad news was the feeling of non-happiness and the feeling of death inside persisting. The book was definitely playing around with my head, no doubt about that, though as they both said, these feelings pre-dated all that. So things like this made it worse but didn't cause it. I was finding writing it all down quite helpful, but of late I hadn't even been doing that. I just wanted it all to end really, and I found myself saying that, and then crying. David felt maybe medication again, F and I not so sure. Maybe give it a few more days. The Iran crisis was deepening, with fifteen UK sailors arrested for allegedly trespassing in Iranian waters.

On the book, after a bit of pressure from me, word finally came back from TB via JoP – go for July. He seemed to think 'If it were done… then 'twere well it were done quickly'. Meeting with Sue Gray, quite relaxed and she had had dinner with Tessa who was clearly pushing the boat out for me. I just wanted to get it sorted now. Royals and [Sir] Nigel Sheinwald [head of Cabinet Office] on the foreign policy front still to come which would be tricky but meanwhile get on with getting ready. Dinner with June Sarpong [broadcaster, charity worker] and her bloke Kit. Seemed quite a nice guy. Italy 2, Scotland 0. England struggled v Andorra [2–0].

Thursday 29 March

Golf with Jamie Rubin. I hit a few half-decent shots but really need to play more to get better. Filling him in about where I was on the book. He felt my timing arguments were a bit self-serving, and he was surprised they were being so accommodating. To a meeting at Random House, but Richard S was not well as now on both radiotherapy and chemo. Then to the Sports Industry Awards. Big media turnout, not least for Becks. I had a little chat with him and with Gary Neville, boring them about Maradona. Brief chat with Arsene Wenger. He asked how I was. 'Surviving.' 'It is all we can do in the modern age.' Big smile. I presented one of the awards, did a little chat, then schmoozed the room a bit with Dick Caborn trying to get people for the Labour dinner. The 'Again?' *Apprentice* moment with Piers had cut through, mentioned by quite a few. Really nice chat with Richard Hill, including about the news that Alfie [Gareth Thomas] was seemingly gay and had left Gemma for a bloke. Incredible. He said it had been a bit of an open secret for a while. Good night. Went to get Rory from Victoria after flight back from Portugal.

Friday 30 March

Did book inserts for Mark then set off for Burnley and the launch of the School Sports Partnership [project to increase quality and quantity of PE and sport]. I did a bit of local media and spoke OK, as did every-one else, but it was all a bit flat and I was annoyed to lose a whole day for it. Calum up with me at hotel. Dinner and then working on book, really need to make the final calls now before hopefully a last meeting with Sue Gray.

Saturday 31 March

Working. Hour run on canal. Then to the match. Chatting to nice Luton board guys and wife who were all saying they had had a taste with Mike Newell [manager] of what I had had in spades and they were really at a loss to know how people under a real spotlight coped. He had been in the headlines for criticising a woman official and also slagging the board, and it had been media mini-frenzy time, they said. Poor match, 0–0 and just nothing there. We hadn't won since November. Home by half-eight.

Sunday 1 April

Problems on book timing still. I just wish it was all over. TB called later. 'How is your saga?' I said no need for a derogatory word. It is a book. He said he was still OK but alarmed re negativity elsewhere. Nigel Shein-wald was the latest to argue that it would damage foreign relations. On the sailors being held by Iran, TB said it was a nightmare because it was not clear what they were asking for or even who was in charge. He was getting hit on it from it all ends – them using it for enormous propaganda, here people saying we should do more. What – like war? And no doubt the same people opposed the Iraq War. It was sad though, and horrible, to see the sailors being used in the TV pictures making confessions of being in their waters. He had been livid when they got one of the women, Faye Turney, to say he ought to withdraw troops from Iraq. All a bit grim. He said the GB situation still not good and the party moving backwards. GB was getting hammered on pensions, papers from the time of his first Budget had been released under FoI and showed the extent of civil service advice he ignored. GB was taking a fairly big hammering generally at the moment. Out to Marine Ices.

Monday 2 April

Sarah Brown round to see Fiona for a chat about 'wife of PM life' so I chatted to her for an hour or so. Fraser was with her. Very cute and smiley. She said though cystic fibrosis kids were living longer, 'it gets them in the end'. I had drafted a letter to send to GB, setting out whens and whys re the book, and thought I might give it to her, but Fiona felt not to send, better to speak. Sarah was keen for me to talk to him anyway about the kind of things he should be thinking of operationally, good personnel to keep and so on. I couldn't quite decide whether she was excited, anxious, a bit overwhelmed, maybe all of the above. I was pushing for Bradders, HC, CR, Doyle, Steve Morris. Also Fiona and I were both emphasising she had to have someone well plugged in to the diary and other decision-making. Fiona felt they were less prepared than we were in '97. Part of it was the lack of trust I guess. He was taking a big hit at the moment as a result of FoI papers on the pensions taxation decision in '97 which *The Times* were really running with, followed by other papers, the Beeb and the Tories, in that order. The Tories were definitely up for following the Bush doctrine on this one – get others to do the dirty work.

Ed Balls was in a bit of bother because he had said that the CBI backed the change, which they hadn't, and he had to retract. They were only just beginning to get used to how it will be. Different order of things. Sarah said it was a pretty vicious campaign. I said it hadn't even started. I was torn. Part of me wanted to help. But I didn't want to commit and I didn't want to give up freedom and I certainly didn't want to get my head back in the vice. She was going to need support though, and so was he. Where he got it from I don't know. In the end I did talk to GB, after she had left, and took him through my thinking. I also sent him the section of the introduction which made clear what I was doing vis a vis him. I said I know you would rather I wasn't doing it all, but I am confident I can do it in a positive way. Also, don't forget that I will be doing media around the book, and will be totally supportive of you and what you do, and helping to set dividing lines with Cameron.

I said the only choices were June/July, or September, and I had decided it was best that it was near as possible to TB departure as possible. I said I wanted to be part of the mix that is shaping the 'first draft of historical judgement around him, at a time of intense focus on his record'. But I said I had thought about him too, and felt that the fact of a new Prime Minister taking office, when for a while everything he does and says will be big news, means that even if the media and our opponents try to make my book a problem, it will be dwarfed by him. If we waited till conference on the other hand, when again he would be hoping to dominate the agenda, I think I could more easily be turned into a distraction. He asked how on earth I found the time to write it. I don't know. I said they are very personal, quite detailed, and they

April '07: AC warns Sarah Tory campaign v GB not even started

do record a lot of the difficulties and disagreements between all the main people, and that includes you and him, you and me from time to time, you and others. But I have basically gone through it and where I have felt inclusion could be used by our opponents to damage you, I have excluded.

In my mind, I have always asked if I could imagine Cameron standing at the Despatch Box using against you something I have written. Where I have had any feeling that he might, I have removed it. He seemed reassured, though I think he probably felt the whole thing was wrong in principle, and he would know that the unsanitised version would be bad. He didn't mention working for him, and I suspect he was hoping to be able to use the book to apply a bit of pressure. I did say I had kept in some of my difficulties with Charlie Whelan, also reference to some policy and strategic disagreements and at times referred to his difficulties with Peter M. I used the line Syd [Young] had suggested – I feel happy I have managed to chronicle the past without jeopardising the future. Out to *Equus*. Good story well told. Girls giggling re [*Harry Potter* star] Daniel Radcliffe's nakedness. But I felt it was a good play and really strong on psychiatrist–patient relationship, which was occupying a lot of my mind right now, me and David S, and also the novel.

Tuesday 3 April

Into town to meet Jeremy Heywood. Mainly small talk re diary, on which he seemed keener than his former colleagues, and on our respective futures. He felt he had learned a lot outside and probably knew more about the City than anyone in government now but he wanted to go back inside. He said he had been close to going back when I was pressing him to do the transition job, but the Tom Watson *Postman Pat* episode had put him off.* Now he was thinking of going back maybe to a beefed-up Cabinet Office. He would definitely get the top job if he went back. He had proved himself to TB and to GB and to the system.

As for me he felt I should not do behind the scenes even though he knew that GB needed help. He felt I was a big national figure and I should be sports minister or maybe a drugs supremo. He felt I was

---

* At the time he wrote his 'Go now' letters to TB, Watson and his wife had visited GB at his home in Scotland. Later he said that apart from a brief chat the couples had only watched *Postman Pat* on DVD and played with their babies.

similarly driven to TB–GB and could sort bureaucracies and make things happen. He felt if I went and tried to do for GB what I had done for TB, it would drive me crazy. GB was not TB, and my relationship with him would never be as harmonious as with TB. It was nice to see him and I was pleased he was going back. Lunch with Stuart Le Gassick and a colleague, who wanted me to get involved in their PFI team. Not sure. I gave a bit of advice but emphasised I just didn't do lobbying. Burnley beat Plymouth 4–0. Dreadful run finally over.

Wednesday 4 April
The Iranian crisis seemed to be resolving itself. Train north to Newcastle. Met by Brendan, drove to the Hilton. Ken Lomas [LRF campaigner and fundraiser] was blissfully unaware that he was going to be inaugurated into the Great North Run Hall of Fame. Really nice hotel and terrific event. Steve Cram and Alison Curbishley. Jonathan Edwards [former athlete]. Also great to see John [TB Sedgefield agent] and Lily Burton, who were both on great form. I was really bigging up Brendan and the GNR in the context of being an amazing example of a simple and brilliant idea which cut through the culture of negativity. Really nice event. Brendan such a top bloke.

Thursday 5 April
Train down. Long meeting with Sue Gray. Still no official royal feedback. She showed me the Sheinwald memo which was really bad. Breach of Official Secrets Act. Fundamental damage to national interest. I read the whole thing and of all the responses it was probably the worst. He felt that in relation to trust with other governments, military planning, and intelligence, it was a real problem. 'Frankly I don't know where to start.' Sue thought it was over the top, and he was blustering. She was going to go back to him and say he couldn't just spray around a blanket desire to say No to everything but had to say more specifically what he objected to and why.

Friday 6 April
Long drive north. M6 traffic a nightmare. Ended up post-Dumfries. Nice enough hotel but off beaten track.

Saturday 7 April

Left after breakfast to collect the kids at Glasgow Airport, then up to Argyll. Lovely day but I hadn't slept well. The book was definitey preying on me. TB called. Said he was up to page 258! Going through line by line. Reckoned he had 'made thirty or so suggested cuts'. He said he could still see advantages but the general establishment view was totally opposed to the whole thing and I had to understand that. He said even on the sanitised GB version it was clear he had tolerated an enormous amount, much more maybe than he should have. Said it had brought back many memories and he felt it was generally OK. He said he was really surprised at the stuff about my depression, that he had no idea it had been so bad. 'I just thought you got a bit grumpy from time to time.' GB still not great. He was sure GB thought that he was pushing 'change and continuity' – with a claim on the record – out of some kind of vanity, when in truth it was because he genuinely felt it was the best strategy for him, GB. As for his own position he felt things would take care of themselves.

I think both of us had been through something of a pain barrier on the media and what they said and thought. He wanted me to go down there next week and go over everything, but I said I was planning to be in Scotland for at least a week. Cue black humour about me going over to GB. We got to the house, absolutely fabulous and in the most beautiful scenery, and then PG and family arrived later. They had been to see GB yesterday en route and Philip said it was really quite depressing. He seemed to have no idea, on any level. He was talking about a 'Bobby Kennedy road to Damascus moment of change' about new politics. But he wasn't clear what it was. PG said all of them came away feeling it really wasn't going to work. Also the Scottish election campaign had been poor. TB had been on good form up here, nobody else, he said. Jack too wooden, GB not firing, all poor. Burnley won at Birmingham [1–0], amazingly, so two wins in a row. Should be safe now.

Sunday 8 April

Really slept badly. Awful dreams. I was with Donald and Graeme [brothers] being cornered inside a building that was collapsing, and Mum was telling me not to do the book, and making me promise not to go back. It was all about the book really. Cold coming on too. Also long periods just lying there, depressed. PG was going on endlessly about the Scottish election campaign, which was clearly going wrong. Calum was working hard. Rory and Zoe up till Tuesday. TB called two or three times, appalled at the MoD allowing captured sailors to sell their stories to the media. Decision taken by head of Navy and agreed to by Des Browne. Ridiculous. You just wonder how something like that can even get past Base One. TB called Saturday to say up to date of King Hussein's [Jordan] funeral, again Monday to say he was up to page 420. He said he wanted to protect me re some of the mental health stuff, felt it was dangerous for me to be so open. I disagreed.

He had one or two specific issues with the transatlantic relationship stuff but agreed with Sue that Sheinwald had gone a bit over he top. We were into a routine of breakfast, walk, golf, lunch, walk, dinner. Not much else. Fiona loved it here. Long chat with Gail. She felt that the pendulum was in danger of swinging too much towards emasculation and sanitisation. Had to watch that. Also, for my own reputation, she said, she was really pushing for the idea of a serial on the website, given to all. I wasn't really very frank with anyone about my own state of mind. I think Fiona just wanted it over and done with, and although I told her about all the doubts and the dreams, I played it down. GB had indicated to Philip he was worried about the timing. I was definitely in catastrophising mode, re the royals, the media into me again, people in party being pissed off, worried re it not being a success. Would the TV series work? Quite a few sleepless nights.

On the Monday evening, thought it was weeks from my birthday, we had a birthday dinner for me. I ended up a total emotional basket case. It was all Philip's idea and he stood up and made the first little speech, and said – news to them – that everyone would say something. He said the three qualities he looked for in people were courage, loyalty and humour. I had all three in spades and he had had cause to benefit from all three. I was the bravest person he'd ever met, never scared of anything. He said he felt privileged to have worked with me and to have become a friend. Georgia then went through some of the key moments in her life. First football shirt, first QPR game, first campaign, how I had always been there for her. How after parents and grandparents I was the one she looked up to.

Then our Gracie. Read out a wonderful little speech that she had prepared, how she loved me even though I could be grumpy and being grumpy was part of being me so it was fine. Sometimes she got mad at me because I could be quiet or angry, but then she remembered how much I did for them. She said she knew there were people out there who hate my guts and 'they should be hung'. She was then in tears talking about me being in tears at Dad's funeral, saying how she had hated to see me cry, and it felt like a terrible thing because I was the one she looked at to be strong, and she realised that grown-ups need parents too. And it made her angry because the people who attack me don't know me and she does and she loves me more than anything. Then Hope [Merritt], saying how important I was to them as a family and I always cheer people up. Fiona, that it had not all been plain sailing, that she had felt our life been a bit of a roller coaster but it was a good life together and she knew it would get better in the next decade, and we were blessed to have the kids and the friends we had.

Gail said she had three powerful impressions she wanted to convey – the first holiday in Majorca and the way I appropriated 'my chair', and how, wherever I go, there is always a chair that becomes mine. The Easter egg hunts I organised down the years which showed humour, caring for kids, inventiveness. And more recently, the charm I turned on in Brussels. 'If he could be that charming all the time, we'd all be happy,' she said. Mark [Johansen] had three points – my ridiculous competitiveness (he felt in the various golf tournaments that it was just easier to lose), the fact I had welcomed him to the family, and above all my relationship with the kids. He said he had never seen kids who were so close to a dad. I was pretty basket case by Grace anyway, but Mark pushed a lot of emotional buttons because he was alluding throughout to John [Merritt], to knowing what a loss that had been, to him knowing it can't have been easy to have a new guy come in like he had, but we had always got on and he had always been made to feel he was part of us straight away.

Zoe made a nice little speech about how I had been welcoming to her and she knew how Rory looked up to me, and how he would always think about what I would think of something. Rory said he was probably seen as a know-it-all nineteen-year-old. He got his best qualities from me and maybe some of the bad ones too. But he was always learning and striving and was aware of where both of us could change. But Mark was right, he didn't know anyone so close to their dad. Then Calum – first he played it for laughs and did a very funny GB impersonation saying why we didn't get on. But then he suddenly got really emotional, said he took the mickey out of me all the time but I was the best person on the planet. He was starting to well up and then cry and then he talked of what he called the best and worst moment of his life – when we went to see Dad's body. He said it was the worst for obvious reasons but he learned more in the moment than he ever had – not just about me but about life and what mattered and he was grateful I gave him that lesson. He was really crying now, hugging me, and I was crying too.

Then Charlie [Calum friend] did a nice little speech about how he had always been close to us all his life, and thanks for producing Calum. Grace G re always being there, Lindsay funny – yes, she said, I could go on about you being a rock in tough times when John and Ellie died, but I am more interested in your world class curmudgeonliness and your never wanting to spend money on clothes. My speech – I started OK but I was a basket case pretty quickly. I said I was really proud to have raised kids who felt and could express the things they had said. I was blessed with the life I had, the kids we had, the job I had done, the opportunities to come. I told them what I had said in one of those theatres Q&As I did, that so long as my parents felt I was a good son, Fiona thought that on balance life was better with me than without, and the kids were as proud of me as I of them, and knew how much I loved them, all the rest could go hang.

What PG and Mark said meant a lot too. I had got used to being controversial and think it was true when I said I didn't care what people thought of me. But I did care what the people here thought. I had reached a stage where I realised that family and friends mattered most. It was quite extraordinary how emotional the evening had become. I don't think people felt embarrassed, perhaps a bit but it seemed OK. It was all very Philip, really human and emotional.

The Goulds, Rory and Zoe left the next day. Mick H and Gabriela came Wednesday. He and I constantly arguing with Lindsay who was sticking up for the PCC. He was still pro-TB but feeling GB losing it. I was still struggling up top and not sleeping well. A big drama on the Friday night when Molly [dog] went missing for four hours. Fiona and Grace total basket cases. We were all imagining the worst. We had seen a couple of guys with binoculars watching the house earlier and I wondered if they had just stolen her. Fiona at one point lying on the sofa just crying and saying she had allowed herself to get too close. We were all really low then Calum went off on another look around the house and found her under our bed. Grace and Fiona ecstatic. On the Saturday 6 a.m. start to get to Leeds v Burnley. There by 12.15. Amazing scenery all the way. Crap game, lost 1–0, bit of aggro at the end. Home by 9. Sorting an Alex article for the *Sunday Mail* for the Scottish elections.

Sunday 15 April

In to see TB as Chelsea and Blackburn went into extra time. Up to the flat. Leo showing me his frogs. Father [Michael] Seed [Catholic priest] leaving as I arrived and was trying to keep me for a chat. TB friendly enough but steely. We went out to the terrace. I said I felt I was being asked to take too much out. The *Peyton Place* issue was definitely a problem, but that was why the foreign policy stuff was so important. The spooks, Sheinwald, FCO, of course there were things in here they felt they would rather not see, but we have passed the point on principle on that. He felt that what people saw in me was a hard man, team player who basically said it as it was so there would be an accurate assumption these were true. And the problem on Iraq was that they could be read to substantiate the main current attack against Bush – that he was going into Iraq come what may. He started to paint a few worse case scenarios – I write something that provokes a real storm, I get called over. Bush gets impeached! Highly unlikely, I said. I don't think anyone will be surprised at what Bush says. Or Bush demands of GB as PM, 'Who is keeping a diary? What are you doing about that?'

He said Bush likes you and you always got on with him. You wouldn't want any of that. One day maybe it is all doable but not now. You could damage yourself and the country and you would not want that. He felt as it stood it drove a coach and horses through the OSA [Official Secrets Act]. He was amazed how much had got through up to now. I said that was because he signalled being relaxed. He wasn't relaxed now. He said some people felt this was just me cashing in and making a name for myself and they were surprised. Others felt it was just not on to do in principle. I said that was an argument to have right at the start, not now. Most of the things he was asking me to take out didn't relate to him, but to family and other leaders. Yeltsin and drink. Bush and some of his little Bushisms. Even Chirac. Some of our discussions on Diana. He still felt on balance, on the principle, OK, and accepted that it could be good for him – though he wanted more re domestic – 'I don't just want to be remembered for NI and wars' – and also said he was surprised how journalistic it was.

Later I sent JoP an email saying I know there is a lot of opposition but it is happening and I really had to get a move on, and also missing deadlines etc. TB chatted a bit re GB again. He said he was worried the public just were not going to buy him at any price. His *Guardian* interview at the weekend saying it was the end of celebrity culture was so wrong at every level. It wasn't true. It didn't matter. And it said out of touch. Where was the beginnings of the big policy agenda? He said he was still trying to help him but it was impossible. Truth is he should have stayed another year and handed to someone younger. If DM stood he thought he would have a chance of winning because the party is beginning to realise the truth. He did not intend to interfere but it was the only way we had a chance. If DM stood we would have a week of him wall-to-wall and we would rocket in the polls because there would be relief. Then the party would see there was a potential winner there. And things would move quickly. He asked after Alex and said maybe he should have listened to him when he said, 'Change your mind – I did.'

Monday 16 April

Working at home, later to Fulham for the interview with Delta. Lovely girl and she was a good talker about the illness. Would work well for LRF. Everything we had suggested so far she had gone for it and done it well. I liked her and her sidekick Georgie. Home and did Monday night football at the school and for once played OK.

Tuesday 17 April

Breakfast with Vijay Solanki of Castrol. They were planning something called the Castrol Index, a statistical basis for player performance analysis for Euro '08, which they were part-sponsoring. Wenger was involved in it. Working out ways I might help them promote, chair sessions on it, get it into the media mix. Could be interesting. Definitely showed how data becoming more central. Then to Battersea for the Delta shoot. Pictures with her, then her solo, and I was writing the piece on my BlackBerry and got clearance all round. She was really lively and bubbly but the shoot didn't work because the clothes weren't right. Lunch with Rory. Not looking forward to going back. Chatting about the book. Interested in Vijay project. Worked on new intro for the book.

Email from JoP, an old one from CB to Sally, saying I was infringing her and kids' rights to a private life. Sue Gray called to appease me a bit, said clearly TB had become more worried but we were on the home straight. Nice chat. She had been brilliant at keeping calm when others were less so. I said I understood all the arguments perfectly well and I certainly did not want to damage national interest or to get caught up in great storms with it, but I felt some of the complaints about specifics were actually just another way of complaining about the general. I watched Man U beat Sheff U as we beat Norwich 3–0. Safe.

Wednesday 18 April

David S. Really just chatting about the holiday, anxieties over the book, and the birthday dinner. He had a very good line: 'When all is said and done, more is said than done.' We did occasionally have a good laugh at these sessions, and I felt generally in better shape than when I went away. But the depression had been deep, the anxieties kept bubbling up in different ways. He felt on the book that all the different players knew me well so they would press the same buttons. TB appealing to my sense of being a team player. GB loyalty to the party. CB importance of family. The civil servant duty. Fiona wanting you to have a calmer life. So when these were all touched at once... it went a bit haywire. Out for a run before all day filming in and around the house. Dull but it has to be done. Judith's partner Louise was terrific, good fun and also even though the work was a bit chore-ish, she and Judith made it bearable.

Grace was around, and being incredibly loving at the moment. I think she knew the recent dive had been grim, and she was really emotional at the birthday dinner. Rory off back to Oxford. I missed him a lot when he was away but what with Zoe, and his poker playing, and generally liking being at home, we had seen more of him since he went to Oxford than I feared we would. Out to do a Battersea CLP fundraiser and pep talk. Usual party crowd but a lot more young people than usual, and a good buzz. Sue Elliott [family friend] had persuaded me to do it for Martin Linton [MP]. Martin felt GB might be OK. His partner not, that TB going to be a big loss. Q&A very friendly, warm, nice evening, good people.

Thursday 19 April

Breakfast with Alan Yentob and Ed [Victor] to go over plans for a Michael Palin event on the lines of the Mel Brooks one. I had bumped into Michael on the Heath and asked if he would do it, and he said yes. Then RH team meeting chaired by Gail. Really tight on deadlines. Went over timing and content. The lawyer felt I had done OK in terms of fighting to keep things in, by conceding in other areas. Still not heard about the royals. Out to a dinner for booksellers. Felt on form. I could certainly sense the excitement about the book. Waterstones and Borders next to me. The German woman from Hatchards said she was so excited about it. Lots of good anecdotes and again I felt if I could just get it over the line and done, it would be fine, and a lot of these worries would go away. TB doing a round of European media, and making clear tricky times ahead on the Treaty, but no referendum.

Friday 20 April

Hackney. All day filming with Louise and Judith. I also did a recorded message to TB for a Radio 5 programme that was going out on the day of his resignation. Jeremy the documentary cameraman heard me doing it, and he said, 'That sounded spot on to me, why do we never hear it?' There was definitely an opening for a different kind of assessment for TB. Judith and Louise good working together and I think both had worked out how best to deal with me. Louise has a touch of the Diana about her. I was trying to help Alex sort a US visa for Park Ji-sung to get a knee operation.

Saturday 21 April

Up at 6 and off with Heinz [Richardson, architect, Zoe's father] to City Challenge, Milton Keynes. A bit too corporate and public schooly for my taste but we got into it as the day wore on. Then first stage was code breaking and we – me, Tim Campbell, Heinz and Cathy's Darren – were useless really. We were 54th out of 54. We just didn't get it really. Drive to the second stage and it was building a self-standing mechanism to move bricks. Darren and Heinz cracked it pretty well but some of them did it in minutes. But at least we were off the bottom. Then third stage running and biking and we got up even higher. To 12th so to our amazement we won 'most improved team' as the day wore on. Good fun day by the end of it, and Heinz was raving about my speech, which I played mainly for laughs with a bit of serious message about the charity and moral purpose.

Sunday 22 April

Sunday Times splashed on 'JoP to be charged'. Felt sick. The cops put their report to the CPS on Friday – ghastly timing for the weekend and elections – and now it looked like they were using the press to pressurise CPS to charge. Sent JoP a note saying hope you're OK. He was a very resilient character, and didn't let things get to him as much as I did, but this was tough. Down to the London Marathon to see Grace run in the mini-race. Fabulous atmosphere. Quite a few people asking why I wasn't doing it. I must get back into it. The trouble was the injuries and also since doing the triathlon I was enjoying the bike far more than the running. I was still getting loads of *Apprentice* comments around the place. I called TB. He said re JoP he felt it was a real abuse by the cops. On the general scene he felt very depressed. David M had ruled out standing. He felt the party was moving back to a position where it ducked the difficult decisions to avoid having to respond to the public. People felt it was GB's turn even if they felt he was wrong for it. It was easier just to let it happen. He said he really felt we were heading to disaster.

He had been through the book and said he had been pretty savage in his suggestions for cuts, particularly Bush calls and meetings. He said the trouble was they were compelling and complete but you were talking about a serving American President. Also, he felt I had to deal with the OSA points on foreign policy. Agreed to meet later. Chatted a bit more re political scene then back to the race. Hot, lovely day, wished I was doing it. We watched Grace come in then wandered around a bit and waited for Mark [Johansen] who was doing it for LRF. I was chatting to Rory about why he wasn't really enjoying Oxford. Nice day. Home, kip then in to see TB, sitting there with the manuscript. CB came in, hostile. 'What are you doing here?' Seeing my editor, I said, trying to make light, but she was in near rage mode.

She said what I was doing was appalling. TB was trying to shush her. I said maybe I should send her some of the stuff I hadn't put in there, or get Fiona to write something, given the way CB had treated her towards the end. TB said there is no point falling out on this. She went out, angry. TB said he had he felt some of the Bush stuff had to go. It was too close in, too potentially neuralgic, just to have verbatim conversations like that. Also the OSA case going on at the moment was a leak of a private TB GWB conversation and I would not want to be in a position where a trial collapsed because the defence successfully argued I was allowed to do what they did.[*] So we had to be able to say I had made changes and responded to OSA concerns. Even with

---

[*] A civil servant and a Labour Party researcher were to be jailed for leaking a confidential memo concerning Iraq between Blair and President George Bush. The contents of the memo remained secret.

cuts, he said it was as complete an account as any one person would do but we had to be careful with it.

He didn't baulk at much. It was the private chat stuff. Also Bill Clinton being negative re Bush. A bit of Putin this time. A bit of swearing. But generally the same as last week. I thanked him for spending the time he had on it, given all else he had to do. Sue had been brilliant, but if it had been left to most people in the system, it would have been shredded. He said he had seen early on that it was an incredible read, but more than that that it could be an important part of the debate not just on legacy but also what politics is becoming, and why. He said it was important it came out well for both of us. If it is bad for me it would be bad for him and vice versa. He said what people think about you is you are hard and loyal and you don't want the book to lose that. It should be the writer not the journalist that comes through. Don't go for big revelations ahead of serious analysis. He felt the lasting benefit of it was showing people what a nightmare politics in the media age had become. I said try to assure CB and that I found it really sad that she and I had not always got on along the way.

One thing I had realised from writing this thing was that we did not always pay sufficient heed to the pressure on families. I had been too hard at times, because I saw so clearly what your interests were, and how to protect them, and I expected people to see things the same way. I was also sad CB and Fiona had fallen out towards the end. He said it was hard because they always felt a bit on the outside. He said he didn't mind the stuff about the kids, he thought they came through well. He was still pretty warm and still trying to help me get the book done. As I left, I wondered if this was the last time we would have one of those little chats up there, and then wondered if the next time I was there, it would be to see GB. It was weird to imagine GB moving in, not to No. 10 so much, but into the flat. I went home and worked on more diary cuts with Mark. RS operation this week. He announced his cancer in his column today. Sad. But Penny said the book was giving him a real purpose and he was loving it.

Monday 23 April

I was finally feeling like we were on the home straight with the book. Richard was in for his big operation tomorrow. We had a long chat, about his illness, about the book, about life and the state of the universe.

I was conscious of not wanting to sound like I thought he would not be working on it much in the future, as in he would not survive, but I told him how brilliant he had been to work with, how his mood and consistency had kept me going at times, and I was going to insist on a bloody big name-check on the main title page. He sounded chuffed about that. He said he had really enjoyed it, it had given him a whole new purpose at a time he needed it, and as someone whose journalistic life was Labour-supporting papers it had been a real privilege to have the access to the material, and be able to shape it. He still wished I had decided just to do the whole thing, GB warts and all, but he understood why I didn't.

He didn't think GB would get near TB in terms of his ability to do the job, and the temperament issues would become a real problem, unless he just was so liberated by getting there that something new and different emerged. 'But my experience is, that as you get older, you find it harder not easier to change. And if you have a generally dark disposition of the world, rather than sunny…' I said his sunny disposition had been a big part of our life and I had particularly appreciated it in recent months. I told him about some of the more recent arguments about content. He said actually he had been surprised there had not been even more push-back and he felt this was just the last shouts, but ultimately 'It's happening, it'll be a great book and I have loved every minute of it'. Burnley on Sky, beat WBA 3–2 after 2–0 down. Car to Brighton, overnight.

Tuesday 24 April
Speech and Q&A to Sussex Enterprise [Chamber of Commerce], Grand Hotel. Nice bunch. Up to see Godric [Smith] at ODA [Olympic Delivery Authority]. Fabulous offices on the twenty-third floor of the Barclays building looking out over the proposed site. GS seemed happy enough though he was not sure it was a successul organisation yet. He liked and respected Seb, and he felt the team being built would be good. He flicked through the book and after a few pages just said, 'Bestseller.' Going to be controversial though, and he felt maybe make a big charity donation from serial. He felt that accusations of 'cashing in' was potentially damaging reputation-wise. He laughed out loud at several points, usually when reminded of an awful episode he had forgotten all about. 'Amazing what memories it revives.' Then he started groaning

a bit, oh no, fuel protests, oh no Martin Sixsmith...* We nipped out for lunch, solid citizen, good to see him in a new setting and clearly a round peg in round hole.

Wednesday 25 April

David S. 'Was I waiting or looking?' He felt I still had one foot in my old life but something stopped me putting the other foot in too, but equally I couldn't remove the foot that was still in there. He felt the external struggle matched an internal one about what kind of person I was, what I wanted, and how I got it. He felt only I could know, but it was better to look than to wait. I was helping PG with some lines for Scotland which was really not looking great. He was trying to give them a last stages strategy but was finding it hard to get them to move on anything. He asked me if I would think about going up there. Long meeting at RH with Caroline to go over pictures. Mark in with the latest version, and though a bit shorter we agreed no need to find additions to match cuts as it would just keep us going round and round for ever.

I did a BBC NI interview for one of the legacy programmes being made about TB. Lunch with Liz Lloyd. She said the argument about me was still raging in there. Some really felt deeply that it was all wrong. I told her about the CB scene on Sunday and said I would probably give the Chequers do [TB farewell] a miss. She seemed a bit down on my project too and I suspect there was more questioning of my motive than I maybe imagined. Sheinwald had been pretty strong in his evidence that it was wrong to divulge these sensitive discussions even if they were discussing things already in the public domain.

Thursday 26 April

Did an interview with *Paris Match* on their elections, but I felt a bit off the pace. I was giving my insights of old situations but their politics is so different. I felt pretty sure Sarkozy would win because he is definitely the one making the weather. Then in to see Sue Gray who said

---

* The former official under Transport Secretary Stephen Byers had attracted widespread criticism when his email advising Byers and press officer Jo Moore not to 'bury' more bad news was leaked to the press. Moore had sent her own departmental email suggesting that the day of the terror attacks in the US was good to get out any stories they wished to bury.

April '07: Liz Lloyd tells AC argument still raging over diaries

after all that, the royals were not nearly as bad as feared. They didn't dispute anything on fact. They would prefer some of the direct quotes to be in reported speech, and they did not want anything that suggested actual knowledge of what happened in the weekly audiences [with the Prime Minister]. Given TB hardly ever talked about them, that was not hard. I think she felt that they had imagined the worst before they read it, and then actually felt it was not a bad account from their perspective. I wondered if Janvrin and [Lord Robert] Fellowes [former private secretary to the Queen] had put a word in. She said don't get me wrong, I think they would rather you weren't doing it, but they did not shout and scream the way that some people have. She was in pretty good form. I asked her if she wanted to be in the acknowledgements, and she screamed out 'NOOOOO!' We were still waiting on the MoD and it was still doing the rounds of the spooks but I felt we were getting there.

Stotty not great. Tumour not operated on. He was starting to eat though and sounded a bit chirpier. Home then out for Cognito Europe [financial PR firm] event. Hedge fund guys. About thirty of them. The speech went fine but they were all pretty right-wing, muttering about going off to Switzerland if anyone tried to regulate them. One guy though clearly a big fan, told me afterwards best speech he'd ever heard, and I should become a full-time evangelist for politics against the media. Also Susan forwarded me email from the Foyle's woman at the RH booksellers' dinner who said it was best of its kind she had ever been to. I felt my public speaking was on form at the moment, if only I could convince myself it actually mattered. I was working on a piece for the *Mirror* for the 10th anniversary of May 1997 [general election], and doing final changes to the Delta piece for *The Observer*.

Friday 27 April
Early start to Swinley Forest [golf club]. Arrived early and chatted with Jamie [Redknapp]. ITV were after him but he was happy enough to stay at Sky, which he thought was the No. 1 for football. Dreadful start, 3 down after 3. Pulled back and I hit some great shots. Par 3 after up and downer then birdied the sixth with a great chip and gimme. Jamie Rubin really improved too. Redders not on fire, despite practicing virtually every day, but good game halved at the end. Bit of work-related stuff. Starting to focus on the copy-edit. Christ there is a lot of work here.

Saturday 28 April

The Times did a story on [former CIA director] George Tenet's book which seemed to be a lot harder on Bush–Cheney than mine, and full of conversations and the like. I sent JoP a note saying Tenet didn't seem to have put his book through the TB–Bush reputation protection committee. When I looked into it, it was way worse than anything I was saying. Basically that the White House and the Pentagon, but especially Cheney and Rumsfeld, were totally determined to attack Iraq, long before 9/11, and also that they constantly 'stretched' the intelligence and tried to insert 'crap' into what they said in public at the time. He said there had never been a proper debate. It was pretty tough stuff. I had always felt able to stand up for TB, justify what we did, but the one part of it that really worried me was this – that we had just been pushed and pulled according to their agenda. He was also pretty clear that Cheney didn't just sex up, but made up, and said people are entitled to their own opinions but not their own facts. Dan Bartlett [Counselor to the President] was out defending Bush and saying he had wrestled with the decision. I set off to deliver the latest MS to Judith in Chelsea so she could get going on the TV version. I was beginning to feel a bit bogged down by the scale of what I needed to do in the next few weeks.

Monday 30 April

Jean Pierre Langellier from *Le Monde* round to discuss French elections. Pretty clear Sarkozy going to win. To Ladbroke Grove to see parts 1 and 2 of the TV, Judith as my voice. Based at Avalon [Management]. A couple of guys editing. They had done not bad jobs, still too tabloid-soapy for me but better than it was. The government machine still chipping away. SG still chasing MoD, Scarlett and royals for final sign-off. Grace's birthday – out with her friends. Slept really badly. Another bout of fundamental doubt re the book, and existence more generally. Also whether I should be doing more for Scotland, with PG nagging me a lot.

Tuesday 1 May

Rowena Skelton from RH round for a copy-editing meeting at home. Not too painful though I told her I was slightly losing the will to live on the whole thing. She said she was not prone to panic but we were really tight on time now. Tenth anniversary of the '97 election. *Mirror* ran piece and looked fine. But most of the ten years coverage was pretty negative. Certainly not what he would have hoped for. Also John Browne was big time in the news, resigned over the High Court saying he had lied about something to do with his relationship with a former gay lover. That twat Peter Wright [editor, *Mail on Sunday*] out and about milking it. John looked pretty broken. I spoke to Anji who was in tears, beating herself up over whether she gave right advice to fight it. She said she felt wretched for TB too, that there was so much negativity around him. She said I must resist GB blandishments – all about keeping me in the tent and it would be bad for the party. We agreed DC was beatable with the right leader, team and strategy. Kate G called too, said she was really down about today, it was such a bad mood compared with '97.

Wednesday 2 May

8.15 saw DS. Told him getting jumpy again re the whole thing and also just not sure what I want to do with the rest of my life. Should I have gone straight back into something? Was I just drifting or hibernating? To Random House for a legal meeting. Felt we were getting there. Martin felt the book had not lost too much as a result of the deletions. Saw Gail briefly. She was in a rage about the John Browne coverage. It was nauseating to see Peter Wright pontificating re his so-called acting in the public interest. What was it about? John was gay. So what? But didn't want people to know. And why should it be known and splashed all over the place? And now he was going to lose his job because of it.

Lunch with Jeremy Paxman at Orso's to discuss his MacTaggart memorial lecture. They had wanted TB and he was second choice, he said. He said he wanted to deliver a few home truths and took notes on my general thesis, much of which he said he accepted. Jeremy always tended to get lumped in with John Humphrys but I never saw him in the same way. I don't think he is a cynic. He is also good at self-mockery. He said he was fifty-seven now and thinking of whether to pack in. He said Robert Harris [author] had said to him, 'Do you really want to have on your tombstone – He presented lots of *Newsnight*s?' He felt TB was formidable, truly exceptional figure and didn't think GB would be in same league but on verra. Sardines and linguine. Good food, nice chat, both of us probably more reflective than in most of our encounters in a studio or discussing being in a studio. Home to do a bit of work then watch dire United performance in Milan [lost 0–3, Champions League].

Thursday 3 May

To see SG to get her latest batch – NIO [Northern Ireland Office] and spooks. Not much from either. Royals agitating a bit re Charles and some of the stuff he said about e.g. the Chinese both at the time of the Hong Kong handover and when Jiang Zemin had his state visit to the UK. I argued much of that was already public. Sue said she wanted to go to the launch party. Home then back in for two speeches. Pri-med [medical education] GPs conference at QEII Centre, one very aggressive question on Iraq, and gave as good as I got. Then to Spencer House for MetLife [insurance company] event. Sixty or so almost all male financial bods. Next to nice US guy who was based in NY, Bill Polpetta. Good enough event and again spiky questions on Iraq. Local elections not looking good but not the meltdown feared. Scotland going to be lost though which was a bit of a disaster. TB legacy stuff not that great but maybe better than expected. I still felt people buying into a lot more re him and even GB than we were led to believe but uphill. Home by 11.

Friday 4 May

Scottish election too close to call and a real mess in the voting. The results bad for us, and we were not that far ahead of the Lib Dems UK vote share-wise, but the Tories were not really doing as well as they need to. Rowena round to go through second batch of queries. SG came on with MoD changes which were basically just to take out references to specific Special Forces operations. Bike ride. Spoke to Ed. Basically decided not to do serial, at all. Sorting loads of bids with Charlotte B. Pix back from CG. Out to Soho House for Ten Years On party. Mainly '97 people, including some I didn't remember.

I did a little speech on how that '97 team was as good a team of people as I had ever known, and I singled out some of those who were there and how brilliant they were – Hilary C, who was a rock, as a whole succession of leaders know, Liz, who was there before anyone knew who TB was and she was still there now, Bradders the world's greatest word machine, PG, living proof that politics and friendship could mix, Doyle because he was slower than me in the marathon, Ben for the time he called and asked me whether I thought the Peter M mortgage [in 1998 with undeclared interest-free loan that led to his resignation as Trade and Industry Secretary] would be a big story, media monitoring and brilliant analyses, Kate and the disaster of St Olave's school visit when she managed to get TB pictured as though on a cross. Carol Linforth [PM's office] for not hating me even though I made her wear a sandwich board, Adrian McMenamin [former press officer] for looking for Oliver Letwin while dressed as Sherlock Holmes. It was a fun night, and even though most of them felt the ten years on coverage had been on balance pretty shit, what I said about them being an amazing team was true. I was chatting mainly to Hilary, who was thinking about what to do next, and Catherine, who was probably going to move on with TB. Mark B got completely pissed. I had seen him tipsy before, but this was like major pissed.

Saturday 5 May

Stables with Grace. Really impressed at the way she didn't go wobbly when Stella [horse] wouldn't come in at first. Out for a run, sluggish, then home to work on captions for the book. Out to David and Louise's for another ten years party. Chatting to D and L mainly about the kids. I think we were both avoiding too much political talk. There was a little bit of an end of an era feel to it all. Nice chat with James Purnell about running. Matthew Taylor funny about the reactions of some of the civil service to the book. Nice enough do. David made a little speech, but it did slightly have the feel of an elephant in the room. There was so much talk around of whether he would or should go up against GB and it was clear he wouldn't and thought he shouldn't. Tessa on good form. SNP really milking it up north, biggest party. Grim and bad for GB as well as TB.

Sunday 6 May

John Reid effectively cleared the last hurdle for GB when he announced he would not be staying on in government under him, and certainly wouldn't be standing for the leadership. Off crack of dawn to Burnley v Coventry, last game of season. Lost 2–1. Poor game. Then to Mum's. TB called. He had just spoken to Sarkozy who won by six per cent. TB was feeling we might still salvage the Scottish elections. He sounded a bit edgy though. He had finally gone snap on announcing his departure this coming Thursday in Sedgefield, and asked me to have a think about how he framed it. Long chat with Anji after the football. She too was a bit unkeen about the Chequers farewell. Still upset re JB fallout. Arsenal draw with Chelsea – Man U champions.

Monday 7 May

Run. Chat with Mum and Calum, then to Bedford for Rory's race at BUSA. He'd run really badly yesterday and dropped out at 300 but did much better in the relay today. Working on acknowledgements and also a briefing script about not doing the serial.

Tuesday 8 May

Most of the day with Rowena going through final chunk. Up to Birmingham in the evening, working on book captions on the way, to Society for British Rheumatology. Like the GPs, a bit chippy and beleaguered, one or two total wankers including a guy who boasted he lied to Milburn to keep open a service planned for closure. Gave as good as I got and quite enjoyable when it kicked off. Nice woman there from Galliard Healthcare PR, quizzing away about TB–GB. Phil Hammond 'celeb GP' chairing. Half and half as to who thought patient care better or worse. A lot of whinging out there though, certainly not a home run re whether we had transformed the NHS for the better. Part of the issue though was never-ending capacity needs. Some tough decisions down the track. I worked on a few lines for TB's speech for Thursday, humble tone, link past to future, but I wasn't motoring. In any event, though he had asked me to help, I knew he would want to do his own thing.

Wednesday 9 May

DS, nothing of real note. I said we were like two blokes chatting in a pub. To DCMS for chaotic and shambolic meeting about the sports fundraiser. We were still short of major sponsors and table sales. Dick [Caborn] full of the usual optimism, but organisers looking worried. Would be a real hard sell from now on in. To Random House for final run through pictures and captions. Ed called and we agreed he should speak to Witherow [*Sunday Times*] and give him the bad news about not doing serial. Not happy, of course. He also felt it was wrong, that the publishers talked rubbish about the relations between sales and serial. 'They ought to pay us, not the other way round.' I spoke to Les Hinton who was surprised and also thought it was the wrong call. He felt the other papers would make it go massive and I would have no redress.

I said I felt that it was the thing that tipped me from doing it for the right reasons, to stop people being able to say 'cashing in'. So though the money was big, I felt it was a reputational hit not worth taking.

Also I felt the argument I made about the modern media was weaker if I took their money and let them control how the book was first seen. I said, 'You think I'm mad, don't you?' LH said I think you're wrong. He said why not do it but give the money to charity? Maybe. Witherow was on with the same arguments, and we had much the same conversation. But once we had talked it over, and they had lobbied me from their perspective, I actually felt I had made the right call. It was not as though I was losing a million, because I had never had it. And the deal Ed had discussed would have had me bound in for years. It just wasn't worth it.

A bit of work, then out to ABC [Australian Broadcasting Corporation] for TB legacy interview before going to Stamford Bridge. Down to see Alex in the tunnel. Ryan Giggs and Gary Neville in suits. I said don't you want to be playing? RG said yes. Looked down. Alex in good form. Playing a weakened team. He said if I had been there half an hour earlier I could have got a game. He was very down on Mourinho, and they had a testy little eyeball exchange when JM emerged. He asked what I had decided re serial. He said if money is not an issue, don't do it. Said that if he had his time again he wouldn't do it. He was on great form, happy and joking with the staff, really pleased at the way the Premiership had gone for Man U [champions]. One of the Chelsea backroom guys came up to me as I was just hanging around talking to Alex, and said, 'Can I say something to you?' and I thought, 'Here we go, Iraq all over again,' and Alex bridled a bit, but I said of course, and he said, 'Tell your mate Tony he is the best we ever had, Britain is a far better place for what you lot have done, and people should stop fucking whingeing.' Hear hear, said Alex. 'Will you tell him for me, yeah?' I said I would and he ran off. Dinner with Joe Hemani. Terry Byrne [David Beckham's agent] there and he was another one saying serial is a killer. He said that every book Becks had done he'd done serial and regretted it. United fans on form.

Thursday 10 May
TB departure announcement day. Bit of work and chat to Calum before heading out for never-ending media round. Irish radio down the line on the way to ITV, 7,500 quid to LRF for the first interview. I watched TB live. Good mood. Short intro from John Burton, then TB in to a great reception. I found it a bit defensive but it probably worked on various levels. It was a bit too downbeat for me and the lines on apology and

mistakes would give the critics too much to feed their own narrative. I stuck pretty much to an achievements script all day, across the piece, plus values, changing the landscape, and being a real person surrounded by the 24/7 rubbish. To Millbank in a cab with Mark Austin, same kind of stuff. All asking about publication date. *WatO* [*World at One* radio programme] with Martha Kearney, William Hague and Charlie Kennedy. News 24 live. Sky. Bloomberg. 5 Live. UTV. Al Jazeera. I got into the rhythm, ending up doing loads more than planned. Then to RH with Charlotte to tidy up a few details on book then back out via Millbank to do Channel 4, quite combative with Jon Snow. Neil K was trying hard to be totally supportive but 'Iraq overshadowed legacy' was his main take-out.

Home then *Newsnight*, and having been asked to do a one on one, which I did, I got talked into staying for a panel discussion after it. Michael Howard one of the panel. We went through TB and Britain, then Iraq and foreign more generally, then general style where Michael Howard really went for me. It was clearly totally pre-prepared, he said he had written in *The Spectator* that I was single-handedly responsible for lowering political debate, a bully and a liar, that TB was probably OK but I had turned him into something he wasn't. I could see Paxman looked genuinely taken aback, and was looking to me to see how I wanted to react. I could feel myself losing it but held back, let Howard drone on, then said they were still in denial, Howard couldn't bring himself to admit he was beaten by a better man and a better party so they preferred to persuade themselves we won through presentation. Get over it. Alan Milburn stepped in with a better line – that it was fine for the Tories to be professional, but not us. Polly Toynbee also stuck up for me, saying the historic bias against Labour was enormous, and they didn't like the fact we managed to correct that and win elections.

Charles Kennedy and David Hare [playwright] staying pretty much out of it. Alan and Polly gave me time to calm internally, then I whacked back more gently. As it wound up, I waited till we were off the set, followed him out, took him to one side and said, 'You ought to remember what Tony said to you once – there is a difference between being nasty and being effective.' He said he felt he had to say it because he had done this piece for *The Spectator*, and I said yes, and the reasons are as I set them out. Get over it. Alan M felt it would go whoosh, and the number of texts coming in suggested it had been quite a moment. I was quite pleased that I managed to keep my temper in check. TB called, I said I thought today he had been a bit too defensive. He felt he had to do it like that and felt it had gone fine, now he would work flat out for a few weeks, particularly on foreign, then off. David M called, said he thought I dealt with Howard well, and asked if I was helping GB with words. He needed words, and he had nobody in there really able to do it. Home half-twelve, stung by Howard, partly because I just hadn't seen it coming, encouraged most people felt I held it together, conscious of end of an era feel, but also that we did have to get behind GB now.

Friday 11 May

Texts galore on the Howard clash. Most seemed to think I handled it fine and he came off worse, as nasty and bitter when most people were being more reflective than usual. Fiona watched it on the net and felt I should have asked what lies he meant and now that I should send a lawyer's letter. Gavin set it up. TB was against, felt best to ignore, especially if people felt I won. Most of the day going through Volume 2 with the TV team to agree the best moments. GB did his campaign launch. Didn't look great. Autocue dominant in the shot as he spoke, not great for their anti-spin line. Overall not bad but a bit same old. Also, Brown for Britain as slogan, not great after ten years! He was also doing too much of the distancing on spin, celebrity etc. And did he really believe that a written Constitution – hinted at – or more powers for civil servants was the way to reconnect? It confirmed to me he was too focused on definition vis a vis TB rather than DC. Audrey called about the autocue, laughing and remembering my 'someone moved the fucking lectern' line in the 1994 diaries, which she was reading. Dinner with Tessa and Fiona at Kalendar. All rallying round GB but no great enthusiasm.

TB got a good enough press today, partly real, partly to build up things against GB. This was the other thing GB had to factor in. They would want to mark up TB as a way of marking him down, a reverse of what he was used to. Fiona felt the Howard attack might be part of a broader strategy to stop me going back. Try to get me discredited so GB would feel I couldn't go back. Tessa was saying how much Sue Gray had enjoyed the book.

Saturday 12 May

Gail had come up with a new idea – maybe do one big interview with the *ST*, one slab of serial, and give all the money to LRF. GB coverage, as entirely predictable, mainly focused on distancing. End of spin, sofa government, review of policy on Iraq. TB called mid-a.m., said he really despaired. It was Clinton–Gore all over again. The problem with distancing was that he was giving the public the sense it was all change, which meant TB lost out on credit for what was achieved, of which GB could present himself as a big part, especially on the economy. And all this constitutional stuff was fine for a narrow range, but not the broader public. We'd done FoI, put the lobby briefings on the record, he had done appearances at the liaison comiittee, monthly press conferences etc. etc. etc. and it had not made a blind bit of difference. Also the one thing the public know about him is the economy but he doesn't own it. Instead he does all this diddling. TB said the people he thinks he can get back by me going will not come back on that diet.

I asked if he thought I should help. He said the problem is they don't really want you for proper strategic advice, but to contain you and to use you in specific circumstances. 'Would you have advised that strategy?' 'No, I advised a very different strategy, continuity and change, in that order at this stage.' 'Exactly, so why is he doing what he did?' 'To define himself against you not DC.' 'Exactly.' He said just as I had done, he had also written him a note with a clear strategy but he was not going to follow it. If he really feels this need to distance, he should be saying we had the right intentions, but we didn't do it all, and he has the energy and experience and commitment to get it done. Got to be about strength. 'He is taking what he thinks is his weakness – the idea of control freakery and intolerance and being selfish – but in trying to address it he has given himself a weakness. It's just not good politics.' Also it was not sensible to be putting out the line of a shift on Iraq. It was all too much 'I am not TB'. But nobody thinks he is. Doesn't look, sound, act like me. Nobody thinks he won't be different, but it's a mistake to overdo.

Also it totally gives Cameron the 'heir to Blair' space he wants. He said Cameron will have watched that with real satisfaction, whereas if GB had done a big thing on here is what we have done, here is what we still want to do, here is where I can make a difference going forward, here is where we need experience and strength, and here is where they are weak and incapable of meeting the challenges of 21st-century Britain, and he would have been in a good place. Instead of which... Jesus! We talked for an hour or so. He said it was not the disloyalty that most annoyed him. In a way he understood that because he had held this grievance for so long. But he felt it was just stupid. The public like loyalty, they don't like this diddling around. The trouble with his own effective endorsement of GB yesterday was there had been no coming together in the run-up. TB had seen Sarkozy yesterday who instinctively got it, got why TB had been the phenomenon he was, was asking why GB was ploughing the furrow he was.

He also saw Chirac, said he looked a bit frail, but they had a good chat and were really warm about each other in private and public. Cf. Schroeder, who he felt had emerged as small-minded post office clerk. He said Sarko was a total tornado. Expect fireworks. He said GB's people were backing Harriet as deputy leader, and her latest thing was about ministers not using their cars. He was seeing GWB next week. I told him to tell him I was going to use the book and media interviews, and serial if I did it, for LRF and I wanted another cheque. As to his own future, he was pretty clear that he felt he should leave Parliament as well as No. 10. He just felt a total clean break was better, and it would not be good for GB if he was hanging around, added to which it would drive him – TB – crazy. He also wanted to get into doing foreign stuff straight away, Middle East for example, but in a different way. The tragedy was that all the other world leaders wanted him to stay around, but GB wanted him off the scene as much as possible. He said the mood was good out and about yesterday, and he felt it had been right to do the apologetic bit. Becks was among those who had put a call in.

I called Les Hinton and said I was thinking interview plus one-shot serial, all to charity. He said not ideal but better than where we were. Told him I would want copy approval including on story projection and ads etc. Witherow called, given an inch but trying for a mile, interview plus panels, 20,000 words for two weeks. Called Ed in Odessa where he was seeing where his mother was raised. He discussed with Gail and agreed interview and a few panels and then one week only. Witherow had said maybe 200k. Would have been 400k if full serial. Read through prog 3 material for TV element then loads of football and nap. A bit of an up and downer with Fiona who was unsurprisingly hacked off at my endless agonising re serial etc., couldn't understand why I had let them reopen the issue having resolved it and then saying that she thought a lot of my angst was because deep down I agreed with her about Iraq, I felt I could have done more to stop it, and I was living with the shame of that. I said that is real transference if I may say so, I supported him and still do, and she just said you have to say that and all the book is doing is making you relive what you think and what you think you are supposed to think, and it is creating all this tension in you.

Sunday 13 May

Final agonise on the serial question. Syd Young said do it and give to charity. Alex: 'Keep life simple and don't upset Fiona.' Bruce felt it was all too close to GB taking over, don't do it. Peter Hyman and HC – don't do serial. PG and Gail round later. Agreed not to do. Wobble over. Loads of football. Play-offs. Premiership last day. Gail round later to discuss how we would set up a new website to promote in detail.

Monday 14 May

Missed GB call first thing. Working on prog 3 in detail. Filming in Battersea. Tim Campbell round for a presentation at WES [William Ellis School]. He did really well, could be a great role model for the young black kids especially. GB called as the presentation began, so we spoke only briefly. He said people were starting to listen to the Tories again. We have something to say but nobody listens. People feeling we are out of touch. Pressing the listen and learn line. I said he had not done enough continuinty amid the change. Asked me to work on lines and arguments. He felt the Tories were vulnerable. Wanting to do long-term challenges. He claimed he was not openly supporting Harriet but e.g. DA and AD backing her.

Tuesday 15 May

Told Les definitely no serial. OK about it considering. Ed spoke to Witherow, not as bad as might have been. We agreed I would do the first big interview with them. To RH at 12 for a meeting on the website. Domain name. Trade pieces. Short release announcing the date. Did so at 3. Home to do French with Calum before his oral tomorrow. Then to Aberdeen Asset [investment management firm] pre-dinner, Martin Gilbert [CEO] top man. I felt people were a lot warmer since TB announced a departure date. Then to PwC event at Chiswell Street Brewery, on public sector reform and how to make change. GB all but confirmed as PM without a contest now, with 308 MPs having nominated him. Nobody else was going to get on the ballot. End of. TB hosting Bertie who was speaking to both Houses of Parliament, first Irish PM ever to do so.

Wednesday 16 May

GB called asking for thoughts on his speech tomorrow. He sent it through later but it was poor. 'Listen and learn' was fine but so limited and it was too passive. PG and I were both trying to get him to put in strength. Also saying to him he must not dump on the past. On the past, it should be to be proud of the record but now facing new challenges. LRF auction. Ian Botham on great form pisstaking most of the evening, and staking out ever more right-wing positions on everything. Daley Thompson [former decathlete] and his wife terrific fun. He was in running gear, despite it being black tie, which he refuses to do. I wished I could do that. One day I will. He said he just refused to wear a suit to anything and if they didn't like it, well he didn't need to be there. Good event, though I ended up spending more than I intended to because a couple of items just weren't getting bids. Six grand for a holiday I wouldn't take.

Rebekah called from Washington, about to see Bush for *The Sun*'s farewell to TB coverage. Wanted tips. I said to get alongside Dan Bartlett before and make clear he loosens him up. If you want to prove you are close to us, start with a joke about the press being bastards. She wanted to get a story – as maybe did TB – about him being asked to do MEPP etc. She had never met him and I was advising being very direct, joke around etc. I worked till 1 doing a response for GB on his draft speech for nominations closing tomorrow. Both PG and I thought it was really poor. It felt passive. Needed more strength. In the end we agreed we should both send him very direct observations. 'Listening and learning' sounds like such an abdication of responsibility for someone wanting to take up the mantle of leadership. Without strength, it means nothing. So we suggested that he start wth Cameron's weaknesses – doesn't understand the problems people face, doesn't have the strength to solve them even if he did. GB understands the challenges, and has strength. That way you link listening and learning, but with strength.

PG sent over a not bad line: 'Leadership is having the humility to listen to the problems of the people, and the strength to act to solve these problems'. We worked on a shorthand. 'The humility to listen, the strength to make a difference'. In truth neither of us thought he should be pushing the listening thing, and it was all part of the distancing from TB and the claim he 'never listens', but we felt if we could at least get him to use it only as a basis for strength. But on listening, if he meant it, he really had to get into the anxieties, frustrations and irritations that people felt. Immigration. People who play by the rules don't get on. Welfare. PC. Housing. Public services taking money but not changing enough. Lack of safety on the streets. 'Don't pander, but do understand.' So listening means understanding all that. Learning means knowing that people are tolerant about immigration, but worry it has gone too far, and public services cannot cope. Compassionate, but not if people choose not to work, and choose not to contribute. People know the government has done a lot, but it not enough, 'not enough for them, not enough for me.' Listening without strength is futile. Strength without listening is arrogance. Our country needs both, my government will provide both.'

In the draft his mantra seemed to be 'Economic stability will be the foundation; Education my passion; The NHS my immediate priority; Affordable housing the new challenge', but it was weak and totally ignored the community respect agenda. There was next to nothing about the past and building on achievements. No real energy, urgency and strength. Next to nothing about tough choices, reform. It was too far gone to fix completely at this late stage. But in the final note I said he must, at a minimum, have a clear message of strength. Must give sense of a new future. Acknowledge past achievements. Acknowledge concerns about immigration, and crime. Must have better more connecting language. We advocated rather than just listening and learning, he say that he has a big programme to meet the challenges of today, that he has experience and strength but if he is to change Britain he cannot do it alone. But even that was just too passive. I said listen and lead would be far better than listen and learn.

Thursday 17 May

Work with Calum, bits and bobs on the book then out for a charity event re comms. All the main charities there, just wanting advice on strategy and comms and how to get government on side. I did an interview with Noreena for the end of her documentary. Home, work on proofs. GB stuff going OK but bit of a problem not having a contest and having two PMs.

Friday 18 May

Tired. Train to Preston working on proofs. Susan called, said Knopf had bought it in the US. Ed felt it was a good deal. Meant going to the US for a week or so shortly after I did the launch here. Rebekah called. Bush had said to pass me a message – he had seen *The Queen* and as I was the only heroic figure he assumed I had done work with the film-makers, and leaned on them. Also joking re bastards and cojones. RW liked him. Bush really fond of all of us and aware of how much grief he had caused us. Chugging through proofs. Also working on getting good people for the next fundraiser.

Pick-up at Preston, to Oaks hotel, then down to Turf Moor for the latest fundraiser we were doing for the club. Some great former players there. David Eyres. Said the 1994 Wembley play-off against Stockport [2–1] was best day of his life. John Angus such a nice guy, and it made me feel a bit old to think I was a child when I first saw him play and now he looked, well, quite old. He said he still loved the ground as much as when he first played there.

John Connelly said he had got a hat trick at every club he played for but never got a match ball. I arranged to get him one at the dinner. Nice chat with Martin Dobson who had just finished a novel about two young footballers. Andy Lochhead was pleased he was in my all-time Burnley eleven. Ditto Dobbo but he felt Angus should have been there ahead of Noble. I was sitting with Ian Wright at the top table who said that even though his time here was late in his career, and short, he absolutely loved it. Brian Mawhinney very supportive of the club and what we stood for. Mawhinney said he felt I had professionalised government comms in a way the Tories wanted to but Major had lacked the bottle to add it to all the fights he had to fight. He added that he felt I did a good job, 'but maybe you went too far!' Good fifteen-minute film on the club's history. I did a Q&A with Wright, and he was excellent. Adrian Heath [former Burnley player and manager] was banging away at me about immigration, said we were losing touch.

Saturday 19 May

Up early and off to Cambridge to see Rory running in the Oxford–Cambridge inter-varsity thing. He didn't run well though and the glandular fever still seemed to be hitting him. TB having done Washington on the day of GB sole nomination was now in Iraq. Did Eamonn Holmes [Sky] interview on the Chelsea charity match next week, during which I came out for Alan Johnson as deputy leader. Godric came down to see us, and said he would read the book properly with a view to working out what stories were most likely to dominate. Home for a crap Cup Final, Chelsea beating Man United 1–0, then out for dinner at La Casalinga, and Grace's face priceless when she saw Paul McCartney walk in, then come over and say hello. He was having dinner with his manager, but chatted for a bit, and Grace and Abi literally sat there open-mouthed. He's still got it.

Monday 21 May

Lunch with Sally and Tom Baldwin [*The Times*]. GB called. He said he wanted to see me before end of the week if possible. We talked a bit but it was too noisy in restaurant. Sal and Tom all a bit small talky. Sally amazed me about a recent Ark [schools charity] fundraiser which raised £29 million. Totally puts me in the shade. She said she was being very good about GB out and about. Tom seemed pretty fed up with journalism. Home for a meeting with Charlotte to put together a media plan and then a conference call with Knopf re a media plan for States late July.

Wednesday 23 May

Construction News [magazine] breakfast at Claridge's which went fine. I was beginning to pick up more doubts about DC from the business community, and not finding it so hard to push a line defending GB. Gave a miss to the DCMS meeting on the Wembley dinner but Carol Linforth was saying they were going to pull the plug unless we hit a tipping point by 1 June. Meeting with the proofreader and Mark B. Trying to sort the cast lists etc. Champions League final. Liverpool lose [to AC Milan, 2–1].

Thursday 24 May

To Chelsea FC for the cystic fibrosis match. Really enjoyed it. We had [Welsh internationals] Neville Southall in goal and Kit Symons alongside me in defence helping me a lot. The one thing I had learned at Soccer Aid was to let these guys take control. Luther Blissett, Warren Barton and Mark Bright [all former top-class players] also playing. Barton couldn't run much but he totally controlled the game. We were playing the MPs as usual, who were not great and we went 3–0 up, then got pegged back but held on for 3–2. Darren Campbell [sprinter] man of the match. I played OK considering but was very sore afterwards. I understood what [Paolo] Maldini [AC Milan and Italy] meant when he said as he got older he needed three days to recover from a match.

Friday 25 May

Birthday. Out to see episode one and two of Judith's diaries film. OK, still a bit tabloidy for my taste. Also hated the 'You' bit when I asked Fiona what Diana was after, and also the reference to 'might top myself' in the bongs at the top. They were doing the editing in what felt like a prison cell at Avalon. Nice team editing and it was getting there for sure. To Random House to go through pictures. Also we had agreed there would be 'running feet', a few words at the bottom of each page to signal the main thing on that page. Richard had done a good job on it but I wanted them in the third not the first person, so we had to go through those. The RH team brought in a nice cake with 'The Campbell Years' on top. They were a really nice bunch, and definitely pushing the boat out. I suddenly announced I had to leave because I was going to see Gordon at the Treasury, and I could tell from the laughter they thought I was joking.

I jumped in a cab, arrived just on time. He looked tired. His second chin was larger. Hair a mess. Nails on right hand not so gnarled but on the left they were bitten right down. He was not in great shape, I would say. He went straight into a thing about how competence was the issue – 'We have lost the NHS as a political argument. All that money but we have lost the argument.' He went through a plan someome had put together for him to revise health care in London as a way of showing how it can be done elsewhere. I said it felt it was too much accepting the culture of negativity but he said if he was out there just defending the record nobody would listen. I felt both were possible. He said he had to be the future. He could not just do the past. I said you have to do both. He had to be continuity and change. One did not work without the other. Also there was not enough of an attack on the Tories.

I was in there for about an hour or so, and it didn't feel great. I felt de-energised by it. He lost it at one point when he raged about how much the party was in debt, how the machine had been allowed to atrophy, '26 million fucking pounds of debt – that is the inheritance.' He was pressing me to work for him and eventually he said he would either like a private arrangement where I offered advice from the background or – what he would prefer – where I would 'run the Labour Party'. He said it would not matter who the general secretary was, he would want me to oversee campaigns and comms. He went into a tirade about how since I left there was nobody bringing it all together, co-ordinating message. Also he wanted me to help him put together a plan to communicate new approach on health. He was very friendly but a lot of anger spilled out at times, and I was trying to persuade him he should be a lot more confident and optimistic. But not easy.

The meeting had to end when he was due to talk to Ban Ki-Moon, UN General Secretary. He ended up keeping him waiting with staff getting agitato. I got a cab home with a guy who was quite political, not one of us but he was sure we would win one more. He said Cameron was not really breaking through. I said what about Gordon? 'He's solid enough.' Home for a bit, a few friends round for a birthday tea, George and Catherine, Gill Keel [family friend], Victoria [neighbour] then out to the Simply Red concert at the Albert Hall. Took Gill to see Mick backstage and she was completely overhwelmed. I think we sometimes took for granted the kind of access we had to people and events. He was really nice to her too. As ever his 'Money too tight to mention' had major resonance.* Everyone was up on their feet by the end. The audience maybe older than I expected in general, but he could still get them going. Nice evening.

Saturday 26 May

To golf at Wentworth with the boys. A bit like watching paint dry. One of those sports definitely better on TV. Andrew Rawnsley doing a bad piece on the diaries, focusing on what I was leaving out, swearing, GB, Iraq. Later took Rory back to Oxford. Still seeming a bit down. Then to Tessa's.

Sunday 27 May

At Tessa and David's. Vile weather. Interesting to see David having got used to living on his own, constantly clearing away and not wanting stuff left around. Jessie's new bloke Louie seemed a good guy. Musician. Tessa going on about the Olympics the whole time, clearly still hoping to be spared extermination when GB took over. She had been at the Chequers do and said it was nice, mainly family and friends from way back, she, JR and Charlie the only senior politicians. Sally too said it was a nice do. Meanwhile a little flurry starting about the book.

I spoke to Rawnsley yesterday who was doing his column on it, focused on someone clearly having briefed on some of the excisions I had been asked to make. Swearing. He had stuff about TB using the c word for Hattersley, also GWB and bits and bobs of other stuff. Front-page story plus his column, the main focus swearing, and TB wanted to tone down the idea he swore like a trooper. Rawnsley's was quite a negative piece, perhaps driven by his desire to have got the first big

---

* In the build-up to his breakdown in the mid-1980s, Campbell listened to 'Money Too Tight to Mention' time and time again when returning home at night, often drunk.

May '07: Diary excisions starting to make news

book out there post-TB, so maybe he was annoyed that I was doing it at all. I spoke to Mike White during the day, who was also clearly being briefed because later Sally called and said he had asked her if it was true that Cherie had threatened me with legal action. It was going to get turbulent again. I didn't feel it was neuralgic and yet it increased nerves and sleeplessness.

Monday 28 May

Mike White ran nothing but it turned out he was doing a bigger number for tomorrow. Went for a swim. Finished David Peace's book on Brian Clough, *The Damned Utd*. Really good, but I kept wanting to know what was real and what wasn't. Alex was also reading it, had some good Cloughie stories, but such a sad ending. Lunch with Rory at Café Rouge. Still not right. Needs to get to a specialist.

Tuesday 29 May

Big piece in *The Guardian* on 'ructions' over the book, a lot of it focused on Cherie being angry about references to her and the family, but also Gus, Sheinwald, Peter M. Gail and PG convinced it was a Peter–Ben W-P operation. A session with DS. He had a really bad cold. He said it was quite strange for him to keep reading about me and then wonder about what of all the things they said I was doing I would raise when I saw him. The book. Again. He was still of the view it was right for me to do it and I was right to insist I was not going back full-time with GB. TB called, just about to leave for Africa. He seemed unaware of all the stuff in the media about the book. Not happy when I told him. He said why get the focus on what is not in it, also it is not good if it looks like 'the family' are falling out. All we need to say is there is a process and you've been punctillious in following it. Beyond that is mischief making. He still felt on balance it was OK and was going to be fine and positive, but not if people kept doing this. He said there was no way CB would have said anything.

Then to GB. TB felt he just didn't know what he wanted to do with the job, and the public was beginning to realise it. So he diddled around on stuff. But it was not breaking through and people were beginning to think it had all been about ambition not vision. I filled him in on my meeting with him. He clearly felt he wasn't really changing and setting himself up for a few falls too. He had to rush because he was leaving for his Africa trip. He said he would instruct the press office to deal with the diary stuff. PG had said yesterday that people who spoke to TB always came away feeling more optimistic. There was something in it. Nice chat, and he was keen to shut it all down.

Kathy Fry the proofreader came round. Lots of little bits and pieces to sort out. Alex called. He wanted advice for Jason [son], who was getting into the event management game again. He was getting Owen Hargreaves. Still trying for [Dimitar] Berbatov [Spurs player] but probably priced out of the market. Alex said he was desperate for his holiday. He was disappointed to have lost the FA Cup Final, but felt the League was always the big one. He said he had seen a good piece somewhere about me not serialising, the right call, he felt people would say it was someone prepared to stand up for what he believed. Chatted over the recent stuff and he said just keep going. Kathy the copy-editor very good and thorough. Worked on it on and off all day, interrupted by a visit from the Nokia people trying to show me how to use a new phone email thing. It was an hour wasted because I just couldnt't do it.

Out early evening to speak at the Shine [charity] event at the Locarno Suite at the FCO. Gus O'Donnell had asked me on behalf of Jim O'Neill [Goldman Sachs economist], and was fine if smallish audience. Did big opportunity and antidote to cynicism message. Went well. Long chat with Gus. He said my book launch coincided with Janvrin's farewell. I said maybe I won't be invited. He said I shouldn't tell you but Robin is quite happy with the book, felt you put a few things straight about that week. So maybe I was right that Robin had put a word in. He too not aware of all the fuss. Very nice chat about that and also re GB. He said he and TB were talking more but he was still doing too much via new so-called initiatives and not big talking points. He also thought it was crazy for GB to be going on about the 'end of spin' when he had Damian McBride on his way in to No. 10. He said GB had a blind spot about some of his own people. Good chat, nice event. Both he and his secretary Jackie were saying what a legend Sue Gray was. She was. Then to see *Das Leben der Anderen* [*The Lives of Others*]. What a film. Brilliant. Liked the Clough book too, which I read in a couple of sittings, so maybe I was into a more fruitful cultural period.

Wednesday 30 May

Most of day on and off working on entries for the website being set up to promote the book. I still wasn't sure I had my head round it all. It was not the kind of thing I got instinctively. With a paper you feel it – have the idea, write it, see it go into print. With this, you are communicating with the ether, but I just had to give it a go. Took me a while then got PG, Gail, RS and others to read. PG very good advice, always watching for my ego taking over and also emphasising the need for a big picture message about 'Why now?' Just about got there. It was quite useful to sit down and write though it all because it meant working through answers to the questions I would get asked endlessly. The web team asked to delay till tomorrow to get it absolutely right. We were calling it 'Diary of a diary', and going over the processes, of keeping the diary, then transcribing, and now all the vetting and other processes. How to get two million plus words in order, then cut to 350,000. How I came to the idea of the single volume, and some of the choices and challenges within that. Why I want to be part of the debate about TB and legacy. Why I still support him.

Richard had a good line, about it being 'a diary, not a paean of praise', so I made clear, it was good days and bad days, things going wrong as well as things going right, fallouts, I also admitted there were some conversations so personal they will never see the light of day. Others borderline, and I have sought the views of others, including TB, before deciding whether to publish. I said I was punctilious in my approach to the vetting process. Into a bit about the media age and the challenge for politics, and how it was TB's fortune and misfortune to be in power as the information and media age became a reality – fortune because he is a superb communicator; misfortune because we have more coverage of politics than ever before, but less understanding of politics and, bizarrely, less real political debate. Also, that the depiction of politics has the superficial appearance of being whole and truthful because of the huge volume of words spoken and written about it, but the humanity of politics is driven out by it all, and I want to give a more rounded picture of what it is actually like.

I talked about the ethical and political responsibilities – to honour the truth, but also to respect and acknowledge the interests of those involved, particularly those still in senior positions of government at home and abroad. How I want to protect and promote TB reputation, and how I do not want to damage GB. Peter Riddell said in *The Times* there was a risk I end up damned for what I leave out and damned for what I leave in. Perhaps. But I was glad to have settled against serialisation, and had decided also not to rebut every piece of stuff about what was in, what wasn't, who was pissed off, who wasn't, because soon they would be done. But I was able to rebut the story about Gus and I having had furious rows about it, and tell of the charity thing I did for him when those rows were meant to be happening.

Thursday 31 May

Hot day and out with Louise, Judy, Jeremy and co, to the car park at the lido on Hampstead Heath, recreated as a French services station! We were on to Iraq in the film and I was filming for the book and reliving the drive down to Marseille Airport when collecting my diaries from a duty clerk after Hutton had asked for them. Judith was stuck in the edit but sent through the three scripts. Overall they were good and I was never going to be able to be happy about the mix, as it was so hard to communicate the hard edge policy drive etc. when there were so many events to cram in. All morning filming. More shots of me writing in, and reading, diaries. How many more can they need? Then onto a train for a few moody staring out of windows shots. As we go through Dalston, a large middle-aged woman who has been reading the *Daily Telegraph* comes over. 'Your farewell tour is rather less glamorous than Vanity Blair's,' she says. She had a rather unpleasant curl to her lip, and snorted something about why was he spending the week in Africa? I thought about engaging with her, telling her that if it hadn't been for TB, Sierra Leone would in a hell of a mess, and explaining how he had got other world leaders to do more to address some of Africa's problems, but she didn't look the type to have her mind changed and in any event the producer was trying to get her to stop blocking the shot.

Home to a rash of messages asking me to comment on [former editor, *News of the World*] Andy Coulson's appointment as Cameron's new communications director. I stayed out of it. The media would focus in on the phone-hacking scandal but the key question was whether he was really political and if he really knew how that world worked.[*] I had my doubts. I had always thought he was sharp, but never had the sense he had deep politics. Cameron was getting into a total muddle on grammar schools, and the question of whether they would allow more, and later Calum and I watched Paxman get David Willetts wriggling as he

---

[*] Coulson resigned as editor of the *News of the World* when the exposure of hacking celebrities' mobile phones resulted in the arrests and subsequent convictions of a reporter and a private detective in the paper's employ.

tried to pretend there was a consistent theme running through what they had been doing. Hopeless. All over the place.

But GB was still not making much of an impact, and the deputy leadership contest was dire. Too much tacking leftwards which to be fair GB picked up on and pointed out in warning against, particularly as Osborne and Cameron were both making 'heir to Blair' noises. Kate G and pals round, and later Jon Sopel, to record my contribution as a German psychiatrist for the farewell film for TB. Very funny, though I said so myself. Really nice evening with Calum, because Fiona and Grace were at the ballet with Lindsay and Hope.

Friday 1 June

Dealing with a stack of enquiries from the proofreaders. Still getting called about Andy Coulson. The Sunday papers seem to have the same idea the dailies had yesterday – that I would want to write a piece on whether he is the new me, or maybe an open letter giving him a bit of friendly advice. Nobody had a whisper of it, though I assume he'd have consulted his closest friends, some of whom are journalists. I was as surprised as anyone else. I've had a few dealings with him in the past, and he has never struck me as a committed Conservative. I can't really recall him expressing a political view at all, at least one independent of the general Murdoch stable line. I didn't do interviews but to those who called I was saying people in the media seem to think that an understanding of the media is the key to these political communications jobs. It's not. It is an understanding of politics. He will also have to get inside Cameron's mind so that he can react instinctively when he is dealing with the media. If the farce over Cameron's ambivalent grammar schools position is anything to go by, that will be easier said than done.

Cameron has had an unbelievably easy ride so far, but when he is forced to make decisions on policy, he really seems to struggle. The problem with Coulson's appointment is not his past excesses, or his salary that will annoy his colleagues. It is that it speaks to a worry people are beginning to develop about Cameron – that, to paraphrase David S, when all is said and done, he is more about saying than doing. Michael Levy called first thing, really grateful that I had said something nice about his Middle East role in the *Jewish Chronicle*. He said that when he saw his and my picture on the front, he thought Oh my God, is he going after me in his book, but what I said was so nice and it really cheered up him and Gilda. He told me some of the nightmare moments of the past fifteen months. Police above the law. Legal bills up to near a million quid. Not sleeping. Felt he had been though a bad dream and it was still ongoing. No idea how it would end but he felt they were totally out to get him. Totally political. I felt for both of them, they just did not deserve what had happened.

Bradders called round and we went over some of his options after leaving. He felt get a base with Tim Allan or Freud and then branch out. He was doing lots for CB, who called for his help with a speech while we were there. He felt once the book was done and dusted I should look to do something bigger in government. But like me he felt a little bit that he wanted his life back and wanted freedom to be with kids more, also not as motivated by GB as TB. Nice to see him, totally solid citizen.

Saturday 2 June

Endless little book queries now. What Rowena called the nit-picking of the arse end, or the arse end of nit-picking. Some tiny, some stuff we should have spotted earlier. Lido, then telly before heading off solo to Chequers dinner, where TB was bringing together a lot of the original team. Anji, Kate, me, PM, PG, JoP, DM, Liz, Tim and Peter Hyman, Sal, Pat, James Purnell, Geoffrey Norris, Sarah Hunter [special advisor], also Roger Liddle [former special advisor on Europe], Patrick Diamond [ex-Policy Unit] and Ben W-P. A few of us met at the Russell Arms in Butler's Cross first. It was a lovely warm evening and an OK mood. Kate had the TV film all done and dusted and was happy with it. Small talky. All the girls arrived first then PG and Pat, Tim and James, finally DM and Pete. We trooped up to Chequers in a convoy. PM etc. already there. TB in blue denim top and fancy beige trousers. CB away, which given our recent exchanges was for the best, Gale there and very friendly.

A Catholic priest there and out on the terrace he was explaining to me the central practical difference between Protestant and Catholic, to do with the significance of the bread and wine. He was quite a nice guy. Clearly close to TB. He had gone with him when TB met the Pope. He had a very funny idea – said once the diaries were done I should do a book explaining that I do God after all. 'Why I now do God! – an instant bestseller … you'll sell half a million just to the Evangelicals.' Nice evening, and everyone saying how much he would miss it all. Peter M wearing a smart suit which he said he bought with Sue Nye years ago. He was a bit wary and distant. I gave him the Clinton snap of BC, PM, PG and AC which Bill had signed individually to the three of us, and which I had found when digging out old pictures.

Lots of chatter re the diaries. TB said he was pleased the fuss around the briefing last week had died down, and said he really didn't like it. 'We don't want any falling out over this.' He was asking what we could do in the future and during the evening several times said the people here could win just about any election campaign. We watched the film, which worked really well. Proper Ten O'Clock News intro, Sopel with the top lines about a man released from captivity, then Adam Boulton in Africa, followed by me as a shrink talking about how hard it will be for him to adapt to freedom, Anji talking about how he would need to re-learn about using money and stopping at red lights, PG in a shop doing a guide to what credit cards are and also people, saying he had made up all the focus groups, Geoffrey N on the need to get back to normality, Kate on how you made your own phone calls. Went down really well.

Dinner. Nice food, good chat. DM and I talking about GB and DC. He felt the public were working out Cameron without too much help from us but agreed there ought to be a bit more punch going in. He was hoping GB might make him Chancellor but felt GB would go for AD [Alistair Darling] or Jack S. Ben was interesting on his Moscow venture [joining a Moscow-based digital media company], really seemed to be doing well. Anji reminiscing about the old days. JoP burnt after a day's sailing. PM made a little speech saying what brought us together – a hope GB (his tone made clear he wasn't hopeful) would take country and party in right direction. A belief in Labour and in Britain. And we all loved TB. Kathryn [Blair, daughter] and Nicky there for part of it. TB looked a bit embarrassed but got up to speak and despite JoP's heckling – e.g. when TB said we were the best people he had ever worked with, Jonathan shouted "better than his chambers – wow". Also when Peter said we had all benefited to greater or lesser degree, JoP said, 'Yes, not all of us will go to jail.'

But TB basically said he could not have done it without us. That he never really went out to get any of us, apart from me everyone came to him and in his usual vague indistinct way he had basically said you may as well stay – for example with DM he didn't remember hiring him, it was just, 'I guess we will be seeing a fair but of each other.' He said did we really ever imagine back in '94 we would be here at Chequers after three election wins? What we achieved we achieved because of this team here and we should all be proud. Said he loved his people and we should know it, and he hoped there was lots we would all do together in the future. Anji was in tears for part of it then stood up to say she felt it had been fantastic and would any of us change anything?

I did a number about how in fact though it was nice of him to say all that, in truth so much of what was achieved was down to him, the fact so many people saw something different and special, also the basic optimism that he managed to keep despite it all. I said he had an ability to make people leave a room feeling better than when they went in. I said he had enormous optimism and resilience and those qualities had been fantastic for achieving what he had done. In the end he must take the lion's share of the credit and whatever else we do in our lives, this has been a big part and, we will always owe him. He seemed genuinely touched, said several times afterwards it really moved him. My sense was that he was now rather dreading going, told a funny story of how Gaddafi kept pressing him on the real reason he was going. 'Why? Why, Tony? Why are you leaving?' And he concluded TB was not telling him the truth. He said we should all help in any way we can for GB to get it right. Nice chat with PH who seemed distant from it, had a new life and career setting up his school but was also as sharp strategically as ever and felt GB was not hitting the right buttons. Good crowd, some really smart people, and even though we had had our ups and downs, e.g. me and Peter, this was a close bunch who had been through a lot together. TB was not really wanting people to leave. He said to me as I left he would be fine and we would be busy. He said again thanks for what you said, it meant a lot, but the truth is I could never have done it without you guys. I left around eleven and PM's car with his diplomatic plates overtook me as we approached Northolt. He was staring out of the back window, lost in thought, didn't see me. It had been a really nice evening, but with a lot of sadness there. For me, it was sad that Fiona wasn't there, mainly because she didn't want to be.

Sunday 3 June

More queries. GB big in press on terror measures. Out to stables. Long run. Endlessly dealing with queries from the proofreaders, which has led me to realise the existence of a whole new hierarchy, or at least a new divide – namely those who are felt to need an explanation in a book, and those who are not. So at Clinton's first mention he is 'President' in brackets, but there is an assumption everyone will know of which country. With Bush, he first appears as a candidate in the US presidential elections, so the context does the explaining for him. Someone like Mugabe has to be given a first name – Robert – and a square bracket explaining that he is President of Zimbabwe. Gaddafi goes without the first name but is square bracketed as Libyan leader, which indeed, as de facto head of state, he is. It gets a bit more random once you get into the famous people who pop up from time to time. Elvis Presley gets a mention when someone does an impersonation of him. He is thought to be so well known no explanation is needed! Noel Gallagher, one of the big names at the No. 10 party in 1997, is thought to be need a square bracket. Ditto Eric Cantona and Roy Keane [footballers]. We are still deciding about [David] Beckham [a footballer].

Monday 4 June

The papers were full of Vladimir Putin reading the riot act to the West, and the Americans in particular. He did the old round table trick – get in a journalist from each of the G8 countries, have something to say, say it with real force, then watch the world sit up and take notice. His warning of a new arms race and a new cold war looked like a carefully delivered 'message'. But his temper is real. Richard said he had been genuinely taken aback by the account of the time Putin invited TB out to Russia, first harangued him in public, then went even harder in private. There will be a chilly atmosphere around him at the G8 this week, and I guess he won't mind.

I was mainly working at home and then into Victoria Street for a meeting with Carol Linforth and team re the Wembley fundraiser. It was not going well. I agreed that if it was a private sector venture we would pull the plug. Two cheques in, lots of promises that came to nothing. Sponsors were being put off by the tough new declaration laws. And there were just too many claims on the corporate pot at the moment. We agreed to give it till Monday but if no traction by then, call it off. Back home to more 'arse end of nitpicking' queries re the book. Rowena now sending them through by the dozen, some tiny and anal, some very good late spots. Football at Gospel Oak and Calum was badly injured in an accidental tackle with Daniel Keel [friend]. To the Royal Free. Not bad treatment, home by just before 12. Not ideal preparation for his first exam tomorrow but he is amazingly resilient.

Tuesday 5 June

Out to Askew Rd W12, audio workshop, to record the audio book. RS, Zoe Howes from RH and I had cut the book to around 60k words which they reckoned would take three days on and off to do. My wretched voice was a problem, constant coughing and clearing of throat but they felt it was going OK. It was quite interesting to read it and get a slightly different feel of it. Lovely producer, a woman called Alexa Moore from Bath. Really pretty and she had a fabulous voice and manner, made it all go easily. It made what could have been a real chore quite pleasant. A typical small studio, no natural light, phone and BlackBerry off because of interference, an endless supply of water and jaffa cakes to keep me going. The edit felt OK, even though there were enormous gaps, at times up to three months. They seemed to enjoy it too, said as some of the others at RH had done that it gave them an insight they had never had before. TB off to G8, Russia the backdrop but climate change took over and a deal of sorts, progress, was done.[*]

Wednesday 6 June

DS. Interesting chat re whether you could apply psychiatry to a society or a country. What did *Big Brother* say about us as a society? What did Beckham, the obsession with celebrity? The desire to build up and knock down. Becks back in for the England match tonight again and on a bit of a roll. Book felt in a better place than a week ago. We talked a bit about the breakdown again, how I used it and so on. Then another day in the studio, voice feeling even weaker. It is a muscle, Alexa says, and like every muscle gets tired. So we need regular breaks. The build-up to the G8 pretty tense and TB big on the news with a tough message for Putin from PMQs about how business will turn against them if they turn their backs on reform and human rights. Home by 5 for Faroes v Scotland [0–2] and England v Estonia. Becks played well in a 3–0 win. Jamie Redknapp called to discuss whether I could help Frank Lampard [Chelsea international] at all, who was getting booed by England fans and getting a bad press. JP meanwhile in hospital with pneumonia.

---

[*] Leaders of the G8 nations, meeting in Heiligendamm, Germany, agreed to seek 'substantial' cuts in greenhouse gas emissions in an effort to tackle climate change.

Thursday 7 June

Out first thing to Paul Moore and the First team in Maida Vale, then to the studio to finish off the audiobook. Done by 12, off to Oxford and spent three hours in lay-by working on the index and the cast lists. Finally felt I was breaking the back of it. Nice call from Stephen Jones [rugby player] who wanted a bit of advice on how to handle the Welsh press who were turning on him a bit. I said don't even let them know you've read it and just imagine you are talking to someone you like. He invited me down to a World Cup game. To the Randolph Hotel and then an event for Mind [mental health charity], which went well. Aso, as I had said to David S yesterday, I found talking about my mental health problems, writing about them, and using them for something more positive, was helpful to me as well as, hopefully, to others. There was definitely a feeling for a lot of the people there today that they didn't know how to talk about it, or weren't meant to, and they felt if people with a profile like mine could, then anyone could.

Out for dinner with Rory and Georgia. Rory really getting into his poker. Someone sent a note over (at Browns) saying they loved my Jon Snow interview on Channel 4 and they loved me anyway. 'Plus don't take offence at bob bob bob jokes.' [A reference to Mike White's chant when learning of the death of Mirror Group proprietor Robert Maxwell, to which AC, then political editor of the *Daily Mirror*, took exception.] Bradders and Bruce called, both livid at a Phil Collins [special advisor] interview in *Telegraph* taking credit for TB's speeches. It led to people sending round spoof jpegs of him doing Moses and Luther King speeches.

Friday 8 June

A long interview with the French news agency AFP, both print and TV, for a series they are doing on how Britain has changed under TB. They are interviewing mainly 'real people' which people in politics are unfairly not assumed to be. I am seemingly the only non-real person they are talking to. Christine Buhagiar, ex of the London bureau, now in Paris, is doing the interview, and I tell her how, when she used to come to briefings, if I was losing my cool, Hilary Coffman used to suggest I direct all my answers at her. It is amazing how a woman's eyes can calm a rising temper. Today she asks all the questions I expected re TB – what I think his legacy will be, what he will do, any regrets, high moments low moments, what did I think of the film *The Queen*, and so on for over an hour, with plenty on the diaries and the book. She had read all the recent stories – some accurate, some way off-beam – about the discussions on content as part of the vetting process. Having had experience of the UK press, she at least had a healthy scepticism about her sources, the newspapers. She was interesting on Sarkozy, said he gave out a real sense of energy and dynamism, but both media and public were very much in 'wait and see' mode.

His presence at the G8 in Germany brought back memories of TB's first G8 in Denver in 1997. TB is the only member of the G8 leaders' group that met then who has served in the same job since. Romano Prodi was Italian PM in Denver and is Italian PM now, but had several years as European Commission President in between. Of the big characters I remember from Denver, Boris Yeltsin is dead, Jacques Chirac recently retired, Helmut Kohl long gone, Bill Clinton six years out of power. And of course soon TB gone too. He had an obviously really tricky meeting with Putin. The mood between them so different to when they first met. Even publicly TB was talking about a deep freeze, and how the world was getting more and more alarmed by Putin. The AFP team gave me a lift into town, to Hyde Park to do some running pictures with Craig Doyle, latest recruit to the Leukaemia Research triathlon team. He is another one who clearly talks about playing with Maradona almost as often as I do. He has got so good at the triathlon he is representing Ireland in his age group – 35–39 – in the world championships in Hamburg in September. He claimed that my personal best would get me in as a qualifier in my age group. The way I felt as we ran around the park, this had the feel of Blarney.

Sunday 10 June

After several days of looking at it and pushing it to one side, today I really will get down to reading the index properly. It is very very long and I think we need to trim it a bit. The entries for TB go on for page after page and I wonder if we need so much detail. What a life being an indexer must be. You could actually take virtually any line in the book and have dozens of index entries. The entry for Fiona includes one that had me laughing out loud ... 'P52, her fruitcake raved about by JP.' I spoke to Richard, who is clearly in a bad way.

Monday 11 June

Litter photocall with Fiona and litter-clearing volunteers on the Heath. Nice bunch. Two Tory councillors though, and really worrying that we lost here. Dan Carrier of the *Camden New Journal* quizzing me on the deputy leadership. Harriet getting good press, Alan Johnson not really breaking through, Hilary Benn seemingly doing best at hustings. Back to a bit of work then in to town to meet David Frost at Bellamy's. Told him he and Murdoch the two main media figures in the book cast lists. I was feeling nervous about it all again, largely because back to the feeling of unsureness about where it all ends. He felt it was all fine, and the worries would go once it was all out there. He was asking me for advice about some of the lines in the film script of *Frost/Nixon* which he felt ratcheted up the carping etc. a bit. I felt not worth worrying about. Keep going with it. We chatted over his idea of a long series of interviews with TB after he had gone. Nice time and as always with David, a good restaurant. He is such a top bloke, and one of those guys who just keeps going, so enthusiastic about everything.

He was talking about some of his *Through The Keyhole* shows as though they were as important as a big interview with a President or PM. He wanted me to do one, but I said even for him... I was already too close to that whole celeb thing and even if the main stuff had been charity, I have to watch it. To Victoria Street for a meeting on sports fundraiser. Dick Caborn with the usual pledges and irrepressible enthusiasm. He said he would get to fifty tables. Peter Watt nervous about it but in the end sided with Margaret McD, who wanted to go ahead with it because enough people out there know about it. It just didn't feel like traction to me still. TB called about half-nine. He was making a speech tomorrow about the press and media culture.

CR had called me earlier and we had discussed some of the arguments. Also she was back on to her theme about my book being bigger and more explosive than I thought. Got me worrying again. TB said he was not sure whether it was sensible to make this speech but he did think it had to be said. I said what is the basic argument? 'That they (the media) are a shower of shits and they make politics next to impossible without any real benefit to anyone.' He felt we had done so much to try to address the problem but in the end they were not interested. They didn't themselves really understand what was going on. He asked me to look at the draft and comment overnight, which I did later. Basically tried to muscularise and get some of the nodalong arguments I used about this area. I felt he gave them too much in saying the media was the most difficult thing to cope with. Also that he didn't set it in broad enough cultural context.

Talked about last Saturday Chequers event. He had really enjoyed the whole evening, felt there was something special about that group of people. Said he got more pissed than he had been for years. G8 was good, he said. And he really felt they had recognsed a lot of the progress had been down to him. Talking up Sarko. Also said his wife-to-be [Carla Bruni] a real firecracker. French elections all one way. Sarko's relationship with Merkel was going to be interesting, such contrasts. On his own future, TB said he was not really on top of it. He did need someone with business acumen, but it was so easy to get trapped into something inappropriate. He was close to sorting out a formal role in MEPP. He felt if he did he could give up his seat. He really didn't want to hang around and he felt that people would understand. It would also be better for GB. He said things were better on that front, and he was treating him with a bit more respect. Maybe GB realised now that he could learn something from him. He said he didn't know whether to be pleased or find it galling. Best to be pleased probably. Home to collect Rory, who was coming home to revise for a few days. Calum's ankle still dreadful a week on. GB in Iraq. Said we had to separate out intelligence and politics. Another dig really.

Tuesday 12 June

GB's Iraq was stuff getting a bit of play. PG sent me a text saying I should put back in stuff re GB. I said, 'Step 1, say era of spin over. 2 put in distance from AC re dossier. 3. Ask AC to come back.' PG said it was such a dissonance between strategy and tactics. He was writing something on it. TB's speech going OK, to predictable responses and rubbishing in most places. They so cannot cope with being commentated on themselves. I was getting loads of bids but asked by JoP etc. not to go on. They said they had their own plan of people up. I did a piece for the blog instead. The main headline was him saying the media were like a 'feral beast', and everyone was assuming I had written it. So weird. I had only been vaguely aware he was doing the speech. It was a good line but in a way too good because it took away from some of the deeper analysis and allowed them to pretend it was just a full frontal attack. Mind you they would have done that anyway. He was certainly speaking from the heart though.

Rowena round am to sort index and cast lists. Revises now due tomorrow. Swim. Run later. Must get in better triathlon shape. Then to see Judith and SP and view part 3 of the TV series. Pretty good. Lots about my state of mind and the family but OK. JP called. On the mend, but said it had been a bit scary. He was not sure about what he would do with himself. Wanted to do the Council of Europe. Felt better but knew he had to slow down.

Wednesday 13 June

DS. Good chat mainly about what I felt as the end of TB's time was nearing. Relief? Sadness? Did I feel I got enough credit? What was I to TB? He to me? Brother rather than boss he felt. Did I ever think it should have been me? No, I don't think so. Still though not any clearer re future plans. To Earl's Court to see Lamda students with writer Robin Soans and Sinead Cusack's friend Max Stafford Clark [director] about their project [*Mixed Up North*] on Burnley. Quite interesting. Not sure how much use I was to him. My main point was that it didn't have a clear post-industrial purpose and that made it depressing. Lacked a context for change. Other places knew what they were for. Revised proofs. Still loads of annoying mistakes. Grace's parents evening. Doing well but one or two saying lippy and chatty.

Thursday 14 June

Shoulder bad. Fixed to see Ron Marx and then physio. Mainly working on proofs then out for speech to a medical insurance firm. Probably plugging the book too much in the Q&A just because it was so front of mind. Also working up the media plan. Getting closer. John Rentoul [*Independent on Sunday*] called, doing profile pre-publication.

Friday 15 June

Fallout continuing re feral beast, and also papers starting to make comparisons between my operation and what they expected under GB. Again, too much definition v TB, not DC.

Sunday 17 June

Loads of good sport. Test v West Indies. US grand prix, Lewis Hamilton wins again. Super League. Becks wins title for Real Madrid. Last round of US Open, Tiger loses to Angel Cabrera. Hamilton amazing stuff, totally hitting a new level.

Monday 18 June

Did a blog on the *Mail,* pegged to the reaction to Tony's feral beast speech and also the *MoS* trying to make out he did the speech because it was similar to things I had said. Lawyer took out a fair bit of the attacks on Dacre. Golf with Jamie R, Phil Babb [ex-Liverpool footballer, now *GolfPunk* magazine) and Matt Dawson. Nice bunch but because we started late I only played nine holes. Not on form. MD much nicer and less chippy than I remembered him. Phil pretty bright. Jamie and I lost by 2. Home after lunch to work on more Rowena queries and checks. Also I was feeling like a bit of a careers advisor, so many of the outgoing No. 10 team looking for work. Paul Allen fixing Bertie for an Irish launch and maybe do an Irish serial. To a pub near Portland hospital to celebrate with Mick H after Romy was finally born. He was well gone, so happy. TB at the Liaison Committee, defending himself on Iraq, and making clear he had never really been that up for an elected Lords.

Tuesday 19 June

Early start and off to the Midlands for a Wella conference. Funny background to the whole thing. When I was first asked I thought it was an event for Deutsche Welle [German TV] and it turned out it was Wella hair products, and by the time I realised I had signed up. So I was talking to a room full of hairdressers. They turned out to be brilliant, really good fun. They started with a weird kind of Chinese exercise thing, had a very funny compere who was like something out of the Chuckle Brothers and who kept them all pumped up. The first question who did more to change Britain and Ireland, TB or Thatcher? Then a woman saying she really liked TB and she wanted to be assured he would be OK when he left! Quite a few on mental health. The questions were almost all friendly and I was on form.

I was unsettled a couple of times today. First Tessa called and said did I have a proper handling plan for the launch because she felt it was going to be a bit rough. She had been with Waheed who said he thought it was immoral. Also with Adam Boulton who had been tearing into me and she said she was so angry she had to walk away. She felt I needed to have people out there and also that TB may have to say something to calm things down. Fiona was angry Tessa had unsettled me but it was a fair point as I was not really devising that kind of political operation, which I almost certainly would had it been happening to someone else. Then Sue Gray called to say GB was after a copy so that

June '07: Tessa urges AC to get proper handling plan for book

unsettled me further. Didn't sleep well at all. He and TB were doing a bit of joint diplomacy today, sharing a call with Sarko on the EU Treaty stuff, which was messy.

Wednesday 20 June

All day recording the TV films. After all the toing and froing they had done a good job. Did a conference call on the Wembley fundraiser which was going better. Took Grace to see Anna Sher [community drama school] then into town to see Mick, Gabriela and the baby. Mick just staring at her. Feeling a bit better but further unsettled by Hilary telling me Neil very opposed to me doing any kind of book at all.

Thursday 21 June

Catherine Mayer from *Time* magazine plus Tom Stoddart [photographer] for a piece. Meeting with Mark Lucas [Labour-supporting filmmaker] and Claire Round [Random House] on revamping the website. Then to the airport with Catherine to fly north. Richard was not returning messages so I was getting worried about him even more. Tried to call Penny too. Not there. The big political story at the moment was GB wanting to put Lib Dems in his government. Not sure what was happening with that. Also trying to work through people who might defend and support me. Mark Lucas had idea of third party endorsers. Flight heaving. To the Marcliffe Hotel [Aberdeen] then run and out for the drinks and dinner. I had forgotten to pack socks so had a last-minute flap on that. Fiona said I needed a valet! The Oilexco [oil and gas production] event was OK. I liked the Canadian CEO, a guy called Arthur Millholland who was really knowledgeable about history and politics. He was a big TB fan, said he couldn't see what benefit we gained from him going.

I did a fairly standard spiel. One guy very agressive about Iraq in the Q&A. A lot about GB. I always seemed to get asked about the *Queen* film at the moment. One from a French guy who said he had read the *Mail* on the way up, and Michael Howard had seemingly had another go at me. I liked his question: 'Do you take it as a compliment?' There was also a guy whose grandad played for Burnley in 1910 or around then. My room was above the entrance and I didn't sleep well because all the late night smokers were out there. When I did sleep, I had a whole succession of dreams which were clearly book-related – TB–GB fighting, Neil shouting, Polly Toynbee on TV saying I had ruined my life! What the hell. Also Catherine Mayer had discovered that it was a US sports coach who was the source of the David S quote I had used, 'When all is said and done, more is said than done.' TB off to Brussels for his last summit after his last Cabinet. Not easy. GB got good play for his last Mansion House speech yesterday, big licks on education. Also, his lot briefing that when he became PM, yes he would wear white tie if he had to! One or two calls about Cabinet. GB had done a totally effusive over-the-top thing about how they would all stand on his shoulders, they presented him with a painting of Chequers and gave him a standing ovation.

Friday 22 June

Bad night's sleep. Just piling in one after the other now. Kamal [Ahmed] called yesterday saying can I do a piece about TB and PMQs. I had a long chat with Catherine who had some good thoughts. Basic approach – how nervous he used to get at the start but how he came to do more and more on his own, and also used the discipline of it to monitor departments. Also how we used PMQs to 'get' five successive Tory leaders, and work them out. It worked as a piece. At the airport I bumped into [NATO general secretary, Sir] George Robertson's son who was overseeing a BAA [British Airports Authority] event with Alex Salmond. On the plane down I was next to an Aussie woman who thought TB was really special and going to be missed big time. There had been a lot of the same feeling last night, and at the Wella thing, and yet some of GB's people seemed to think our lift was down to TB going and GB coming on the scene. As PG said, they had been feeding themselves a diet of that basic view for ten years, that TB was unpopular and GB not. Absolute nonsense.

Long chat with Alan Milburn later. He said he had had approaches via Charles Clarke and John Hutton about whether he would have a conversation with GB. Of course I will, he said, but nothing came of it. He thought he would call him on Wednesday and offer him a job. Alan would only take something big and he felt that those were all gone. He was probably going to stay as an MP but do other stuff too. He felt GB now knew he had to adopt a Blairite position, but he had three problems – he was fighting against his own position, he was fighting against his own people who had poor judgement and were hoping to get tribal, and he was fighting against his own character. We agreed that TB's optimism was the thing that really made him special for that

June '07: TB's last Cabinet, then last summit

position. It meant he didn't get too down and he was always thinking solutions not problems.

GB and his people start so many sentences 'The problem is...' He felt I would be mad to get involved with him, other than maybe as something in the election campaign. He was very friendly about the book, said I deserved to do with it whatever I wanted given all I had done, and he would go out and speak for me if it got messy. I had a chat about the same thing with Sally who was really nice about it, said I needed to do for myself what I normally did for others, get a few people together and brief them on lines and arguments to promote when talking to the hacks. She felt it should be OK but there was a fair bit of 'Why is he doing it?' around the place. I didn't see *Newsnight* – GB with John Simpson, Nick Robinson [BBC political editor] and Evan Davis [BBC economics editor] – but PG said it was awful. He doesn't know what he is, he said. He apologised endlessly for the Iraq dossier intelligence etc. He congratulated Simpson on his reports from Afghanistan. He was a bit all over the place. There was no big clear message.

Saturday 23 June

Observer happy with the PMQs piece and more pisstaking re hairdressers after the Wella event. Kamal and Roger both saying TB going to be missed big time. I said I felt the poll jump was in part because there had been so much focus on us and on TB and his last few weeks had been good. TB been at the EU summit for two days and seemed to get an OK deal. GB's lot briefing against him, saying they had to sort a capitulation to Sarkozy that TB was about to make. I worked on a Q&A for people who would do interviews re the book. Bike then lido. TB called around 7. He was just back from Rome. He had had 45 minutes' sleep after Brussels then off to the Vatican. He said he was definitely converting some time in the future. I said, 'Soon?' He said you don't just do it overnight, has to be a process. But as soon as feasible. It clearly meant so much to him, but I still couldn't fully understand why.

Then we went into joking mode... There would be a process, he said. The NEC Catholic conversion committee would have to give their view. Jack Dromey would have to give his blessing. And so on. Said the summit was OK, and GB only called him after it was sorted. Livid at the briefing. Also that GB was so tactical rather than strategic. Filled him in on *Newsnight*. He said on the one hand he is asking me to tell Bush he won't wobble and on the other he sends out different signals here. It is all tactics, no strategy. Said he was not exactly looking forward to tomorrow now. There was a very good piece in the *Times* magazine by Robert Crampton, with Nick Danziger snaps, and it really caught him well. He said Peter M and I were geniuses which was nice of him, though JP told me he had seen a Barry Cox [TV executive and Blair friend] interview with Rawnsley saying in the end TB had pushed me out.

Sunday 24 June

It was a bit like the old days in terms of the phone going with Switch and various people, mainly TB and JP. *Observer* gave a good show for the PMQs piece alongside a nice little piece from Charles Kennedy, less so from Iain Duncan Smith and Ann Treneman [*Times* sketchwriter]. I spoke to TB as I started a long run. He said on the deputy leadership he feared AJ was not going to win, and Harriet would win on Cruddas' second preferences, what DM would call a Faustian pact. He said Deborah Mattinson [pollster] had given them this tomfool polling allegedly showing Harriet helped GB in the south. What he needs in the south is people in the south thinking he understands them and their lives. But if they can make a strategic misjudgement based on that, there will be others.

He said he was glad he was going now. It felt like the right time but he really did worry once the going got a bit rougher, and the temperament questions started to get asked, that GB would be found wanting. At the moment it is easy. Mistakes will be forgiven. He will get the benefit of the doubt. But when the pressures and problems start, it will be tough. That being said he intended simply to say he had all the qualities to be a great Prime Minister. There was absolutely no point in doing the back-seat driver thing, or even commenting other than to be positive. I said I felt TB had done well these past few weeks, that actually lots of focus on him, and on the record, had helped contribute to the rise in the polls. He said we are leaving having delivered the right position and now GB can build on that. He intended to say also that we had shown we could deliver on the stable and orderly transition. Then he did his Northern accent... 'Right you are, Ali, better go. Off to Manchester.'

Long run, then a text from Carol Linforth saying the buzz was Harriet had definitely won. Sally confirmed that was what people thought. I called JP who said it was all rumour. He said he would find it very hard to welcome it. He really didn't buy into anything positive about her at all. But the truth is Alan Johnson had not really wanted it enough and so HH came through. JP was in fairly jovial form but that was because he said his gut still said Johnson. When the result came she went over to John and he was very steely to the point of being rude. He just couldn't hide what he thought. TB was very big in what he said about GB. There was a moment when he mentioned GB's 'character' and paused and for a moment it looked like he was going to say what he thought, but was fine. He said he had the character to be a great PM. He called me later and said the statement was true but incomplete.

He said he had felt fine letting go, that the time was about right. We had delivered the right position and now it was up to GB to make it work. He felt short-term HH was not a problem but it could become one over time. It would all depend on policy positions in the end. You had to hand it to Harriet on the resilience front though. I suppose I would have to add her to my list of people who get there by just keeping going. She looked and sounded a bit patronising, and she got a great round of applause for whacking spin. Nonetheless, she was deputy leader now and I went upstairs and took out four or five bad references to her in the book, including the time JP suggested we ensure her shadow Cabinet survival by getting everyone who loathed her to vote for her. JP called again, said GB was agitating about JP staying in Admiralty Arch for a while after Wednesday. He had been on, saying the press were on to it and JP said didn't he have better things to worry about?

He said we should get together to cry on each other's shoulders. It was not a good day though GB did fine. He said he thought he was fine without being outstanding. Just a few days to go now and then TB was gone. Then the book and I was dreading it even more now. HH was named party chairman and DA election co-ordinator, so maybe it would make my choices easier. I'm not sure Harriet would want me around too much. I told JP about GB asking me to go back. He agreed part of it was just keeping me onside. Godric called with a pretty good assessment re book. He felt TB came out well. A bit too much duopoly and he felt so far – halfway through – that some of the things Diana said would be the main immediate focus. Then a long chat with Helle about her biographer who was coming to see me tomorrow.

Monday 25 June

Jakob Nielsen [journalist] came to interview me about Helle. He stayed for an hour and a half or so, and I sensed he liked her. I was pushing her human side, her humour, also her resilience and her ability to stay upbeat, but also the fact she got our politics so much. Richard called. He had been listening to the audiobook and he loved it. He sounded terrible. He was clearly not good but said he had lain there for six hours with Christopher [son] listening to it and he felt it was going to be a huge hit. I was now just hoping he would survive long enough to see the physical book done and dusted. Watched [Tim] Henman v [Carlos] Moya. Great stuff. I sent a message to Jan Felgate [agent] and got a nice reply from Henman saying he appreciated the support. I really admired how he just kept going. People saying retire and he just played on. Not seeing much news at the moment. Quite a good Nick Robinson piece on GB in Kirkaldy.

Tuesday 26 June

I decided not to have a launch party. I just couldn't face it. Rowena off to Scotland to do the final changes on site and get the thing printed. I phoned through one or two and there were a few last-minute legal changes as well. In to see Bruce, full of good advice and wisdom as usual, then to meet party people at HoC then through for Caborn meeting. Fifty tables. Need a few more performers now. Also what to do re prizes, and whether I should do the auction. I was worrying it would be a bit of a problem if I did it in the midst of a media storm. If GB got a fantastic honeymoon and I somehow buggered it. To No. 10 through 70 Whitehall for the Steve Morris, Tom Kelly, Nigel Sheinwald, Kim Darroch [Cabinet Office, appointed Permanent Representative to the EU] and Gareth Evans [No. 10 official] farewell. Good mood. TB made a nice speech covering all five and Tom made a terrific speech in response about what a great guy TB was to work for. Really nice mood. Robin Janvrin there, insisted I went to his farewell and also introduced me to his successor.

Scarlett there and we had a longish chat. He felt it was a terrific read and would be a success. I explained why I wanted to do it, why I felt I had to in a way. He was perfectly nice, said we should meet up. Sheinwald was edgy and asking me if Republicans and Democrats would be OK with it. I hoped so. Steve Morris and his Irish wife and friends really nice. Little chat with Peter M and [Sir] Bill Jeffrey [Permanent Secretary for Defence] and his wife. Usual flirting away with the garden room girls and the duty clerks etc. Taking the piss out of Martin Sheehan going back to the SCU [Strategic Communication Unit] under GB. I said don't forget you only have one boss. Home, sorted the last legals and the book finally went to press late p.m. Out to Merrill Lynch. Speech and Q&A on depression and general mental health issues.

Then to Hilary Armstrong's farewell via a chat with Alex re the Labour dinner and people we need to get there. Charles Clarke and Charlie Falconer quizzing me re the book. CC against in principle. Even if not serialising, he just felt it was the wrong thing to do. And as the DB book showed it poses people with questions re whether they should come back. He was appalled at the idea of everyone diarising. CF had a different concern. He felt that I would do the most complete and best written account and therefore mine would become the one that identified the government. I disagreed, said it would just be part of it and I was entitled to be part of it as much as anyone. Bruce and Sally being more supportive but I sensed it was going to be problem. Charles was really quite heavy about it. Then loads of the young women from the Cabinet Office wanting their pictures taken. Nice do and HA so solid a citizen. Tessa there on tenterhooks, as were most of them waiting for GB to take over, taking me aside to tell me what she thought would happen. Home. Feeling a bit discombobulated. I was dreading the book more every day. I wish there was a way of doing it without the hoo-ha and without all these competing pressures.

Wednesday 27 June

Pretty big day really. TB out, GB in. David S first thing. Told him re being discombobulated. Also about CF telling me last night I had to get a proper job. 'You can't just go on interviewing Lance Armstrong for the rest of your life.' Charlie said I had too much talent and energy to waste away, and he reckoned I had gone a bit bonkers since leaving. DS felt maybe they were transferring their own anxieties. He asked how I felt as TB left. Privileged to have been there. Proud at what I was able to do. Unique in having been central to the TB–GB transition, but anxious about it. Regretful I didn't see it all through but above all privileged. Still not ready for a real proper job, and conflicted about politics. I needed the freedom I had and I needed the space. Maybe when he went I would find something worthwhile to do, but part of me doubted it. I had come to realise the family really was the most important thing, and I had to keep that in mind. Also, the mental health stuff was showing me there are different ways to make a difference.

I said I felt sure that if GB really wanted me to help him, I would find it hard just to tell him No, I won't. I needed something in my life to fire my zeal and enthusiasm and even TB at times could cast me down, so with GB... not easy. These sessions with David had made me much more aware of the things that could hit my moods, for good and bad, and I just had to be careful, I knew that. Mark Lucas and team round to do web stuff and pictures. Such a nice guy and so good at what he does. Then basically I watched telly all day. PMQs. Good stuff. TB's Au revoir, auf wiedersehen, arrivederci. Swatting a Lib Dem who asked what advice would TB give to GB re relationship between state and faith by saying he can't be bothered with answering. Had to acknowledge the latest Iraq casualties, and there were a few war demonstrations around, but he had a great ending: 'That is that, the end.' Then a standing ovation from the whole House, started on our side, DC quickly up. Great theatre. He went back to No. 10 and it was when he was doing the farewells that I felt I ought to have been there. Also that I should have done a proper farewell myself maybe. But it was not helped by the fact that CB and FM ended as they did.

Cherie had a little pop at the press as they left. TB off to the Palace and it all felt very different to when we went in '97. Now just on my own watching at home. TB and GB the main guys. Yet I had been so close to one and responsible in part for getting him to accept the other as successor. TB then off to Sedgefield by train and lots of talk of the Middle East Quartet [UK, EU, Russia, UN] envoy job beckoning. Then GB applauded out of the Treasury and off to the Palace. In there 55 minutes. Looked good if nervous when he got to the street. He spoke really well. Without notes and good message. Change but rooted in values. School motto – do our utmost. He looked OK too and Alison said later he spoke really well to the staff and spent proper time with them. HC saying it had all been very moving. Lots of media calls. I decided not to do anything. I got a message from GB, just saying thanks for having helped him, and I decided to write a short note rather than call when I knew he would be so busy. I am not sure I fully believed every word, but it had happened and as TB said at Chequers, we had to do what we could to make it work now.

Index

The ubiquity of Tony Blair and Gordon Brown in the foregoing pages precludes their inclusion in the index. The letter n indicates a footnote.

9/11 98, 224, 248, 389, 392, 394, 568

1997 election 3, 305, 508n, 539, 552, 567, 568, 569, 570

2001 election 3, 124n, 195, 528

2005 election 3–7, 9, 106, 121, 133, 142, 147–8, 159, 195, 226, 228, 254, 277

   press coverage 4–6, 8

Abbott, Paul 285, 437, 466

Adams, Gerry 500, 549

Adonis, Andrew 5, 6–7, 8, 123, 193, 214, 542

Afghanistan 143, 156, 217, 226, 248, 278, 365–6, 367, 392, 445

Africa 53, 97–8, 99, 279, 470, 484

Ahern, Bertie 70, 72, 291, 505, 578

Aldred, Dave 22, 23, 26, 40, 47, 48, 51, 77

Alexander, Douglas 178, 201, 206, 210, 228, 256, 298–9, 395, 445, 496

Allan, Tim 10, 12, 113, 382, 384, 437, 442

Allardyce, Sam 239–40, 242, 266, 337

Allawi, Ayad 114

Alton, Roger 377, 392

Armstrong, Hilary 161, 166, 262, 607

Armstrong, Lance 105, 111, 379, 607

Arsenal 18, 20, 24, 28, 31

Ashley, Jackie 176, 211

Ashton, [Baroness] Cathy 381

Austin, Ian 264

Back, Neil 20, 30, 36, 38, 55, 65, 80, 84, 88, 89, 92, 102

Baker, Jim 257–8, 467

Balls Ed 4–5, 10, 105–7, 120–22, 130, 135, 139, 141, 154, 167, 171, 181, 186, 201–2, 203, 204–5, 212, 220–21, 225, 228–9, 231, 236, 243, 258, 264–5, 275, 357, 433, 552

Balshaw, Iain 16

Banks, Tony, funeral of 215–16

Barnes, Stuart 29, 76, 93, 95

Barroso, José Manuel 63–4

Barwick, Brian 165

Basu, Parna 8, 9, 27, 103, 123, 151, 246, 279

Beaumont, Bill 15, 34, 36, 39, 43, 51, 64, 86, 87, 90, 97, 98, 99, 241

   ill 87, 94, 96

Becker, Boris 369

Beckett, Margaret 215, 265–6, 266–7, 306, 363–4, 382, 391, 443

Beckham, David 94, 313, 352, 354, 550, 573, 577, 593, 594, 599

Beecham, Jeremy 271, 278

Begg, Ann 345

Bell, Tim 122

Benn, Hilary 90, 177, 195, 247, 390–91, 597

Benn, Melissa 133, 175–6, 200, 211, 525

Benn, Tony 176, 216, 525

Bennett, David 120

Bennett, Mark 120, 131, 133

Bennett, Nigel 448, 460, 491

Berlusconi, Silvio 242, 244, 262, 294

Best, George 134, 160, 165

Bickerstaffe, Rodney 215

bird flu 291, 293

Bird, Jackie 139
Biscombe, Tony 19, 30, 99, 153
Blackmore, Keith 282, 338
Blair, Cherie 27, 94, 137, 143, 187, 227,
    322, 326, 417–18, 419, 431, 485, 537–8,
    542, 563, 564, 585
Blair, Euan 22, 525, 563
Blair, Ian 385
Blairites 6, 403, 409, 422, 432, 475
Blears, Hazel 371
Blunkett, David 4, 122, 136+n, 137, 138,
    139, 207, 220, 224, 286, 502
Bogdanor, Vernon 232–3, 304, 518
Booth, Gale 449
Bostock, Tom 222–4, 529–30
Boulton, Adam 4, 135, 233, 302, 303,
    371, 381, 591, 600
Bradshaw, David 58, 174, 420
Brand, Jo 468, 470–71, 475, 543
Bridge, Jerry 107
Brind, Don 215
British Grand Prix 351–2
British Lions 7, 9–11, 13–36, 61, 74, 108,
    117, 135, 169
    All Blacks 6, 34–5, 38, 47, 50–51, 55,
        65, 67, 69, 74, 76, 83, 94, 101, 153
    first match against 78–80
    second match against 91
    'spear tackle' 78–9, 80–81, 88, 90
    third match against 100
    anthem 24, 26, 27, 28, 29, 30, 32, 33,
        34, 39, 42, 43, 49, 52
    Argentina match 17, 25, 29–30
    drinking 21, 23, 32, 33, 49–50, 74, 88,
        92, 101–2
    New Zealand tour 5–6, 9, 13, 15–17,
        25–6, 29, 30, 33–53, 53–8, 63–4,
        139, 153, 287, 312, 345
    pre-match routines 29
    press response/coverage 30, 32–3,
        36–8, 40–43, 45, 49, 52–4, 56–8, 64,
        67, 70, 71, 73–4, 78–84, 91–3, 97,
        101–2
Brooks, Mel 268, 410, 447, 453, 455,
    460–61
Brown, Colin 119
Browne, Des 4, 371, 480, 556
Browne, John 307, 340, 347, 349, 357,
    363, 370–71, 383, 384, 391, 423–4, 569
Bulloch, Gordon 28, 39, 57+n, 100

Bush, George W. 96, 98, 99, 116+n, 200,
    225, 325, 354, 378–9, 382–3, 385, 387,
    391, 451, 453, 509–10, 515, 552, 579
    and Afghanistan 143
    and Campbell/Diaries 51, 53, 138,
        394, 497, 522, 529–30, 540, 559,
        563, 564, 568, 580–81
    and Iraq 68–9, 140, 318, 446, 454, 465,
        478, 528+n, 544, 559, 563n, 568
    and MEPP 53, 249, 386, 389–90, 395,
        397, 398, 410, 458, 480, 527
Butler, Eddie 92
Butler, Nick 347, 349, 357, 370, 383, 410,
    423
Butler, Robin 232
by-elections 232+n, 235, 248, 365
Byers, Stephen 121, 409, 432
Byrne, Shane 23, 48, 65–6, 80, 100

Cable, Vince 146
Caborn, Dick 94, 168, 215, 352, 369, 426,
    463, 546, 550, 572, 597, 606
Cahn, Andrew 204
Cameron, David 167, 168, 169–71, 174,
    177–9, 183, 184, 185, 219–20, 279,
    347–8
    becomes Tory leader 165–6
    friendly press 231
    as heir to Blair 140, 198, 199–200,
        225–6, 259, 348, 353, 398, 422, 576,
        589
    Labour tactics against 127, 135, 143,
        156–7, 173, 186, 189, 192, 206,
        210–11, 231, 270, 295, 353, 444
    nerves 178–9
    pitch for centre ground 133, 142,
        148, 188, 221, 229, 348, 353, 435,
        466, 499
    policy v rhetoric 130, 145, 237, 348,
        353, 378, 432, 434–5, 589
    runs for Tory leadership 62, 115–16,
        120, 122, 123–4, 126–7, 129, 139,
        141
Campbell, Alastair
    in analysis 115, 128, 130, 131, 132,
        133, 140, 141, 149, 154, 161, 164,
        181, 185, 310–11
    medication 113, 152, 154, 155, 162–3,
        164, 175, 185, 208, 218, 223–4, 274,
        404, 435–6, 459, 545, 550

Campbell, Alastair *cont.*
  sessions 125–6, 144, 155–6, 166,
    183–4, 191, 193, 209, 267, 273, 279,
    283, 291, 309, 344–5, 355, 376, 437,
    490, 496, 505, 512, 519, 545, 561,
    566, 607–8
  'demons' 126, 152, 155–6, 163, 175,
    183–4, 223–4
  with family 424
  with Millar 137, 151–2, 162–3, 175,
    197–8, 219, 380, 392, 549–50
  breakdown 35, 57, 77, 144, 209, 363,
    436, 450, 584n, 594
  conflicted over work commitment
    207, 208, 238, 267, 274, 289, 339,
    394, 412–14, 422, 433, 514–16, 607
  depression 104–5, 109, 113, 114, 129,
    131, 149, 150, 152, 164, 224, 261,
    273, 377, 544–5
  Diaries 61, 108, 110, 111, 112, 113,
    117, 118, 120, 178, 185, 193, 194,
    263, 286, 294, 296, 309, 360, 410,
    412, 438, 453, 469, 486, 502, 508,
    513, 516, 517, 586–8
  index 542, 595, 596
  television tie-in 460, 467, 527, 535,
    546, 548–9, 562, 568, 582–3, 588,
    601
  volume 1 54, 105–6, 107, 152, 286,
    383, 395–6, 490, 511, 521–3, 525–6,
    529–30, 532–3, 534–5, 536–8. 547–
    8, 552–3, 556, 559, 563–4, 572–3
  volume 2 etc. 14, 27, 41, 52, 56, 63,
    70, 84, 104, 125, 131, 134, 136,
    144–5, 150, 151, 155, 156, 184, 186,
    194, 218, 273, 277, 297, 317–18,
    349, 383
  drinking 57, 126, 132, 144, 155, 166,
    191, 326, 376, 437, 450–51, 490,
    496, 584n
  media attacks 33, 44, 53, 90, 92, 94,
    95, 102, 104, 292
  note to Gordon Brown 252–5, 256,
    259, 415, 429
  Brown's response 255–6
  self-analysis 111–13, 380, 396
  self-harming 208, 209
  thoughts of suicide 131, 166, 209,
    260, 445
  see also mental health

Campbell, Calum (son) 15, 111, 131,
  140, 153, 184–5, 204, 268–9, 323, 337,
  352, 355, 371, 372, 373, 396, 424, 486,
  519, 521–2, 557, 558, 593, 598
Campbell, Dave 24, 38, 39
Campbell, Grace (daughter) 7, 9, 11,
  15, 18, 19, 34, 44, 66, 80, 82, 104, 111,
  134, 139, 168, 205, 208, 249, 304, 318,
  396, 424, 430, 436, 543, 557, 558, 561,
  581, 599
Campbell, Nicky 351
Campbell, Rory (son) 4, 13, 14, 24, 32,
  57, 62, 80, 92, 94, 111, 130, 139, 140,
  164, 166–7, 168, 181, 185, 190, 194,
  213–14, 232–3, 240–41, 320, 336, 347,
  378, 385, 395, 415, 423, 424, 430, 445,
  466, 522, 557, 563, 572, 595
  unwell 345, 350, 351, 353, 355, 365,
    581, 585
Campese, David 312–13, 319, 320–21,
  323, 326–7, 329
Capaldi, Jim 495
Carling, Will 40
Carrick, Michael 361, 409
Carter, Dan 91
Carter, Jimmy 395
Carter, Matt 119, 272, 283
Cash, Mel 379, 455
Channel 5 News 163–4
charity 28, 112, 122, 132, 318
  'Audience with' 72, 97
  Leukaemia Research Fund 104, 113,
    124–5, 130, 169, 185, 250, 268, 309,
    328, 360, 362, 378, 411, 438, 460
  Red campaign 222, 223
  Soccer Aid 271, 279–80, 296–7, 302,
    306, 307, 311–14, 317, 319–39, 345,
    347, 354, 582
Charlton, Bobby 328, 336–7, 476
Cheetham, Louisa 6, 11, 15, 17, 24–8, 30,
  38, 41–3, 45, 52–4, 64, 69, 70, 73, 75,
  78, 85, 86
Chirac, Jacques 22n, 41, 46, 56, 63, 90,
  94, 98, 103, 123, 180, 183, 212, 298–9,
  350, 467, 541, 577, 596
Clark, Helen 86, 456
Clarke, Charles 3, 118, 128, 144, 145,
  186, 195, 233, 236, 278, 282, 291, 297,
  299, 300, 301, 303, 304, 306, 308,
  362–3, 364, 366, 375n, 376, 390, 607

Clarke, Ken 115, 120, 126, 169, 364+n
Clarke, Nita 525
Cleary, Mick 18, 57
Clifford, Max 302
Clifford, Simon 23
climate change/global warming 53, 99, 296, 391, 425, 453, 484, 487, 510, 528, 594+n
Clinton, Bill 27–8, 158, 174, 230, 251, 253, 317–18, 422–3, 424–5, 451, 453, 596
Clinton, Hillary 158, 244, 245, 392
Clough, Brian 20, 585–6
Cockerell, Michael 523, 527
Coe, Seb 94, 124+n, 125, 500–501, 513–14
Coffman, Hilary 114, 177, 526, 570, 571, 595, 601
Cole, Ashley 470, 474, 475
Cole, Cheryl 469–70
Collins, Patrick 25
Collins, Phil 120, 595
Collins, Ray 142
Comic Relief 461, 463, 464, 468–9, 470–76, 485, 489, 503, 542–3, 545
Cook, Robin 8, 13, 21, 22, 109+n–10, 115, 263, 395
Cooper, Gareth 37
Cooper, Yvette 8, 186
Corry, Martin 24, 26, 27, 33, 37, 41, 42, 50, 51, 54, 65, 76, 77, 78, 83, 84, 88, 89–90
council tax 104, 186, 187, 196
Cowell, Simon 367, 468–9, 475, 497
Cracknell, David 216, 263
Cracknell, James 426
Crampton, Robert 9, 604
Crerand, Paddy 22, 301
Cueto, Mark 16, 30, 32, 39, 46, 97, 102
Curtis, Richard 470
Cusiter, Chris 20, 24, 31, 38–9, 54, 71, 84
Cusworth, Les 29

Dacre, Paul 254, 264, 600
Daily Mail 18, 26, 27, 30, 32, 37, 58, 89, 90, 92, 93, 246, 254, 267–8, 303, 399, 421, 438–9
Dallaglio, Lawrence 20, 22–3, 31, 32, 33, 34, 42, 43, 48, 49, 50, 51, 55
d'Arcy, Gordon 24, 33, 92

Davies, Brian 215
Davies, David 23, 165, 242, 271, 440
Davies, Eddie 239
Davies, Gavyn 489
Davis, David 9, 62, 116, 120, 122, 123–4, 126–7, 130, 139, 141, 145, 165, 166, 169
Dawson, Judith 495, 535
Dawson, Matt 23–4, 28, 31, 49, 65, 76, 85, 95, 103, 132, 153, 600
Deacon, Sarah 138
Dearlove, Sir Richard 521, 531
Dell'Olio, Nancy 23, 242, 249, 251, 252, 271, 309
Desailly, Marcel 321, 323, 324, 326, 329, 330, 333, 335–6, 337, 345
devolution 496, 498, 533–4
Dewar, Donald 52
Dobson, Frank 13, 145, 200
Docherty, Amanda 31
domestic reforms 5–7, 60, 104, 108, 116, 122, 127, 130, 143, 270
Doyle, Craig 312, 321, 393, 596
Doyle, Matthew 122, 180, 496, 552, 570
Drayson, Paul 8
Drogba, Didier 216
Dromey, Jack 271–2, 273, 274, 275, 278, 280, 281, 282, 290, 297, 341, 344
Dunphy, Eamon 18
Dunstone, Charles 219
Duvall, Len 458
Dyke, Greg 217

Ecclestone, Bernie 351–2, 476, 507, 508n
education policy 5, 6–7, 15, 61, 128, 129, 130, 131, 148, 150, 154, 156, 157, 161, 166, 168, 170+n, 174, 180, 181, 186, 187, 191–2, 193, 200
    party rebellion 248
    sex offenders in schools 202–3, 204
    tuition fees 61, 183
    white paper/bill 203, 259, 269–70, 271, 279
    location of votes 221–2, 272
election in future 105, 127, 135, 149, 172, 176, 189, 196, 236, 309, 357, 402, 408, 603
elections generally 77, 83, 96
elections (winning three) 309–10, 384, 574, 591

energy policy 147, 154, 156, 218, 290, 315–16, 350–51, 353, 360
Ennis, Jeff 166
Enstone-Watts, Charlie 164
Eriksson, Sven-Göran 23, 165, 205, 239, 242, 249, 251, 271, 307, 352, 440
Esquire 54, 102
European Union (EU) 37, 40–41, 45, 46, 56, 60, 62, 63–4, 69, 74+n, 86–7, 115, 123, 149, 157, 169, 177, 180, 562
British Presidency 22, 40–41, 56, 63, 90, 159, 182
Brussels summit 492
Common Agricultural Policy (CAP) 62–3, 90, 149
Dutch referendum 40, 44, 45, 46, 63
French referendum 38, 40, 41, 45, 46, 63
Hampton Court summit 123, 134, 157
Spanish referendum 46
UK rebate 22, 52, 62–3, 69, 163, 165, 177, 179, 180, 181, 182
Evans, Huw 174, 192
Everett, Rupert 470–71

Falconer, Charlie 260–61, 262, 263, 276, 366, 385, 607
Farthing, Alison 125
Farthing, Michael 125
Feehan, John 41, 69, 91, 95
Ferdinand, Rio 16, 20, 352
Ferguson, Alex 8, 185, 190, 239–40, 279–80, 352, 369, 374, 424, 438, 454–5, 477, 541
and Manchester United 11, 18, 20, 23, 24, 153, 272, 301, 321, 361–2, 369, 409, 454, 477
Fitzpatrick, Sean 136
Fletcher, Darren 16, 20, 541
Fletcher, Paul 252, 467
Fletcher, Tom 298
Ford, Mike 16, 51, 71, 84
Foster, Brendan 6, 116, 159, 197, 301, 379, 404, 413, 426, 491, 554
Freud, Emma 461, 470, 543
Freud, Matthew 297, 412
Frost/Nixon 502–3, 597

G7/8 53, 60, 146n, 279, 378, 379, 593, 594+n, 596
Gleneagles summit 53, 96, 97–8, 101, 103, 104
Galloway, George 98, 219
Gartside, Phil 239
Garvey, Kate 126, 173, 178, 279
Gascoigne, Paul 'Gazza' 314, 327, 329, 336, 337, 354, 362, 368–9
Gerrard, Steven 141
Gibbon, Gary 249
Gibbons, Jo 119
Gieve, Sir John 225
Giggs, Ryan 16, 20–21, 573
Gill, David 153, 165, 336
Gilman, Cathy 207, 250, 268, 309, 318, 346, 438
Gimson, Andrew 169
Gimson, Sally 169
Ginola, David 321, 324, 326, 327, 328, 329, 330, 331, 333, 335, 336–7, 339, 349, 375, 396
Glazer, Malcolm 11, 18, 20
Goldsmith, Ben 473
Goldsmith, Lord Peter 475
Goodrem, Delta 326, 328, 367, 500, 545, 560, 567
Gore, Al 230, 361, 424–5, 453, 576
Gould, Bryan 92
Gould, Georgia 13, 347
Gould, Grace 115
Gould, Philip 10, 105, 123, 126–8, 131, 146, 149, 162, 196–7, 201, 227, 245, 247, 251, 293, 298, 311, 384, 414, 556, 587
focus groups 159, 167, 230, 245, 248, 384
his house 120, 222
overview 111–13, 245–6, 427–30
on therapy 57, 111, 113, 114, 125, 154, 164
Gould, Victoria 289, 443
Grant, Linda 244
Gray, Andy 135, 450
Gray, Sue 493, 500–501, 503, 513, 517–19, 523, 526, 532–3, 542, 546, 550–51, 554, 560, 567, 575, 586, 600
Greenwood, Will 30–31, 38–9, 65, 71–2, 86, 267–8
Greenstock, Jeremy 106, 524

Grewcock, Danny 39, 73–4, 79–80, 81–2, 96
Griffiths, Nigel 12–13
Grip, Tord 242
Grocott, Bruce 7, 112–13, 120, 154, 193–4, 201, 391, 413–14, 607
on education policy 215
The Guardian 27, 84, 119, 135, 175, 181, 200, 229, 272, 273, 285, 344, 347, 355, 364, 415, 442, 559, 585
Gullit, Ruud 280, 312, 313, 319, 321, 322, 323, 324, 325, 327, 328, 329, 331, 333, 334, 335, 336–7

Hain, Peter 351–2, 395
Hague, William 124+n, 178, 182, 216
Hands, David 37
Hanna, Conor 367
Hansen, Alan 367
Hanson, Lord James 455
Hargreaves, Owen 487, 586
Harman, Harriet 272, 316, 342, 344, 350, 501, 577, 578, 597, 604–5
Harper, Ross 52
Harrison, Patrick 31
Harrison, Miles 29, 70, 76
Harverson, Paddy 25–6, 31, 38
Hattersley, Roy 120, 584
Hayes, John 57n, 68, 72, 102
Hayward, Paul 95
Hayward, Tony 371
health policy 270, 287, 294, 296
Healey, Austin 93
Hehir, Peter 52
Hemani, Joe 249–50, 301, 573
Henry, Graham 6, 36, 44, 74, 76, 78, 90–91
Henry, Thierry 486
Henson, Gavin 18, 22, 31–4, 38–9, 43, 55, 64–73, 80, 82, 86, 98+n–9, 102, 135, 150, 322–3, 328
Hertz, Noreena 462, 477, 487, 492, 497, 520, 580
Heseltine, Michael 233
Hewitt, Lleyton 355
Hewitt, Patricia 134–5, 297, 299, 300, 301–2, 316
Hickie, Denis 16, 18, 88–9
Hignell, Alastair 45, 92
Hill, David 5, 72, 113–14, 177, 276–7, 289, 403, 419, 529

Holmes, Eamonn 436, 581
Holmes, Sir John 211, 213, 297
Hook, George 94
Hoon, Geoff 13, 268–9, 306
Horgan, Shane 16, 18, 32, 35, 65, 88–9
House of Lords 108–9, 237–8, 400, 533
Howard, Michael 9, 16, 98, 108, 120, 122, 129, 144, 166, 247, 273, 275, 380, 574–5
Hucknall, Mick 272, 298, 320, 381, 434, 471, 474, 518
Hughes, Simon 219
Humphrys, John 113, 375, 507, 569
Hunter, Anji 114, 158, 198, 279, 347, 357, 370, 371, 381–2, 489, 498, 535, 569, 571, 591, 592
Hutton, John 4, 9, 136–7, 142, 147, 280, 445–6, 497–8
Hutton Inquiry 77+n, 184n, 322, 325, 377, 451, 453, 489+n, 531

ID cards 15, 37–8, 192, 205, 210, 217, 233–5, 248, 353, 425–6
immigration 3, 9, 397, 398, 419, 443
Ingram, Adam 371
Iran 347, 399, 457–8, 511, 550, 551, 556
Iraq 23–4, 105, 108, 144, 223, 270–71, 275, 290, 291, 377, 392, 449, 454, 456, 461, 498, 574, 608
Blair/Bush relationship 53, 68–9, 285, 392, 397, 446, 478, 528+n, 547, 559, 563n, 568
Blair visits 184, 321, 325, 349, 409, 477, 581
and Brown 225, 229, 291, 307, 308–9, 461, 467, 576, 598
and Campbell 297, 363, 445, 525, 577, 584, 588
and Chirac 212, 467
dossier 244, 603
fate of Saddam Hussein 454, 487, 488, 490
post-war governance 114, 217, 315, 318, 325, 349, 378–9, 393, 398, 445, 447, 487
troops withdrawal (or not) 98, 223, 248, 278, 285, 318, 321, 359, 490, 522–3, 551

Iraq *cont.*
  war opposition/fall-out 3, 4, 8–9,
    68–9, 86, 98, 109, 139, 168, 184,
    199, 215, 222, 263, 269, 328, 345,
    363, 382, 392, 399, 410, 411, 428,
    438–9, 457–8, 462, 482, 509, 551,
    570, 601
  Weapons of Mass Destruction
    (WMD) 77, 184n, 534
Irish Republican Army (IRA) 107, 151,
  291
Irish Times 23, 112
  Campbell's column 44, 52, 63, 83,
    114
Ishak, Magdy 241, 261, 363, 409
Israel (and Lebanon, Palestine) 249,
  379+n, 384, 385, 386, 389–92, 394–5,
  397, 399, 409, 426

Jackson, Darren 328
Jackson, Glenda 266–7
Jackson, General Sir Mike 382
Jackson, Peter 18, 43, 58, 91–2
James, David 352
Jansa, Marcus 11, 48
Jeffrey, Sir Bill 606
Jenkins, Gareth 19–20, 48, 70, 72
Jenkins, Gethin 28, 66
Jenkins, Katherine 29
Johnson, Alan 123, 142, 147, 160, 215,
  246, 306, 346, 395, 581, 597, 604–5
Johnson, Scott 71–2, 75–6, 86
Jones, Stephen 33, 42, 45, 56, 65–6, 74,
  77, 81, 85, 88, 93, 96, 98, 100, 102,
  150, 194, 320, 322, 595
Jonsson, Ulrika 251
Jowell, Tessa 14, 25–6, 94, 96, 101, 103,
  105, 118, 144, 161, 180, 197, 224, 257,
  261–3, 265–7, 268, 269, 274, 283, 344,
  356–7, 370, 373, 382, 385, 387, 388,
  413, 468, 510
  on education policy 215
  see also Mills, David
Juncker, Jean-Claude 63

Kay, Ben 27, 37, 89, 92, 95
Kay, Katie 9
Keane, Roy 16, 18, 20–21, 152–4, 155,
  165, 354, 409
Keating, Paul 41

Keating, Ronan 50
Keen, Ann 394
Keller, Nick 443, 473
Kellner, Peter 381
Kelly, Ruth 6, 161, 174, 191–2, 202–3,
  204, 205, 210, 214, 215, 252, 306, 315,
  366, 372, 490
Kemp, Ross 138, 470, 476
Kennedy, Charles 98, 108, 111, 144,
  177–8, 196
  drinking 174, 194, 294
Kenny, Siobhan 269
Kerr-Dineen, Tim 133
Kettle, Martin 176
Khan, Sadiq 213
Kilfoyle, Peter 200
Kinnock, Neil 54, 55, 112–13, 119, 150,
  185, 193, 194, 200, 211, 214, 217, 220,
  270, 308–9, 358, 391–2, 485, 574
  on centre ground 204–5
  public criticism of Blair 200–201, 203

Labour Party 3, 8, 10, 11, 12, 23, 37,
  59–61, 77, 103, 105, 112–13, 127, 129,
  156, 165, 343, 356, 504
  Clause Four 8+n, 272
  loans for honours 271–3, 274–5,
    276, 278, 283–4n, 289, 290, 295,
    359, 376, 384, 386, 456, 458, 473,
    475, 476, 480–81, 493–4+n, 503–4,
    506–9, 511, 533, 547, 562
  New Labour 4, 5, 16, 75, 115, 116,
    118, 119, 127, 130, 134, 145, 146–7,
    148, 156, 159, 175, 176, 182, 184,
    191, 199
  Parliamentary Labour Party (PLP) 5,
    6, 7, 8, 9, 12–13, 161, 174, 183, 270,
    273, 275, 307, 316, 384, 402
  Progress (group) 406
Larder, Phil 44, 51, 85
Latham, Sara 9, 317, 422
Laws David165
Lawson, Neal 133, 211
Lee, Sammy 240
Levy, Michael 272, 376, 377, 378, 458,
  475, 476, 478, 481, 494, 504, 505, 506,
  509, 512, 533, 537, 589–90
Lewis, Damian 336, 338
Liberal Democrats 61, 181, 198, 199,
  206, 601

Lipman, Maureen 469–71, 475, 543
Livermore, Spencer 141, 246
Lloyd, Liz 120, 156, 169–70, 173, 179,
    182, 183, 192, 193, 221, 229, 230, 231,
    235, 237, 238, 246, 357, 385, 443, 445
local elections 223, 248, 285, 287, 288,
    291, 296, 297, 300, 302, 303–5, 570
Lombardi, Vince 46
London bombings (7/7) 97+n–8, 99,
    101, 102, 103, 104, 105, 108, 138
London Olympics (bid) 14, 15, 25–6, 94,
    96, 101, 102, 103, 104, 123, 138, 161,
    279, 370, 373, 398, 501
Lowe, Rupert 21, 164
Lowther-Pinkerton, Jamie 25, 30, 31

Macallister, Gary 323
Macari, Lou 22
McBride, Damian 229, 307, 413, 475, 586
McCartney, Ian 119
McCartney, Paul 581
McConnell, Jack 491
McDonagh, Margaret 104, 138, 260, 417
McElhone, Natascha 437, 473
McFadden, Brian 311, 321, 331
McFadden, Pat 6, 8, 154–5, 173, 273,
    315, 444, 445, 504
McFall, John 182, 305, 308
McGeechan, Ian 17, 18, 27, 29–30, 37,
    42, 47, 48, 51, 64, 68, 70, 78, 83, 85,
    100
McGrory, Danny 527
McGuinness, Martin 203
McHugh, David 76, 84
McManaman, Steve 162
McTernan, John 192, 504, 511
Mail on Sunday 25, 115, 116, 252, 264–5,
    267, 287, 301, 302–3, 339, 356–7, 569
Manchester United 6, 11, 16, 20, 140,
    242, 251, 573
    Cup Final 16, 18, 20, 22, 24, 26, 28
    see also Ferguson, Alex
Manningham-Buller, Eliza 212–3, 456
Mandela, Nelson 124, 129
Mandelson, Peter 108, 143, 173, 194–6,
    198, 233, 263, 288–9, 357–9, 382
    and Campbell Diaries 508, 534–5
    and John Prescott 302–3
    and John Smith 189–90
    resignations 122–3+n, 158, 289

Maradona, Diego 322, 323, 324, 328,
    329, 330, 331–4, 336, 338, 339+n, 341,
    345, 360, 379, 550, 596
Marr, Andrew 176, 217, 235, 244, 256,
    350, 408, 412, 417–18, 426
Mawhinney, Lord Brian 530, 581
Mbeki, Thabo 325
Meads, Colin 76
Mealamu, Kevin 79
Mellor, David 215–16, 302, 540
mental health 241–2, 277, 434, 435,
    436–8, 441, 443–4, 445, 505, 556
Merkel, Angela 125, 134, 159, 177, 180,
    183, 218, 346, 348, 373–4, 375, 467,
    598
Merritt, John 13
Meyer, Christopher 140, 144, 154, 176,
    518
Middle East 27, 248–9, 378, 391, 393,
    476, 577, 608
    Peace Process (MEPP), 53, 285, 363,
    400, 446, 457–8, 467, 478, 480, 494,
    579, 598
Milburn, Alan 121, 139, 148, 158, 159,
    160, 161, 273, 385, 386, 387, 409, 432,
    602–3
Miliband, David 4, 118, 123, 128, 169,
    177, 190, 195, 217, 246, 252, 281–2,
    305, 306, 346–7, 382, 387+n, 391,
    395–6, 402, 406, 433, 487, 517, 519–20,
    528, 560
Miliband, Ed 176, 205, 206, 210, 259,
    433
Miliband, Isaac 169
Millar, Audrey 111, 120, 169, 184, 211,
    393, 411, 442, 480, 548, 575
Millar, Fiona 18, 34, 58, 62, 69, 84, 114,
    120, 141, 155, 185, 240, 275, 302, 304,
    354, 365, 394, 396, 429, 466, 498, 500,
    551–2, 557, 558, 564, 575
    arguments with 3, 55, 105, 116, 120,
    133–4, 150, 163, 181–2, 203, 207–8,
    279, 384–5, 577
    Blair as 'the other woman' 14, 105,
    184, 222, 224, 380, 479, 488–9
    and the Campbell Diaries 450, 453,
    490, 495, 508, 556, 563, 577, 582
    education campaigning 73, 129–30,
    131, 133, 166–7, 193, 200–201, 246,
    262, 272, 384–5, 388, 542

Millar, Fiona *cont.*
　　Compass event 207, 208–9, 211, 214,
　　　　220
　　emotional tensions with 7, 10, 11, 13,
　　　　56–7, 109, 113, 125
　　and Mandelson 194, 195–6
　　mooted as MP 61, 173, 174, 185, 309,
　　　　396–7
　　political tensions with 3, 10, 111, 132,
　　　　197, 207, 224, 256, 258, 261, 266, 267,
　　　　274, 343–4, 430, 459, 484, 592, 600
Millar, Gavin 575
Mills, Bob 134
Mills, David 103, 105, 161, 180, 197, 204,
　　225, 263, 265, 267, 278, 285–6, 287,
　　359, 382
　　and Silvio Berlusconi story 242+n–3,
　　　　244, 252, 259–60, 261–2
Mills, Keith 94
Mitchell, Andrew 115, 130, 166, 169
Moody, Lewis 24, 33, 39
Morgan, Albert 20
Morgan, Piers 179, 367, 463, 467,
　　468–74, 475, 477, 485, 489, 543, 550
Morgan, Sally 8, 9, 106, 119–20, 159,
　　168, 174–5, 191, 192, 220, 273, 316,
　　384, 386, 387, 395, 445, 542, 603
Morris, Estelle 174, 211, 215
Morton, Andrew 133
Mosey, Roger 165
Mowlam, Mo 110–11
Murdoch, James 177, 488
Murdoch, Rupert/Murdoch press 41,
　　54, 139, 148, 310, 387, 389, 391
Muslims/Islam 136, 162, 163, 213,
　　224–5+n, 230+n, 245, 248, 278, 285,
　　286, 394, 440–41, 456, 466, 467
　　Islamic 'extremism' 97n, 248, 271,
　　　　379n, 410, 478

Nadal, Rafa 355
National Policy Forum 104
Naughtie, Jim 461, 486
Neil, Andrew 122, 133, 225, 268
Neville, Gary 24, 477, 487, 492, 497, 550,
　　573
Nicholson, Lindsay 13
Northern Ireland 125, 134, 229, 258,
　　287, 291, 494, 500, 504–5, 549
　　Good Friday Agreement 14, 462

Nye, Sue 158, 221, 229, 405, 470, 477,
　　489, 496, 516, 590

Oborne, Peter 33, 34, 217
O'Callaghan, Donncha 30–31, 64, 213
O'Connell, Paul 28, 33, 38–9, 56, 65–6,
　　74, 78
O'Donnell, Gus 129, 248, 259–60, 405,
　　493, 586
O'Driscoll, Brian 16, 19, 20, 21, 23, 24,
　　27, 28, 33, 34, 36, 37, 39, 43, 46, 49,
　　51, 65–7, 73, 76, 78–83, 85–6, 88, 89,
　　95, 132, 135, 155
O'Driscoll, Gary 24
O'Gara, Ronan 16, 23, 26, 44, 49, 50, 51,
　　67, 71, 72, 76–7, 79, 84, 91, 271, 322
O'Kelly, Mal 21, 22, 39, 44–5, 45–6
O'Neill, Jim 586
O'Neill, Martin 239
Osborne, George 9, 123–4, 126, 166,
　　177–9, 188, 211–12, 213, 279, 447, 473,
　　499, 506
　　on Blair and Brown 177, 180
Osman, Louise 527
O'Sullivan, Eddie 19, 21, 29, 34, 37, 426
Owen, Michael 16, 17, 20, 28–9, 30, 31,
　　54, 55, 71

Palin, Michael 430, 561
Paxman, Jeremy 137, 420, 569, 574,
　　588
Peat, Michael 165
Peel, Dwayne 32, 42, 49, 65, 77, 91
Pendry, Tom 24
Penn, Mark 104, 112, 199–200, 244–5,
　　283, 297,
pensions policy 160, 165, 167, 178, 270,
　　280, 287, 295–6, 315
　　Turner Report 156+n–7, 159, 167,
　　　　213, 288, 291
Philipps, Ros 338
policy ('big stuff') 236, 237–8, 245, 249,
　　287–8
Pound, Stephen 215, 341
Powell, Jonathan 99, 108–9, 110–11, 135,
　　167, 203, 259, 284, 290, 364, 382, 403,
　　444, 445, 484, 525
　　and Campbell Diaries 517, 518, 520,
　　　　521, 522, 523, 524, 526, 528, 532–3,
　　　　534, 535, 538, 547–8, 550, 560

Powell, Jonathan *cont.*
  and loans investigation 376, 380,
    385, 458, 476, 478, 481, 496, 507,
    508, 511, 512, 518, 533, 547, 562–3
Poyet, Gus 312, 313, 314, 319, 323, 324,
  325, 328, 337, 338
Prebble, Stuart 447, 490
Prescott, John 3, 60, 88+n, 119, 127, 129,
  130, 142, 149, 154, 180, 181, 186–7,
  196, 224, 232, 257, 289, 290, 310,
  339–44, 345, 346, 366, 371, 372, 373,
  375, 381, 382, 385, 386–7, 395, 415,
  418, 421–2, 457, 460, 604–5
  on education policy 215, 217
  extramarital affair 297+n, 299,
    300–301, 302–3, 317
Price, Lance 106, 113–14, 115, 116, 122,
  176, 377, 502, 518
Prideaux, Charles 268
Primarolo, Dawn 229
Prince William 9, 15, 25–6, 27, 30, 31,
  34, 58, 86, 88, 89, 94
Pryce, Vicky 211
Public Administration Select
  Committee (PASC) 155, 163, 167,
  176, 532
Purves, Libby 266–7
Putin, Vladimir 160, 378, 379, 464, 465,
  593, 594, 596

The Queen 436, 441, 451, 454–5, 580, 595,
  601
Queen's Speech 14–15, 16, 106, 425, 459,
  460, 461
Queiroz, Carlos 20, 362

Ramsay, Gordon 312, 321
Ramsay, Louise 39, 45, 48, 49, 69, 72, 75,
  78, 86
Rawnsley, Andrew 140, 238, 465, 584
Rebuck, Gail 13, 179, 393, 395, 396, 401,
  486, 569
  and Campbell Diaries 111, 178, 294,
    296, 309, 383, 413, 508–9, 513, 521,
    527, 536, 539, 548, 556, 557, 575–6,
    578
Reddaway, David 465
Redgrave, Steve 94
Redknapp, Jamie 320, 325, 327, 329,
  340, 343, 344, 354, 359, 457

Rees, Merlyn 194
Reid, John 121, 134–5, 144, 161, 177,
  229, 246, 291, 306, 317, 348–9, 362–3,
  375, 376, 379, 382, 386, 395, 406, 424,
  426, 432, 443, 459, 571
Reiss, Charles 134
reshuffles 4, 5, 6, 12, 13, 50, 106, 121,
  143, 204, 237, 248, 275, 290, 303–6,
  311
Rickman, Alan 185
Risdale, Peter 456
Robinson, Andy 19, 37, 64, 71, 74, 83, 91
Robinson, Jason 30–31, 55
Robson, James 22, 26, 44, 87, 96, 100
Rogers, Dave 72, 98
Rogers, Heather 497
Rose, Stuart 497
Rowntree, Graeme 16, 96
Rubin, Jamie 115, 153, 277, 359, 380,
  412, 550, 567
Rusbridger, Alan 347

Sandon, Susan 62, 383, 438, 490, 533
Sarkozy, Nicolas 218, 298, 299, 326, 364,
  541, 546, 566–7, 568, 571, 577, 596,
  598, 601, 603
Schmeichel, Peter 320–21, 322, 325, 327,
  330, 335, 336, 337–8, 487
Schroeder, Gerhard 90, 94, 116, 134, 160,
  348, 467, 577
Scott, Gavin 34, 52
Scottish National Party (SNP) 251–2,
  278, 284+n, 376, 491–2, 493–4, 506,
  571
security/terrorism policy 104, 108, 139,
  140, 141, 143, 145, 148, 178, 278
  Commons defeat 144, 146, 150, 154
Sheerman, Barry 266
Sheridan, Andrew 102
Shetty, Shilpa 492, 515
Short, Clare 145, 223, 360, 442, 502
Shriver, Bobby 222–3
Smith, Chris 215
Smith, Delia 281
Smith, Jacqui 371, 372, 442, 482
Smith, Jim 29
Smith, John 189–90, 214, 485
Smith, Richard 16, 20, 24, 52, 79, 84,
  87, 153
Sopel, Jon 269, 589

Souster, Mark 81
Southgate, Gareth 165
Spacey, Kevin 158, 263, 377–8, 402, 439
Spelman, Caroline 187
Stevenson, Dennis 104, 211
Stevenson, Wilf 475
Stewart, James 275
Stott, Richard 54, 62, 105–6, 107, 152,
    155, 156, 194, 198, 286, 325–6, 359–60,
    377, 383, 412, 414, 430, 438, 449–50,
    490–91, 508, 550, 564–5, 606
Straw, Jack 3, 97, 135, 288+n, 306, 315,
    342, 350, 366, 389–90, 440–41
Sturgeon, David
    see Campbell, Alastair: in analysis
Sugar, Alan 471, 472, 474, 475, 476, 543
Sumption, Johnathan 451
The Sun 34, 88, 139, 221, 230, 381
Symons, Liz 363

Taylor, Matthew 156, 167, 170, 238, 316,
    498, 571
Taylor, Simon 21–2, 37, 54–5
Timms, Stephen 355
Thatcher, Margaret 22n, 269, 292, 305–6,
    308, 362, 376, 428, 430, 482, 485
Theakston, Jamie 179
Thomas, Gareth 'Alfie' 43, 46, 56, 65,
    66, 77, 80–83, 85, 86, 88, 91, 96, 100,
    102, 132, 150, 322–4, 326–7, 328, 329,
    330, 333, 336, 337, 338, 550
Thomas, Geoff 104, 169, 241, 378
Thomas, Paul 41
Thompson, Steve 21, 28, 32, 37, 73, 100
Thorning-Schmidt, Helle 132–3, 134,
    321, 438, 487, 605–6
The Times 6, 8, 9, 13, 37, 62, 81, 112, 119,
    139, 154, 230, 236, 265, 288, 291, 400,
    401, 408
    Campbell's columns 18, 25, 26, 31,
        36, 50–51, 75, 84, 89, 111, 114, 115,
        140, 266, 267, 268, 282, 284, 320,
        338, 366–7, 372, 373, 411, 440, 488,
        499
Thuram, Lilian 369
Todeschini, Federico 29
Torry, Peter 370, 373–4, 375
Toulmin, Tim 464
Townsend, Andy 337
Toynbee, Polly 215, 422, 574, 601

Trenaman, Ann 604
Trian, Marianna 464
Trident 360, 383, 480, 542
Turner, Ruth 104, 119, 170, 277, 358
    and loans investigation 275–6, 359,
        458, 476, 481, 493–4, 496, 499, 504,
        507, 509, 512, 513, 533
Tydesley, Clive 337, 380

Umaga, Tana 78–9, 80, 82–3, 85–6, 88,
    89, 91, 92–3, 95, 100

Vaz, Keith 352, 385
Victor, Ed 135, 185, 263, 266, 268, 286,
    294, 296, 309, 412, 413, 447, 534–5,
    577
de Villepin, Dominique 298–9
Vine, Jeremy 166, 437
Viner Brian 169

Wade, Rebekah 34, 120, 138, 139, 179,
    229, 470, 526+n, 579, 580
Wallace, Richard 367
Wallis, Neil 380
Walters, Humphrey 7, 10, 22, 452
Walters, Mark 18
'war on terror' 398–9
Watson, Tom 402–3, 410, 414, 415,
    553+n
Watt, Peter 350, 464, 597
Webster, Phil 6, 62, 215, 229, 265, 383,
    534
Wegg-Prosser, Ben 179
Wenger, Arsene 24, 31, 290, 490, 550,
    560
White, Julian 73
Wilkinson, Jonny 5–6, 11, 17, 19, 21,
    24–39, 42–8, 51, 55, 56, 58, 65, 75, 82,
    83, 86, 91, 93, 97, 100
Williams, Martyn 28, 39, 49, 77, 93
Williams, Robbie 271, 311, 319, 325, 326,
    329
Williams, Shane 34, 65, 82, 84
Willmott, Richard 331, 338
Wilson, Ben 7, 11, 15, 16, 26–8, 32, 33,
    36, 51–4, 58, 67, 76, 78, 81
Wilson, Bob 311
Wilson, Dean 68
Wilson, Harold 452
Wilson, Richard 302

Winner, Michael 474
Winterton, Rosie 317, 340, 344, 437
Woodall, Trinny 469–78, 542–3,
Woodcock, John 9, 280
Woodward, Clive 5–6, 7, 10, 15–58,
    64–8, 70–99, 101–5, 164, 188, 213–14,
    283, 312, 345
Woodward, Jayne 9, 21–2, 26, 30, 32, 33,
    76, 80, 93, 103
Worsley, Joe 20

Yelland, David 268

Zidane, Zinedine 366, 369, 374
Zola, Gianfranco 319, 321, 322–4,
    328–30, 334–7

Index